Theory of Codes

This is a volume in
PURE AND APPLIED MATHEMATICS

A Series of Monographs and Textbooks

Editors: SAMUEL EILENBERG AND HYMAN BASS

A list of recent titles in this series appears at the end of this volume.

THEORY OF CODES

JEAN BERSTEL

Université Paris VI

DOMINIQUE PERRIN

Université Paris VII

1985

ACADEMIC PRESS, INC.

(Harcourt Brace Jovanovich, Publishers)

Orlando San Diego New York London
Toronto Montreal Sydney Tokyo

ACADEMIC PRESS, INC.
Orlando, Florida 32887

United Kingdom Edition published by
ACADEMIC PRESS INC. (LONDON) LTD.
24/28 Oval Road, London NW1 7DX

Library of Congress Cataloging in Publication Data

Berstel, Jean, Date
Theory of codes.

(Pure and applied mathematics ;)
Bibliography: p.
1. Coding theory. I. Perrin, Dominique. II. Title.
III. Series: Pure and applied mathematics (Academic Press) ; .
QA3.P8 [QA268] 510 s [519.4] 84-12445
ISBN 0-12-093420-5 (alk. paper)

PRINTED IN THE UNITED STATES OF AMERICA

85 86 87 88 9 8 7 6 5 4 3 2 1

to Mahar

Contents

CHAPTER 2 Prefix Codes

CHAPTER 3 Biprefix Codes

CHAPTER 4 Automata

CHAPTER 5 Groups of Biprefix Codes

CHAPTER 6 Densities

CHAPTER 7 Conjugacy

CHAPTER 8 Polynomial of a Code

Preface

The theory of codes takes its origin in the theory of information devised by Shannon in the 1950s. In the past thirty years, this theory has developed in several directions, one of which is the theory of entropy, a branch of probability theory. Another is the theory of error-correcting codes which is one of the beautiful applications of commutative algebra. This volume presents a comprehensive study of the theory of variable length codes, and provides a systematic exposition of the topic.

The theory of codes, as presented here, uses both combinatorial and algebraic methods. Due to the nature of the questions raised and solved, this theory is now clearly a part of theoretical computer science and is strongly related to combinatorics on words, automata theory, formal languages, and the theory of semigroups.

The object of the theory of codes is, from an elementary point of view, the study of the properties concerning factorizations of words into a sequence of words taken from a given set. Thus it is related to syntactic analysis, even though the connection seems loose at first glance. One of the basic techniques used in this book is constructing special automata that perform certain kinds of parsing.

It is quite remarkable that the problem of encoding as treated here admits a rather simple mathematical formulation: it is the study of embeddings of one free monoid into another. We may consider this to be a basic problem of algebra. There are related problems in other algebraic structures. For instance, if we replace free monoids by free groups, the study of codes reduces to that of subgroups of a free group. However, the situation is quite different at the very beginning. In fact, according to the Nielsen–Schreier theorem, any subgroup of a free group is itself free, whereas the corresponding statement is false for free monoids. Nevertheless the relationship between codes and groups is more than an analogy, and we shall see in this book how the study of a group associated with a code can reveal some of its properties. It was M.P. Schützenberger's discovery that coding theory is closely related to classical algebra. He has been the main architect of this theory. The main basic results are due to him and most further developments were stimulated by his conjectures.

The aim of the theory of codes is to give a structural description of the codes in a way that allows their construction. This is easily accomplished for prefix codes, as shown in Chapter 2. The case of biprefix codes is already much more difficult, and the complete structural description given in Chapter 3 is one of the highlights of the theory. However, the structure of general codes (neither prefix nor suffix) still remains unknown to a large extent. For example, no systematic method is known for constructing all finite codes. The result given in Chapter 8 about the factorization of the commutative polynomial of a code must be considered (despite the difficulty of its proof) as an intermediate step toward the understanding of codes.

Many of the results given in this book are concerned with extremal properties, the interest in which comes from the interconnection that appears between different concepts. But it also goes back to the initial investigations on codes considered as communication tools. Indeed, these extremal properties in general reflect some optimization in the encoding process. Thus a maximal code uses, in this sense, the whole capacity of the transmission channel.

Primarily, two types of methods are used in this book: direct methods on words and syntactic methods. Direct methods consist of a more or less refined analysis of the sequencing of letters and factors within a word. Syntactic methods, as used in Chapters 4–8, include the study of special automata associated with codes and of the corresponding monoids of relations.

As usual during the preparation of a book, we had to make choices about the material to be covered. We have included mainly results concerning codes themselves. We have neglected in particular their relationship with varieties of languages and semigroups and also with free Lie algebras. We have not treated the developments leading toward ergodic theory. On the other hand, we have included results of combinatorial nature such as the description of comma-free codes or bisections and trisections of free monoids.

There were other choices to be made, beyond terminology and notation which of course vary through the research papers. These concern the degree of generality of the exposition. It appears that many facts discovered for finite codes remain true for recognizable codes and even for a larger class of codes (thin codes) encountered in the literature. In general, the transition from finite to recognizable codes does not imply major changes in the proof. However, changing to thin codes may imply some rather delicate computations. This is clearly demonstrated in Chapters 4 and 6, where the summations to be made become infinite when the codes are no longer recognizable. But this approach leads to a greater generality and, as we believe, to a better understanding by focusing attention on the main argument. Moreover, the characterization of the monoids associated with thin codes given in Chapter 4 may be considered to be a justification of our choice.

The organization of the book is as follows: A preliminary chapter (Chapter 0) is intended mainly to fix notation and should be consulted only when necessary. The book is composed of three major parts: part one consisting of Chapters 1–3, part two of Chapters 4–6, and part three of Chapters 7 and 8, which are independent of each other.

Chapters 1–3 constitute an elementary introduction to the theory of codes in the sense that they primarily make use of direct methods. Chapter 1 contains the definition, the relationship with submonoids, the first results on measure, and the introduction of the notions of complete, maximal, and thin codes. Chapter 2 is devoted to a systematic study of prefix codes, developed at a very elementary level. Indeed, this is the most intuitive and easy part of the theory of codes and certainly deserves considerable discussion. We believe that its interest largely goes beyond the theory of codes. The chapter ends with the well-known theorem on deciphering delay.

Chapter 3 is also elementary, although more dense. Its aims are to describe the structure of maximal biprefix codes and to give methods for constructing the finite ones. The use of formal power series is of great help. The presentation of the results, frequently scattered or unpublished, appears to be new.

The next three chapters contain what is known about codes but can be proved only by syntactic methods. Chapter 4 is devoted to these techniques, using a more systematic treatment. Instead of the frequently encountered monoids of functions we study monoids of unambiguous relations which do not favor left or right. Chapter 4 concludes with a first illustration of these techniques: the proof of the theorem of synchronization of semaphore codes.

Chapter 5 deals with the groups of biprefix codes. Chapter 6 shows how to compute the density of the submonoid generated by a code by transferring the computation into the associated monoid of unambiguous relations. The formula of densities, linking together the density of the submonoids, the degree of the code, and the densities of the contexts, is the most striking result.

As previously mentioned, Chapter 7 is very combinatorial in nature. It contains for circular codes a systematic theory that leads to the study of the well-known comma-free codes. It is followed by the study of factorizations of a free monoid and more importantly of the characterization of the codes that may appear as factors.

Chapter 8 contains the proof and discussion of the theorem of the factorization of the polynomial of a finite maximal code. Many of the results of the preceding chapters are used in the proof of this theorem which contains the most current detailed information about the structure of general codes. The book ends with the connection between maximal biprefix codes and semisimple algebras.

The book is written at an elementary level. In particular, the knowledge required is covered by a basic mathematical culture. Complete proofs are given and the necessary results of automata theory or theory of semigroups are presented in Chapter 0.

Each chapter is followed by an exercise section which frequently complements the material covered in the text. As is customary, difficult exercises are starred or double starred. The chapters end with notes containing references for the more important results, bibliographic discussions, complementary material, and references for the exercises.

It seems impossible to cover the whole text in a one-year course; however, the book contains enough material for several courses, at various levels, in undergraduate or graduate curricula. Moreover, several chapters are largely independent and can be lectured on separately. As an example, we taught a course based solely on Chapter 7. In addition, a one-year lecture at the undergraduate level may be composed of Chapter 1, Chapter 2 without the last section, Chapter 3, and the first two sections of Chapter 4. The methods used there are all elementary and semigroup theory is not employed. Because of the extensive use of trees, Chapter 2 by itself might constitute an interesting complement to a course in the theory of programming.

Chapters 4 and 5, which rely on the structure of monoids of unambiguous relations, are an excellent illustration for a course in algebra. Similarly, Chapter 6 can be used as an adjunct to a course on probability theory.

During the four years of preparation of this book, we have received help and collaboration from many people. It is a pleasure for us to express our thanks to them. First, several colleagues who offered to read preliminary versions of several chapters, discovered errors and suggested improvements and complements. We are greatly indebted to A. de Luca, G. Hansel, J.-E. Pin, C. Reutenauer, and A. Restivo. We also appreciated the invaluable help of S. W. Margolis and P. E. Schupp.

Needless to say, we are greatly indebted to M.P. Schützenberger. The project of writing this book stems from him and he has encouraged us constantly in many discussions.

In addition, the typing of the manuscript, first in French then in English, involved the talents of Claudine Beaujean, Anne Berstel, Maryse Brochot, Zoé Civange, Martine Chaumard, Rosa De Marchi, and Arlette Dupont. Their help is gratefully acknowledged.

Finally, this work was accomplished at the Laboratoire d'Informatique et Programmation, which provided moral and technical support.

CHAPTER 0

Preliminaries

0. INTRODUCTION

In this preliminary chapter, we give a short but complete account of some basic notions which will be used throughout the book. This chapter is not designed for a systematic reading but rather as a reference.

The first three sections contain our notation and basic vocabulary. Each of the four subsequent sections is an introduction to a topic which is not completely treated in this book. These sections are concerned mainly with the theory of automata. Kleene's theorem is given and we show how to construct a minimal automaton from a given automaton. Syntactic monoids are defined. These concepts and results will be discussed in another context in Chapter IV.

1. NOTATION

As usual, $\mathbb{N}$, $\mathbb{Z}$, $\mathbb{Q}$, $\mathbb{R}$, and $\mathbb{C}$ denote the sets of nonnegative integers, integers, and rational, real, and complex numbers, respectively. By convention, $0 \in \mathbb{N}$. We set

$$\mathbb{R}_+ = \{x \in \mathbb{R} \mid x \geq 0\}.$$

Next,

$$\binom{n}{p} = \frac{n!}{p!(n-p)!}$$

denotes the binomial coefficient of n and p.

Given two subsets X, Y of a set Z, we define

$$X - Y = \{z \in Z \mid z \in X, z \notin Y\}.$$

An element x and the singleton set $\{x\}$ will usually not be distinguished. The set of all subsets of a set X is denoted by $\mathfrak{P}(X)$.

The function symbols are usually written on the left of their arguments but with some exceptions: When we consider the composition of actions on a set, the action is written on the right. In particular, permutations are written on the right.

A partition of a set X is a family $(X_i)_{i \in I}$ of *nonempty* subsets of X such that

(i) $X = \bigcup_{i \in I} X_i$
(ii) $X_i \cap X_j = \varnothing, \qquad (i \neq j)$.

We usually define a partition as follows: "Let $X = \bigcup_{i \in I} X_i$ be a partition of X." We denote the cardinality of a set X by $\text{Card}(X)$.

2. MONOIDS

A *monoid* is a set M equipped with an associative binary operation and has a neutral element. The operation is usually written multiplicatively. The neutral element is unique and is denoted by 1_M or simply by 1.

For any monoid M, the set $\mathfrak{P}(M)$ is given a monoid structure by defining, for $X, Y \subset M$,

$$XY = \{xy \mid x \in X, y \in Y\}.$$

The neutral element is $\{1\}$.

A *submonoid* of M is a subset N which is stable under the operation and which contains the neutral element of M

$$NN \subset N, \tag{2.1}$$

$$1_M \in N. \tag{2.2}$$

Note that a subset N of M satisfying (2.1) does not always satisfy $1_M = 1_N$ and therefore may be a monoid without being a submonoid of M.

A *morphism* from a monoid M into a monoid N is a function

$$\varphi\colon \quad M \to N$$

which satisfies, for all $m, m' \in M$,

$$\varphi(mm') = \varphi(m)\varphi(m'),$$

and furthermore

$$\varphi(1_M) = 1_N.$$

A *congruence* on a monoid M is an equivalence relation θ on M such that, for all $m, m' \in M, u, v \in M$

$$m \equiv m' \bmod \theta \quad \Rightarrow \quad umv \equiv um'v \bmod \theta.$$

Let φ be a morphism from M onto N. The equivalence θ defined by $m \equiv m' \bmod \theta$ iff $\varphi(m) = \varphi(m')$ is a congruence. It is called the *nuclear congruence* induced by φ. Conversely, if θ is a congruence on the monoid M, the set M/θ of the equivalence classes of θ is equipped with a monoid structure, and the canonical function from M onto M/θ is a monoid morphism.

An *idempotent* of a monoid M is an element e of M such that

$$e = e^2.$$

For each idempotent e of a monoid M, the set

$$M(e) = eMe$$

is a monoid contained in M. It is easily seen that it is the largest monoid contained in M having e as a neutral element. It is called the monoid *localized* at e.

It will sometimes be convenient to use the term *semigroup* to denote a set equipped with an associative operation but without the requirement of the existence of a neutral element. The notions of subsemigroup and semigroup morphism are then defined in the same way as the corresponding notions for monoids.

Let M be a monoid. The set of (left and right) invertible elements of M is a group called the *group of units* of M.

A *cyclic monoid* is a monoid with just one generator, i.e.,

$$M = \{a^n \mid n \in \mathbb{N}\}$$

with $a^0 = 1$. If M is infinite, it is isomorphic to the additive monoid $\mathbb{N}$ of nonnegative integers. If M is finite, the *index* of M is the smallest integer $i \geq 0$ such that there exists an integer $r \geq 1$ with

$$a^{i+r} = a^i. \tag{2.3}$$

The smallest integer r such that (2.3) holds is called the *period* of M. The pair composed of index i and period p determines a monoid having $i + p$ elements,

$$M_{i,p} = \{1, a, a^2, \ldots, a^{i-1}, a^i, \ldots, a^{i+p-1}\}.$$

Its multiplication is conveniently represented in Fig. 0.1.

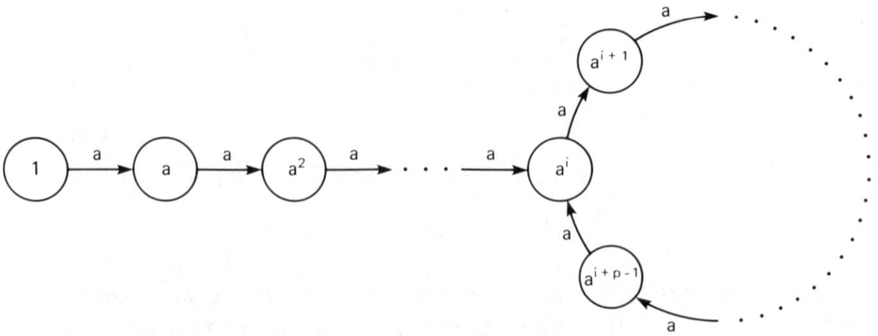

Fig. 0.1 The monoid $M_{i,p}$.

The monoid $M_{i,p}$ contains two idempotents (provided $a \neq 1$). Indeed, assume that $a^j = a^{2j}$. Then either $j = 0$ or $j \geq i$ and j and $2j$ have the same residue mod p, hence $j \equiv 0 \bmod p$. Conversely, if $j \geq i$ and $j \equiv 0 \bmod p$, then $a^j = a^{2j}$.

Consequently, the unique idempotent $e \neq 1$ in $M_{i,p}$ is $e = a^j$, where j is the unique integer in $\{i, i+1, \ldots, i+p-1\}$ which is a multiple of p.

Let M be a monoid. For $x, y \in M$, we define

$$x^{-1}y = \{z \in M \mid xz = y\} \qquad \text{and} \qquad xy^{-1} = \{z \in M \mid x = zy\}.$$

For subsets X, Y of M, this notation is extended to

$$X^{-1}Y = \bigcup_{x \in X} \bigcup_{y \in Y} x^{-1}y \qquad \text{and} \qquad XY^{-1} = \bigcup_{x \in X} \bigcup_{y \in Y} xy^{-1}.$$

The following identities hold for subsets X, Y, Z of M:

$$(XY)^{-1}Z = Y^{-1}(X^{-1}Z) \qquad \text{and} \qquad X^{-1}(YZ^{-1}) = (X^{-1}Y)Z^{-1}.$$

Given a subset X of a monoid M, we define

$$F(X) = M^{-1}XM^{-1}$$

to be the set of *factors* of elements in X. We have

$$F(X) = \{m \in M \mid \exists u, v \in M : umv \in X\}.$$

We sometimes use the notation $\bar{F}(X)$ to denote the complement of $F(X)$ in M,

$$\bar{F}(X) = M - F(X).$$

3. WORDS

Let A be a set, which we call an *alphabet*. A *word* w on the alphabet A is a finite sequence of elements of A

$$w = (a_1, a_2, \ldots, a_n), \qquad a_i \in A.$$

The set of all words on the alphabet A is denoted by A^* and is equipped with the associative operation defined by the concatenation of two sequences

$$(a_1, a_2, \ldots, a_n)(b_1, b_2, \ldots, b_m) = (a_1, a_2, \ldots, a_n, b_1, b_2, \ldots, b_m).$$

This operation is associative. This allows us to write

$$w = a_1 a_2 \cdots a_n$$

instead of $w = (a_1, a_2, \ldots, a_n)$, by identifying each element $a \in A$ with the sequence (a). An element $a \in A$ is called a *letter*. The empty sequence is called the *empty word* and is denoted by 1. It is the neutral element for concatenation. Thus the set A^* of words is equipped with the structure of a monoid. The monoid A^* is called the *free monoid* on A. The set of nonempty words on A is denoted by A^+. Thus we have $A^+ = A^* - 1$.

The *length* $|w|$ of the word $w = a_1 a_2 \cdots a_n$ with $a_i \in A$ is the number n of letters in w. Clearly, $|1| = 0$. The function $w \mapsto |w|$ is a morphism from A^* onto the additive monoid $\mathbb{N}$. For $n \geq 0$, we use the notation

$$A^{(n)} = \{w \in A^* \mid |w| \leq n - 1\}$$

and also

$$A^{[n]} = \{w \in A^* \mid |w| \leq n\}.$$

In particular, $A^{(0)} = \varnothing$ and $A^{[0]} = \{1\}$.

For a subset B of A, we let $|w|_B$ denote the number of letters of w which are in B. Thus

$$|w| = \sum_{a \in A} |w|_a.$$

For a word $w \in A^*$, the set

$$\text{alph}(w) = \{a \in A \mid |w|_a > 0\}$$

is the set of all letters occurring at least once in w. For a subset X of A^*, we set

$$\text{alph}(X) = \bigcup_{x \in X} \text{alph}(x).$$

A word $w \in A^*$ is a *factor* of a word $x \in A^*$ if there exist $u, v \in A^*$ such that $x = uwv$.

The relation *is a factor of* is a partial order on A^*. A factor w of x is *proper* if $w \neq x$.

A word $w \in A^*$ is a *left factor* of a word $x \in A^*$ if there is a word $u \in A^*$ such that $x = wu$. The factor w is called *proper* if $w \neq x$. The relation *is a left factor of* is again a partial order on A^* called the *prefix ordering*. We write $w \leq x$ when w *is a left factor of* x and $w < x$ whenever $w \leq x$ and $w \neq x$. This order has the following fundamental property. If for some x,

$$w \leq x, \qquad w' \leq x,$$

then w and w' are comparable, i.e.,

$$w \leq w' \qquad \text{or} \qquad w' \leq w.$$

In other words, if $vw = v'w'$, then either there exists $s \in A^*$ such that $v = v's$ (and also $sw = w'$) or there exists $t \in A^*$ such that $v' = vt$ (and then $w = tw'$).

In an entirely symmetric manner we define a right factor w of a word x by $x = vw$ for some $v \in A^*$. A set $P \subset A^*$ is called *prefix-closed* if it contains the left factors of its elements: $uv \in P \Rightarrow u \in P$. A suffix-closed set is defined symmetrically.

The *reverse* w of a word $w = a_1 a_2 \cdots a_n$, $a_i \in A$, is

$$\tilde{w} = a_n \cdots a_2 a_1.$$

The notations $\tilde{w}$ and $w^{\sim}$ are equivalent. Note that for all $u, v \in A^*$,

$$(uv)^{\sim} = \tilde{v}\tilde{u}.$$

The *reverse* $\tilde{X}$ of a set $X \subset A^*$ is the set $\tilde{X} = \{\tilde{x} \mid x \in X\}$.

A *factorization* of a word $w \in A^*$ is a sequence $(u_1, u_2, \ldots, u_n)$ of $n \geq 0$ words in A^* such that

$$w = u_1 u_2 \cdots u_n.$$

For a subset X of A^*, we denote by X^* the submonoid generated by X,

$$X^* = \{x_1 x_2 \cdots x_n \mid n \geq 0, x_i \in X\}.$$

Similarly, we denote by X^+ the subsemigroup generated by X,

$$X^+ = \{x_1 x_2 \cdots x_n \mid n \geq 1, x_i \in X\}.$$

We have

$$X^+ = \begin{cases} X^* - 1 & \text{if } 1 \notin X, \\ X^* & \text{otherwise.} \end{cases}$$

By definition, each word w in X^* admits at least one factorization $(x_1, x_2, \ldots, x_n)$ whose elements are all in X. Such a factorization is called an X-factorization. We frequently use the pictorial representation of an X-factorization given in Fig. 0.2.

A word $x \in A^*$ is called *primitive* if it is not a power of another word. Thus x is primitive iff $x = y^n$ with $n \geq 0$ implies $x = y$. Observe that the empty word is not primitive.

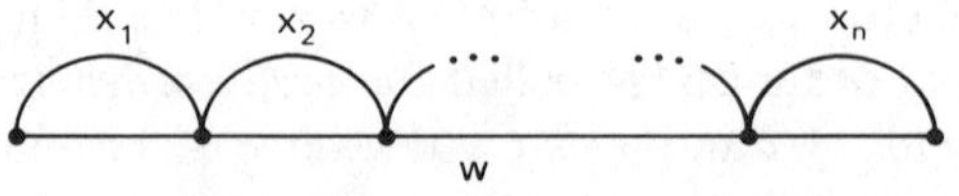

Fig. 0.2 An X-factorization of w.

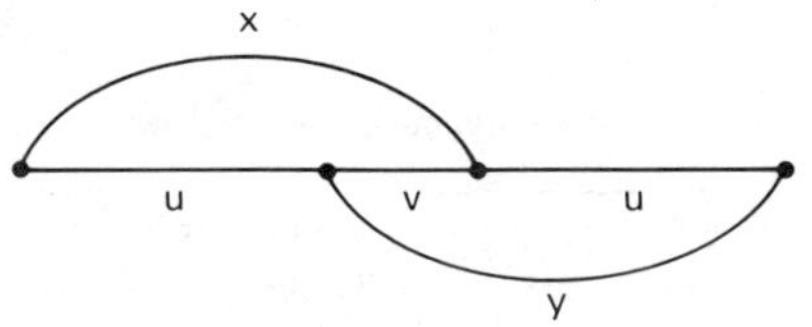

Fig. 0.3 Two conjugate words.

Two words x, y are called *conjugate* if there exists words u, v such that $x = uv$, $y = vu$. (See Fig. 0.3.) We frequently say that y is a conjugate of x. Two conjugate words are obtained from each other by a cyclic permutation. More precisely, let γ be the function from A^* into itself defined by

$$\gamma(1) = 1 \qquad \text{and} \qquad \gamma(av) = va \tag{3.1}$$

for $a \in A, v \in A^*$. It is clearly a bijection from A^* onto itself. Two words x and y are conjugate iff there exists an integer $n \geq 0$ such that

$$x = \gamma^n(y).$$

This easily implies that the conjugacy relation is an equivalence relation. A *conjugacy class* is a class of this equivalence relation.

PROPOSITION 3.1 *Each nonempty word is a power of a unique primitive word.*

Proof Let $x \in A^+$ and δ be the restriction of the function γ defined by (3.1) to the conjugacy class of x. Then $\delta^k = 1$ iff x is a power of some word of length k.

Let p be the order of δ, i.e., the g.c.d. of the integers k such that $\delta^k = 1$. Since $\delta^p = 1$, there exists a word r of length p such that $x = r^e$ with $e \geq 1$. The word r is primitive, otherwise there would be a word s of length q dividing p such that $r \in s^*$, which in turn implies that $x \in s^*$, contrary to the definition of p. This proves the existence of the primitive word. To show unicity, consider a word $t \in A^*$ such that $x \in t^*$ and let $k = |t|$. Since $\delta^k = 1$, the integer k is a multiple of p. Consequently $t \in r^*$. Thus if t is primitive, we have $t = r$. □

Let $x \in A^+$. The unique primitive word r such that $x = r^n$ for some integer n is called the *root* of x. The integer n is the *exponent* of x. We sometimes write

$$r = \sqrt{x}.$$

PROPOSITION 3.2 *Two nonempty conjugate words have the same exponent and their roots are conjugate.*

Proof Let $x, y \in A^+$ be two conjugate words, and let i be an integer such that $y = \gamma^i(x)$. Set $r = \sqrt{x}$ and $s = \sqrt{y}$ and let $x = r^n$. Then

$$y = \gamma^i(r^n) = (\gamma^i(r))^n.$$

TABLE 0.1

The Number $l_n(k)$ of Primitive Conjugacy Classes over a k-Letter Alphabet

n	1	2	3	4	5	6	7	8	9	10	11	12
$l_n(2)$	2	1	2	3	6	9	18	30	56	99	186	335
$l_n(3)$	3	3	8	18	48	116						
$l_n(4)$	4	6	20									

This shows that $\gamma^i(r) \in s^*$. Interchanging the roles of x and y, we have $\gamma^j(s) \in r^*$. It follows that $\gamma^i(r) = s$ and $\gamma^j(s) = r$. Thus r and s are conjugate and consequently x and y have the same exponent. □

PROPOSITION 3.3 *All words in a conjugacy class have the same exponent. If C is a conjugacy class of words of length n with exponent e, then*

$$\text{Card}(C) = n/e.$$

Proof Let $x \in A^n$ and C be its conjugacy class. Let δ be the restriction of γ to C and p be the order of δ. The root of x is the word r of length p such that $x = r^e$. Thus $n = pe$. Now $C = \{x, \delta(x), \ldots, \delta^{p-1}(x)\}$. These elements are distinct since p is the order of δ. Thus $\text{Card}(C) = p$. □

We now compute the number of conjugacy classes of words of given length over a finite alphabet. Let A be an alphabet with k letters. For all $n \geq 1$, the number of conjugacy classes of primitive words in A^* of length n is denoted by $l_n(k)$. The notation is justified by the fact that this number depends only on k and not on A.

The first values of this function, for $k = 2, 3, 4$, are given in Table 0.1. Clearly $l_n(1) = 1$ if $n = 1$, and $l_n(1) = 0$, otherwise. Now for $n \geq 1$

$$k^n = \sum_{d|n} d l_d(k), \tag{3.2}$$

where d runs over the divisors of n. Indeed, every word of length n belongs to exactly one conjugacy class of words of length n. Each class has $d = n/e$ elements, where e is the exponent of its words. Since there are as many classes whose words have exponent n/e as there are classes of primitive words of length $d = n/e$, the result follows. □

We can obtain an explicit expression for the numbers $l_n(k)$ by using the classical technique of Mobius inversion which we now recall.

The *Möbius function* is the function

$$\mu\colon\ \mathbb{N} - \{0\} \to \mathbb{N}$$

defined by

$$\mu(1) = 1$$

and

$$\mu(n) = \begin{cases} (-1)^i & \text{if } n \text{ is the product of } i \text{ distinct prime numbers,} \\ 0 & \text{otherwise.} \end{cases}$$

PROPOSITION 3.4 (Möbius Inversion Formula) *Let α, β be two functions from $\mathbb{N} - \{0\}$ into $\mathbb{N}$. Then*

$$\alpha(n) = \sum_{d|n} \beta(d) \qquad (n \geq 1) \tag{3.3}$$

iff

$$\beta(n) = \sum_{d|n} \mu(d)\alpha(n/d) \qquad (n \geq 1). \tag{3.4}$$

Proof Define a product on the set $\mathscr{S}$ of functions from $\mathbb{N} - \{0\}$ into $\mathbb{N}$ by setting, for $f, g \in \mathscr{S}$,

$$f * g(n) = \sum_{n=de} f(d)g(e).$$

It is easily verified that $\mathscr{S}$ is a commutative monoid for this product. Its neutral element is the function $\mathit{1}$ taking the value 1 for $n = 1$ and 0 elsewhere.

Let $\iota \in \mathscr{S}$ be the constant function with value 1. Let us verify that

$$\iota * \mu = \mathit{1}. \tag{3.5}$$

Indeed $\iota * \mu(1) = 1$; for $n \geq 2$, let $n = p_1^{k_1} p_2^{k_2} \cdots p_m^{k_m}$ by the prime decomposition of n. If d divides n, then $\mu(d) \neq 0$ iff

$$d = p_1^{l_1} p_2^{l_2} \cdots p_m^{l_m}$$

with all $l_i = 0$ or 1. Then $\mu(d) = (-1)^t$ with $t = \sum_{i=1}^m l_i$. It follows that

$$\iota * \mu(n) = \sum_{d|n} \mu(d) = \sum_{t=0}^{m} (-1)^t \binom{m}{t} = 0.$$

Now let $\alpha, \beta \in \mathscr{S}$. Then formula (3.3) is equivalent to $\alpha = \iota * \beta$ and formula (3.4) is equivalent to $\beta = \mu * \alpha$. By (3.5) these two formulas are equivalent. □

PROPOSITION 3.5 *The number of conjugacy classes of primitive words of length n over an alphabet with k letters is*

$$l_n(k) = \sum_{d|n} \mu(n/d) k^d.$$

Proof This is immediate from formula (3.2) by Möbius inversion. □

A word $w \in A^+$ is called *unbordered* if no proper nonempty left factor of w is a right factor of w. In other words, w is unbordered iff

$$w \in uA^+ \cap A^+u \qquad \text{implies} \quad u = 1.$$

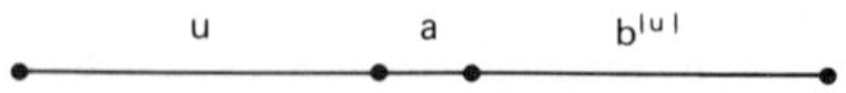

Fig. 0.4 The word $uab^{|u|}$.

If w is unbordered, then

$$wA^* \cap A^*w = wA^*w \cup w.$$

The following property holds.

PROPOSITION 3.6 *Let A be an alphabet with at least two letters. For each word $u \in A^+$, there exists $v \in A^*$ such that uv is unbordered.*

Proof Let a be the first letter of u, and let $b \in A - a$. Let us verify that the word $w = uab^{|u|}$ is unbordered (Fig. 0.4). A nonempty left factor t of w starts with the letter a. It cannot be a right factor of w unless $|t| > |u|$. But then we have $t = sab^{|u|}$ for some $s \in A^*$, and also $t = uab^{|s|}$. Thus $|s| = |u|$, hence $t = w$. □

Let A be an alphabet. The *free group* $A^{®}$ on A is defined as follows: Let $\bar{A}$ be an alphabet in bijection with A and disjoint from A. Denote by

$$a \mapsto \bar{a}$$

the bijection from A onto $\bar{A}$. This notation is extended by setting, for all $a \in A \cup \bar{A}$,

$$\bar{\bar{a}} = a.$$

Let δ be the symmetric relation defined for $u, v \in (A \cup \bar{A})^*$ and $a \in A \cup \bar{A}$ by

$$ua\bar{a}v \equiv uv \bmod \delta.$$

Let ρ be the reflexive and transitive closure of δ. Then ρ is a congruence. The quotient $A^{®} = (A \cup \bar{A})^*/\rho$ is a group. Indeed, for all $a \in A \cup \bar{A}$,

$$a\bar{a} \equiv 1 \bmod \rho.$$

Thus the images of the generators are invertible in $A^{®}$. The group $A^{®}$ is called the free group on A.

4. AUTOMATA

Let A be an alphabet. An *automaton* over A is composed of a set Q (the set of *states*), a subset I of Q (the *initial* states), a subset T of Q (the *terminal* or final states), and a set

$$\mathscr{F} \subset Q \times A \times Q$$

called the set of *edges*. The automaton is denoted by

$$\mathscr{A} = (Q, I, T)$$

The automaton is *finite* when the set Q is finite.

A *path* in the automaton $\mathscr{A}$ is a sequence $c = (f_1, f_2, \ldots, f_n)$ of consecutive edges

$$f_i = (q_i, a_i, q_{i+1}), \qquad 1 \le i \le n.$$

The integer n is called the length of the path c. The word $w = a_1 a_2 \cdots a_n$ is the *label* of the path c. The state q_1 is the *origin* of c, and the state q_{n+1} the *end* of c. A useful notation is

$$c\colon\ q_1 \xrightarrow{w} q_{n+1}.$$

By convention, there is, for each state $q \in Q$, a path of length 0 from q to q. Its label is the empty word.

A path $c\colon i \to t$ is *successful* if $i \in I$ and $t \in T$. The set *recognized* by $\mathscr{A}$, denoted by $L(\mathscr{A})$, is defined as the set of labels of successful paths.

A state $q \in Q$ is *accessible* (resp. *coaccessible*) if there exists a path $c\colon i \to q$ with $i \in I$ (resp. a path $c\colon q \to t$ with $t \in T$). An automaton is *trim* if each state is both accessible and coaccessible. Let P be the set of accessible and coaccessible states, and let $\mathscr{A}^\circ = (P, I \cap P, T \cap P)$. Then it is easy to see that $\mathscr{A}^\circ$ is trim and

$$L(\mathscr{A}) = L(\mathscr{A}^\circ).$$

An automaton $\mathscr{A} = (Q, I, T)$ is *deterministic* if $\mathrm{Card}(I) = 1$ and if

$$(p, a, q), (p, a, r) \in \mathscr{F} \quad \Rightarrow \quad q = r.$$

Thus for each $p \in Q$ and $a \in A$, there is at most one state q in Q such that $p \xrightarrow{a} q$. For $p \in Q$, and $a \in A$, define

$$p \cdot a = \begin{cases} q & \text{if } \ (p, a, q) \in \mathscr{F}, \\ \varnothing & \text{otherwise.} \end{cases}$$

The partial function

$$Q \times A \to Q$$

defined in this way is extended to words by setting, for all $p \in Q$,

$$p \cdot 1 = p,$$

and, for $w \in A^*$and $a \in A$,

$$p \cdot wa = (p \cdot w) \cdot a.$$

This function is called the *transition function* or next-state function of $\mathscr{A}$. With this notation, we have with $I = \{i\}$,

$$L(\mathscr{A}) = \{w \in A^* \mid i \cdot w \in T\}.$$

An automaton is *complete* if for all $p \in Q$, $a \in A$, there exists at least one $q \in Q$ such that $p \xrightarrow{a} q$.

PROPOSITION 4.1 *For each automaton $\mathscr{A}$, there exists a complete deterministic automaton $\mathscr{B}$ such that*

$$L(\mathscr{A}) = L(\mathscr{B}).$$

If $\mathscr{A}$ is finite, then $\mathscr{B}$ can be chosen to be finite.

Proof Set $\mathscr{A} = (Q, I, T)$. Define $\mathscr{B} = (R, u, V)$ by setting $R = \mathfrak{P}(Q)$, $u = I$,

$$V = \{S \subset Q \mid S \cap T \neq \varnothing\}.$$

Define the transition function of $\mathscr{B}$, for $S \in R$, $a \in A$ by

$$S \cdot a = \{q \in Q \mid \exists s \in S : s \xrightarrow{a} q\}.$$

The automaton $\mathscr{B}$ is complete and deterministic. It is easily seen that $L(\mathscr{A}) = L(\mathscr{B})$. □

Let $\mathscr{A} = (Q, i, T)$ be a deterministic automaton. For each $q \in Q$, let

$$L_q = \{w \in A^* \mid q \cdot w \in T\}.$$

Two states $p, q \in Q$ are called *inseparable* if

$$L_p = L_q;$$

they are *separable* otherwise. A deterministic automaton is *reduced* if two distinct states are always separable.

Let X be a subset of A^*. We define a special automaton $\mathscr{A}(X) = (Q, i, T)$ in the following way. The states of $\mathscr{A}(X)$ are the nonempty sets

$$u^{-1}X$$

for $u \in A^*$. The initial state is $X = 1^{-1}X$, and the final states are those containing the empty word. The transition function is defined for a state $Y = u^{-1}X$ and a letter $a \in A$ by

$$Y \cdot a = a^{-1}Y.$$

Observe that this indeed defines a partial function. We have

$$L(\mathscr{A}(X)) = X.$$

Indeed, an easy induction shows that for $w \in A^*$

$$X \cdot w = w^{-1}X.$$

Consequently

$$w \in L(\mathscr{A}(X)) \quad \Leftrightarrow \quad 1 \in X \cdot w \quad \Leftrightarrow \quad 1 \in w^{-1}X \quad \Leftrightarrow \quad w \in X.$$

The automaton $\mathscr{A}(X)$ is reduced. Indeed, for $Y = u^{-1}X$,

$$L_Y = \{v \in A^* \mid Y \cdot v \in T\} = \{v \in A^* \mid uv \in X\}.$$

Thus

$$L_Y = Y.$$

The automaton $\mathscr{A}(X)$ is called the *minimal automaton* of X. This terminology is justified by the following proposition.

PROPOSITION 4.2 *Let $\mathscr{A} = (Q, i, T)$ be a trim deterministic automaton and let $X = L(\mathscr{A})$. Let $\mathscr{A}(X) = (P, j, S)$ be the minimal automaton of X. The function from Q into P defined by*

$$\varphi\colon \quad q \to L_q$$

is surjective and satisfies

$$\varphi(q \cdot a) = \varphi(q) \cdot a.$$

Proof Let $q \in Q$. Let $u \in A^*$ such that $i \cdot u = q$. Then

$$L_q = \{w \in A^* \mid q \cdot w \in T\} = u^{-1}X.$$

Since $\mathscr{A}$ is trim, $L_q \neq \varnothing$. This shows that $L_q \in P$. Thus φ is a function from Q into P. Next, let us show that φ is surjective. Let $u^{-1}X \in P$. Then $u^{-1}X \neq \varnothing$. Thus $i \cdot u \neq \varnothing$ and setting $q = i \cdot u$, we have $L_q = u^{-1}X = \varphi(q)$. Thus φ is surjective.

Finally, for $q = i \cdot u$,

$$\varphi(q \cdot a) = L_{q \cdot a} = (ua)^{-1}X = (u^{-1}X) \cdot a = L_q \cdot a. \quad \square$$

Assume furthermore that the automaton $\mathscr{A}$ in the proposition is reduced. Then the function φ is a bijection, which identifies $\mathscr{A}$ with the minimal automaton. In this sense, there exists just one reduced automaton recognizing a given set.

Let $\mathscr{A} = (Q, i, T)$ be a deterministic automaton. Consider the set $\mathscr{T}$ of partial functions from Q into Q. These functions are written on the right: if $q \in Q$ and $m \in \mathscr{T}$, then the image of q by m is denoted by qm. Composition is defined by

$$q(mn) = (qm)n.$$

Thus $\mathscr{T}$ has a monoid structure.

Let φ be the function which to a word $w \in A^*$ associates the partial function from Q into Q defined by

$$q\varphi(w) = q \cdot w.$$

The function φ is a morphism from A^* into the monoid $\mathcal{T}$. The submonoid $\varphi(A^*)$ of $\mathcal{T}$ is called the *transition monoid* of the automaton $\mathcal{A}$.

Observe that, setting $X = L(\mathcal{A})$, we have

$$\varphi^{-1}\varphi(X) = X. \tag{4.1}$$

Indeed $w \in \varphi^{-1}\varphi(X)$ iff $\varphi(w) \in \varphi(X)$ which is equivalent to $i\varphi(w) \in T$, i.e., to $w \in X$.

A morphism φ from A^* onto a monoid M is said to *recognize* a subset X of A^* if

$$\varphi^{-1}\varphi(X) = X.$$

Let X be a subset of A^*. For $w \in A^*$, set

$$\Gamma(w) = \{(u, v) \in A^* \times A^* \mid uwv \in X\}.$$

The *syntactic congruence* of X is the equivalence relation σ_X on A^* defined by

$$w \equiv w' \mod \sigma_X \iff \Gamma(w) = \Gamma(w').$$

It is easily verified that σ_X is a congruence. The quotient of A^* by σ_X is, by definition, the *syntactic monoid* of X. We denote it by $\mathcal{M}(X)$, and we denote by φ_X the canonical morphism from A^* onto $\mathcal{M}(X)$.

PROPOSITION 4.3 *Let X be a subset of A^*, and let $\varphi: A^* \to M$ be a surjective morphism. If φ recognizes X, then there exists a morphism ψ from M onto the syntactic monoid $\mathcal{M}(X)$ such that*

$$\varphi_X = \psi \circ \varphi.$$

Proof It suffices to show that

$$\varphi(w) = \varphi(w') \Rightarrow \varphi_X(w) = \varphi_X(w'). \tag{4.2}$$

Indeed, if (4.2) holds, then for an element $m \in M$, $\psi(m)$ is defined as the unique element in $\varphi_X(\varphi^{-1}(m))$. To show (4.2), we consider $(u, v) \in \Gamma(w)$. Then $uwv \in X$. Thus $\varphi(u)\varphi(w)\varphi(v) \in \varphi(X)$. From $\varphi(w) = \varphi(w')$, it follows that $\varphi(u)\varphi(w')\varphi(v) \in \varphi(X)$. Since φ recognizes X, this implies that $uw'v \in X$. Thus $(u, v) \in \Gamma(w')$. □

PROPOSITION 4.4 *Let X be a subset of A^*. The syntactic monoid of X is isomorphic to the transition monoid of the minimal automaton $\mathcal{A}(X)$.*

Proof Let M be the transition monoid of the automaton $\mathcal{A}(X) = (Q, i, T)$ and let $\varphi: A^* \to M$ be the canonical morphism. By (4.1), the morphism φ recognizes X. By Proposition 4.3, there exists a morphism ψ from M onto the syntactic monoid $\mathcal{M}(X)$ such that $\varphi_X = \psi \circ \varphi$.

It suffices to show that ψ is injective. For this, consider $m, m' \in M$ such that $\psi(m) = \psi(m')$. Let $w, w' \in A^*$ such that $\varphi(w) = m$, $\varphi(w') = m'$. Then $\varphi_X(w) = \varphi_X(w')$. To prove that $\varphi(w) = \varphi(w')$, we consider a state $p \in Q$, and let $u \in A^*$ be such that $p = u^{-1}X$. Then

$$p\varphi(w) = p \cdot w = (uw)^{-1}X = \{v \in A^* \mid (u, v) \in \Gamma(w)\}.$$

Since $\Gamma(w) = \Gamma(w')$, we have $p\varphi(w) = p\varphi(w')$. Thus $\varphi(w) = \varphi(w')$, i.e., $m = m'$. □

We now turn to the study of properties which are specific to finite automata.

THEOREM 4.5 *Let $X \subset A^*$. The following conditions are equivalent.*

(i) *The set X is recognized by a finite automaton.*
(ii) *The minimal automaton $\mathscr{A}(X)$ is finite.*
(iii) *The family of sets*

$$u^{-1}X,$$

for $u \in A^*$, is finite.
(iv) *The syntactic monoid $\mathscr{M}(X)$ is finite.*
(v) *The set X is recognized by a morphism from A^* onto a finite monoid.*

Proof (i) ⇒ (ii) Let $\mathscr{A}$ be a finite automaton recognizing X. By Proposition 4.1, we can assume that $\mathscr{A}$ is deterministic. By Proposition 4.2, the minimal automaton $\mathscr{A}(X)$ also is finite.

(ii) ⇔ (iii) is clear.

(ii) ⇒ (iv) holds by Proposition 4.4 and by the fact that the transition monoid of a finite automaton is always finite.

(iv) ⇒ (v) is clear.

(v) ⇒ (i) Let $\varphi: A^* \to M$ be a morphism onto a finite monoid M, and suppose that φ recognizes X. Let $\mathscr{A} = (M, 1, \varphi(X))$ be the deterministic automaton with transition function defined by

$$m \cdot a = m\varphi(a).$$

Then $1 \cdot w \in \varphi(X)$ iff $\varphi(w) \in \varphi(X)$, thus iff $w \in X$. Consequently $L(\mathscr{A}) = X$. □

A subset X of A^* is called *recognizable* if it satisfies one of the equivalent conditions of Theorem 4.5.

PROPOSITION 4.6 *The family of recognizable subsets of A^* is closed under all boolean operations: union, intersection, complementation.*

Proof Let $X, Y \subset A^*$ be two recognizable subsets of A^*. Let $\mathscr{A} = (P, i, S)$ and $\mathscr{B} = (Q, j, T)$ be complete deterministic automata such that $X = L(\mathscr{A})$,

$Y = L(\mathscr{B})$. Let

$$\mathscr{C} = (P \times Q, (i, j), R)$$

be the complete deterministic automaton defined by

$$(p, q) \cdot a = (p \cdot a, q \cdot a).$$

For $R = (S \times Q) \cup (P \times T)$, we have $L(\mathscr{C}) = X \cup Y$. For $R = S \times T$, we have $L(\mathscr{C}) = X \cap Y$. Finally, for $R = S \times (Q - T)$, we have $L(\mathscr{C}) = X - Y$. □

Consider now a slight generalization of the notion of automaton. An *asynchronous automaton* on A is an automaton $\mathscr{A} = (Q, I, T)$, the edges of which may be labeled by either a letter or the empty word. Therefore the set of its edges satisfies

$$\mathscr{F} \subset Q \times (A \cup 1) \times Q.$$

The notions of a path or a successful path extend in a natural way so that the notion of the set recognized by the automaton is clear.

PROPOSITION 4.7 *For any finite asynchronous automaton $\mathscr{A}$, there exists a finite automaton $\mathscr{B}$ such that $L(\mathscr{A}) = L(\mathscr{B})$.*

Proof Let $\mathscr{A} = (Q, I, T)$ be an asynchronous automaton. Let $\mathscr{B} = (Q, I, T)$ be the automaton, the edges of which are the triples (p, a, q) such that there exists a path $p \xrightarrow{a} q$ in $\mathscr{A}$. We have

$$L(\mathscr{A}) \cap A^+ = L(\mathscr{B}) \cap A^+.$$

If $I \cap T \neq \varnothing$, both sets $L(\mathscr{A})$ and $L(\mathscr{B})$ contain the empty word and are therefore equal. Otherwise, the sets are equal up to the empty word and the result follows from Proposition 4.6 since the set $\{1\}$ is recognizable. □

The notion of an asynchronous automaton is useful to prove the following result.

PROPOSITION 4.8 *If $X \subset A^*$ is recognizable, then X^* is recognizable. If $X, Y \subset A^*$ are recognizable, then XY is recognizable.*

Proof Since $X^* = (X - 1)^*$ and since $X - 1$ is recognizable, we may suppose that $1 \notin X$. Let $\mathscr{A} = (Q, I, T)$ be a finite automaton recognizing X. Let $\mathscr{F}$ be the set of its edges. Since $1 \notin X$, we have $I \cap T = \varnothing$. Let $\mathscr{B} = (Q, I, T)$ be the asynchronous automaton with edges

$$\mathscr{F} \cup (T \times \{1\} \times I).$$

Then $L(\mathscr{B}) = X^+$. In fact, the inclusion $X^* - 1 \subset L(\mathscr{B})$ is clear. Conversely, let $c: i \xrightarrow{w} j$ be a successful path in $\mathscr{B}$. By the definition of $\mathscr{B}$, this path has the form

$$c: \quad i_1 \xrightarrow{w_1} t_1 \xrightarrow{1} i_2 \xrightarrow{w_2} t_2 \cdots i_n \xrightarrow{w_n} t_n$$

with $i = i_1, j = t_n$ and where no path $c_k: i_k \xrightarrow{w_k} t_k$ contains an edge labeled by the empty word. Then $w_1, w_2, \ldots, w_n \in X$ and therefore $w \in X^+$.

Now let $\mathscr{A} = (P, I, S)$ and $\mathscr{B} = (Q, J, T)$ be two finite automata with sets of edges $\mathscr{F}$ and $\mathscr{G}$, respectively. Let $X = L(\mathscr{A})$ and let $Y = L(\mathscr{B})$. One may assume that $P \cap Q = \varnothing$. Let $\mathscr{C} = (P \cup Q, I, T)$ be the asynchronous automaton with edges

$$\mathscr{F} \cup \mathscr{G} \cup (S \times \{1\} \times J).$$

Then $L(\mathscr{C}) = XY$ as we may easily check. □

We shall now give another characterization of recognizable subsets of A^*.

Let M be a monoid. The family of *rational subsets* of M is the smallest family $\mathscr{R}$ of subsets of M such that

(i) any finite subset of M is in $\mathscr{R}$,
(ii) if $X, Y \in \mathscr{R}$, then $X \cup Y \in \mathscr{R}$ and $XY \in \mathscr{R}$,
(iii) if $X \in \mathscr{R}$, then $X^* \in \mathscr{R}$.

THEOREM 4.9 *Let A be a finite alphabet. A subset of A^* is recognizable iff it is rational.*

Proof Denote by $\text{Rec}(A^*)$ the family of recognizable subsets of A^* and by $\text{Rat}(A^*)$ that of rational subsets of A^*. Let us first prove the inclusion $\text{Rat}(A^*) \subset \text{Rec}(A^*)$. In fact, any finite subset X of A^* is clearly recognizable. Moreover, Propositions 4.6 and 4.8 show that the family $\text{Rec}(A^*)$ satisfies conditions (ii) and (iii) of the definition of $\text{Rat}(A^*)$. This proves the inclusion.

To show that $\text{Rec}(A^*) \subset \text{Rat}(A^*)$, let us consider a recognizable subset X of A^*. Let $\mathscr{A} = (Q, I, T)$ be a finite automaton recognizing X. Set $Q = \{1, 2, \ldots, n\}$ and for $1 \le i, j \le n$,

$$X_{i,j} = \{w \in A^* \mid i \xrightarrow{w} j\}.$$

We have

$$X = \bigcup_{i \in I} \bigcup_{j \in T} X_{i,j}.$$

It is therefore enough to prove that each $X_{i,j}$ is rational. For $k \in \{0, 1, \ldots, n\}$, denote by $X_{i,j}^{(k)}$ the set of those $w \in A^*$ such that there exists a path $c: i \xrightarrow{w} j$ passing only through states $l \le k$ except perhaps for i, j. In other words we have $w \in X_{i,j}^{(k)}$ iff $w = a_1 a_2 \cdots a_m$ with

$$c: \quad i \xrightarrow{a_1} i_1 \xrightarrow{a_2} i_2 \longrightarrow \cdots i_{m-1} \xrightarrow{a_m} j$$

and $i_1 \le k, \ldots, i_{m-1} \le k$. We have the formulas

$$X_{i,j}^{(0)} \subset A \cup 1, \tag{4.3}$$

$$X_{i,j}^{(n)} = X_{i,j}, \tag{4.4}$$

$$X_{i,j}^{(k+1)} = X_{i,j}^{(k)} \cup X_{i,k+1}^{(k)}(X_{k+1,k+1}^{(k)})^* X_{k+1,j}^{(k)} \qquad (0 \le k < n). \tag{4.5}$$

Since A is finite, $X_{i,j}^{(0)} \in \mathrm{Rat}(A^*)$ by (4.3). Then (4.5) shows by induction on $k \ge 0$ that $X_{i,j}^{(k)} \in \mathrm{Rat}(A^*)$. Therefore $X_{i,j} \in \mathrm{Rat}(A^*)$ by (4.4). □

5. IDEALS IN A MONOID

Let M be a monoid. A *right ideal* of M is a nonempty subset R of M such that

$$RM \subset R$$

or equivalently such that for all $r \in R$ and all $m \in M$, we have $rm \in R$. Since M is a monoid, we then have $RM = R$ because M contains a neutral element.

A *left ideal* of M is a nonempty subset L of M such that

$$ML \subset L.$$

A *two-sided ideal* (also called an ideal) is a nonempty subset I of M such that

$$MIM \subset I.$$

A two-sided ideal is therefore both a left and a right ideal. In particular, M itself is an ideal of M.

An element 0 of M is a *zero* if $0 \neq 1$ and for all $m \in M$

$$0m = m0 = 0.$$

If M contains a zero it is unique and the set $\{0\}$ is a two-sided ideal which is contained in any ideal of M.

An ideal I (resp., a left, right ideal) is called *minimal* if for any ideal J (resp., left, right ideal)

$$J \subset I \quad \Rightarrow \quad J = I.$$

If M contains a minimal two-sided ideal, it is unique because any nonempty intersection of ideals is again an ideal. If M contains a 0, the set $\{0\}$ is the minimal two-sided ideal of M. An ideal $I \neq 0$ (resp., a left, right ideal) is then called 0-*minimal* if for any ideal J (resp., left, right ideal)

$$J \subset I \quad \Rightarrow \quad J = 0 \qquad \text{or} \qquad J = I.$$

For any $m \in M$, the set

$$R = mM$$

is a right ideal. It is the smallest right ideal containing m. In the same way, the set

$$L = Mm$$

is the smallest left ideal containing m and the set

$$I = MmM$$

is the smallest two-sided ideal containing m.

We now define in a monoid M four equivalence relations $\mathscr{R}$, $\mathscr{L}$, $\mathscr{J}$ and $\mathscr{H}$ as

$$m\mathscr{R}m' \quad \text{iff} \quad mM = m'M,$$

$$m\mathscr{L}m' \quad \text{iff} \quad Mm = Mm',$$

$$m\mathscr{J}m' \quad \text{iff} \quad MmM = Mm'M,$$

$$m\mathscr{H}m' \quad \text{iff} \quad mM = m'M \quad \text{and} \quad Mm = Mm'.$$

Therefore, we have for instance, $m\mathscr{R}m'$ iff there exist $u, u' \in M$ such that

$$m' = mu, \qquad m = m'u'.$$

We have $\mathscr{R} \subset \mathscr{J}$, $\mathscr{L} \subset \mathscr{J}$, and $\mathscr{H} = \mathscr{R} \cap \mathscr{L}$.

PROPOSITION 5.1 *The two equivalence $\mathscr{R}$ and $\mathscr{L}$ commute*:

$$\mathscr{R}\mathscr{L} = \mathscr{L}\mathscr{R}.$$

Proof Let $m, n \in M$ be such that $m\mathscr{R}\mathscr{L}n$. There exists $p \in M$ such that $m\mathscr{R}p$, $p\mathscr{L}n$ (see Fig. 0.5).

There exist by the definitions, $u, u', v, v' \in M$ such that $p = mu$, $m = pu'$, $n = vp$, $p = v'n$.

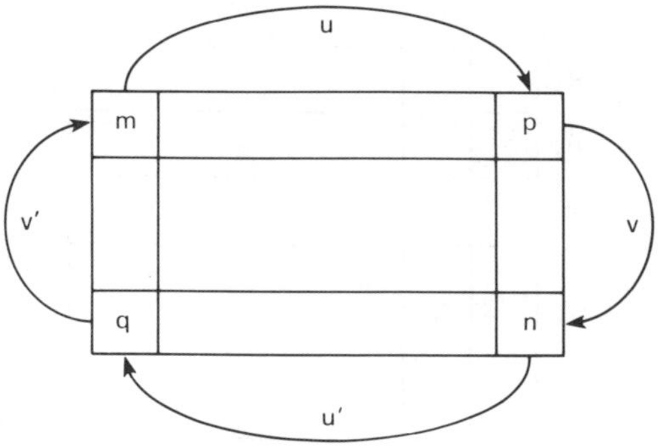

Fig. 0.5 $\mathscr{R}\mathscr{L} = \mathscr{L}\mathscr{R}$.

Set $q = vm$. We then have

$$q = vm = v(pu') = (vp)u' = nu',$$

$$n = vp = v(mu) = (vm)u = qu.$$

This shows that $q\mathscr{R}n$. Furthermore, we have

$$m = pu' = (v'n)u' = v'(nu') = v'q.$$

Since $q = vm$ by the definition of q, we obtain $m\mathscr{L}q$. Therefore $m\mathscr{L}q\mathscr{R}n$ and consequently $m\mathscr{L}\mathscr{R}n$.

This proves the inclusion $\mathscr{R}\mathscr{L} \subset \mathscr{L}\mathscr{R}$. The proof of the converse inclusion is symmetrical. □

Since $\mathscr{R}$ and $\mathscr{L}$ commute, the relation

$$\mathscr{D} = \mathscr{R}\mathscr{L} = \mathscr{L}\mathscr{R}$$

is an equivalence relation. We have the inclusions

$$\mathscr{H} \subset \mathscr{R},\ \mathscr{L} \subset \mathscr{D} \subset \mathscr{J}.$$

The classes of the relation $\mathscr{D}$, called $\mathscr{D}$-classes, can be represented by a schema called an "egg-box" as in Fig. 0.6.

The $\mathscr{R}$-classes are figured by rows and the $\mathscr{L}$-classes by columns. The squares at the intersection of an $\mathscr{R}$-class and an $\mathscr{L}$-class are the $\mathscr{H}$-classes.

We denote by $L(m)$, $R(m)$, $D(m)$, $H(m)$, respectively, the $\mathscr{L}$, $\mathscr{R}$, $\mathscr{D}$, and $\mathscr{H}$ classes of an element $m \in M$. We have

$$H(m) = R(m) \cap L(m) \qquad \text{and} \qquad R(m),\quad L(m) \subset D(m).$$

PROPOSITION 5.2 *Let M be a monoid. Let $m, m' \in M$ be $\mathscr{R}$-equivalent. Let u, $u' \in M$ be such that*

$$m = m'u', \qquad m' = mu.$$

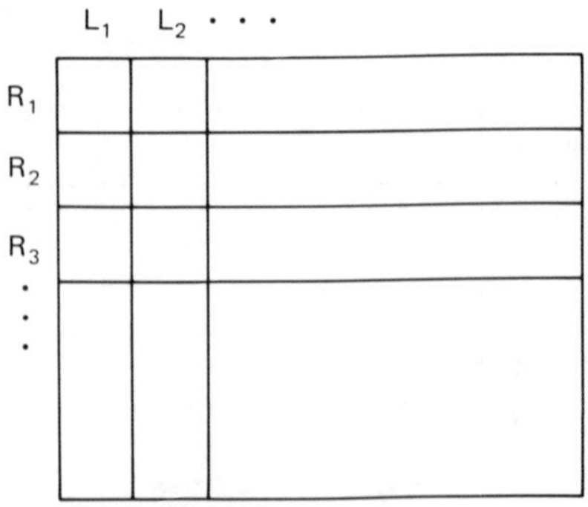

Fig. 0.6 A $\mathscr{D}$-class.

The mappings

$$\rho_u\colon \quad q \to qu, \qquad \rho_{u'}\colon \quad q' \to q'u'$$

are bijections from $L(m)$ *onto* $L(m')$ *inverse to each other. Moreover they preserve* $\mathscr{R}$-classes.

Proof We first verify that ρ_u maps $L(m)$ into $L(m')$. If $q \in L(m)$, then $Mq = Mm$ and therefore $Mqu = Mmu = Mm'$. Hence $qu = \rho_u(q)$ is in $L(m')$. Analogously, $\rho_{u'}$ maps $L(m')$ into $L(m)$.

Let $q \in L(m)$ and compute $\rho_u\rho_{u'}(q)$. Since $q\mathscr{L}m$, there exist $v, v' \in M$ such that $q = vm$, $m = v'q$ (see Fig. 0.7). We have

$$\begin{aligned}\rho_u\rho_{u'}(q) &= quu' = (vm)uu'\\ &= v(mu)u' = vm'u'\\ &= vm = q.\end{aligned}$$

This shows that $\rho_u\rho_{u'}$ is the identity on $L(m)$. We show in the same way that $\rho_u\rho_{u'}$ is the identity on $L(m')$.

Finally, since $quu' = q$ for all $q \in L(m)$, the elements q and $\rho_u(q)$ are in the same $\mathscr{R}$ class. □

Proposition 5.2 has the following consequence which justifies the *regular* shape of Fig. 0.7.

PROPOSITION 5.3 *Any two* $\mathscr{H}$*-classes contained in the same* $\mathscr{D}$*-class have the same cardinality.* □

We now come to the point of locating the idempotents in an ideal. The first result describes the $\mathscr{H}$-class of an idempotent.

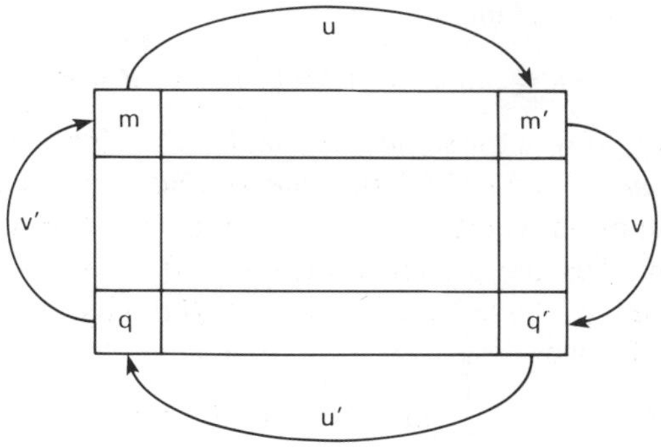

Fig. 0.7 The reciprocal bijections.

PROPOSITION 5.4 *Let M be a monoid and let $e \in M$ be an idempotent. The $\mathscr{H}$-class of e is the group of units of the monoid.*

$$M(e) = eMe.$$

Proof Let $m \in H(e)$. Then, we have for some $u, u', v, v' \in M$

$$e = mu, \qquad m = eu', \qquad e = vm, \qquad m = v'e.$$

Therefore $em = e(eu') = eu' = m$ and in the same way $me = m$. This shows that $m \in M(e)$. Since

$$m(eue) = mue = e, \qquad (eve)m = evm = e.$$

the element m is both right and left invertible in M. Hence, m belongs to the group of units of $M(e)$. Conversely, if $m \in M(e)$ is right and left invertible, we have

$$mu = vm = e$$

for some $u, v \in M(e)$. Since $m = em = me$, we obtain $m\mathscr{H}e$. □

PROPOSITION 5.5 *An $\mathscr{H}$-class of a monoid M is a group iff it contains an idempotent.*

Proof Let H be an $\mathscr{H}$-class of M. If H contains an idempotent e, then $H = H(e)$ is a group by Proposition 5.4. The converse is obvious. □

PROPOSITION 5.6 *Let M be a monoid and $m, n \in M$. Then*

$$mn \in R(m) \cap L(n)$$

iff $R(n) \cap L(m)$ contains an idempotent.

Proof If $R(n) \cap L(m)$ contains an idempotent e, then

$$e = nu, \qquad n = eu', \qquad e = vm, \qquad m = v'e$$

for some $u, u', v, v' \in M$. Hence

$$mnu = m(nu) = me = (v'e)e = v'e = m$$

so that $mn\mathscr{R}m$. We show in the same way that $mn\mathscr{L}n$. Hence $mn \in R(m) \cap L(n)$.

Conversely, if $mn \in R(m) \cap L(n)$, then $mn\mathscr{R}m$ and $n\mathscr{L}mn$. By Proposition 5.2 the multiplication on the right by n is a bijection from $L(m)$ onto $L(mn)$. Since $n \in L(mn)$, this implies the existence of $e \in L(m)$ such that $en = n$. Since n preserves $\mathscr{R}$ classes, we have additionally $e \in R(n)$. Hence there exists $u \in M$ such that $e = nu$. Hence

$$nunu = enu = nu$$

and $e = nu$ is an idempotent in $R(n) \cap L(m)$. □

PROPOSITION 5.7 *Let M be a monoid and let D be a $\mathscr{D}$-class of M. The following conditions are equivalent.*

(i) *D contains an idempotent.*
(ii) *Each $\mathscr{R}$-class of D contains an idempotent.*
(iii) *Each $\mathscr{L}$-class of D contains an idempotent.*

Proof Obviously, only (i) $\Rightarrow$ (ii) requires a proof. Let $e \in D$ be an idempotent. Let R be an $\mathscr{R}$ class of D and let $n \in L(e) \cap R$. (See Fig. 0.8). Since $n\mathscr{L}e$, there exist $v, v' \in M$ such that

$$n = ve, \qquad e = v'n.$$

Let $m = ev'$. Then $mn = e$ because

$$mn = (ev')n = e(v'n) = ee = e.$$

Moreover, we have $m\mathscr{R}e$ since $mn = e$ and $m = ev'$. Therefore, $e = mn$ is in $R(m) \cap L(n)$. This implies, by Proposition 5.6, that R contains an idempotent. □

A $\mathscr{D}$-class D satisfying one of the conditions of Proposition 5.7 is called *regular*.

PROPOSITION 5.8 *Let M be a monoid and let H be an $\mathscr{H}$-class of M. The two following conditions are equivalent.*

(i) *There exist $h, h' \in H$ such that $hh' \in H$.*
(ii) *H is a group.*

Proof (i) $\Rightarrow$ (ii) If $hh' \in H$, then by Proposition 5.6, H contains an idempotent. By Proposition 5.5, it is a group.

(ii) $\Rightarrow$ (i) is obvious. □

We now study the minimal and 0-minimal ideals in a monoid. Recall that if M contains a minimal ideal, it is unique. However, it may contain several 0-minimal ideals.

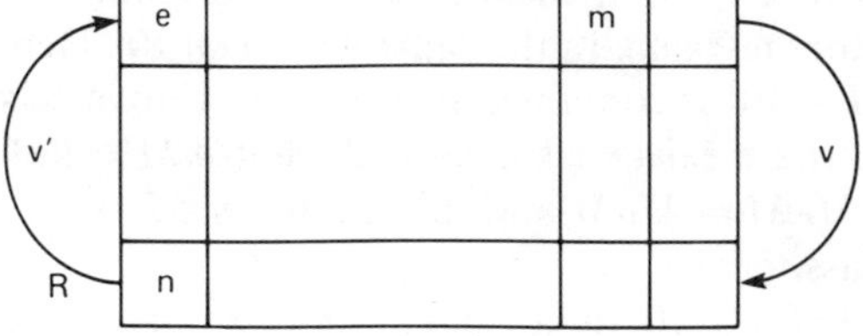

Fig. 0.8 Finding an idempotent in *R*.

Let M be a monoid containing a zero. We say that M is *prime* if for any m, $n \in M - 0$, there exists $u \in M$ such that

$$mun \neq 0.$$

PROPOSITION 5.9 *Let M be a prime monoid.*

1. *If M contains a 0-minimal ideal, it is unique.*
2. *If M contains a 0-minimal right (resp., left) ideal, then M contains a 0-minimal ideal; this ideal is the union of all minimal right (resp. left) ideals of M.*
3. *If M both contains a 0-minimal right ideal and a 0-minimal left ideal, its 0-minimal ideal is composed of a regular $\mathscr{D}$-class and zero.*

Proof

1. Let I, J be two 0-minimal ideals of M. Let $m \in I - 0$ and let $n \in J - 0$. Since M is prime, there exist $u \in M$ such that $mun \neq 0$. Then $mun \in I \cap J$ implies $I \cap J \neq 0$. Since $I \cap J$ is an ideal, we obtain $I \cap J = I = J$.

2. Let R be a 0-minimal right ideal. We first show that for all $m \in M$, either $mR = \{0\}$ or the set mR is a 0-minimal right ideal. In fact, mR is clearly a right ideal. Suppose $mR \neq 0$ and let $R' \neq 0$ be a right ideal contained in mR. Set $S = \{r \in R \mid mr \in R'\}$. Then $R' = mS$ and $S \neq \{0\}$ since $R' \neq \{0\}$. Moreover, S is a right ideal because R' is a right ideal. Since $S \subset R$, the fact that R is a 0-minimal right ideal implies the equality $S = R$. This shows that $mR = R'$ and consequently that mR is a 0-minimal right ideal.

Let I be the union of all the minimal right ideals. It is a right ideal, and by the preceding discussion, it is also a left ideal. Let $J \neq \{0\}$ be an ideal of M. Then for any 0-minimal right ideal R of M,

$$RJ \subset R \cap J \subset R.$$

We have $RJ \neq \{0\}$ since for any $r \in R$ and $m \in J - 0$, there exists $u \in M$ such that $rum \neq 0$ whence $rum \in RJ - \{0\}$. Since R is a 0-minimal right ideal and $R \cap J$ is a right ideal distinct from $\{0\}$, we have $R \cap J = R$. Hence $R \subset J$. This shows that $I \subset J$. Hence I is contained in any nonzero ideal of M and therefore is the 0-minimal ideal of M.

3. Let I be the 0-minimal ideal of M. Let $m, n \in I - \{0\}$. By 2 the right ideal mM and the left ideal Mn are 0-minimal. Since M is prime, there exists $u \in M$ such that $mun \neq 0$. The right ideal mM being 0-minimal, we have $mM = munM$ and therefore $m\mathscr{R}mun$. In the same way, $mun\mathscr{L}n$. Hence we have $m\mathscr{D}n$. This shows that $I - \{0\}$ is contained in a $\mathscr{D}$-class. Conversely, if $m \in I - \{0\}$, $n \in M$ and $m\mathscr{D}n$, there exists a $k \in M$ such that $mM = kM$ and $Mk = Mn$. Hence $MmM = MkM = MnM$ and this implies $n \in I - \{0\}$. This shows that $I - \{0\}$ is a $\mathscr{D}$-class.

Let us show that $I - \{0\}$ is a regular $\mathscr{D}$-class. By Proposition 5.7, it is enough to prove that $I - \{0\}$ contains an idempotent. Let m, $n \in I - \{0\}$.

Since M is prime, there exists $u \in M$ such that $mun \neq 0$. Since the right ideal mM is 0-minimal and since $mun \neq 0$, we have $mM = muM = munM$. Whence $mun \in R(mu)$. Symmetrically, since Mn is a 0-minimal left ideal, we have $Mn = Mun = Mmun$, whence $mun \in L(n)$. Therefore $mun \in R(mu) \cap L(n)$ and by Proposition 5.6, this implies that $R(n) \cap L(mu)$ contains an idempotent. This idempotent belongs to the $\mathscr{D}$ class of m and n and therefore to $I - \{0\}$. □

COROLLARY 5.10 *Let M be a prime monoid. If M contains a 0-minimal right ideal and a 0-minimal left ideal, then M contains a unique 0-minimal ideal I which is the union of all the 0-minimal right (resp., left) ideals. This ideal is composed with a regular $\mathscr{D}$ class and 0. Moreover, we have the following computational rules.*

1. *For $m \in I - \{0\}$ and $n \in M$ such that $mn \neq 0$, we have*

$$m \mathscr{R} mn.$$

2. *For $m \in I - \{0\}$ and $n \in M$ such that $nm \neq 0$, we have*

$$m \mathscr{L} nm.$$

3. *For any $\mathscr{H}$ class $H \subset I - \{0\}$ we have*

$$H^2 = H \qquad \text{or} \qquad H^2 = \{0\}.$$

Proof The first group of statements is an easy consequence of Proposition 5.9. Let us prove 1. We have $mnM \subset mM$. Since mM is a 0-minimal right ideal and $mn \neq 0$, this forces the equality $mnM = mM$. The proof of 2 is symmetrical. Finally, to prove 3, let us suppose $H^2 \neq \{0\}$. Let $h, h' \in H$ be such that $hh' \neq 0$. Then, by 1 and 2, $h \mathscr{R} hh'$ and $h' \mathscr{L} hh'$. Since $h \mathscr{L} h'$ and $h' \mathscr{L} hh'$, we have $h \mathscr{L} hh'$. Therefore $hh' \in H$ and H is a group by Proposition 5.8. □

We finally give the statements corresponding to Proposition 5.9 and Corollary 5.10 for minimal ideals instead of 0-minimal ideals. This is of course of interest only in the case where the monoid does not have a zero.

PROPOSITION 5.11 *Let M be a monoid.*

1. *If M contains a minimal right (resp., left) ideal, then M contains a minimal ideal which is the union of all the minimal right (resp., left) ideals.*
2. *If M contains a minimal right ideal and a minimal left ideal, its minimal ideal I is a $\mathscr{D}$-class. All the $\mathscr{H}$-classes in I are groups.*

Proof Let 0 be an element that does not belong to M and let

$$M_0 = M \cup 0$$

be the monoid whose law extends that of M in such a way that 0 is a zero. The monoid M_0 is prime.

An ideal I (resp., a right ideal R, a left ideal L) of M is minimal iff $I \cup \{0\}$ (resp., $R \cup \{0\}$, $L \cup \{0\}$) is a 0-minimal ideal (resp., right ideal, left ideal) of M_0. Moreover the restriction to M of the relations $\mathcal{R}, \mathcal{L}, \mathcal{D}, \mathcal{H}$ in M_0 coincide with the corresponding relations in M. Therefore statements 1 and 2 can be deduced from Proposition 5.9 and Corollary 5.10. □

COROLLARY 5.12 *Let M be a monoid containing a minimal right ideal and a minimal left ideal. Then M contains a minimal ideal which is the union of all the minimal right (resp., left) ideals. This ideal is a $\mathcal{D}$ class and all its $\mathcal{H}$ classes are groups.* □

6. SEMIRINGS AND MATRICES

A *semiring* K is a set equipped with two operations denoted $+$ and $\cdot$ satisfying the following axioms:

(i) The set K is a commutative monoid for $+$ with a neutral element denoted 0.

(ii) The set K is a monoid for multiplication $\cdot$ with a neutral element denoted by 1.

(iii) Multiplication is distributive on addition.

(iv) For all $x \in K$, $0 \cdot x = x \cdot 0 = 0$.

Clearly, any ring with unit is a semiring. Other examples of semirings are as follows.

The boolean semiring $\mathcal{B}$ is composed of two elements 0 and 1. The axioms imply

$$0 + 0 = 0, \qquad 0 + 1 = 1 + 0 = 1,$$

$$0 \cdot 1 = 1 \cdot 0 = 0 \cdot 0 = 0, \qquad 1 \cdot 1 = 1.$$

The semiring $\mathcal{B}$ is specified by

$$1 + 1 = 1.$$

The other possibility, viz., $1 + 1 = 0$, defines the field $\mathbb{Z}/2\mathbb{Z}$. $\mathbb{N}$ is the semiring of natural integers and $\mathbb{R}_+$ is the semiring of nonnegative real numbers.

For any monoid M, the set $\mathfrak{P}(M)$ is a semiring for the operations of union and set product.

A semiring K is called *ordered* if it is given with a partial order $\leq$ satisfying the following properties:

(i) 0 is the smallest element of K;

(ii) the following implications hold:

$$x \leq y \quad \Rightarrow \quad x + z \leq y + z,$$

$$x \leq y \quad \Rightarrow \quad xz \leq yz, \quad zx \leq zy.$$

The semirings $\mathscr{B}$, $\mathbb{N}$, $\mathbb{R}_+$, are ordered by the usual ordering.

$$x \leq y \quad \Leftrightarrow \quad x = y + z.$$

An ordered semiring is said to be *complete* if any subset X of K admits a least upper bound in K. It is the unique element k of K such that

(i) $x \in X \Rightarrow x \leq k$,
(ii) if $x \leq k'$ for all $x \in X$, then $k \leq k'$.

We denote $k = \sup(X)$ or $k = \sup\{x \mid x \in X\}$ or $k = \sup_{x \in X}(x)$. Semiring $\mathscr{B}$ is complete. Semirings $\mathbb{N}$, $\mathbb{R}_+$ are not complete. They may be completed according to the following general procedure:

Let K be an ordered semiring whose order is total. Let

$$\mathscr{K} = K \cup \infty,$$

where $\infty \notin K$. The operations of K are extended to $\mathscr{K}$ by setting for $x \in K$,

(i) $x + \infty = \infty + x = \infty$,
(ii) if $x \neq 0$; then $x\infty = \infty x = \infty$,
(iii) $\infty\infty = \infty, 0\infty = \infty 0 = 0$.

Extending the order of K to $\mathscr{K}$ by $x \leq \infty$ for all $x \in K$, the set $\mathscr{K}$ becomes a totally ordered semiring. It is a complete semiring because any subset has an upper bound and therefore also a least upper bound. We define

$$\mathscr{N} = \mathbb{N} \cup \infty, \qquad \mathscr{R}_+ = \mathbb{R}_+ \cup \infty$$

to be the complete semirings obtained by applying this construction to $\mathbb{N}$ and $\mathbb{R}_+$. If $\mathscr{K}$ is a complete semiring, the sum of an infinite family $(x_i)_{i \in I}$ of elements of $\mathscr{K}$ is defined by

$$\sum_{i \in I} x_i = \sup\left\{\sum_{j \in J} x_j \mid J \subset I,\ J \text{ finite}\right\}. \tag{6.1}$$

In the case of semiring $\mathscr{R}_+$, this gives the usual notion of a summable family: A family $(x_i)_{i \in I}$ of elements in $\mathbb{R}_+$ is summable if sum (6.1) is finite.

In particular, for a sequence $(x_n)_{n \geq 0}$ of elements of a complete semiring, we have

$$\sum_{n \geq 0} x_n = \sup_{n \geq 0}\left\{\sum_{i \leq n} x_i\right\} \tag{6.2}$$

since any finite subset of $\mathbb{N}$ is contained in some interval $\{0, 1, \ldots, n\}$. Moreover, if $I = \bigcup_{j \in J} I_j$ is a partition of I, then

$$\sum_{i \in I} x_i = \sum_{j \in J}\left(\sum_{i \in I_j} x_i\right). \tag{6.3}$$

Consider, for instance, a mapping $\pi: A^* \to \mathbb{R}_+$. Let X be a subset of A^* and let

$$X_n = \{x \in X \mid |x| \leq n\}.$$

Then

$$\sum_{x \in X} \pi(x) = \sup_{n \geq 0} \left\{ \sum_{x \in X_n} \pi(x) \right\}.$$

Formulas (6.1)–(6.3) lead to results of the following kind:

PROPOSITION 6.1 *Let $(a_n)_{n \geq 0}$ be a sequence of elements of $\mathbb{R}_+$. Let, for $r \in \mathbb{R}_+$,*

$$a(r) = \sum_{n \geq 0} a_n r^n.$$

If $a(r) < \infty$ for $r \in [0, 1[$, then

$$\sup\{a(r) \mid r \in [0, 1[\} = a(1).$$

Proof The mapping $a: r \mapsto a(r)$ from $\mathbb{R}_+$ into $\mathbb{R}_+$ is nondecreasing. By successive applications of (6.2), (6.3), and then (6.2), we have

$$\begin{aligned}
\sup\{a(r) \mid r \in [0, 1[\} &= \sup_{r \in [0,1[} \left(\sup_{n \geq 0} \sum_{i \leq n} a_i r^i \right) \\
&= \sup_{n \geq 0} \left(\sup_{r \in [0,1[} \sum_{i \leq n} a_i r^i \right) \\
&= \sup_{n \geq 0} \left(\sum_{i \leq n} a_i \right) \\
&= \sum_{n \geq 0} a_n = a(1). \quad \square
\end{aligned}$$

Let P, Q be two sets and let K be a semiring. A $P \times Q$-*matrix* with coefficients in K is a mapping

$$m: \quad P \times Q \to K.$$

We denote indistinctly by

$$(p, m, q) \qquad \text{or} \qquad m_{p,q}$$

the value of m on $(p, q) \in P \times Q$. We also say that m is a K-*relation* between P and Q. If $P = Q$, we say that it is a K-relation *over* Q. The set of all K-relations between P and Q is denoted by $K^{P \times Q}$.

Let $m \in K^{P \times Q}$ be a K-relation between P and Q. For $p \in P$, the *row* of index p of m is denoted by m_{p*}. It is the element of K^Q defined by

$$(m_{p*})_q = m_{pq}.$$

Similarly, the *column* of index q, of m is denoted by m_{*q}. It is an element of K^P. Let P, Q, R be three sets and let K be a complete semiring. For $m \in K^{P \times Q}$ and $n \in K^{Q \times R}$, the product mn is defined as the following element of $K^{P \times R}$. Its value on $(p, r) \in P \times R$ is

$$(mn)_{p,r} = \sum_{q \in Q} m_{p,q} n_{q,r}.$$

When $P = Q = R$, we thus obtain an associative multiplication which turns $K^{Q \times Q}$ into a monoid. Its identity is denoted I_Q.

A *monoid* of K-*relations* over Q is a submonoid of $K^{Q \times Q}$. It contains in particular the identity I_Q.

7. FORMAL SERIES

Let A be an alphabet and let K be a semiring. A *formal series* (or just *series*) over A with coefficients in K is a mapping

$$\sigma\colon \quad A^* \to K.$$

The value of σ on $w \in A^*$ is denoted (σ, w). We indifferently denote by

$$K^{A^*} \qquad \text{or} \qquad K\langle\langle A \rangle\rangle$$

the set of formal series over A. We denote by $K\langle A \rangle$ the set of formal series $\sigma \in K\langle\langle A \rangle\rangle$ such that $(\sigma, w) = 0$ for all but a finite number of $w \in A^*$. An element of $K\langle A \rangle$ is called a *polynomial.* A series $\sigma \in K\langle\langle A \rangle\rangle$ can be extended to a linear function from $K\langle A \rangle$ into K by linearity. For $p \in K\langle A \rangle$,

$$(\sigma, p) = \sum_{w \in A^*} (\sigma, w)(p, w).$$

This definition makes sense because p is a polynomial. Let $\sigma, \tau \in K\langle\langle A \rangle\rangle$ and $k \in K$. We define the formal series $\sigma + \tau$, $\sigma\tau$, and $k\sigma$ by

$$(\sigma + \tau, w) = (\sigma, w) + (\tau, w), \tag{7.1}$$

$$(\sigma\tau, w) = \sum_{uv = w} (\sigma, u)(\tau, v), \tag{7.2}$$

$$(k\sigma, w) = k(\sigma, w). \tag{7.3}$$

In (7.2), the sum runs over the $1 + |w|$ pairs (u, v) such that $w = uv$. It is therefore a finite sum. The set $K\langle\langle A \rangle\rangle$ contains two special elements denoted 0 and 1 defined by

$$(0, w) = 0, \qquad (1, w) = \begin{cases} 1 & \text{if } w = 1, \\ 0 & \text{else.} \end{cases}$$

As usual, we denote $\sigma^n = \sigma\sigma \cdots \sigma$ (n times) and $\sigma^0 = 1$. With the operations defined by (7.1) and (7.2) the set $K\langle\langle A\rangle\rangle$ is a semiring. It may be verified that when K is complete $K\langle\langle A\rangle\rangle$ is also complete.

The *support* of a series $\sigma \in K\langle\langle A\rangle\rangle$ is the set

$$\operatorname{supp}(\sigma) = \{w \in A^* \mid (\sigma, w) \neq 0\}.$$

The mapping $\sigma \mapsto \operatorname{supp}(\sigma)$ is an isomorphism from $\mathscr{B}\langle\langle A\rangle\rangle$ onto $\mathfrak{P}(A^*)$.

A family $(\sigma_i)_{i\in I}$ of series is said to be *locally finite* if for all $w \in A^*$, the set

$$\{i \in I \mid (\sigma_i, w) \neq 0\}$$

is finite. In this case, a series σ denoted

$$\sigma = \sum_{i\in I} \sigma_i$$

can be defined by

$$(\sigma, w) = \sum_{i\in I} (\sigma_i, w). \tag{7.4}$$

This notation makes sense because in the sum (7.4) all but a finite number of terms are different from 0. We easily check that for a locally finite family $(\sigma_i)_{i\in I}$,

$$\tau\left(\sum_{i\in I} \sigma_i\right) = \sum_{i\in I} \tau\sigma_i.$$

Let $\sigma \in K\langle\langle A\rangle\rangle$ be a series such that

$$(\sigma, 1) = 0.$$

Then the family $(\sigma^n)_{n\geq 0}$ is locally finite. In fact, the support of σ^n does not contain words of length less than n. We denote

$$\sigma^* = \sum_{n\geq 0} \sigma^n, \qquad \sigma^+ = \sum_{n\geq 1} \sigma^n.$$

Then

$$\sigma^* = 1 + \sigma^+, \qquad \sigma^*\sigma = \sigma\sigma^* = \sigma^+.$$

PROPOSITION 7.1 *Let K be a ring with unit and let $\sigma \in K\langle\langle A\rangle\rangle$ be a series such that $(\sigma, 1) = 0$. Then $1 - \sigma$ is invertible and*

$$\sigma^* = (1 - \sigma)^{-1}. \tag{7.5}$$

Proof We have

$$1 = \sigma^* - \sigma^+ = \sigma^* - \sigma^*\sigma = \sigma^*(1 - \sigma).$$

Symmetrically, $1 = (1 - \sigma)\sigma^*$, hence the result. □

For $X \subset A^*$, we denote by $\underline{X}$ the *characteristic series* of X defined by

$$(\underline{X}, x) = \begin{cases} 1 & \text{if} \quad x \in X, \\ 0 & \text{else.} \end{cases}$$

We consider the characteristic series $\underline{X}$ of X as an element of $\mathbb{N}\langle\langle A \rangle\rangle$. When $X = \{x\}$ we usually write x instead of $\underline{x}$. In particular, since the family $(x)_{x \in X}$ is locally finite, we have $\underline{X} = \sum_{x \in X} x$. More generally, we have for any series $\sigma \in K\langle\langle A \rangle\rangle$,

$$\sigma = \sum_{w \in A^*} (\sigma, w) w.$$

PROPOSITION 7.2 *Let X, $Y \subset A^*$. Then*

$$(\underline{X} + \underline{Y}, w) = \begin{cases} 0 & \textit{if} \quad w \notin X \cup Y, \\ 1 & \textit{if} \quad w \in (X - Y) \cup (Y - X), \\ 2 & \textit{if} \quad w \in X \cap Y. \end{cases}$$

In particular, with $Z = X \cup Y$,

$$\underline{X} + \underline{Y} = \underline{Z} \qquad \textit{iff} \quad X \cap Y = \varnothing. \quad \square$$

Given two sets X, $Y \subset A^*$, the product XY is said to be *unambiguous* if any word $w \in XY$ has only one factorization $w = xy$ with $x \in X$, $y \in Y$.

PROPOSITION 7.3 *Let X, $Y \subset A^*$. Then*

$$(\underline{X}\,\underline{Y}, w) = \operatorname{Card}\{(x, y) \in X \times Y \mid w = xy\}.$$

In particular, with $Z = XY$,

$$\underline{Z} = \underline{X}\,\underline{Y}$$

iff the product XY is unambiguous. $\square$

The following proposition approaches very closely the main subject of this book.

PROPOSITION 7.4 *For $X \subset A^+$, we have*

$$((\underline{X})^*, w) = \operatorname{Card}\{(x_1, \ldots, x_n) \mid n \geq 0,\, x_i \in X,\, w = x_1 x_2 \cdots x_n\}. \tag{7.6}$$

Proof By the definition of $(\underline{X})^*$ we have

$$((\underline{X})^*, w) = \sum_{k \geq 0} ((\underline{X})^k, w).$$

Applying Proposition 7.2, we obtain

$$((\underline{X})^k, w) = \operatorname{Card}\{(x_1, x_2, \ldots, x_k) \mid x_i \in X,\, w = w_1 x_2 \cdots x_k\},$$

whence formula (7.6). $\square$

EXAMPLE 7.1 $\underline{A}^* = (1 - \underline{A})^{-1} = \sum_{w \in A^*} w$ and $(\underline{A}^*\underline{A}^*, w) = 1 + |w|$.

We now define the *Hadamard product* of two series σ, $\tau \in K\langle\langle A \rangle\rangle$ as the series $\sigma \odot \tau$ given by

$$(\sigma \odot \tau, w) = (\sigma, w)(\tau, w).$$

This product is distributive over addition, viz.

$$\sigma \odot (\tau + \tau') = \sigma \odot \tau + \sigma \odot \tau'.$$

If the semiring K satisfies $xy = 0 \Rightarrow x = 0$ or $y = 0$, then

$$\mathrm{supp}(\sigma \odot \tau) = \mathrm{supp}(\sigma) \cap \mathrm{supp}(\tau)$$

In particular, for X, $Y \subset A^*$ and $Z = X \cap Y$,

$$\underline{Z} = \underline{X} \odot \underline{Y}.$$

Given two series σ, $\tau \in \mathbb{Z}\langle\langle A \rangle\rangle$ we write $\sigma \leq \tau$ when $(\sigma, w) \leq (\tau, w)$ for all $w \in A^*$.

8. PERMUTATION GROUPS

In this section we give some elementary results and definitions on permutation groups. Let G be a group and let H be a subgroup of G. The *right cosets* of H in G are the sets Hg for $g \in G$. The equality $Hg = Hg'$ holds iff $gg'^{-1} \in H$. Hence the right cosets of H in G are a partition of G.

When G is finite. $[G:H]$ denotes the index of H in G. This number is both equal to $\mathrm{Card}(G)/\mathrm{Card}(H)$ and to the number of right cosets of H in G.

Let Q be a set. The *symmetric group* over Q composed of all the permutations of Q is denoted by $\mathfrak{S}_Q$. For $Q = \{1, 2, \ldots, n\}$ we write $\mathfrak{S}_n$ instead of $\mathfrak{S}_{\{1,2,\ldots,n\}}$. A permutation is written to the right of its argument. Thus for $g \in \mathfrak{S}_Q$ and $q \in Q$ the image of q by g is denoted by qg.

A *permutation group* over Q is any subgroup of $\mathfrak{S}_Q$. For instance, the *alternating group* over $\{1, 2, \ldots, n\}$, denoted by $\mathfrak{A}_n$, is the permutation group composed of all even permutations.

Let G be a permutation group over Q. The *stabilizer of* $q \in Q$ is the subgroup of G composed of all permutations of G fixing q,

$$H = \{h \in G \mid qh = q\}.$$

A *permutation group* over Q is any subgroup of $\mathfrak{S}_Q$. For instance, the exists $g \in G$ such that $pg = q$.

PROPOSITION 8.1

1. *Let G be a group and let H be a subgroup of G. Let Q be the set of right cosets of H in G.*

$$Q = \{Hg \mid g \in G\}.$$

Let φ be the mapping from G into $\mathfrak{S}_Q$ defined for $g \in G$ and $Hk \in Q$ by

$$(Hk)\,\varphi(g) = H(kg).$$

The mapping φ is a morphism from G into $\mathfrak{S}_Q$ and the permutation group $\varphi(G)$ is transitive. Moreover, the subgroup $\varphi(H)$ is the stabilizer of the point $H \in Q$.

2. *Conversely, let G be a transitive permutation group over Q, let $q \in Q$ and let H be the stabilizer of q.*

The mapping γ from G into Q defined by

$$\gamma\colon\ g \mapsto qg$$

induces a bijection α from the set of right cosets of H onto Q and for all $k \in G$, $g \in G$,

$$\alpha(Hk)\,g = \alpha(Hkg).$$

Proof

1. The mapping φ is well defined because $Hk = Hk'$ implies $Hkg = Hk'g$. It is a morphism since $\varphi(1) = 1$ and

$$(Hk)\varphi(g)\varphi(g') = (Hkg)\varphi(g') = Hkgg' = (Hk)\varphi(gg').$$

The permutation group $\varphi(G)$ is transitive since for $k,k' \in G$, we have $(Hk)\varphi(k^{-1}k') = Hk'$. Finally, for all $h \in H$, $\varphi(h)$ fixes the coset H and conversely, if $\varphi(g)$ $(g \in G)$ fixes H, then $Hg = H$ and thus $g \in H$.

2. Assume that $Hg = Hg'$. Then $gg'^{-1} \in H$, thus $qgg'^{-1} = q$, showing that $qg = qg'$. Thus $\gamma(g) = \gamma(g')$. This shows that we can define a function α by setting $\alpha(Hg) = \gamma(g)$. Since G is transitive, γ is surjective and therefore also α is surjective. To show that α is injective, assume that $\alpha(Hg) = \alpha(Hg')$. Then $qg = qg'$, whence $qgg'^{-1} = q$. Thus gg'^{-1} fixes q. Consequently $gg'^{-1} \in H$, whence $Hg = Hg'$.

The last formula is a direct consequence of the fact that both sides are equal to qkg. □

Let G be a transitive permutation group over a finite set Q. By definition, the *degree of* G is the number $\operatorname{Card}(Q)$.

PROPOSITION 8.2 *Let G be a transitive permutation group over a finite set Q. Let $q \in Q$ and let H be the stabilizer of q. The degree of G is equal to the index of H in G.*

Proof The function $\alpha\colon Hg \mapsto qg$ of Proposition 8.1(2) is a bijection from the set of right cosets of H onto Q. Consequently $\operatorname{Card}(Q) = [G : H]$. □

Two permutation groups G over Q and G' over Q' are called *equivalent* if there exists a bijection α from Q onto Q' and an isomorphism φ from G onto G' such that for all $q \in Q$ and $g \in G$,

$$\alpha(qg) = \alpha(q)\varphi(g)$$

or equivalently, for $q' \in Q'$ and $g \in G$,

$$q'\varphi(g) = \alpha((\alpha^{-1}(q'))g).$$

As an example, consider a permutation group G over Q and let H be the stabilizer of some q in Q. According to Proposition 8.1(2) this group is equivalent to the permutation group over the set of right cosets of H obtained by the action of G on the cosets of H.

Another example concerns any two stabilizers H and H' of two points q and q' in a transitive permutation group G over Q. Then H and H' are equivalent. Indeed, since G is transitive, there exists $g \in G$ such that $qg = q'$. Then g defines a bijection α from Q onto itself by $\alpha(p) = pg$. The function $\varphi: H \to H'$ given by $\varphi(h) = g^{-1} hg$ is an isomorphism and for all $p \in Q$, $h \in H$,

$$\alpha(ph) = \alpha(p)\, \varphi(h).$$

Let G be a transitive permutation group over Q. An *imprimitivity equivalence* of G is an equivalence relation θ over Q that is stable for the action of G, i.e., such that for all $g \in G$,

$$p \equiv q \mod \theta \quad \Rightarrow \quad pg \equiv qg \mod \theta$$

The partition associated with an imprimitivity equivalence is called an *imprimitivity partition.*

Let θ be an imprimitivity equivalence of G. The action of G on the classes of θ defines a transitive permutation group denoted by G_θ called the *imprimitivity quotient* of G for θ.

For any element q in Q, denote by $[q]$ the equivalence class of $q \bmod \theta$, and let K_q be the transitive permutation group over $[q]$ formed by the restrictions to $[q]$ of the permutations g that globally fix $[q]$, i.e., such that $[q]g = [q]$. The group K_q is the group induced by G on the class $[q]$.

We prove that the groups K_q, $q \in Q$ all are equivalent. Indeed let $q,q' \in Q$ and $g \in G$ be such that $qg = q'$. The restriction α of g to $[q]$ is a bijection from $[q]$ onto $[q']$. Clearly, α is injective. It is surjective since if $p \equiv q' \bmod \theta$, then $pg^{-1} \equiv q \bmod \theta$ and $\alpha(pg^{-1}) = p$. Let φ be the isomorphism from K_q onto $K_{q'}$ defined for $k \in K_q$ by $p'\varphi(k) = \alpha(\alpha^{-1}(p')k)$. This shows that the groups K_q and $K_{q'}$ are equivalent. In particular, all equivalence classes mod θ have the same number of elements.

Any of the equivalent groups K_q are called the *induced groups* of G on the classes of θ and are denoted by G^θ.

Let $d = \operatorname{Card} Q$ be the degree of G, e the degree of G_θ, and f the degree of G^θ. Then

$$d = ef.$$

Indeed, e is the number of classes of θ and f is the common cardinality of each of the classes mod θ.

Let G be a transitive permutation group over Q. Then G is called *primitive* if the only imprimitivity equivalences of G are the equality relation and the universal relation over Q.

PROPOSITION 8.3 *Let G be a transitive permutation group over Q. Let $q \in Q$ and H be the stabilizer of q. Then G is primitive iff H is a maximal subgroup of G.*

Proof Assume first that G is primitive. Let K be a subgroup of G such that $H \subset K \subset G$. Consider the family of subsets of Q having the form qKg for $g \in G$. Any two of these subsets are either disjoint or identical. Suppose indeed that for some $k, k' \in K$ and $g, g' \in G$, we have $qkf = qk'g'$. Then $qkg\,g'^{-1}k'^{-1} = q$, showing that $kgg'^{-1}k'^{-1} \in H \subset K$. Thus $gg'^{-1} \in K$, whence $Kg = Kg'$ and consequently $qKg = qKg'$. Thus the sets qKg form a partition of Q which is clearly an imprimitivity partition. Since G is primitive this implies that either $qK = \{q\}$ or $qK = Q$. The first case means that $K = H$. In the second case, $K = G$ since for any $g \in G$ there is some $k \in K$ with $qk = qg$ showing that $gk^{-1} \in H \subset K$ which implies $g \in K$. This proves that H is a maximal subgroup.

Conversely, let H be a maximal subgroup of G and let θ be an imprimitivity equivalence of G. Let K be the subgroup

$$K = \{k \in G \mid qk \equiv q \bmod \theta\}.$$

Then $H \subset K \subset G$, which implies that $K = H$ or $K = G$. If $K = H$, then the class of q is reduced to q and θ is therefore reduced to the equality relation. If $K = G$, then the class of q is equal to Q and θ is the universal equivalence. Thus G is primitive. □

Let G be a transitive permutation group on Q. Then G is said to be *regular* if all elements of $G - \{1\}$ have no fixed point. It is easily verified that in this case $\mathrm{Card}(G) = \mathrm{Card}(Q)$.

PROPOSITION 8.4 *Let G be a transitive permutation group over Q and let $q \in Q$. The group G is regular iff the stabilizer of q is a singleton.* □

Let $k \geq 1$ be an integer. A permutation group G over Q is called *k-fold transitive* (or k-transitive) if for all k-tuples $(p_1, p_2, \ldots, p_k) \in Q^k$ and $(q_1, q_2, \ldots, q_k) \in Q^k$ composed of distinct elements, there is a $g \in G$ such that $p_1 g = q_1, p_2 g = q_2, \ldots, p_k g = q_k$.

The 1-transitive groups are just the transitive groups. Any k-transitive group for $k \geq 2$ is clearly also $(k - 1)$ transitive. The group $\mathfrak{S}_n$ is n-fold transitive.

PROPOSITION 8.5 *Let $k \geq 2$ be an integer. A permutation group G over Q is k-transitive iff G is transitive and if the restriction to the set $Q - \{q\}$ of the stabilizer of $q \in Q$ is $(k - 1)$-transitive.*

Proof The condition is clearly necessary. Conversely assume that the condition is satisfied and let $(p_1, p_2, \ldots, p_k) \in Q^k$, and $(q_1, q_2, \ldots, q_k) \in Q^k$ be k-tuples composed of distinct elements. Since G is transitive, there exists a $g \in G$ such that $p_1 g = q_1$. Let H be the stabilizer of q_1. Since the restriction of H to the set $Q - \{q_1\}$ is $(k-1)$-fold transitive, there is an $h \in H$ such that $p_2 gh = q_2, \ldots, p_k gh = q_k$. Since $p_1 gh = q_1$, the permutation $g' = gh$ satisfies $p_1 g' = q_1, \ldots, p_k g' = q_k$. This shows that G is k transitive. □

A 2-transitive group is also called *doubly transitive*.

PROPOSITION 8.6 *A doubly transitive permutation group is primitive.*

Proof Let G be a doubly transitive permutation group over Q and consider an imprimitivity equivalence θ on G. If θ is not the equality on Q, then there are two distinct elements $q, q' \in Q$ such that $q \equiv q' \bmod \theta$. Let $q'' \in Q$ be distinct from q. Since G is 2-fold transitive, there exist $g \in G$ such that $qg = q$ and $q'g = q''$. Since θ is an imprimitivity equivalence we have $q \equiv q'' \bmod \theta$. Thus θ is the universal relation on Q. This shows that G is primitive. □

The converse of Proposition 8.6 is false. Indeed, for any prime number p, the cyclic group generated by the permutation $(12 \cdots p)$ is primitive but is not doubly transitive. An interesting case where the converse of Proposition 8.6 is true is described in a famous theorem of Schur that will be stated in Chapter 5.

NOTES

Each of the subjects treated in this chapter is part of a theory that we have considered only very superficially. A more complete exposition about words can be found in Lothaire (1983). For automata (Sect. 4) we follow the notation of Eilenberg (1974). Theorem 4.9 is due to S. Kleene. Our presentation of ideals in monoids (Sect. 5) is developed with more detail in Clifford and Preston (1961) or Lallement (1979). The notion of a prime monoid is not classical but it is well fitted to the situation that we shall find in Chapter IV. The 0-minimal ideals of prime monoids are usually called completely 0-simple semigroups. For semirings and formal series see Eilenberg (1974) or Berstel and Reutenauer (1984). Our definition of a complete semiring is less general than that of Eilenberg (1974) but it will be enough for our purposes. A classical textbook on permutation groups is Wielandt (1964).

CHAPTER I

Codes

0. INTRODUCTION

The definitions and some important general properties of codes are presented in this chapter. The first two sections contain several equivalent definitions of codes and free submonoids. In Section 3 we give a method for verifying that a given set of words is a code. A more appropriate framework to answer this question will be given in Chapter IV where automata with multiplicities will be considered.

In Section 4 we introduce the notion of a Bernoulli distribution over an alphabet. This allows us to give a necessary condition for a set to be a code (Theorem 4.2). The questions about probabilities raised in this and in the following section will be developed in more depth in Chapter VI.

Section 5 introduces the concept of a complete set. This is in some sense a notion dual to that of a code. The main result of this chapter (Theorem 5.10) describes complete codes by using results on Bernoulli distributions developed previously. In the last section the operation of composition of codes is introduced and several properties of this operation are established.

1. DEFINITIONS

This section contains the definitions of the notions of code, prefix (suffix, biprefix) code, maximal code, and coding morphism and gives examples.

Let A be an alphabet. A subset X of the free monoid A^* is a *code* over A if for all $n, m \geq 1$ and $x_1, \ldots, x_n, x'_1, \ldots, x'_m \in X$, the condition

$$x_1 x_2 \cdots x_n = x'_1 x'_2 \cdots x'_m \tag{1.1}$$

implies

$$n = m \quad \text{and} \quad x_i = x'_i \quad \text{for} \quad i = 1, \ldots, n. \tag{1.2}$$

In other words, a set X is a code if any word in X^+ can be written *uniquely* as a product of words in X, that is, has a unique factorization in words in X. Since $1.1 = 1$, a code never contains the empty word 1. It is clear that any subset of a code is a code. In particular, the empty set is a code.

The definition of a code can be rephrased as follows:

PROPOSITION 1.1 *If a subset X of A^* is a code, then any morphism β: $B^* \to A^*$ which induces a bijection of some alphabet B onto X is injective. Conversely, if there exists an injective morphism β: $B^* \to A^*$ such that $X = \beta(B)$, then X is a code.*

Proof Let β: $B^* \to A^*$ be a morphism such that β is a bijection of B onto X. Let $u, v \in B^*$ be words such that $\beta(u) = \beta(v)$. If $u = 1$, then $v = 1$; indeed, $\beta(b) \neq 1$ for each letter $b \in B$ since X is a code. If $u \neq 1$ and $v \neq 1$, set $u = b_1 \cdots b_n, v = b'_1 \cdots b'_m$, with $n, m \geq 1, b_1, \ldots, b_n, b'_1, \ldots, b'_m \in B$. Since β is a morphism, we have

$$\beta(b_1) \cdots \beta(b_n) = \beta(b'_1) \cdots \beta(b'_m).$$

But X is a code and $\beta(b_i), \beta(b'_j) \in X$. Thus $n = m$ and $\beta(b_i) = \beta(b'_i)$ for $i = 1, \ldots, n$. Now β is injective on B. Thus $b_i = b'_i$ for $i = 1, \ldots, n$, and $u = v$. This shows that β is injective.

Conversely, if β: $B^* \to A^*$ is an injective morphism, and if

$$x_1 \cdots x_n = x'_1 \cdots x'_m \tag{1.3}$$

for some $n, m \geq 1$, $x_1, \ldots, x_n$, $x'_1, \ldots, x'_m \in X = \beta(B)$, then we consider the letters b_i, b'_j in B such that $\beta(b_i) = x_i, \beta(b'_j) = x'_j, i = 1, \ldots, n, j = 1, \ldots, m$. Since β is injective, Eq. (1.3) implies that $b_1 \cdots b_n = b'_1 \cdots b'_m$. Thus $n = m$ and $b_i = b'_i$, whence $x_i = x'_i$ for $i = 1, \ldots, n$. □

A morphism β: $B^* \to A^*$ which is injective and such that $X = \beta(B)$, is called a *coding morphism for X*. For any code $X \subset A^*$, the existence of a coding morphism for X is straightforward: it suffices to take any bijection of a set B onto X and to extend it to a morphism from B^* into A^*.

Proposition 1.1 is the origin for the terminology since the words in X encode the letters of the set B. The coding procedure consists of associating to a word $b_1 b_2 \cdots b_n (b_i \in B)$ which is the text in plain language an encoded or enciphered message $\beta(b_1) \cdots \beta(b_n)$ by the use of the coding morphism β. The fact that β is injective ensures that the coded text can be deciphered in a unique way to get back the original text.

EXAMPLE 1.1 For any alphabet A, the set $X = A$ is a code. More generally, if $p \geq 1$ is an integer, then $X = A^p$ is a code called the *uniform code* of words of length p. Indeed, if elements of X satisfy Eq. (1.1), then the constant length of words in X implies the conclusion (1.2).

EXAMPLE 1.2 Over an alphabet A consisting of a single letter a, a nonempty subset $X \subset a^*$ is a code iff X is a singleton distinct from 1 ($=a^0$).

EXAMPLE 1.3 The set $X = \{aa, baa, ba\}$ over $A = \{a, b\}$ is a code. Indeed, suppose the contrary. Then there exists a word w in X^+, of minimal length, that has two distinct factorizations,

$$w = x_1 x_2 \cdots x_n = x'_1 x'_2 \cdots x'_m$$

$(n, m \geq 1, x_i, x'_j \in X)$. Since w is of minimal length, we have $x_1 \neq x'_1$. Thus x_1 is a proper left factor of x'_1 or vice versa. Assume that x_1 is a proper left factor of x'_1. By inspection of X, this implies that $x_1 = ba$, $x'_1 = baa$. This in turn implies that $x_2 = aa$, $x'_2 = aa$ (see Fig. 1.1). Thus $x'_1 = x_1 a$, $x'_1 x'_2 = x_1 x_2 a$, and if we assume that $x'_1 x'_2 \cdots x'_p = x_1 x_2 \cdots x_p a$, it necessarily follows that $x_{p+1} = aa$ and $x'_{p+1} = aa$. Thus $x'_1 x'_2 \cdots x'_{p+1} = x_1 x_2 \cdots x_{p+1} a$. But this contradicts the existence of two factorizations.

EXAMPLE 1.4 The set $X = \{a, ab, ba\}$ is not a code since the word $w = aba$ has two distinct factorizations

$$w = (ab)a = a(ba).$$

The following corollary to Proposition 1.1 is useful.

COROLLARY 1.2 *Let $\alpha: A^* \to C^*$ be an injective morphism. If X is a code over A, then $\alpha(X)$ is a code over C. If Y is a code over C, then $\alpha^{-1}(Y)$ is a code over A.*

Proof Let $\beta: B^* \to A^*$ be a coding morphism for X. Then $\alpha(\beta(B)) = \alpha(X)$, and since $\alpha \circ \beta: B^* \to C^*$ is an injective morphism, Proposition 1.1 shows that $\alpha(X)$ is a code.

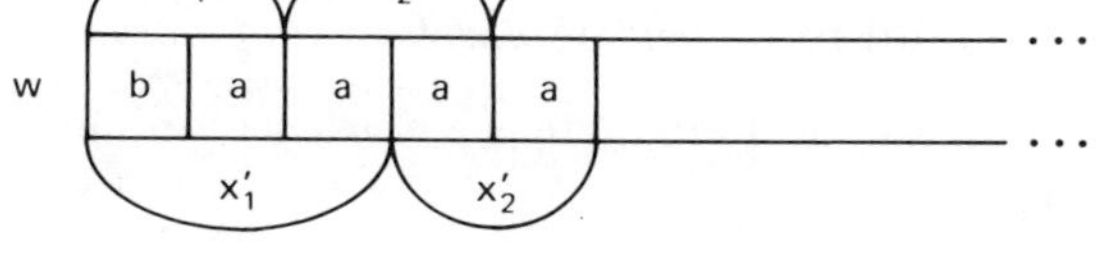

Fig. 1.1 A double factorization starting.

Conversely, let $X = \alpha^{-1}(Y)$, let $n, m \geq 1, x_1, \ldots, x_n, x'_1, \ldots, x'_m \in X$ be such that

$$x_1 \cdots x_n = x'_1 \cdots x'_m.$$

Then

$$\alpha(x_1) \cdots \alpha(x_n) = \alpha(x'_1) \cdots \alpha(x'_m).$$

Now Y is a code; therefore $n = m$ and $\alpha(x_i) = \alpha(x'_i)$ for $i = 1, \ldots, n$. The injectivity of α implies that $x_i = x'_i$ for $i = 1, \ldots, n$, showing that X is a code. □

COROLLARY 1.3 *If $X \subset A^*$ is a code, then X^n is a code for all integers $n > 0$.*

Proof Let $\beta: B^* \to A^*$ be a coding morphism for X. Then $X^n = \beta(B^n)$. But B^n is a code. Thus the conclusion follows from Corollary 1.2. □

EXAMPLE 1.5 We show that the product of two codes is not a code in general. To do this, we consider the sets $X = \{a, ba\}$ and $Y = \{a, ab\}$ which are easily seen to be codes over the alphabet $A = \{a, b\}$. Then

$$Z = XY = \{aa, aab, baa, baab\}.$$

The word $w = aabaab$ has two distinct factorizations,

$$w = (aa)(baab) = (aab)(aab).$$

Thus Z is not a code.

An important class of codes is the class of prefix codes to be introduced now. Let X be a subset of A^*. Then X is a *prefix* set if no element of X is a proper left factor of another element in X. In an equivalent manner, X is prefix if for all x, x' in X,

$$x \leq x' \quad \Rightarrow x = x'. \tag{1.4}$$

This may be rephrased as: two distinct elements in X are incomparable in the prefix ordering.

It follows immediately from (1.4) that a prefix set X containing the empty word just consists of the empty word. Suffix sets are defined in a symmetric way. A subset X of A^* is *suffix* if no word in X is a proper right factor of another word in X. A set is *biprefix* if it is both prefix and suffix. Clearly, a set of words X is suffix iff $\tilde{X}$ is prefix.

PROPOSITION 1.4 *Any prefix (suffix, biprefix) set of words $X \neq \{1\}$ is a code.*

Proof If X is not a code, then there is a word w of minimal length having two factorizations

$$w = x_1 x_2 \cdots x_n = x'_1 x'_2 \cdots x'_m \qquad (x_i, x'_j \in X).$$

Both x_1, x'_1 are nonempty, and since w has minimal length, they are distinct. But then $x_1 < x'_1$ or $x'_1 < x_1$ contradicting the fact that X is prefix. Thus X is a code. The same argument holds for suffix sets. □

A *prefix code* (*suffix code*, *biprefix code*) is a prefix set (suffix, biprefix set) which is a code, that is distinct from $\{1\}$.

EXAMPLE 1.6 Uniform codes are biprefix. The sets X and Y of Example 1.5 are a prefix and a suffix code.

EXAMPLE 1.7 The sets $X = a^*b$ and $Y = \{a^n b^n : n \geq 1\}$ over $A = \{a, b\}$ are prefix, thus prefix codes. The set Y is suffix, thus biprefix, but X is not. This example shows the existence of infinite codes over a finite alphabet.

A code X is *maximal* over A if X is not properly contained in any other code over A, that is, if

$$X \subset X', \qquad X' \text{ code} \quad \Rightarrow \quad X = X'.$$

The maximality of a code depends on the alphabet over which it is given. Indeed, if $X \subset A^*$ and $A \subsetneq B$, then $X \subset B^*$ and X is certainly not maximal over B, even if it is a maximal code over A. The definition of a maximal code gives no algorithm that allows us to verify that it is satisfied. However, maximality is decidable, at least for recognizable codes (see Section 5).

EXAMPLE 1.8 Uniform codes A^n are maximal over A. Suppose the contrary. Then there is a word $u \in A^+ - A^n$ such that $Y = A^n \cup \{u\}$ is a code. The word $w = u^n$ belongs to Y^*, and it is also in $(A^n)^*$ because its length is a multiple of n. Thus $w = u^n = x_1 x_2 \cdots x_{|u|}$ for some $x_1, \ldots, x_{|u|} \in A^n$. Now $u \notin A^n$. Thus the two factorizations are distinct, Y is not a code and A^n is maximal.

PROPOSITION 1.5 *Any code X over A is contained in some maximal code over A.*

Proof Let $\mathscr{F}$ be the set of codes over A containing X, ordered by set inclusion. To show that $\mathscr{F}$ contains a maximal element, it suffices to demonstrate, in view of Zorn's lemma, that any chain $\mathscr{C}$ (i.e., any totally ordered subset) in $\mathscr{F}$ admits a least upper bound in $\mathscr{F}$.

Consider a chain C of codes containing X; then

$$\hat{Y} = \bigcup_{Y \in \mathscr{C}} Y$$

is the least upper bound of C. It remains to show that $\hat{Y}$ is a code. For this, let $n, m \geq 1$, $y_1, \ldots, y_n, y'_1, \ldots, y'_m \in \hat{Y}$ be such that

$$y_1 \cdots y_n = y'_1 \cdots y'_m.$$

Each of the y_i, y'_j belongs to a code of the chain $\mathscr{C}$ and this determines $n + m$ elements (not necessarily distinct) of $\mathscr{C}$. One of them, say Z, contains all the others. Thus $y_1, \cdots, y_n, y'_1, \cdots, y'_m \in Z$, and since Z is a code, we have $n = m$ and $y_i = y'_i$ for $i = 1, \ldots, n$. This shows that $\hat{Y}$ is a code. □

Proposition 1.5 is no longer true if we restrict ourselves to finite codes. There exist finite codes which are contained in no finite maximal code. An example of such a code will be given in Section 5 (Example 5.11).

The fact that a set $X \subset A^*$ is a code admits a very simple expression in the terminology of formal power series.

PROPOSITION 1.6 *Let X be a subset of A^+, and let $M = X^*$ be the submonoid generated by X. Then X is a code iff $\underline{M} = (\underline{X})^*$ or equivalently $\underline{M} = (1 - \underline{X})^{-1}$.*

Proof According to Proposition 0.7.3, the coefficient $((\underline{X})^*, w)$ of a word w in $(\underline{X})^*$ is equal to the number of distinct factorizations of w in words in X. By definition, X is a code iff this number takes only the values 0 and 1 for any word in A^*. But this is equivalent to saying that $(\underline{X})^*$ is the characteristic series of its support, that is, $(\underline{X})^* = \underline{M}$. □

2. CODES AND SUBMONOIDS

The submonoid X^* generated by a code X is sometimes easier to handle than the code itself. The fact that X is a code (prefix code, biprefix code) is equivalent to the property that X^* is a free monoid (a right unitary, biunitary monoid). These latter properties may be verified directly on the submonoid without any explicit description of its base. Thus we can prove that sets are codes by knowing only the submonoid they generate.

We start with a general property.

PROPOSITION 2.1 *Let A be an alphabet. Any submonoid M of A^* has a unique minimal set of generators $X = (M - 1) - (M - 1)^2$.*

Proof Set $Q = M - 1$. First, we verify that X generates M, i.e., that $X^* = M$. Since $X \subset M$, we have $X^* \subset M$. We prove the opposite inclusion by induction on the length of words. Of course, $1 \in X^*$. Let $m \in Q$. If $m \notin Q^2$, then $m \in X$. Otherwise $m = m_1 m_2$ with $m_1, m_2 \in Q$ both strictly shorter than m. Therefore m_1, m_2 belong to X^* and $m \in X^*$.

Now let Y be a set of generators of M. We may suppose that $1 \notin Y$. Then each $x \in X$ is in Y^* and therefore can be written as

$$x = y_1 y_2 \cdots y_n \qquad (y_i \in Y, n \geq 0).$$

The facts that $x \neq 1$ and $x \notin Q^2$ force $n = 1$ and $x \in Y$. This shows that $X \subset Y$. Thus X is a minimal set of generators and such a set is unique. □

EXAMPLE 2.1 Let $A = \{a, b\}$ and let $M = \{w \in A^* \mid |w|_a \equiv 0 \bmod 2\}$. Then we compute $X = (M - 1) - (M - 1)^2 = b \cup ab^*a$.

We now turn to the study of the submonoid generated by a code. By definition, a submonoid M of A^* is *free* if there exists an isomorphism

$$\alpha: \quad B^* \to M$$

of a free monoid B^* onto M.

PROPOSITION 2.2 *If M is a free submonoid of A^*, then its minimal set of generators is a code. Conversely, if $X \subset A^*$ is a code, then the submonoid X^* of A^* is free and X is its minimal set of generators.*

Proof Let α: $B^* \to M$ be an isomorphism. Then α, considered as a morphism from B^* into A^*, is injective. By Proposition 1.1, the set $X = \alpha(B)$ is a code. Next $M = \alpha(B^*) = (\alpha(B))^* = X^*$. Thus X generates M. Furthermore $B = B^+ - B^+B^+$ and $\alpha(B^+) = M - 1$. Consequently $X = (M - 1) - (M - 1)^2$, showing that X is the minimal set of generators of M.

Conversely, assume that $X \subset A^*$, is a code and consider a coding morphism $\alpha: B^* \to A^*$ for X. Then α is injective and α is a bijection from B into X. Thus α is a bijection from B^* onto $\alpha(B^*) = X^*$. Consequently X^* is free. Now α is a bijection, thus $B = B^+ - B^+B^+$ implies $X = X^+ - X^+X^+$, showing by Proposition 2.1 that X is the minimal set of generators of M. □

The code X which generates a free submonoid M of A^* is called the *base* of M.

COROLLARY 2.3 *Let X and Y be codes over A. If $X^* = Y^*$, then $X = Y$.*

EXAMPLE 2.1 (*continued*) The set X is a (biprefix) code, thus M is a free submonoid of A^*.

According to Proposition 2.2, we can distinguish two cases where a set X is not a code. First, when X is not the minimal set of generators of $M = X^*$, that is, there exists an equality

$$x = x_1 x_2 \cdots x_n$$

with $x, x_i \in X$ and $n \geq 2$. Note that despite this fact, M might be free. The other case holds when X is the minimal set of generators, but M is not free (this is the case of Example 1.4).

We now give a characterization of free submonoids of A^* which is intrinsic in the sense that it does not rely on the bases. Another slightly different characterization is given in the exercises.

Let M be a monoid. A submonoid N of M is *stable* (in M) if for all $u, v, w \in M$,

$$u,\ v,\ uw,\ wv \in N \quad \Rightarrow \quad w \in N. \tag{2.1}$$

The hypotheses of (2.1) may be written as

$$w \in N^{-1}N \cap NN^{-1},$$

thus the condition for stability becomes

$$N^{-1}N \cap NN^{-1} \subset N$$

or simply

$$N^{-1}N \cap NN^{-1} = N, \tag{2.2}$$

since $1 \in N$ and therefore $N \subset N^{-1}N \cap NN^{-1}$.

Figure 1.2 gives a pictorial representation of condition (2.1) when the elements u, v, w are words. The membership in N is represented by an arch.

Stable submonoids have interesting properties. As a result, they appear in almost all of the chapters in this book. A reason for this is Proposition 2.4 which yields a remarkable characterization of free submonoids of a free monoid. As a practical application, the proposition is used to prove that some submonoids are free, and consequently, that their bases are codes without knowing the bases.

PROPOSITION 2.4 *A submonoid N of A^* is stable iff it is free.*

Proof Assume first that N is stable. Set $X = (N - 1) - (N - 1)^2$. To prove that X is a code, suppose the contrary. Then there is a word $z \in N$ of minimal length having two distinct factorizations in words of X,

$$z = x_1x_2 \cdots x_n = y_1y_2 \cdots y_m$$

with $x_1, \ldots, x_n, y_1, \ldots, y_m \in X$. We may suppose $|x_1| < |y_1|$. Then $y_1 = x_1w$ for some nonempty word w. It follows that

$$x_1, \quad y_2 \cdots y_m, \quad x_1w = y_1, \quad wy_2 \cdots y_m = x_2 \cdots x_n$$

are all in N. Since N is stable, w is in N. Consequently $y_1 = x_1w \notin X$, which yields the contradiction. Thus X is a code.

Conversely, assume that N is free and let X be its base. Let $u, v, w \in A^*$ and suppose that

$$u, v, uw, wv \in N.$$

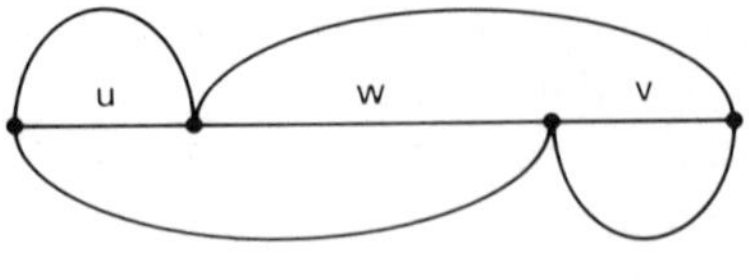

Fig. 1.2 Representation of stability.

Set

$$u = x_1 \cdots x_k, \qquad wv = x_{k+1} \cdots x_r,$$

$$uw = y_1 \cdots y_l, \qquad v \;= y_{l+1} \cdots y_s,$$

with x_i, y_j in X. The equality $u(wv) = (uw)v$ implies

$$x_1 \cdots x_k x_{k+1} \cdots x_r = y_1 \cdots y_l y_{l+1} \cdots y_s.$$

Thus $r = s$ and $x_i = y_i$ $(i = 1, \ldots, s)$ since X is a code. Moreover, $l \geq k$ because $|uw| \geq |u|$, showing that

$$uw = x_1 \cdots x_k x_{k+1} \cdots x_l = u x_{k+1} \cdots x_l,$$

hence $w = x_{k+1} \cdots x_l \in N$. Thus N is stable. □

For a prefix code X, the submonoid X^* is free, as we have seen, but has a stronger property. Those submonoids which are generated by prefix codes, can also be characterized by a condition which is independent of the base.

Let M be a monoid and let N be a submonoid of M. Then N is *right unitary* (in M) if for all $u, v \in M$,

$$u,\ uv \in N \quad \Rightarrow \quad v \in N.$$

In a symmetric way, N is *left unitary* if for all $u, v \in M$,

$$u,\ vu \in N \quad \Rightarrow \quad v \in N.$$

The conditions may be rewritten as follows: N is right unitary iff $N^{-1}N = N$, and N is left unitary iff $NN^{-1} = N$

The submonoid N of M is *biunitary* if it is both left and right unitary.

The four properties stable, left unitary, right unitary, and biunitary are of the same nature. Their relationships can be summarized as

$$\begin{array}{ccc} & \text{stable:}\quad N^{-1}N \cap NN^{-1} = N & \\ \nearrow & & \nwarrow \\ \text{left unitary:}\quad NN^{-1} = N & & N^{-1}N = N:\quad \text{right unitary} \\ \nwarrow & & \nearrow \\ & \text{biunitary:}\quad N^{-1}N = NN^{-1} = N & \end{array}$$

Example 2.1 (*continued*) The submonoid M is biunitary. Indeed, if u, $uv \in M$ then $|u|_a$ and $|uv|_a = |u|_a + |v|_a$ are even numbers; consequently $|v|_a$ is even and $v \in M$. Thus M is right unitary.

Example 2.2 In group theory, the concepts stable, unitary and biunitary collapse and coincide with the notion of subgroup. Indeed, let H be a stable submonoid of a group G. For all $h \in H$, both hh^{-1} and $h^{-1}h$ are in H. Stability implies that h^{-1} is in H. Thus H is a subgroup. If H is a subgroup, then conversely $HH^{-1} = H^{-1}H = H$, showing that H is biunitary.

The following proposition shows the relationship between the submonoids we defined and codes.

PROPOSITION 2.5 *A submonoid M of A^* is right unitary (resp., left unitary, biunitary) iff its minimal set of generators is a prefix code (suffix code, biprefix code). In particular, a right unitary (left unitary, biunitary) submonoid of A^* is free.*

Proof Let $M \subset A^*$ be a submonoid, $Q = M - 1$ and let $X = Q - Q^2$ be its minimal set of generators. Suppose M is right unitary.

To show that X is prefix, let x, xu be in X for some $u \in A^*$. Then $x, xu \in M$ and thus $u \in M$. If $u \neq 1$, then $u \in Q$; but then $xu \in Q^2$ contrary to the assumption. Thus $u = 1$ and X is prefix.

Conversely, suppose X is prefix. Let $u, v \in A^*$ be such that $u, uv \in M = X^*$. Then

$$u = x_1 \cdots x_n, \qquad uv = y_1 \cdots y_m$$

for some $x_1, \ldots, x_n, y_1, \ldots, y_m \in X$. Consequently

$$x_1 x_2 \cdots x_n v = y_1 \cdots y_m.$$

Since X is prefix, neither x_1 nor y_1 is a proper left factor of the other. Thus $x_1 = y_1$, and for the same reason $x_2 = y_2, \ldots, x_n = y_n$. This shows that $m \geq n$ and $v = y_{n+1} \cdots y_m$ belongs to M. Thus M is right unitary. □

Let M be a submonoid of A^*. Then M is *maximal* if $M \neq A^*$ and M is not properly contained in any other submonoid excepted A^*.

PROPOSITION 2.6 *If M is a maximal free submonoid of A^*, then its base X is a maximal code.*

Proof Let Y be a code on A with $X \subsetneq Y$. Then $X^* \subset Y^*$ and $X^* \neq Y^*$ since otherwise $X = Y$ by Corollary 2.3. Now X^* is maximal. Thus $Y^* = A^*$ and $Y = A$. Thus $X \subsetneq A$. Let $b \in A - X$. The set $Z = X \cup b^2$ is a code and $M \subsetneq Z^* \subsetneq A^*$ since $b^2 \notin M$ and $b \notin Z^*$. This contradicts the maximality of M. □

Note that the converse of the proposition is false since uniform codes A^n $(n \geq 1)$ are maximal. But if $k, n \geq 2$, we have $(A^{kn})^* \subsetneq (A^n)^* \subsetneq A^*$. showing that $(A^{nk})^*$ is not maximal.

We now introduce a family of biprefix codes called group codes which have interesting properties. Before we give the definition, let us consider the following situation.

Let G be a group, H be a subgroup of G, and

$$\varphi: \quad A^* \to G \tag{2.3}$$

be a morphism. The submonoid

$$M = \varphi^{-1}(H) \tag{2.4}$$

is biunitary. Indeed, if, for instance, $p, pq \in M$, then $\varphi(p), \varphi(pq) \in H$, therefore $\varphi(p)^{-1}\varphi(pq) = \varphi(q) \in H$ and $q \in M$. The same proof shows that M is left unitary. Thus the base, say X, of M is a biprefix code.

The definition of the submonoid M in (2.4) is equivalent to a description as the intersection of A^* with a subgroup of the free group $A^{\circledast}$ on A. Indeed, the morphism φ in (2.3) factorizes in a unique way in

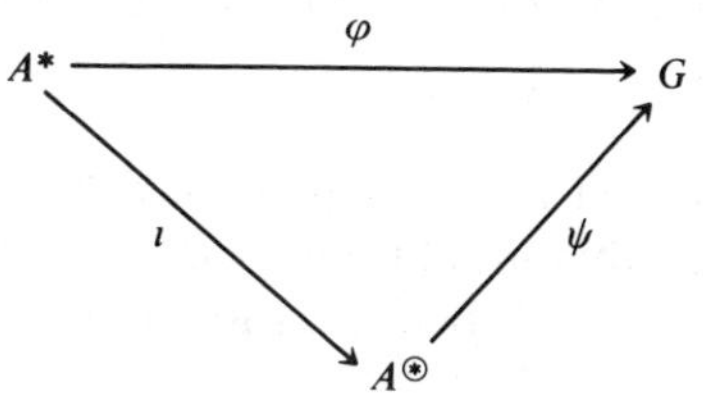

with ι the canonical injection. Setting $Q = \psi^{-1}(H)$, we have

$$M = Q \cap A^*.$$

Conversely if Q is a subgroup of $A^{\circledast}$ and $M = Q \cap A^*$, then

$$M = \iota^{-1}(Q).$$

A *group code* is the base X of a submonoid $M = \varphi^{-1}(H)$, where φ is a morphism given by (2.3) which, moreover, is supposed to be *surjective*. Then X is a biprefix code and X is a maximal code. Indeed, if $M = A^*$, then $X = A$ is maximal. Otherwise take $w \in A^* - M$ and setting $Y = X \cup w$, let us verify that Y is not a code. Set $m = \varphi(w)$. Since φ is surjective, there is word $\bar{w} \in A^*$ such that $\varphi(\bar{w}) = m^{-1}$. The words $u = w\bar{w}$, $v = \bar{w}w$ both are in M, and $w\bar{w}w = uw = wv \in Y^*$. This word has two distinct factorizations in words in Y, namely, uw formed of words in X followed by a word in Y, and wv which is composed the other way round. Thus Y is not a code and X is maximal.

We give now three examples of group codes.

EXAMPLE 2.3 Let $A = \{a, b\}$ and consider the set

$$M = \{w \in A^* \mid |w|_a \equiv 0 \bmod 2\}$$

of Example 2.1. We have $M = \varphi^{-1}(0)$, where

$$\varphi\colon\quad A^* \to \mathbb{Z}/2\mathbb{Z}$$

is the morphism given by $\varphi(a) = 1$, $\varphi(b) = 0$. Thus the base of M, namely the code $X = b \cup ab^*a$, is a group code, hence maximal.

EXAMPLE 2.4 The uniform code A^m over A is a group code. The monoid $(A^m)^*$ is indeed the kernel of the morphism of A^* onto Z/mZ mapping all letters on the number 1.

EXAMPLE 2.5 Let $A = \{a, b\}$, and consider now the submonoid

$$\{w \in A^* \mid |w|_a = |w|_b\} \tag{2.5}$$

composed of the words on A having as many a's as b's. Let

$$\delta: \quad A^* \to \mathbb{Z}$$

be the morphism defined by $\delta(a) = 1$, $\delta(b) = -1$. Clearly

$$\delta(w) = |w|_a - |w|_b$$

for all $w \in A^*$. Thus the set (2.5) is equal to $\delta^{-1}(0)$. The base of $\delta^{-1}(0)$ is denoted by D or D_1, the submonoid itself by D^* or $D_1{}^*$. Words in D are called *Dyck-primes*, D is the *Dyck code* over A. The set D^* is the *Dyck set* over A.

EXAMPLE 2.6 More generally, let $A = B \cup \bar{B}$ ($B \cap \bar{B} = \emptyset$) be an alphabet with $2n$ letters, and let $\delta: A^* \to B^*$ be the morphism of A^* onto the free group $B^{\circledast}$ defined by $\delta(b) = b$, $\delta(\bar{b}) = b^{-1}$ for $b \in B, \bar{b} \in \bar{B}$. The base of the submonoid $\delta^{-1}(1)$ is denoted by D_n and is called the *Dyck code* over A or over n letters.

We now turn to a slightly different topic and consider the free submonoids of A^* containing a given submonoid. We start with the following observation which easily follows from Proposition 2.4.

PROPOSITION 2.7 *The intersection of an arbitrary family of free submonoids of A^* is a free submonoid.*

Proof Let $(M_i)_{i \in I}$ be a family of free submonoids of A^*, and set $M = \bigcap_{i \in I} M_i$. Clearly M is a submonoid, and it suffices to show that M is stable. If

$$u, vw, uv, w \in M,$$

then these four words belong to each of the M_i. Each M_i being stable, w is in M_i for each $i \in I$. Thus $w \in M$. □

Proposition 2.7 leads to the following considerations. Let X be a subset of A^*. As we have just seen, the intersection of all free submonoids of A^* containing X is again a free submonoid. It is the smallest free submonoid of A^* containing X. We call it the *free hull* of X. If X^* is a free submonoid, then it coincides of course with its free hull.

Let X be a subset of A^*, let N be its free hull and let Y be the base of N. If X is not a code, then $X \neq Y$. The following result, known as the *defect theorem* gives an interesting relationship between X and Y.

THEOREM 2.8 *Let X be a subset of* A^*, *and let Y be the base of the free hull of X. If X is not a code, then*

$$\mathrm{Card}(Y) \le \mathrm{Card}(X) - 1.$$

The following result is a consequence of the theorem. It can be proved directly as well (Exercise 2.1).

COROLLARY 2.9 *Let* $X = \{x_1, x_2\}$. *Then X is not a code iff* x_1 *and* x_2 *are powers of the same word*: $x_1 = y^p$, $x_2 = y^q$ *for some* $y \in A^+$, $p, q \ge 0$.

Note that this corollary entirely describes the codes with two elements. The case of sets with three words is already much more complicated.

For the proof of Theorem 2.8, we first show the following result.

PROPOSITION 2.10 *Let* $X \subset A^*$ *and let Y be the base of the free hull of X. Then*

$$Y \subset X(Y^*)^{-1} \cap (Y^*)^{-1}X,$$

i.e., each word in Y appears as the first (resp., last) factor in the factorization of some word $x \in X$ *in words belonging to Y.*

Proof Suppose that a word $y \in Y$ is not in $(Y^*)^{-1}X$. Then $X \subset 1 \cup Y^*(Y - y)$. Setting

$$Z = y^*(Y - y),$$

we have $Z^+ = Y^*(Y - y)$, thus $X \subset Z^*$. Now Z^* is free. Indeed, any word $z \in Z^*$ has a unique factorization

$$z = y_1 y_2 \dots y_n, \qquad y_1, \dots, y_n \in Y, \quad y_n \ne y,$$

and therefore can be written uniquely as

$$z = y^{p_1} z_1 y^{p_2} z_2 \cdots y^{p_r} z_r, \qquad z_1, \dots, z_r \in Y - y, \quad p_i \ge 0.$$

Now $X \subset Z^* \subsetneq Y^*$, showing that Y^* is not the free hull of X. This yields the contradiction. □

Proof of Theorem 2.8 If X contains the empty word, then X and $X' = X - 1$ have same free hull Y^*. If the result holds for X', it also holds for X, since if X' is a code, then $Y = X$ and $\mathrm{Card}(Y) = \mathrm{Card}(X) - 1$, and otherwise $\mathrm{Card}(Y) \le \mathrm{Card}(X') - 1 \le \mathrm{Card}(X) - 2$. Thus we may assume that $1 \notin X$. Let $\alpha: X \to Y$ be the mapping defined by

$$\alpha(x) = y \qquad \text{if} \quad x \in yY^*.$$

This mapping is uniquely defined since Y is a code; it is everywhere defined since $X \subset Y^*$. In view of Proposition 2.10, the function α is surjective. If X is not a code, then there exists a relation

$$x_1x_2\cdots x_n = x'_1x'_2\cdots x'_m, \qquad x_i, x'_j \in X \tag{2.6}$$

with $x_1 \neq x'_1$. However, Y is a code, and by (2.6) we have

$$\alpha(x_1) = \alpha(x'_1).$$

Thus α is not injective. This proves the inequality. □

3. A TEST FOR CODES

It is not always easy to verify that a given set of words is a code. The test described in this section is not based on any new property of codes but consists merely in a systematic organization of the computations required to verify that a set of words satisfies the definition of a code.

In the case where X is finite, or more generally if X is recognizable, the amount of computation is finite. In other words, it is effectively decidable whether a finite (recognizable) set is a code.

Before starting the description of the algorithm, let us consider

EXAMPLE 3.1. Let $A = \{a, b\}$, and $X = \{b, abb, abbba, bbba, baabb\}$. This set is not a code. For instance, the word

$$w = abbbabbbaabb$$

has two factorizations (see Fig. 1.3)

$$w = (abbba)(bbba)(abb) = (abb)(b)(abb)(baabb).$$

These two factorizations define a sequence of left factors of w, each one corresponding to an attempt at a double factorization. We give this list, together with the attempt at a double factorization:

$$\begin{aligned}
(\mathrm{abbba}) &= (\mathrm{abb})\mathit{ba}\\
(\mathrm{abbba}) &= (\mathrm{abb})(\mathrm{b})\mathit{a}\\
(\mathrm{abbba})\mathit{bb} &= (\mathrm{abb})(\mathrm{b})(\mathrm{abb})\\
(\mathrm{abbba})(\mathrm{bbba}) &= (\mathrm{abb})(\mathrm{b})(\mathrm{abb})\mathit{ba}\\
(\mathrm{abbba})(\mathrm{bbba})\mathit{abb} &= (\mathrm{abb})(\mathrm{b})(\mathrm{abb})(\mathrm{baabb})\\
(\mathrm{abbba})(\mathrm{bbba})(\mathrm{abb}) &= (\mathrm{abb})(\mathrm{b})(\mathrm{abb})(\mathrm{baabb}).
\end{aligned}$$

Each but the last one of these attempts fails, because of the *rest* corresponding to the italicized right factor, which remains after the factorization.

The algorithm presented here computes all the *remainders* in all attempts at a double factorization. It discovers a double factorization by the fact that the empty word is one of the remainders.

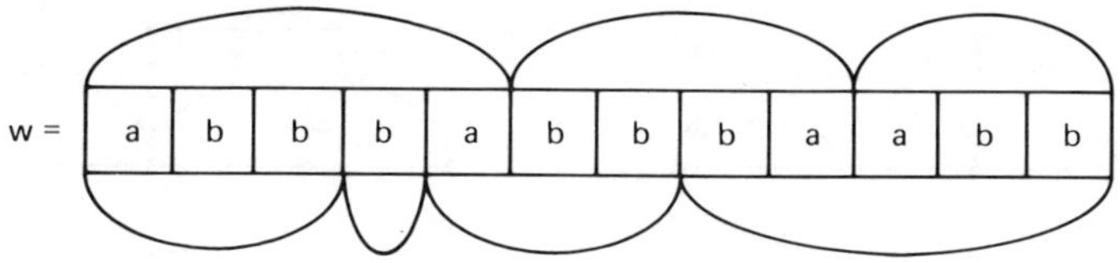

Fig. 1.3 Two factorizations.

Formally, the computations are organized as follows. Let X be a subset of A^+, and let

$$U_1 = X^{-1}X - 1,$$
$$U_{n+1} = X^{-1}U_n \cup U_n^{-1}X \qquad \text{for} \quad n \geq 1.$$

Then we have the following result:

THEOREM 3.1 *The set $X \subset A^+$ is a code iff none of the sets U_n defined above contains the empty word.*

EXAMPLE 3.1 (*continued*) The word ba is in U_1, next $a \in U_2$, then $bb \in U_3$ and $ba \in U_4$, finally $abb \in U_5$ and since $1 \in U_6$, the set X is not a code, according to Theorem 3.1.

The proof of Theorem 3.1 is based on the following lemma.

LEMMA 3.2 *Let $X \subset A^+$ and let $(U_n)_{n\geq 1}$ be defined as above. For all $n \geq 1$ and $k \in \{1,\dots,n\}$, we have $1 \in U_n$ iff there exist a word $u \in U_k$ and integers i, $j \geq 0$ such that*

$$uX^i \cap X^j \neq \varnothing, \qquad i + j + k = n. \tag{3.1}$$

Proof We prove the statement for all n by descending induction on k. Assume, first $k = n$. If $1 \in U_n$, taking $u = 1$, $i = j = 0$, Eq. (3.1) is satisfied. Conversely, if (3.1) holds, then $i = j = 0$. This implies $u = 1$ and consequently $1 \in U_n$.

Now let $n > k \geq 1$, and suppose that the equivalence holds for n, $n - 1,\dots,k + 1$. If $1 \in U_n$, then by induction hypothesis, there exists $v \in U_{k+1}$ and two integers $i,j \geq 0$ such that

$$vX^i \cap X^j \neq \varnothing, \qquad i + j + k + 1 = n.$$

Thus there are words $x \in X^i$, $y \in X^j$ such that $vx = y$. Now $v \in U_{k+1}$, and there are two cases. Either there is a word $z \in X$ such that

$$zv = u \in U_k,$$

or there exist $z \in X$, $u \in U_k$ such that

$$z = uv.$$

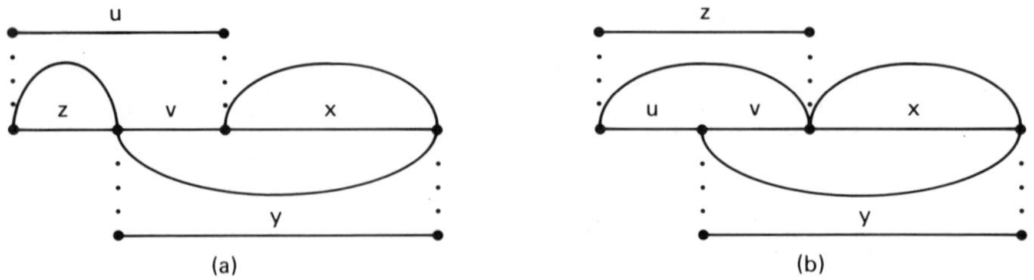

Fig. 1.4 The two cases.

In the first case [see Fig. 1.4a], one has $ux = zy$, thus

$$uX^i \cap X^{j+1} \neq \varnothing, \qquad u \in U_k.$$

In the second case [see Fig. 3.2(b)], one has $zx = uvx = uy$, thus

$$uX^j \cap X^{i+1} \neq \varnothing, \qquad u \in U_k.$$

In both cases, Formula (3.1) is satisfied.

Conversely, assume that there are $u \in U_k$ and $i, j \geq 0$ with

$$uX^i \cap X^j, \qquad i + j + k = n.$$

Then

$$ux_1x_2\cdots x_i = y_1y_2\cdots y_j$$

for some x_r, y_s in X. If $j = 0$, then $i = 0$ and $k = n$. Thus $j \geq 1$. Once more, we distinguish two cases, according to the length of u compared to the length of y_1.

If $u = y_1v$ for some $v \in A^+$, then $v \in X^{-1}U_k \subset U_{k+1}$ and further

$$vx_1x_2\cdots x_i = y_2\cdots y_j.$$

Thus $vX^i \cap X^{j-1} \neq \varnothing$ and by the induction hypothesis $1 \in U_n$.

If $y_1 = uv$ for some $v \in A^+$, then $v \in U_k^{-1}X \subset U_{k+1}$ and

$$x_1x_2\cdots x_i = vy_2\cdots y_i,$$

showing that $X^i \cap vX^{j-1} \neq \varnothing$. Thus again $1 \in U_n$ by the induction hypothesis. This concludes the proof. ▯

It may be noteworthy that the nature of U_1 did not play any role in the proof of the lemma. In other words, the lemma remains true if U_1 is replaced by any set Y, provided that for $n > 1$, the sets U_n are defined as before. However, the definition of U_1 is essential in the proof of Theorem 3.1 itself.

Proof of Theorem 3.1 If X is not a code, then there is a relation

$$x_1x_2\cdots x_p = y_1y_2\cdots y_q, \qquad x_i, y_j \in X, \quad x_1 \neq y_1.$$

Assume $|y_1| < |x_1|$. Then $x_1 = y_1 u$ for some $u \in A^+$. But then

$$u \in U_1 \qquad \text{and} \qquad uX^{p-1} \cap X^{q-1} \neq \varnothing.$$

According to the lemma, $1 \in U_{p+q-1}$.

Conversely, if $1 \in U_n$, take $k = 1$ in the lemma. There exists $u \in U_1$ and integers $i, j \geq 0$, such that $uX^i \cap X^j \neq \varnothing$. Now $u \in U_1$ implies that $xu = y$ for some $x, y \in X$. Furthermore $x \neq y$ since $u \neq 1$. It follows from $xuX^i \cap xX^j \neq \varnothing$ that $yX^i \cap xX^j \neq \varnothing$, showing that X is not a code. This establishes the theorem. □

Proposition 3.3 shows that Theorem 3.1 provides an algorithm for testing whether a recognizable set is a code.

PROPOSITION 3.3 *If $X \subset A^+$ is a recognizable set, then the set of all U_n $(n \geq 0)$ is finite.*

This statement is straightforward for a finite set X since each U_n is composed of right factors of words in X.

Proof Let σ be the syntactic congruence of X, defined by

$$w \equiv w' \mod \sigma \qquad \text{iff} \quad (\forall u, v \in A^*, uwv \in X \Leftrightarrow uw'v \in X).$$

Let μ be the congruence of A^* with the two classes $\{1\}$ and A^+. Let $\iota = \sigma \cap \mu$. We use the following general fact.

If $L \subset A^*$ is a union of equivalence classes of a congruence θ, then for any subset Y of A^*, $Y^{-1}L$ is a union of congruence classes mod θ. (Indeed, let $z \in Y^{-1}L$ and $z' \equiv z \bmod \theta$. Then $yz \in L$ for some $y \in Y$, whence $yz' \in L$. Thus $z' \in Y^{-1}L$).

We prove that each U_n is a union of equivalence classes of ι by induction on $n \geq 1$. For $n = 1$, X is a union of classes of σ, thus $X^{-1}X$ also is a union of classes for σ, and finally $X^{-1}X - 1$ is a union of classes of ι. Next, if U_n is a union of classes of ι, then by the previous fact both $U_n^{-1}X$ and $X^{-1}U_{n-1}$ are unions of classes of ι. Thus U_{n+1} is a union of classes of ι. The fact that X is recognizable implies that ι has finite index. The result follows. □

EXAMPLE 3.1 (*continued*) For $X = \{b, abb, abbba, bbba, baabb\}$, we obtain

$U_1 = \{ba, bba, aabb\}$; $\quad X^{-1}U_1 = \{a, ba\}$; $\quad U_1^{-1}X = \{abb\}$;

$U_2 = \{a, ba, abb\}$; $\quad X^{-1}U_2 = \{a, 1\}$; $\quad U_2^{-1}X = \{bb, bba, abb, 1, ba\}$.

Thus $1 \in U_3$ and X is not a code.

Example 3.2 Let $X = \{a, ab, ba\}$ and $A = \{a, b\}$. We have

$$U_1 = \{b\}; \qquad U_2 = \{a\}; \qquad U_3 = \{1, b\}; \qquad U_4 = X; \qquad U_5 = U_3.$$

The set U_3 contains the empty word. Thus X is not a code.

Example 3.3 Let $X = \{aa, ba, bb, baa, bba\}$ and $A = \{a, b\}$. We obtain $U_1 = \{a\}$, $U_2 = U_1$. Thus $U_n = \{a\}$ for all $n \geq 1$ and X is a code.

If $X \subset A^+$ is prefix (thus a code), then $U_1 = X^{-1}X - 1 = \emptyset$. Thus the algorithm ends immediately for such codes. On the other hand, if X is suffix, the algorithm does not stop after one step. This asymmetrical behavior is due of course to the definition of the U_n which favors computing from left to right.

4. MEASURE OF A CODE

In this section, we give a precise formulation to the idea that a code has only few words, by introducing the notion of the measure of a code.

A *Bernoulli distribution* on A^* is a function

$$\pi: \quad A^* \to \mathbb{R}_+,$$

which is a morphism into the multiplicative monoid $\mathbb{R}_+$ of nonnegative real numbers, and which moreover satisfies

$$\sum_{a \in A} \pi(a) = 1.$$

A distribution is *positive* if $\pi(a) > 0$ for all $a \in A$. It follows from the definition that

$$\pi(1) = 1$$

and that

$$\sum_{u \in A^n} \pi(u) = 1, \qquad n \geq 1.$$

Indeed, for $u \in A^n$, we have

$$\sum_{a \in A} \pi(ua) = \pi(u) \sum_{a \in A} \pi(a) = \pi(u),$$

thus

$$\sum_{u \in A^{n+1}} \pi(u) = \sum_{v \in A^n} \pi(v) \sum_{a \in A} \pi(a) = \sum_{v \in A^n} \pi(v).$$

Thus π defines a probability distribution on each set A^n. We extend π to $\mathfrak{P}(A^*)$ by setting for $L \subset A^*$

$$\pi(L) = \sum_{l \in L} \pi(l).$$

Then π becomes a function

$$\pi\colon \quad \mathfrak{P}(A^*) \to \mathscr{R}$$

and satisfies the following properties:

$$\pi(L) \geq 0 \qquad \text{for all } L \subset A^*; \qquad \pi(\varnothing) = 0;$$

for any family $(L_i)_{i \in I}$ of subsets of A^*

$$\pi\left(\bigcup_{i \in I} L_i\right) \leq \sum_{i \in I} \pi(L_i); \tag{4.1}$$

if the sets L_i are pairwise disjoint, then

$$\pi\left(\bigcup_{i \in I} L_i\right) = \sum_{i \in I} \pi(L_i). \tag{4.2}$$

The value $\pi(L)$ is the *measure* of the set L relative to π. It is a nonnegative number or $+\infty$.

There is a special case of these formulas which is useful for the computation of the measure of a set.

Let $L \subset A^*$, and for $n \geq 0$ set

$$s_n = \pi\{w \in L \mid |w| \leq n\}.$$

Then the following formula holds in $\mathscr{R}$:

$$\pi(L) = \sup_{n \geq 0} s_n. \tag{4.3}$$

EXAMPLE 4.1 Let A be a finite nonempty set, and

$$\pi(a) = \frac{1}{\mathrm{Card}(A)}, \qquad a \in A.$$

Then π defines a Bernoulli distribution on A^* called the *uniform* distribution.

EXAMPLE 4.2 Let $A = \{a, b\}$ and $X = \{a, ba, bb\}$. Let $\pi\colon A^* \to \mathbb{R}_+$ be a distribution. Setting as usual

$$\pi(a) = p, \qquad \pi(b) = q = 1 - p,$$

we have

$$\pi(X) = p + pq + q^2 = p + pq + (1 - p)q = p + q = 1.$$

If L, M are subsets of A^*, then

$$LM = \bigcup_{l \in L} \bigcup_{m \in M} \{lm\}. \tag{4.4}$$

It follows from (4.1) that

$$\pi(LM) \le \sum_{l\in L}\sum_{m\in M}\pi(l)\pi(m) = \sum_{l\in L}\pi(l)\sum_{m\in M}\pi(m) = \pi(L)\pi(M). \tag{4.5}$$

The inequality in (4.5) may be strict if the union in (4.4) is not disjoint.

For any subset X of A^*, Eqs. (4.1) and (4.5) imply that

$$\pi(X^*) \le \sum_{n\ge 0}\pi(X^n) \le \sum_{n\ge 0}\pi(X)^n. \tag{4.6}$$

Thus if $\pi(X) < 1$, then $\pi(X^*) < \infty$. Proposition 4.1 shows that for codes, the converse implication holds, and that the inequalities in (4.6) are equalities.

Proposition 4.1 *Let $X \subset A^+$ and let π be a Bernoulli distribution on A^*.*

(1) *If X is a code, then*

$$\pi(X^n) = \pi(X)^n \quad \textit{for} \quad n \ge 1; \tag{4.7}$$

$$\pi(X^*) = \sum_{n\ge 0}\pi(X)^n;$$

and in particular

$$\pi(X^*) < \infty \quad \textit{iff} \quad \pi(X) < 1.$$

(2) *Conversely, if π is positive, if $\pi(X)$ is finite, and if*

$$\pi(X^n) = \pi(X)^n \quad \textit{for all} \quad n \ge 1, \tag{4.8}$$

then X is a code.

Proof For $n \ge 1$, let S_n be the n-fold Cartesian product of X: $S_n = X \times X \times \cdots \times X$.

(1) Assume that X is a code. Then the function

$$(x_1, \ldots, x_n) \mapsto x_1 \cdots x_n$$

is a bijection of S_n onto X^n. Consequently

$$\pi(X)^n = \sum_{(x_1,\ldots,x_n)\in S_n}\pi(x_1)\cdots\pi(x_n) = \sum_{x\in X^n}\pi(x) = \pi(X^n).$$

This shows (4.7). Next the sets $(X^n)_{n\ge 0}$ are pairwise disjoint. Thus

$$\pi(X^*) = \sum_{n\ge 0}\pi(X^n).$$

This together with (4.7) proves the second equality. The last one is an immediate consequence.

(2) Assume that X is not a code. Then there is a word $u \in X^*$ having two distinct factorizations in words in X, say

$$u = x_1x_2\cdots x_n = x'_1x'_2\cdots x'_m,$$

with $n, m \geq 1$ and $x_i, x'_j \in X$. The word $w = uu$ has two factorizations:

$$u = x_1 x_2 \cdots x_n x'_1 \cdots x'_m = x'_1 x'_2 \cdots x'_m x_1 x_2 \cdots x_n$$

of the same length $k = n + m$. It follows that

$$\pi(X)^k = \sum_{(y_1,\ldots,y_k) \in S_k} \pi(y_1 \cdots y_k) \geq \pi(X^k) + \pi(w).$$

But the finiteness of $\pi(X)$ and condition (4.8) imply $\pi(w) \leq 0$, hence $\pi(w) = 0$. This contradicts the hypothesis that π is positive. □

THEOREM 4.2 *Let X be a code over A. For all Bernoulli distributions π on A^*, we have $\pi(X) \leq 1$.*

In the case where the alphabet A is finite and where the distribution π is uniform, we obtain,

COROLLARY 4.3 *Let X be a code over an alphabet with k letters; then*

$$\sum_{x \in X} k^{-|x|} \leq 1. \quad \square$$

Proof of Theorem 4.2 We prove the statement first in the case where the numbers $|x|$, for $x \in X$, are bounded. (This is the case of a finite code, but a code satisfying the condition is not necessarily finite when the alphabet is infinite.) Thus we assume that there is some integer $k \geq 1$ with

$$X \subset A \cup A^2 \cup \cdots \cup A^k.$$

It follows that for $n \geq 1$, $X^n \subset A \cup A^2 \cup \cdots \cup A^{nk}$, hence

$$\pi(X^n) \leq nk.$$

Arguing by contradiction, assume now that $\pi(X) > 1$, that is,

$$\pi(X) = 1 + \varepsilon$$

for some $\varepsilon > 0$. Then by Eq. (4.7), for $n \geq 1$

$$\pi(X)^n = (1 + \varepsilon)^n.$$

In view of (4.9), we have for all $n \geq 1$

$$(1 + \varepsilon)^n \leq kn,$$

which is impossible. Thus $\pi(X) \leq 1$.

If X is an arbitrary code, set for $n \geq 1$

$$X_n = \{x \in X \mid |x| \leq n\}.$$

The set X_n is a code satisfying the conditions of the first part of the proof. Consequently

$$\pi(X_n) \leq 1.$$

This shows, in view of Eq. (4.3), that

$$\pi(X) = \sup_{n \geq 1} \pi(X_n) \leq 1. \quad \square$$

EXAMPLE 4.3 Let $A = \{a, b\}$, and $X = \{b, ab, ba\}$. Define π by $\pi(a) = \frac{1}{3}$, $\pi(b) = \frac{2}{3}$. Then

$$\pi(X) = \tfrac{2}{3} + \tfrac{2}{9} + \tfrac{2}{9} = \tfrac{10}{9},$$

thus X is not a code. Note that for $\pi(a) = \pi(b) = \frac{1}{2}$, we get $\pi(X) = 1$. Thus it is impossible to conclude that X is not a code from the second distribution.

The following example shows that the converse of Theorem 4.2 is false.

EXAMPLE 4.4 Let $A = \{a, b\}$, and $X = \{ab, aba, aab\}$. The set X is not a code since

$$(aba)(ab) = (ab)(aab).$$

However, any Bernoulli distribution π gives $\pi(X) < 1$. Indeed, let $\pi(a) = p$, $\pi(b) = q$. Then

$$\pi(X) = pq + 2p^2q.$$

It is easily seen that we always have $pq \leq \frac{1}{4}$ and also $p^2q \leq \frac{4}{27}$, provided that $p + q = 1$. Consequently

$$\pi(X) \leq \tfrac{1}{4} + \tfrac{8}{27} < 1.$$

This example gives a good illustration of the limits of Theorem 4.2 in its use for testing whether a set is a code. Indeed, the set X of Example 4.4, where the test fails, is obtained from the set of Example 4.3, where the test is successful, simply by replacing b by ab. This shows that the counting argument represented by a Bernoulli distribution takes into account the lengths as well as the number of words. In other words, Theorem 4.2 allows us to conclude that X is not a code only if there are "too many too short words."

Proposition 4.4 is very useful for proving that a code is maximal. The direct method for proving maximality, based on the definition, indeed is usually much more complicated than the verification of the conditions of the proposition. A more precise statement, holding for a large class of codes, will be given in the next section (Theorem 5.10).

PROPOSITION 4.4 *Let X be a code over A. If there exists a positive Bernoulli distribution π on A^* such that $\pi(X) = 1$, then the code X is maximal.*

Proof Assume that X is not maximal. Then there is some word $y \in X$ such that $Y = X \cup y$ is a code. By Theorem 4.1, we have $\pi(Y) \leq 1$. On the other hand,

$$\pi(Y) = \pi(X) + \pi(y) = 1 + \pi(y).$$

Thus $\pi(y) = 0$, which is impossible since π is positive. □

EXAMPLE 4.2 *(continued)* Since $\pi(X) = 1$ and X is prefix, X is a maximal code.

EXAMPLE 4.5 We examine again the Dyck code D over $A = \{a, b\}$ of Example 2.5. Let $\pi: A^* \to \mathbb{R}_+$ be a positive Bernoulli distribution, and let

$$\pi(a) = p, \qquad \pi(b) = q,$$

$$d_n = \pi(D \cap A^n), \qquad d_n^{(*)} = \pi(D^* \cap A^n), \qquad n \geq 0.$$

In view of computing the measure of D, consider the formal power series

$$d(t) = \sum_{n \geq 0} d_n t^n, \qquad d^{(*)}(t) = \sum_{n \geq 0} d_n^{(*)} t^n.$$

We have for $n \geq 0$

$$d_{2n}^{(*)} = \binom{2n}{n} p^n q^n; \qquad d_{2n+1}^{(*)} = 0.$$

On the other hand, $\pi(L \cap A^n) \leq 1$ for any $L \subset A^*$ and for all n. In particular, $d_{2n}^{(*)} \leq 1$ for all $n \geq 0$, and consequently the series $\sum_{n \geq 0} d_n^{(*)} z^n$ converges in the region $\{z \in \mathbb{C} \mid |z| < 1\}$. In fact

$$d^{(*)}(z) = \frac{1}{\sqrt{1 - 4pqz^2}} \qquad \text{for} \quad |z| < 1 \tag{4.10}$$

since in this region, the (generalized) binomial formula gives

$$\frac{1}{\sqrt{1 - 4pqz^2}} = \sum_{n \geq 0} (-1)^n \binom{-\frac{1}{2}}{n} 4^n p^n q^n z^{2n},$$

and an elementary verification shows that

$$\binom{2n}{n} = (-1)^n \binom{-\frac{1}{2}}{n} 4^n. \tag{4.11}$$

Each word in $D^* \cap A^n$ has a unique factorization into words in D. Thus

$$d_n^{(*)} = \sum_{k \geq 0} \sum_{m_1 + \cdots + m_k = n} d_{m_1} d_{m_2} \cdots d_{m_k}.$$

For the corresponding generation functions, this gives

$$d^{(*)}(t) = \frac{1}{1 - d(t)}. \tag{4.12}$$

Consequently we have, for $|z| < 1$,

$$d(z) = \sum_{n \geq 0} d_n z^n = 1 - \frac{1}{d^*(z)} = 1 - \sqrt{1 - 4pqz^2}. \tag{4.13}$$

It follows that

$$\begin{aligned}\pi(D) = \sum_{n \geq 0} d_n &= \lim_{\substack{z \to 1 \\ z \in [0,1[}} \sum_{n \geq 0} d_n z^n \\ &= \lim_{\substack{z \to 1 \\ z \in [0,1[}} 1 - \sqrt{1 - 4pqz^2} = 1 - \sqrt{1 - 4pq}.\end{aligned}$$

It is easily seen that $1 - \sqrt{1 - 4pq} = 1 - |p - q|$. Thus we get

$$\pi(D) = 1 - |p - q| = 1 - |\pi(a) - \pi(b)|.$$

For $\pi(a) = \pi(b) = \frac{1}{2}$, we have $\pi(D) = 1$. This gives another proof that D is a maximal code (Example 2.5). Note that $\pi(D) < 1$ for any other Bernoulli distribution.

By Formula (4.12), we have (using again the binomial formula)

$$d_{2n} = (-1)^{n+1} \binom{\frac{1}{2}}{n} 4^n p^n q^n.$$

Since $\binom{\frac{1}{2}}{n} = (1/2n)\binom{-\frac{1}{2}}{n-1}$ we obtain [using again Formula (4.11)]

$$d_{2n} = \frac{2}{n}\binom{2n-2}{n-1} p^n q^n. \tag{4.14}$$

This gives as a byproduct the following formula

$$\mathrm{Card}(D \cap A^{2n}) = \frac{2}{n}\binom{2n-2}{n-1}.$$

Let $D' = D \cap aA^* = D \cap A^*b$. The set D'^* is exactly the set of well parenthesized strings when letter a stands for '(' and letter b for ')'. The previous formulae allow us to compute easily its length distribution. Let $D'' = D \cap bA^* = D \cap A^*a$ and

$$d'_n = \pi(D' \cap A^n), \qquad d''_n = \pi(D'' \cap A^n)$$

let $d'(t)$, $d''(t)$ be the series $d'(t) = \sum_{n \geq 0} d'_n t^n$, $d''_n(t) = \sum_{n \geq 0} d''_n t^n$. We have $\tilde{D}' = D''$ and $d'(t) = d''(t)$. Since $d(t) = d'(t) + d''(t)$, we obtain $d'(t) = \frac{1}{2}d(t)$. Let $d'^{(*)}_n = \pi(D'^* \cap A^n)$ and $d'^{(*)}(t) = \sum_{n \geq 0} d'^{(*)}_n t^n$. Then, as for (4.12)

$$d'^{(*)}(t) = \frac{1}{1 - d'(t)}.$$

Since $d'(t) = \frac{1}{2}d(t)$, we obtain from (4.13)

$$d'^{(*)}(z) = \frac{2}{1 + \sqrt{1 - 4pqz^2}} = \frac{d(z)}{2pqz^2}.$$

Therefore by (4.14)

$$d'^{(*)}_{2n} = \frac{1}{n+1}\binom{2n}{n}p^n q^n$$

and also

$$\mathrm{Card}(D'^* \cap A^{2n}) = \frac{1}{n+1}\binom{2n}{n}. \tag{4.15}$$

The numbers $\gamma_n = (1/(n+1))\binom{2n}{n}$ for $n \geq 0$ are called the *Catalan numbers.* Their first values are given below

n	0	1	2	3	4	5
γ_n	1	1	2	5	14	42

EXAMPLE 4.6 The set $X = \bigcup_{n \geq 0} a^n bA^n$ is prefix, and therefore is a code over $A = \{a, b\}$. It is a maximal code. Let indeed π be a positive Bernoulli distribution, and set $p = \pi(a)$. Then

$$\pi(a^n bA^n) = p^n(1 - p)$$

hence

$$\pi(X) = \sum_{n \geq 0} p^n(1 - p) = (1/(1 - p))(1 - p) = 1.$$

5. COMPLETE SETS

Any subset of a code is itself a code. Consequently, it is important to know the structure of maximal codes. Many of the results contained in this book are about maximal codes.

The notion of complete sets introduced in this section is in some sense dual to that of a code. For instance, any set containing a complete set is itself complete. Even if the duality is not perfectly balanced, it allows us to formulate maximality in terms of completeness, thus replacing an extremal property by a combinatorial one.

Let M be a monoid and let P be a subset of M. An element $m \in M$ is *completable in* P if there exist u, v in M such that

$$umv \in P.$$

It is equivalent to say that P meets the two-sided ideal MmM,

$$MmM \cap P \neq \emptyset,$$

or, in other words, that

$$m \in F(P) = M^{-1}PM^{-1}.$$

A word which is not completable in P is incompletable. The set of words completable in P is of course $F(P)$; the set $\bar{F}(P) = M - F(P)$ of incompletable words is a two-sided ideal of M which is disjoint from P.

A subset P of M is *dense* in M if all elements of M are completable in P, thus if $F(P) = M$ or, in an equivalent way, if P meets all (two-sided) ideals in M. Clearly, each superset of a dense set is dense.

The use of the adjective *dense* is justified by the fact that dense subsets of M are exactly the dense sets relative to some topology on M (see Exercise 5.3).

EXAMPLE 5.1 Let $A = \{a\}$. The dense subsets of A^* are the infinite subsets.

EXAMPLE 5.2 In a group G, any nonempty subset is dense, since $GmG = G$ for m in G.

EXAMPLE 5.3 The Dyck code D over $A = \{a, b\}$ is dense in A^*. Indeed, if $w \in A^*$, then $v = a^{2|w|_b}wb^{|w|}$ is easily seen to be in D^*. Furthermore, no proper nonempty left factor of v is in D^*. Thus v is is D, showing that w is completable in D.

It is useful to have a special term for codes X such that the submonoid X^* is dense. A subset P of M is called *complete* in M if the submonoid generated by P is dense. Every dense set is also complete. Next a subset X of A^* is complete iff $F(X^*) = A^*$.

EXAMPLE 5.4 Any nonempty subset of a^+ is complete, since it generates an infinite submonoid.

The following theorem is of fundamental importance.

THEOREM 5.1 *Any maximal code is complete.*

To prove this result, we first describe a method for embedding any code in a complete code.

PROPOSITION 5.2 *Let $X \subset A^+$ be a code. Let $y \in A^*$ be an unbordered word such that $A^*yA^* \cap X^* = \emptyset$. Let*

$$U = A^* - X^* - A^*yA^*. \tag{5.1}$$

Then the set

$$Y = X \cup y(Uy)^* \tag{5.2}$$

is a complete code.

Proof Let

$$V = A^* - A^*yA^*.$$

Then by assumption $X^* \subset V$ and $U = V - X^*$. Let us first observe that the set

$$Z = Vy$$

is a prefix code.

Assume indeed that $vy < v'y$ for two words v and v' in V. Since y is unbordered, vy must be a left factor of v'. But then v' is in A^*yA^*, a contradiction. Thus Z is prefix.

Now we show that Y is a code. Assume the contrary and consider a relation

$$y_1y_2\cdots y_n = y'_1y'_2\cdots y'_m$$

with $y_1,\ldots,y'_m \in Y$, and $y_1 \neq y'_1$. The set X being a code, one of these words must be in $Y - X$. Assume that one of $y_1,\ldots,y_n$ is in $Y - X$, and let p be the smallest index such that $y_p \in y(Uy)^*$. From $y \notin F(X^*)$ it also follows that $y_p \notin F(X^*)$. Consequently one of $y'_1,\ldots,y'_m$ is in $y(Uy)^*$. Let q be the smallest index that $y'_q \in y(Uy)^*$. Then

$$y_1\cdots y_{p-1}y, \qquad y'_1y'_2\cdots y'_{q-1}y \in Z$$

whence $y_1\cdots y_{p-1} = y'_1\cdots y'_{q-1}$ since Z is prefix. The set X is a code, thus from $y_1 \neq y'_1$ it follows that $p = q = 1$. Set

$$y_1 = yu_1y\cdots yu_ky,$$

$$y'_1 = yu'_1y\cdots yu'_ly,$$

with $u_1,\ldots,u_k,u'_1,\ldots,u'_l \in U$. Assume $y_1 < y'_1$. Since Z is prefix, the set Z^* is right unitary. From $U \subset V$, it follows that each u_iy, u'_iy is in Z. Consequently

$$u_1 = u'_1,\ldots,u_k = u'_k.$$

Let $t = u'_{k+1}y\cdots yu'_ly$. We have

$$y_2\cdots y_n = ty'_2\cdots y'_m.$$

The word y is a factor of t, and thus occurs also in $y_2\cdots y_n$. This shows that one of $y_2,\ldots,y_n$, say y_r, is in $y(Uy)^*$. Suppose r is chosen minimal. Then $y_2\cdots y_{r-1}y \in Z$ and $u'_{k+1}y \in Z$ are left factors of the same word. With the set Z being prefix, we have

$$u'_{k+1} = y_2\cdots y_{r-1}.$$

Thus $u'_{k+1} \in X^*$, in contradiction with the hypothesis $u'_{k+1} \in U$. This shows that Y is a code.

Finally, let us show that Y is complete. Let $w \in A^*$ and set

$$w = v_1yv_2y\cdots yv_{n-1}yv_n$$

with $n \geq 1$ and $v_i \in A^* - A^*yA^*$. Then

$$ywy \in Y^*.$$

Indeed let $v_{i_1}, v_{i_2}, \ldots, v_{i_k}$ be those v_i's which are in X^*. Then

$$ywy = (yv_1 y \cdots yv_{i_1-1}y)v_{i_1}(yv_{i_1+1}y \cdots yv_{i_2-1}y)$$
$$\times \cdots \times v_{i_k}(yv_{i_k+1}y \cdots yv_n y).$$

Each of the parenthesized words is in Y. Thus the whole word is in Y^*. □

Proof of Theorem 5.1 Let $X \subset A^+$ be a code which is not complete. If $\mathrm{Card}(A) = 1$, then $X = \varnothing$, and X is not maximal. If $\mathrm{Card}(A) \geq 2$, consider a word $u \notin F(X^*)$. According to Proposition 3.6 of Chapter 0, there is a word $v \in A^*$ such that $y = uv$ is unbordered. We still have $y \notin F(X^*)$. If follows then from Proposition 5.2 that $X \cup y$ is a code. Thus X is not maximal. □

EXAMPLE 5.5 Let $A = \{a, b\}$ and $X = \{bb, bbab, babb\}$. The word $y = aba$ is incompletable in X^*. However, $X \cup y$ is not a code, since

$$(bb)(aba)(babb) = (bbab)(aba)(bb).$$

This example shows that Proposition 5.2 is false without the assumption that y is unbordered.

EXAMPLE 5.6 We are able now to verify one of the claims made in Section 1, namely that there do exist finite codes which are not contained in a maximal finite code.

Let $X = \{a^5, ba^2, ab, b\}$. It is a code over $A = \{a, b\}$. Any maximal code containing X is infinite. Indeed, let Y be a maximal code over A containing X, and assume Y finite. Set $m = \max\{|y| \mid y \in Y\}$ and let

$$u = b^m a^{4+5m} b^m.$$

The maximality of Y implies its completeness. Thus u is a factor of a word in Y^*. Neither b^m nor a^{4+5m} can be proper factors of a word in Y. Thus there exist $y, y' \in Y \cup 1$ and integers $p, q, r \geq 0$ such that

$$u = b^p y a^q y' b^r$$

with $a^q \in Y^*$ (see Fig. 1.5). The word a^5 is the only word in Y which does not contain b; thus q is a multiple of 5; this implies that $|y|_a + |y'|_a \equiv 4 \bmod 5$.

Let $y = b^h a^{5s+i}$ and $y' = a^{j+5t} b^k$ with $0 \leq i, j \leq 4$. We have $i + j \equiv 4 \bmod 5$ whence $i + j = 4$. We will show that any choice of i, j leads to the conclusion that Y is not a code. This yields the contradiction.

If $i = 0, j = 4$, then $k \geq 1$ and we have $ba^2 \cdot a^{5t+4} b^k = b \cdot a^{5(t+1)} \cdot ab \cdot b^{k-1}$.

If $i = 1, j = 3$, then $b^h a^{5s+1} \cdot b = b^h \cdot a^{5s} \cdot ab$.

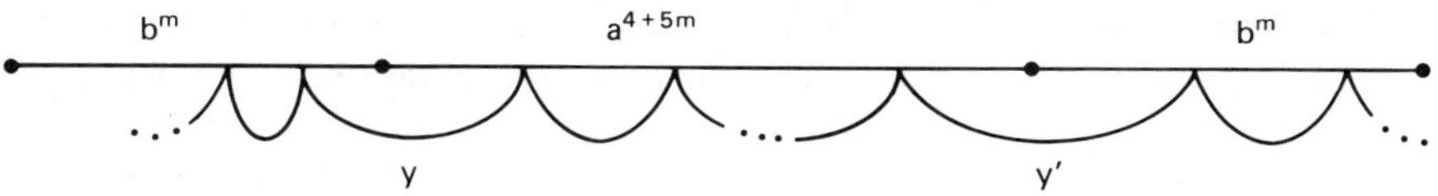

Fig. 1.5 The factorization of $b^m a^{4+5m} b^m$ in words in Y.

If $i = 2, j = 2$, then $b \cdot a^{2+5t} b^k = ba^2 \cdot a^{5t} \cdot b^k$.

If $i = 3, j = 1$, then $h \geq 1$ and $b^h a^{5s+3} \cdot b = b^{h-1} \cdot ba^2 \cdot a^{5s} \cdot ab$.

Finally,

$$\text{if } i = 4, j = 0, \text{ then } b^h a^{5s+4} \cdot ab = b^h \cdot a^{5(s+1)} \cdot b.$$

This example is a particular case of a general construction (see Exercise 5.2).

The converse of Theorem 5.1 is false (see Example 5.7). However, it is true under an additional assumption that relies on the following definition.

A subset P of a monoid M which is not dense is called *thin*. If P is thin, there is at least one element m in M which is incompletable in P, i.e., such that $MmM \cap P = \varnothing$, or equivalently $F(P) \neq M$.

The use of the adjective *thin* is justified by results like Proposition 5.3 or 5.6.

PROPOSITION 5.3 *Let M be a monoid and $P, Q \subset M$. Then the set $P \cup Q$ is thin iff P and Q are thin. If R is dense and P is thin, then $R - P$ is dense.*

Proof If P and Q are thin, then there exist $m, n \in M$ such that

$$MmM \cap P = \varnothing, \qquad MnM \cap Q = \varnothing.$$

Then mn is incompletable in $P \cup Q$ and therefore $P \cup Q$ is thin. Conversely if $P \cup Q$ is thin, there exists $m \in M$ which is uncompletable in $P \cup Q$ and therefore incompletable in P and also in Q. Hence P and Q are thin. If R is dense in M and P is thin, then $R - P$ cannot be thin since otherwise $R = (R - P) \cup P$ would also be thin by the above statement. ☐

Thin subsets of a free monoid have additional properties. In particular, any finite subset of A^* is clearly thin. Furthermore, if X, Y are thin subsets of A^* then the set

$$XY$$

is thin. In fact, if $u \notin F(X)$, $v \notin F(Y)$, then $uv \notin F(XY)$.

EXAMPLE 5.7 The Dyck code D over $A = \{a, b\}$ is dense (See Example 5.3). It is a maximal code since it is a group code (see Example 2.5). For each $x \in D$, the code $D - x$ remains dense, in view of Proposition 5.3, and thus remains complete. But of course $D - x$ is no more a maximal code. This example shows that the converse of Theorem 5.1 does not hold in general.

Theorem 5.1 admits a converse in the case of codes which are both thin and complete. Before going on to prove this, we give some useful properties of these sets.

PROPOSITION 5.4 *Let $X \subset A^*$ be a thin and complete set. Let w be a word incompletable in X. Then*

$$A^* = \bigcup_{\substack{d \in D \\ g \in G}} d^{-1}X^*g^{-1} = D^{-1}X^*G^{-1}, \tag{5.3}$$

where D and G are the sets of right (resp. left) factors of w.

Note that the set $D \times G$ is finite.

Proof Let $z \in A^*$. Since X^* is dense, the word wzw is completable in X^*, thus for some $u, v \in A^*$

$$uwzwv \in X^*.$$

Now w is not a factor of a word in X. Thus there exist two factorizations

$$w = g_1 d = g d_1$$

such that

$$ug_1, dzg, d_1 v \in X^*.$$

This shows that $z \in d^{-1}X^*g^{-1}$. □

PROPOSITION 5.5 *Let X be a thin and complete subset of A^*. For any positive Bernoulli distribution π on A^*, we have*

$$\pi(X) \geq 1.$$

Proof We have $\pi(A^*) = \infty$. In view of Eq. (5.3), there exists a pair $(d, g) \in D \times G$ such that $\pi(d^{-1}X^*g^{-1}) = \infty$. Now

$$d(d^{-1}X^*g^{-1})g \subset X^*.$$

This implies

$$\pi(d)\pi(d^{-1}X^*g^{-1})\pi(g) \leq \pi(X^*).$$

The positivity of π shows that $\pi(dg) \neq 0$. Thus $\pi(X^*) = \infty$. Now

$$\pi(X^*) \leq \sum_{n \geq 0} \pi(X^n) \leq \sum_{n \geq 0} (\pi(X))^n.$$

Assuming $\pi(X) < 1$, we get $\pi(X^*) < \infty$. Thus $\pi(X) \geq 1$. □

Note the following property showing, as already claimed before, that a thin set has only *few* words.

PROPOSITION 5.6 *Let $X \subset A^*$ be a thin set. For any positive Bernoulli distribution on A^*, we have*

$$\pi(X) < \infty.$$

Proof Let w be a word which is not a factor of a word in $X : w \notin F(X)$. Set $n = |w|$. We have $n \geq 1$. For $0 \leq i \leq n-1$, consider

$$X_i = \{x \in X \mid |x| \equiv i \bmod n\}.$$

It suffices to show that $\pi(X_i)$ is finite for $i = 0, \ldots, n-1$. Now

$$X_i \subset A^i(A^n - w)^*.$$

Since $A^n - w$ is a code, we have

$$\pi[(A^n - w)^*] = \sum_{k \geq 0} (\pi(A^n - w))^k = \sum_{k \geq 0} (1 - \pi(w))^k.$$

The positivity of π implies $\pi(w) > 0$, and consequently

$$\pi[(A^n - w)^*] = \frac{1}{\pi(w)}.$$

Thus $\pi(X_i) \leq 1/\pi(w)$. □

We are now ready to prove

THEOREM 5.7 *Any thin and complete code is maximal.*

Proof Let X be a thin, complete code and let π be a positive Bernoulli distribution. By Proposition 5.5, $\pi(X) \geq 1$, and by Theorem 4.2, we have $\pi(X) \leq 1$. Thus $\pi(X) = 1$. But then Proposition 4.4 shows that X is maximal. □

Theorems 5.1 and 5.7 can be grouped together to give

THEOREM 5.8 *Let X be a code over A. Then X is complete iff X is dense or maximal.*

Proof Assume X is complete. If X is not dense, then it is thin, and consequently X is maximal by the previous theorem. Conversely, a dense set is complete, and a maximal code is complete by Theorem 5.1. □

Before giving other consequences of these statements, let us present a first application of the combinatorial characterization of maximality.

PROPOSITION 5.9 *Let $X \subset A^*$ be a finite maximal code. For any nonempty subset B of A, the code $X \cap B^*$ is a maximal code over B. In particular, for each letter $a \in A$, there is an integer n such that $a^n \in X$.*

Proof The second claim results from the first one by taking $B = \{a\}$. Let $n = \max \{|x| \mid x \in X\}$ be the maximal length of words in X, and let $\emptyset \neq B \subset A$. To show that $Y = X \cap B^*$ is a maximal code over B, it suffices to show,

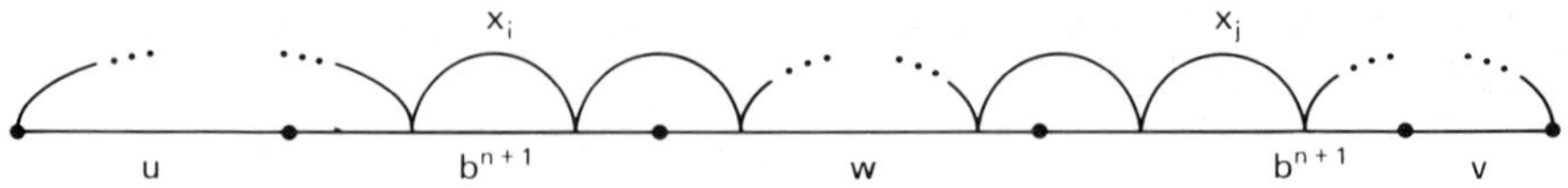

Fig. 1.6 The factorization of $ub^{n+1}wb^{n+1}v$.

in view of Theorem 5.7, that Y is complete (in B^*). Let $w \in B^*$ and $b \in B$. Consider the word

$$w' = b^{n+1}wb^{n+1}.$$

The completeness of X gives words $u, v \in A^*$ such that

$$uw'v = x_1x_2 \cdots x_k$$

for some $x_1, x_2, \ldots, x_k \in X$. But by the definition of n, there exist two integers i, j $(1 \le i < j \le k)$ such that

$$x_ix_{i+1} \cdots x_j = b^rwb^s$$

for some $r, s \in \{1, \ldots, n\}$ (see Fig. 1.6). But then $x_i, x_{i+1}, \ldots, x_j \in X \cap B^* = Y$. This shows that w is completable in Y^*. □

Let $X \subset A^+$ be a finite maximal code, and let $a \in A$ be a letter. The (unique) integer n such that $a^n \in X$ is called the *order* of a relative to X.

THEOREM 5.10 *Let X be a thin code. The following conditions are equivalent:*

(i) *X is a maximal code.*
(ii) *There exists a positive Bernoulli distribution π with $\pi(X) = 1$.*
(iii) *For any positive Bernoulli distribution π, we have $\pi(X) = 1$.*
(iv) *X is complete.*

Proof (i) ⇒ (iv) is Theorem 5.1. (iv) ⇒ (iii) is a consequence of Theorem 4.2 and Proposition 5.5. (iii) ⇒ (ii) is not very hard, and (ii) ⇒ (i) is Proposition 4.4. □

Theorem 5.10 gives a surprisingly simple method to test whether a thin code is maximal. It suffices to take any positive Bernoulli distribution and to check whether the measure of the code equals 1.

EXAMPLE 5.8. The Dyck code D over $A = \{a, b\}$ is maximal and complete, but satisfies $\pi(D) = 1$ only for one Bernoulli distribution (see Example 4.5). Thus the conditions (i) + (ii) + (iv) do not imply (iii) for dense codes.

EXAMPLE 5.9 The prefix code $X = \bigcup_{n \ge 0} a^nbA^n$ over $A = \{a, b\}$ is dense since for all $w \in A^*$, $a^{|w|}bw \in X$. It satisfies (iii), as we have seen in Example 4.6. Thus X satisfies the four conditions of the theorem without being thin.

THEOREM 5.11 *Let X be a thin subset of A^+, and let π be a positive Bernoulli distribution. Any two among the three following conditions imply the third*

(i) *X is a code,*
(ii) *$\pi(X) = 1$,*
(iii) *X is complete.*

Proof (i) + (ii) $\Rightarrow$ (iii). The condition $\pi(X) = 1$ implies that X is a maximal code, by Proposition 4.4. Thus by Theorem 5.1, X is complete.

(i) + (iii) $\Rightarrow$ (ii) Theorem 4.2 and condition (i) imply that $\pi(X) \leq 1$. Now X is thin and complete; in view of Proposition 5.5, we have $\pi(X) \geq 1$.

(ii) + (iii) $\Rightarrow$ (i) Let $n \geq 1$ be an integer. First, we verify that X^n is thin and complete. To see completeness, let $u \in A^*$, and let $v, w \in A^*$ be such that $vuw \in X^*$. Then $vuw \in X^k$ for some $k \geq 0$. Thus $(vuw)^n \in (X^n)^k \subset (X^n)^*$. This shows that u is completable in $(X^n)^*$. Further, since X is thin and because the product of two thin sets is again thin, the set X^n is thin.

Thus, X^n is thin and complete. Consequently, $\pi(X^n) \geq 1$ by Proposition 5.5. On the other hand, we have $\pi(X^n) \leq \pi(X)^n$ and thus $\pi(X^n) \leq 1$. Consequently $\pi(X^n) = 1$. Thus for all $n \geq 1$

$$\pi(X^n) = \pi(X)^n.$$

Proposition 4.1 shows that X is a code. □

Thin codes constitute a very important class of codes. They will be characterized by some finiteness condition in Chapter IV. We anticipate these results by proving a particular case which shows that the class of thin codes is quite a large one.

PROPOSITION 5.12 *Any recognizable code is thin.*

Proof Let $X \subset A^*$ be a recognizable code, and let $\mathcal{A} = (Q, i, T)$ be a deterministic complete automaton recognizing X. Associate to a word w, the number

$$\rho(w) = \operatorname{Card}(Q \cdot w) = \operatorname{Card}\{q \cdot w \mid q \in Q\}.$$

We have $\rho(w) \leq \operatorname{Card} Q$ and for all u, v,

$$\rho(uwv) \leq \rho(w).$$

Let J be the set of words w in A^* with minimal $\rho(w)$. The inequality above shows that J is a two-sided ideal of A^*.

Let $w \in J$, and let $P = Q \cdot w$. Then $P \cdot w = P$. Indeed $P \cdot w \subset Q \cdot w = P$, and on the other hand, $P \cdot w = Q \cdot w^2$. Thus $\operatorname{Card}(P \cdot w) = \rho(w^2)$. Since $\rho(w)$ is minimal, $\rho(w^2) = \rho(w)$, whence the equality. This shows that the mapping $p \mapsto p \cdot w$ from P onto P is a bijection. It follows that there is some integer n with the property with the mapping $p \mapsto p \cdot w^n$ is the identity mapping on P.

Since $P = Q \cdot w$, we have

$$q \cdot w = q \cdot w^{n+1} \qquad \text{for all} \quad q \in Q.$$

To show that X is thin, it suffices to show that X does not meet the two-sided ideal J. Assume that $J \cap X \neq \emptyset$ and let $x \in X \cap J$. Then

$$i \cdot x = t \in T.$$

Next $x \in J$ and, by the previous discussion, there is some integer $n \geq 1$ such that $i \cdot x^{n+1} = t$. This implies that $x^{n+1} \in X$. But this is impossible, since X is a code. □

The converse of Proposition 5.12 is false:

EXAMPLE 5.10 The code $X = \{a^n b^n \mid n \geq 1\}$ is thin (e.g., ba is not a factor of X), but X is not recognizable.

EXAMPLE 5.11 In one interesting case, the converse of Proposition 5.12 holds: *Any thin group code is recognizable.* Indeed let $X \subset A^*$ be a group code. Let $\varphi: A^* \to G$ be a surjective morphism onto a group G, and let H be a subgroup of G such that $X^* = \varphi^{-1}(H)$. By assumption, X is thin. Let m be a word that is incompletable in X. We show that H has finite index in G, and more precisely that

$$G = \bigcup_{p \leq m} H[\varphi(p)]^{-1},$$

(where p runs over the left factors of m). Indeed let $g \in G$ and $w \in \varphi^{-1}(g)$. Let $u \in A^*$ be such that $\varphi(u)$ is the group inverse of $g\varphi(m)$. Then $\varphi(wmu) = g\varphi(m)\varphi(u) = 1$, whence $wmu \in X^*$. Now m is incompletable in X. Thus m is not factor of a word in X and consequently there is a factorization $m = pq$ such that wp, $qu \in X^*$. But then $h = \varphi(wp) \in H$. Since $h = g\varphi(p)$, we have $g \in H\varphi(p)^{-1}$. This proves the formula.

The formula shows that there are finitely many right cosets of H in G. Thus the permutation group on the right cosets, say K, is also finite. Let $\alpha: G \to K$ be the canonical morphism defined by $Hr\alpha(g) = Hrg$ (see Section 0.8). Then, setting $N = \{\sigma \in K \mid H\sigma = H\}$, we have $H = \alpha^{-1}(N) = \alpha^{-1}(\alpha(H))$. Thus $X^* = \psi^{-1}\psi(X^*)$, where $\psi = \alpha \cdot \varphi$. Since K is finite, this shows that X^* is recognizable. Consequently, X is also recognizable (Exercise 2.7).

Remark We have used in the preceding paragraphs arguments which rely essentially on two techniques: measures on the one hand which allowed us to prove especially Theorem 5.7 and direct *combinatorial* arguments on words on the other (as in the proof of Theorem 5.1).

It is interesting to note that some of the proofs can be done by using just one of the two techniques. A careful analysis shows that all preceding statements with the exception of those involving maximality can be established by using only arguments on measures. As an example, the implication (ii) ⇒ (iv) in Theorem 5.10 can be proved as follows without using the maximality of X. If X is not complete, then X^* is thin. Thus, by Proposition 5.6, $\pi(X^*) < \infty$ which implies $\pi(X) < 1$ by Proposition 4.1.

Conversely, there exist, for some of the results given here, *combinatorial* proofs which do not rely on measures. This is the case for Theorem 5.8, where the proof given relies heavily on arguments about measures. Another proof of this result will be given in Chapter IV (Corollary 5.5). This proof is based on the fact that if $X \subset A^+$ is a thin complete code, then all words $w \in A^*$ satisfy

$$(X^*wX^*)^+ \cap X^* \neq \emptyset.$$

This implies Theorem 5.8, because according to this formula, $X \cup w$ is not a code for $w \notin X$ and thus X is a maximal code.

6. COMPOSITION

We now introduce a partial binary operation on codes called composition. This operation associates to two codes Y and Z satisfying a certain compatibility condition a third code denoted by $Y \circ Z$.

There is a twofold interest in this operation. First, it gives a useful method for constructing more complicated codes from simpler ones. Thus we will see that the composition of a prefix and a suffix code can result in a code that is neither prefix nor suffix.

Second, and this constitutes the main interest for composition, the converse notion of decomposition allows us to study the structure of codes. If a code X decomposes into two codes Y and Z, then these codes are generally simpler.

Let $Z \subset A^*$ and $Y \subset B^*$ be two codes with $B = \text{alph}(Y)$. Then the codes Y and Z are *composable* if there is a bijection from B onto Z. If β is such a bijection, then Y and Z are called composable *through* β. Then β defines a morphism $B^* \to A^*$ which is injective since Z is a code (Proposition 1.1). The set

$$X = \beta(Y) \subset Z^* \subset A^* \tag{6.1}$$

is obtained by *composition* of Y and Z (by means of β). We denote it by

$$X = Y \circ_\beta Z \qquad \text{or} \qquad X = Y \circ Z,$$

when the context permits it. Since β is injective, X and Y are related by bijection, and in particular $\text{Card}\, X = \text{Card}\, Y$. The words in X are obtained just by replacing, in the words of Y, each letter b by the word $\beta(b) \in Z$. The injectivity of β, the Corollary 1.2 and (6.1) show the following result

PROPOSITION 6.1 *If Y and Z are two composable codes, then $X = Y \circ Z$ is a code.* □

EXAMPLE 6.1 Let $A = \{a, b\}$, $B = \{c, d, e\}$ and

$$Z = \{a, ba, bb\} \subset A^*, \qquad Y = \{cc, d, dc, e, ec\} \subset B^*.$$

The code Z is prefix, and Y is suffix. Further Card B = Card Z. Thus Y and Z are composable, in particular by means of the morphism $\beta: B^* \to A^*$ defined by

$$\beta(c) = a, \qquad \beta(d) = ba, \qquad \beta(e) = bb.$$

Then $X = Y \circ Z = \{aa, ba, baa, bb, bba\}$. This code X is neither prefix nor suffix. Now choose

$$\beta': \quad B^* \to A^*,$$

$$\beta'(c) = ba, \qquad \beta'(d) = a, \qquad \beta'(e) = bb.$$

Then $X' = Y \circ_{\beta'} Z = \{baba, a, aba, bb, bbba\}$. This example shows that the composed code $Y \circ_\beta Z$ depends essentially on the mapping β.

Let $X \subset A^*$ be a code, with $A = \text{alph}(X)$. Since A is a code over itself and $X = \iota(X)$, with $\iota: A^* \to A^*$ the identity mapping, we have

$$X = X \circ_\iota A.$$

Let $\beta: B^* \to A^*$ be a coding morphism for X. Then $X = \beta(B)$ and thus

$$X = B \circ_\beta X.$$

These examples show that every code is obtained in at least two ways as a composition of codes.

The two expressions $X = X \circ A$ and $X = B \circ X$ are exactly the particular cases obtained by replacing one of the two codes by the alphabet in the expression

$$X = Y \circ Z.$$

Indeed, if $Y = B$, then $Z = \beta(B) = X$; if now $Z = A$, then B can be identified with A, and Y can be identified with X.

Notice also the formula

$$X = Y \circ_\beta Z \Rightarrow X^n = Y^n \circ_\beta Z \qquad n \geq 2.$$

Indeed, Y^n is a code (Corollary 1.3) and

$$Y^n \circ Z = \beta(Y^n) = X^n.$$

PROPOSITION 6.2 *Let $X \subset C^*$, $Y \subset B^*$, and $Z \subset A^*$ be three codes, and assume that X and Y are composable through γ and that Y and Z are composable through β. Then*

$$(X \circ_\gamma Y) \circ_\beta Z = X \circ_{\beta \circ \gamma} (Y \circ_\beta Z).$$

Proof We may suppose that $C = \text{alph}(X)$, $B = \text{alph}(Y)$. By hypothesis, the injective morphisms

$$\gamma\colon\ C^* \to B^*, \qquad \beta\colon\ B^* \to A^*$$

satisfy

$$\gamma(C) = Y, \qquad \beta(B) = Z.$$

Let $\delta\colon D^* \to C^*$ be a coding morphism for X; thus $\delta(D) = X$. Then

$$D^* \xrightarrow{\delta} C^* \xrightarrow{\gamma} B^* \xrightarrow{\beta} A.$$

and $\beta\gamma\delta(D) = \beta\gamma(X) = X \circ_{\beta\gamma} \beta\gamma(C) = X \circ_{\beta\gamma} (Y \circ_\beta Z)$, and also $\beta\gamma\delta(D) = \beta(\gamma\delta(D)) = \gamma\delta(D) \circ_\beta \beta(B) = (X \circ_\gamma Y) \circ Z$. □

Some of the properties of codes are preserved under composition.

PROPOSITION 6.3 *Let Y and Z be composable codes, and let $X = Y \circ Z$.*

1. *If Y and Z are prefix (suffix) codes, then X is a prefix (suffix) code.*
2. *If Y and Z are complete, then X is complete.*
3. *If Y and Z are thin, then X is thin.*

The proof of (3) uses Lemma 6.4 which cannot be established before Chapter IV, where more powerful tools will be available.

LEMMA 6.4 *Let Z be a thin complete code over A. For each word $u \in Z^*$ there exists a word $w \in Z^*uZ^*$ having the following property. If $mwn \in Z^*$, then there exists a factorization $w = sut$ with $ms, tn \in Z^*$.*

Proof of Proposition 6.3 Let $Y \subset B^*$, $Z \subset A^*$, and let $\beta\colon B^* \to A^*$ be an injective morphism with $\beta(B) = Z$. Thus $X = \beta(Y) = Y \circ_\beta Z$.

1. Assume Y and Z are prefix codes. Consider $x, xu \in X$ with $u \in A^*$. Since $X \subset Z^*$, we have $x, xu \in Z^*$ and since Z^* is right unitary, this implies $u \in Z^*$. Let $y = \beta^{-1}(x), v = \beta^{-1}(u) \in B^*$. Then $y, yv \in Y$ and Y is prefix; thus $v = 1$ and consequently $u = 1$. This shows that X is prefix. The case of suffix codes is handled in the same way.

2. Let $w \in A^*$. The code Z is complete, thus $uwv \in Z^*$ for some $u, v \in A^*$. Let $h = \beta^{-1}(uwv) \in B^*$. There exist, by the completeness of Y, two words $\bar{u}, \bar{v} \in B^*$ with $\bar{u}h\bar{v} \in Y^*$. But then $\beta(\bar{u})uwv\beta(\bar{v}) \in X^*$. This proves the completeness of X.

3. If Z is not complete, then $F(X) \subset F(Z^*) \neq A^*$ and X is thin. Assume now that Z is complete. The code Y is thin. Consequently $F(Y) \neq B^*$. Let $\bar{u} \in B^* - F(Y)$, and $u = \beta(\bar{u})$. Let w be the word associated to u in Lemma 6.4. Then $w \notin F(X)$. Indeed, assuming the contrary, there exist words $m, n \in A^*$ such that

$$x = mwn \in X \subset Z^*.$$

In view of Lemma 6.4,

$$x = msutn, \qquad \text{with} \quad ms, tn \in Z^* = \beta(B^*).$$

Setting $p = \beta^{-1}(ms)$, $q = \beta^{-1}(tn)$, we have $p\bar{u}q \in Y$. Thus $\bar{u} \in F(Y)$, contrary to the assumption. This shows that w is not in X, and thus X is thin. □

We now consider the second aspect of the composition operation, namely the decomposition of a code into simpler ones. For this, it is convenient to extend the notation alph in the following way: let $Z \subset A^*$ be a code, and $X \subset A^*$. Then

$$\mathrm{alph}_Z(X) = \{z \in Z \mid \exists u, v \in Z^* : uzv \in X\}.$$

In other words, $\mathrm{alph}_Z(X)$ is the set of words in Z which appear at least once in a factorization of a word in X as a product of words in Z. Of course, $\mathrm{alph}_A = \mathrm{alph}$. The following proposition describes the condition for the existence of a decomposition.

Proposition 6.5 *Let $X, Z \subset A^*$ be codes. There exists a code Y such that*

$$X = Y \circ Z$$

iff

$$X \subset Z^* \qquad \text{and} \qquad \mathrm{alph}_Z(X) = Z. \tag{6.2}$$

The second condition in (6.2) means that all words in Z appear in at least one factorization of a word in X as product of words in Z.

Proof Let $X = Y \circ_\beta Z$, where $\beta: B^* \to A^*$ is an injective morphism, $Y \subset B^*$ and $B = \mathrm{alph}(Y)$. Then $X = \beta(Y) \subset \beta(B^*) = Z^*$ and further $\beta(B) = \mathrm{alph}_{\beta(B)}(\beta(Y))$, that is, $Z = \mathrm{alph}_Z(X)$.

Conversely, let $\beta: B^* \to A^*$ be a coding morphism for Z, and set $Y = \beta^{-1}(X)$. Then $X \subset \beta(B^*) = Z^*$ and $\beta(Y) = X$. By Corollary 1.2, Y is a code. Next $\mathrm{alph}(Y) = B$ since $Z = \mathrm{alph}_Z(X)$. Thus Y and Z are composable and $X = Y \circ_\beta Z$. □

We have already seen that there are two distinguished decompositions of a code $X \subset A^*$ as $X = Y \circ Z$, namely $X = B \circ X$ and $X = X \circ A$. They are obtained by taking $Z = X$ and $Z = A$ in Proposition 6.5 [and assuming $A = \mathrm{alph}(X)$]. These decompositions are not interesting. We will call *indecomposable* a code which has no other decompositions. Formally, a code $X \subset A^*$ with $A = \mathrm{alph}(X)$ is called *indecomposable* if $X = Y \circ Z$ and $B = \mathrm{alph}(Y)$ imply $Y = B$ or $Z = A$. If X is decomposable, and if Z is a code such that $X = Y \circ Z$, and $Z \neq X, A$, then we say that X decomposes *over* Z.

Example 6.1 (*continued*) The code X decomposes over Z. On the contrary, the code $Z = \{a, ba, bb\}$ is indecomposable. Indeed, let T be a code such that

$Z \subset T^*$, and suppose $T \neq A$. Necessarily, $a \in T$. Thus $b \notin T$. But then $ba, bb \in T$, whence $Z \subset T$. Now Z is a maximal code (Example 4.2), thus $Z = T$.

PROPOSITION 6.6 *For any finite code X, there exist indecomposable codes $Z_1, \ldots, Z_n$ such that*

$$X = Z_1 \circ \cdots \circ Z_n.$$

To prove this proposition, we introduce a notation. Let X be a finite code, and let

$$l(X) = \sum_{x \in X} (|x| - 1) = \sum_{x \in X} |x| - \mathrm{Card}(X).$$

For each $x \in X$, we have $|x| \geq 1$. Thus $l(X) \geq 0$, and moreover

$$l(X) = 0 \quad \text{iff} \quad X \quad \text{is a subset of the alphabet.}$$

PROPOSITION 6.7 *If $X, Z \subset A^*$ and $Y \subset B^*$ are finite codes such that $X = Y \circ Z$, then $l(X) \geq l(Y) + l(Z)$.*

Proof Let $\beta: B^* \to A^*$ be the injective morphism such that

$$X = Y \circ_\beta Z.$$

From $\mathrm{Card}(X) = \mathrm{Card}(Y)$ it follows that

$$l(X) - l(Y) = \sum_{x \in X} |x| - \sum_{y \in Y} |y| = \sum_{y \in Y} (|\beta(y)| - |y|).$$

Now $|\beta(y)| = \sum_{b \in B} |\beta(b)| \cdot |y|_b$. Thus

$$\begin{aligned} l(X) - l(Y) &= \sum_{y \in Y} \left(\sum_{b \in B} (|\beta(b)|\,|y|_b - |y|_b) \right) \\ &= \sum_{y \in Y} \left(\sum_{b \in B} (|\beta(b)| - 1) \cdot |y|_b \right) \\ &= \sum_{b \in B} (|\beta(b)| - 1) \cdot \left(\sum_{y \in Y} |y|_b \right). \end{aligned}$$

By assumption $\mathrm{B} = \mathrm{alph}(Y)$, whence $\sum_{y \in Y} |y|_b \geq 1$ for all b in B. Further $|\beta(b)| \geq 1$ for $b \in B$ by the injectivity of β. Thus

$$l(X) - l(Y) \geq \sum_{b \in B} (|\beta(b)| - 1) = \sum_{z \in Z} (|z| - 1) = l(Z). \quad \square$$

Proof of Proposition 6.6 The proof is by induction on $l(X)$. If $l(X) = 0$, then X is composed of letters, and thus is indecomposable. If $l(X) > 0$ and X is decomposable, then $X = Y \circ Z$ for some codes Y, Z. Further Y and Z are not formed of letters only, and thus $l(Y) > 0$, $l(Z) > 0$. By Proposition 6.7, we have

$l(Y) < l(X)$ and $l(Z) < l(X)$. Thus Y and Z are compositions of indecomposable codes. Thus X also is such a composition. □

Proposition 6.6 shows the existence of a decomposition of codes. This decomposition needs not be unique. This is shown in

EXAMPLE 6.2 Consider the codes

$$X = \{aa, ba, baa, bb, bba\}$$

and

$$Y = \{cc, d, dc, e, ec\}, \qquad Z = \{a, ba, bb\}$$

of Example 6.1. As we have seen, $X = Y \circ Z$. There is also a decomposition

$$X = Y' \circ_\gamma Z'$$

with

$$Y' = \{cc, d, cd, e, ce\}, \qquad Z' = \{aa, b, ba\},$$

and

$$\gamma: B^* \to A^* \quad \text{defined by } \gamma(c) = b, \quad \gamma(d) = aa, \quad \gamma(e) = ba.$$

The code Z is undecomposable, the code Z' is obtained from Z by interchanging a and b, and by taking then the reverse. These operations do not change indecomposability.

EXAMPLE 6.3 This example shows that in decompositions of a code in indecomposable codes, even the number of components need not be unique. For $X = \{a^3b\}$, we have

$$X = \{cd\} \circ \{a^2, ab\} = \{cd\} \circ \{u^2, v\} \circ \{a, ab\}$$

and also

$$X = \{cd\} \circ \{a^3, b\}.$$

This gives two decompositions of length 3 and 2, respectively.

The code X in Example 6.2 is neither prefix nor suffix, but is composed of such codes. We may ask whether any (finite) code can be obtained by composition of prefix and suffix codes. This is not the case, as shown in

EXAMPLE 6.4 The code $X = \{b, ba, a^2b, a^3ba^4\}$ does not decompose over a prefix or a suffix code.

Assume the contrary. Then $X \subset Z^*$ for some prefix (or suffix) code $Z \neq A$. Thus Z^* is right unitary (resp. left unitary). From $b, ba \in Z^*$, it follows that $a \in Z^*$, whence $A = \{a, b\} \subset Z^*$ and $A = Z$. Assuming Z^* left unitary, b,

$a^2b \in Z^*$ implies $a^2 \in Z^*$. It follows that $a^3b \in Z^*$, whence $a^3 \in Z^*$ and finally $a \in Z^*$. Thus again $Z = A$.

We now give a list of properties of codes which are inherited by the factors of a decomposition. Proposition 6.8 is in some sense dual to Proposition 6.3.

PROPOSITION 6.8 *Let X, Y, Z be codes with $X = Y \circ Z$.*

1. *If X is prefix (suffix), then Y is prefix (suffix).*
2. *If X is maximal, then Y and Z are maximal.*
3. *If X is complete, then Z is complete.*
4. *If X is thin, then Z is thin.*

Proof We assume that $X, Z \subset A^*$, $Y \subset B^*$, $\beta: B^* \to A^*$ an injective morphism with $\beta(B) = Z$, $\beta(Y) = X$.

1. Let $y, yu \in Y$. Then $\beta(y)$, $\beta(y)\beta(u) \in X$, and since X is prefix, $\beta(u) = 1$. Now β is injective, whence $u = 1$.

2. If Y is not maximal, let $Y' = Y \cup y$ be a code for some $y \notin Y$. Then $\beta(Y') = \beta(Y) \cup \beta(y)$ is a code which is distinct from X by the injectivity of β. Thus X is not maximal.

Assume now that Z is not maximal. Set $Z' = Z \cup z$ for some $z \notin Z$ such that Z' is a code. Extend B to $B' = B \cup b$ $(b \notin B)$ and define β over B'^* by $\beta(b) = z$. Then β is injective by Proposition 1.1 because Z' is a code. Further $Y' = Y \cup b$ is a code, and consequently $\beta(Y') = X \cup z$ is a code, showing that X is not maximal.

3. is clear from $X^* \subset Z^*$.

4. Any word in Z is a factor of a word in X. Thus $F(Z) \subset F(X)$. By assumption, $F(X) \neq A^*$. Thus $F(Z) \neq A^*$ and Z is thin. □

PROPOSITION 6.9 *Let X, Y, Z be three codes such that $X = Y \circ Z$. Then*

X is thin and complete $\Leftrightarrow$ Y and Z are thin and complete.

Proof By Proposition 6.3, the code X is thin and complete, provided Y and Z are. Assume conversely that X is thin and complete. Proposition 6.8 shows that Z is thin and complete. In view of Theorem 5.8, X is a maximal code. By Proposition 6.8, Y is maximal, and thus Y is complete (Theorem 5.2). It remains to show that Y is thin. With the notations of the proof of Proposition 6.8, consider a word $u \notin F(X)$. Since Z^* is dense, $sut \in Z^*$ for some words $s, t \in A^*$. Thus $sut = \beta(w)$ for some $w \in B^*$. But now w is not completable in Y, since otherwise $hwk \in Y$ for some $h, k \in B^*$, giving $\beta(h)\, sut\, \beta(k) \in X$, whence $u \in F(X)$. Thus Y is thin. □

By Proposition 6.9, for thin codes Y, Z, the code $Y \circ Z$ is maximal iff Y and Z are maximal. We have no example showing that this becomes false without the assumption that Y and Z are thin.

PROPOSITION 6.10 *Let X be a maximal code over A. For any code $Z \subset A^*$, the following equivalence holds:*

$$X \text{ decomposes over } Z \text{ iff } X^* \subseteq Z^*.$$

In particular,

$$X \text{ is indecomposable iff } X^* \text{ is a maximal submonoid of } A^*.$$

Proof If X decomposes over Z, then $X^* \subset Z^*$. Conversely, if $X^* \subset Y^*$, let $\bar{Z} = \text{alph}_Z(X)$. Then $X \subset \bar{Z}^*$, and of course $\bar{Z} = \text{alph}_{\bar{Z}}(X)$. By Proposition 6.5, X decomposes over $\bar{Z}$. In view of Proposition 6.8, the code $\bar{Z}$ is maximal. By $\bar{Z} \subset Z$, we have $\bar{Z} = Z$. □

EXAMPLE 6.5 Let A be an alphabet. We show that the uniform code A^n decomposes over Z iff $Z = A^m$ and m divides n. In particular, A^n is indecomposable for n prime and for $n = 1$.

Indeed, let $A^n = X = Y \circ_\beta Z$, where $Y \subset B^*$ and $\beta: B^* \to A^*$. The code X is maximal and biprefix, and thus Y also is maximal and biprefix and Z is maximal. Let $y \in Y$ be a word of maximal length, and set $y = ub$ with $b \in B$. Then $Y \cup uB$ is prefix. Let indeed $y' = ub'$, $b' \in B$. Any proper left factor of y' is also a proper left factor of y, and therefore is not in $Y \cup uB$; next if y' is a left factor of some y'' in $Y \cup uB$, then by the maximality of the length of y, we have $|y'| = |y''|$ and $y' = y''$. Thus $Y \cup uB$ is a code. Hence $Y \cup uB = Y$, because Y is maximal. It follows that $\beta(uB) = \beta(u) Z \subset X$. Now X is a uniform code, thus all words in Z have the same length, say m. Since Z is maximal, $Z = A^m$. It follows that $n = m \cdot |y|$. □

EXERCISES

SECTION 1

1.1. Let $n \geq 1$ be an integer. Let I, J be two sets of nonnegative integers such that for $i, i' \in I$ and $j, j' \in J$,

$$i + j \equiv i' + j' \mod n$$

implies $i = i', j = j'$. Let

$$Y = \{a^i b a^j \mid i \in I, j \in J\}$$

and $X = Y \cup a^n$. Show that X is a code.

SECTION 2

2.1. Show directly (i.e., without using Theorem 2.8) that a set $X = \{x, y\}$ is a code iff x and y are not powers of a single word.

2.2. Let K be a field and A an alphabet. Denote by $K\langle A \rangle$ the subalgebra of $K\langle\langle A \rangle\rangle$ formed by the series $\sigma \in K\langle\langle A \rangle\rangle$ such that $(\sigma, w) = 0$ for all but a finite number of words $w \in A^*$. Let $X \subset A^+$ be a code and β: $B^* \to A^*$ be a coding morphism for X. Extend β by linearity to a morphism from $K\langle B\rangle$ into $K\langle A\rangle$. Show that β defines an isomorphism between $K\langle B\rangle$ and the subalgebra of $K\langle A\rangle$ generated by the elements of X.

2.3. Show that a submonoid N of a monoid M is stable iff for all $m, n \in M$ we have

$$nm, n, mn \in N \quad \Rightarrow \quad m \in N.$$

2.4. Let M be a commutative monoid. Show that a submonoid of M is stable iff it is biunitary.

2.5. For $X \subset A^+$ let Y be the base of the smallest right unitary submonoid containing X.

(a) Show that $Y \subset (Y^*)^{-1}X$.

(b) Deduce that $\mathrm{Card}(Y) \leq \mathrm{Card}(X)$, and give an example showing that equality might hold.

***2.6.** Let X be a subset of A^+. Define a sequence $(S_n)_{n\geq 0}$ of subsets of A^* by setting

$$S_0 = X^*, \qquad S_{n+1} = [S_n^{-1}S_n \cap S_nS_n^{-1}]^*.$$

Set $S(X) = \bigcup_{n\geq 0} S_n$. Show that $S(X)$ is the free hull of X. Show that when X is recognizable, the free hull of X is recognizable.

2.7. Let M be a submonoid of A^* and let

$$X = (M - 1) - (M - 1)^2$$

be its minimal set of generators. Show that X is recognizable iff M is recognizable.

2.8. Let M be a monoid. Show that M is free iff it satisfies the following conditions:

(i) there is a morphism

$$\lambda: \ M \to \mathbb{N}$$

into the additive monoid $\mathbb{N}$ such that $\lambda^{-1}(0) = 1$,

(ii) for all $x, y, z, t \in M$, we have

$$xy = zt$$

iff there exists $u \in M$ such that $xu = z, y = ut$ or $x = zu, uy = t$.

Section 3

3.1. Let X be a subset of A^+ such that $X \cap XX^+ = \varnothing$. Define a relation $\rho \subset A^* \times A^*$ by $(u, v) \in \rho$ iff there exists $x \in X^*$ such that

$$uxv \in X, \qquad ux \neq 1, \qquad uv \neq 1, \qquad xv \neq 1.$$

Show that X is a code iff $(1,1) \notin \rho^+$, where ρ^+ denotes the transitive closure of ρ.

Section 4

4.1. Let D be the Dyck code over $A = \{a, b\}$.

(a) Show that the following equality holds

$$\underline{D} = a\underline{D}_a{}^*b + b\underline{D}_b{}^*a$$

with $D_a = D \cap aA^*b$, $D_b = D \cap bA^*a$.

(b) Derive from the previous equality another proof of

$$d(t) = 1 - \sqrt{1 - 4pqt^2},$$

where $d(t)$ is the series defined in Example 4.5.

4.2. Let $n \geq 1$ be an integer and I, J be two subsets of $\{0, 1, \ldots, n-1\}$ such that for each integer p in $\{0, 1, \ldots, n-1\}$ there exist a unique pair $(i, j) \in I \times J$ such that

$$p = i + j \mod n.$$

Let

$$V = \{i + j - n \mid i \in I, j \in J, i + j \geq n\}.$$

For a set K of integers, let

$$a^K = \{a^k \mid k \in K\}.$$

Let $X \subset \{a, b\}^*$ be the set

$$X = a^I(ba^V)^*ba^J \cup a^n.$$

Show that X is a maximal code.

Section 5

5.1. Show that the set $X = \{a^3, b, ab, ba^2, aba^2\}$ is complete and that no proper subset of X is complete. Show that X is not a code.

***5.2.** Let $p \geq 5$ be a prime number. Let I, J be two subsets of $\{0, 1, \ldots, p-2\}$ such that for each integer q in $\{0, 1, \ldots, p-2\}$ there exists a unique pair $(i, j) \in I \times J$ such that $q = i + j$.

(a) Show that $X = a^p \cup \{a^iba^j \mid i \in I, j \in J\}$ is a code.

(b) Show that if $\text{Card}(I) \geq 2$ and $\text{Card}(J) \geq 2$, then X is not contained in any finite code.

5.3. Let M be a monoid. Let $\mathscr{F}$ be the family of subsets of M which are two-sided ideals of M or empty.

(a) Show that there is a topology on M for which $\mathscr{F}$ is the family of open sets.
(b) Show that a subset P of M is dense in M with respect to this topology iff $F(P) = M$, i.e., if P is dense in the sense of the definition given in Section 5.

5.4. With the notations of Proposition 5.2, and $V = A^* - A^*yA^*$, show successively that

$$\underline{A}^* = (\underline{V}y)^*\underline{V} = (\underline{U}y)^*(\underline{X}^*y(\underline{U}y)^*)^*\underline{V} = (\underline{U}y)^*\underline{V} + (\underline{U}y)^*(\underline{Y})^*y(\underline{U}y)^*\underline{V}.$$

(Use the identity $(\sigma + \tau)^* = \tau^*(\sigma\tau^*)^* = (\sigma^*\tau)^*\sigma^*$ for two power series σ, τ having no constant term). Derive directly from these equations the fact that Y is a code and that Y is complete.

5.5. Show that each recognizable code is contained in a maximal recognizable code.

5.6. Show that each thin code is contained in a maximal thin code.

SECTION 6

6.1. Let $\psi: A^* \to G$ be a morphism from A^* onto a group G. Let H be a subgroup of G and let X the group code defined by $X^* = \psi^{-1}(H)$. Show that X is indecomposable iff H is a maximal subgroup of G.

NOTES

The concept of a code originated in the theory of communication initiated by C. Shannon in the late 1940s. In this framework, the development of coding theory lead to a detailed study of constant length codes in connection with problems of error detection and correction. An account of this research can be found in McWilliams and Sloane (1977) or Van Lindt (1982). A classical book on information and communication theory is Ash (1965). See also Csiszár and Körner (1981) and McEliece (1977).

Variable-length codes were investigated in depth for the first time by Schützenberger (1955) and also by Gilbert and Moore (1959). The direction followed by Schützenberger consists in linking the theory of codes with classical noncommutative algebra. The results presented in this book represent this point of view. An early account of it can be found in Nivat (1966).

The notion of a stable submonoid appears for the first time in Schützenberger (1955) which contains Proposition 2.4. The same result is also given in Shevrin (1960), Cohn (1962) and Blum (1965). A detailed proof of Proposition 2.7 appears in Tilson (1972). The defect theorem (Theorem 2.8) has been proved in several formulations in Lentin (1972), Makanin (1976), and

Ehrenfeucht and Rozenberg (1978). Some generalizations are discussed in Berstel *et al.* (1979). For related questions see also Spehner (1976).

The test for codes given in Section 3 goes back to Sardinas and Patterson (1953) and is in fact usually known as the Sardinas and Patterson algorithm. The proof of correctness is surprisingly involved and has motivated a number of papers Bandyopadhyay (1963), Levenshtein (1964), Riley (1967), and De Luca (1976). The design of an efficient algorithm is described in Spehner (1976). See also Rodeh (1982) and Apostolico and Giancarlo (1984). The problem of testing whether a recognizable set is a code is a special case of a well-known problem in automata theory, namely testing whether a given rational expression is unambiguous. Standard decision procedures exist for this question (see Eilenberg, 1974 and Aho *et al.* 1975). These techniques will be used in Chapter IV. The connection between codes and rational expressions has been pointed out in Brzozowski (1967). Further, a characterization of those codes whose coding morphism preserves the star height of rational expressions is given in Hashiguchi and Honda (1976a).

The results of Section 4 are well known in information theory. The full statement of the Kraft–McMillan theorem (McMillan, 1956) includes a converse of Corollary 4.3 which will be proved in Chapter VII (Proposition VII.3.1).

The main results of Section 5 are from Schützenberger (1955). Our presentation is slightly more general. Proposition 5.2 and Exercise 5.5 are due to Ehrenfeucht and Rozenberg (1983). They answer a question of Restivo (1977). Theorem 5.12 appears in Boë *et al.* (1980). Example 5.11 is a special case of a construction due to Restivo (1977), Exercise 2.6 is from Berstel *et al.* (1979), Exercise 2.8 is known as Levi's lemma (Levi, 1944), Exercise 3.1 is from Spehner (1975). Exercise 5.2 is from Restivo (1977). It exhibits a class of codes which are not contained in any finite maximal code. Further results in this direction can be found in De Felice and Restivo (1984).

CHAPTER **II**

Prefix Codes

0. INTRODUCTION

Undoubtedly the prefix codes are the easiest to construct. The verification that a given set of words is a prefix code is straightforward. However, most of the interesting problems on codes can be raised for prefix codes. In some sense, these codes form a family of *models* of codes: frequently, it is easier to gain intuition about prefix codes rather than general codes. However, we can observe that the reasoning behind prefix codes is often valid in the general case.

For this reason we now present a chapter on prefix codes. In the first section, we comment on their definition and give some elementary properties. We also show how to draw the picture of a prefix code as a tree (the literal representation of prefix codes).

In Section 2, a construction of the automata associated to prefix codes is given. These automata are deterministic, and we will see in Chapter IV how to extend their construction to general codes.

The third section deals with maximal prefix codes. Characterizations in terms of completeness are given. Section 4 presents the usual operations on prefix codes. Most of them have an easy interpretation as operations on trees.

An important family of prefix codes is introduced in Section 5. They have many combinatorial properties which illustrate the notions presented previously. The synchronization of prefix codes is defined in Section 6. In fact, this notion will be generalized to general codes in Chapter IV where the relationship with groups will be established. The notion of measure of a prefix code can be amplified by a definition of average length. This is done in Section 7, where a combinatorial equivalence of average length is given.

The last section contains an important result. The deciphering delay is introduced to extend the notion of prefix code to more general codes. Prefix codes are codes with deciphering delay zero. We give a combinatorial proof of the fact that for a finite maximal code the deciphering delay is either infinite or zero, which means that in the latter case the code is prefix.

1. PREFIX CODES

This introductory section contains equivalent formulations of the definition of a prefix code together with the description of the tree associated to a prefix code. We then show how any prefix code induces in a natural way a factorization of the free monoid. Of course, all results in this chapter transpose to suffix codes by using the reverse operation.

It is convenient to have a shorthand for the proper left factors (resp., proper right factors) of the words of a set X. For this we use

$$XA^- = X(A^+)^{-1} \qquad \text{and} \qquad A^-X = (A^+)^{-1}X.$$

A subset X of A^* is *prefix* if $X \cap XA^+ = \varnothing$. If X contains the empty word 1, then $X = \{1\}$. In the other cases, X is a code (Proposition I.1.4). There is a series of equivalent definitions, all of which will be useful.

PROPOSITION 1.1 *For any subset X of A^*, the following conditions are equivalent:*

(i) $X \cap XA^+ = \varnothing$,
(ii) $X \cap XA^- = \varnothing$,
(iii) XA^-, X, XA^+ *are pairwise disjoint,*
(iv) *if $x, xu \in X$, then $u = 1$,*
(v) *if $xu = x'u'$ and $x, x' \in X$, then $x = x'$ and $u = u'$.* □

The following proposition can be considered as describing a way to construct prefix codes. It also shows a useful relationship between prefix codes and right ideals.

PROPOSITION 1.2

1. *Let L be a subset of A^*, and let*

$$X = L - LA^+. \tag{1.1}$$

Then X is prefix, and it is a code iff $1 \notin L$. Moreover

$$XA^* = LA^*, \tag{1.2}$$

that is, X and L generate the same right ideal.

2. *Let X be a prefix set, and let M be a subset of A^* such that $XA^* = MA^*$. Then $X = M - MA^+$. In particular $X \subset M$, and X is the minimal set of generators of the right ideal MA^*.*

Proof 1. From $X \subset L$, it follows that $XA^+ \subset LA^+$, whence $X \cap XA^+ \subset X \cap LA^+ = \emptyset$. Further $1 \in X$ iff $1 \in L$. This proves the first statement. Next, we claim that

$$L \subset XA^*. \tag{1.3}$$

Indeed let $u \in L$. If $u \in X$, then $u \in XA^*$. Otherwise $u \in LA^+$, whence $u = u'w$ for some $u' \in L$, $w \in A^+$. Arguing by induction on the length, we get that $u' \in XA^*$. Thus, u also is in XA^*.

From (1.3), it follows that $LA^* \subset XA^*$. The reverse inclusion is clear. This proves (1.2).

2. Let x be an element of X. Then $x = mu$ for some $m \in M$, $u \in A^*$. Similarly, $m = x'u$ for some $x' \in X$, $u \in A^*$. It follows that $x = x'vu$, whence $vu = 1$, since X is prefix. Thus $X \subset M$. Next $(XA^*)A = (MA^*)A$, showing that $XA^+ = MA^+$. This implies that $X \subset M - MA^+$. To show the converse inclusion, let $m \in M - MA^+$. Then $m = xu$ for some $x \in X$, $u \in A^*$. Assuming $u \neq 1$, it follows that $m \in XA^+ = MA^+$, which is not the case. Thus, $u = 1$ and $m \in X$. This completes the proof. □

The set $X = L - LA^+$ is called the *initial part* of L or also the *base* of the right ideal LA^*.

COROLLARY 1.3 *Let X and Y be prefix subsets of A^*. If $XA^* = YA^*$, then $X = Y$.* □

EXAMPLE 1.1 Let $A = \{a, b\}$ and let $L = A^*aA^*$ be the set of words containing at least one occurrence of the letter a. Then

$$X = L - LA^+ = b^*a.$$

EXAMPLE 1.2 Let $A = \{a, b\}$ and let $X = A^*ab - A^*abA^+$. Clearly X is a prefix code. It is the set of words ending with ab that do not contain another occurence of the factor ab. Thus, $X = b^*a^*ab$. This code, as does the previous one, belongs to the family of semaphore codes that are studied in Section 5.

We now give a useful graphic representation of codes, especially of prefix codes over an alphabet with 2 or 3 letters. It consists of associating a tree with each prefix code in such a way that the leaves of the tree represent the words in the code.

First, we associate an infinite tree with the set A^* of words over an alphabet A as follows. The alphabet is totally ordered, and words of equal length are ordered lexicographically Each node of the tree represents a word in A^*. Words of small length are to the left of words of greater length, and words of equal length are disposed vertically according to lexical ordering. There is an edge from u to v iff $v = ua$ for some letter $a \in A$. The tree obtained in this way is the *literal representation* of A^* (see Figs. 2.1 and 2.2).

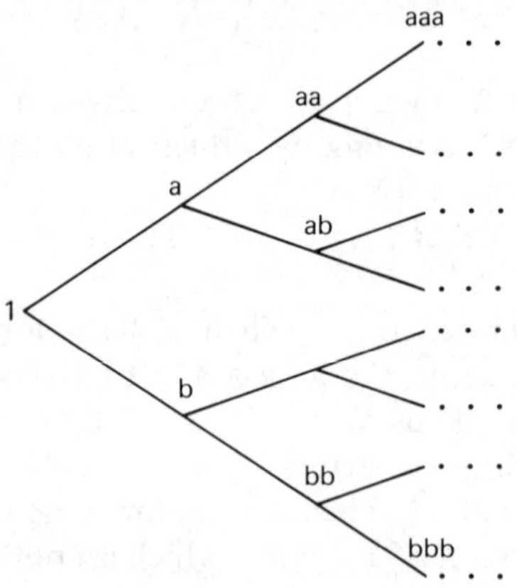

Fig. 2.1 The literal representation of $\{a, b\}^*$.

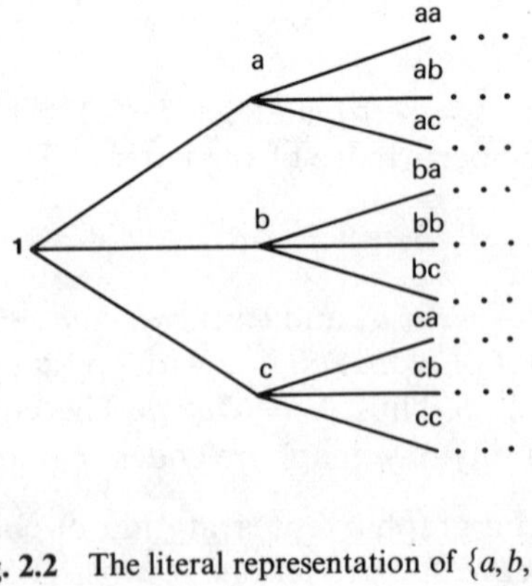

Fig. 2.2 The literal representation of $\{a, b, c\}^*$.

To a given subset X of A^* we associate a subtree of the literal representation of A^* as follows. We keep just the nodes corresponding to the words in X and all the nodes on the paths from the root to these nodes. Nodes corresponding to words in X are marked if necessary. The tree obtained in this way is the *literal representation* of X. Figures 2.3–2.6 give several examples.

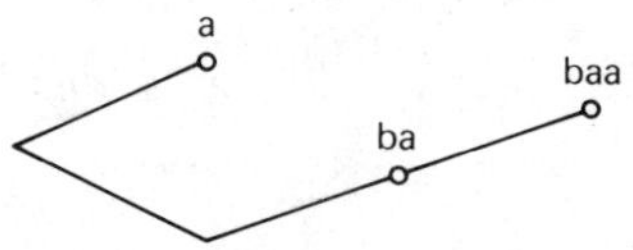

Fig. 2.3 Literal representation of $X = \{a, ba, baa\}$.

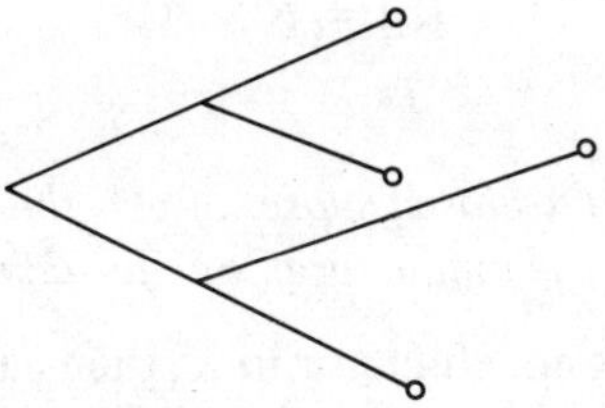

Fig. 2.4 Literal representation of $X = \{aa, ab, baa, bb\}$.

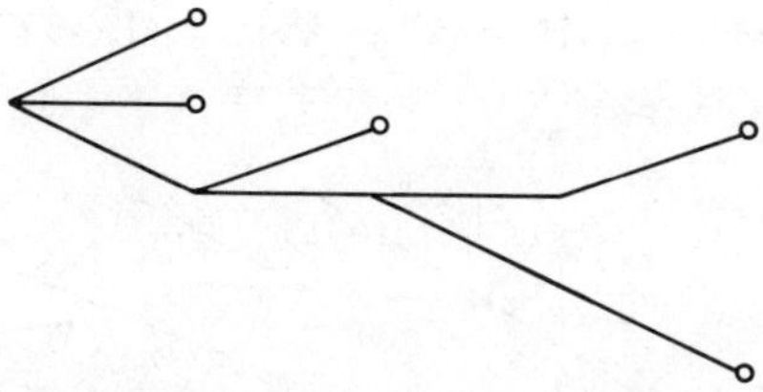

Fig. 2.5 Literal representation of $X = \{a, b, ca, cbba, cbcc\}$.

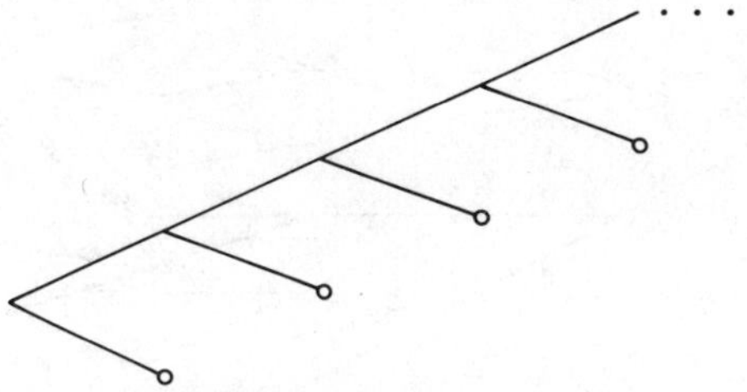

Fig. 2.6 Literal representation of $X = a^*b$.

It is easily seen that a code X is prefix iff in the literal representation of X, the nodes corresponding to words in X are all leaves of the tree.

The advantage of the literal representation, compared to simple enumeration, lies in the easy readability. Contrary to what might seem to happen, it allows a compact representation of relatively big codes (see Fig. 2.7).

After this digression, let us state the factorization theorem announced at the beginning of this section.

THEOREM 1.4 *Let X be a prefix code over A, and let*

$$R = A^* - XA^*.$$

Then R is prefix closed and nonempty. Further,

$$\underline{X} - 1 = \underline{R}(\underline{A} - 1), \tag{1.4}$$

$$1 + \underline{R}\underline{A} = \underline{R} + \underline{X}, \tag{1.5}$$

$$\underline{A}^* = \underline{X}^*\underline{R}. \tag{1.6}$$

Conversely, if R is a prefix-closed subset of A^*, then $X = RA - R$ is a prefix code. If $R \neq \varnothing$, then it is the unique prefix code such that $R = A^* - XA^*$.

Proof If a word w has no left factor in X, then each of the left factors of w shares this property. Thus, R is prefix closed. The set R is nonempty because $X \neq \{1\}$. The product of X and A^* is unambiguous in view of Proposition 1.1(v). Thus, $\underline{XA^*} = \underline{X}\,\underline{A}^*$ and

$$\underline{R} = \underline{A^* - XA^*} = \underline{A}^* - \underline{X}\,\underline{A}^* = (1 - \underline{X})\underline{A}^*. \tag{1.7}$$

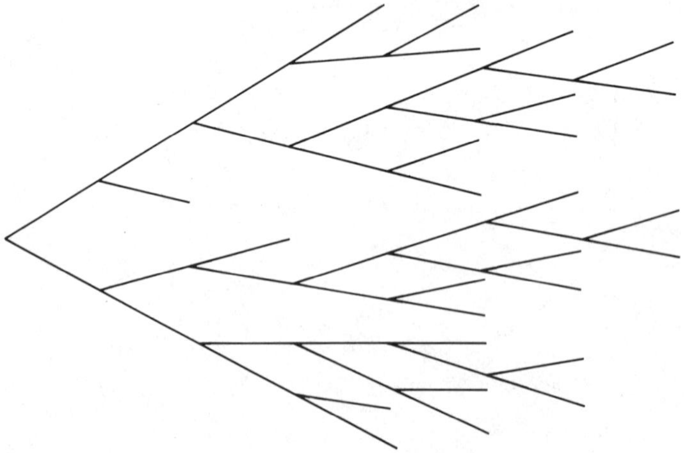

Fig. 2.7 A code with 26 elements.

From this equation and

$$(1 - \underline{A})^{-1} = \underline{A}^*,$$

we get, by multiplying (1.7) by $1 - \underline{A}$,

$$\underline{R}(1 - \underline{A}) = 1 - \underline{X},$$

which is formula (1.4). This also gives

$$\underline{R} - \underline{R}\underline{A} = 1 - \underline{X},$$

from which (1.5) follows. Finally, note that

$$\underline{X}^* = (1 - \underline{X})^{-1}$$

by Proposition 6.1 of Chapter I. Multiplication of (1.7) by X^* gives

$$\underline{X}^*\underline{R} = \underline{X}^*(1 - \underline{X})\underline{A}^* = \underline{A}^*.$$

This proves (1.6).

Conversely, let R be a prefix closed subset of A^*. If $R = \varnothing$, then $X = RA - R = \varnothing$ is a prefix code; thus we may assume R nonempty. Let $X = RA - R$. Then X is prefix. Indeed if $x \in X$, then $x = ra$ for some $r \in R$, $a \in A$. Each proper left factor u of x is a left factor of r, thus, it is in R and therefore not in X. This shows that $X \cap XA^- = \varnothing$.

With R being prefix-closed, 1 belongs to R and

$$\underline{X} = \underline{R}\underline{A} - \underline{R} + 1.$$

Indeed the product RA is unambiguous, and furthermore $1 \notin RA$. It successively follows from the formula that

$$\underline{X} - 1 = \underline{R}(\underline{A} - 1), \quad \underline{R} = (1 - \underline{X})\underline{A}^* = \underline{A}^* - \underline{X}\underline{A}^* = \underline{A^* - XA^*}.$$

The last equality holds because X is prefix. Assume finally that there is a prefix code Y such that

$$R = A^* - YA^* = A^* - XA^*.$$

Then $YA^* = XA^*$, whence $Y = X$ by Corollary 1.3. This proves uniqueness. □

Note the following combinatorial interpretations of formulas (1.5) and (1.6). The first says that a word in R followed by a letter is either in R or in X and that each word in X is composed of a word in R followed by a letter. The second formula says that each word $w \in A^*$ admits a unique factorization

$$w = x_1 x_2 \cdots x_n u, \qquad x_1, \ldots, x_n \in X, \qquad u \in R.$$

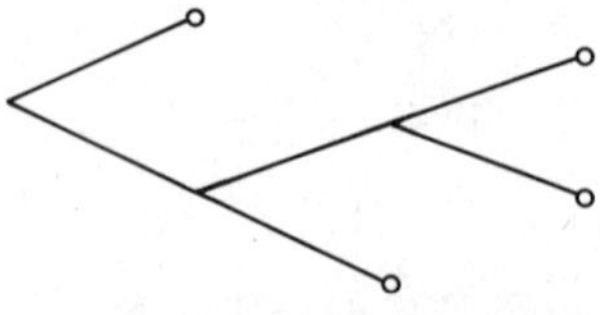

Fig. 2.8 A prefix code.

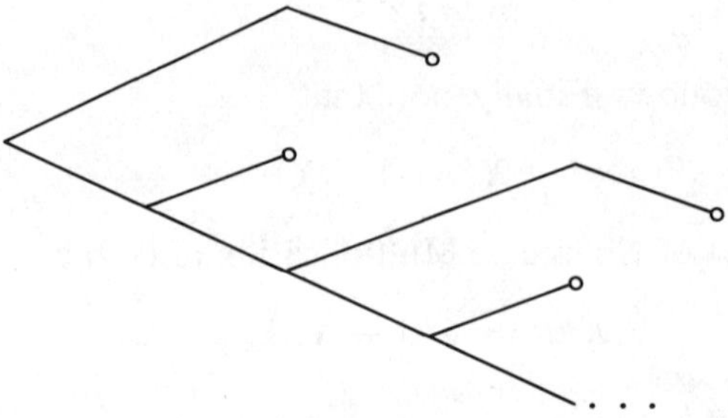

Fig. 2.9 Another prefix code.

EXAMPLE 1.3 Let $X = \{a, baa, bab, bb\} \subset A^+$ be the code represented in Fig. 2.8. Here $R = \{1, b, ba\} = XA^-$, and $\underline{X} - 1 = (1 + b + ba)(\underline{A} - 1)$. The equality between R and XA^- characterizes maximal prefix codes, as we will see in Section 3.

EXAMPLE 1.4 Let $X = (b^2)^*\{a^2b, ba\}$, as given in Fig. 2.9. Here $R = R_1 \cup R_2$, where $R_1 = XA^- = (b^2)^*(1 \cup a \cup b \cup a^2)$ is the set of proper left factors of X, and $R_2 = XA^+ - X - XA^- = (b^2)^*(abA^* \cup a^3A^*)$. Thus Eq. (1.4) now becomes

$$\underline{X} - 1 = (b^2)^*(1 + a + b + a^2 + ab\underline{A}^* + a^3\underline{A}^*)(\underline{A} - 1).$$

2. THE AUTOMATON OF A PREFIX CODE

The literal representation yields an easy method for verifying whether a word w is in X^* for some fixed prefix code X. It suffices to follow the path starting at the root through the successive letters of w. Whenever a leaf is reached, the corresponding factor of w is split away and the procedure is restarted.

We will consider several automata derived from the literal representation and relate them to the minimal automaton. The study which is initiated here will be generalized to arbitrary codes in Chapter IV. The particular case of prefix codes is interesting in itself because it is the origin of most of the general results of Chapter IV.

Recall (Chapter 0) that for any subset $X \subset A^*$, we denote by $\mathscr{A}(X)$ the minimal deterministic automaton recognizing X.

PROPOSITION 2.1 *Let X be a subset of A^*. The following conditions are equivalent:*

(i) *X is prefix.*
(ii) *The minimal automaton $\mathscr{A}(X)$ either is empty or has a single final state t and $t \cdot A = \varnothing$.*
(iii) *There exists a deterministic automaton $\mathscr{A} = (Q, i, T)$ recognizing X with $T \cdot A = \varnothing$.*

Proof (i) $\Rightarrow$ (ii) Suppose that X is nonempty. Set $\mathscr{A}(X) = (Q, i, T)$. First, we claim that for $q \in T$, we have $\{w \in A^* \mid q \cdot w \in T\} = \{1\}$. Indeed let $x \in X$ and $w \in A^*$ be words such that $i \cdot x = q$ (remember that $q \in T$) and $q \cdot w \in T$. Then $xw \in X$, whence $w = 1$. This shows the claim.

Thus, two final states are not separable and from the minimality of $\mathscr{A}(X)$, it follows that $\mathscr{A}(X)$ has just one final state, say t. Assume that $t \cdot A \neq \varnothing$, and that $t \cdot a = p$ for some letter $a \in A$ and some state p. Since p is coaccessible, we have $p \cdot v = t$ for some $v \in A^*$. Thus $t \cdot av = t$, whence $av = 1$, a contradiction.

(ii) $\Rightarrow$ (iii) clear.

(iii) $\Rightarrow$ (i) From $T \cdot A = \varnothing$, it follows that $T \cdot A^+ = \varnothing$. Thus, if $x \in X$, and $w \in A^+$, then $i \cdot xw = \varnothing$ and $xw \notin X$. Thus $X \cap XA^+ = \varnothing$. □

It is easy to construct an automaton for a prefix code by starting with the literal representation. This automaton, call it the *literal automaton* of a prefix code X, is the deterministic automaton

$$\mathscr{A} = (XA^- \cup X, 1, X)$$

defined by

$$u \cdot a = \begin{cases} ua & \text{if } ua \in XA^- \cup X, \\ \varnothing & \text{otherwise.} \end{cases}$$

Since $XA^- \cup X$ is prefix-closed, we immediately see that $1 \cdot u \in X$ iff $u \in X$, that is $L(\mathscr{A}) = X$. The pictorial representation of a literal automaton corresponds, of course, to the literal representation of the code.

EXAMPLE 2.1 The code $X = \{ab, bab, bb\}$ over $A = \{a, b\}$ has the literal representation given in Fig. 2.10a and the literal automaton given in Fig. 2.10b.

The literal automaton $\mathscr{A}$ of a prefix code X is trim but is not minimal in general. For infinite codes, it is always infinite. Let us consider two states of $\mathscr{A}$. It is equivalent to consider the two left factors of words of X, say u and v, leading to these states. These two states are unseparable iff

$$u^{-1}X = v^{-1}X.$$

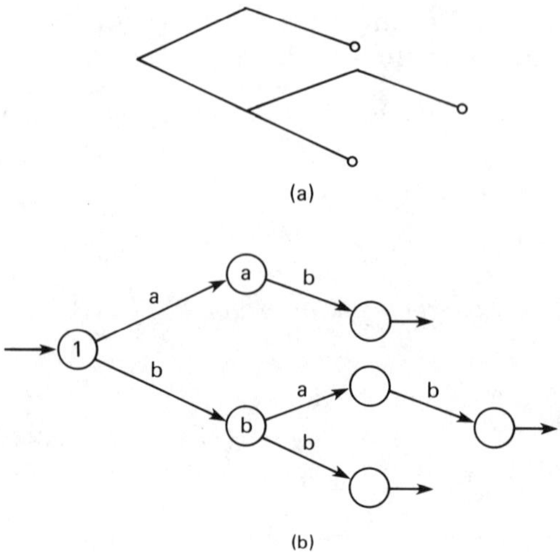

Fig. 2.10 (a) Literal representation of X, (b) Literal automaton of X.

Note that this equality means, on the literal representation of X that the two subtrees with roots u and v, respectively, are the same. This yields an easy procedure for the computation of the minimal automaton: first, all final states are labeled, say with label 0. If labels up to i are defined we consider subtrees such that all nodes except the roots are labeled. Then roots are labeled identically iff the (labeled) subtrees are isomorphic. Taking the labels as states, we obtain the minimal automaton. The procedure is described in Example 2.1–2.3.

EXAMPLE 2.1 (*continued*) The three terminal states are unseparable by Proposition 2.1. The states a and ba are unseparable since $a^{-1}X = (ba)^{-1}X = b$. No other relation exists, thus the minimal automaton is as given in Fig. 2.11.

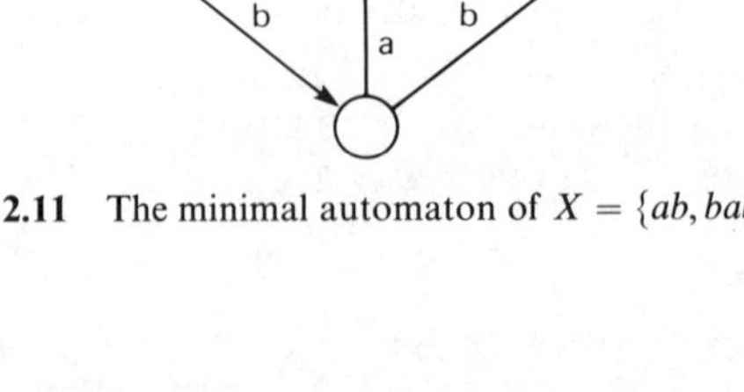

Fig. 2.11 The minimal automaton of $X = \{ab, bab, bb\}$.

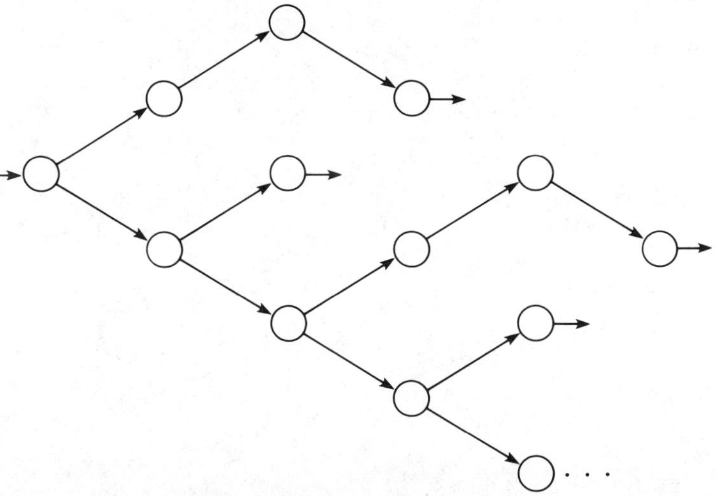

Fig. 2.12 A literal automaton.

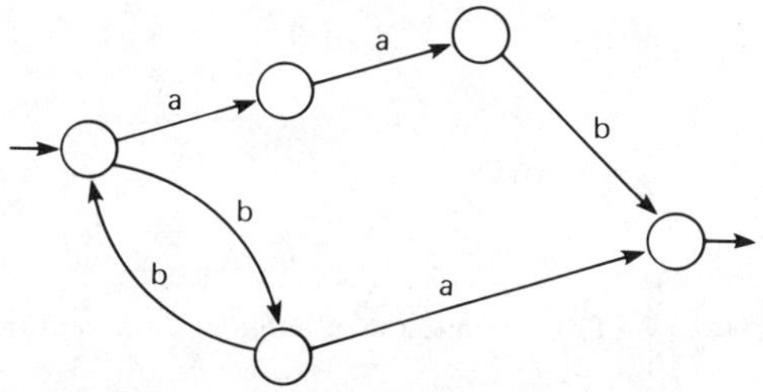

Fig. 2.13 Minimal automaton corresponding to Fig. 2.12.

EXAMPLE 2.2 The literal automaton of $X = (b^2)^*(a^2b \cup ba)$ is given in Fig. 2.12. Clearly the final states are equivalent, and also the predecessors of final states and their predecessors. On the main diagonal, however, the states are only equivalent with a step 2. This gives the minimal automaton of Fig. 2.13.

EXAMPLE 2.3 In Fig. 2.14 the labeling procedure has been carried out for the 26 element code of Fig. 2.7. This gives the subsequent minimal automaton of Fig. 2.15.

We now consider automata recognizing the submonoid X^* generated by a prefix code X. Recall that X^* is right unitary (Proposition I.2.5). Proposition 2.2 is the analogue of Proposition 2.1.

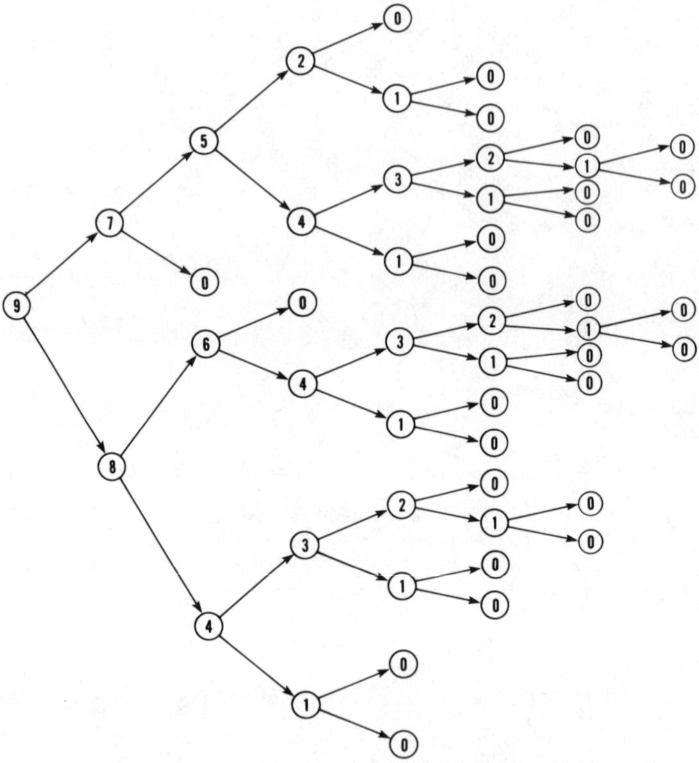

Fig. 2.14 The computation of a minimal automaton.

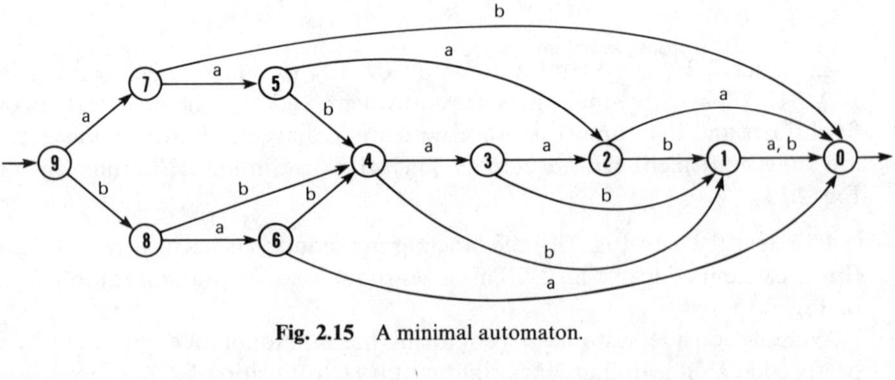

Fig. 2.15 A minimal automaton.

PROPOSITION 2.2 *Let P be a subset of A^*; the following conditions are equivalent*:

(i) *P is a right unitary submonoid.*
(ii) *The minimal automaton $\mathcal{A}(P)$ has a unique final state, namely the initial state.*
(iii) *There exists a deterministic automaton recognizing P having the initial state as the unique final state.*

Proof (i) $\Rightarrow$ (ii) The states in $\mathcal{A}(P)$ are the nonempty sets $u^{-1}P$, for $u \in A^*$. Now if $u \in P$, then $u^{-1}P = P$ because $uv \in P$ iff $v \in P$.

Thus, there is only one final state in $\mathcal{A}(P)$, namely P which is also the initial state.

(ii) $\Rightarrow$ (iii) clear.

(iii) $\Rightarrow$ (i) Let $\mathcal{A} = (Q, i, i)$ be the automaton recognizing P. The set P then is a submonoid since the final state and the initial state are the same. Further let u, $uv \in P$. Then $i \cdot u = i$ and $i \cdot uv = i$. This implies that $i \cdot v = i$ because $\mathcal{A}$ is deterministic. Thus, $v \in P$, showing that P is right unitary. □

If $\mathcal{A} = (Q, i, T)$ is any deterministic automaton over A, the *stabilizer* of a state q is the submonoid

$$\mathrm{Stab}(q) = \{w \in A^* \mid q \cdot w = q\}.$$

PROPOSITION 2.3 *The stabilizer of a state of a deterministic automaton is a right unitary submonoid. Every right unitary submonoid is the stabilizer of a state of some deterministic automaton.*

Proof It is an immediate consequence of the proof of Proposition 2.2. □

This proposition shows the importance of right unitary submonoids and of prefix codes in automata theory. Proposition 2.4 presents a method for deriving the minimal automaton $\mathcal{A}(X^*)$ of X^* from the minimal automata $\mathcal{A}(X)$ of the prefix code X.

PROPOSITION 2.4 *Let X be a nonempty prefix code over A, and let $\mathcal{A}(X) = (Q, i, t)$ be the minimal automaton of X. Then the minimal automaton of X^* is*

$$\mathcal{A}(X^*) = \begin{cases} (Q, t, t) & \text{if} \quad \mathrm{Stab}(i) \neq 1, \qquad (2.1) \\ (Q - i, t, t) & \text{if} \quad \mathrm{Stab}(i) = 1; \qquad (2.2) \end{cases}$$

the action of $\mathcal{A}(X^*)$, denoted by $\circ$, is given by

$$q \circ a = q \cdot a \qquad \text{for} \quad q \neq t, \tag{2.3}$$

$$t \circ a = i \cdot a. \tag{2.4}$$

Proof Let $\mathscr{B} = (Q, t, t)$ be the automaton obtained from $\mathscr{A}(X)$, defining the action $\circ$ by (2.3) and (2.4). Then clearly

$$L(\mathscr{B}) = \{w \mid t \circ w = t\} = X^*.$$

Let us verify that the automaton $\mathscr{B}$ is reduced. For this, consider two distinct states p and q. Since $\mathscr{A}(X)$ is reduced, there is a word u in A^* separating p and q, i.e., such that, say

$$p \cdot u = t, \qquad q \cdot u \neq t. \tag{2.5}$$

It follows that $p \circ u = t$, and furthermore $p \circ v \neq$ t for all $v < u$. If $q \circ u \neq t$, then u separates p and q in the automaton $\mathscr{B}$ also. Otherwise, there is a smallest left factor v of u such that $q \circ u = t$. For this v, we have $q \cdot v = t$. In view of (2.5), $v \neq u$. Thus, $v < u$. But then $q \circ v = t$ and $p \circ v \neq t$, showing the p and q are separated by v.

Each state in $\mathscr{B}$ is coaccessible because this is the case in $\mathscr{A}(X)$. From $1 \notin X$, we have $i \neq t$. The state i is accessible in $\mathscr{B}$ iff the set $\{w \mid t \circ w = i\}$ is nonempty, thus iff $\mathrm{Stab}(i) \neq 1$. If this holds, $\mathscr{B}$ is the minimal automaton of X^*. Otherwise, the accessible part of $\mathscr{B}$ is its restriction to $Q - i$. □

The automaton $\mathscr{A}(X^*)$ always has the form given by (2.2) if X is finite. In this case, it is obtained by identifying the initial and the final state. The classification of the prefix codes according to the form of the minimal automaton $\mathscr{A}(X^*)$ goes through the notion of chain.

A prefix code X is a *chain* if there exist disjoint nonempty sets Y, Z such that $Y \cup Z$ is prefix and

$$X = Y^*Z.$$

PROPOSITION 2.5 *Let X be a nonempty prefix code over A, and let $\mathscr{A}(X) = (Q, i, t)$ be the minimal automaton of X. The following conditions are equivalent*:

(i) $\mathrm{Stab}(i) \neq 1$;
(ii) *X is a chain,*
(iii) *there exists a word $u \in A^+$ such that $u^{-1}X = X$.*

Proof (i) ⇒ (ii) By Proposition 2.3, $\mathrm{Stab}(i)$ is a right unitary submonoid. Its base, say Y, is a prefix code which is nonempty because $\mathrm{Stab}(i) \neq 1$. Let Z be the set of words defined as follows: $z \in Z$ iff $i \cdot z = t$ and $i \cdot z' \neq i$ for all nonempty left factors z' of z. From $t \cdot A = \varnothing$, it follows that Z is a prefix code. Further $Y \cap Z = \varnothing$, by $i \neq t$. Finally $X = Y^*Z$. It remains to verify that $V = Y \cup Z$ is prefix. A proper left factor of a word in Z is neither in Z nor in Y, the latter by definition. A proper left factor w of a word y in Y cannot be in Z, since otherwise $i \cdot w = t$ whence $i \cdot y = \varnothing$. Thus V is prefix and X is a chain.

(ii) ⇒ (iii) Assume that $X = Y^*Z$ with $V = Y \cup Z$ prefix and $Y \cap Z = \varnothing$. Consider a word $u \in Y$. The code V being prefix, we have $u^{-1}Z = \varnothing$. Thus $u^{-1}X = u^{-1}(Y^*Z) = u^{-1}Y^*Z = Y^*Z = X$.

(iii) ⇒ (i) The automaton $\mathscr{A}(X)$ being minimal, the states of $\mathscr{A}(X)$ are in bijective correspondence with the nonempty sets $v^{-1}X$, where v runs over A^*. The bijection is given by associating the state $i \cdot v$ to $v^{-1}X$. Thus, the equality $u^{-1}X = X$ expresses precisely that $i \cdot u = i$. Consequently $u \in \mathrm{Stab}(i)$. □

EXAMPLE 2.1 *(continued)* The minimal automaton of X^* is given in Fig. 2.16. The finite code X is not a chain.

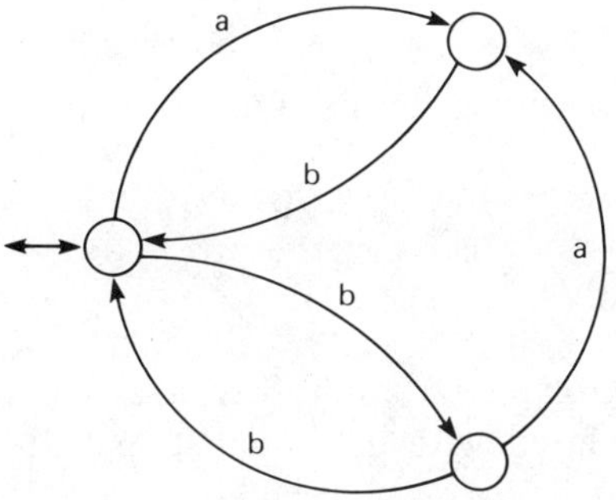

Fig. 2.16 The minimal automaton of X^*.

EXAMPLE 2.2 *(continued)* This code is a chain. The automaton $\mathscr{A}(X^*)$ is obtained without suppressing the initial state of $\mathscr{A}(X)$. See Fig. 2.17.

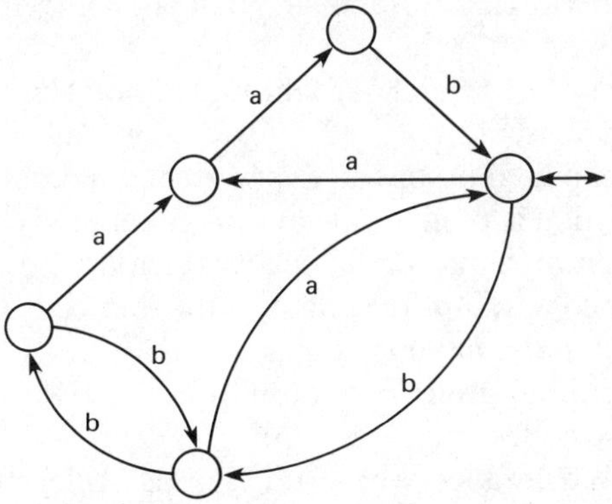

Fig. 2.17 The minimal automaton of X^*, with $X = (b^2)^*(a^2b \cup ba)$.

EXAMPLE 2.4 Consider the code $X = ba^*b$ over $A = \{a, b\}$. Its minimal automaton is given in Fig. 2.18a. The stabilizer of the initial state is just 1. The minimal automaton $\mathscr{A}(X^*)$ given in Fig. 2.18b is derived from formula (2.2).

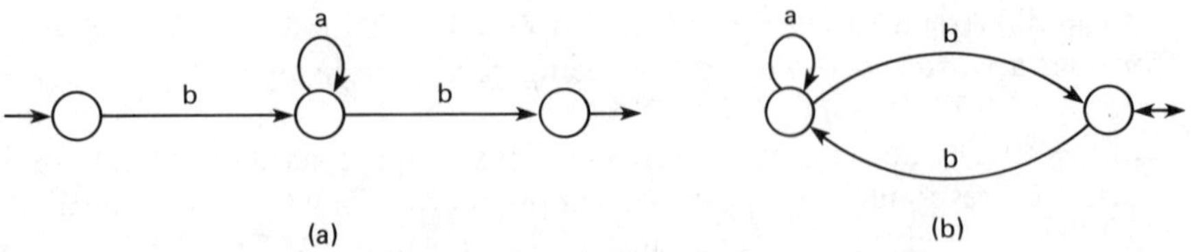

Fig. 2.18 (a) The minimal automaton of $X = ba^*b$, and (b) of X^*.

A construction which is analogous to that of Proposition 2.4 allows us to define the *literal automaton* of X^* for a prefix code X. It is the automaton

$$\mathscr{A} = (XA^-, 1, 1)$$

whose states are the proper left factors of words in X, and with the action given by

$$u \cdot a = \begin{cases} ua & \text{if} \quad ua \in XA^-, \\ 1 & \text{if} \quad ua \in X, \\ \varnothing & \text{otherwise.} \end{cases} \tag{2.6}$$

This automaton is obtained from the literal automaton for X by identifying all final states of the latter with the initial state 1. It is immediate that this automaton recognizes X^*.

3. MAXIMAL PREFIX CODES

A subset X of A^* is a *maximal prefix* set if it is prefix and if it is properly contained in no other prefix subset of A^*, that is, if $X \subset Y \subset A^*$ and Y prefix imply $X = Y$.

As for maximal codes, a reference to the underlying alphabet is necessary for the definition to make sense.

The set $\{1\}$ is a maximal prefix set. Every other maximal prefix set is a code. A maximal code which is prefix is always maximal prefix. The converse does not hold: there exist maximal prefix codes which are not maximal as codes. However, under mild assumptions, namely for thin codes, we will show that maximal prefix codes are maximal codes.

The study of maximal prefix codes uses a left-to-right oriented version of dense and complete codes.

Let M be a monoid, and let N be a subset of M. An element $m \in M$ is *right-completable* in N if $mw \in N$ for some w in M. It is equivalent to say that N meets the right ideal mM. A subset N is *right dense* if every $m \in M$ is right completable in N, i.e., if N meets all right ideals. The set N is *right complete* if the submonoid generated by N is right dense. The set N is *right thin* if it is not right dense. Of course, all these definition make sense if right is replaced by left.

The following implications hold for a subset N of a monoid M:

$$N \text{ right dense} \quad\Rightarrow\quad N \text{ dense}$$
$$N \text{ right complete} \quad\Rightarrow\quad N \text{ complete}$$
$$N \text{ thin} \quad\Rightarrow\quad N \text{ right thin.}$$

In the case of a free monoid A^*, a subset N of A^* is right dense iff every word in A^* is a left factor of some word in N. Thus every (nonempty) left ideal is right dense. Similarily, N is right complete if every word w in A^* can be written as

$$w = m_1 m_2 \cdots m_r p$$

for some $r \geq 0$, $m_1, \ldots, m_r \in N$, and p a left factor of some word in N.

PROPOSITION 3.1 *For any subset $X \subset A^*$ the following conditions are equivalent.*

(i) *XA^* is right dense,*
(ii) *$A^* = XA^- \cup X \cup XA^+$,*
(iii) *for all $w \in A^*$, there exist $u, v \in A^*$, $x \in X$ with $wu = xv$.*

Proof (i) $\Rightarrow$ (iii) Let $w \in A^*$. Since XA^* is right dense, it meets the right ideal wA^*. Thus $wu = xv$ for some $u, v \in A^*$, and $x \in X$.

(iii) $\Rightarrow$ (ii) If $wu = xv$, then $w \in XA^-$, $w \in X$ or $w \in XA^+$ according to $w < x$, $w = x$, or $w > x$.

(ii) $\Rightarrow$ (i) The set of left factors of XA^* is $XA^- \cup X \cup XA^+$. □

PROPOSITION 3.2 *Let $X \subset A^+$ be a subset that does not contain the empty word. Then XA^* is right dense iff X is right complete.*

Proof Suppose first that XA^* is right dense and consider a word $w \in A^*$. If $w \in XA^- \cup X$, then $wu \in X$ for some $u \in A^*$. Otherwise $w \in XA^+$ by Proposition 3.1. Thus, $w = xw'$ for some $x \in X$, $w' \in A^+$. Since $x \neq 1$, we have $|w'| < |w|$. Arguing by induction, $w'u \in X^*$ for some u in A^*. Thus, w is a left factor of some word in X^*.

Conversely, let $w \in A^*$, and assume that $wu \in X^*$ for some $u \in A^*$. Multiplying if necessary by some word in X, we may assume that $wu \neq 1$. Then $wu \in X^+ \subset XA^*$. □

Note that Proposition 3.2 does not hold for $X = \{1\}$. In this case, $XA^* = A^*$ is right dense, but $X^* = \{1\}$ is, of course, not.

THEOREM 3.3 *Let X be a prefix subset of A^*. The following conditions are equivalent:*

(i) *X is a maximal prefix set,*
(ii) *XA^* is right dense.*

Further, if $X \neq \{1\}$, they are equivalent to
(iii) *X is right complete.*

Observe that the equivalence of prefix maximality and right completeness given in this statement is stronger than the result for general codes (Theorem I.5.10). In the general case, the restriction to thin codes is necessary.

Proof By Proposition 3.2, conditions (ii) and (iii) are equivalent. Let us show that (i) and (ii) are equivalent. Let $u \in A^+$. The set $X \cup u$ is prefix iff $(X \cup u) \cap (X \cup u)A^+ = \varnothing$, thus, iff

$$(u \cap XA^+) \cup (X \cap uA^+) = \varnothing,$$

or iff $u \notin XA^+$ and $u \notin XA^-$. Denote by U the set of all words u such that $X \cup u$ is prefix. Then

$$U = A^* - (XA^+ \cup XA^-). \tag{3.1}$$

Clearly X is maximal prefix iff $X = U$; thus, by (3.1) and in view of Proposition 3.1, this is equivalent to X being right dense. □

The following corollary appears to be useful.

Corollary 3.4 *Let $L \subset A^+$ and let $X = L - LA^+$. Then L is right complete iff X is a maximal prefix code.*

Proof L is right complete iff LA^* is right dense (Proposition 3.2). From $XA^* = LA^*$ (Proposition 1.2) and Theorem 3.3, the statement follows. □

We now give the statement corresponding to the first part of Theorem 1.4, but for maximal prefix codes.

Theorem 3.5 *Let X be a prefix code over A, and let $P = XA^-$ be the set of proper left factors of words in X. Then X is maximal prefix iff one of the following equivalent conditions hold:*

$$\underline{X} - 1 = \underline{P}(\underline{A} - 1), \tag{3.2}$$

$$1 + \underline{P}\underline{A} = \underline{P} + \underline{X}, \tag{3.3}$$

$$\underline{A}^* = \underline{X}^*\underline{P}. \tag{3.4}$$

Proof Set $R = A^* - XA^*$. If X is maximal prefix, then XA^* is right dense and $R = P$ by Proposition 3.1. The conclusion then follows directly from Theorem 1.4. Conversely, if $\underline{X} - 1 = \underline{P}(\underline{A} - 1)$, then by Eq. (1.4)

$$\underline{P}(\underline{A} - 1) = \underline{R}(\underline{A} - 1).$$

Since $A - 1$ is invertible we get $P = R$, showing that XA^* is right dense. □

In the case of a finite maximal prefix code, Eq. (3.2) gives a factorization of $\underline{X} - 1$ into two polynomials. Formula (3.3) has an interpretation on the literal representation of a code X which makes the verification of maximality very easy: if p is a node which is not in X, then for each $a \in A$, there must exist a node pa in the literal representation of X.

The following statement corresponds to the other part of Theorem 1.4 and characterizes those prefix-closed sets which define maximal prefix codes.

PROPOSITION 3.6 *Let R be a nonempty prefix-closed subset of A^*, and let $X = RA - R$. Then X is a maximal prefix code iff R contains no right ideal. If this is the case, $R = XA^-$.*

Proof By Theorem 1.4, X is prefix and

$$R = A^* - XA^*.$$

From this, it follows that R contains no right ideal iff XA^* meets all right ideals, i.e., iff XA^* is right dense. Thus the equivalence follows from Theorem 3.3. The last observation is a consequence of $A^* = XA^* \cup XA^-$. ☐

We now come to the relation existing between maximal prefix codes and maximal codes which are prefix.

THEOREM 3.7 *Let X be a thin subset of A^+. The following conditions are equivalent:*

(i) *X is a maximal prefix code,*
(ii) *X is prefix and a maximal code,*
(iii) *X is right complete and a code.*

Proof (ii) ⇒ (i) is clear. (i) ⇒ (iii) follows from Theorem 3.3. It remains to prove (iii) ⇒ (ii). Let $Y = X - XA^+$. By Proposition 1.2 $YA^* = XA^*$. Thus Y is right complete. Consequently Y is complete. The set Y is also thin, since $Y \subset X$. Thus Y is a maximal code by Theorem I.5.7. From the inclusion $Y \subset X$, we have $X = Y$. ☐

EXAMPLE 3.1 This example shows that Theorem 3.7 does not hold without the assumption that the code is thin. Let $X = \{uba^{|u|} \mid u \in A^*\}$ over $A = \{a, b\}$ be the reversal of the code given in Example I.4.6. It is a maximal code which is right dense, whence right complete. However, X is not prefix. From Corollary 3.4, it follows that $Y = X - XA^+$ is a maximal prefix code. Of course, $Y \neq X$, and thus, Y is not maximal.

PROPOSITION 3.8 *Let X be a thin subset of* A^+. *The following conditions are equivalent*:

(i) *X is a maximal prefix code.*
(ii) *X is prefix, and there exists a positive Bernoulli distribution* π *such that* $\pi(X) = 1$.
(iii) *X is prefix, and* $\pi(X) = 1$ *for all positive Bernoulli distributions* π.
(iv) *X is right complete, and there exists a positive Bernoulli distribution such that* $\pi(X) = 1$.
(v) *X is right complete, and* $\pi(X) = 1$ *for all positve Bernoulli distributions* π.

Proof It is an immediate consequence of Theorem 3.7 and of Theorem I.5.10. □

In the previous section, we gave a description of prefix codes by means of the bases of the stabilizers in a deterministic automaton. Now we consider maximal prefix codes. Let us introduce the following definition. A state q of a deterministic automaton $\mathscr{A} = (Q, i, T)$ over A is *recurrent* if for all $u \in A^*$, there is a word $v \in A^*$ such that $q \cdot uv = q$. This implies in particular that $q \cdot u \neq \emptyset$ for all u in A^*.

PROPOSITION 3.9 *Let X be a prefix code over A. The following conditions are equivalent.*

(i) *X is maximal prefix.*
(ii) *The minimal automaton of* X^* *is complete.*
(iii) *All states of the minimal automaton of* X^* *are recurrent.*
(iv) *The initial state of the minimal automaton of* X^* *is recurrent.*
(v) X^* *is the stabilizer of a recurrent state in some deterministic automaton.*

Proof (i) ⇒ (ii) Let $\mathscr{A}(X^*) = (Q, i, i)$ be the minimal automaton of X^*. Let $q \in Q$, $a \in A$. There is some word $u \in A^*$ such that $i \cdot u = q$. The code X being right complete, $uav \in X^*$ for some word v. Thus $i = i \cdot uav = (q \cdot a) \cdot v$, showing that $q \cdot a \neq \emptyset$. Thus $\mathscr{A}(X^*)$ is complete.

(ii) ⇒ (iii) Let $q \in Q$, $u \in A^*$; then $q' = q \cdot u \neq \emptyset$ since $\mathscr{A}(X^*)$ is complete. $\mathscr{A}(X^*)$ being minimal, q' is coaccessible, and q is accessible. Thus $q' \cdot v = q$, for some $v \in A^*$, showing that q is recurrent.

(iii) ⇒ (iv) ⇒ (v) is clear.

(v) ⇒ (i) Let $\mathscr{A} = (Q, i, T)$ be a deterministic automaton and $q \in Q$ be a recurrent state such that $X^* = \mathrm{Stab}(q)$. For all $u \in A^*$ there is a word $v \in A^*$ with $q \cdot uv = q$, thus $uv \in X^*$. This shows that X is right complete. The set X being prefix, the result follows from Theorem 3.3. □

4. OPERATIONS ON PREFIX CODES

Prefix codes are closed under some simple operations. We start with a general result which will be used several times.

PROPOSITION 4.1 *Let $X, (Y_i)_{i \in I}$ be nonempty subsets of A^* and let $(X_i)_{i \in I}$ be a partition of X. Set*

$$Z = \bigcup_{i \in I} X_i Y_i.$$

1. *If X and the Y_i's are prefix (maximal prefix), then Z is prefix (maximal prefix).*
2. *If Z is prefix, then all Y_i are prefix.*
3. *If X is prefix and Z is maximal prefix, then X and the Y_i's are maximal prefix.*

Proof 1. Assume that $z, zu \in Z$. Then

$$z = xy, \qquad zu = x'y'$$

for some $i, j \in I$, $x \in X_i$, $y \in Y_i$, $x' \in X_j$, $y' \in Y_j$. From

$$xyu = x'y'$$

it follows that $x = x'$, because X is prefix, whence $i = j$ and $y = y'$. Thus, $u = 1$ and Z is prefix. Assume now that XA^* and the Y_iA^* are right dense. Let $w \in A^*$. Then $ww' = xv$ for some $w', v \in A^*$, $x \in X$. Let x belong to X_i. Since Y_iA^* is right dense, $vv' \in Y_iA^*$ for some $v' \in A^*$. Thus $ww'v' \in X_iY_iA^*$ whence $ww'v' \in ZA^*$. Thus Z is maximal prefix.

2. Let $y, yu \in Y_i$ and $x \in X_i$. Then $xy, xyu \in Z$, implying that $u = 1$.

3. From $ZA^* \subset XA^*$ we get that XA^* is right dense. Consequently X is maximal prefix. To show that Y_iA^* is right dense, let $w \in A^*$. For any $x \in X_i$, xw is right-completable in ZA^*. Thus, $xw = zw'$ for some $z \in Z$. Setting $z = x'y'$ with $x' \in X_j$, $y' \in Y_j$ gives $xw = x'y'w'$. The code X being prefix, we get $x = x'$, whence $w = y'w'$, showing that w is in Y_iA^*. □

For Card(I) = 1, we obtain, in particular,

COROLLARY 4.2 *If X and Y are prefix codes (maximal prefix), then XY is a prefix code (maximal prefix).* □

The converse of this corollary holds only under rather restrictive conditions and will be given in Proposition 4.10.

COROLLARY 4.3 *Let $X \subset A^+$, and $n \geq 1$. Then X is (maximal) prefix iff X^n is (maximal) prefix.*

Proof By Corollary 4.2, X^n is maximal prefix for a maximal prefix code X. Conversely, setting $Z = X^n = X^{n-1}X$, it follows from Proposition 4.1(2) that X is prefix. Writing $Z = XX^{n-1}$, we see by Proposition 4.1(3) that X (and X^{n-1}) are maximal prefix if Z is. □

Corollary 4.3 is a special case of Proposition 4.8, to be proved later.

COROLLARY 4.4 *Let X and Y be prefix codes, and let $X = X_1 \cup X_2$ be a partition. Then $Z = X_1 \cup X_2 Y$ is a prefix code and Z is maximal prefix iff X and Y are maximal prefix.*

Proof With $Y' = \{1\}$, we have $Z = X_1 Y' \cup X_2 Y$. The result follows from *is prefix and Z is maximal prefix if X and Y are.* □

There is a special case of this corollary which deserves attention. It constitutes an interesting operation on codes viewed as trees.

COROLLARY 4.5 *Let X and Y be prefix codes, and $x \in X$. Then*

$$Z = (X - x) \cup xY$$

is prefix and Z is maximal prefix if X and Y are. □

The operation performed on X and Y is sketched in Fig. 2.19. We now turn to the converse operation.

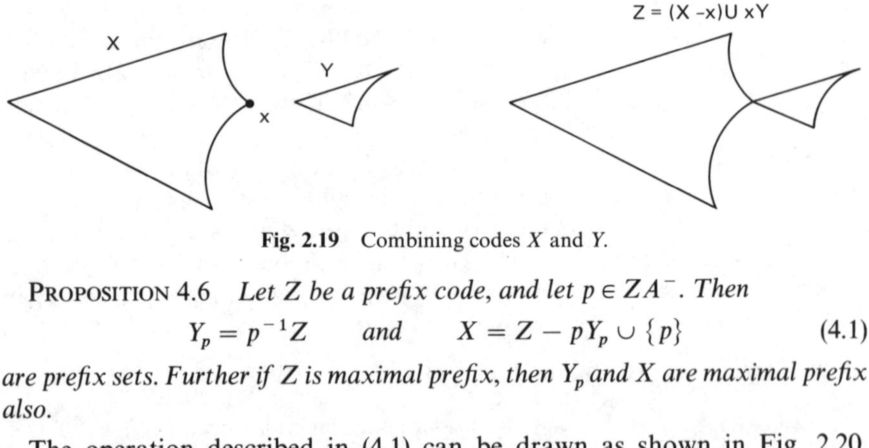

Fig. 2.19 Combining codes X and Y.

PROPOSITION 4.6 *Let Z be a prefix code, and let $p \in ZA^-$. Then*

$$Y_p = p^{-1}Z \qquad \text{and} \qquad X = Z - pY_p \cup \{p\} \tag{4.1}$$

are prefix sets. Further if Z is maximal prefix, then Y_p and X are maximal prefix also.

The operation described in (4.1) can be drawn as shown in Fig. 2.20. Proposition 4.6 is a special case of the following result.

PROPOSITION 4.7 *Let Z be a prefix code, and let Q be a prefix subset of ZA^-. For each $p \in ZA^-$, the set $Y_p = p^{-1}Z$ is a prefix code; further*

$$X = Q \cup \left(Z - \bigcup_{p \in Q} pY_p\right)$$

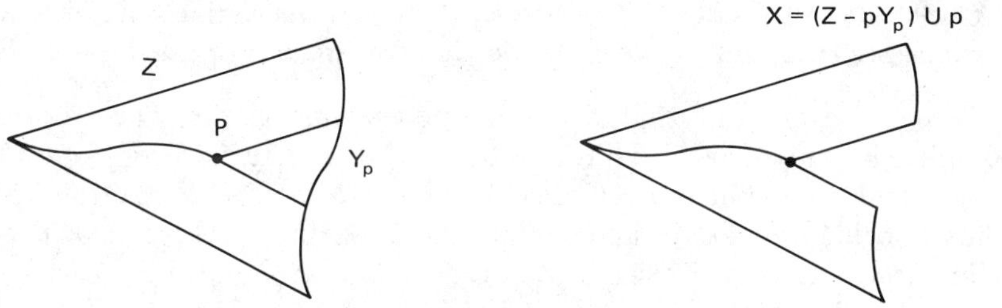

Fig. 2.20 Separating Z and Y_p.

is a prefix set. If Z is maximal prefix, then X and the Y_p $(p \in Q)$ are maximal prefix.

Proof Set $X_0 = Z - \bigcup_{p \in Q} pY_p$, $Y_0 = \{1\}$, $X_p = \{p\}$; then

$$Z = X_0 Y_0 \cup \bigcup_{p \in Q} X_p Y_p.$$

Thus, to derive the result from Proposition 4.1, it suffices to show that X is prefix.

Let $x, xu \in X$ with $u \in A^+$. These words cannot both be in the prefix set Z nor can they both be in the prefix set Q. Since $Q \subset ZA^-$, we have $x \in Q$, $xu \in Z$. Thus $u \in Y_x$ and xu is not in X. □

Propositions 4.1 and 4.7 can be used to enumerate some maximal prefix sets. Let us illustrate the computation in the case of $A = \{a, b\}$. If Z is maximal prefix and $Z \neq 1$, then both

$$X = a^{-1}Z, \qquad Y = b^{-1}Z$$

are maximal prefix and

$$Z = aX \cup bY. \tag{4.2}$$

Conversely, if X and Y are maximal prefix, then so is Z. Thus, Eq. (4.2) defines a bijection from maximal prefix codes onto pairs of maximal prefix sets. Further

$$\text{Card}(Z) = \text{Card}(X) + \text{Card}(Y).$$

Let α_n be the number of maximal prefix sets with n elements. Then by Eq. (4.2), for $n \geq 2$,

$$\alpha_n = \sum_{k+l=n} \alpha_k \alpha_l.$$

These numbers are related to the Catalan numbers already encountered in Section I.4 (see Exercise 4.1):

$$\alpha_{n+1} = \frac{1}{n+1}\binom{2n}{n}.$$

PROPOSITION 4.8 *Let Y, Z be composable codes and $X = Y \circ Z$. Then X is a maximal prefix and thin code iff Y and Z are maximal prefix and thin codes.*

Proof Assume first that X is thin and maximal prefix. Then X is right complete by Theorem 3.3. Thus X is thin and complete. By Proposition I.6.9, both Y and Z are thin and complete. Further Y is prefix (Proposition I.6.8(i)). Thus Y (being thin, prefix, and complete) is a maximal prefix code. Next X is right dense and $X \subset Z^*$. Thus Z is right dense. Consequently Z is a right complete, thin code. By Theorem 3.7, Z is maximal prefix.

Conversely, Y and Z being prefix, X is prefix by Proposition I.6.3, and Y, Z being both thin and complete, X is also thin and complete by Proposition I.6.9. Thus X is a maximal prefix code. □

PROPOSITION 4.9 *Let Z be a prefix code over A, and let $Z = X \cup Y$ be a partition. Then $T = X^*Y$ is a prefix code, and further T is maximal prefix iff Z is a maximal prefix code.*

Proof Let B be an alphabet bijectively associated to Z, and let $B = C \cup D$ be the partition of B induced by the partition $Z = X \cup Y$. Then

$$T = C^*D \circ Z.$$

The code C^*D clearly is prefix. Thus, T is prefix by Proposition I.6.3. Next, $T^* = 1 \cup Z^*Y$ showing that T is right complete iff Z is right complete. The second part of the statement thus results from Theorem 3.3. □

Note that the codes of this proposition are the *chains* of Section 2. We conclude this section by the proof of a converse to Corollary 4.2. This result will be of use later (Section 8).

PROPOSITION 4.10 *Let X and Y be finite nonempty subsets of A^* such that the product XY is unambiguous. If XY is a maximal prefix code, then X and Y are maximal prefix codes.*

The following example shows that the conclusion fails for infinite codes. However, it is not known whether the hypothesis of unambiguity is necessary.

EXAMPLE 4.2 Consider $X = \{1, a\}$ and $Y = (a^2)^*b$ over $A = \{a, b\}$. Here X is not prefix, and Y is not maximal prefix. However, $XY = a^*b$ is maximal prefix and the product is unambiguous.

Proof Let $Z = XY$ and $n = \max\{|y| \mid y \in Y\}$. The proof is by induction on n. For $n = 0$, we have $Y = \{1\}$ and $Z = X$. Thus, the conclusion clearly holds. Assume $n \geq 1$ and set

$$T = \{y \in Y \mid |y| = n\}, \qquad Q = \{q \in YA^- \mid qA \cap T \neq 0\}.$$

By construction, $T \subset QA$. In fact $T = QA$. Indeed, let $q \in Q$, $a \in A$ and let $x \in X$ be a word of maximal length. Then xq is a left factor of a word in Z, and xqa is right-completable in ZA^*. The code Z being prefix, no proper left factor of xqa is in Z. Consequently

$$xqav = x'y'$$

for some $x' \in X$, $y' \in Y$, and $v \in A^*$. Now $n = |qa| \geq |y'|$, and $|x| \geq |x'|$. Thus $x = x'$, $y' = qa$, $u = 1$. Consequently $qa \in Y$ and $T = QA$.

Now let

$$Y' = (Y - T) \cup Q, \qquad Z' = XY'.$$

We verify that Z' is prefix. Assume the contrary. Then

$$xy'u = x'y''$$

for some $x, x' \in X$, $y', y'' \in Y'$, $u \neq 1$. Let a be the first letter of u. Then either y' or $y'a$ is in Y. Similarly either y'' or $y''b$ (for any b in A) is in Y. Assume $y' \in Y$. Then $xy' \in Z$ is a proper left factor of $x'y''$ or $x'y''b$, one of them being in Z. This contradicts the fact that Z is prefix. Thus $y'a \in Y$. As before, $xy'a$ is not a proper left factor of $x'y''$ or $x'y''b$. Thus necessarily $u = a$ and $y'' \in Y$, and we have

$$xy'a = x'y''$$

with $y'a$, $y'' \in Y$. The unambiguity of the product XY shows that $x = x'$, $y'a = y''$. But then $y'' \notin Y'$. This yields the contradiction.

To see that Z' is maximal prefix, observe that $Z \subset Z' \cup Z'A$. Thus $ZA^* \subset Z'A^*$ and the result follows from Theorem 3.3. Finally, it is easily seen that the product XY' is unambiguous: if $xy' = x'y''$ with $x, x' \in X$, $y', y'' \in Y'$, then either $y', y'' \in Y - T$ or $y', y'' \in Q$, the third case being ruled out by the prefix character of Z.

Of course, $\max\{|y| \mid y \in Y'\} = n - 1$. By the induction hypothesis, X and Y' are maximal prefix. Since

$$Y = (Y' - Q) \cup QA,$$

the set Y is maximal prefix by Corollary 4.4. □

It is also possible to give a completely different proof of Proposition 4.10 using the fact that, under the hypotheses of the Proposition, we have $\pi(X)\pi(Y) = 1$ for all Bernoulli distributions π (see Exercise VIII.4.2).

5. SEMAPHORE CODES

This section contains a detailed study of semaphore codes which constitute an interesting subclass of the prefix codes. This investigation also illustrates the techniques introduced in the preceding sections.

Proposition 5.1 *For any nonempty subset S of A^+, the set*

$$X = A^*S - A^*SA^+ \tag{5.1}$$

is a maximal prefix code.

Proof The set $L = A^*S$ is a left ideal, and thus, is right dense. Consequently, L is right complete, and by Corollary 3.4, the set $X = L - LA^+$ is maximal prefix. □

A code X of the form given in Eq. (5.1) is called a *semaphore code*, the set S being a set of semaphores for X. The terminology stems from the following observation: a word is in X iff it ends with a semaphore, but none of its proper left factors ends with a semaphore. Thus, reading a word from left to right, the first appearance of a semaphore gives a "signal" indicating that what has been read up to now is in the code X.

Example 5.1 Let $A = \{a, b\}$ and $S = \{a\}$. Then $X = A^*a - A^*aA^+$ whence $X = b^*a$. Note that we also have $X = A^*a^+ - A^*a^+A^+$ showing that a semaphore code admits several sets of semaphores (see also Proposition 5.7).

Example 5.2 For $A = \{a, b\}$ and $S = \{aa, ab\}$, we have $A^*S = A^*aA$. Thus $A^*S - A^*SA^+ = b^*aA$.

The following proposition characterizes semaphore codes among prefix codes.

Proposition 5.2 *Let $X \subset A^+$. Then X is a semaphore code iff X is prefix and*

$$A^*X \subset XA^*. \tag{5.2}$$

Proof Let $X = A^*S - A^*SA^+$ be a semaphore code. Then X is prefix and it remains to show (5.2). Let $w \in A^*X$. Since $w \in A^*S$, w has a factor in S. Let w' be the shortest left factor of w which is in A^*S. Then w' is in X. Consequently, $w \in XA^*$.

Conversely, assume that a prefix code X satisfies (5.2). Set $M = XA^*$. In view of Proposition 1.2, and by the fact that X is prefix, we have

$$X = M - MA^+.$$

Equation (5.2) implies that

$$A^*M = A^*XA^* \subset XA^* = M,$$

thus, $M = A^*M$ and

$$X = A^*M - A^*MA^+. \quad □$$

Example 5.3 The code $Y = \{a^2, aba, ab^2, b\}$ is a maximal prefix code over A. However, Y is not a semaphore code, since $ab \in A^*Y$ but $ab \notin YA^*$.

A semaphore code is maximal prefix, thus, right complete. The following proposition describes those right complete sets which are semaphore codes.

Proposition 5.3 *Let $X \subset A^+$. Then X is a semaphore code iff X is right complete and*

$$X \cap A^*XA^+ = \varnothing. \tag{5.3}$$

Proof A semaphore code is maximal prefix, thus also right complete. Further, by (5.2),

$$A^*XA^+ \subset XA^+$$

thus

$$X \cap A^*XA^+ \subset X \cap XA^+ = \varnothing,$$

showing Eq. (5.3).

Conversely, if a set X satisfies (5.3), then X is prefix. To show that X is semaphore, we verify that (5.2) holds. Let $w = ux \in A^*X$ with $u \in A^*$, $x \in X$. The code X being right complete, we have $uxv = x'yv$ for some $x' \in X$, $y \in X^*$, $v \in A^*$. Now Eq. (5.3) shows that ux is not a proper left factor of x'. Thus $ux \in x'A^*$. □

Corollary 5.4 *Let $X \subset A^+$ be a semaphore code and let $P = XA^-$. Then $PX \subset XP \cup X^2$.*

Proof (*See Fig.* 2.21) Let $p \in P$, $x \in X$. By Eq. (5.2), $px = yu$ for some $y \in X$, $u \in A^*$. The code X is prefix, thus $|p| < |y|$. Consequently, u is a right factor of x, and by (5.3), $u \notin XA^+$. The code X is maximal prefix, therefore $u \in XA^- \cup X$. □

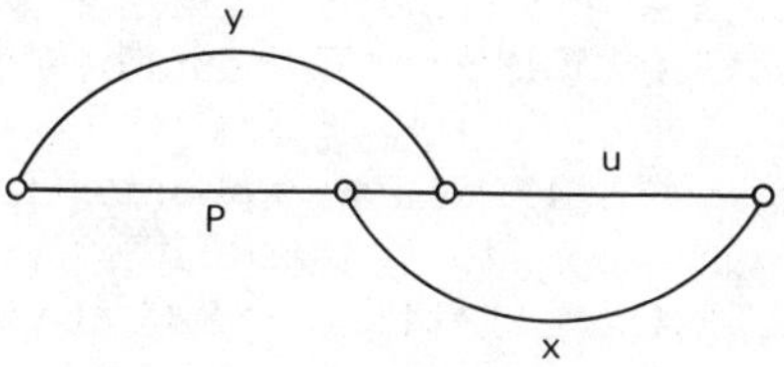

Fig. 2.21 Proof of Corollary 5.4.

Formula (5.3) expresses a property of semaphore codes which is stronger than the prefix condition: for a semaphore code X, and two elements $x, x' \in X$, the only possible way for x to occur as a factor in x' is to be a right factor of x'. We now use this fact to characterize semaphore codes among maximal prefix codes.

Proposition 5.5 *Let $X \subset A^+$, and let $P = XA^-$ be the set of proper left factors of words in X. Then X is a semaphore code iff X is a maximal prefix code and P is suffix-closed.*

Of course, P is always prefix closed. Thus P is suffix closed iff it contains the factors of its elements.

Proof Let X be a semaphore code. Then X is a maximal prefix code (Proposition 5.1). Next, let $p = uq \in P$ with $u,q \in A^*$. Let $v \in A^+$ be a word such that $pv \in X$. Then $q \notin XA^*$, since otherwise $pv = uqv \in X \cap A^*XA^+$, violating Proposition 5.3. Thus $q \in XA^- = P$.

Conversely, assume that X is maximal prefix and that $X \cap A^*XA^+ \neq \emptyset$. Let $x \in X \cap A^*XA^+$. Then $x = ux'v$ for some $u \in A^*$, $x' \in X$, $v \in A^+$. It follows that $ux' \in P$ and, P being suffix-closed, also $x' \in P$ which is impossible. Thus X is a semaphore code by Proposition 5.3. □

Another consequence of Proposition 5.3 is

PROPOSITION 5.6 *Any semaphore code is thin.*

Proof By Formula (5.3), no word in XA^* is a factor of a word in X. □

COROLLARY 5.7 *Any semaphore code is a maximal code.*

Proof A semaphore code is a maximal prefix code and thin by Propositions 5.1 and 5.6. Thus by Theorem 3.7, such a code is maximal code. □

Now we determine the sets of semaphores giving the same semaphore code.

PROPOSITION 5.8 *Two nonempty subsets S and T of A^+ define the same semaphore code iff $A^*SA^* = A^*TA^*$. For each semaphore code X, there exists a unique minimal set of semaphores, namely $T = X - A^+X$.*

Proof Let $X = A^*S - A^*SA^+$, $Y = A^*T - A^*TA^+$. By Proposition 1.2, we have $XA^* = A^*SA^*$, $YA^* = A^*TA^*$, and by Corollary 1.3, $X = Y$ iff $A^*SA^* = A^*TA^*$.

Next, let $X = A^*S - A^*SA^+$ be a semaphore code. By the definition of $T = X - A^+X$, we may apply to T the dual of Proposition 1.2. Thus, $A^*T = A^*X$. Since $A^*TA^* = A^*XA^* = A^*SA^*$, the set T is indeed a set of semaphores for X.

Finally, let us verify that $T \subset S$. Let $t \in T$; then $t = usv$ for some $u, v \in A^*$, $s \in S$, and $s = u't'v'$ for some $u', v' \in A^*, t' \in T$. Thus, $t = uu't'v'v$. Note that $T \subset X$. Thus, formula (5.3) applies, showing that $v'v = 1$. Since T is a suffix code, we have $uu' = 1$. Thus, $t = s \in S$. □

We now study some operations on semaphore codes.

PROPOSITION 5.9 *If X and Y are semaphore codes, then XY is a semaphore code. Conversely, if XY is a semaphore code and if X is a prefix code, then X is a semaphore code.*

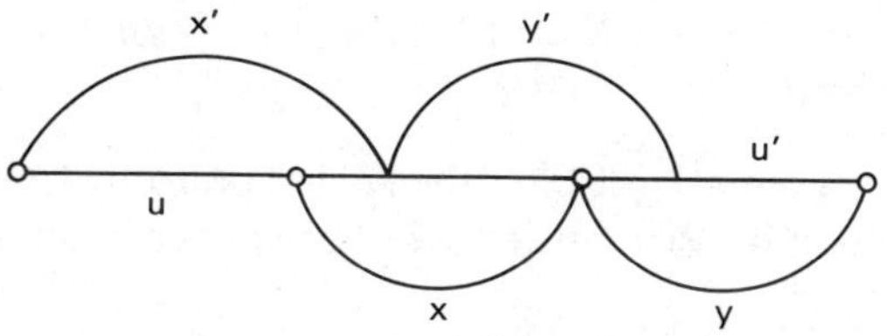

Fig. 2.22 Proof of Proposition 5.9.

Proof If X, Y are semaphore codes, then by Corollary 4.2, XY is a prefix code. Further by Proposition 5.2.

$$A^*XY \subset XA^*Y \subset XYA^*.$$

thus XY is a semaphore code.

Assume now that XY is a semaphore code, and that X is a prefix code. We show that $A^*X \subset XA^*$. For this, let $w = ux \in A^*X$, with $u \in A^*$, $x \in X$, and let y be a word in Y of minimal length. Then

$$wy = uxy = x'y'u'$$

for some $x' \in X$, $y' \in Y$, $u' \in A^*$ (see Fig. 2.22). By the choice of y, we have $|y| \leq |y'| \leq |y'u'|$, thus, $|ux| \geq |x'|$, showing that $ux \in XA^*$. □

The following example shows that if XY is a semaphore code, then Y need not be semaphore, even if it is maximal prefix.

EXAMPLE 5.4 Over $A = \{a, b\}$, let $X = a^*b$, and $Y = \{a^2, aba, ab^2, b\}$. Then X is a semaphore code, and Y is a maximal prefix code. However, Y is not semaphore (Example 5.3). On the other hand the code $Z = XY$ is semaphore. Indeed, Z is maximal prefix, and the set

$$P = ZA^- = a^*\{1, b, ba, bab\}$$

is suffix-closed. The conclusion follows from Proposition 5.4 (see Fig. 2.23).

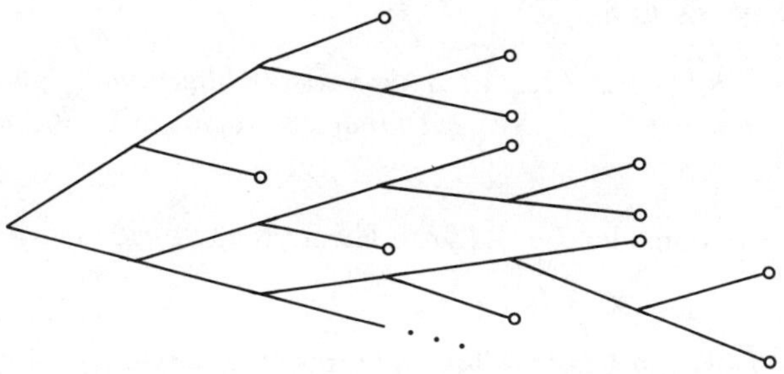

Fig. 2.23 The code $a^*b\{a^2, aba, ab^2, b\}$.

Corollary 5.10 *For any $X \subset A^+$ and $n \geq 1$, the set X is a semaphore code iff X^n is a semaphore code.*

Proof If X^n is a semaphore core, then X is a prefix by Corollary 4.3 and X is a semaphore code by Proposition 5.9. The converse follows directly from Proposition 5.9. □

Example 5.5 The code $X = \{a, baa, baba, bab^2, b^2\}$ represented in Fig. 2.24 is a maximal prefix code but not semaphore. Indeed, the word a has an inner occurrence in bab^2, contradicting formula (5.3). However, X decomposes into two semaphores codes

$$X = Y \circ Z$$

with $Y = \{c, dc, d^2, de, e\}$ and $Z = \{a, ba, b^2\}$.

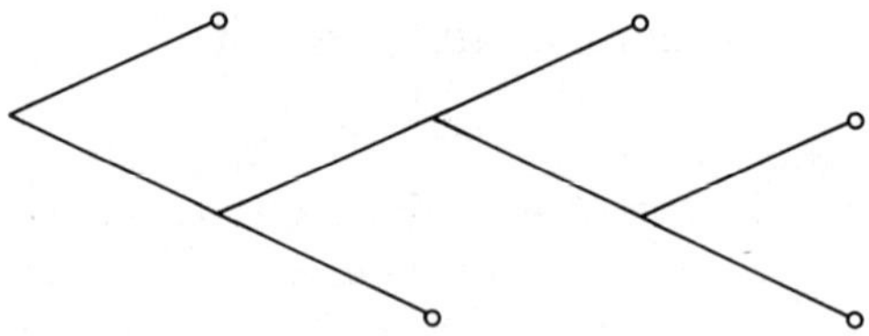

Fig. 2.24 The code X.

Given a semaphore code

$$X = A^*S - A^*SA^+,$$

it is natural to consider

$$Y = SA^* - A^+SA^*.$$

The code Y is a maximal suffix code; its reverse $\tilde{Y} = A^*\tilde{S} - A^*\tilde{S}A^+$ is a semaphore code with semaphores $\tilde{S}$. The following result shows a strong relation between X and Y.

Proposition 5.11 *Let $S \subset A^+$. There exists a bijection β from $X = A^*S - A^*SA^+$ onto $Y = SA^* - A^+SA^*$ such that, for each $x \in X$, $\beta(x)$ is a conjugate of x.*

Proof First, consider $J = A^*SA^*$. Then J is a two-sided ideal, and further

$$X = J - JA^+, \qquad Y = J - A^+J.$$

Indeed, $J = JA^* = (A^*S)A^*$. Thus, A^*S and J generate the same right ideal. By Proposition 1.2, $J - JA^+ = X$. The same arguments hold for Y.

Now we define, for each $x \in X$,

$$D(x) = \{d \in A^+ \mid \text{there is some } g \in A^* \text{ with } x = gd \text{ and } dg \in J\}.$$

Thus, $D(x)$ is composed of nonempty right factors of x. Further $D(x)$ is nonempty since x is in $D(x)$. Thus, each $D(x)$ contains some shortest element. This will be used to define β as follows. For $x \in X$,

$$\beta(x) = dg, \tag{5.4}$$

where d is the shortest word in $D(x)$ and g is such that

$$x = gd. \tag{5.5}$$

Thus, $\beta(x)$ is a conjugate of x, and $\beta(x) \in J$. We show that

$$\beta(x) \in J - A^+J = Y.$$

Assume the contrary. Then

$$\beta(x) = dg = uj \tag{5.6}$$

for some $u \in A^+$, $j \in J$.

Next g is a proper left factor of x. Consequently, $g \notin J$, since $J = JA^* = XA^*$, and thus, any word in J has a left factor in X. This shows that $|g| < |j|$, since otherwise g would belong to the ideal generated by j, thus $g \in J$.

It follows from this and from (5.6) that $|d| > |u|$, thus, $d = ud'$ for some $d' \in A^*$. Moreover $d' \in D(x)$, since $d'(gu) = ju \in J$ and $(gu)d' = gd = x \in X$. This yields a contradiction by the fact that d' is strictly shorter than d. Thus, $\beta(x) \in Y$.

Consider the converse mapping γ from Y into X defined by considering for y in Y

$$G(y) = \{e \in A^+ \mid y = eh \text{ and } he \in J\}$$

and by setting $\gamma(y) = he$, with $e \in G(y)$ of minimal length.

If $y = \beta(x) = dg$ is given by (5.4) and (5.5) and if $\gamma(y) = he$ with $e \in G(y)$, $eh = y$, then

$$dg = \beta(x) = eh. \tag{5.7}$$

Note that $gd \in J$. Thus, $d \in G(y)$. Consequently, $|d| \geq |e|$. Now the word e is not a proper left factor of d. Otherwise, setting $d = eu$, $ug = h$ in (5.7) with $u \in A^+$, we get

$$geu = gd = x, \qquad uge = he \in J,$$

showing that $u \in D(x)$ and contradicting the minimality of $|d|$. Thus $d = e$, $g = h$, and $\gamma(\beta(x)) = x$. An analogous proof shows that $\beta(\gamma(y)) = y$ for y in Y. Thus, β and γ are reciprocal bijections from X onto Y. □

TABLE 2.1

The X–Y Correspondance

X	D	Y
aa	a, aa	aa
aba	a, ba, aba	aab
abb	b, bb, abb	bab
ba	ba	ba
bb	b, bb	bb

EXAMPLE 5.6 Let us illustrate the construction of Proposition 5.11 by considering, over $A = \{a, b\}$, the set of semaphores $S = \{a^2, ba, b^2\}$. Then

$$X = A^*S - A^*SA^+ = \{a^2, ba, b^2, aba, ab^2\},$$

$$Y = SA^* - A^+SA^* = \{a^2, a^2b, ba, bab, b^2\}.$$

Table 2.1 lists on each row an element $x \in X$, the corresponding set $D(x)$ and the element $\beta(x) \in Y$.

Proposition 5.11 shows that any semaphore code can be transformed into a suffix code by a bijection which conjugates words. This property does not hold for arbitrary prefix codes, as shown by

EXAMPLE 5.7 Let $X = \{ab, ba, c, ac, bca\}$. Assume that there exists a bijection β which transforms X into a suffix code Y by conjugating the words in X. Then Y necessarily contains c, and ab, ba. Further Y contains ca (with c and ac, Y would not be suffix!). All the words conjugate to bca now have a right factor equal to one of c, ab, ba, ca. Thus, Y is not suffix.

In fact, X cannot be completed into a semaphore code, since c is a factor of bca.

We end this section with the following result which shows that biprefix codes are not usually semaphore codes.

PROPOSITION 5.12 *Let X be a biprefix semaphore code. Then $X = A^n$ for some $n \geq 1$.*

Proof It is sufficient to show that $X \subset A^n$ for some n. Let $x, y \in X$. For each right factor q of x, we have $qy \in A^*X \subset XA^*$. Thus there is, in view of Proposition 5.3, a left factor p of y such that $qp \in X$.

In this way we define a mapping from the set of right factors of x into the set of left factors of y. The set X being suffix, the mapping is injective; it follows that $|x| \leq |y|$. Interchanging x and y, we get $|y| \leq |x|$. Thus, all words in X have the same length. □

For semaphore codes, the above result is a particular case of the theorem of synchronization of semaphores to be stated in the next section. For biprefix codes, it is an easy consequence of Theorem III.4.2.

6. SYNCHRONOUS CODES

Let X be a maximal prefix code over A, and let x be a word. The word x is said to *synchronize* a word $u \in A^*$ if $ux \in X^*$. The word $x \in A^+$ is called *synchronizing* for X if it synchronizes every word in A^*, i.e., iff

$$A^*x \subset X^*. \tag{6.1}$$

It follows from (6.1) that a synchronizing word x is in X^* and further that xy (with $y \in X^*$) is synchronizing if x is synchronizing.

A maximal prefix code X is *synchronous* iff there exists a word which is synchronizing. Otherwise the code is called *asynchronous*.

EXAMPLE 6.1 The code $X = b^*a$ is synchronous. Indeed, a is a synchronizing word, since $A^*a \subset X^*$.

EXAMPLE 6.2 A biprefix code X over A is asynchronous if $X \neq A$. Assume indeed that $x \in X^*$ is synchronizing. For any $u \in A^*$, we have $ux \in X^*$. The monoid X^* being left unitary, it follows that $u \in X^*$. Thus $A^* = X^*$.

The terminology is derived from the following observation: let w be a word which has to be factored into words of some prefix code X. The appearance, in the middle of the word w, of some synchronizing word x, i.e., the existence of a factorization

$$w = uxv$$

implies that ux is in X^*. Thus we may start the decoding at the beginning of the word v. Since X^* is right unitary, we have indeed $w \in X^*$ iff $v \in X^*$. That means that the whole word is in X^* iff the final part can be decoded.

Note that any code X over A satisfying (6.1) is maximal prefix. Indeed, let $y, yu \in X$. Then $ux \in X^*$, and $y(ux)$, $(yu)x$ are two X factorizations which are distinct iff $u \neq 1$. Thus $u = 1$. Next, (6.1) shows that X is right complete.

Any synchronous code is thin. Indeed, if x is a synchronizing word for a code X, then x^2 is not a factor of a word in X, since otherwise $uxxv \in X$ for some $u, v \in A^*$. From $ux \in X^+$, it would follow that X is not prefix.

The fact that a code X is synchronous is well reflected by the automata recognizing X. Let us give a definition. Let

$$\mathscr{A} = (Q, i, T)$$

be a deterministic automaton on A. The *rank* of a word $x \in A^*$ in $\mathcal{A}$ is defined by

$$\operatorname{rank}_{\mathcal{A}}(x) = \operatorname{Card}(Q \cdot x).$$

It is an integer or $+\infty$. Clearly

$$\operatorname{rank}_{\mathcal{A}}(uxv) \leq \operatorname{rank}_{\mathcal{A}}(x).$$

PROPOSITION 6.1 *Let X be a maximal prefix code over A, and let $x \in X^*$. The following conditions are equivalent*:

(i) *x is synchronizing for X.*
(ii) *For the minimal automaton $\mathcal{A}(X^*)$, we have* $\operatorname{rank}_{\mathcal{A}(X^*)}(x) = 1$
(iii) *There exists a deterministic automaton $\mathcal{A}$ recognizing X^* such that* $\operatorname{rank}_{\mathcal{A}}(x) = 1$.

Proof (i) $\Rightarrow$ (ii) Let $\mathcal{A}(X^*) = (Q, i, i)$. Let $q \in Q$, and let $u \in A^*$ with $i \cdot u = q$. From $ux \in X^*$, it follows that $q \cdot x = i$. Thus $Q \cdot x = \{i\}$, showing that $\operatorname{rank}_{\mathcal{A}(X^*)}(x) = 1$.

(ii) $\Rightarrow$ (iii) is clear.

(iii) $\Rightarrow$ (i) Let $\mathcal{A} = (Q, i, T)$ and let $q_0 = Q \cdot x$. Then $q_0 \in T$. We verify that x is synchronizing. Let $u \in A^*$, and set $q = i \cdot u$. From $q \cdot x = q_0$, we have $ux \in X^*$. $\square$

PROPOSITION 6.2 *Let X be a thin maximal prefix code over A, and let $P = XA^-$. Then X is synchronous iff for all $p \in P$, there exists $x \in X^*$ such that $px \in X^*$.*

Note that the existence of a unique word synchronizing all left factors is not required in the hypotheses of the proposition.

Proof The condition is clearly necessary. It is also sufficient. Let $w \in A^*$ be such that w is not a factor of a word in X. Let $K = \{p_1, p_2, \ldots, p_n\}$ be the set of right factors of w which are in P.

The set K is not empty since $1 \in K$. Define a sequence $x_1, \ldots, x_n$ of words in X^* as follows: x_1 is a word in X^* such that $p_1 x_1 \in X^*$. If $x_1, \ldots, x_{i-1}$ are defined, there exist, because X is right complete, words $y \in X^*$, $p \in P$ with

$$p_i x_1 \cdots x_{i-1} = yp.$$

Then x_i is defined to be a word in X^* such that $px_i \in X^*$. It follows that for $i = 1, \ldots, n$,

$$p_i x_1 \cdots x_{i-1} x_i \in X^*. \tag{6.2}$$

The word $z = wx_1x_2 \cdots x_n$ is synchronizing for X. Indeed let $u \in A^*$. Then

$$uw = y'p'$$

for some $y' \in X^*$ and $p' \in P$. The word p' is right factor of w, since otherwise w would be a factor of a word in X. Thus, $p' = p_i$ for some $p_i \in K$. Using (6.2), we obtain

$$uz = y'(p_i x_1 \cdots x_i)(x_{i+i} \cdots x_n) \in X^*. \quad \square$$

PROPOSITION 6.3 *Let X, Y, Z be maximal prefix codes with $X = Y \circ Z$. Then X is synchronous iff Y and Z are synchronous.*

Proof Let $Y \subset B^*$, $X, Z \subset A^*$, and $\beta: B^* \to A^*$ be such that

$$X = Y \circ_\beta Z.$$

First, assume that Y and Z are synchronous, and let $y \in Y^*$, $z \in Z^*$ be synchronizing words. Then $B^*y \subset Y^*$ and $A^*x \subset Z^*$, whence

$$A^*z\beta(y) \subset Z^*\beta(y) = \beta(B^*y) \subset \beta(Y^*) = X^*,$$

showing that $z\beta(y)$ is a synchronizing word for X.

Conversely, assume that $A^*x \subset X^*$ for some $x \in X^*$. Then $x \in Z^*$ and $X^* \subset Z^*$; thus, x is also synchronizing for Z. Next, let $y = \beta^{-1}(x) \in Y^*$. Then

$$\beta(B^*y) = Z^*x \subset A^*x \subset X^* = \beta(Y^*).$$

The mapping β being injective, it follows that $B^*y \subset Y^*$. Consequently, Y is synchronous. $\square$

EXAMPLE 6.3 The code $X = (A^2 - b^2) \cup b^2A^2$ is asynchronous, since it decomposes over the code A^2 which is asynchronous (Example 6.2). It is also directly clear that a word $x \in X^*$ can never synchronize words of odd length.

EXAMPLE 6.4 For any maximal prefix code Z and $n \geq 2$, the code $X = Z^n$ is asynchronous. Indeed, such a code has the form $X = B^n \circ Z$ for some alphabet B, and B^n is synchronous only for $n = 1$ (Example 6.2).

We now give a result on prefix codes which will be generalized when other techniques will be available (Theorem III.3.6). The present proof is elementary. Recall from Chapter I that for a finite code X, the *order* of a letter a is the integer n such that a^n is in X.

The existence of the order of a results from Proposition I.5.9. Note that for a finite maximal prefix code, it is an immediate consequence of the inclusion $a^+ \subset X^*P$, with $P = XA^-$.

THEOREM 6.4 *Let $X \subset A^+$ be a finite maximal prefix code. If the orders of the letters $a \in A$ are relatively prime, then X is synchronous.*

Proof Let $P = XA^-$ and let $\mathcal{A} = (P, 1, 1)$ be the literal automaton of X^*. This automaton is complete since X is maximal prefix. Recall that its action is given by

$$p \cdot a = \begin{cases} pa & \text{if} \quad pa \in P, \\ 1 & \text{if} \quad pa \in X. \end{cases}$$

For all $w \in A^*$, define

$$Q(w) = P \cdot w.$$

Then for $w, w' \in A^*$,

$$Q(w'w) \subset Q(w), \qquad \operatorname{Card} Q(w'w) \leq \operatorname{Card} Q(w'). \tag{6.3}$$

Observe that for all $W \in A^*$, $\operatorname{Card}(Q(w)) = \operatorname{rank}_{\mathscr{A}}(w)$.

Let $u \in A^*$ be a word such that $\operatorname{Card}(Q(u))$ is minimal. The code X being right complete, there exists $v \in A^*$ such that $w = uv \in X^+$. By (6.3), $\operatorname{Card}(Q(w))$ is minimal. Further $w \in X^+$ implies

$$1 \in Q(w). \tag{6.4}$$

We will show that $\operatorname{Card}(Q(w)) = 1$. This proves the theorem in view of Proposition 6.1.

Let $a \in A$ be a fixed letter, and let n be the positive integer such that $a^n \in X$. We define two sets of integers I and K by

$$I = \{i \in \mathbb{N} \mid Q(w)a^i \cap X \neq \varnothing\},$$
$$K = \{k \in \{0, \ldots, n-1\} \mid a^k w \in X^*\}.$$

First, we show that

$$\operatorname{Card} I = \operatorname{Card} Q(w). \tag{6.5}$$

Indeed, consider a word $p \in Q(w) (\subset P)$. There is an integer i such that $pa^i \in X$, since X is finite and maximal. This integer is unique since otherwise X would not be prefix. Thus there is a mapping which associates to each p in $Q(w)$ the integer i such that $pa^i \in X$. This is clearly a surjective mapping onto I. We verify that it is also injective. Assume the contrary. Then $pa^i \in X$ and $p'a^i \in X$ for $p, p' \in Q(w)$, $p \neq p'$. This implies $\operatorname{Card}(Q(wa^i)) < \operatorname{Card}(Q(w))$, contradicting the minimality of $\operatorname{Card}(Q(w))$. Thus the mapping is bijective. This proves (6.5).

Next set

$$m = \max\{i + k \mid i \in I, k \in K\}.$$

Clearly $m \leq \max I + \max K \leq \max I + n - 1$. Let

$$R = \{m, m+1, \ldots, m+n-1\}.$$

We shall find a bijection from $I \times K$ onto R. For this, let $r \in R$ and for each $p \in Q(w)$, let

$$v(p) = p \cdot a^r w.$$

Then

$$\nu(p) = (p \cdot a^r) \cdot w \in P \cdot w = Q(w).$$

Thus $\nu(Q(w)) \subset Q(w)$ and $\nu(Q(w)) = Q(w)$ by the minimality of $Q(w)$. Thus ν is a bijection from $Q(w)$ onto itself. It follows by (6.4) that there exists a unique $p_r \in Q(w)$ such that $p_r a^r w \in X^*$. Let i_r be the unique integer such that $p_r a^{1_r} \in X$. Then $i_r \in I$, whence $i_r \leq m \leq r$. Set

$$r = i_r + \lambda n + k_r \tag{6.6}$$

with $\lambda \in \mathbb{N}$ and $0 \leq k_r < n$. This uniquely defines k_r and we have

$$p_r w = (p_r a^{i_r})(a^n)^\lambda (a^{k_r} w).$$

Since $p_r a^{i_r} \in X$ and X^* is right unitary, we have $(a^n)^\lambda (a^{k_r} w) \in X^*$ and also $a^{k_r} w \in X^*$. Thus, $k_r \in K$. The preceding construction defines a mapping

$$R \to I \times K, \qquad r \mapsto (i_r, k_r) \tag{6.7}$$

first by determining i_r, then by computing k_r by means of (6.6). This mapping is injective. Indeed, if $r \neq r'$, then either $i_r \neq i_{r'}$, or it follows from (6.6) and from $r \not\equiv r' \bmod n$ that $k_r \neq k_{r'}$.

We now show that the mapping (6.7) is surjective. Let $(i, k) \in I \times K$, and let $\lambda \in \mathbb{N}$ be such that

$$r = i + \lambda n + k \in R.$$

By definition of I, there is a (unique) $q \in Q(w)$ such that $qa^i \in X$, and by the definition of K, we have

$$qa^r w \in X.$$

Thus, $q = p_r$, $i = i_r$, $k = k_r$, showing the surjectivity.

It follows from the bijection that

$$n = \mathrm{Card}(R) = \mathrm{Card}(I) \cdot \mathrm{Card}(K).$$

This in turn implies, by (6.5), that Card $Q(w)$ divides the integer n. Thus Card $Q(w)$ divides the order of each letter in the alphabet. Since these orders are relatively prime, necessarily $\mathrm{Card}(Q(w)) = 1$. The proof is complete. □
complete. □

We will prove later (Section IV.7) the following important theorem.

THEOREM 6.5 *Let X be a semaphore code. Then there exists a synchronous semaphore code Z and an integer d such that*

$$X = Z^d.$$

This result admits Proposition 5.12 as a special case. Consider indeed a biprefix semaphore code $X \subset A^+$. Then according to Theorem 6.5, we have

TABLE 2.2

The Transitions of $\mathscr{A}(X^*)$

Q	1	2	3	4	5	6	7	8	9
a	2	3	1	1	3	8	9	3	1
b	4	6	7	5	1	4	1	5	1

$X = Z^d$ with Z synchronous. The code X being biprefix, Z is also biprefix (Proposition 4.9); but a biprefix synchronous code is trivial by Example 6.2. Thus, $Z = A$ and $X = A^d$.

Theorem 6.5 describes in a simple manner the structure of asynchronous semaphore codes. Indeed, if $X = Z^d$ with Z synchronous, then X is asynchronous iff $d \geq 2$ (see also Example 6.4).

We may ask whether such a description exists for general maximal prefix codes: is it true that an indecomposable maximal prefix code X is either biprefix or synchronous? Unfortunately, it is not the case, even when X is finite, as shown by

EXAMPLE 6.5 Let $A = \{a, b\}$, and let X be the prefix code with automaton $\mathscr{A}(X) = (Q,1,1)$ whose transitions are given in Table 2.2. The automaton $\mathscr{A}(X^*)$ is complete, thus X is maximal prefix. In fact, X is finite; it is given in Fig. 2.25.

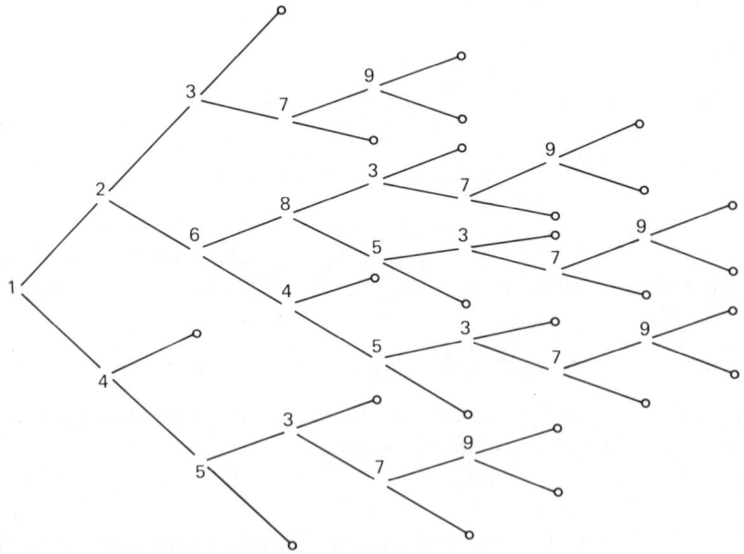

Fig. 2.25 An asynchronous indecomposable code.

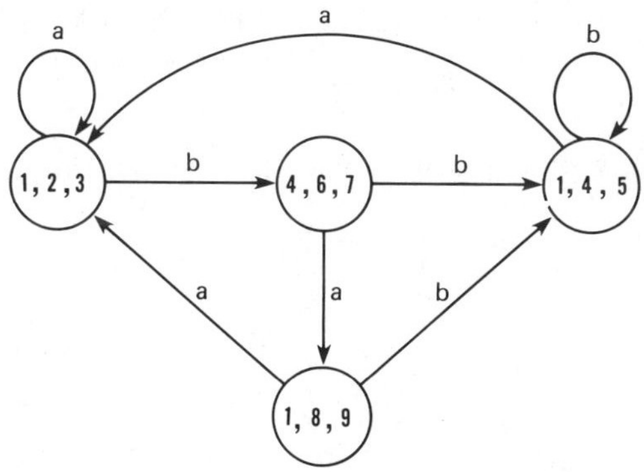

Fig. 2.26

To show that X is asynchronous, observe that the action of the letters a and b preserves globally the sets of states

$$\{1,2,3\}, \quad \{1,4,5\}, \quad \{4,6,7\}, \quad \{1,8,9\}$$

as shown in Fig. 2.26. This implies that X is asynchronous. Assume indeed that $x \in X^*$ is a synchronizing word. Then by definition $A^*x \subset X^*$, whence $q \cdot x = 1$ for all states in $q \in Q$. Thus for each three element subset I, we would have $I \cdot x = \{1\}$.

Further X is not biprefix since b^3, $ab^4 \in X$. Finally, the inspection of Fig. 2.25 shows that X is indecomposable.

7. AVERAGE LENGTH

The results of Chapter I concerning the measure of a code apply of course to prefix codes. However, for these codes, considerable extensions exist in two directions. First, the properties proved in Chapter I hold for measures which are much more general than those defined by Bernoulli distributions. Second, there exists a remarkable combinatorial interpretation of the average length of a prefix code by means of the measure of its proper left factors (Proposition 7.2).

A function

$$\pi: \quad A^* \to \,]0,1]$$

is a (positive) *cylindric measure* if the two following conditions are satisfied:

$$\pi(1) = 1 \tag{7.1}$$

and for all $w \in A^*$,

$$\pi(w) = \sum_{a \in A} \pi(wa). \tag{7.2}$$

The function π is extended to subsets of A^* by setting, for $L \subset A^*$,

$$\pi(L) = \sum_{u \in L} \pi(u).$$

Thus, (7.2) may be written as $\pi(w) = \pi(wA)$. Note that this implies, in view of (7.1), that

$$\pi(A) = 1.$$

More generally, for $n \geq 0$

$$\pi(A^n) = 1,$$

since

$$\pi(A^{n+1}) = \sum_{w \in A^n} \pi(wA) = \sum_{w \in A^n} \pi(w) = \pi(A^n).$$

A positive Bernoulli distribution is of course a cylindric measure. The converse is false. Example 7.1 shows that cylindric measures are quite general.

EXAMPLE 7.1 Let $A = \{a, b\}$, and let $(\alpha_n)_{n \geq 0}$ be a sequence of positive real numbers such that the series $\sum_{n \geq 0} \alpha_n$ converges and

$$\sum_{n \geq 0} \alpha_n = \alpha < 1. \tag{7.3}$$

Define a sequence $(\beta_n)_{n \geq 0}$ by $\beta_0 = 1$ and for $n \geq 1$,

$$\beta_n = 1 - \sum_{i=0}^{n-1} \alpha_i.$$

Then by construction

$$0 < \beta_n < 1 \quad (n \geq 1), \qquad \alpha_n + \beta_{n+1} = \beta_n \quad (n \geq 0).$$

We define a cylindric measure on A^* by setting for $n \geq 0$,

$$\pi(b^n a) = \alpha_n, \qquad \pi(b^n) = \beta_n$$

and for

$$w = b^n a u$$

with $n \geq 0$ and $u \in A^+$,

$$\pi(w) = \alpha_n 2^{-|u|}.$$

It is easily verified that π is indeed a cylindric measure. Let $X = b^*a$. The real numbers α_n, β_n are reported on the literal representation of X (Fig. 2.27). Note that

$$\pi(X) = \sum_{n \geq 0} \alpha_n = \alpha.$$

EXAMPLE 7.2 Let π: $A^* \to]0, 1]$ be a cylindric measure, and let $u \in A^*$.

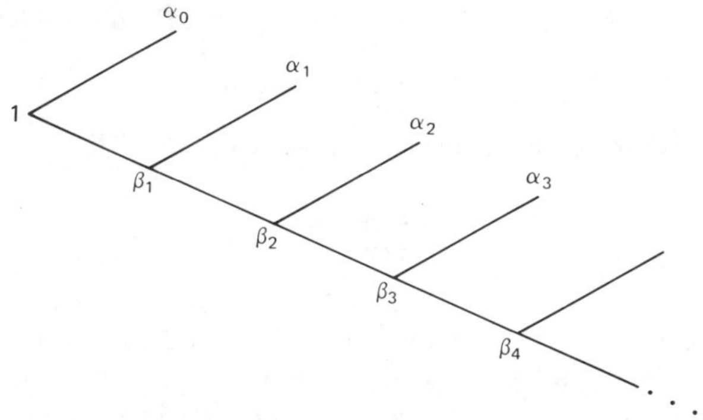

Fig. 2.27 Some values of the cylindric measure.

Define a function $\rho: A^* \to]0, 1]$ by

$$\rho(w) = \frac{\pi(uw)}{\pi(u)}, \qquad w \in A^*.$$

Then ρ is a cylindric measure since $\pi(1) = 1$ and

$$\sum_{a \in A} \rho(wa) = \frac{1}{\pi(u)} \sum_{a \in A} \pi(uwa) = \frac{\pi(uw)}{\pi(u)} = \rho(w).$$

PROPOSITION 7.1 *Let π be a cylindric measure on A^*.*

1. *For any prefix code X, we have*

$$\pi(X) \leq 1.$$

2. *For any finite maximal prefix code, we have*

$$\pi(X) = 1.$$

For Bernoulli distributions, this follows from Theorems I.4.2 and I.5.10 and from the fact that a finite set is thin.

Proof We first show 2. If $\text{Card}(A) = 1$, or $X = A$, then the result is clear. Otherwise, let $x \in X$ be a word of maximal length, and let $t \in A^*$, $a \in A$ be such that $x = ta$. Then by the maximality of x, $tA \subset X$. If $t = 1$, then $X = A$. Thus, $t \neq 1$. The set $Y = (X - tA) \cup t$ is a maximal prefix code (Proposition 4.6). Next, Y has strictly fewer elements than X; this comes from $\text{Card}(A) \geq 2$. Further

$$\pi(Y) = \pi(X) - \pi(tA) + \pi(t) = \pi(X).$$

This shows that $\pi(X) = 1$ by induction of the cardinality.

To prove statement 1, let X be an arbitrary prefix code and let

$$X_n = \{x \in X \mid |x| \leq n\}.$$

According to what we just proved, we have $\pi(X_n) \leq 1$. Thus,

$$\pi(X) = \sup_{n \geq 0} \pi(X_n) \leq 1. \quad \square$$

EXAMPLE 7.1 *(continued)*. The code $X = b^*a$ is maximal prefix. Nevertheless, $\pi(X) = \alpha < 1$. This shows that the second part of Proposition 7.1 does not hold for infinite codes. In addition, since any number $\alpha \in]0, 1[$ can be written in the form given by (7.3), the cylindric measure of the infinite maximal prefix code X can take any value in the interval $]0, 1]$.

Given a prefix code $X \subset A^+$ and a cylindric measure π on A^* such that $\pi(X) = 1$, the *average length* of X (relatively to π) is defined by

$$\lambda(X) = \sum_{x \in X} |x| \, \pi(x).$$

It is a nonnegative real number or infinite. The context always indicates which is the underlying cylindric measure. We therefore omit the reference to it in the notation.

The quantity $\lambda(X)$ is in fact the mean of the random variable assigning to each $x \in X$ its length $|x|$.

PROPOSITION 7.2 *Let X be a prefix code and let $P = XA^-$. Further, let π be a cylindric measure such that $\pi(X) = 1$. Then $\lambda(X) = \pi(P)$.*

Proof We start the proof by showing that each $p \in P$ satisfies

$$\pi(pA^* \cap X) = \pi(p). \tag{7.4}$$

Consider indeed the function $\rho: A^* \to]0, 1]$ defined by

$$\rho(w) = \pi(pw)/\pi(p).$$

In view of Example 7.2, it is a cylindric measure. On the other hand

$$pA^* \cap X = p(p^{-1}X),$$

and by Proposition 4.6, the set $p^{-1}X$ is a prefix code. Proposition 7.1 therefore implies that $\rho(p^{-1}X) \leq 1$. From

$$\rho(p^{-1}X) = \pi(pA^* \cap X)/\pi(p)$$

it follows that

$$\pi(p) \geq \pi(pA^* \cap X). \tag{7.5}$$

Next let

$$Y = (X - (pA^* \cap X)) \cup p.$$

By the same Proposition 4.6, the set Y is a prefix code; according to Proposition 7.1, $\pi(Y) \leq 1$. Thus,

$$\pi(X) - \pi(pA^* \cap X) + \pi(p) \leq 1.$$

By assumption, $\pi(X) = 1$. Consequently

$$\pi(p) \leq \pi(pA^* \cap X).$$

Together with (7.5), this yields (7.4).

Now, we observe the following identity concerning formal power series

$$\sum_{x \in X} |x| x = \sum_{p \in P} \underline{(pA^* \cap X)}. \tag{7.6}$$

Indeed, the multiplicity of a word $x \in X$ on the right-hand side of (7.6) is the number of its left factors in P. This number is precisely its length. It follows from (7.6) that

$$\sum_{x \in X} |x| \pi(x) = \sum_{p \in P} \pi(pA^* \cap X).$$

The left-hand side is $\lambda(X)$, and by (7.4), we obtain

$$\lambda(X) = \sum_{p \in P} \pi(p) = \pi(P). \quad \square$$

For a finite maximal prefix code, the cylindrical measure equals 1. Thus,

COROLLARY 7.3 *Let X be a finite maximal prefix code and $P = XA^-$. For any cylindric measure π on A^*, the following holds:*

$$\lambda(X) = \pi(P). \quad \square$$

For a Bernoulli distribution, the finiteness condition can be replaced by the condition to be thin.

COROLLARY 7.4 *Let X be a thin maximal prefix code, and $P = XA^-$. For any positive Bernoulli distribution π on A^*, we have*

$$\lambda(X) = \pi(P).$$

Further, the average length $\lambda(X)$ is finite.

Proof The code X being maximal, Theorem I.5.11 shows that $\pi(X) = 1$; thus, the equality $\lambda(X) = \pi(P)$ follows from Proposition 7.2. Moreover, P is thin since each factor of a word in P is also a factor of a word in X. By Proposition I.5.6, $\pi(P)$ is finite. $\square$

We shall see in Chapter VI that the average length is still finite in the more general case of thin maximal codes.

EXAMPLE 7.3 Let $A = \{a, b\}$ and $X = a^*b$. For any positive Bernoulli distribution π, let $\pi(a) = p$, $\pi(b) = q$. Then

$$\lambda(X) = \pi(a^*) = 1/q.$$

EXAMPLE 7.4 Let D be the Dyck code over $A = \{a, b\}$ (see Example I.4.5). We have seen that for a Bernoulli distribution given by $\pi(a) = p$, $\pi(b) = q$, the following formula holds:

$$\pi(D) = 1 - |p - q|.$$

Further, setting $d_n = \pi(D \cap A^n)$, we have by formula (I.4.14),

$$d_{2n} = \frac{2}{n}\binom{2n-2}{n-1} p^n q^n, \qquad d_{2n+1} = 0 \qquad (n \geq 1).$$

It follows that, for $p = q = \frac{1}{2}$, we have $\pi(D) = 1$ and

$$\lambda(D) = \sum_{n \geq 0} 2nd_{2n} = \sum_{n \geq 0} 2^{2-2n}\binom{2n-2}{n-1}.$$

This series diverges since, according to Stirling's formula,

$$2^{-2n+2}\binom{2n-2}{n-1} \sim \frac{2}{\sqrt{\pi(n-1)}}.$$

Thus, the average length of D is infinite for $p = q = \frac{1}{2}$.

The next example concerns the computation of the average length of semaphore codes. We start with an interesting identity.

PROPOSITION 7.5 *Let $X \subset A^+$ be a semaphore code, $P = XA^-$ and let S be the minimal set for which $X = A^*S - A^*SA^+$. For $s, t \in S$, let*

$$X_s = X \cap A^*s \text{ and } R_{s,t} = \{w \in A^* \mid sw \in A^*t \text{ and } |w| < |t|\}.$$

Then for all $t \in S$,

$$\underline{P}\underline{t} = \sum_{s \in S} \underline{X}_s \underline{R}_{st}. \tag{7.7}$$

Proof First, we observe that each product $X_s R_{st}$ is unambiguous, since X_s is prefix. Further any two terms of the sum are disjoint, since $X = \bigcup X_s$ is prefix. Thus, it suffices to show that

$$Pt = \bigcup_{s \in S} X_s R_{st}.$$

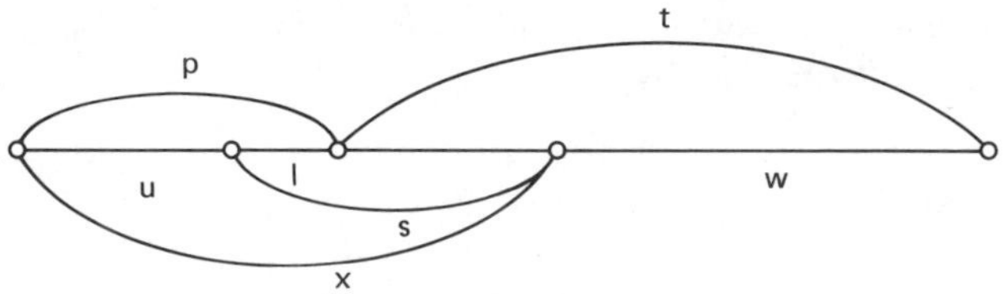

Fig. 2.28 Factorizations of pt.

First let $p \in P$, and let x be the shortest left factor of pt, which is in $A^* S$. Then $x \in X$ and

$$pt = xw$$

for some $w \in A^*$. Next $x \in X_s$ for some $s \in S$. Set $x = us$. The word p being in P, we have $|p| < |x|$, whence $|w| < |t|$ (see Fig. 2.28). Now p cannot be a proper left factor of u, since otherwise s would be a proper factor of t, contradicting Proposition 5.7 and the minimality of S. Thus, u is a left factor of p and $sw \in A^*t$, showing that $w \in R_{st}$.

Conversely, let $x \in X_s$ and $w \in R_{st}$ for some $s, t \in S$. Then $x = us$ and $sw = lt$ for a proper left factor l of s. Then ul is a proper left factor of $us = x$; thus, $ul \in P$ and $xw = ult \in Pt$. □

Corollary 7.6 *With the notations of Proposition 7.5, we have for any Bernoulli distribution π, the following system of equations:*

$$\lambda(X)\pi(t) = \sum_{s \in S} \pi(X_s)\pi(R_{st}), \qquad (t \in S), \tag{7.8}$$

$$\sum_{s \in S} \pi(X_s) = 1. \quad \square$$

For the case of a finite set S, the system (7.8) is a set of $1 + \mathrm{Card}(S)$ linear equations in the $1 + \mathrm{Card}(S)$ unknown variables $\pi(X_s)$ and $\lambda(X)$. The sets R_{st} being finite, the coefficients $\pi(R_{st})$ are easily computed. This yields the desired expression of $\lambda(X)$. In the special case where S is a singleton, we get

Corollary 7.7 *Let $s \in A^+$, let $X = A^*s - A^*sA^+$ and $R = \{w \in A^* \mid sw \in A^*s \text{ and } |w| < |s|\}$. Then for any positive Bernoulli distribution π, we have*

$$\lambda(X) = \pi(R)/\pi(s). \quad \square$$

Example 7.5 Let $A = \{a, b\}$ and consider $s = aba$. The corresponding set R is $R = \{1, ba\}$. If $\pi(a) = p$ and $\pi(b) = q = 1 - p$, then for $X = A^*aba - A^*abaA^+$, we get

$$\lambda(X) = \frac{1 + pq}{p^2 q}.$$

Now choose $s' = baa$. The corresponding R' is the set $R' = \{1\}$. Thus, for $X' = A^*baa - A^*baaA^+$, we have

$$\lambda(X) = \frac{1}{qp^2}$$

For $p = q = \frac{1}{2}$, this gives $\lambda(X) = 10$, $\lambda(X') = 8$. This is an interesting paradox: we have to wait longer for the first appearance of *aba* than for the first appearance of *baa*!

8. DECIPHERING DELAY

Let X be a subset of A^+. Then X is said to have *finite deciphering delay* if there is an integer $d \geq 0$ such that

$$\forall x, x' \in X, \quad \forall y \in X^d, \quad \forall u \in A^*, \qquad xyu \in x'X^* \quad \Rightarrow \quad x = x'. \qquad (8.1)$$

If (8.1) holds for some integer d, then it holds for all $d' \geq d$. If X has finite deciphering delay, then the smallest integer d satisfying (8.1) is the *deciphering delay* of X. This notion is clearly oriented from left to right; it is straightforward to define a dual notion (working from right to left).

The terminology is justified by the following consideration: let $w \in A^*$ be a word having two left factors in X^+, and such that the shorter one is in X^{1+d}. If (8.1) holds, then the two X-factorizations start with the same word in X. Thus, the "delay" between the moment when, reading from left to right, a possible factor of an X-factorization is discovered, and the moment when these factors are definitively valid, is bounded.

It follows from the definition that the sets with delay $d = 0$ are the prefix codes. This is the reason why prefix codes are also called instantaneous codes. In this sense, codes with finite delay are a natural generalization of prefix codes.

PROPOSITION 8.1 *A subset X of A^+, which has a finite deciphering delay, is a code.*

Proof Let d be the deciphering delay of X. Assume that X is not a code. Then there is an equality

$$w = x_1 x_2 \cdots x_n = y_1 y_2 \cdots y_m, \quad x_1 \neq y_1$$

with $n, m \geq 1$, $x_1, \ldots, x_n, y_1, \ldots, y_m \in X$. Let $z \in X$. Then $wz^d \in y_1 X^*$. By (8.1), we have $x_1 = y_1$. Thus, X is a code. $\square$

EXAMPLE 8.1 The suffix code $X = \{aa, ba, b\}$ has an infinite deciphering delay. Indeed, for all $d \geq 0$, the word $b(aa)^d \in X^{1+d}$ is a left factor of $y(aa)^d$ with $y = ba \neq b$.

We now study maximal codes with finite deciphering delay. The following result is similar to Proposition I.5.2. However, it is less general and we do not know of a simple construction to embed a code with finite deciphering delay into a complete one.

PROPOSITION 8.2 *Let X be a subset of A^+ which has finite deciphering delay. If $y \in A^+$ is an unbordered word such that*

$$X^*yA^* \cap X^* = \varnothing,$$

then

$$Y = X \cup y$$

has finite deciphering delay.

Proof Consider the set $V = X^*y$. It is a prefix code. Indeed, assume that $v = xy$ and $v' = x'y$ with $x, x' \in X^*$, and $v < v'$. Then necessarily $v \leq x'$ since y is unbordered. But then $x' \in X^*yA^*$, a contradiction. Note also that

$$V^+A^* \cap X^* = \varnothing$$

since $V^+A^* \subset VA^*$. □

Let d be the deciphering delay of X and let

$$e = d + |y|.$$

We show that the deciphering delay of Y is at most e. For this, let us consider a relation

$$w = y_1y_2 \cdots y_{e+1}u = y'_1y'_2 \cdots y'_n$$

with $y_1, \ldots, y_{e+1}, y'_1, \ldots, y'_n \in Y$, $u \in A^*$ and, arguing by contradiction, assume that $y_1 \neq y'_1$.

First, let us verify that one of $y_1, \ldots, y_{e+1}$ is equal to y. Assume the contrary. Then $y_1 \cdots y_{d+1} \in X^{d+1}$. Let q be the smallest integer such that (Fig. 2.29)

$$y_1 \cdots y_{d+1} \leq y'_1 \cdots y'_q.$$

The delay of X being d, and $y_1 \neq y'_1$, one among $y'_1, \ldots, y'_q$ must be equal to

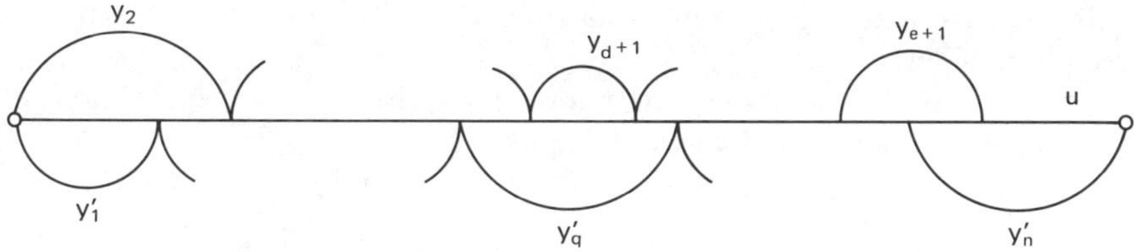

Fig. 2.29

y. We cannot have $y'_i = y$ for an index $i < q$, since otherwise $y_1 \cdots y_{d+1} \in V^+A^* \cap X^*$. Thus, $y'_q = y$ and $y'_1 \cdots y'_q \in V$. Note that

$$y'_1 \cdots y'_{q-1} \leq y_1 \cdots y_{d+1}.$$

Next $|y_{d+2} \cdots y_{e+1}| \geq e - d = |y|$. It follows that

$$y'_1 \cdots y'_q \leq y_1 \cdots y_{e+1}.$$

But then $y_1 \cdots y_{e+1} \in X^* \cap X^*yA^*$, which is impossible. This shows the claim, namely, that one of $y_1, \ldots, y_{e+1}$ is equal to y.

It follows that w has a left factor $y_1 y_2 \cdots y_p$ in V with $y_1, \ldots, y_{p-1} \in X$ and $y_p = y$. By the hypothesis, one of $y'_1, \ldots, y'_n$ must be equal to y. Thus w has also a left factor $y'_1 y'_2 \cdots y'_q$ in V with $y'_1, \ldots, y'_{q-1} \in X$ and $y'_q = y$. The code V being prefix, we have

$$y_1 y_2 \cdots y_{p-1} = y'_1 y'_2 \cdots y'_{q-1}.$$

Since X is a code, this and the assumption $y_1 \neq y'_1$ imply that $p = q = 1$. But then $y_p = y = y_q$. This yields the final contradiction. □

Proposition 8.2 has the following interesting consequence.

THEOREM 8.3 *Let X be a thin subset of A^+. If X has finite deciphering delay, then the following conditions are equivalent*

(i) *X is a maximal code,*
(ii) *X is maximal in the family of codes with finite deciphering delay.*

Proof The case where A has just one letter is clear. Thus, we suppose that $\operatorname{Card}(A) \geq 2$. It suffices to prove (ii) ⇒ (i). For this, it is enough to show that X is complete. Assume the contrary and consider a word u which is not a factor of a word in X^*. According to Proposition 0.3.6, there exists $v \in A^*$ such that $y = uv$ is unbordered. But then $A^*yA^* \cap X^* = \varnothing$ and by Proposition 8.2, $X \cup y$ has finite deciphering delay. This yields the contradiction. □

We now state and prove the main result of this section.

THEOREM 8.4 *Any finite maximal code with finite deciphering delay is prefix.*

In an equivalent manner, a maximal finite code either is prefix or has infinite deciphering delay.

The proof of the theorem is rather long. It requires new concepts which will be illustrated in a different way in Chapter VI.

Let X be a subset of A^+. A word $s \in A^*$ is *simplifying* (for X) if for all $x \in X^*$, $v \in A^*$,

$$xsv \in X^* \quad \Rightarrow \quad sv \in X^*.$$

The set of simplifying words is denoted by S(X) or S. It is a right ideal. Further X^* is right unitary iff $1 \in$ S, thus, iff S $= A^*$.

A word p is *extendable* (for X) if, for all $u \in A^*$, there exists $v \in A^*$ such that $puv \in X^*$. Clearly, an extendable word is right completable. The set of extendable words is denoted by E(X) or E. As for S, it is a right ideal. Further, X is right complete iff $1 \in$ E; thus, iff E $= A^*$.

Of course the notions of simplifying and extendable words are left-to-right oriented, just as the notion of deciphering delay.

PROPOSITION 8.5 *Let $X \subset A^+$ be a code. If both* E *and* S *are nonempty, then* E = S.

Proof Let us show first the inclusion S $\subset$ E. Let $s \in$ S, $p \in$ E. Note that $pt \in X^*$ for some word t and that pt still is extendable. Thus, we may assume that $p \in$ E $\cap$ X*. Consider any word $u \in A^*$. Since $p \in$ E, the word psu can be completed: there is a word $v \in A^+$ such that $psuv \in X^*$. But p is in X^* and s is simplifying. Thus, $suv \in X^*$, showing that s is extendable.

Conversely, let $s \in$ S, $p \in$ E. To show that p is simplifying, let $x \in X^*$, $v \in A^*$ such that $xpv \in X^*$. Since the word pvs is right completable, we have $pvsw \in X^*$ for some $w \in A^*$. But then $xpvsw \in X^*$ also and since s is simplifying, we have $sw \in X^*$. Thus, finally, the four words x, $x(pv)$, $(pv)(sw)$, and sw are in X^*. The set X^* is stable, thus $pv \in X^*$. This shows that p is simplifying. □

Let $X \subset A^+$ be a code and let $w \in A^*$. A *right context* of w is a word $v \in A^*$ such that there exist $x_1, \ldots, x_n \in X$ with

1. $wv = x_1 x_2 \cdots x_n$
2. v is a proper right factor of x_n.

The set of right contexts of w is denoted by $C_r(w)$. This set is nonempty iff w is right-completable in X^*. Further $1 \in C_r(w)$ iff $w \in X^*$.

Recall that if S(X) $\neq \varnothing$, then it is a right ideal. Its initial part

$$U = \mathrm{S} - \mathrm{S}\,A^+$$

is prefix and

$$UA^* = \mathrm{S}.$$

PROPOSITION 8.6 *Let X be a code such that* S = E $\neq \varnothing$ *and let* $U =$ S $-$ S A^+. *For all $w \in A^*$, we have*

1. *The set $C_r(w)U$ is prefix.*
2. *The product $C_r(w)U$ is unambiguous.*
3. *If $w \in S$, then $C_r(w)U$ is maximal prefix.*

Proof We first verify the following property:

if $vuz = v'u'$ *for* $v, v' \in C_r(w)$, $u, u' \in U$, *and* $z \in A^*$,
then $v = v'$, $u = u'$, $z = 1$ (*)

Indeed, first note that $u \in$ E. Thus, there exists $t \in A^*$ such that $uzt \in X^*$. Then

$$(wv)(uzt) = (wv')(u't). \tag{8.2}$$

Each one of the first three parenthesized words is in X^*. Now the fourth word, namely $u't$, is also in X^*, because u' is simplifying. The set X being a code, the word in (8.2) has a unique factorization in words in X, starting with wv, and also with wv'. It follows that $v = v'y$ or $v' = vy$ for some $y \in X^*$. This implies that $v = v'$ as follows: assume, for instance, that $v = v'y$, and set $wv = x_1x_2 \cdots x_n$, $wv' = x'_1 \cdots x'_m$, $y = y_1 \cdots y_p$, with $x_1, \ldots, x_n$, $x'_1, \ldots, x'_m$, $y_1, \ldots, y_p \in X$. Then $|x_n| > |v|$ and assuming $p > 0$, we have on the one hand (Fig. 2.30)

$$|y_p| \le |y| \le |v| < |x_n|,$$

and on the other hand, by

$$x_1x_2 \cdots x_n = x'_1 \cdots x'_m y_1 \cdots y_p,$$

we have $x_n = y_p$. Thus $p = 0$, $y = 1$, and $v = v'$. Going back to (8.2), this gives $uz = u'$. Now U is prefix. Consequently $z = 1$ and $u = u'$. This proves property (*).

It follows immediately from (*) that $C_r(w)U$ is prefix, and also, taking $z = 1$, that the product $C_r(w)U$ is unambiguous. This proves 1 and 2. To prove 3, we show that $C_r(w)$S is right dense. For this, consider a word $t \in A^*$. The word

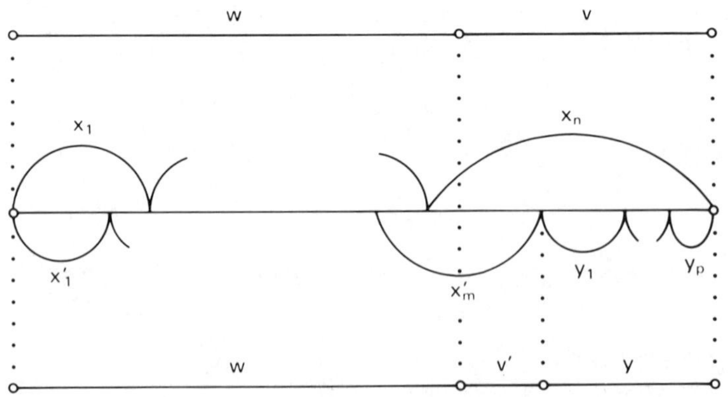

Fig. 2.30 Factorization of $wv = wv'y$.

wt is right completable, since $w \in \mathrm{E}$. Thus, $wtt' \in X^*$ for some $t' \in A^*$. Thus, tt' is in $w^{-1}X^*$. Consequently $tt' = vy$ for some $v \in C_r(w)$, $y \in X^*$. Now observe that $w \in \mathrm{E}$, and consequently also $yw \in \mathrm{E}$. Thus, $tt'w = vyw \in C_r(w)\mathrm{S}$. This shows that $C_r(w)\mathrm{S}$ is right complete. From $C_r(w)\mathrm{S} = C_r(w)UA^*$ it follows then by Theorem 3.3 that the prefix set $C_r(w)U$ is maximal prefix. □

To be able to use these propositions in the proof of the theorem, we verify that the hypothesis of the propositions are satisfied: we show that S and E are nonempty.

PROPOSITION 8.7 *Let X be a code with finite deciphering delay. Then* $X^d \subset \mathrm{S}(X)$.

Proof Let $x \in X^d$, let further $x_1, x_2, \ldots, x_p \in X$ and $v \in A^*$, be such that $x_1 x_2 \cdots x_p x v \in X$. Thus

$$x_1 x_2 \cdots x_p x v = y_1 y_2 \cdots y_q$$

for some $y_1, \ldots, y_q \in X$. From the fact that X has delay d, it follows that $x_1 = y_1, x_2 = y_2, \ldots, x_p = y_p$, whence $q \geq p$ and $xv = y_{p+1} \cdots y_q$. Thus, $xv \in X^*$. This shows that x is simplifying. □

PROPOSITION 8.8 *Let X be a maximal code with finite deciphering delay d. Then* $X^d \subset \mathrm{E}(X)$.

Proof The case of a one letter alphabet is clear. Thus, assume that $\mathrm{Card}(A) \geq 2$. Let $x \in X^d$ and $u \in A^*$. By Proposition 0.3.6, there is a word $v \in A^*$ such that $y = xuv$ is unbordered. This implies that

$$X^*yA^* \cap X^* \neq \varnothing.$$

Indeed, otherwise $X \cup y$ would be a code by Proposition 8.2, contradicting the maximality of X.

Consequently, there exist $z \in X^*$, $w \in A^*$ such that $zyw \in X^*$. By Proposition 8.7, x is simplifying; thus, $zyw = zxuvw \in X^*$ implies $xuvw \in X^*$. This shows that x is extendable. □

Proof of Theorem 8.4. Let X be a maximal finite code with finite deciphering delay d. According to Propositions 8.7 and 8.8, both $\mathrm{S}(X)$ and $\mathrm{E}(X)$ are nonempty. Thus by Proposition 8.5, they are equal. Set

$$S = \mathrm{S}(X) = \mathrm{E}(X).$$

Then $X^d \subset S$, further S is a right ideal, and the prefix set

$$U = S - SA^+$$

satisfies

$$S = UA^*.$$

We claim that U is a finite set. Indeed, set

$$\delta = d \cdot \max_{x \in X} |x|$$

and let us verify that a word in U has length $\leq \delta$. For this, let $s \in S$ with $|s| > \delta$. The word s being extendable, there is a word $w \in A^*$ such that $sw \in X^*$. By the choice of δ, the word sw is a product of at least $d + 1$ words in X, and s has a proper left factor, say s', in X^d. From $X^d \subset S$, we have $s \in SA^+$; thus, $s \notin U$. This proves the claim.

Now, we fix a word $x \in X^d$, and consider the set $C_r(x)$ of right contexts of x. The set $C_r(x)$ is finite since each element of $C_r(x)$ is a right factor of some word in the finite set X.

By Proposition 8.6(3), the set $Z = C_r(x)U$ is a maximal prefix set, since $x \in X^d \subset S$. Further, Z is the unambiguous product of the finite sets $C_r(x)$ and U. By Proposition 4.10, both $C_r(x)$ and U are maximal prefix sets. Since $1 \in C_r(x)$, we have $C_r(x) = \{1\}$.

Thus, we have shown that $C_r(x) = \{1\}$ for $x \in X^d$. This implies as follows that X is prefix. Assume that $y, y' \in X$ and $yt = y'$ for some $t \in A^*$. Let $x = y^d$. Then $xt = y^d t = y^{d-1} y'$ and $|t| < |y'|$ show that $t \in C_r(x)$. Since $x \in X^d$, we have $t = 1$. Thus, X is a prefix code. □

The following examples show that Theorem 8.4 is optimal in several directions.

EXAMPLE 8.2 The suffix code $X = \{aa, ba, b\}$ is a finite maximal code and has infinite deciphering delay.

EXAMPLE 8.3 The code $\{ab, abb, baab\}$ has deciphering delay 1. It is neither prefix nor maximal: indeed, the word $bbab$, for instance, can be added to it.

EXAMPLE 8.4 The code $X = ba^*$ is maximal and suffix. It has deciphering delay 1. It is not prefix, but it is infinite.

EXERCISES

SECTION 1

1.1. Let A be a finite alphabet, and let P be a prefix-closed subset of A^*. Show that P is infinite iff there exists an infinite sequence $(p_n)_{n \geq 1}$ of elements in P such that

$$p_1 < p_2 < p_3 < \cdots .$$

1.2. Let A be a finite alphabet and let $X \subset A^+$ be a prefix code. Set $R = A^* - XA^*$. Show that for all $n \geq 1$,

$$A^n = (R \cap A^n) \cup (XA^* \cap A^n), \qquad (*)$$

where the union is disjoint. Let $k = \mathrm{Card}(A)$ and $\alpha_n = \mathrm{Card}(X \cap A^n)$ for $n \geq 1$. Derive from $(*)$ that

$$\sum_{n \geq 1} \alpha_n k^{-n} \leq 1.$$

(This gives an elementary proof of Corollary I.4.3 for prefix codes. See also Proposition 7.1.)

SECTION 2

2.1. Let $X \subset A^+$ be a prefix code. Let $P = XA^-$ and let

$$\mathscr{A} = (P, 1, 1)$$

be the literal automaton of X^*. Consider an automaton

$$\mathscr{A} = (Q, i, i)$$

which is deterministic, trim, and such that $X^* = \mathrm{Stab}(i)$. Show that there is a function

$$\rho: \quad P \rightarrow Q$$

with $\rho(1) = i$ and such that for $a \in A$,

$$\rho(p \cdot a) = \rho(p) \cdot a.$$

SECTION 3

3.1. Let $X \subset A^+$ be a finite maximal prefix code and $P = XA^-$. Show that

$$\mathrm{Card}(X) - 1 = \mathrm{Card}(P)\big(\mathrm{Card}(A) - 1\big).$$

3.2. Let A be an alphabet, and let $M(A)$ be the monoid of prefix subsets of A^* equipped with the induced product. Show that $M(A)$ is a free monoid and that the set of maximal (resp., recognizable) prefix sets is a free submonoid of $M(A)$. (Use Exercise I.2.2. and set $\gamma(X) = \min_{x \in X} |x|$).

SECTION 4

4.1. Let $A = \{a, b\}$. Associate to each maximal prefix set $Z \subset A^*$, a word $\gamma(Z) \in A^*$ as follows:

$$\gamma(\{1\}) = 1$$

and if $Z = aX \cup bY$,

$$\gamma(Z) = a\gamma(X)b\gamma(Y).$$

Let $D \subset A^+$ be the Dyck code and $D_a = D \cap aA^*$. Show that γ is a bijection of the set of maximal prefix sets onto D_a^* and further that

$$|\gamma(Z)| = 2\,\mathrm{Card}(Z) - 2.$$

Derive from this that the number of maximal prefix sets with n elements is $\mathrm{Card}(D_a^* \cap A^{2n-2}) = (1/n)\binom{2n-2}{n-1}$ (cf. Example I.4.5).

4.2. Let X and Y be two prefix codes over A, and

$$P = A^* - XA^*, \qquad Q = A^* - YA^*.$$

Set

$$R = P \cap Q.$$

Show that there exists a unique prefix code $Z = X \wedge Y$ such that

$$Z = RA - R.$$

Show that

$$Z = (X \cap Q) \cup (X \cap Y) \cup (P \cap Y).$$

Show that if X and Y are maximal prefix sets, then so is Z.

4.3. Let A be a finite alphabet. Show that the family of recognizable maximal prefix codes is the least family $\mathscr{F}$ of subset of A^* such that

(i) $A \in \mathscr{F}$,

(ii) if $X, Y \in \mathscr{F}$ and if $X = X_1 \cup X_2$ is a partition in recognizable sets X_1, X_2, then

$$Z = X_1 \cup X_2 Y \in \mathscr{F}.$$

(iii) if $X \in \mathscr{F}$ and if $X = X_1 \cup X_2$ is a partition in recognizable sets, then

$$Z = X_1^* X_2 \in \mathscr{F}.$$

SECTION 5

5.1. Let $X \subset A^*$ be a prefix code. Show that the following conditions are equivalent.

(i) $A^*X = X^+$.

(ii) X is a semaphore code, and the minimal set of semaphores

$$S = X - A^+X$$

satisfies

$$SA^* \cap A^*S = SA^*S \cup S.$$

Note that for a code

$$X = A^*w - A^*wA^+,$$

the conditions are satisfied provided w is unbordered

5.2. Let $J \subset A^+$ be a two-sided ideal. For each $x \in J$, denote by $\|x\|$ the greatest integer n such that

$$x \in J^n$$

and set $\|x\| = 0$ for $x \notin J$.

Show that, for all $x,\ y \in A^*$

$$\|x\| + \|y\| \leqslant \|xy\| \leqslant \|x\| + \|y\| + 1$$

SECTION 6

6.1. Let $X \subset A^+$ be a finite maximal prefix code. Show that if X contains a letter $a \in A$, then there is an integer $n \geq 1$ such that a^n is synchronizing.

6.2. Let $X \subset A^*$ be a synchronous prefix code. Assume that the automaton $\mathscr{A}(X^*)$ has n states. Show that there exists a synchronizing word of length at most n^3.

SECTION 7

7.1. Let $X \subset A^*$ be a maximal prefix code, and let $\alpha: X \to]0, 1]$ be a function such that

$$\sum_{x \in X} \alpha(x) = 1.$$

Show that there is a cylindric measure on A^* such that $\pi(x) = \alpha(x)$ for $x \in X$. Show that, moreover, π may be chosen such that $\pi(xy) = \pi(x)\pi(y)$ for all $x,\ y \in X^*$.

7.2. Let $X \subset A^+$ be a code and let $\pi: X \to]0, 1]$ be a function such that

$$\sum_{x \in X} \pi(x) = 1.$$

Define the *entropy* of X (relatively to π) to be

$$H(X) = -\sum_{x \in X} \pi(x) \log_k \pi(x),$$

where $k = \operatorname{Card}(A)$. Set $\lambda(X) = \sum_{x \in X} |x| \pi(x)$.

Show that

$$H(X) \leq \lambda(X)$$

and that the equality holds iff

$$\pi(x) = k^{-|x|} \qquad \text{for} \quad x \in X.$$

Show that if X is finite and has n elements, then

$$H(X) \leq \log_k n.$$

7.3. Let B be a finite set and let $\pi: B \to \mathbb{R}_+$ be a function. Also, let $A = \{a, b\}$. For every function $\alpha: B \to A^*$ set

$$\lambda(\alpha) = \sum_{b \in B} |\alpha(b)|\pi(b).$$

We consider injective functions α such that $\alpha(B)$ is prefix, and we look for such a function with $\lambda(\alpha)$ minimal. Such a function is called a *Huffman encoding* of (B, π).

Show that the following algorithm allows us to obtain a Huffman two elements of B such that $\pi(c_1), \pi(c_2) \leq \pi(c)$ for all c in $B - \{c_1, c_2\}$. Let

$$B' = B - \{c_1, c_2\} \cup \{d\}$$

with $d \notin B$ and define $\pi': B' \to \mathbb{R}_+$ by $\pi'(c) = \pi(c)$ for all $c \in B' - \{d\}$ and $\pi'(d) = \pi(c_1) + \pi(c_2)$.

Let α' be a Huffman encoding of (B', π') and let α be the function from B into A^* defined by

$$\alpha(c) = \alpha'(c) \qquad \text{for} \quad c \in B - \{c_1, c_2\},$$
$$\alpha(c_1) = \alpha'(d)a, \qquad \alpha(c_2) = \alpha'(d)b.$$

Show that α is a Huffman encoding of (B, π).

SECTION 8

8.1. For a set $X \subset A^+$, define, as in Section I.3, a sequence $(U_n)_{n \geq 0}$ of subsets of A^* by setting

$$U_1 = X^{-1}X - 1, \qquad U_{n+1} = X^{-1}U_n \cup U_n^{-1}X, \qquad n \geq 1.$$

Show that X has finite deciphering delay iff all sets U_n are empty for sufficiently large n.

8.2. Let Y and Z be composable codes with finite deciphering delay $d(Y)$ and $d(Z)$. Show that $X = Y \circ Z$ has finite delay $d(X) \leq d(Y) + d(Z)$. (Hint: show that for $y \in X^{d(Y)}$, $z \in X^{d(Z)}$, we have $yz \in S(X)$.)

8.3. Let $X = \{x, y\}$ be a two-element code. Show that the deciphering delay of X is at most one.

8.4. Let $X \subset A^*$ be a finite code.

(a) Show that there exists a smallest submonoid $M \subset X^*$ such that M is generated by a code with finite deciphering delay.

(b) Let $Y \subset A^*$ be the base of the submonoid whose existence is asserted in (a). Show by a proof analogous to that of Proposition I.2.10 that

$$Y \subset X(Y^*)^{-1} \cap (Y^*)^{-1}X.$$

Deduce from this if X does not have finite deciphering delay,

$$\mathrm{Card}(Y) \leq \mathrm{Card}(X) - 1.$$

NOTES

The results of the first four sections belong to folklore, and they are known to readers familiar with automata theory or with trees.

Semaphore codes were introduced in Schützenberger (1964) under the name of $\mathscr{J}$ codes. All the results presented in Section 5 can be found in that paper which also contains Theorem 6.5. and Proposition 7.5.

The notion of synchronous prefix code has been extensively studied in the context of automata theory. Let us mention Černy's problem which can be formulated as follows in our context: given a synchronous prefix code X whose minimal automaton $\mathscr{A}(X^*)$ has n states, what upper bound can be given to the length of the shortest synchronizing word as a function of n? See Exercise 6.2, Moore (1956), Černy (1964), and Pin (1978). Example 6.5 is obtained by a construction of Perrin (1977a) (see Exercise VIII.4.1). The synchronization properties of a special class of prefix codes called *inclusion codes* have been studied by Bobrow and Hakimi (1969) and Boë (1972).

The results of Section 7 are given in another terminology in Feller (1957). The pair formed by a prefix code X and a cylindric measure π such that $\pi(xy) = \pi(x)\pi(y)$ for all $x, y \in X^*$ defines what Feller calls a *recurrent event*.

The notion of deciphering delay appears at the very beginning of the theory of codes (Gilbert and Moore, 1959; Levenshtein, 1964). Theorem 8.4 is due to Schützenberger (1966). It was conjectured in Gilbert and Moore (1959). An incomplete proof appears in Markov (1962). A proof of a result which is more general than Theorem 8.4 has been given in Schützenberger (1966). A characterisation of the coding morphism for a code with finite deciphering delay is given in Choffrut (1979).

The monoid of prefix subsets defined in Exercise 3.2 has been further studied by Lassez (1973). The description of the Huffman algorithm (Exercise 7.3) is commented on in Knuth (1973) which also contains other interesting algorithms on trees. Exercise 8.4 is from Berstel *et al.* (1979). An analogous result is proved in Salomaa (1981).

Let us mention the following result which has not been reported here: For a three-element code $X = \{x, y, z\}$, there exists at most one right infinite word with two distinct X-factorizations (Karhumäki, 1983).

CHAPTER III

Biprefix Codes

0. INTRODUCTION

The object of this chapter is to describe the structure of maximal biprefix codes. This family of codes has quite remarkable properties and can be described in a rather satisfactory manner.

As in the rest of this book, we will work here within the family of *thin* codes. As we will see, this family contains all the usual examples, and most of the fundamental properties extend to this family when they hold in the simple (i.e., finite or recognizable) case.

To each thin maximal biprefix code, two basic parameters will be associated: its *degree* and its *kernel*. The degree is a positive integer which is, as we will see in Chapter IV, the degree of a permutation group associated with the code. The kernel is the set of code words which are proper factors of some code word. We shall prove that these two parameters characterize a thin maximal biprefix code.

In the first section, we introduce the notion of a *parse* of a word with respect to a biprefix code. It allows us to define an integer-valued function called the *indicator* of a biprefix code. This function will be quite useful in the sequel.

In the second section, we give a series of equivalent conditions for a thin code to be maximal biprefix. The fact that thin maximal biprefix codes are extremal objects is reflected in the observation that a subset of their properties suffices to characterize them completely. We also give a transformation (called *internal transformation*) which preserves the family of maximal biprefix codes.

Section 3 contains the definition of the degree of a thin maximal biprefix code. It is defined as the number of *interpretations* of a word which is not a factor of a code word. This number is independent of the word chosen. This fact will be used to prove most of the fundamental properties of biprefix codes. We will prove that the degree is invariant under internal transformation.

In the fourth section, a construction of the thin maximal biprefix code having a given degree and kernel is described. We also describe the *derived code* of a thin maximal biprefix code. It is a code whose degree is one less than the degree of the original code. Both constructions are consequences of a fundamental result (Theorem 4.3) which characterizes those sets of words which can be completed in a finite maximal biprefix code without modification of the kernel.

Section 5 is devoted to the study of *finite* maximal biprefix codes. It is shown that for a fixed degree and a fixed size of the alphabet, there exists only a finite number of such codes. Further it is proved that, on this finite set, the internal transformation acts transitively.

1. PARSES

A *biprefix* code is a subset X of A^+ which is both prefix and suffix. In other words, we have

$$XA^+ \cap X = \emptyset, \qquad A^+X \cap X = \emptyset. \tag{1.1}$$

An *X-parse* (or simply a parse) of a word $w \in A^*$ is a triple (v, x, u) (see Fig. 3.1) such that $w = vxu$ and

$$v \in A^* - A^*X, \qquad x \in X^*, \qquad u \in A^* - XA^*.$$

An *interpretation* of $w \in A^*$ is a triple (v, x, u) such that $w = vxu$ and

$$v \in A^-X, \qquad x \in X^*, \qquad u \in XA^-.$$

Since the code X is biprefix, we have $A^-X \subset A^* - A^*X$, and $XA^- \subset A^* - XA^*$, thus any interpretation of w is also a parse of w.

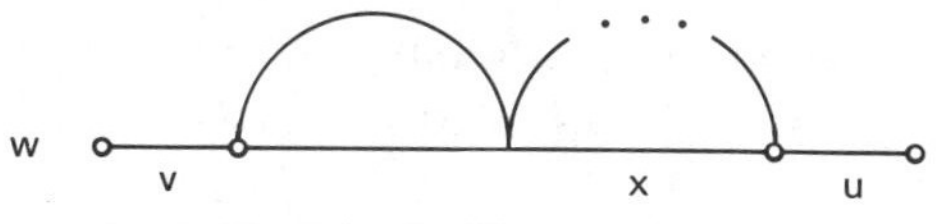

Fig. 3.1 An X-parse of w.

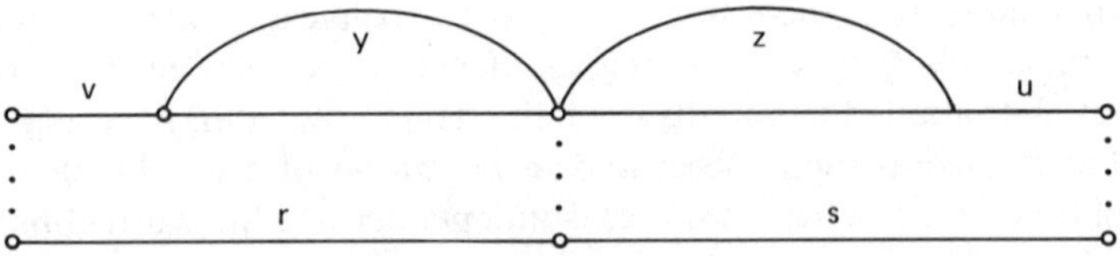

Fig. 3.2 A parse of w passing through the point (r, s).

A *point* in a word $w \in A^*$ is a pair $(r, s) \in A^* \times A^*$ such that $w = rs$. A word w thus has $|w| + 1$ points. A parse (v, x, u) of w is said to *pass* through the point (r, s) provided $x = yz$ for some $y, z \in X^*$ such that $r = vy$, $s = zu$ (see Fig. 3.2).

PROPOSITION 1.1 *Let $X \subset A^+$ be a biprefix code. For each point of a word $w \in A^*$, there is one and only one parse passing through this point.*

Proof Let (r, s) be a point of $w \in A^*$. The code X being prefix, there is a unique $z \in X^*$, and a unique $u \in A^* - XA^*$ such that $s = zu$ (Theorem II.1.4). Since X is suffix, we have $r = vy$ for a unique $v \in A^* - A^*X$ and a unique $y \in X^*$. Clearly (v, yz, u) is a parse of w passing through (r, s). The uniqueness follows from the uniqueness of the factorizations of s and r. □

PROPOSITION 1.2 *Let $X \subset A^+$ be a biprefix code. For any $w \in A^*$, there are bijections between the following sets:*

1. *the set of parses of w,*
2. *the set of left factors of w which have no right factor in X,*
3. *the set of right factors of w which have no left factor in X.*

Proof Set $V = A^* - A^*X$, $U = A^* - XA^*$. For each parse (v, x, u) of w, the word v is in V and is a left factor of w. Thus v is in the set described in 2. Conversely, if $w = vw'$ and $v \in V$, set $w' = xu$ with $x \in X^*$ and $u \in U$ (this is possible since X is prefix). Then (v, x, u) is a parse. The uniqueness of the factorization $w' = xu$ shows that the mapping $(v, x, u) \mapsto u$ is a bijection from the set of parses on the set described in 3. □

Let X be a biprefix code over A. The *indicator* of X is the formal power series L_X (or simply L) which associates to any word w the number (L, w) of X-parses of w.

Setting $U = A^* - XA^*$, $V = A^* - A^*X$, we have the result

$$L = \underline{V}\underline{X}^*\underline{U} \tag{1.2}$$

Note that $\underline{XA^*} = \underline{X}\underline{A}^*$ since X is prefix, and $\underline{A^*X} = \underline{A}^*\underline{X}$ since X is suffix. Thus $\underline{U} = \underline{A}^* - \underline{X}\underline{A}^* = (1 - \underline{X})\underline{A}^*$ and $\underline{V} = \underline{A}^*(1 - \underline{X})$. Substituting this in (1.2), we obtain

$$L = \underline{A}^*(1 - \underline{X})\underline{A}^*. \tag{1.3}$$

This can also be written as

$$L = \underline{V}\underline{A}^* = \underline{A}^*\underline{U}. \tag{1.4}$$

Note that this is a compact formulation of Proposition 1.2.

From formula (1.3), we obtain a convenient expression for the number of parses of a word $w \in A^*$:

$$(L, w) = |w| + 1 - (\underline{A}^*\underline{X}\underline{A}^*, w). \tag{1.5}$$

The term $(\underline{A}^*\underline{X}\underline{A}^*, w)$ equals the number of occurrences of words in X as factors of w. Thus we see from (1.5) that for any biprefix codes X, Y the following implication holds:

$$Y \subset X \quad \Rightarrow \quad L_X \leq L_Y. \tag{1.6}$$

(Recall that the notation $L_X \leq L_Y$ means that $(L_X, w) \leq (L_Y, w)$ for all w in A^*).

PROPOSITION 1.3 *Let $X \subset A^+$ be a biprefix code, let $U = A^* - XA^*$, $V = A^* - A^*X$, and let L be the indicator of X. Then*

$$\underline{V} = L(1 - \underline{A}), \qquad \underline{U} = (1 - \underline{A})L, \tag{1.7}$$

$$1 - \underline{X} = (1 - \underline{A})L(1 - \underline{A}). \tag{1.8}$$

Proof Formula (1.7) follows from (1.4), and (1.8) is an immediate consequence of (1.3). □

PROPOSITION 1.4 *Let $X \subset A^+$ be a biprefix code and let L be its indicator. Then for all $w \in A^*$*

$$0 \leq (L, w) - 1 \leq |w|. \tag{1.9}$$

In particular, $(L, 1) = 1$. Further, for all $u, v, w \in A^*$,

$$(L, v) \leq (L, uvw). \tag{1.10}$$

Proof For a given word w, there are at most $|w| + 1$ and at least one (namely, the empty word) left factors of w which have no right factor in X. Thus (1.9) is a consequence of Proposition 1.2.

Next any parse of u can be extended to a parse of uvw. This parse of uvw is uniquely determined by the parse of v (Proposition 1.1). This shows (1.10). □

EXAMPLE 1.1 The indicator L of the biprefix code $X = \varnothing$ satisfies $(L, w) = |w| + 1$ for all $w \in A^*$.

EXAMPLE 1.2 For the biprefix code $X = A$, the indicator has value $(L, w) = 1$ for all $w \in A^*$.

The following proposition gives a characterization of formal power series which are indicators.

PROPOSITION 1.5 *A formal power series $L \in \mathbb{Z}\langle\langle A \rangle\rangle$ is the indicator of a biprefix code iff it satisfies the following conditions:*

(i) *For all $a \in A$, $w \in A^*$,*

$$0 \le (L, aw) - (L, w) \le 1, \tag{1.11}$$

$$0 \le (L, wa) - (L, w) \le 1. \tag{1.12}$$

(ii) *For all $a, b \in A$ and $w \in A^*$,*

$$(L, aw) + (L, wb) \ge (L, w) + (L, awb). \tag{1.3}$$

(iii) $(L, 1) = 1$.

Proof Assume that L is the indicator of some biprefix code X. It follows from formula (1.7) that the coefficients of the series $L(1 - \underline{A})$ and $(1 - \underline{A})L$ are 0 or 1. For a word $w \in A^*$ and a letter $a \in A$, we have $(L(1 - \underline{A}), wa) = (L, wa) - (L, w)$. Thus, (1.12) holds. The same holds for (1.11). Finally, formula (1.8) gives for the empty word, the equality $(L, 1) = 1$, and for $a, b \in A$, $w \in A^*$,

$$-(\underline{X}, awb) = (L, awb) - (L, aw) - (L, wb) + (L, w),$$

showing (1.13).

Conversely, assume that L satisfies the three conditions. Set $S = (1 - \underline{A})L$. Then $(S, 1) = (L, 1) = 1$. Next for $a \in A$, $w \in A^*$, we have

$$(S, aw) = (L, aw) - (L, w).$$

By (1.11), $0 \le (S, aw) \le 1$, showing that S is the characteristic series of some set U containing the empty word 1. Next, if $a, b \in A$, $w \in A^*$, then by (1.13)

$$(S, aw) = (L, aw) - (L, w) \ge (L, awb) - (L, wb) = (S, awb).$$

Thus, $awb \in U$ implies $aw \in U$, showing that U is prefix-closed.

According to Theorem II.1.4, the set $X = UA - U$ is a prefix code and $1 - \underline{X} = \underline{U}(1 - \underline{A})$.

Symmetrically, the series $T = L(1 - \underline{A})$ is the characteristic series of some nonempty suffix-closed set V, the set $Y = AV - V$ is a suffix code and $1 - \underline{Y} = (1 - \underline{A})\underline{V}$.

Finally

$$1 - \underline{X} = \underline{U}(1 - \underline{A}) = (1 - \underline{A})L(1 - \underline{A}) = (1 - \underline{A})\underline{V} = 1 - \underline{Y}.$$

Thus, $X = Y$ and X is biprefix with indicator L. □

2. MAXIMAL BIPREFIX CODES

A code $X \subset A^+$ is a maximal biprefix code if, for any biprefix code $Y \subset A^+$, the inclusion $X \subset Y$ implies that $X = Y$. As in the preceding chapter, it is convenient to note that the set $\{1\}$ is a maximal biprefix set without being a code. We start by giving a series of equivalent conditions for a thin code to be maximal biprefix.

PROPOSITION 2.1 *Let X be a thin subset of A^+. The following conditions are equivalent*:

(i) *X is a maximal code and biprefix.*
(ii) *X is a maximal biprefix code.*
(iii) *X is a maximal prefix code and a maximal suffix code.*
(iv) *X is a prefix left complete code.*
(iv′) *X is a suffix right complete code.*
(v) *X is a left complete and right complete code.*

Proof (i) $\Rightarrow$ (ii) is clear. (ii) $\Rightarrow$ (iii). If X is maximal prefix, then by Theorem II.3.7, X is a maximal code, therefore X is maximal suffix. Similarly, if X is maximal suffix, it is maximal prefix. Thus, assume that X is neither maximal prefix nor maximal suffix. Let $y, z \in X$ be such that $X \cup y$ is prefix and $X \cup z$ is suffix. Then $X \cup yz$ is biprefix. However, $yz \notin X$ (since otherwise $X \cup y$ would not be prefix). This contradicts (ii).

(iii) $\Rightarrow$ (iv′) is a consequence of Theorem II.3.3 stating that a maximal prefix code is right-complete (similarly for the implication (iii) $\Rightarrow$ (iv)).

(iv) $\Rightarrow$ (v) The code X is complete and thin. Thus, it is maximal. This shows that it is maximal prefix, which in turn implies that it is right complete.

(v) $\Rightarrow$ (i) A complete, thin code is maximal. By Theorem II.3.7 a right-complete thin code is prefix. Similarly, X is suffix. ▯

A code which is both maximal prefix and maximal suffix is always maximal biprefix, and the converse holds, as we have seen, for thin codes. However, this may become false for codes that are not thin (see Example 2.3).

EXAMPLE 2.1 A group code is a biprefix and a maximal code (Section I.2).

EXAMPLE 2.2 Let $A = \{a, b\}$ and

$$X = \{a^3, a^2ba, a^2b^2, ab, ba^2, baba, bab^2, b^2a, b^3\}.$$

By inspection of the literal representation (Fig. 3.3), X is seen to be a maximal prefix code.

The reverse code $\tilde{X}$ is also maximal prefix (Fig. 3.4). Thus X is a maximal biprefix code. Observe that $\tilde{X}$ is equal to the set obtained from X by interchanging a and b (reflection with respect to the horizontal axis). This is an exceptional fact, which will be explained later (Example 5.1).

EXAMPLE 2.3 Let $A = \{a, b\}$ and

$$X = \{wab^{|w|} \mid w \in A^*\}$$

(see Examples I.4.6 and II.3.1). It is a maximal, right-dense code which is suffix

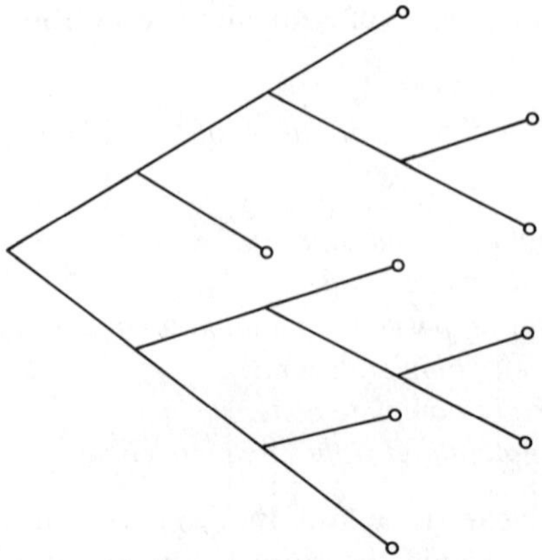

Fig. 3.3 The literal representation of X.

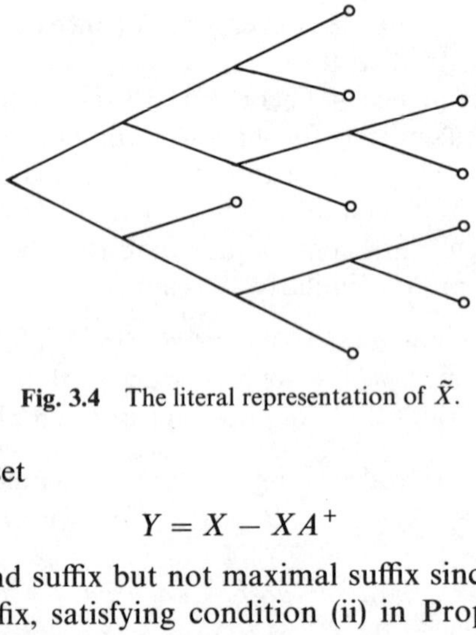

Fig. 3.4 The literal representation of $\tilde{X}$.

but not prefix. The set

$$Y = X - XA^+$$

is maximal prefix and suffix but not maximal suffix since $Y \subsetneq X$. Thus, Y is also maximal biprefix, satisfying condition (ii) in Proposition 2.1 without satisfying condition (iii).

The following result gives a different characterization of maximal biprefix codes within the family of thin codes.

PROPOSITION 2.2 *A thin code X is maximal biprefix iff for all $w \in A^*$, there exists an integer $n \geq 1$ such that $w^n \in X^*$.*

Proof Assume that for all $w \in A^*$, we have w^n in X^* for some $n \geq 1$. Then X clearly is right-complete and left-complete. Thus, X is maximal biprefix by Proposition 2.1.

Conversely, let X be a maximal biprefix code, and let $w \in A^*$. Consider a word $u \in \bar{F}(X)$, i.e., which is not a factor of a word in X. The code X being right-complete, for all $i \geq 1$ there exists a word v_i such that

$$w^i u v_i \in X^*.$$

Since $u \in \bar{F}(X)$, there exists a left factor s_i of u such that $w^i s_i \in X^*$.

Let k, m with $k < m$ be two integers such that $s_k = s_m$. Then setting $n = m - k$, we have $w^k s_k \in X^*$, $w^m s_m = w^n w^k s_k \in X^*$.

Since X^* is left-unitary, this implies that $w^n \in X^*$. □

We now describe an operation which makes it possible to construct maximal biprefix codes by successive transformations.

Proposition 2.3 *Let X be a code which is maximal prefix and maximal suffix, and let $w \in A^*$. Set*

$$\begin{aligned} G &= Xw^{-1}, & D &= w^{-1}X, \\ G_0 &= (wD)w^{-1}, & D_0 &= w^{-1}(Gw), \\ G_1 &= G - G_0, & D_1 &= D - D_0. \end{aligned} \tag{2.1}$$

If $G_1 \neq \varnothing$ and $D_1 \neq \varnothing$, then the set

$$Y = (X \cup w \cup G_1(wD_0^*)D_1) - (Gw \cup wD) \tag{2.2}$$

is a maximal prefix and maximal suffix code. Further,

$$\underline{Y} = \underline{X} + (1 - \underline{G})w(1 - \underline{D}_0^* \underline{D}_1). \tag{2.3}$$

Proof If $D_1 \neq \varnothing$, then D is nonempty. Further $1 \notin D$, since otherwise $w \in X$, and X being biprefix, this implies $G = D = \{1\}$, and $D_0 = \{1\}$ and finally $D_1 = \varnothing$, a contradiction. Thus, w is a proper left factor of a word in X, and by Proposition II.4.6, the sets D and

$$Y_1 = (X \cup w) - wD$$

are maximal prefix codes.

Next, $Gw = X \cap A^*w$, also $G_0 w = wD \cap A^*w$; similarly for D and D_0. Thus,

$$wA^* \cap A^*w \cap X = Gw \cap wD = wD_0 = G_0 w. \tag{2.4}$$

Now note that $G = G_0 \cup G_1$. From this and (2.4), we get

$$\begin{aligned} Gw \cup wD &= G_0 w \cup G_1 w \cup wD \\ &= wD_0 \cup G_1 w \cup wD \\ &= G_1 w \cup wD, \end{aligned}$$

since $D_0 \subset D$. Similarly

$$Gw \cup wD = Gw \cup wD_1.$$

Thus

$$Y = (Y_1 \cup G_1 wD_0^* D_1) - G_1 w.$$

Since $D = D_1 \cup D_0$ is a maximal prefix code and $D_1 \neq \varnothing$, the set $D_0^* D_1$ is a maximal prefix code (Proposition II.4.9). This and the fact that Y_1 is maximal prefix imply, according to Proposition II.4.4, that Y is maximal prefix.

Symmetrically, it may be shown successively that $Y_2 = (X \cup w) - wG$ and $Y' = (Y_2 - wD_1) \cup G_1 G_0^* wD_1$ are maximal suffix codes. From (2.4), we obtain by induction that $G_0^* w = wD_0^*$. Thus, $Y' = Y$ and consequently Y is also maximal suffix.

To prove (2.3), set

$$\sigma = \underline{X} + (1 + \underline{G})w(1 - \underline{D}_0^* \underline{D}_1)$$

Then

$$\sigma = \underline{X} + \underline{w} - \underline{G}w - w\underline{D}_0^* \underline{D}_1 + \underline{G}w\underline{D}_0^* \underline{D}_1,$$

$$\sigma = \underline{X} + w - \underline{G}w - w\underline{D}_0^* \underline{D}_1 + \underline{G}_0 w\underline{D}_0^* \underline{D}_1 + \underline{G}_1 w\underline{D}_0^* \underline{D}_1.$$

Since $\underline{G}_0 w = w\underline{D}_0$, we obtain

$$\begin{aligned}\sigma &= \underline{X} + w - \underline{G}w - w\underline{D}_0^* D_1 + w\underline{D}_0 \underline{D}_0^* D_1 + \underline{G}_1 w\underline{D}_0^* \underline{D}_1 \\ &= \underline{X} + w - \underline{G}w - w\underline{D}_1 + \underline{G}_1 w\underline{D}_0^* \underline{D}_1.\end{aligned}$$

The sets $G_1 w$, D_0, D_1 are prefix, and $D_0 \neq 1$ (since otherwise $w \in X$). Thus, the products in the above expression are unambiguous. Next it follows from (2.4) that

$$G_1 w \cap wD = \varnothing.$$

Consequently

$$\underline{Gw \cup wD} = \underline{G}_1 w + w\underline{D}.$$

Thus

$$\sigma = \underline{X} + w + \underline{G_1 wD_0^* D_1} - \underline{Gw \cup wD} = \underline{Y}. \quad \square$$

The code Y is said to be obtained from X by *internal transformation* (with respect to w).

EXAMPLE 2.4 Let $A = \{a, b\}$, and consider the uniform code $X = A^2$. Let $w = a$. Then $G = D = A$ and $G_0 = D_0 = \{a\}$. Consequently, the code Y defined by formula (2.2) is

$$Y = a \cup ba^*b.$$

Note that Y is a group code as is X.

From formula (2.2), it is clear that for a finite code X, the code Y is finite iff $D_0 = \varnothing$. This case deserves particular attention.

PROPOSITION 2.4 *Let X be a finite maximal biprefix code and let $w \in A^*$. Set*

$$G = Xw^{-1}, \qquad D = w^{-1}X. \tag{2.5}$$

If $G \neq \varnothing$, $D \neq \varnothing$ and $Gw \cap wD = \varnothing$, then

$$Y = (X \cup w \cup GwD) - (Gw \cup wD) \tag{2.6}$$

is a finite maximal biprefix code, and

$$\underline{Y} = \underline{X} + (\underline{G} - 1)w(\underline{D} - 1). \tag{2.7}$$

Conversely, let Y be a finite maximal biprefix code. Let $w \in Y$ be a word such that there exists a maximal prefix code D, and a maximal suffix code G with

$$GwD \subset Y.$$

Then

$$X = (Y - w - GwD) \cup (Gw \cup wD) \tag{2.8}$$

is a finite maximal biprefix code, and further (2.5), (2.6), *and* (2.7) *hold.*

Proof If $Gw \cap wD = \varnothing$, then we have, with the notations of Proposition 2.3, $G_0 = D_0 = \varnothing$ by formula (2.4). Then (2.2) simplifies into (2.6). Formula (2.7) is a direct consequence of formula (2.3).

Conversely, let us first show that X is a maximal prefix code. Set

$$Z = (Y - w) \cup wD.$$

Since Y is maximal prefix by Proposition 2.1. and since D is maximal prefix and $w \in Y$, Corollary II.4.5. implies that the set Z is a maximal prefix code. Next observe that

$$X = (Z - GwD) \cup Gw.$$

The set $Q = Gw$ is contained in ZA^-, since $Gw \subset (X - w)A^-$. Next Q is prefix: assume indeed that $gw = g'wt$ for some $g, g' \in G, t \in A^*$. Let d be a word in D of maximal length.

The set D being maximal prefix, either $td \in DA^-$, or $td \in DA^+$ or finally $td \in D$. The two first cases are ruled out by the property of Y to be prefix. Thus, $td \in D$, and since d has maximal length, we get $t = 1$. This proves the claim.

Further, for all $g \in G$, we have $D = (gw)^{-1}Z$. Indeed, the inclusion $gwD \subset Z$ implies $D \subset (gw)^{-1}Z$, and D being a maximal prefix code, the equality follows.

In view of Proposition II.4.7, the set X consequently is a maximal prefix code. Symmetrically, it may be shown that X is maximal suffix. Since X is finite, it is maximal biprefix.

It remains to show that Y is obtained from X by internal transformation. First, the inclusion $Gw \subset X$ follows from (2.8), implying $G \subset Xw^{-1}$, and G being a maximal suffix code, this enforces the equality

$$G = Xw^{-1}.$$

Symmetrically $D = w^{-1}X$. Moreover, $G \neq \emptyset$, $D \neq \emptyset$, because they are maximal codes. Let us show that

$$Gw \cap wD = \emptyset.$$

If $gw = wd$ for some $g \in G$, $d \in D$, then $ggw = gwd \in GwD \subset Y$. Thus w, $ggw \in Y$; this is impossible, since Y is suffix.

From $w \in Y$ we get the result that $Gw \cap Y = \emptyset$; otherwise Y would not be suffix. Similarly $wD \cap Y = \emptyset$, because Y is prefix. Then as a result of (2.8), $X - (Gw \cup wD) = Y - (w \cup GwD)$, implying (2.6). □

EXAMPLE 2.5 Let $A = \{a, b\}$ and $X = A^3$. Consider the word $w = ab$. Then $G = D = A$ and $Gw \cap wD = \emptyset$. Thus Proposition 2.4 yields a finite code Y. This code is obtained by dropping in Fig. 3.5 the dotted lines and by adjoining the heavy lines. The result is the maximal biprefix code of Example 2.2.

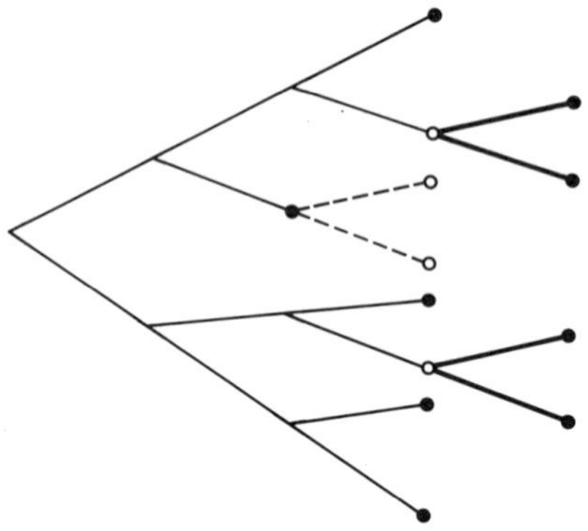

Fig. 3.5 An internal transformation.

3. DEGREE

In this section, we examine the indicator of thin maximal biprefix codes. For these biprefix codes, some simplifications occur.

Let $X \subset A^+$ be a biprefix code, set $U = A^* - XA^*$, $V = A^* - A^*X$ and let $L = \underline{V}\underline{X}^*\underline{U}$ be the indicator of X. If X is a maximal prefix code, then $U = P$ where $P = XA^-$ is the set of proper left factors of words in X. In the same way, for a maximal suffix code, we have $V = S$ where $S = A^-X$ is the set of proper right factors of words in X. It follows that if X is maximal prefix and maximal suffix, each parse of a word is an interpretation. Then we have

$$L = \underline{S}\underline{X}^*\underline{P} = \underline{S}\underline{A}^* = \underline{A}^*\underline{P}. \tag{3.1}$$

This basic formula will be used frequently. It means that the number of parses of a word is equal to the number of its right factors which are in P, or equivalently the number of its left factors which are in S.

Let X be a subset of A^+. Denote by

$$H(X) = A^- X A^- = \{w \in A^* \mid A^+ w A^+ \cap X \neq \varnothing\}$$

the set of *internal factors* of words in X. Let

$$\bar{H}(X) = A^* - H(X).$$

Clearly, each internal factor is a factor of a word in X. The converse may be false. The set $H(X)$ and the set

$$F(X) = \{w \in A^* \mid A^* w A^* \cap X \neq \varnothing\}$$

of factors of words in X are related by

$$F(X) = H(X) \cup XA^- \cup A^- X \cup X$$

and for $\bar{F}(X) = A^* - F(X)$,

$$A^+ \bar{H}(X) A^+ \subset \bar{F}(X) \subset \bar{H}(X).$$

These relations show that $\bar{H}(X)$ is nonempty iff $\bar{F}(X)$ is nonempty; thus X is thin iff $\bar{H}(X) \neq \varnothing$.

THEOREM 3.1 *Let $X \subset A^+$ be a biprefix code. Then X is a thin maximal code iff its indicator L is bounded. In this case,*

$$\bar{H}(X) = \{w \in A^* \mid (L, w) = d\}, \tag{3.2}$$

where d is defined as $d = \max\{(L, w) \mid w \in A^*\}$.

Proof Let X be a thin maximal biprefix code. Let $w \in \bar{H}(X)$ and $w' \in A^*$. According to formula (3.1), $(L, ww') = (\underline{S}\underline{A}^*, ww')$. Thus the number of parses of ww' is equal to the number of left factors of ww' which are in $S = A^- X$. Since $w \in \bar{H}(X)$, it follows that no such left factor in S is strictly longer than w. Thus all these left factors are left factors of w. Again using formula (3.1), this shows that

$$(L, ww') = (L, w).$$

Now by Proposition 1.4, we have $(L, ww') \geq (L, w')$. Thus we get

$$(L, w') \leq (L, w)$$

showing that L is bounded on A^* by its value for a word in $\bar{H}(X)$. This shows also that L is constant on $\bar{H}(X)$. Thus

$$\bar{H}(X) \subset \{w \in A^* \mid (L, w) = d\}.$$

To show the converse inclusion, consider an internal factor $w \in H(x)$. Then there exist $p, s \in A^+$ such that $w' = pws \in X$. This implies that

$$(L, w') \geq (L, w) + 1.$$

Indeed, each parse of w can be extended in a parse of w', and w' has an additional parse, namely $(1, w', 1)$. This shows that for an internal factor w, the number (L, w) is strictly less than the maximal value d. Thus formula (3.2) is proved.

Assume now conversely that X is a biprefix code with bounded indicator L, let $d = \max\{(L, w) \mid w \in A^*\}$ and let $v \in A^*$ be a word such that $(L, v) = d$. We use formula (1.3) which can be rewritten as

$$\underline{X}\underline{A}^* = \underline{A}^* + (\underline{A} - 1)L.$$

Let $w \in A^+$ be any nonempty word, and set $w = au$, with $a \in A, u \in A^*$. Then

$$(\underline{X}\underline{A}^*, wv) = (\underline{A}^* + (\underline{A} - 1)L, auv) = 1 + (L, uv) - (L, auv).$$

By Proposition 1.4, both (L, uv) and (L, auv) are greater than or equal to (L, v). By the choice of v, we have $(L, uv) = (L, auv) = d$.

Thus $(\underline{X}\underline{A}^*, wv) = 1$. Thus we have proved that for all $w \in A^+$, $wv \in XA^*$. This shows that X is right complete. This shows also that X is thin. Indeed, we have $v \in \bar{H}(X)$ since for all $g, d \in A^+$ we have $gv \in XA^*$ and therefore $gvd \notin X$. Thus X is a thin maximal prefix code. Symmetrically, it can be shown that X is maximal suffix. This gives the result by Proposition 2.1. □

Let X be a thin maximal biprefix code, and let L be its indicator. The *degree* of X, noted $d(X)$ or simply d, is the number

$$d(X) = \max\{(L, w) \mid w \in A^*\}$$

According to Theorem 3.1, the degree d is the number of parses of any word which is not an internal factor of X. Before going on, let us illustrate the notion of degree with several examples.

EXAMPLE 3.1 Let φ be a morphism of A^* onto a group G, and let G' be a subgroup of G. Let X be the group code for which $X^* = \varphi^{-1}(G')$. We have seen that X is a maximal biprefix code, and that X is thin iff G' has finite index in G (Example I.5.11).

The degree of X is equal to the index of G' in G. Indeed let $w \in \bar{H}(X)$ be a word which is not an internal factor of X, and consider the function ψ which associates, to each word $u \in A^*$, the unique word $p \in P = XA^-$ such that $uw \in X^*p$. Each p obtained in such a way is a proper right factor of w. The set $\psi(A^*)$ is the set of right factors of w in P. Since $w \in \bar{H}(X)$, we have Card $\psi(A^*) = d(X)$. Next, we have for $u, v \in A^*$,

$$\psi(u) = \psi(v) \Leftrightarrow G'\varphi(u) = G'\varphi(v).$$

Indeed, if $\psi(u) = \psi(v) = p$, then uw, $vw \in X^*p$, and consequently $\varphi(u)$, $\varphi(v) \in G'\varphi(p)\varphi(w)^{-1}$. Conversely, if $G'\varphi(u) = G'\varphi(v)$, let $r \in A^*$ be a word such that $uwr \in X^*$. Then $\varphi(vwr) \in G'\varphi(u)\varphi(wr) \subset G'$, whence $vwr \in X^*$. Thus $\psi(u) = \psi(v)$.

This shows that the index of G' in G is $d(X)$. By Proposition 0.8.1, $d(X)$ is also equal to the degree of the permutation group corresponding to the action of G on the cosets of G', as defined in Section 0.8.

EXAMPLE 3.2 The only maximal biprefix code with degree 1 over A is $X = A$.

EXAMPLE 3.3 Any maximal biprefix code of degree 2 over an alphabet A has the form

$$X = C \cup BC^*B, \tag{3.3}$$

where A is the disjoint union of B and C, with $B \neq \emptyset$.

Indeed, let $C = A \cap X$ and $B = A - C$. Each $b \in B$ has two parses, namely $(1, 1, b)$ and $(b, 1, 1)$. Thus, a word which is an internal factor of a word $x \in X$ cannot contain a letter in B, since otherwise x would have at least three parses. Thus, the set H of internal factors of X satisfies $H \subset C^*$. Next consider a word x in X. Either it is a letter, and then it is in C, or otherwise it has the form $x = aub$ with $a, b \in A$ and $u \in H \subset C^*$. X being biprefix, neither a nor b is in C. Thus $X \subset C \cup BC^*B$. The maximality of X implies the equality.

This shows that any maximal biprefix code of degree 2 is a group code. Indeed, the code given by (3.3) is obtained by considering the morphism from A^* onto $\mathbb{Z}/2\mathbb{Z}$ defined by $\varphi(B) = \{1\}$, $\varphi(C) = \{0\}$.

EXAMPLE 3.4 Consider the set

$$Y = \{a^n b^n \mid n \geq 1\}.$$

It is a biprefix code which is not maximal since $Y \cup ba$ is biprefix. Also Y is thin since $ba \in \bar{F}(Y)$. The code Y is not contained in a thin maximal biprefix code. Suppose indeed that X is a thin maximal biprefix code of degree d containing Y. For any $n \geq 0$, the word a^n then has $n + 1$ parses, since it has $n + 1$ right factors which all are proper left factors of a word in Y, whence in X. Since $d \leq n$, this is impossible. In fact, Y is contained in the Dyck code over $\{a, b\}$ (see Example I.2.5).

EXAMPLE 3.5 Let $X, Y \subset A^+$ be two thin maximal biprefix codes. Then XY is maximal biprefix and thin and

$$d(XY) = d(X) + d(Y).$$

The first part of the claim follows indeed from Corollary II.4.2. Next, let $w \in \bar{H}(XY)$ be a word which is not an internal factor of XY. Then, $w \in \bar{H}(X)$ and $w \in \bar{H}(Y)$. The left factors of w which are also proper right factors of XY are of two kinds: first there are $d(Y)$ left factors which are proper right factors of Y, then there are $d(X)$ left factors uy with $u \in A^- X$, $y \in Y$. These are the only left factors of w which are in $A^-(XY)$. Since w has $d(XY)$ parses with respect to XY, this gives the formula.

We now define a formal power series associated to a code X and which plays a fundamental role in the following. Let X be a thin maximal biprefix code over A. The *tower* over X is the formal power series T_X (also written T when no confusion is possible) defined by

$$(T_X, w) = d - (L_X, w). \tag{3.4}$$

The following proposition states some useful elementary facts about the series T.

PROPOSITION 3.2 *Let X be a thin maximal biprefix code of degree d over A, set $P = XA^-$, $S = A^- X$, and let T be the tower over X. Then*

$$(T, w) = 0 \quad \textit{iff} \quad w \in \bar{H}(X),$$

and for $w \in H(X)$,

$$1 \leq (T, w) \leq d - 1. \tag{3.5}$$

Further

$$(T, 1) = d - 1$$

and

$$\underline{X} - 1 = (\underline{A} - 1)T(\underline{A} - 1) + d(\underline{A} - 1), \tag{3.6}$$

$$\underline{P} = (\underline{A} - 1)T + d, \tag{3.7}$$

$$\underline{S} = T(\underline{A} - 1) + d. \tag{3.8}$$

Proof According to Theorem 3.1, $(T, w) = 0$ iff $w \in \bar{H}(X)$. For all other words, $1 \leq (T, w)$. Also $(T, w) \leq d - 1$ since all words have at least one parse, and $(T, 1) = d - 1$ since the empty word has exactly one parse.

Next by definition of T, we have $T + L = dA^*$, whence

$$T(1 - \underline{A}) + L(1 - \underline{A}) = d = (1 - \underline{A})T + (1 - \underline{A})L.$$

The code X is maximal; consequently $P = A^* - XA^*$ and $S = A^* - A^*X$. Thus we can apply Proposition 1.3 with $P = U$, $S = V$. Together with the equation above, this yields formulas (3.7), (3.8), and also (3.6) since

$$\underline{X} - 1 = \underline{P}(A - 1) = ((\underline{A} - 1)T + d)(\underline{A} - 1). \quad \square$$

Proposition 3.2 shows that the support of the series T is contained in the set $H(X)$.

Note that two thin maximal biprefix codes X and X' having the same tower are equal. Indeed, by Proposition 3.2, they have the same degree since

$$(T, 1) = d(X) - 1 = d(X') - 1.$$

But then Eq. (3.6) implies that $X = X'$.

Whenever some thin maximal biprefix code of degree $d = d(X)$ satisfies some equation

$$\underline{X} - 1 = (\underline{A} - 1)T(\underline{A} - 1) + d(\underline{A} - 1),$$

then T must be the tower on X. The next result gives a sufficient condition to obtain the same conclusion without knowing that the integer d is equal to $d(X)$.

PROPOSITION 3.3 *Let $T, T' \in \mathbb{Z} \ll A \gg$ and let $d, d' \geq 1$ be integers such that*

$$(\underline{A} - 1)T(\underline{A} - 1) + d(\underline{A} - 1) = (\underline{A} - 1)T'(\underline{A} - 1) + d'(\underline{A} - 1). \quad (3.9)$$

If there is a word $w \in A^*$ such that $(T, w) = (T', w)$, then $T = T'$ and $d = d'$.

Proof After multiplication on both sides by $\underline{A}^* = (1 - \underline{A})$, Eq. (3.9) becomes

$$T - d\underline{A}^* = T' - d'\underline{A}^*.$$

If $(T, w) = (T', w)$, then $(d\underline{A}^*, w) = (d/\underline{A}^*, w)$. Thus, $d = d'$, which implies $T = T'$. $\square$

We now observe the effect of an internal transformation (Proposition 2.3) on the tower of a thin maximal biprefix code X. Recall that, provided w is a word such that G_1, D_1 are both nonempty, where

$$G = Xw^{-1}, \qquad D = w^{-1}X, \qquad G_0 = (wD)w^{-1}, \qquad D_0 = w^{-1}(Gw),$$

$$G_1 = G - G_0, \qquad D_1 = D - D_0,$$

the code Y defined by

$$\underline{Y} = \underline{X} + (1 - \underline{G})w(1 - \underline{D}_0^*\underline{D}_1)$$

is maximal biprefix. By Proposition II.4.6, the sets $G = Xw^{-1}$ and $D = w^{-1}X$ are maximal suffix and maximal prefix. Let U be the set of proper right factors of G, and let V be the set of proper left factors of D. Then $D_0^* V$ is the set of proper left factors of words in $D_0^* D_1$, since $D = D_0 \cup D_1$. Consequently

$$\underline{G} - 1 = (\underline{A} - 1)\underline{U}, \qquad \underline{D}_0^* \underline{D}_1 - 1 = \underline{D}_0^* \underline{V}(\underline{A} - 1).$$

Going back to Y, we get

$$\underline{Y} - 1 = \underline{X} - 1 + (\underline{A} - 1)\underline{U} w \underline{D}_0^* V(\underline{A} - 1).$$

Let T be the tower over X. Then using Eq. (3.6), we get

$$\underline{Y} - 1 = (\underline{A} - 1)(T + \underline{U} w \underline{D}_0^* \underline{V})(\underline{A} - 1) + d(\underline{A} - 1).$$

Observe that since X is thin, both G and D are thin. Consequently also U and V are thin. Since $D_1 = D - D_0 \neq \emptyset$, D_0 is not a maximal code. As a subset of D, the set D_0 is thin. By Theorem I.5.7, D_0 is not complete. Thus D_0^* is thin. Thus $UwD_0^* V$, as a product of thin sets, is thin. Next $\text{supp}(T) \subset H(X)$ is thin. Thus $\text{supp}(T) \cup UwD_0^* V$ is thin.

Let u be a word which is not a factor of a word in this set. Then

$$(T + \underline{U} w D_0^* \underline{V}, u) = 0$$

On the other hand, formula (2.2) shows that since $G_1(wD_0^*)D_1$ is thin, the set Y is thin. Thus, the support of the tower T_Y over Y is thin. Let v be such that $(T_Y, v) = 0$, then

$$(T + \underline{U} w \underline{D}_0^* \underline{V}, \text{uv}) = (T_Y, uv) = 0,$$

showing that Proposition 3.3 can be applied. Consequently,

$$d(X) = d(Y) \qquad \text{and} \qquad T_Y = T + \underline{U} w \underline{D}_0^* \underline{V}.$$

Thus, the degree of a thin maximal biprefix code remains invariant under internal transformations.

Example 3.6 The finite maximal biprefix code $X = \{a^3, a^2ba, a^2b^2, ab, ba^2, baba, bab^2, b^2a, b^3\}$ over $A = \{a, b\}$ of Example 2.2 has degree 3. This can be seen by observing that no word has more than 3 parses, and the word a^3 has 3 parses, or also by the fact (Example 2.5) that X is obtained from the uniform code A^3 by internal transformation with respect to the word $w = ab$. Thus $d(X) = d(A^3) = 3$.

In this example, $D\ (= w^{-1}A^3) = G\ (= A^3 w^{-1}) = A$. Thus

$$T_X = T_{A^3} + w.$$

Clearly

$$T_{A^3} = 2 + a + b.$$

Consequently

$$T_X = 2 + a + b + ab.$$

We now give a characterization of the formal power series that are the tower over some thin maximal biprefix code.

PROPOSITION 3.4 *A formal power series $T \in \mathbb{N} \langle\langle A \rangle\rangle$ is the tower over some thin maximal biprefix code iff it satisfies the following conditions.*

(i) *for all $a \in A$, $v \in A^*$,*

$$0 \leq (T, v) - (T, av) \leq 1, \tag{3.10}$$

$$0 \leq (T, v) - (T, va) \leq 1; \tag{3.11}$$

(ii) *for all $a, b \in A$, $v \in A^*$,*

$$(T, av) + (T, vb) \leq (T, v) + (T, avb); \tag{3.12}$$

(iii) *there exists a word $v \in A^*$ such that*

$$(T, v) = 0.$$

Proof Let X be a thin maximal biprefix code of degree d, let L be its indicator, and let $T = d\underline{A}^* - L$. Then Eqs. (3.10), (3.11), and (3.12) are direct consequences of Eqs. (1.11), (1.12), and (1.13). Further (iii) holds for all $v \in \bar{H}(X)$, and this set is nonempty.

Conversely, assume that $T \in \mathbb{N} \langle\langle A \rangle\rangle$ satisfies the conditions of the proposition. Define

$$d = (T, 1) + 1, \qquad L = d\underline{A}^* - T.$$

Then by construction, L satisfies the conditions of Proposition 1.5, and consequently L is the indicator of some biprefix code X. Next by assumption, T has nonnegative coefficients. Thus for all $w \in A^*$, we have $(T, w) = d - (L, w) \geq 0$. Thus, L is bounded. In view of Theorem 3.1, the code X is maximal and thin. Since $(T, v) = 0$ for at least one word v, we have $(L, v) = d$ and $d = \max\{(L, w) \mid w \in A^*\}$. Thus, d is the degree of X and $T = d\underline{A}^* - L$ is the tower over X. □

The preceding result makes it possible to disassemble the tower over a biprefix code.

PROPOSITION 3.5 *Let T be the tower over a thin maximal biprefix code X of degree $d \geq 2$. The series*

$$T' = T - \underline{H(X)}$$

is the tower of some thin maximal biprefix code of degree $d - 1$.

Proof First observe that T' has nonnegative coefficients. Indeed, by Proposition 3.2, $(T, w) \geq 1$ iff $w \in H(X)$. Consequently $(T', w) \geq 0$ for $w \in H(X)$, and $(T', w) = (T, w) = 0$ otherwise.

Next, we verify the three conditions of Proposition 3.4.

(i) Let $a \in A$, $v \in A^*$. If $av \in H(X)$, then $v \in H(X)$. Thus $(T', av) = (T, av) - 1$ and $(T', v) = (T', av) - 1$. Therefore the inequality results from the corresponding inequality for T. On the other hand, if $av \notin H(X)$, then $(T, av) = (T', av) = 0$. Consequently $(T, v) \leq 1$ whence $(T', v) = 0$. Thus the inequality (3.10) holds for T'.

(ii) Let a, $b \in A$ and $v \in A^*$. If $avb \in H(X)$, then $(T', av) = (T, w) - 1$ for each of the four words $w = avb$, av, vb, and v. Thus, the inequality

$$(T', av) + (T', vb) \leq (T', v) + (T', avb)$$

results, in this case, from the corresponding inequality for T. On the other hand, if $avb \notin H(X)$, then as before $(T, av), (T, vb) \leq 1$ and $(T', av) = (T', vb) = 0$. Thus (3.12) holds for T'.

Condition (iii) of Proposition 3.4 is satisfied clearly for T' since $(T', w) = 0$ for $w \in H(X)$. Thus T' is the tower over some thin maximal biprefix code. Its degree is $(T', 1)$. Since $1 \in H(X)$, we have $(T', 1) = d - 2$. This completes the proof. □

Let X be a thin maximal biprefix code of degree $d \geq 2$, and let T be the tower over X. Let X' be the thin maximal biprefix code with tower $T' = T - \underline{H(X)}$. Then X' has degree $d - 1$. The code X' is called the *code derived* from X. Since for the indicators L and L' of X and X', we have $L = d\underline{A}^* - T$ and $L' = (d - 1)\underline{A}^* - T'$, it follows that

$$L' = L - \underline{\bar{H}(X)}. \tag{3.14}$$

We let $X^{(n)}$ denote the code derived from $X^{(n-1)}$ for $d(X) \geq n + 1$.

PROPOSITION 3.6 *The tower of a thin maximal biprefix code X of degree $d \geq 2$ satisfies*

$$T = \underline{H}(X) + \underline{H}(X') + \cdots + \underline{H}(X^{(d-2)}).$$

Proof By induction, we have from Proposition 3.5

$$T = H(X) + H(X') + \cdots + H(X^{(d-2)}) + \hat{T},$$

where $\hat{T}$ is the tower over a code of degree 1. This code is the alphabet, and consequently $\hat{T} = 0$. This proves the result. □

We now describe the set of proper left factors and the set of proper right factors of words of the derived code of a thin maximal biprefix code.

Proposition 3.7 *Let $X \subset A^+$ be a thin maximal biprefix code of degree $d \geq 2$. Let*

$$S = A^- X, \quad P = XA^- \qquad \text{and} \qquad H = A^- XA^-, \quad \bar{H} = A^* - H.$$

1. *The set $S \cap \bar{H}$ is a thin maximal prefix code. The set H is the set of its proper left factors, i.e., $S \cap \bar{H} = HA - H$.*
2. *The set $P \cap \bar{H}$ is a thin maximal suffix code. The set H is the set of its proper right factors, i.e., $P \cap \bar{H} = AH - H$.*
3. *The set $S \cap H$ is the set of proper right factors of the derived code X'.*
4. *The set $P \cap H$ is the set of proper left factors of the derived code X'.*

Proof We first prove 1. Let T be the tower over X, and let T' be the tower over the derived code X'. By Proposition 3.5, $T = T' + \underline{H}$, and by Proposition 3.2

$$\underline{S} = T(\underline{A} - 1) + d.$$

Thus, $\underline{S} = T'(\underline{A} - 1) + d - 1 + \underline{H}(\underline{A} - 1) + 1$. The code X' has degree $d - 1$. Thus, the series $T'(\underline{A} - 1) + d - 1$ is, by formula (3.8), the characteristic series of the set $S' = A^- X'$ of proper right factors of words of X'. Thus,

$$\underline{S} = \underline{H}(\underline{A} - 1) + 1 + \underline{S}' \qquad \text{and} \qquad \underline{S}' = T'(\underline{A} - 1) + d - 1.$$

The set H is prefix-closed and nonempty. We show that H contains no right ideal. Indeed, the set X is a maximal prefix code by Proposition 2.1. By Proposition II.3.6, the set P contains no right ideal and consequently $H = A^- P$ contains no right ideal. Again by Proposition II.3.6, the set $Y = HA - H$ is a maximal prefix code, and $H = YA^-$. Thus

$$\underline{Y} = \underline{H}(\underline{A} - 1) + 1.$$

Further, H being also suffix-closed, the set Y is in fact a semaphore code by Proposition II.5.5. We now verify that $Y = S \cap \bar{H}$.

Assume that $y \in Y$. Then, from the equation $\underline{S} = \underline{Y} + \underline{S}'$, it follows that $y \in S$. Since $H = YA^-$, we have $y \notin H$. Thus $y \in S \cap \bar{H}$. Conversely, assume that $y \in S \cap \bar{H}$. Then $y \neq 1$, since $d \geq 2$ implies that $H \neq \varnothing$ and consequently $1 \in H$. Further, each proper left factor of y is in $SA^- = A^- XA^- = H$, thus is an internal factor of X. In particular, considering just the longest proper left factor, we have $y \in HA$. Consequently, $y \in HA - H = Y$.

The second claim is proved in a symmetric way. To show 3, observe that by what we proved before, we have

$$\underline{S} = \underline{Y} + \underline{S}'. \tag{3.15}$$

Next $S = (S \cap H) \cup (S \cap \bar{H}) = Y \cup (S \cap H)$, since $Y = S \cap \bar{H}$. Moreover, the union is disjoint, thus $\underline{S} = \underline{Y} + \underline{S \cap H}$. Consequently $S' = S \cap H$. In the same way, we get point 4. □

THEOREM 3.8 *Let X be a thin maximal biprefix code of degree d. Then the set S' of its proper right factors is a disjoint union of d maximal prefix sets.*

Proof If $d = 1$, then $X = A$ and the set $S = \{1\}$ is a maximal prefix set. If $d \geq 2$, then the set $Y = S \cap \bar{H}$, where $H = A^- X A^-$ and $\bar{H} = A^* - H$, is maximal prefix by Proposition 3.7. Further, the set $S' = S \cap H$ is the set of proper right factors of the code derived from X. Arguing by induction, the set S' is a disjoint union of $d - 1$ maximal prefix sets. Thus $S = Y \cup S'$ is a disjoint union of d maximal prefix sets. □

It must be noted that the decomposition, in Theorem 3.8, of the set S into disjoint maximal prefix sets is not unique (see Exercise 3.2). The following corollary to Theorem 3.8 is rather surprising.

COROLLARY 3.9 *Let $X \subset A^+$ be a thin maximal biprefix code having degree d. For any positive Bernoulli distribution π on A^*, the average length of X is equal to d.*

Proof Let π be a positive Bernoulli distribution on A^*, and let $\lambda(X)$ be the average length of X. By Corollary II.7.4, the average length $\lambda(X)$ is finite and $\lambda(X) = \pi(S)$, where $S = A^- X$ is the set of proper right factors of X. In view of Theorem 3.8, we have

$$\underline{S} = \underline{Y}_1 + \underline{Y}_2 + \cdots + \underline{Y}_d,$$

where each Y_i is a maximal prefix code. As a set of factors of X, each Y_i also is thin. Thus $\pi(Y_i) = 1$ for $i = 1, \ldots, d$ by Theorem I.5.10. Consequently,

$$\lambda(X) = \sum_{i=i}^{d} \pi(Y_i) = d. \quad \square$$

Note that Corollary 3.9 can also be proved directly by starting with formula 3.7. However, the proof we have given here is the most natural one.

We now prove a converse of Theorem 3.8.

PROPOSITION 3.10 *Let X be a thin maximal suffix code. If the set of its proper right factors is a disjoint union of d maximal prefix sets, then X is biprefix and has degree d.*

Proof Let $S = A^- X$. By assumption $\underline{S} = \underline{Y}_1 + \cdots + \underline{Y}_d$, where $Y_1, \ldots, Y_d$ are maximal prefix sets. Let U_i be the set of proper left factors of Y_i. Then $\underline{A}^* = \underline{Y}_i^* \underline{U}_i$, and thus $(1 - \underline{Y}_i)\underline{A}^* = \underline{U}_i$, whence

$$\underline{A}^* = \underline{U}_i + \underline{Y}_i \underline{A}_i^*.$$

Summing up these equalities gives

$$d\underline{A}^* = \sum_{i=i}^{d} \underline{U}_i + \underline{S}\underline{A}^*.$$

Multiply on the left by $\underline{A} - 1$. Then, since $(\underline{A} - 1)\underline{S} = \underline{X} - 1$,

$$d = \sum_{i=i}^{d} (\underline{A} - 1)\underline{U}_i + (\underline{X} - 1)\underline{A}^*,$$

whence

$$\underline{X}\underline{A}^* = \underline{A}^* - \sum_{i=i}^{d} (\underline{A} - 1)\underline{U}_i + d.$$

From this formula, we derive the fact that XA^* is right dense. Indeed, let $w \in A^+$, and set $w = au$, with $a \in A$. Each of the sets Y_i is maximal prefix. Thus, each Y_iA^* is right dense. There exists a word v such that simultaneously $auv \in Y_iA^*$ for all $i \in \{1, \ldots, d\}$ and also $uv \in Y_iA^*$ for all $i \in \{1, \ldots, d\}$. Thus for each $i \in \{1, \ldots, d\}$

$$\begin{aligned}((\underline{A} - 1)\underline{U}_i, wv) &= (\underline{A}\underline{U}_i, wv) - (\underline{U}_i, wv) \\ &= (\underline{U}_i, uv) - (\underline{U}_i, wv) = 1 - 1 = 0.\end{aligned}$$

Consequently

$$(\underline{X}\underline{A}^*, wv) = (\underline{A}^*, wv) = 1.$$

Thus, $wv \in XA^*$. Consequently XA^* is right dense or equivalently, X is right complete. In view of Proposition 2.1, this means that X is maximal biprefix.

Let $w \in \bar{H}(X)$ be a word which is not an internal factor of X. Then $w \in U_i$ for $1 \leq i \leq d$. The set Y_i being maximal prefix, we have $w \in Y_iA^*$ for $1 \leq i \leq d$. Consequently, w has exactly d left factors which are right factors of words in X, one in each Y_i. Thus X has degree d. □

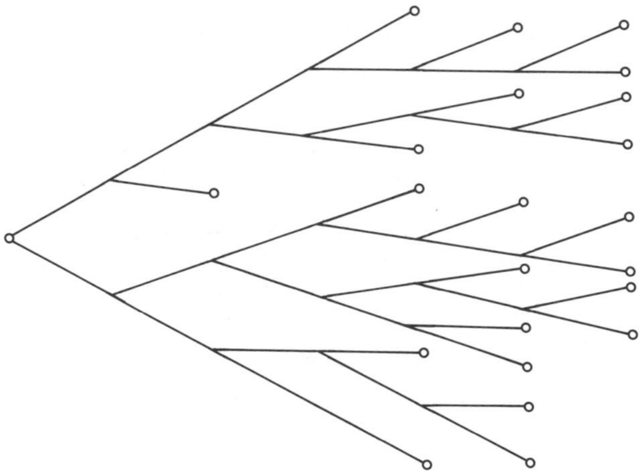

Fig. 3.6 A maximal biprefix code of degree 4.

EXAMPLE 3.7 Let X be the finite maximal biprefix code given in Fig. 3.6. The tower T over X is given by Fig. 3.7 (by its values on the set $H(X)$). The derived code X' is the maximal biprefix code of degree 3 of Examples 2.2 and 3.6. The set S', or proper right factors of X', is indicated in Fig. 3.8. The set S of proper right factors of X is indicated in Fig. 3.9. The maximal prefix code $Y = S \cap \bar{H}$ is the set of words indicated in the figure by ($\odot$). It may be verified by inspection of Figs. 3.7, 3.8, and 3.9 that $S' = S \cap H$.

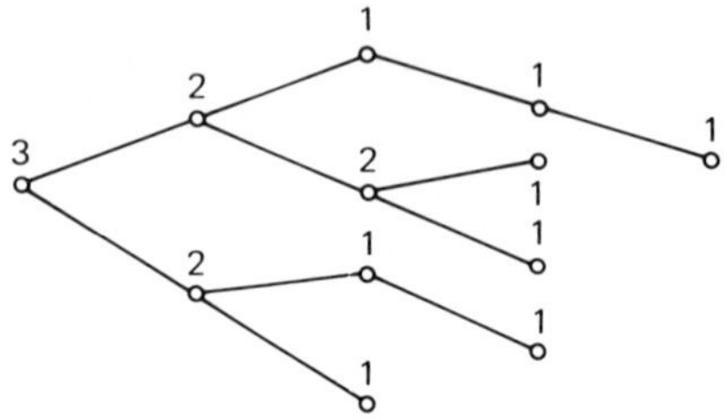

Fig. 3.7 The tower T over X.

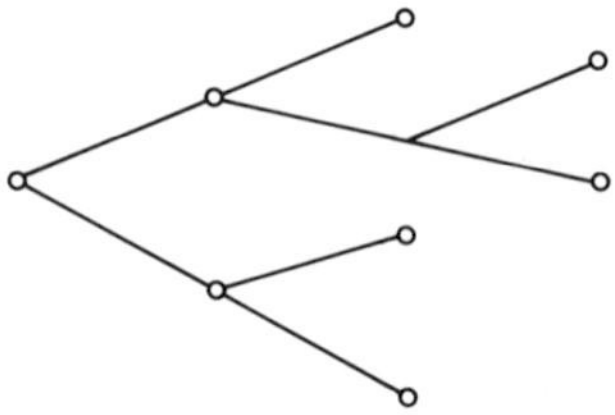

Fig. 3.8 The set S' of proper right factor of X'.

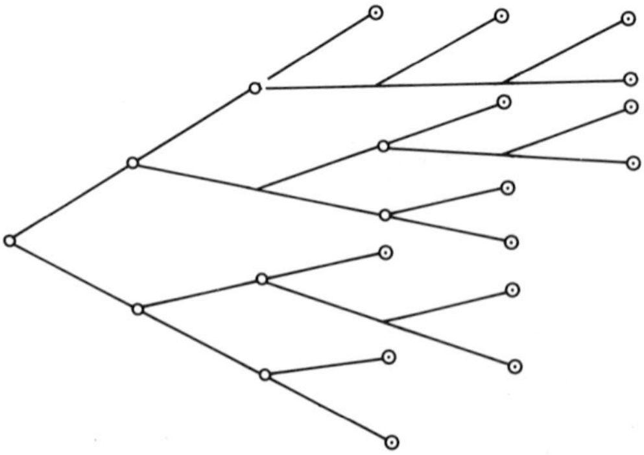

Fig. 3.9 The set S of proper right factors of X.

4. KERNEL

Let $X \subset A^+$, and let $H = A^- X A^-$ be the set of internal factors of X. The *kernel* of X, denoted $K(X)$, or K if no confusion is possible, is the set

$$K = X \cap H.$$

Thus a word is in the kernel if it is both in the code and an internal factor of the code. As we will see in this section, the kernel is one of the main characteristics of a maximal biprefix code.

We start by showing how the kernel is related to the computation of the indicator.

PROPOSITION 4.1 *Let $X \subset A^+$ be a thin maximal biprefix code of degree d and let K be the kernel of X. Let Y be a set such that*

$$K \subset Y \subset X.$$

Then for all $w \in H(X) \cup Y$,

$$(L_Y, w) = (L_X, w). \tag{4.1}$$

For all $w \in A^*$,

$$(L_X, w) = \min\{d, (L_Y, w)\}. \tag{4.2}$$

Proof By formula (1.3), we have

$$L_X = \underline{A}^*(1 - \underline{X})\underline{A}^*, \; L_Y = \underline{A}^*(1 - \underline{Y})\underline{A}^*.$$

Let $w \in A^*$, and let $F(w)$ be the set of its factors. For any word $x \in A^*$, the number $(\underline{A}^* x \underline{A}^*, w)$ is the number of occurrences of x as a factor of w. It is nonzero only if $x \in F(w)$. Thus

$$(\underline{A}^*\underline{X}\underline{A}^*, w) = \sum_{x \in F(w) \cap X} (\underline{A}^* x \underline{A}^*, w)$$

showing that if $F(w) \cap X = F(w) \cap Y$, then $(L_X, w) = (L_Y, w)$. Thus, it suffices to show that $F(w) \cap X = F(w) \cap Y$ for all $w \in H(X) \cup Y$. From the inclusion $Y \subset X$, we get $F(w) \cap Y \subset F(w) \cap X$ for all $w \in A^*$. If $w \in H(X)$, then $F(w) \subset H(X)$ and $F(w) \cap X \subset K(X)$. Thus $F(w) \cap X \subset F(w) \cap Y$ in this case. If $w \in Y$, then no proper left nor right factor of w is in X, since X is biprefix. Thus $F(w) \cap X = \{w\} \cup (A^- w A^- \cap X) \subset \{w\} \cup K(X) \subset Y$. Consequently $F(w) \cap X \subset F(w) \cap Y$ in this case also. This shows (4.1).

Now let $w \in H(X)$ be an internal factor of X. Then $(L_X, w) < d$ by Theorem 3.1. Consequently, $(L_X, w) = (L_Y, w)$ by formula (4.1). Next let $w \in \bar{H}(X)$. Then $(L_X, w) = d$. By formula (1.6), $(L_X, w) \le (L_Y, w)$. This proves (4.2). □

Given two power series σ and τ, we denote by $\min\{\sigma, \tau\}$ the series defined by

$$(\min\{\sigma, \tau\}, w) = \min\{(\sigma, w), (\tau, w)\}.$$

THEOREM 4.2 *Let X be a thin maximal biprefix code with degree d, and let K be its kernel. Then*

$$L_X = \min\{d\underline{A}^*, L_K\}.$$

In particular, a thin maximal biprefix code is determined by its degree and its kernel.

Proof Take $Y = K(X)$ in the preceding proposition. Then the formula follows from (4.2). Assume that there are two codes X and X' of same degree d and $K(X) = K(X')$. Then $L_{K(X)} = L_{K(X')}$, whence $L_X = L_{X'}$ which in turn implies $X = X'$. This completes the proof. □

Clearly, the kernel of a biprefix code is itself a biprefix code. However, not every biprefix code is the kernel of some biprefix code. We now give characterization of those biprefix codes which are a kernel of some thin maximal biprefix code. For this, it is convenient to introduce a notation: for a subset Y of A^+, let

$$\mu(Y) = \max\{(L_Y, y) \mid y \in Y\};$$

it is a nonegative integer or infinity. By convention, $\mu(\varnothing) = 0$.

THEOREM 4.3 *A biprefix code Y is the kernel of some thin maximal biprefix code of degree d iff*

(i) *Y is not maximal biprefix,*
(ii) *$\mu(Y) \le d - 1$.*

Proof Let X be a thin maximal biprefix code of degree d, and let $Y = K(X)$ be its kernel. Let us verify conditions (i) and (ii). To verify (i), consider a word $x \in X$ such that $(L_X, x) = \mu(X)$; we claim that $x \notin H(X)$. Thus, $x \notin K(X)$, showing that $Y \subsetneq X$. Assume the claim is wrong. Then $uxv \in X$ for some u, $v \in A^+$. Consequently, $(L_X, uxv) \ge 1 + (L_X, x)$ since the word uxv has the interpretation $(1, uxv, 1)$ which passes through no point of x. This contradicts the choice of x, and proves the claim. Next, for all $y \in Y$, we have $(L_X, y) = (L_Y, y)$ by formula (4.1). Since $(L_X, y) \le d - 1$ because $y \in H(X)$, condition (ii) is also satisfied.

Conversely, let Y be a biprefix code satisfying conditions (i) and (ii). Let $L \in \mathbb{N} \ll A \gg$ be the formal power series defined for $w \in A^*$ by

$$(L, w) = \min\{d, (L_Y, w)\}.$$

Let us verify that L satisfies the three conditions of Proposition 1.5. First, let $a \in A$ and $w \in A^*$. Then

$$0 \le (L_Y, aw) - (L_Y, w) \le 1.$$

If follows that if $(L_Y, w) < d$, then $(L_Y, aw) = (L, aw)$; on the other hand, if

$(L_Y, w) \geq d$, then $(L, aw) = (L, w) = d$. Thus

$$0 \leq (L, aw) - (L, w) \leq 1.$$

The symmetric inequality

$$0 \leq (L, wa) - (L, w) \leq 1$$

is shown in the same way. Thus the first of the conditions of Proposition 1.5 is satisfied.

Next, for $a, b \in A$, $w \in A^*$, $(L_Y, aw) + (L_Y, wb) \geq (L_Y, w) + (L_Y, awb)$. Consider first the case where $(L_Y, w) \geq d$. Then $(L, aw) = (L, wb) = (L, w) = (L, awb) = d$, and the inequality

$$(L, aw) + (L, wb) \geq (L, w) + (L, awb)$$

is clear. Assume now that $(L_Y, w) < d$. Then $(L_Y, aw) \leq d$ and $(L_Y, wb) \leq d$. Consequently

$$\begin{aligned}(L, aw) + (L, wb) &= (L_Y, aw) + (L_Y, wb)\\ &\geq (L_Y, w) + (L_Y, awb)\\ &\geq (L, w) + (L, awb)\end{aligned}$$

since $L \leq L_Y$. This shows the second condition.

Finally, we have $(L_Y, 1) = 1$, whence $(L, 1) = 1$.

Thus, according to Proposition 1.5, the series L is the indicator of some biprefix code X. Further, L being bounded, the code X is thin and maximal biprefix by Theorem 3.1. By the same argument, the code Y being nonmaximal, the series L_Y is unbounded. Consequently, $\max\{(L, w) \mid w \in A^*\} = d$, showing that X has degree d.

We now prove that $Y = X \cap H(X)$, i.e., Y is the kernel of X. First, we have the inclusion $Y \subset H(X)$. Indeed, if $y \in Y$, then $(L, y) \leq (L_Y, y) \leq \mu(Y) \leq d - 1$. Thus, by Theorem 3.1, $y \in H(X)$. Next, observe that it suffices to show that $X \cap H(X) = Y \cap H(X)$; this is equivalent to showing that

$$(\underline{X}, w) = (\underline{Y}, w)$$

for all $w \in H(X)$. Let us prove this by induction on $|w|$. Clearly, the equality holds for $|w| = 0$. Next, let $w \in H(X) - 1$. Then $(L, w) \leq d - 1$. Thus, $(L, w) = (L_Y, w)$. This in turn implies

$$(\underline{A}^* \underline{X} \underline{A}^*, w) = (A^* \underline{Y} \underline{A}^*, w).$$

But $F(w) \subset H(X)$. Thus, by the induction hypothesis, $(\underline{X}, s) = (\underline{Y}, s)$ for all proper factors of w. Thus the equation reduces to $(\underline{X}, w) = (\underline{Y}, w)$. □

We now describe the relation between the kernel and the operation of derivation.

PROPOSITION 4.4 *Let X be a thin maximal biprefix code of degree $d \geq 2$, and let $H = A^{-}XA^{-}$. Set*

$$K = X \cap H, \qquad Y = HA - H, \qquad Z = AH - H.$$

Then the code X' derived from X is

$$X' = K \cup (Y \cap Z). \tag{4.3}$$

Further,

$$K = X \cap X'. \tag{4.4}$$

Proof Let $S = A^{-}X$ and $P = XA^{-}$ be the sets of proper right factors and of proper left factors of words in X. Let $S' = S \cap H$ and $P' = P \cap H$. According to Proposition 3.7, S' is the set of proper right factors of words in X' and similarly for P'. Thus,

$$\underline{X}' - 1 = (\underline{A} - 1)\underline{S}' = \underline{A}\underline{S}' - \underline{S}'.$$

From $S' = S \cap H$, we have $AS' = AS \cap AH$, and

$$\underline{A}\underline{S}' = \underline{A}\underline{S} \odot \underline{A}\underline{H},$$

where $\odot$ denotes the Hadamard product (see Section 0.6). Thus,

$$\underline{X}' - 1 = (\underline{A}\underline{S} \odot \underline{A}\underline{H}) - \underline{S}'.$$

Now observe that, by Proposition 3.7, the set Z is a maximal suffix code with proper right factors H. Thus, $(\underline{Z} - 1) = (\underline{A} - 1)\underline{H}$ and

$$\underline{A}\underline{H} = \underline{Z} - 1 + \underline{H}.$$

Similarly, from $\underline{X} - 1 = (\underline{A} - 1)\underline{S}$ we get

$$\underline{A}\underline{S} = \underline{X} - 1 + \underline{S}.$$

Substitution gives

$$\begin{aligned}\underline{X}' - 1 &= (\underline{X} - 1 + \underline{S}) \odot (\underline{Z} - 1 + \underline{H}) - \underline{S}' \\ &= \underline{X \cap Z} + \underline{S \cap Z} + \underline{X \cap H} + \underline{S \cap H} + 1 - (1 \odot \underline{H}) - (\underline{S} \odot 1) - \underline{S}'.\end{aligned}$$

Indeed, the other terms have the value 0 since neither X nor Z contains the empty word. Now $Z = P \cap \bar{H}$ (Proposition 3.7), whence $X \cap Z = X \cap P \cap \bar{H} = \varnothing$. Also by definition $S' = S \cap H$ and $K = X \cap H$. Thus the equation becomes

$$\underline{X}' - 1 = \underline{S \cap Z} + \underline{K} - 1.$$

Finally, note that by Proposition 3.7, $Y = S \cap \bar{H}$. Thus,

$$S \cap Z = S \cap P \cap \bar{H} = Y \cap Z,$$

and

$$X' = K \cup (Y \cap Z),$$

showing (4.3). Next

$$X \cap X' = (K \cap X) \cup (X \cap Y \cap Z).$$

Now $X \cap Y \cap Z = X \cap P \cap S \cap \bar{H} = \emptyset$, and $K \cap X = K$. Thus,

$$X \cap X' = K$$

as claimed. □

PROPOSITION 4.5 *Let X be a thin maximal biprefix code of degree $d \geq 2$ and let X' be the derived code. Then*

$$K(X') \subset K(X) \subsetneq X'. \tag{4.5}$$

Proof First, we show that $H(X') \subset H(X)$. Indeed, let $w \in H(X')$. Then we have $(T_{X'}, w) \geq 1$, where $T_{X'}$ is the tower over X'. By Proposition 3.5, $(T_{X'}, w) = (T_X, w) - (H(X), w)$. Thus, $(T_X, w) \geq 1$. This in turn implies that $w \in H(X)$ by Proposition 3.2.

By definition, $K(X') = X' \cap H(X')$. Thus, $K(X') \subset X' \cap H(X)$. By Proposition 4.4, $X' = K(X) \cup T$, where T is a set disjoint from $H(X)$. Thus $X' \cap H(X) = K(X)$. This shows that $K(X') \subset K(X)$. Next, formula (4.4) also shows that $K(X) \subset X'$. Finally, we cannot have the equality $K(X) = X'$, since by Theorem 4.3, the set $K(X)$ is not a maximal biprefix code. □

The following theorem is a converse of Proposition 4.5.

THEOREM 4.6 *Let X' be a thin maximal biprefix code. For each set Y such that*

$$K(X') \subset Y \subsetneq X' \tag{4.6}$$

there exists a unique thin maximal biprefix code X such that

(i) $K(X) = Y$,
(ii) $d(X) = 1 + d(X')$.

Moreover, the code X' is derived from X.

Proof We first show that Y is the kernel of some biprefix code. For this, we verify the conditions of Theorem 4.3. The strict inclusion $Y \subsetneq X'$ shows that Y is not a maximal code. Next, by Proposition 4.1, $(L_Y, y) = (L_{X'}, y)$ for $y \in Y$. Thus, setting $d = d(X') + 1$, we have $\mu(Y) \leq d(X') = d - 1$.

According to Theorem 4.3, there is a thin maximal biprefix code X having degree d such that $K(X) = Y$. By Theorem 4.2, this code is unique. It remains to show that X' is the derived code of X. Let Z be the derived code of X. By

Proposition 4.5, $K(Z) \subset K(X) = Y \subsetneq Z$. Thus we may apply Proposition 4.1, showing that for all $w \in A^*$,

$$(L_Z, w) = \min\{d - 1, (L_Y, w)\}.$$

The inclusions of formula 4.6 give, by Proposition 4.1,

$$(L_{X'}, w) = \min\{d - 1, (L_Y, w)\}$$

for all $w \in A^*$. Thus $L_{X'} = L_Z$, whence $Z = X'$. □

Proposition 4.5 shows that the kernel of a code is located in some "interval" determined by the derived code. Theorem 4.6 shows that all of the "points" of this interval can be used effectively.

More precisely, Proposition 4.5 and Theorem 4.6 show that there is a bijection between the set of thin maximal biprefix codes of degree $d \geq 2$, and the pairs

$$(X', Y)$$

composed of a thin maximal biprefix code X' of degree $d - 1$ and a set Y satisfying (4.6). The bijection associates to a code X the pair $(X', K(X))$, where X' is the derived code of X.

EXAMPLE 4.1 We have seen in Example 3.3 that any maximal biprefix code of degree 2 has the form

$$X = C \cup BC^*B,$$

where the alphabet A is the disjoint union of B and C, and $B \neq \emptyset$. This observation can also be established by using Theorem 4.6. Indeed, the derived code of a maximal biprefix code of degree 2 has degree 1 and therefore is A. Then for each proper subset C of A there is a unique maximal biprefix code of degree 2 whose kernel is C. This code is clearly the code given by the above formula.

EXAMPLE 4.2 The number of maximal biprefix codes of degree 3 over a finite alphabet A having at least two letters is infinite. Indeed, consider an infinite thin maximal biprefix code X' of degree 2. Its kernel $K(X')$ is a subset of A and consequently is finite. In view of Theorem 4.6, each set K containing $K(X')$ and strictly contained in X' is the kernel of some maximal biprefix code of degree 3. Thus, there are infinitely many of them.

5. FINITE MAXIMAL BIPREFIX CODES

Finite maximal biprefix codes have quite remarkable properties which make them fascinating objects.

PROPOSITION 5.1 *Let $X \subset A^+$ be a finite maximal biprefix code of degree d. Then for each letter $a \in A$,*

$$a^d \in X.$$

With the terminology introduced in Chapter I, this is equivalent to saying that the order of each letter is the degree of the code.

Proof Let $a \in A$. According to Proposition 2.2, there is an integer $n \geq 1$ such that $a^n \in X$. Since X is finite, there is an integer k such that a^k is not an internal factor of X. The number of parses of a^k is equal to d. It is also the number of right factors of a^k which are proper left factors of words in X, that is n. Thus $n = d$. □

Note as a consequence of this result that it is, in general, impossible to complete a finite biprefix code into a maximal biprefix code which is finite. Consider, for example, $A = \{a, b\}$ and $X = \{a^2, b^3\}$. A finite maximal biprefix code containing X would have simultaneously degree 2 and degree 3.

We now show the following result:

THEOREM 5.2 *Let A be a finite set, and let $d \geq 1$. There are only a finite number of finite maximal biprefix codes over A with degree d.*

Proof The only maximal biprefix code over A, having degree 1 is the alphabet A. Arguing by induction on d, assume that there are only finitely many finite maximal biprefix codes of degree d. Each finite maximal biprefix code of degree $d + 1$ is determined by its kernel which is a subset of X'. Since X' is a finite maximal biprefix code of degree d there are only a finite number of kernels and we are finished. □

Denote by $\beta_k(d)$ the number of finite maximal biprefix codes of degree d over a k letter alphabet A.

Clearly $\beta_k(1) = 1$. Also $\beta_k(2) = 1$; indeed $X = A^2$ is, in view of Example 2.3, the only finite maximal biprefix code of degree 2. It is also clear that $\beta_1(d) = 1$ for all $d \geq 1$.

EXAMPLE 5.1 Let us verify that

$$\beta_2(3) = 3. \tag{5.1}$$

Let indeed $A = \{a, b\}$, and let $X \subset A^+$ be a finite maximal biprefix code of degree 3. The derived code X' is necessarily $X' = A^2$, since it is the only finite maximal biprefix code of degree 2. Let $K = X \cap X'$ be the kernel of X. Thus $K \subset A^2$.

According to Proposition 5.1, both $a^3, b^3 \in X$. Thus K cannot contain a^2 or b^2. Consequently, $K \subset \{ab, ba\}$. We next rule out the case $K = \{ab, ba\}$. Suppose indeed that this equality holds. For each $k \geq 1$, the word $(ab)^k$ has exactly two X parses. But X being finite, there is an integer k such that $(ab)^k \in H(X)$, and $(ab)^k$ should have three X parses. This is the contradiction.

Thus there remain three candidates for K: $K = \varnothing$ which correspond to $X = A^3$, then $K = \{ab\}$, which gives the code X of Example 2.2, and $K = \{ba\}$ which gives the reverse $\tilde{X}$ of the code X of Example 2.2. This shows (5.1). Note also that this explains why $\tilde{X}$ is obtained from X by exchanging the letters a and b: this property holds whenever it holds for the kernel.

We now show how to construct all finite maximal biprefix codes by a sequence of internal transformations, starting with a uniform code.

THEOREM 5.3 *Let A be a finite alphabet and $d \geq 1$. For each finite maximal biprefix code $X \subset A^+$ of degree d, there is a finite sequence of internal transformations which, starting with the uniform code A^d, yields X.*

Proof Let K be the kernel of X. If $K = \varnothing$, then $X = A^d$ and there is nothing to prove. This holds also if $\mathrm{Card}(A) = 1$. Thus we assume $K \neq \varnothing$ and $\mathrm{Card}(A) \geq 2$. Let $x \in K$ be a word which is not a factor of another word in K. We show that there exist a maximal suffix code G and a maximal prefix code D such that

$$GxD \subset X. \tag{5.2}$$

Assume the contrary. Let $P = XA^-$. Since $x \in K$, x is an internal factor. Thus the set Px^{-1} is not empty. Then for all words $g \in Px^{-1}$, there exist two words d, d' such that

$$gxd, \quad gxd' \in X \qquad \text{and} \qquad X(xd)^{-1} \neq X(xd')^{-1}.$$

Suppose the contrary. Then for some $g \in Px^{-1}$, all the sets $X(xd)^{-1}$, with d running over the words such that $gxd \in X$, are equal. Let $D = \{d \mid gxd \in X\}$ and let $G = X(xd)^{-1}$, where d is any element in D. Then $GxD \subset X$, contradicting our assumption. This shows the existence of d, d'.

Among all triples (g, d, d') such that

$$gxd, \quad gxd' \in X \quad \text{and} \quad X(xd)^{-1} \neq X(xd')^{-1},$$

let us choose one with $|d| + |d'|$ minimal. For this fixed triple (g, d, d'), set

$$G = X(xd)^{-1} \qquad \text{and} \qquad G' = X(xd')^{-1}.$$

Then G and G' are distinct maximal suffix codes. Take any word $h \in G - G'$. Then either h is a proper right factor of a word in G' or has a word in G' as a proper right factor. Thus, interchanging if necessary G and G', there exist words $u, g' \in A^+$ such that

$$g' \in G, \qquad ug' \in G'.$$

Note that this implies

$$g'xd \in X, \qquad ug'xd' \in X.$$

Now consider the word $ug'xd$. Of course, $ug'xd \notin X$. Next $ug'xd \notin P$, since otherwise $g'xd \in K$, and x would be a factor of another word in K, contrary to the assumption. Since $ug'xd \notin P \cup X$, it has a proper left factor in X. This left factor cannot be a left factor of $ug'x$, since $ug'xd' \in X$. Thus it has $ug'x$ as a proper left factor. Thus there is a factorization

$$d = d''v$$

with $d'', v \in A^+$, and $ug'xd'' \in X$.

Now we observe that the triple (ug', d', d'') has the same properties as (g, d, d'). Indeed, both words $ug'xd'$ and $ug'xd''$ are in X. Also $X(xd')^{-1} \neq X(xd'')^{-1}$ since $gxd' \in X$, but $gxd'' \notin X$: this results from the fact that gxd'' is a proper left factor of $gxd \in X$ (Fig. 3.10). Thus, (ug', d', d'') satisfies the same constraints as (g, d, d'): however, $|d'| + |d''| < |d'| + |d|$. This yields the contradiction and proves (5.2). Let

$$Y = (X \cup Gx \cup xD) - (x \cup GxD). \tag{5.3}$$

In view of Proposition 2.4, the set Y is a finite maximal biprefix code, and moreover, the internal transformation with respect to x transforms Y into X.

Finally (5.3) shows that

$$\begin{aligned}\mathrm{Card}(Y) &= \mathrm{Card}(X) + \mathrm{Card}(G) + \mathrm{Card}(D) - 1 - \mathrm{Card}(G)\,\mathrm{Card}(D)\\ &= \mathrm{Card}(X) - (\mathrm{Card}(G) - 1)(\mathrm{Card}(D) - 1).\end{aligned}$$

The code G being maximal suffix and $\mathrm{Card}(A) \geq 2$, we have $\mathrm{Card}(G) \geq 2$. For the same reason, $\mathrm{Card}(D) \geq 2$. Thus

$$\mathrm{Card}(Y) \leq \mathrm{Card}(X) - 1. \tag{5.4}$$

Arguing by induction on the number of elements, we can assume that Y is obtained from A^d by a finite number of internal transformations. This completes the proof. □

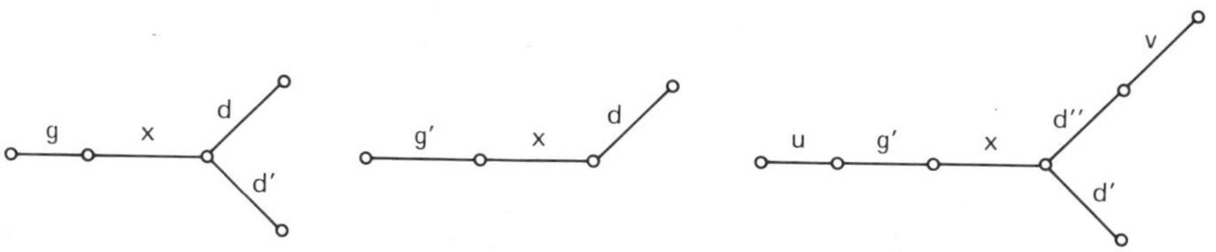

Fig. 3.10 From triple (g, d, d') to triple (ug', d', d'').

Observe that by this theorem [and formula (5.4)] each finite maximal biprefix code $X \subset A^+$ of degree d satisfies

$$\mathrm{Card}(X) \geq \mathrm{Card}(A^d) \tag{5.5}$$

with an equality iff $X = A^d$. This result can be proved directly as follows (see also Exercise II.7.2).

Let X be a finite maximal prefix code, and

$$\lambda = \sum_{x \in X} |x| k^{-|x|}$$

with $k = \mathrm{Card}(A)$. The number λ is the average length of X with respect to the uniform Bernoulli distribution on A^*.
Let us show the inequality

$$\mathrm{Card}(X) \geq k^\lambda. \tag{5.6}$$

For a maximal biprefix code X of degree d, we have $\lambda = d$ (Corollary 3.9), and thus (5.5) is a consequence of (5.6).

To show (5.6), let $n = \mathrm{Card}(X)$. Then

$$\lambda = \sum_{x \in X} k^{-|x|} \log_k k^{|x|},$$

$$\log_k n = \sum_{x \in X} k^{-|x|} \log_k n.$$

The last equality follows from $1 = \sum_{x \in X} k^{-|x|}$, which holds by the fact that X is a finite maximal prefix code. Thus,

$$\lambda - \log_k n = \sum_{x \in X} k^{-|x|} \log_k (k^{|x|}/n).$$

The function log being concave, we have

$$\lambda - \log_k n \leq \log_k \left(\sum_{x \in X} \frac{1}{n} \right) = 0.$$

This shows (5.6).

EXAMPLE 5.2 Let $A = \{a, b\}$ and let X be the finite maximal biprefix code of degree 4 with literal representation given in Fig. 3.11. The kernel of X is $K = \{ab, a^2b^2\}$. There is no pair (G, D) composed of a maximal suffix code G and a maximal prefix code D such that $GabD \subset X$. On the other hand

$$Aa^2b^2A \subset X.$$

The code X is obtained from the code Y given in Fig. 3.12 by internal transformation relatively to a^2b^2. The code Y is obtained from A^4 by the sequence of internal transformations relatively to the words aba, ab^2, and ab.

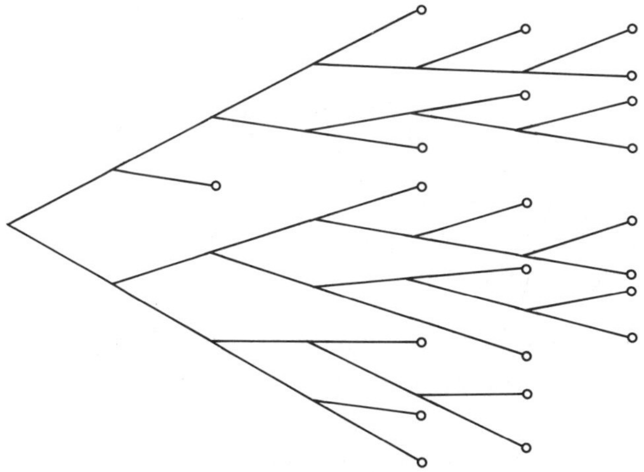

Fig. 3.11 The code X.

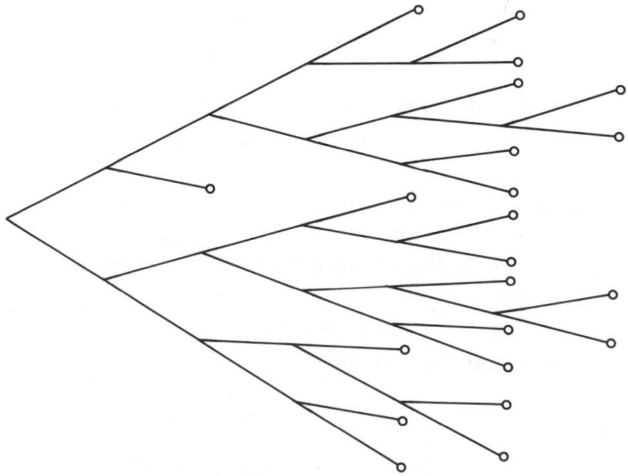

Fig. 3.12 The code Y.

We now describe the construction of a finite maximal biprefix code from its derived code.

Let $Y \subset A^+$ be a biprefix code. A word $w \in A^*$ is called *full* (with respect to Y) if there is an interpretation passing through any point of w. It is equivalent to saying that w is full if any parse of w is an interpretation.

The biprefix code Y is *insufficient* if the set of full words with respect to Y is finite.

PROPOSITION 5.4 *A thin maximal biprefix code over a finite alphabet A is finite iff its kernel is insufficient.*

Proof Suppose first that X is finite. Let d be its degree, and let K be its kernel. Consider a word w in $\bar{H}(X)$. Then w has exactly d X-interpretations. These are not all K-interpretations, because K is a subset of the derived code of X, which has degree $d-1$. Thus, there is a point of w through which no K-interpretation passes. Thus, w is not full (for K). This shows that the set of full words (with respect to K) is contained in $H(X)$. Since $H(X)$ is finite, the set K is insufficient.

Conversely, suppose that X is infinite. Since the alphabet A is finite, there is an infinite sequence $(a_n)_{n\geq 0}$ of letters such that, setting $P = XA^{-1}$, we have for all $n \geq 0$,

$$p_n = a_0 a_1 \cdots a_n \in P.$$

Note that there are at most $d(X)$ integers n for which p_n is a proper right factor of a word in X. Similarly, there exist at most $d(X)$ integers n such that for all $m \geq 1$,

$$a_{n+1} a_{n+2} \cdots a_{n+m} \in P.$$

Indeed, each such integer n defines an interpretation of each word $a_0 a_1 \cdots a_r$ ($r > n$), which is distinct from the interpretations associated to the other integers.

These observations show that there exists an integer k such that for all $n \geq k$, the following hold: $p_n \in A^*X$ and $a_{n+1}a_{n+2}\cdots a_{n+m} \in X$ for some $m \geq 1$. The first property implies by induction that for all $n \geq k$, there is an integer $i \leq k$ such that $a_i \cdots a_n \in X^*$.

Let $w_l = a_k a_{k+1} \cdots a_{k+l}$ for $l \geq 1$. We show that through each point of w_l passes a K-interpretation. Indeed, let

$$u = a_k a_{k+1} \cdots a_n, \qquad v = a_{n+1} a_{n+2} \cdots a_{k+l}$$

for some $k \leq n \leq k + l$. There exists an integer $i \leq k$ such that $a_i \cdots a_{k-1}$, $u \in X^*$, and there is an integer $m \geq k + l$ such that $va_{k+1} \cdots a_m \in X^*$. In fact, these two words are in $H(X) \cap X^*$ and consequently they are in K^*. This shows that K is a sufficient set and completes the proof. □

The previous proposition yields the following result.

THEOREM 5.5 *Let X' be a finite maximal biprefix code of degree $d-1$ and with kernel K'. For each insufficient subset K of X' containing K', there exists a unique finite maximal biprefix code X of degree d, having kernel K. The derived code of X is X'.*

Proof Since K is insufficient, K is not a maximal biprefix code. Thus $K' \subset K \subsetneq X'$. In view of Theorem 4.6, there is a unique thin maximal biprefix code X of degree d and kernel K. The derived code of X is X'. By Proposition 5.4, the code X is finite. □

The following corollary gives a method for the construction of all finite maximal biprefix codes by increasing degrees.

COROLLARY 5.6 *For any integer $d \geq 2$, the function*

$$X \mapsto K(X)$$

is a bijection of the set of finite maximal biprefix codes of degree d onto the set of all insufficient subsets K of finite maximal biprefix codes X' of degree $d - 1$ such that

$$K(X') \subset K \subsetneq X'. \quad \square$$

EXAMPLE 5.3 Let $A = \{a, b\}$. For each integer $n \geq 0$, there exists a unique finite maximal biprefix code $X_n \subset A^+$ of degree $n + 2$ with kernel

$$K_n = \{a^i b^i \mid 1 \leq i \leq n\}.$$

For $n = 0$, we have $K_0 = \emptyset$ and $X_0 = A^2$. Arguing by induction, assume X_n constructed. Then $K_n \subset X_n$ and also $a^{n+2}, b^{n+2} \in X_n$, since $d(X_n) = n + 2$. We show that $a^{n+1}b^{n+1} \in X_n$. Indeed, no proper left factor of $a^{n+1}b^{n+1}$ is in X_n since each has a right factor in X_n or is a proper right factor of a^{n+2}. Consider now a word $a^{n+1}b^{n+k}$ for a large enough integer k. Since X_n is finite, there is some left factor $a^{n+1}b^{n+r} \in X_n$ for some $r \geq 1$. If $r \geq 2$, then b^{n+2} is a right factor of this word. Thus $r = 1$, and $a^{n+1}b^{n+1} \in X_n$.

Clearly $K_n \subset K_{n+1}$. The set K_{n+1} is insufficient. In fact, a has no K_{n+1} interpretation passing through the point $(a, 1)$ and b has no interpretation passing through the point $(1, b)$. Therefore, the set of full words is $\{1\}$. Finally

$$K_n \subset K_{n+1} \subsetneq X_n.$$

This proves the existence and unicity of X_{n+1}, by using Theorem 5.5.

The code X_1 is the code of degree 3 given in Example 2.2. The code X_2 is the code of degree 4 of Example 5.2.

EXERCISES

SECTION 1

1.1. Let $X \subset A^+$ be a biprefix code and $L = L_X$ its indicator. Show that if for $u, v \in A^*$ we have $(L, uvu) = (L, u)$, then for all $m \geq 0$, $(L, (uv)^m u) = (L, u)$.

Section 2

2.1. Let $X \subset A^+$ be a thin maximal biprefix code. To each word $w \in \bar{F}(X)$, we will associate a function ρ_w from $\{1, 2, \ldots, |w|\}$ into itself. Let

$$w = a_1 a_2 \cdots a_n, \qquad a_i \in A.$$

(a) Show that for each integer i in $\{1, 2, \ldots, n\}$, there exists a unique integer $k \in \{1, 2, \ldots, n\}$ such that either $a_i a_{i+1} \cdots a_k$ or $a_i a_{i+1} \cdots a_n a_1 \cdots a_k$ is in X. Set

$$\rho_w(i) = k.$$

This defines, for each $w \in \bar{F}(X)$, a mapping ρ_w from $\{1, 2, \ldots, |w|\}$ into itself.

(b) Show that X is suffix iff the function ρ_w is injective for all $w \in \bar{F}(X)$.

(c) Show that X is left complete iff the function ρ_w is a surjection for all $w \in \bar{F}(X)$.

(d) Derive from this that a thin maximal prefix code is suffix iff it is left complete (cf. the proof of Proposition 2.1).

2.2. Let $P = \{w\tilde{w} \mid w \in A^*\}$ be the set of *palindrome* words.

(a) Show that P^* is biunitary. Let X be the biprefix code for which $X^* = P^*$. Then X is called the set of *palindrome primes.*

(b) Show that X is left complete and right complete.

2.3. Show that two maximal biprefix codes which are obtained one from the other by internal transformation are either both recognizable or both not recognizable.

Section 3

3.1. Let $P, S \in \mathbb{Z}\langle A \rangle$ be polynomials such that

$$P(1 - \underline{A}) = (1 - \underline{A})S.$$

Show that there exist an integer $d \in \mathbb{Z}$ and a polynomial $Q \in \mathbb{Z}\langle A \rangle$ such that

$$P = (1 - \underline{A})Q + d; \qquad S = Q(1 - \underline{A}) + d$$

(Hint: show for this that if two homogeneous polynomials $P, Q \in \mathbb{Z}\langle A \rangle$ satisfy $P\underline{A} = \underline{A}Q$, then $P = \underline{A}R$, $Q = R\underline{A}$ for some polynomial R.)

3.2. Let X be a thin maximal biprefix code of degree d. Let $w \in \bar{H}(X)$ and let

$$1 = p_1, p_2, \ldots, p_d$$

be those of the right factors of w which are proper left factors of X. Set

$$Y_i = p_i^{-1}X \qquad \text{for} \quad 2 \le i \le d, \quad Y_1 = 1.$$

Show that each Y_i is a maximal suffix set, and that the set S of proper right factors of X is the disjoint union of the Y_i's (cf. Theorem 3.8).

3.3. Let X be a thin maximal biprefix code of degree d and let S be the set of its proper right factors. Show that there exists a unique partition of S into a disjoint union of d prefix sets Y_i satisfying

$$Y_{i-1} \subset Y_i A^- \qquad \text{for} \quad 2 \le i \le d.$$

(Hint: Set $Y_d = S \cap \bar{H}(X)$.)

Section 4

4.1. Let X be a finite biprefix code. Show, using Theorem 4.3, that there exists a recognizable maximal biprefix code containing X.

4.2. Show that if X is a recognizable maximal biprefix code of degree $d \ge 2$, then the derived code is recognizable.

4.3. Let X be a thin maximal biprefix code of degree $d \ge 2$. Let $w \in \bar{H}(X)$, and let s be the longest left factor of w which is a proper right factor of X. Further, let x be the left factor of w which is in X. Show that the shorter one of s and x is in the derived code X'.

4.4. Let X_1 and X_2 be two thin maximal biprefix codes having same kernel: $K(X_1) = K(X_2)$. Set

$$X = X_1 \wedge X_2$$

(cf. Exercise II.4.2). Show that X is thin, maximal and biprefix. Use this to give a direct proof of the fact that two thin maximal biprefix codes with same kernel and same degree are equal.

Section 5

5.1. Let X be a finite maximal biprefix code. Show that if a word $w \in A^+$ satisfies

$$pwq = rws \in X \tag{6.1}$$

for some $p, q, r, s \in A^+$, and $p \ne r$, then $w \in H(X')$, when X' is the derived code of X. (Hint: Start with a longest word satisfying (6.1) and use Proposition 3.7.)

5.2. For a finite code X, let $l(X) = \max\{|x| \mid x \in X\}$. Show, using Exercise 5.1, that if X is a finite maximal biprefix code over a k letter alphabet, then

$$l(X) \le l(X') + k^{l(X')-1}$$

with X' denoting the derived code of X.

Denote by $\lambda(k, d)$ the maximum of the lengths of the words of all finite maximal biprefix codes of degree d over a k letter alphabet. Show that for $d \geq 2$

$$\lambda(k, d) \leq \lambda(k, d-1) + k^{\lambda(k,d-1)-1}.$$

Compare with the bound given by Theorem 5.2.

5.3. Let $X \subset A^+$ be a finite maximal biprefix code of degree d. Let $a, b \in A$, and define a function φ from $\{0, 1, \ldots, d-1\}$ into itself by

$$a^i b^{d-\varphi(i)} \in X.$$

Show that φ is a bijection.

5.4. Show that for each $k \geq 2$, the number $\beta_k(d)$ of finite maximal biprefix codes of degree d over a k letter alphabet is unbounded as a function of d.

5.5. A *quasipower* of order n is defined by induction as follows: a quasipower of order 0 is an unbordered word. A quasipower of order $n+1$ is a word of the form uvu, where u is a quasipower of order n. Let k be an integer and let α_n be the sequence inductively defined by

$$\alpha_1 = k + 1,$$
$$\alpha_{n+1} = \alpha_n(k^{\alpha_n} + 1) \qquad (n \geq 1).$$

Show that any word over a k letter alphabet with length at least equal to α_n has a factor which is a quasipower of order n.

5.6. Let X be a finite maximal biprefix code of degree $d \geq 2$ over a k letter alphabet. Show that

$$\max_{x \in X} |x| \leq \alpha_{d-1} + 2,$$

where (α_n) is the sequence defined in Exercise 5.5. (Hint: Use Exercise 1.1.) Compare with the bound given by Exercise 5.2.

5.7. Show that the number of finite maximal biprefix codes of degree 4 over a two-letter alphabet is

$$\beta_2(4) = 73.$$

NOTES

The idea to study biprefix codes goes back to Schützenberger (1956) and Gilbert and Moore (1959). These papers already contain significant results. The first systematic study is in Schützenberger (1961b,c).

Propositions 2.1 and 2.2 are from Schützenberger (1961c). The internal transformation appears in Schützenberger (1961b). The fact that all finite maximal biprefix codes can be obtained from the uniform codes by internal transformation (Theorem 5.3) is from Césari (1972). The fact that the average length of a thin maximal biprefix code is an integer (Corollary 3.9) is already in Gilbert and Moore (1959). It is proved in Schützenberger (1961b) with the methods developed in Chapter VI. Theorem 3.8 and its converse (Proposition 3.1) appear in Perrin (1977a). The notion of derived code is due to Césari (1979). The presentation of the results given here, using the indicator and the tower, appears to be new.

The results of Section 4 are a generalization to thin codes of results in Césari (1979). The methods of this section are used in Perrin (1982) to prove that any finite biprefix code is contained in a recognizable maximal biprefix code (Exercise 4.1). It is unknown whether any recognizable biprefix code is contained in a recognizable maximal biprefix code.

Theorem 5.2 appears already in Schützenberger (1961b) with a different proof (see Exercise 5.6). The rest of this section is due to Césari (1979). The enumeration of finite maximal biprefix codes over a two-letter alphabet has been pursued by computer. A first program was written in 1975 by C. Precetti using internal transformations. It produced several thousands of them for $d = 5$. In 1984, a program written by M. Léonard using the method of Corollary 5.6 gave the exact number of finite maximal biprefix codes of degree 5 over a two-letter alphabet. This number is 5,056 783.

Exercise 3.1 is a very special case of a result of Cohn called "weak Euclidian algorithm" in Cohn (1971). Exercises 3.3, 4.4, 5.1, and 5.2 are from Césari (1979).

CHAPTER **IV**

Automata

0. INTRODUCTION

In Chapters II and III, we studied special families of codes. We now return to the study of general codes. In the present chapter, we introduce a new technique: unambiguous automata. The main idea is to replace computations on words by computations on paths labeled by words. This is a technique which is well known in formal language theory. It will be used here in a special form related to the characteristic property of codes.

Within this frame, the main fact is the equivalence between codes and unambiguous automata. The uniqueness of paths in unambiguous automata corresponds to the uniqueness of factorizations for a code. Unambiguous automata appear to be a generalization of deterministic automata in the same manner as the notion of a code extends the notion of a prefix code.

To each unambiguous automaton corresponds a monoid of relations which is also called unambiguous. A relation in this monoid corresponds to each word and the computations on words are replaced by computations on relations.

The principal result of this chapter (Theorem 5.1) shows that very thin codes are exactly the codes for which the associated monoid satisfies a finiteness condition: it contains relations of finite rank. This result explains why thin codes constitute a natural family containing the recognizable codes. It makes it possible to prove properties of thin codes by reasoning in finite structures. As a consequence, we shall give, for example, an alternative proof of the maximality of thin complete codes which does not use measures.

The main result also allows us to define, for each thin code, some important parameters: the degree and the group of the code. The group of a thin code is a finite permutation group. The degree of the code is the number of elements on which this group acts. These parameters reflect properties of words by means of "interpretations." For example, the synchronous codes in the sense of Chapter II are those having degree 1.

One of the applications of the notions introduced in this chapter is the proof of the theorem on the synchronization of semaphore codes announced in Chapter II. A direct combinatorial proof of this result would certainly be extremely difficult.

This chapter is organized in the following manner. In the first section, the notion of unambiguous automaton is introduced. The basic result on the correspondence between codes and unambiguous automata is Proposition 1.5.

In the second section, we study various types of unambiguous automata which can be associated with a code. In particular, the flower automaton is defined and it is shown that this is some kind of universal automaton in the sense that any unambiguous automaton associated with a code can be obtained by a reduction of the flower automaton of this code. We also show how to decompose the flower automaton of the composition of two codes.

In Section 3, basic properties of unambiguous monoids of relations are proved. These monoids constantly appear in the sequel, since each unambiguous automaton gives rise to an unambiguous monoid of relations. In particular, we define two representations of unambiguous monoids of relations, called the $\mathscr{R}$- and $\mathscr{L}$-representations. These representations are relative to a fixed idempotent chosen in the monoid, and they describe the way the elements of the monoid act by right or left multiplication on the $\mathscr{R}$-class and the $\mathscr{L}$-class of the idempotent.

The notion of rank of a relation is defined in Section 4. The most important result in this section states that the minimal ideal of an unambiguous monoid of relations is formed of the relations having minimal rank, provided that rank is finite (Theorem 4.5). Moreover, in this case the minimal ideal has a well-organized structure.

In Section 5 we return to codes. We define the notion of a very thin code which is a refinement of the notion of thin code. The two notions coincide for a complete code. Then we prove the fundamental theorem: A code X is very thin iff the associated unambiguous monoid of relations contains elements of finite positive rank (Theorem 5.1). Several consequences of this result on the structure of codes are given.

Section 6 contains the definition of the group and the degree of a code. The definition is given through the flower automaton, and then it is shown that it is independent of the automaton considered. We also show how the degree may be expressed in terms of interpretations of words. Then synchronous codes are defined, and it is shown that these are the codes with degree 1. We prove then that the composition of codes corresponds to a classical operation on their groups. The case of prefix codes is studied in some more detail.

In Section 7, we give the proof of the theorem on the synchronization of semaphore codes (Theorem 7.1) which has been mentioned in Chapter II (Theorem II.6.5).

1. AUTOMATA

Let A be an alphabet. Recall from Section 0.4 that an *automaton* over A

$$\mathscr{A} = (Q, I, T)$$

consists of a set Q of *states*, of two subsets I and T of Q called sets of *initial* and *terminal* states, respectively, and of a set

$$\mathscr{F} \subset Q \times A \times Q$$

whose elements are called *edges*. An edge

$$f = (p, a, q)$$

is also denoted by

$$f: \quad p \xrightarrow{a} q.$$

The letter $a \in A$ is called the *label* of the edge.

A *path* in $\mathscr{A}$ is a finite sequence

$$c = c_1 c_2 \cdots c_n$$

of consecutive edges $c_i: p_i \xrightarrow{a_i} q_i$ (i.e., such that $q_i = p_{i+1}$ for $1 \le i \le n-1$). We shall also write

$$c: \quad p_1 \xrightarrow{w} q_n,$$

where

$$w = a_1 a_2 \cdots a_n$$

is the *label* of the path c. The path is said to start at p_1 and end at q_n. The length of the path is the number n of edges which compose it. For each state $q \in Q$, we introduce also the *null path* beginning and ending at q, denoted by $1_q: q \to q$. Its length is 0, and its label is $1 \in A^*$.

With each automaton $\mathscr{A} = (Q, I, T)$ over A is associated a function denoted by $\varphi_{\mathscr{A}}$ (or φ for short, if the context allows it)

$$\varphi: \quad A \to \mathscr{N}^{Q \times Q}$$

defined by

$$(p, \varphi(a), q) = \begin{cases} 1 & \text{if} \quad (p, a, q) \in \mathscr{F}, \\ 0 & \text{otherwise.} \end{cases}$$

This function extends into a morphism, still denoted φ, from A^* into the monoid $\mathscr{N}^{Q \times Q}$ of $\mathscr{N}$-relation over Q (see Section 0.6). In particular, we have

$$\varphi(1) = I_Q,$$

and for $u, v \in A^*$

$$(p, \varphi(uv), q) = \sum_{r \in Q} (p, \varphi(u), r)(r, \varphi(v), q).$$

The morphism $\varphi = \varphi_{\mathscr{A}}$ is called the *representation associated* with $\mathscr{A}$.

PROPOSITION 1.1 *Let $\mathscr{A} = (Q, I, T)$ be an automaton over A. For all $p, q \in Q$ and $w \in A^*$, $(p, \varphi_{\mathscr{A}}(w), q)$ is the (possibly infinite) number of paths from p to q with label w.* □

An automaton $\mathscr{A} = (Q, I, T)$ over A is *unambiguous* if for all $p, q \in Q$ and $w \in A^*$,

$$(p, \varphi_{\mathscr{A}}(w), q) \in \{0, 1\}.$$

Thus an automaton is unambiguous iff for all $p q \in Q$ and $w \in A^*$, there is at most one path from p to q with label w.

A path $c: i \to t$ is called *successful* if $i \in I$ and $t \in T$. The *behavior* of the automaton $\mathscr{A} = (Q, I, T)$ is the formal power series $|\mathscr{A}|$ defined by

$$(|\mathscr{A}|, w) = \sum_{\substack{i \in I \\ t \in T}} (i, \varphi_{\mathscr{A}}(w), t). \tag{1.1}$$

The set *recognized* by $\mathscr{A}$ is the support of $|\mathscr{A}|$. It is just the set of all labels of successful paths. It is denoted by $L(\mathscr{A})$, as in Section 0.4.

PROPOSITION 1.2 *Let $\mathscr{A} = (Q, I, T)$ be an automaton over A. For all $w \in A^*$, $(|\mathscr{A}|, w)$ is the (possibly infinite) number of successful paths labeled by w.* □

A more compact writing of formula 1.1 consists in

$$(|\mathscr{A}|, w) = I\varphi(w)\, T. \tag{1.2}$$

Here, the element $I \in \mathscr{N}^Q$ is considered as a row vector and $T \in \mathscr{N}^Q$ as a column vector.

EXAMPLE 1.1 Let $\mathscr{A}$ be the automaton given by Fig. 4.1, with $I = T = \{1\}$. Its behavior is the series

$$|\mathscr{A}| = \sum_{n \geq 0} f_n a^n,$$

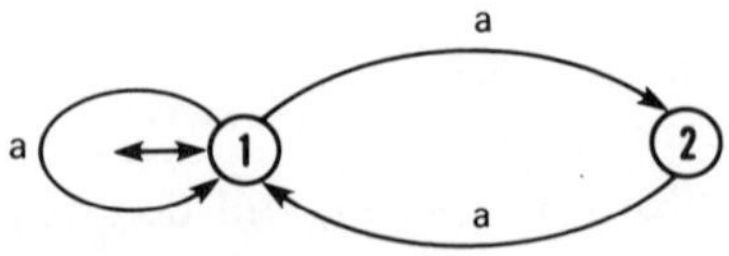

Fig. 4.1 The Fibonacci automaton.

where f_n is the nth Fibonacci number. These numbers are defined by

$$f_0 = f_1 = 1,$$
$$f_{n+1} = f_n + f_{n-1}, \qquad n \geq 1.$$

For $n \geq 1$, we have

$$\varphi_{\mathscr{A}}(a^n) = \begin{bmatrix} f_n & f_{n-1} \\ f_{n-1} & f_{n-2} \end{bmatrix},$$

with $f_{-1} = 0$.

Let $\mathscr{A} = (Q, I, T)$ be an automaton. A state $q \in Q$ is *accessible* (resp., *coaccessible*) if there exists a path $c: i \to q$ with $i \in I$ (resp., a path $c: q \to t$ with $t \in T$). An automaton is *trim* if all states are both accessible and coaccessible.

The *trim part* of $\mathscr{A} = (Q, I, T)$ is the automaton

$$\mathscr{A}^0 = (P, I \cap P, T \cap P),$$

which is the restriction of $\mathscr{A}$ to the set P of states of $\mathscr{A}$ which are both accessible and coaccessible. It is easily seen that

$$|\mathscr{A}^0| = |\mathscr{A}|.$$

PROPOSITION 1.3 *Let $\mathscr{A} = (Q, i, t)$ be a trim automaton with a unique initial and a unique final state. Then $\mathscr{A}$ is unambiguous iff $|\mathscr{A}|$ is a characteristic series.*

Proof If $\mathscr{A}$ is unambiguous, then clearly $|\mathscr{A}|$ is a characteristic series. Conversely, if

$$(p, \varphi_{\mathscr{A}}(w), q) \geq 2$$

for some $p, q \in Q$ and $w \in A^*$, then choosing paths $i \xrightarrow{u} p$ and $q \xrightarrow{v} t$, we have

$$(|\mathscr{A}|, uwv) \geq 2. \quad \square$$

If $\mathscr{A}$ is an unambiguous automaton, we usually identify the series $|\mathscr{A}|$ with the set $L(\mathscr{A})$ recognized by $\mathscr{A}$.

To each automaton $\mathscr{A} = (Q, I, T)$, we associate an automaton $\mathscr{A}^*$ by a canonical construction consisting of the two following steps. Let $\omega \notin Q$ be a new state, and let

$$\mathscr{B} = (Q \cup \omega, \omega, \omega) \tag{1.3}$$

be the automaton with edges

$$\mathscr{G} = \mathscr{F} \cup \mathscr{I} \cup \mathscr{T} \cup \mathscr{O}$$

where $\mathscr{F}$ is the set of edges of $\mathscr{A}$, and

$$\mathscr{I} = \{(\omega, a, q) \mid \exists i \in I : (i, a, q) \in \mathscr{F}\}, \tag{1.4}$$

$$\mathscr{T} = \{(q, a, \omega) \mid \exists t \in T : (q, a, t) \in \mathscr{F}\}, \tag{1.5}$$

$$\mathscr{O} = \{(\omega, a, \omega) \mid \exists i \in I, t \in T : (i, a, t) \in \mathscr{F}\}. \tag{1.6}$$

By definition, the automaton $\mathscr{A}^*$ is the trim part of $\mathscr{B}$.

PROPOSITION 1.4 *Let $X \subset A^+$, and let $\mathscr{B}$ be an automaton such that $|\mathscr{A}| = \underline{X}$. Then*

$$|\mathscr{A}^*| = (\underline{X})^*. \tag{1.7}$$

Proof Since $\mathscr{A}^*$ is the trim part of the automaton $\mathscr{A}$ defined by formula 1.3, it suffices to show that $|\mathscr{B}| = |\mathscr{A}|^*$.

A path $c: \omega \to \omega$ in $\mathscr{B}$ is called *simple* if it is not the null path, and if no interior node is equal to ω. Each path $c: \omega \to \omega$ is a product, in a unique manner, of simple paths from ω to ω.

Let S be the power series defined as follows: for all $w \in A^*$, (S, w) is the number of simple paths from ω to ω labeled with w. By the preceding remarks, we have

$$|\mathscr{B}| = S^*.$$

Thus it remains to prove that

$$S = \underline{X}.$$

Let $w \in A^*$. If $w = 1$, then

$$(S, 1) = (\underline{X}, 1) = 0,$$

since a simple path is not null. If $w = a \in A$, then $(S, a) = 1$ iff $a \in X$, according to formula (1.6). Assume now $|w| \geq 2$. Set $w = aub$ with $a, b \in A$ and $u \in A^*$. Each simple path $c: \omega \xrightarrow{w} \omega$ factorizes uniquely into

$$c: \quad \omega \xrightarrow{a} p \xrightarrow{u} q \xrightarrow{b} \omega$$

for some $p, q \in Q$. There exists at least one successful path

$$i \xrightarrow{a} p \xrightarrow{u} q \xrightarrow{b} t$$

in $\mathscr{A}$. This path is unique because the behavior of $\mathscr{A}$ is a characteristic series. If there is another simple path $c': \omega \xrightarrow{w} \omega$ in $\mathscr{B}$, then there is also another successful path labeled w in $\mathscr{A}$; this is impossible. Thus there is at most one simple path $c: \omega \xrightarrow{w} \omega$ in $\mathscr{B}$ and such a path exists iff $w \in X$. Consequently, $S = \underline{X}$, which was to be proved. □

EXAMPLE 1.2 Let $X = \{a, a^2\}$. Then $\underline{X} = |\mathscr{A}|$ for the automaton given in Fig. 4.2, with $I = \{1\}$, $T = \{3\}$. The automaton $\mathscr{A}^*$ is the automaton of Fig. 4.1 up to a renaming of ω. Consequently, for $n \geq 0$

$$((\underline{X})^*, a^n) = f_n.$$

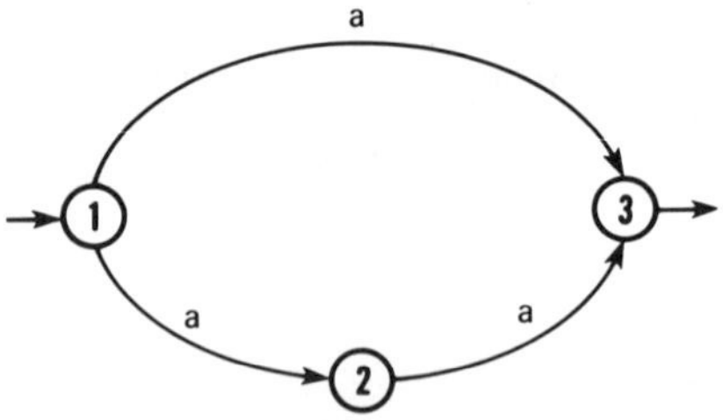

Fig. 4.2

EXAMPLE 1.3 Let $X = \{aa, ba, baa, bb, bba\}$. We have $\underline{X} = |\mathscr{A}|$ for the automaton $\mathscr{A}$ of Fig. 4.3, with $I = \{1\}$, $T = \{4\}$. The corresponding automaton $\mathscr{A}^*$ is given in Fig. 4.4.

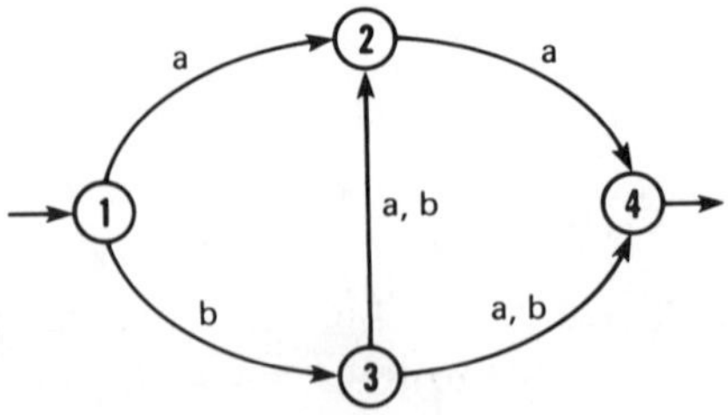

Fig. 4.3

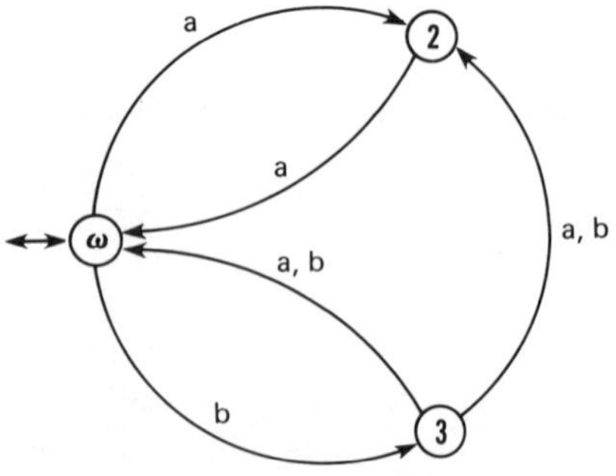

Fig. 4.4

PROPOSITION 1.5 *Let $X \subset A^+$ and let $\mathscr{A}$ be an automaton such that $|\mathscr{A}| = \underline{X}$. Then X is a code iff $\mathscr{A}^*$ is unambiguous.*

Proof According to Proposition 1.4, we have $|\mathscr{A}^*| = (\underline{X})^*$. Since $\mathscr{A}$ is trim, Proposition 1.3 shows that $\mathscr{A}^*$ is unambiguous iff $|\mathscr{A}^*|$ is a characteristic series. Since $L(\mathscr{A}) = X^*$, this means that $\mathscr{A}^*$ is unambiguous iff $\underline{X}^* = (\underline{X})^*$. Thus we get the proposition from Proposition I.6.1. □

In view of Proposition 1.5, we can determine whether a set X given by an unambiguous automaton $\mathscr{A}$ is a code, by computing $\mathscr{A}^*$ and testing whether $\mathscr{A}^*$ is unambiguous. For doing this, we may use the following method.

Let $\mathscr{A} = (Q, I, T)$ be an automaton over A. Define the *square* of $\mathscr{A}$

$$\mathscr{S}(\mathscr{A}) = (Q \times Q, I \times I, T \times T)$$

by defining

$$(p_1, p_2) \xrightarrow{a} (q_1, q_2)$$

to be an edge of $\mathscr{S}(\mathscr{A})$ iff

$$p_1 \xrightarrow{a} q_1 \qquad \text{and} \qquad p_2 \xrightarrow{a} q_2$$

to be an edge of $\mathscr{S}(\mathscr{A})$ iff

PROPOSITION 1.6 *An automaton $\mathscr{A} = (Q, I, T)$ is unambiguous iff there is no path in $\mathscr{S}(\mathscr{A})$ of the form*

$$(p, p) \xrightarrow{u} (r, s) \xrightarrow{v} (q, q) \tag{1.8}$$

with $r \neq s$.

Proof The existence of a path of the form (1.8) in $\mathscr{S}(\mathscr{A})$ is equivalent to the existence of the pair of paths

$$p \xrightarrow{u} r \xrightarrow{v} q \qquad \text{and} \qquad p \xrightarrow{u} s \xrightarrow{v} q$$

with the same label uv in $\mathscr{A}$. □

To decide whether a recognizable set X (given by an unambiguous finite automaton) is a code, it suffices to compute $\mathscr{A}^*$ and to test whether $\mathscr{A}^*$ is unambiguous by inspecting the finite automaton $\mathscr{S}(\mathscr{A}^*)$, looking for paths of the form (1.8).

EXAMPLE 1.4 Consider again the automaton $\mathscr{A}^*$ of Example 1.3 (Fig. 4.4). The automaton $\mathscr{S}(\mathscr{A}^*)$ is given in Fig. 4.5, where only the part accessible from the states (q, q) is drawn. It shows that $\mathscr{A}^*$ is unambiguous.

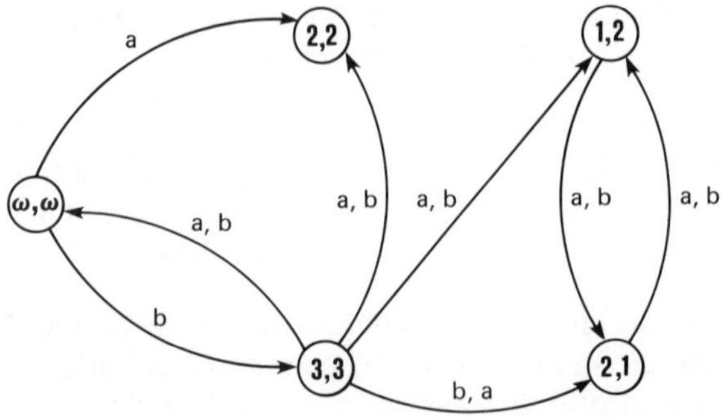

Fig. 4.5 Part of the square of the automaton of Fig. 4.4.

The following proposition is the converse of Proposition 1.5.

PROPOSITION 1.7 *Let $\mathscr{A} = (Q, 1, 1)$ be an unambiguous automaton over A with a single initial and final state. Then its behavior $|\mathscr{A}|$ is the characteristic series of some free submonoid of A^*.*

Proof Let $M \subset A^*$ be such that $|\mathscr{A}| = \underline{M}$. Clearly the set M is a submonoid of A^*. We shall prove that M is a stable submonoid. For this, suppose that

$$u, wv, uw, v \in M.$$

Then there exist in $\mathscr{A}$ paths

$$1 \xrightarrow{u} 1, \qquad 1 \xrightarrow{wv} 1, \qquad 1 \xrightarrow{uw} 1, \quad 1 \xrightarrow{v} 1.$$

The two middle paths factorize as

$$1 \xrightarrow{w} p \xrightarrow{v} 1, \qquad 1 \xrightarrow{u} q \xrightarrow{w} 1$$

for some $p, q \in Q$. Thus there exist two paths

$$1 \xrightarrow{u} 1 \xrightarrow{w} p \xrightarrow{v} 1$$

$$1 \xrightarrow{u} q \xrightarrow{w} 1 \xrightarrow{v} 1.$$

Since $\mathscr{A}$ is unambiguous, these paths coincide, whence $1 = p = q$. Consequently $w \in M$. Thus M is stable, and by Proposition I.2.4, M is free. $\square$

The following terminology is convenient for automata of the form $\mathscr{A} = (Q, 1, 1)$ having just one initial state which is also the unique final state.

A path

$$c\colon \quad p \xrightarrow{w} q$$

is called *simple* if it is not the null path (i.e., $w \in A^+$) and if for any factorization

$$c: \quad p \xrightarrow{u} r \xrightarrow{v} q$$

of the path c into two nonnull paths, we have $r \neq 1$. We have already used, in the proof of Proposition 1.4, the fact that each path from 1 to 1 decomposes in a unique manner into a product of simple paths from 1 to 1. More generally, any path c from p to q either is the null path, is simple, or decomposes in a unique manner as

$$c: \quad p \xrightarrow{u} 1 \xrightarrow{x_1} 1 \xrightarrow{x_2} 1 \cdots 1 \xrightarrow{x_n} 1 \xrightarrow{v} q,$$

where each of these $n + 2$ paths is simple.

We end this section by showing how to test (by means of an automaton) whether a code is complete.

PROPOSITION 1.8 *Let $X \subset A^+$ be a code, and let $\mathscr{A} = (Q, 1, 1)$ be an unambiguous trim automaton recognizing X^*. Then X is complete iff the monoid $\varphi_{\mathscr{A}}(A^*)$ does not contain the null relation.*

Proof If X is complete, then there exist, for each $w \in A^*$, two words $u, v \in A^*$ such that $uwv \in X^*$. Then there exists a path

$$1 \xrightarrow{u} p \xrightarrow{w} q \xrightarrow{v} 1,$$

and consequently $\varphi_{\mathscr{A}}(w)$ is not null.

Conversely, if $\varphi_{\mathscr{A}}(A^*)$ does not contain the null relation, then for each $w \in A^*$, there exists at least one path $p \xrightarrow{w} q$. Since $\mathscr{A}$ is trim, there exist two paths $1 \xrightarrow{u} p$ and $q \xrightarrow{v} 1$. Then $uwv \in X^*$. Thus X is complete. □

2. FLOWER AUTOMATON

We describe in this section the construction of a "universal" automaton recognizing a submonoid of A^*.

Let X be an arbitrary subset of A^+. We define an automaton

$$\mathscr{A}_D(X) = (Q, I, T)$$

by

$$Q = \{(u, v) \in A^* \times A^* \mid uv \in X\},$$

$$I = 1 \times X, \qquad T = X \times 1,$$

with edges

$$(u, v) \xrightarrow{a} (u', v')$$

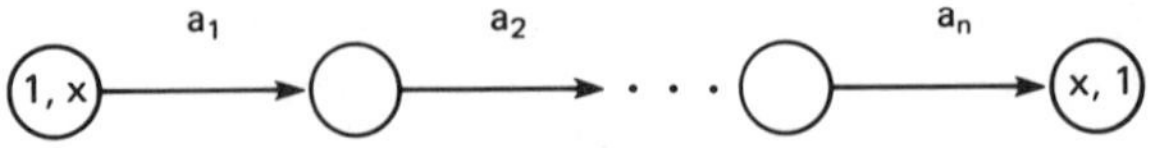

Fig. 4.6 The edges of $\mathscr{A}_D(X)$ for $x = a_1 a_2 \cdots a_n$.

iff $ua = u'$ and $v = av'$. In other words, the edges of $\mathscr{A}_D$ are

$$(u, av) \xrightarrow{a} (ua, v), \qquad uav \in X.$$

It is equivalent to say that the set of edges of the automaton $\mathscr{A}_D$ is the disjoint union of the sets of edges given by Fig. 4.6 for each $x = a_1 a_2 \cdots a_n$ in X. The automaton $\mathscr{A}_D(X)$ is unambiguous and recognizes X, i.e.,

$$|\mathscr{A}_D(X)| = \underline{X}.$$

The *flower automaton* of X is by definition the automaton $(\mathscr{A}_D(X))^*$ obtained from $\mathscr{A}_D(X)$ by applying the construction described in Section 1, [formulas (1.4)–(1.6)]. It is denoted by $\mathscr{A}_D^*(X)$ rather than $(\mathscr{A}_D(X))^*$. We denote by φ_D the associated representation. Thus, following the construction of Section 1, the automaton $\mathscr{A}_D^*(X)$ is obtained in two steps as follows. Starting with $\mathscr{A}_D(X)$, we add a new state ω, and the edges

$$\begin{aligned} \omega &\xrightarrow{a} (a, v) && \text{for} \quad av \in X, \\ (u, a) &\xrightarrow{a} \omega && \text{for} \quad ua \in X, \\ \omega &\xrightarrow{a} \omega && \text{for} \quad a \in X. \end{aligned}$$

This automaton is now trimmed. The states in $1 \times X$ and $X \times 1$ are no longer accessible or coaccessible and consequently disappear. Usually, the state ω is denoted by $(1, 1)$. Then $\mathscr{A}_D^*(X)$ takes the form

$$\mathscr{A}_D^*(X) = (P, (1, 1), (1, 1))$$

with

$$P = \{(u, v) \in A^+ \times A^+ \mid uv \in X\} \cup \{(1, 1)\},$$

and there are four types of edges

$$\begin{aligned} (u, av) &\xrightarrow{a} (ua, v) && \text{for} \quad uav \in X, \quad (u, v) \neq (1, 1), \\ (1, 1) &\xrightarrow{a} (a, v) && \text{for} \quad av \in X, \quad v \neq 1, \\ (u, a) &\xrightarrow{a} (1, 1) && \text{for} \quad ua \in X, \quad u \neq 1, \\ (1, 1) &\xrightarrow{a} (1, 1) && \text{for} \quad a \in X. \end{aligned}$$

The terminology is inspired by the graphical representation of this automaton. Indeed each word $x \in X$ defines a simple path

$$(1,1) \xrightarrow{x} (1,1)$$

in $\mathscr{A}_D^*(X)$. If $x = a \in A$, it is the edge

$$(1,1) \xrightarrow{a} (1,1).$$

If $x = a_1 a_2 \cdots a_n$ with $n \geq 2$, it is the path

$$(1,1) \xrightarrow{a_1} (a_1, a_2 \cdots a_n) \xrightarrow{a_2} (a_1 a_2, a_3 \cdots a_n) \longrightarrow \cdots \xrightarrow{a_n} (1,1).$$

EXAMPLE 2.1 Let $X = \{aa, ba, bb, baa, bba\}$. The flower automaton is given in Fig. 4.7.

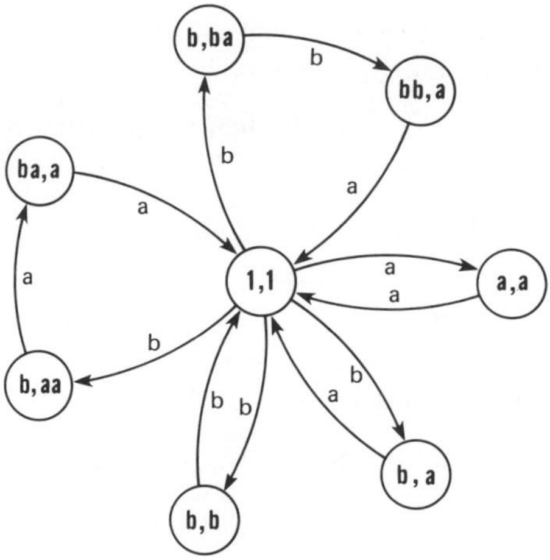

Fig. 4.7 The flower automaton of X.

THEOREM 2.1 *Let X be a subset of A^+. The following conditions are equivalent*:

(i) *X is a code.*

(ii) *For any unambiguous automaton $\mathscr{A}$ recognizing X, the automaton $\mathscr{A}^*$ is unambiguous.*

(iii) *The flower automaton $\mathscr{A}_D^*(X)$ is unambiguous.*

(iv) *There exists an unambiguous automaton $\mathscr{A} = (Q, 1, 1)$ recognizing X^* and X is the minimal set of generators of X^*.*

Proof (i) $\Rightarrow$ (ii) is Proposition 1.5. The implication (ii) $\Rightarrow$ (iii) is clear. To prove (iii) $\Rightarrow$ (iv) it suffices to show that X is the minimal generating set of X^*. Assume the contrary, and let $x \in X$, $y, z \in X^+$ be words such that $x = yz$. Then there exists in $\mathscr{A}_D^*(X)$ a simple path $(1,1) \xrightarrow{x} (1,1)$ and a path $(1,1) \xrightarrow{y} (1,1) \xrightarrow{z} (1,1)$ which is also labeled by x. These paths are distinct, so $\mathscr{A}_D^*(X)$ is ambiguous. (iv) ⇒ (i) By Proposition 1.7, X^* is free; thus X is a code. □

We shall now describe explicitly the paths in the flower automaton of a code X.

Proposition 2.2 *Let $X \subset A^+$ be a code. The following conditions are equivalent for all words $w \in A^*$ and all states (u, v), (u', v') in the automaton $\mathscr{A}_D^*(X)$:*

(i) *There exists in $\mathscr{A}_D^*(X)$ a path*

$$c: \quad (u, v) \xrightarrow{w} (u', v'),$$

(ii) $w \in vX^*u'$ *or* ($uw = u'$ *and* $v = wv'$),
(iii) $uw \in X^*u'$ *and* $wv' \in vX^*$.

Proof (i) ⇒ (ii) If c is a simple path, then it is a path in $\mathscr{A}_D$. Consequently, $uw = u'$ and $v = wv'$ (Fig. 4.8(a)). Otherwise c decomposes into

$$c: \quad (u, v) \xrightarrow{v} (1,1) \xrightarrow{x} (1,1) \xrightarrow{v'} (u', v')$$

with $w = vxu'$ and $x \in X^*$ (Fig. 4.8(b)).

(ii) ⇒ (iii) If $w \in vX^*u'$, then $uw \in uvX^*u' \subset X^*u'$ and $w \in vX^*u'v' \subset vX^*$, since $uv, u'v' \in X \cup 1$. If $uw = u'$ and $v = wv'$, then the formulas are clear.

(iii) ⇒ (i) By hypothesis, there exist $x, y \in X^*$ such that

$$uw = xu', \qquad wv' = vy.$$

Let $z = uwv'$. Then

$$z = uwv' = xu'v' = uvy \in X^*.$$

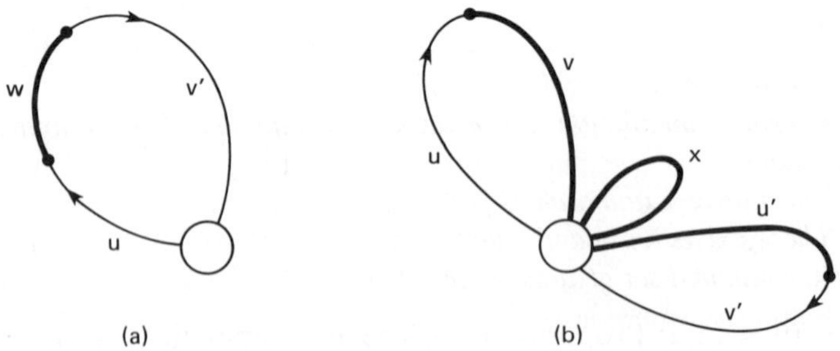

Fig. 4.8 Paths in the flower automaton.

Each of these three factorizations determines a path in $\mathscr{A}_D^*(X)$:

$$c:\quad (1,1) \xrightarrow{u} (\bar{u},\bar{v}) \xrightarrow{w} (\bar{u}',\bar{v}') \xrightarrow{v'} (1,1),$$

$$c':\quad (1,1) \xrightarrow{x} (1,1) \xrightarrow{u'} (u',v') \xrightarrow{v'} (1,1),$$

$$c'':\quad (1,1) \xrightarrow{u} (u,v) \xrightarrow{v} (1,1) \xrightarrow{y} (1,1).$$

(The paths $(1,1) \xrightarrow{u} (u,v) \xrightarrow{v} (1,1)$ and $(1,1) \xrightarrow{u'} (u',v') \xrightarrow{v'} (1,1)$ may have length 0.) Since X is a code, the automaton $\mathscr{A}_D^*(X)$ is unambiguous and consequently $c = c' = c''$. We obtain that $(u,v) = (\bar{u},\bar{v})$ and $(\bar{u}',\bar{v}') = (u',v')$. Thus

$$(u,v) \xrightarrow{w} (u',v'). \quad \square$$

The flower automaton of a code has "many" states. In particular, the flower automaton of an infinite code is infinite, even though there exist finite unambiguous automata recognizing X^* when the code X is recognizable. We shall show that in some sense which will be made more precise now, $\mathscr{A}_D^*(X)$ is universal among the automata recognizing X^*.

Consider two unambiguous automata

$$\mathscr{A} = (P, 1, 1) \qquad \text{and} \qquad \mathscr{B} = (Q, 1, 1)$$

and their associated representations $\varphi_{\mathscr{A}}$ and $\varphi_{\mathscr{B}}$. A function

$$\rho: \quad P \to Q$$

is a *reduction of* $\mathscr{A}$ onto $\mathscr{B}$ if it is surjective, $\rho(1) = 1$ and if, for all $w \in A^*$,

$$(q, \varphi_{\mathscr{B}}(w), q') = 1$$

iff there exist $p, p' \in P$ with

$$(p, \varphi_{\mathscr{A}}(w), p') = 1, \qquad \rho(p) = q, \quad \rho(p') = q'.$$

The definition means that if $p \xrightarrow{w} p'$ is a path in $\mathscr{A}$, then $\rho(p) \xrightarrow{w} \rho(p')$ is a path in $\mathscr{B}$. Conversely, a path $q \xrightarrow{w} q'$ can be "lifted" in some path $p \xrightarrow{w} p'$ with $p \in \rho^{-1}(q)$, $p' \in \rho^{-1}(q')$.

Another way to see the definition is the following. The matrix $\varphi_{\mathscr{B}}(w)$ can be obtained from $\varphi_{\mathscr{A}}(w)$ by partitioning the latter into blocs indexed by a pair of classes of the equivalence defined by ρ, and then by replacing null blocs by 0, and nonnull blocs by 1.

Observe that if ρ is a reduction of $\mathscr{A}$ onto $\mathscr{B}$, then for all $w, w' \in A^*$, the following implication holds:

$$\varphi_{\mathscr{A}}(w) = \varphi_{\mathscr{A}}(w') \quad \Rightarrow \quad \varphi_{\mathscr{B}}(w) = \varphi_{\mathscr{B}}(w').$$

Thus there exists a unique morphism

$$\hat{\rho}: \quad \varphi_{\mathscr{A}}(A^*) \to \varphi_{\mathscr{B}}(A^*)$$

such that

$$\varphi_{\mathscr{B}} = \hat{\rho} \circ \varphi_{\mathscr{A}}.$$

The morphism $\hat{\rho}$ is called the morphism associated with the reduction ρ.

PROPOSITION 2.3 *Let $\mathscr{A} = (P, 1, 1)$ and $\mathscr{B} = (Q, 1, 1)$ be two unambiguous trim automata. Then there exists at most one reduction of $\mathscr{A}$ onto $\mathscr{B}$. If $\rho: P \to Q$ is a reduction, then*

1. $|\mathscr{A}| \subset |\mathscr{B}|$,
2. $|\mathscr{A}| = |\mathscr{B}|$ *iff* $\rho^{-1}(1) = 1$.

Proof Let $\rho, \rho': P \to Q$ be two reductions of $\mathscr{A}$ onto $\mathscr{B}$. Let $p \in P$, and let $q = \rho(p)$, $q' = \rho'(p)$. Let $u, v \in A^*$ be words such that $1 \xrightarrow{u} p \xrightarrow{v} 1$ in the automaton $\mathscr{A}$. Then we have, in the automaton $\mathscr{B}$, the paths

$$1 \xrightarrow{u} q \xrightarrow{v} 1, \qquad 1 \xrightarrow{u} q' \xrightarrow{v} 1.$$

Since $\mathscr{B}$ is unambiguous, $q = q'$. Thus $\rho = \rho'$.

1. If $w \in |\mathscr{A}|$, there exists a path $1 \xrightarrow{w} 1$ in $\mathscr{A}$; thus there is a path $1 \xrightarrow{w} 1$ in $\mathscr{B}$. Consequently $v \in |\mathscr{B}|$.

2. Let $w \in |\mathscr{B}|$. Then there is a path $p \xrightarrow{w} p'$ in $\mathscr{A}$ with $\rho(p) = \rho(p') = 1$. If $1 = \rho^{-1}(1)$, then this is a successful path in $\mathscr{A}$ and $w \in |\mathscr{A}|$. Conversely, let $p \neq 1$. Let $1 \xrightarrow{u} p \xrightarrow{v} 1$ be a simple path in $\mathscr{A}$. Then $uv \in X$, where X is the base of $|\mathscr{A}|$. Now in $\mathscr{B}$, we have $1 \xrightarrow{u} \rho(p) \xrightarrow{v} 1$. Since $|\mathscr{B}| = |\mathscr{A}|$, we have $\rho(p) \neq 1$. Thus $\rho^{-1}(1) = 1$. □

PROPOSITION 2.4 *Let $X \subset A^+$ be a code, and let $\mathscr{A}_D^*(X)$ be its flower automaton. For each unambiguous trim automaton $\mathscr{A}$ recognizing X^*, there exists a reduction of $\mathscr{A}_D^*(X)$ onto $\mathscr{A}$.*

Proof Let $\mathscr{A}_D^*(X) = (P, (1, 1), (1, 1))$ and $\mathscr{A} = (Q, 1, 1)$. Define a function

$$\rho: \quad P \to Q$$

as follows. Let $p = (u, v) \in P$. If $p = (1, 1)$, then set $\rho(p) = 1$. Otherwise $uv \in X$, and there exists a unique path

$$c: \quad 1 \xrightarrow{u} q \xrightarrow{v} 1 \qquad \text{in} \quad \mathscr{A}.$$

Then set $\rho(p) = q$.

The function ρ is surjective. Let indeed $q \in Q$, $q \neq 1$. Let

$$c_1: \quad 1 \xrightarrow{u} q, \qquad c_2: \quad q \xrightarrow{v} 1$$

be two simple paths in $\mathscr{A}$. Then $uv \in X$, and $p = (u, v) \in P$ satisfies $\rho(p) = q$.

We now verify that ρ is a reduction. For this, assume first that for a word $w \in A^*$, and $q, q' \in Q$,

$$(q, \varphi_{\mathscr{A}}(w), q') = 1.$$

Consider two simple paths in $\mathscr{A}$, $e: 1 \xrightarrow{u} q$, $e': q' \xrightarrow{v'} 1$. Then in $\mathscr{A}$, there is a path

$$1 \xrightarrow{u} q \xrightarrow{w} q' \xrightarrow{v'} 1.$$

Consequently $uwv' \in X^*$. Thus for some $x_i \in X$, $uwv' = x_1 x_2 \cdots x_n$. Since e is simple, u is a left factor of x_1, and similarly v' is a right factor of x_n. Setting

$$x_1 = uv, \qquad x_n = u'v',$$

we have

$$uwv' = uvx_2 \cdots x_n = x_1 \cdots x_{n-1} u'v',$$

whence

$$uw \in X^*u', \qquad wv' \in uX^*.$$

In view of Proposition 2.2, $((u, v), \varphi_D(w), (u', v')) = 1$.

Suppose now conversely that

$$(p, \varphi_D(w), p') = 1 \tag{2.1}$$

for some $p = (u, v)$, $p' = (u', v')$, and $w \in A^*$. Let $q = \rho(p)$, $q' = \rho(p')$. By construction, there are in $\mathscr{A}$ paths

$$1 \xrightarrow{u} q \xrightarrow{v} 1 \quad \text{and} \quad 1 \xrightarrow{u'} q' \xrightarrow{v'} 1 \tag{2.2}$$

In view of Proposition 2.2, formula (2.1) is equivalent to

$$(uw = u' \quad \text{and} \quad v = wv') \quad \text{or} \quad (w = vxu' \quad \text{for some} \quad x \in X^*).$$

In the first case, $uv = uwv' = u'v'$. Thus the two paths (2.2) coincide, giving the path in $\mathscr{A}$,

$$1 \xrightarrow{u} q \xrightarrow{w} q' \xrightarrow{v'} 1.$$

In the second case, there is in $\mathscr{A}$ a path

$$q \xrightarrow{v} 1 \xrightarrow{x} 1 \xrightarrow{u'} q'.$$

Thus, $(q, \varphi_{\mathscr{A}}(w), q') = 1$ in both cases. □

EXAMPLE 2.2 For the code $X = \{aa, ba, bb, baa, bba\}$, the flower automaton is given in Fig. 4.9.

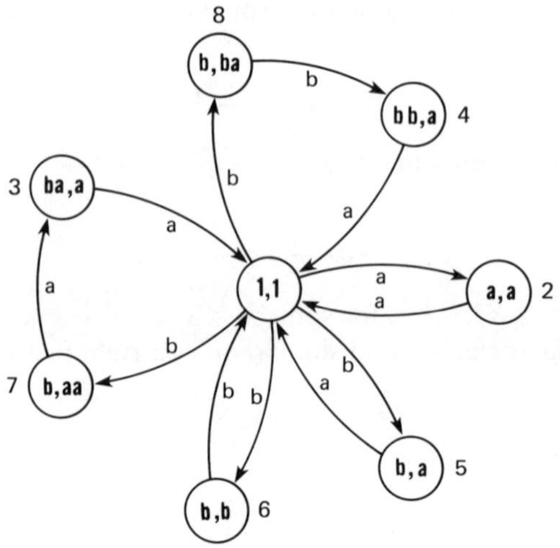

Fig. 4.9 The flower automaton of X.

Consider the automaton given in Fig. 4.10. The function $\rho: P \to \{1,2,3\}$ is given by

$$\rho((a,a)) = \rho((ba,a)) = \rho((bb,a)) = 2,$$
$$\rho((b,a)) = \rho((b,b)) = \rho((b,aa)) = \rho((b,ba)) = 3,$$
$$\rho((1,1)) = 1.$$

The matrices of the associated representations (with the states numbered as indicated in Figs. 4.9 and 4.10)

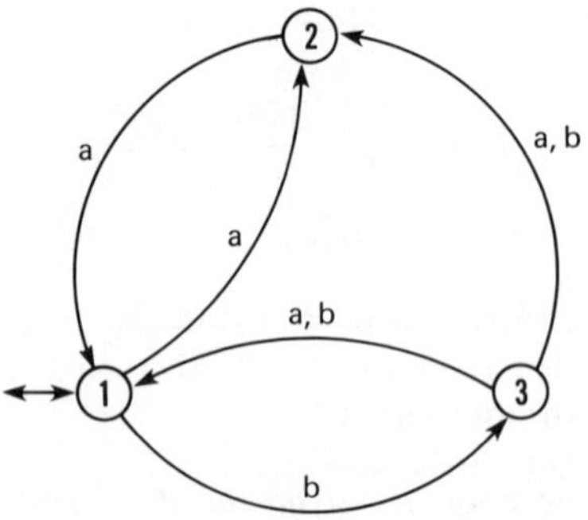

Fig. 4.10 Another automaton recognizing X^*.

$$\varphi_D(a) = \begin{array}{c} 1 \\ 2 \\ 3 \\ 4 \\ 5 \\ 6 \\ 7 \\ 8 \end{array}\left[\begin{array}{c:ccc:cccc} 0 & 1 & 0 & 0 & 0 & 0 & 0 & 0 \\ \hdashline 1 & & & & & & & \\ 1 & & 0 & & & & 0 & \\ 1 & & & & & & & \\ \hdashline 1 & 0 & 0 & 0 & & & & \\ 0 & 0 & 0 & 0 & & & & \\ 0 & 0 & 1 & 0 & & & 0 & \\ 0 & 0 & 0 & 0 & & & & \end{array}\right], \qquad \varphi(a) = \begin{bmatrix} 0 & 1 & 0 \\ 1 & 0 & 0 \\ 1 & 1 & 0 \end{bmatrix},$$

$$\varphi_D(b) = \begin{array}{c} 1 \\ 2 \\ 3 \\ 4 \\ 5 \\ 6 \\ 7 \\ 8 \end{array}\left[\begin{array}{c:ccc:cccc} 0 & 0 & 0 & 0 & 1 & 1 & 1 & 1 \\ \hdashline 0 & & & & & & & \\ 0 & & 0 & & & & 0 & \\ 0 & & & & & & & \\ \hdashline 0 & 0 & 0 & 0 & & & & \\ 1 & 0 & 0 & 0 & & & & \\ 0 & 0 & 0 & 0 & & & 0 & \\ 0 & 0 & 0 & 1 & & & & \end{array}\right], \qquad \varphi(b) = \begin{bmatrix} 0 & 0 & 1 \\ 0 & 0 & 0 \\ 1 & 1 & 0 \end{bmatrix}.$$

The concept of a reduction makes it possible to indicate a relation between the flower automata of a composed code and those of its components.

PROPOSITION 2.5 *Let $Y \subset B^+$, $Z \subset A^+$ be two composable codes and let $X = Y \circ_\beta Z$. If Y is complete, then there exists a reduction of $\mathscr{A}_D^*(X)$ onto $\mathscr{A}_D^*(Z)$. Moreover, $\mathscr{A}_D^*(Y)$ can be identified, through β, with the restriction of $\mathscr{A}_D^*(X)$ to the states in $Z^* \times Z^*$.*

Proof Let P and S be the sets of states of $\mathscr{A}_D^*(X)$ and $\mathscr{A}_D^*(Z)$, respectively, and let φ_X and φ_Z be the representations associated to $\mathscr{A}_D^*(X)$ and $\mathscr{A}_D^*(Z)$.

We define the function

$$\rho\colon \quad P \to S$$

as follows. First, let $\rho((1,1)) = (1,1)$. Next, consider $(u, v) \in P - (1,1)$. Then $uv \in Z^+$. Consequently, there exist unique $z, \bar{z} \in Z^*$, and $(r, s) \in S$ such that

$$u = zr, \qquad v = s\bar{z}$$

(see Fig. 4.11). Then let $\rho(u, v) = (r, s)$. The function ρ is surjective. Indeed, each word in Z appears in at least one word in X; thus each state in S is reached in a refinement of a state in P.

To show that ρ is a reduction, suppose that

$$((u, v), \varphi_X(w), (u', v')) = 1.$$

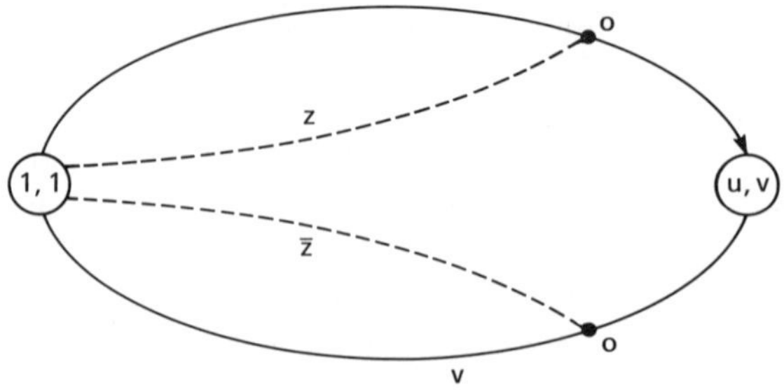

Fig. 4.11 Decomposing a petal.

Let $(r, s) = \rho((u, v))$, $(r', s') = \rho((u', v'))$, and let $z, \bar{z}, z', \bar{z}' \in Z^*$ be such that

$$u = zr, \qquad v = s\bar{z}, \qquad u' = z'r', \qquad v' = s'\bar{z}'.$$

By Proposition 2.2, $uw \in X^*u'$, $wv' \in vX^*$. Thus $zrw \in Z^*r'$, $ws'\bar{z}' \in sZ^*$, implying that $zrws' \in Z^*$ and $rws'\bar{z} \in Z^*$. This in turn shows, in view of the stability of Z^*, that $rws' \in Z^*$. Set $zrw = \hat{z}r'$, with $\hat{z} \in Z^*$. Then

$$\hat{z}(r's') = z(rws')$$

and each of the four factors in this equation is in Z^*. Thus Z being a code, either $\hat{z} = zt$ or $z = \hat{z}t$ for some $t \in Z^*$. In the first case, we get $tr's' = rws'$, whence $rw \in Z^*r'$. The second case implies $r's' = trws'$. Since $r's' \in 1 \cup Z$, this forces $t = 1$ or $rws' = 1$. In both cases, $rw \in Z^*r'$. Thus $rw \in Z^*r'$, and similarly $ws' \in sZ^*$. By Proposition 2.2,

$$((r, s), \varphi_Z(w), (r', s')) = 1.$$

Assume conversely that

$$((r, s), \varphi_Z(w), (r', s')) = 1.$$

Then by Proposition 2.2

$$rw = zr', \qquad ws' = sz'$$

for some $z, z' \in Z^*$. Then $rws' \in Z^*$, and Y being complete, there exist $t, t' \in Z^*$ such that $m = trws't' \in X^*$. Let

$$m = trws't' = trsz't' = tzr's't' = x_1 \cdots x_n$$

with $n \geq 1$, $x_1, \ldots, x_n \in X$. We may assume that t and t' have been chosen of minimal length, so that t is a proper left factor of x_1 and t' is a proper right factor of x_n. But then, since $m \in Z^*$ and also $trs \in Z^*$, trs is a left factor of x_1 and $r's't'$ is a right factor of x_n (Fig. 4.12). Define

$$x_1 = uv \qquad \text{with } u = tr, \quad v \in sZ^*,$$

$$x_n = u'v' \qquad \text{with } u' = t'r', \quad v \in s'Z^*.$$

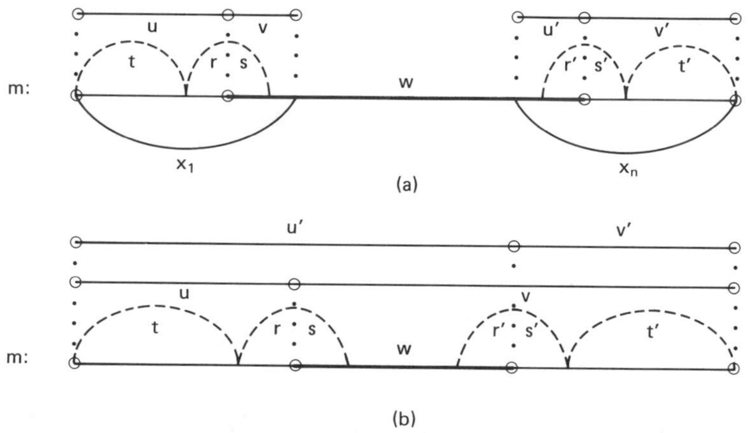

Fig. 4.12 The cases of (a) $n > 1$ and (b) $n = 1$.

Then (u, v) and (u', v') are states of $\mathscr{A}_D^*(X)$, and moreover

$$\rho((u, v)) = (r, s), \qquad \rho((u', v')) = (r', s'),$$

and

$$m = uwv' = uvx_2 \cdots x_n = x_1 \cdots x_{n-1}u'v'.$$

Thus

$$uw \in X^*u' \qquad \text{and} \qquad wv' \in vX^*.$$

Finally, consider the set R of states of $\mathscr{A}_D^*(Y)$. Then R can be identified with

$$R' = \{(u, v) \in P \mid u, v \in Z^*\}.$$

The edges of $\mathscr{A}_D^*(Y)$ correspond to those paths $(u, v) \to (u', v')$ of $\mathscr{A}_D^*(X)$ with endpoints in R', and with label in Z. □

EXAMPLE 2.3 Recall from Chapter I that the code $X = \{aa, ba, bb, baa, bba\}$ is a composition of $Y = \{cc, d, e, dc, ec\}$ and $Z = \{a, ba, bb\}$.

The flower automaton $\mathscr{A}_D^*(X)$ is given in Fig. 4.13. The flower automaton $\mathscr{A}_D^*(Z)$ is given in Fig. 4.14. It is obtained from $\mathscr{A}_D^*(X)$ by the reduction

$$\rho(1) = \rho(2) = \rho(3) = \rho(4) = \bar{1},$$

$$\rho(6) = \rho(8) = \bar{6},$$

$$\rho(5) = \rho(7) = \bar{7}.$$

The flower automaton $\mathscr{A}_D^*(Y)$ is given in Fig. 4.15.

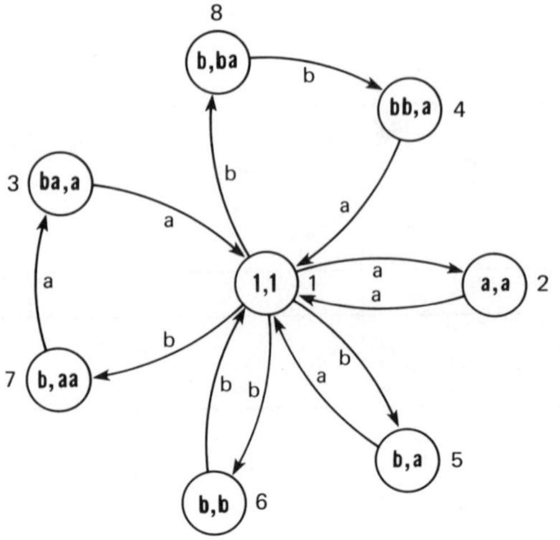

Fig. 4.13 The flower automaton of X.

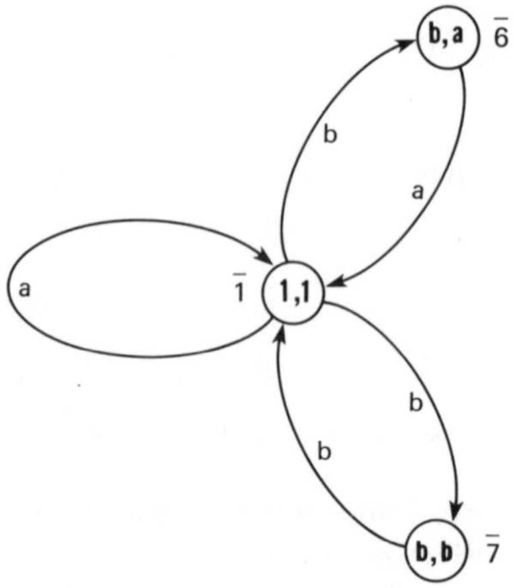

Fig. 4.14 The flower automaton of Z.

Let $X \subset A^+$ be a code and let $\beta: B^* \to A^*$ be a coding morphism for X. Since β is injective, there exists a partial function,

$$\gamma: \quad A^* \to B^*$$

with domain X^* and such that $\gamma(\beta(u)) = u$ for all $u \in B^*$. We say that γ is a *decoding function* for X.

Such a decoding function can be computed by an automaton with output called a decoding automaton. The construction goes as follows. Let

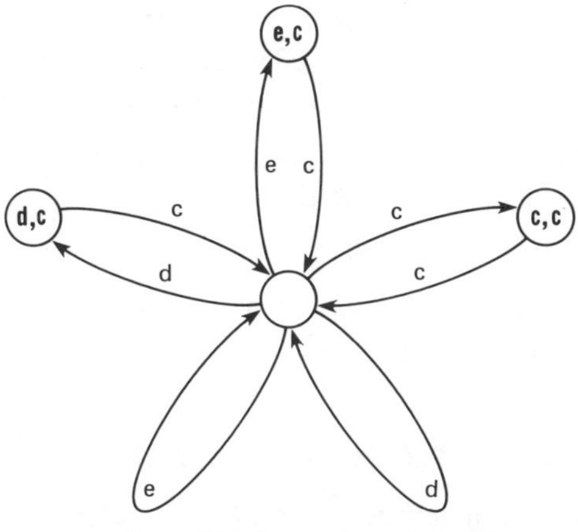

Fig. 4.15 The flower automaton of Y.

$\mathscr{A}_D^*(X) = (P, (1,1), (1,1))$ be the flower automaton of X. We define for each edge e of this automaton an *output label* $\sigma(e) \in B \cup 1$. Let $e = ((u, v), a, (u', v'))$ be an edge of $\mathscr{A}_D^*(X)$. Then we set

$$\sigma(e) = \begin{cases} \beta^{-1}(ua) & \text{if} \quad (u', v') = (1, 1), \\ 1 & \text{otherwise.} \end{cases}$$

The output label $\sigma(c)$ of a path c is the product of the output labels of the edges that c is formed of. Then, for all $x \in X^*$,

$$\gamma(x) = \sigma(c),$$

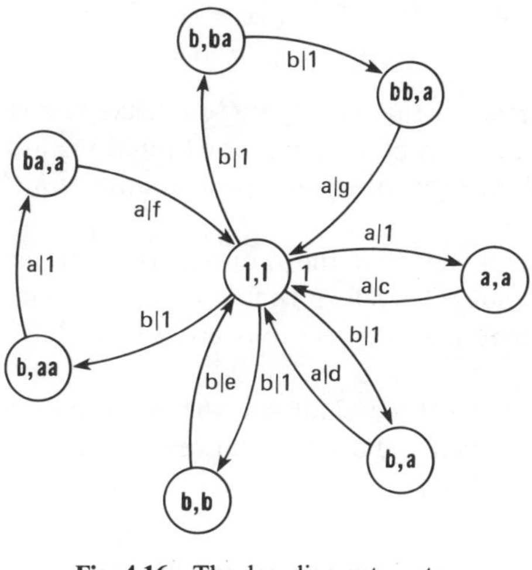

Fig. 4.16 The decoding automaton.

where c is the unique successful path with (input) label x. Thus γ can be computed using the automaton $\mathscr{A}_D^*(X)$. This is especially interesting when X is finite since, in this case, the corresponding flower automaton is also finite.

EXAMPLE 2.4 Let $X = \{aa, ba, bb, baa, bba\}$ be the code of Example 2.3. Let β be the coding morphism for X defined by

$$\beta(c) = aa, \qquad \beta(d) = ba, \qquad \beta(e) = bb, \qquad \beta(f) = baa, \qquad \beta(g) = bba.$$

The output labels of the automaton $\mathscr{A}_D^*(X)$ are represented in Fig. 4.16 with $p \xrightarrow{a|\sigma(e)} q$ denoting that the edge $e = (p, a, q)$ has output label $\sigma(e)$.

3. MONOIDS OF UNAMBIGUOUS RELATIONS

Let m be an $\mathscr{N}$-relation between P and Q. It is called *unambiguous* if

$$m \in \{0, 1\}^{P \times Q},$$

that is to say, if the coefficients of m are zero or one. An unambiguous $\mathscr{N}$-relation will simply be called an *unambiguous relation*.

A *monoid of unambiguous relations* over Q is a submonoid of $\mathscr{N}^{Q \times Q}$ such that all its elements are unambiguous. As a submonoid of $\mathscr{N}^{Q \times Q}$, it contains the identity I_Q.

Let M be a monoid of unambiguous relations over Q. Any element $m \in M$ can be considered as a $Q \times Q$-matrix with coefficients zero or one. It is important to observe that these coefficients 0, 1 belong to $\mathbb{N}$ and not to the Boolean semiring $\mathscr{B}$.

Let $m, n \in M$ and $p, q \in Q$ be such that $(p, mn, q) = 1$. Then there exists a unique $r \in Q$ such that

$$(p, m, r) = (r, n, q) = 1.$$

This shows in particular that two $Q \times Q$-matrices m, n with coefficients 0, 1 which belong to a monoid of unambiguous relations are related by a very strong condition: if l is a row of m, and c is a column of n, there is at most one $r \in Q$ such that $l_r = c_r = 1$.

We shall sometimes say that the monoid M itself, as a monoid of $\mathscr{N}$-relations, is *unambiguous*. Therefore an unambiguous monoid of $\mathscr{N}$-relations and a monoid of unambiguous relations are, fortunately for the reader, the same thing.

For $m \in M$ and $p, q \in Q$ we shall use the notation pmq to express that $(p, m, q) = 1$. This compact and useful notation is introduced in the analogy of (Boolean) binary relations. However, we should keep in mind that, by unambiguity,

$$pmrnq, \qquad pmsnq$$

imply $r = s$.

A monoid M of unambiguous relations over Q is said to be *transitive* if for all $p, q \in Q$, there exists $m \in M$ such that pmq. The first result indicates the connection between monoids of unambiguous relations and unambiguous automata.

PROPOSITION 3.1 *Let $\mathscr{A}$ be an automaton over A. Then $\mathscr{A}$ is unambiguous iff $\varphi_{\mathscr{A}}(A^*)$ is unambiguous. Moreover, if $\mathscr{A} = (Q, 1, 1)$, then $\mathscr{A}$ is trim iff $\varphi_{\mathscr{A}}(A^*)$ is transitive.*

Proof The first equivalence results from Proposition 1.1. Next let $\mathscr{A} = (Q, 1, 1)$ be a trim automaton. Let $p, q \in Q$. Let $u, v \in A^*$ be such that $p \xrightarrow{u} 1$, and $1 \xrightarrow{v} q$ are paths. Then $p \xrightarrow{uv} q$ is a path and consequently $p\varphi_{\mathscr{A}}(uv)q$. The converse is clear. □

Let m be an unambiguous relation between P and Q. Then m is a *function* if there is a function f from P into Q such that pmq iff $f(p) = q$. If f is a bijection, then m will be called a bijection; further if $P = Q$, then m is a *permutation.* If m is an $\mathscr{N}$ relation over Q, then m is *idempotent* if $mm = m$, and m is *invertible* if there is a relation n over Q such that $mn = nm = I_Q$.

PROPOSITION 3.2 *Let m be an unambiguous relation over Q. Then m is invertible iff m is a permutation.*

Proof Let m be an invertible relation, and let n be a relation such that $mn = nm = I_Q$. For all $p \in Q$, there exists $q \in Q$ such that pmq, since from $pmnp$ we get $pmqnp$ for some $q \in Q$. This element q is unique: if pmq', then $qnpmq' = qI_Qq'$, whence $q = q'$. This shows that m is a function. Now if pmq and $p'mq$, then $pmqnp$ and $p'mqnp$, implying $p' = p$. Thus m is injective. Since $nm = I_Q$, m is also surjective. Thus m is a permutation. The converse is clear. □

Observe that we did not make use of the unambiguity in this proof.

Let m be an unambiguous relation over a set Q. A *fixed point* of m is an element $q \in Q$ such that qmq. In matrix form, the fixed points are the indices q such that $m_{q,q} = 1$, thus such that there is a 1 on the diagonal. We denote by $\text{Fix}(m)$ the set of fixed points of m.

PROPOSITION 3.3 *Let M be a monoid of unambiguous relations over Q. Let $m \in M$ and let $S = \text{Fix}(m)$. The following conditions are equivalent:*

(i) *m is idempotent.*

(ii) *For all $p, q \in Q$, we have pmq iff there exists an $s \in S$ such that pms and smq.*

(iii) *We have*

$$m = cl \qquad \text{and} \qquad lc = I_S, \tag{3.1}$$

where $c \in \{0, 1\}^{Q \times S}$ and $l \in \{0, 1\}^{S \times Q}$ are the restrictions of m to $Q \times S$ and $S \times Q$, respectively.

If m is idempotent, then moreover, we have in matrix form

$$c = \begin{bmatrix} I_S \\ c' \end{bmatrix}, \qquad l = [I_S \quad l'], \qquad m = \begin{bmatrix} I_S & l' \\ c' & c'l' \end{bmatrix}$$

with $c' \in \{0,1\}^{(Q-S)\times S}$, $l' \in \{0,1\}^{S\times(Q-S)}$, *and* $l'c' = 0$.

The decomposition (3.1) of an idempotent relation is called the *column–row decomposition* of the relation.

Proof (i) ⇒ (ii) Let $p, q \in Q$ be such that pmq. Then pm^3q. Consequently, there are $s, t \in Q$ such that $pmsmtmq$. It follows that $pmsmq$ and $pmtmq$. Since M is unambiguous, we have $s = t$, whence sms and $s \in S$. The converse is clear.

(ii) ⇒ (iii) Let c and l be the restrictions of m to $Q \times S$ and $S \times Q$, respectively. If pmq, then there exists $s \in S$ such that pms and smq. Then pcs and slq. Conversely if pcs and slq, then we have $pmsmq$, thus pmq. Since this fixed point s is unique, we have $m = cl$.

Now let $r, s \in S$ with $rlcs$. Then $rlqcs$ for some $q \in Q$. Thus rmq and qms. Moreover, rmr and sms, whence

$$rmrmqms, \qquad rmqmsms$$

The unambiguity implies that $r = q = s$. Conversely we have $slcs$ for all $s \in S$. Thus $lc = I_S$.

(iii) ⇒ (i) We have $m^2 = clcl = c(lc)l = cl = m$. Thus m is idempotent.

(iv) Assume that m is idempotent. The restriction of m to $S \times S$ is the identity. Indeed sms holds for all $s \in S$, and if smr with $s, r \in S$, then $smsmr$ and $smrmr$, implying $s = r$ by unambiguity. This shows that c and l have the indicated form. Finally, the product lc is

$$lc = I_S + l'c'.$$

Since $lc = I_S$, this implies that $l'c' = 0$, which concludes the proof. □

Let M be a monoid of unambiguous relations over Q and let $e \in M$ be an idempotent. Then $M(e) = eMe$ is a monoid, and e is the neutral element of $M(e)$, since for all $m \in M(e)$, $em = me = eme = m$. It is the greatest monoid contained in M and having neutral element e. It is called the *monoid localized* at e (cf. Section 0.2). We denote by $G(e)$ the group of units of the monoid $M(e)$, which is also the $\mathscr{H}$-class of e (Proposition 0.5.4).

Note that $M(e)$ is not a monoid of unambiguous relations in our sense, since the relation I_Q is not in $M(e)$, except when $e = I_Q$. However, the following proposition shows that $M(e)$ is naturally isomorphic to a monoid of unambiguous relations M_e over the set of fixed points of e.

PROPOSITION 3.4 *Let M be a monoid of unambiguous relations over Q, let e be an idempotent in M and let* $S = \mathrm{Fix}(e)$ *be the set of fixed points of e. The* *restriction γ of the elements of $M(e)$ to $S \times S$ is an isomorphism of $M(e)$ onto a monoid of unambiguous relations M_e over S. If $e = cl$ is the column–row decomposition of e, this isomorphism is given by*

$$\gamma\colon \quad m \mapsto lmc. \tag{3.2}$$

In particular, $G_e = lG(e)c$ is a permutation group over S.

Further, if M is transitive, then M_e is transitive.

Proof Let γ be the function defined by (3.2). If $m \in eMe$, then for $s, t \in S$,

$$(s, \gamma(m), t) = (s, lmc, t) = (s, m, t),$$

because we have sls and tct. Thus $\gamma(m)$ is the restriction of the elements in eMe to $S \times S$. Further, γ is a morphism since

$$\gamma(e) = lec = I_S$$

and for $m, n \in eMe$,

$$\gamma(mn) = \gamma(men) = l(men)c = lmclnc = \gamma(m)\gamma(n).$$

Finally γ is injective since if $\gamma(m) = \gamma(n)$ for some $m, n \in eMe$, then also $c\gamma(m)l = c\gamma(n)l$. But $c\gamma(m)l = clmcl = eme = m$. Thus $m = n$. The monoid

$$M_e = \gamma(eMe)$$

is a monoid of $\mathcal{N}$-relations over S since it contains the relation I_S. Its elements, as restrictions of unambiguous relations, are themselves unambiguous. Finally $G_e = \gamma(G(e))$ is composed of invertible relations. By Proposition 3.2, it is a permutation group over S.

If M is transitive, consider $s, t \in S$. There exists $m \in M$ such that smt. Then also $(se)m(et)$. Taking the restriction to S, we have $s\gamma(eme)t$. Since $\gamma(eme) \in M_e$, this shows that M_e is transitive. □

EXAMPLE 3.1 Consider the $\mathcal{N}$-relation given in matrix form by

$$m = \begin{bmatrix} 0 & 1 & 0 & 0 \\ 1 & 0 & 1 & 0 \\ 0 & 0 & 0 & 0 \\ 1 & 0 & 1 & 0 \end{bmatrix}.$$

Then

$$m^2 = \begin{bmatrix} 1 & 0 & 1 & 0 \\ 0 & 1 & 0 & 0 \\ 0 & 0 & 0 & 0 \\ 0 & 1 & 0 & 0 \end{bmatrix}$$

and $m^3 = m$.

Thus m^2 is an idempotent relation. The monoid $M = \{1, m, m^2\}$ is a monoid of unambiguous relations.

The fixed points of the relation $e = m^2$ are 1 and 2, and its column–row decomposition is

$$e = \begin{bmatrix} 1 & 0 \\ 0 & 1 \\ 0 & 0 \\ 0 & 1 \end{bmatrix} \begin{bmatrix} 1 & 0 & 1 & 0 \\ 0 & 1 & 0 & 0 \end{bmatrix} = cl.$$

We have

$$m = c \begin{bmatrix} 0 & 1 \\ 1 & 0 \end{bmatrix} l$$

and the restriction of m to the set $\{1, 2\}$ is the transposition (12). The monoid M_e is equal to the group G_e which is isomorphic to $\mathbb{Z}/2\mathbb{Z}$.

Let M be an arbitrary monoid. We compare now the localized monoids of two idempotents of a $\mathscr{D}$-class. Let e, e' be two $\mathscr{D}$-equivalent idempotents of M. Then there exists an element $d \in M$ such that $e \mathscr{R} d \mathscr{L} e'$. By definition of these relations, there exists a quadruple

$$(a, a', b, b') \tag{3.3}$$

of elements of M such that

$$ea = d, \qquad da' = e, \qquad bd = e', \qquad b'e' = d \tag{3.4}$$

(see Fig. 4.17). The quadruple (3.3) is a *passing system* from e to e'.

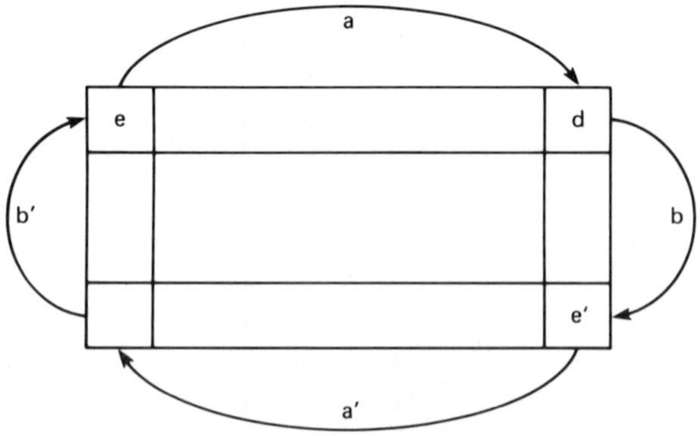

Fig. 4.17 The passing system.

The following formulas are easily derived from (3.4):

$$eaa' = e, \qquad bb'e' = e'$$
$$bea = e' \qquad b'e'a' = e,$$
$$ea = b'e', \qquad be = e'a'$$

(the last formula is obtained by $be = bb'e'a' = e'a'$). If e and e' are idempotents, then the following hold also:

$$eabe = e, \qquad e'a'b'e' = e'.$$

(Note that most of these identities appear in Section 0.5.)

Two monoids of $\mathcal{N}$-relations M over Q and M' over Q' are *equivalent* if there exists a relation $\theta \in \{0,1\}^{Q \times Q'}$ which is a bijection from Q onto Q' such that the function

$$m \mapsto \theta^t m \theta$$

is an isomorphism from M onto M' (θ^t is the transposed of θ). Since θ is a bijection, we have $\theta^t = \theta^{-1}$. Therefore, in the case where M and M' are permutation groups, this definition coincides with that given in Section 0.8.

PROPOSITION 3.5 *Let M be a monoid of unambiguous relations over Q, and let $e, e' \in M$ be two $\mathcal{D}$-equivalent idempotents. Then the monoids $M(e)$ and $M(e')$ are isomorphic, the monoids M_e and $M_{e'}$ an equivalent, and the groups G_e and $G_{e'}$ are equivalent permutation groups.*

More precisely, let $S = \text{Fix}(e)$, $S' = \text{Fix}(e')$, let $e = cl$, $e' = c'l'$ be their column–row decompositions, let γ and γ' be the restrictions to $S \times S$ and $S' \times S'$ and let (a, a', b, b') be a passing system from e to e'. Then

1. *The function $\tau: m \mapsto bma$ is an isomorphism from $M(e)$ onto $M(e')$.*
2. *The relation $\theta = lac' = lb'c' \in \{0,1\}^{S \times S'}$ is a bijection from S onto S'.*
3. *The function $\tau': n \mapsto \theta^t n \theta$ is an isomorphism from M_e onto $M_{e'}$.*
4. *The following diagram is commutative*

$$\begin{array}{ccc} M(e) & \xrightarrow{\tau} & M(e') \\ \gamma \downarrow & & \downarrow \gamma' \\ M_e & \xrightarrow{\tau'} & M_{e'}. \end{array}$$

Proof

1. Let $m \in M(e)$. Then $\tau(m) = bma = bemea = e'a'mb'e'$, showing that $\tau(m)$ is in $M(e')$. Next $\tau(e) = bea = e'$. For $m, m' \in M(e)$,

$$\tau(m)\tau(m') = bmabm'a = bmeabem'a = bmem'a = bmm'a = \tau(mm').$$

Thus τ is a morphism. Finally, it is easily seen that

$$m' \mapsto b'm'a'$$

is the inverse function of τ; thus τ is an isomorphism from $M(e)$ onto $M(e')$.

2. We have $eae' = eb'e'$. Consequently $leae'c' = leb'e'c'$. Since $le = l, e'c' = c'$, we get that

$$\theta = lac' = lb'c'.$$

The relation θ is left-invertible since

$$(l'bc)\theta = l'bclac' = l'beac' = l'e'c' = I_{S'}$$

and it is right-invertible, since we have

$$\theta(l'a'c) = lb'c'l'a'c = lb'e'a'c = lec = I_S.$$

Thus θ is invertible and consequently is a bijection, and

$$\theta^t = l'a'c = l'bc.$$

4. For $m \in M(e)$, we have

$$\tau'\gamma(m) = (l'bc)(lmc)(lac') = l'bemeac' = l'(bma)c' = \gamma'\tau(m),$$

showing that the diagram is commutative.

3. Results from the commutativity of the diagram and from the fact that γ, τ, γ' are isomorphisms. □

Example 3.2 Consider the matrices

$$u = \begin{bmatrix} 0 & 0 & 0 & 1 \\ 1 & 0 & 1 & 0 \\ 0 & 0 & 0 & 0 \\ 0 & 1 & 0 & 0 \end{bmatrix}, \qquad v = \begin{bmatrix} 0 & 0 & 1 & 0 \\ 1 & 0 & 1 & 0 \\ 1 & 0 & 0 & 0 \\ 0 & 1 & 0 & 0 \end{bmatrix}.$$

They generate a monoid of unambiguous relations (as we may verify by using, for instance, the method of Proposition 2.4). The matrix

$$uv = \begin{bmatrix} 0 & 1 & 0 & 0 \\ 1 & 0 & 1 & 0 \\ 0 & 0 & 0 & 0 \\ 1 & 0 & 1 & 0 \end{bmatrix}$$

is the matrix m of Example 3.1. The element

$$e = (uv)^2 = \begin{bmatrix} 1 & 0 & 1 & 0 \\ 0 & 1 & 0 & 0 \\ 0 & 0 & 0 & 0 \\ 0 & 1 & 0 & 0 \end{bmatrix}$$

is an idempotent. $\mathrm{Fix}(e) = \{1,2\}$, and the column–row decomposition is

$$e = \begin{bmatrix} 1 & 0 \\ 0 & 1 \\ 0 & 0 \\ 0 & 1 \end{bmatrix} \begin{bmatrix} 1 & 0 & 1 & 0 \\ 0 & 1 & 0 & 0 \end{bmatrix} = cl.$$

The matrix

$$e' = (vu)^2 = \begin{bmatrix} 0 & 0 & 0 & 0 \\ 1 & 0 & 1 & 0 \\ 1 & 0 & 1 & 0 \\ 0 & 0 & 0 & 1 \end{bmatrix}$$

is also an idempotent. We have $\mathrm{Fix}(e') = \{3,4\}$, and e' has the column–row decomposition

$$e' = \begin{bmatrix} 0 & 0 \\ 1 & 0 \\ 1 & 0 \\ 0 & 1 \end{bmatrix} \begin{bmatrix} 1 & 0 & 1 & 0 \\ 0 & 0 & 0 & 1 \end{bmatrix} = c'l'.$$

The idempotents e and e' lie in the same $\mathscr{D}$-class. Indeed, we may take as a passing system from e to e' the elements

$$a = b' = u, \qquad a' = b = vuv.$$

The bijection $\theta = lac'$ from the set $\mathrm{Fix}(e) = \{1,2\}$ onto the set $\mathrm{Fix}(e') = \{3,4\}$ is

$$\theta\colon\ 1 \mapsto 4, \quad 2 \mapsto 3$$

We now describe a useful method for computing the group G_e of an idempotent e in a monoid of unambiguous relations. This method requires us to make a choice between "left" and "right." We first present the right-hand case.

Let M be a monoid of unambiguous relations, and let e be an idempotent element in M. Let R be the $\mathscr{R}$-class of e, let Λ be the set of $\mathscr{H}$-classes of R and let $G = G(e)$ be the $\mathscr{H}$-class of e.

For each $H \in \Lambda$, choose two elements $a_H, a'_H \in M$ such that

$$ea_H \in H, \qquad ea_H a'_H = e;$$

with the convention that

$$a_G = a'_G = e.$$

(see Figure 4.18). Such a set of pairs $(a_H, a'_H)_{H\in\Lambda}$ is called a *system of coordinates* of R relatively to the idempotent e. Then $Ga_H = H$ and $Ha'_H = G$. The elements a_H, a'_H realize two reciprocal bijections from G onto H.

Let $e = cl$ be the column–row decomposition of e, and set

$$l_H = la_H \qquad \text{and} \qquad c_H = a'_H c \qquad \text{for} \quad H \in \Lambda. \tag{3.5}$$

Note that then $l_H = lea_H$ follows from $l = le$.

Each $m \in M$ defines a partial right action on the set Λ by setting, for all $H \in \Lambda$

$$H \cdot m = \begin{cases} Hm & \text{if} \quad Hm \in \Lambda, \\ \varnothing & \text{otherwise.} \end{cases} \tag{3.6}$$

Now we define a partial function from $\Lambda \times M$ into G by setting

$$H * m = \begin{cases} l_H m c_{H'}, & \text{if} \quad H \cdot m = H' \in \Lambda, \\ \varnothing & \text{if} \quad H \cdot m = \varnothing \end{cases} \tag{3.7}$$

First, observe that $H \cdot m \neq \varnothing$ implies $H * m \in G_e$. Indeed set $H' = Hm$. From $ea_H \in H$ we get $ea_H m \in H'$, showing that

$$ea_H m a'_{H'} \in G.$$

It follows that

$$\begin{aligned} H * m = l_H m c_{H'} &= (lea_H)m(a'_{H'}c) \\ &= l(ea_H m a'_{H'})c \in G_e. \end{aligned}$$

Note that for $g \in G$, we have $G * g = lgc$; this is the element of G_e canonically associated to g, and indeed $a_G = a'_G = e$.

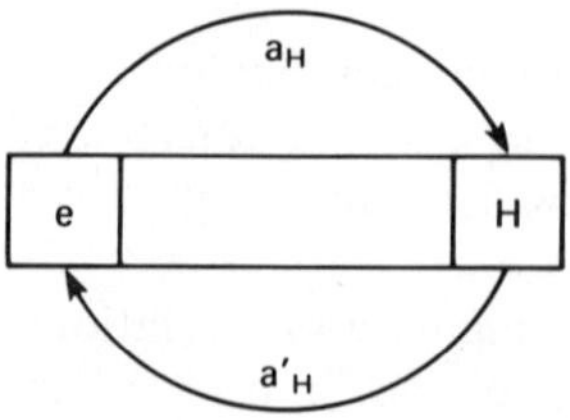

Fig. 4.18 Two coordinates.

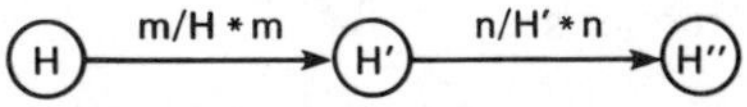

Fig. 4.19 Composition of outputs.

Before stating the result, let us show the following relation. For all $m, n \in M$,

$$(H * m)(H \cdot m * n) = H * mn. \tag{3.8}$$

To verify formula (3.8), let $H' = Hm$, $H'' = Hmn$ (the cases where $H \cdot m = \varnothing$ or $H \cdot mn = \varnothing$ are straightforward). See Fig. 4.19. We have

$$\begin{aligned}(H * m)(H' * n) &= l_H m c_{H'} l_{H'} n c_{H''} \\ &= l a_H m a'_{H'} e a_{H'} n a'_{H''} c \\ &= l((e a_H m a'_{H'})e) a_{H'} n a'_{H''} c.\end{aligned}$$

Since $e a_H m a'_{H'} \in G$, we have $e a_H m a'_{H'} e = e a_H m a'_{H'}$. Thus

$$(H * m)(H' * n) = l((e a_H m) a'_{H'} a_{H'}) n a'_{H''} c.$$

Since $e a_H m \in H'$ and the multiplication on the right by $a'_{H'} a_{H'}$ is the identity on H', we get

$$\begin{aligned}(H * m)(H' * n) &= l e a_H m n a'_{H''} c \\ &= l_H m n c_{H''} \\ &= H * mn.\end{aligned}$$

This proves formula (3.8). As a consequence, we have the following result:

PROPOSITION 3.6 *Let M be a monoid of unambiguous relations generated by a set T. Let e be an idempotent of M, let R be its $\mathscr{R}$-class, let Λ be the set of $\mathscr{H}$-classes of R and let $(a_H, a'_H)_{H \in \Lambda}$ be a system of coordinates of R relatively to e. Then the group G_e is generated by the elements of the form $H * t$, for $H \in \Lambda$, $t \in T$, and $H * t \neq \varnothing$.*

Proof The elements $H * t$, for $H \in \Lambda$ and $t \in T$ either are $\varnothing$ or are in G_e. Now let g be an element of $G(e)$. Then

$$g = t_1 t_2 \cdots t_n, \qquad t_i \in T,$$

because T generates M. Let $G = G(e)$ and let

$$H_i = G t_1 t_2 \cdots t_i, \qquad 1 \le i \le n.$$

From $Gg = G$ it follows that $H_i t_{i+1} \cdots t_n = G$. Thus $H_i \in \Lambda$. By (3.8),

$$G * g = (G * t_1)(H_1 * t_2) \cdots (H_{n-1} * t_n).$$

But $G * g = lgc$. This shows the result. $\square$

The pair of partial functions

$$\Lambda \times M \to \Lambda, \qquad \Lambda \times M \to G_e$$

defined by (3.6) and (3.7) is called the *$\mathscr{R}$-representation* of M relatively to e and to the coordinate system $(a_H, a'_H)_{H \in \Lambda}$.

Observe that the function

$$\mu: \quad M \to (G_e \cup 0)^{\Lambda \times \Lambda},$$

where 0 is a new element, which associates to each $m \in M$ the $\Lambda \times \Lambda$-matrix defined by

$$(\mu m)_{H,H'} = \begin{cases} H * m & \text{if} \quad Hm = H', \\ 0 & \text{otherwise,} \end{cases}$$

is a morphism from M into the monoid of row-monomial $\Lambda \times \Lambda$-matrices with elements in $G_e \cup 0$. This is indeed an equivalent formulation of formula (3.8).

Symmetrically, we define the *$\mathscr{L}$-representation* of M relatively to e as follows. Let L be the $\mathscr{L}$-class of e, and let Γ be the set of its $\mathscr{H}$-classes. For each $H \in \Gamma$, choose two elements $b_H, b'_H \in M$ such that

$$b_H e \in H, \qquad b'_H b_H e = e,$$

with $b_G = b'_G = e$. Such a set of pairs $(b_H, b'_H)_{H \in \Gamma}$ is called a *system of coordinates* of L with respect to e. As in (3.5), we set $c_H = b_H c$, $l_H = l b'_H$ for $H \in \Gamma$.

For each $m \in M$, we define a partial left action on Γ by setting, for $H \in \Gamma$,

$$m \cdot H = \begin{cases} mH & \text{if} \quad mH \in \Gamma, \\ \varnothing & \text{otherwise,} \end{cases}$$

and a partial function from $M \times \Gamma$ into G_e by setting

$$m * H = \begin{cases} l_{H'} m c_H & \text{if} \quad mH = H' \in \Gamma, \\ \varnothing & \text{otherwise.} \end{cases}$$

Then formula (3.8) becomes

$$(n * m \cdot H)(m * H) = nm * H \tag{3.9}$$

and Proposition 3.7 holds mutatis mutandis.

Remark For the computation of the $\mathscr{L}$-classes and the $\mathscr{R}$-classes of a monoid of unambiguous relations, we can use the following observation, whose verification is straightforward: If $m \mathscr{L} n$ (resp., if $m \mathscr{R} n$), then each row (resp., column) of m is a sum of rows (resp., columns) of n and vice versa. This yields an easy test to conclude that two elements are in *distinct* $\mathscr{L}$-classes (resp., $\mathscr{R}$-classes).

EXAMPLE 3.3 Let us consider again the unambiguous monoid of Example 3.2, generated by the matrices

$$u = \begin{bmatrix} 0 & 0 & 0 & 1 \\ 1 & 0 & 1 & 0 \\ 0 & 0 & 0 & 0 \\ 0 & 1 & 0 & 0 \end{bmatrix}, \qquad v = \begin{bmatrix} 0 & 0 & 1 & 0 \\ 1 & 0 & 1 & 0 \\ 1 & 0 & 0 & 0 \\ 0 & 1 & 0 & 0 \end{bmatrix}.$$

We consider the idempotent

$$e = (uv)^2 = \begin{bmatrix} 1 & 0 & 1 & 0 \\ 0 & 1 & 0 & 0 \\ 0 & 0 & 0 & 0 \\ 0 & 1 & 0 & 0 \end{bmatrix}.$$

Its $\mathscr{R}$-class R is formed of three $\mathscr{H}$-classes, numbered 0, 1, 2. In Fig. 4.20 a representative is given for each of these $\mathscr{H}$-classes. The fact that the $\mathscr{L}$-classes

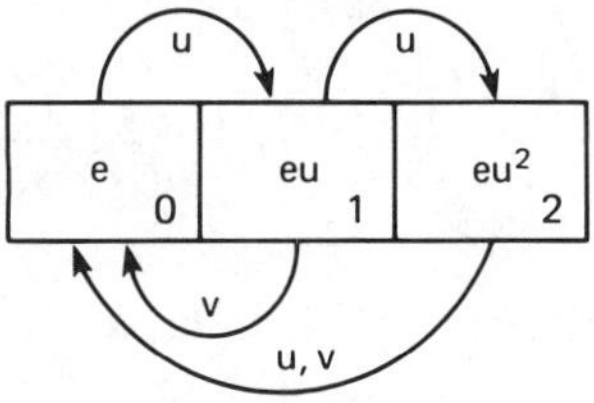

Fig. 4.20 The $\mathscr{R}$-class of idempotent e.

are distinct is verified by inspecting the rows of e, eu, eu^2. Next, we compute that $eu^3 = eu^2v = e$, showing that these elements are $\mathscr{R}$-equivalent. Further, $euv = (uv)^3 \mathscr{H} e$. Finally

$$ev = \begin{bmatrix} 1 & 0 & 1 & 0 \\ 1 & 0 & 1 & 0 \\ 0 & 0 & 0 & 0 \\ 1 & 0 & 1 & 0 \end{bmatrix}$$

has only one nonnull row (column) and consequently cannot be in the $\mathscr{D}$-class of e. We have reported in Fig. 4.20 the effect of the right multiplication by u and v.

We choose a system of coordinates of R by setting

$$a_0 = a'_0 = e,$$
$$a_1 = u, \qquad a'_1 = vuv,$$
$$a_2 = u^2, \qquad a'_2 = u.$$

Then

$$l_0 = \begin{bmatrix} 1 & 0 & 1 & 0 \\ 0 & 1 & 0 & 0 \end{bmatrix}, \qquad c_0 = \begin{bmatrix} 1 & 0 \\ 0 & 1 \\ 0 & 0 \\ 0 & 1 \end{bmatrix},$$

$$l_1 = \begin{bmatrix} 0 & 0 & 0 & 1 \\ 1 & 0 & 1 & 0 \end{bmatrix}, \qquad c_1 = \begin{bmatrix} 0 & 0 \\ 0 & 1 \\ 0 & 1 \\ 1 & 0 \end{bmatrix},$$

$$l_2 = \begin{bmatrix} 0 & 1 & 0 & 0 \\ 0 & 0 & 0 & 1 \end{bmatrix}, \qquad c_2 = \begin{bmatrix} 0 & 1 \\ 1 & 0 \\ 0 & 0 \\ 0 & 1 \end{bmatrix}.$$

Let us denote by

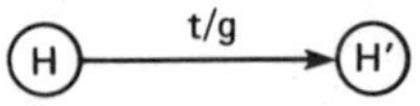

the fact that $H \cdot t = H'$ and $H * t \cdot g$. Then the $\mathscr{R}$-representation of M relatively to e and to this system of coordinates is obtained by completing Fig. 4.20 and is given in Fig. 4.21. We set

$$i = \begin{bmatrix} 1 & 0 \\ 0 & 1 \end{bmatrix}, \qquad j = \begin{bmatrix} 0 & 1 \\ 1 & 0 \end{bmatrix}.$$

The group G_e is of course $\mathfrak{S}_2$. □

The concepts introduced in this paragraph are greatly simplified when we consider the case of a monoid of (total) *functions* from Q into itself, instead of a monoid of unambiguous relations.

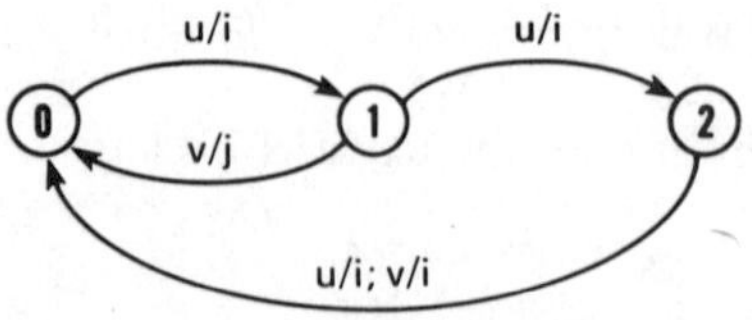

Fig. 4.21 The $\mathscr{R}$-representation of M.

For $a \in M$, write $pa = q$ instead of $(p, a, q) = 1$.

The *image* of a, denoted $\mathrm{Im}(a)$, is the set of $q \in Q$ such that $pa = q$ for some $p \in Q$.

The *nuclear equivalence* of a, denoted $\mathrm{Ker}(a)$, is the equivalence relation on Q defined by $p \equiv q \bmod \mathrm{Ker}(a)$ iff $pa = qa$.

If $b \in Ma$, then $\mathrm{Im}(b) \subset \mathrm{Im}(a)$. If $b \in aM$, then $\mathrm{Ker}(a) \subset \mathrm{Ker}(b)$ (note the inversion of inclusions).

A function $e \in M$ is idempotent iff its restriction to its image is the identity. Thus, its image is in this case equal to its set of fixed points: $\mathrm{Im}(e) = \mathrm{Fix}(e)$.

As a result of what precedes, if $a\mathscr{L}b$, then $\mathrm{Im}(a) = \mathrm{Im}(b)$ and if $a\mathscr{R}b$, then $\mathrm{Ker}(a) = \mathrm{Ker}(b)$. This allows us to "separate" functions.

To compute the $\mathscr{R}$-class of an idempotent function e over a finite set, we may use the following observation, where $S = \mathrm{Fix}(e)$. If the restriction of m to S is a permutation on S, then $e\mathscr{H}em$. Indeed, we have in this case $eme = em$ since $\mathrm{Im}(em) = S$ and e is the identity on S. It follows that $(em)^k e = em^k$ for $k \geq 1$, whence $(em)^k = em^k$ for $k \geq 1$. Thus $(em)^p = e$, with $p = \mathrm{Card}(S)!$ and this shows the claim.

EXAMPLE 3.4 Let M be the monoid of functions from the set

$$Q = \{1, 2, \ldots, 8\}$$

into itself generated by the two functions u and v given in the following array

	1	2	3	4	5	6	7	8
u	4	5	4	5	8	1	8	1
v	2	3	4	5	6	7	8	1

where each column contains the images by u and v of the element of Q placed on the top of the column.

The function $e = u^4$ is idempotent and has the set of fixed points $S = \{1, 4, 5, 8\}$,

	1	2	3	4	5	6	7	8
u^4	1	4	1	4	5	8	5	8

We get the pattern of Fig. 4.22 for the $\mathscr{R}$-class R of e. These four $\mathscr{H}$-classes are distinct because the images of e, ev, ev^2, ev^3 are distinct. For the edges going back to the $\mathscr{H}$-class of e, we use the observation stated above; it suffices to verify that the restrictions to S of the functions u, vu, v^2u, v^3u, v are permutations.

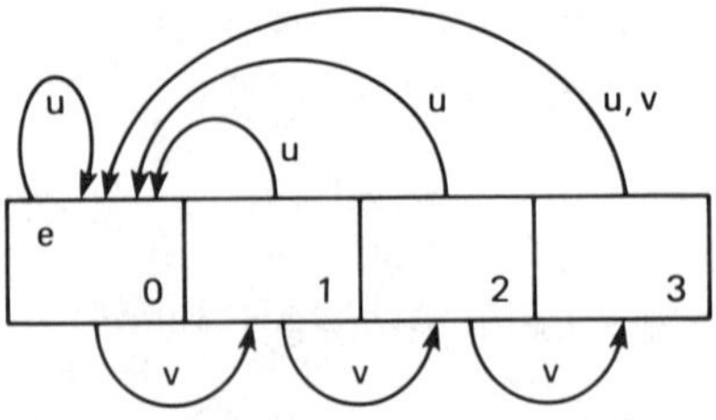

Fig. 4.22 The $\mathscr{R}$-class of e.

Choose a system of coordinates of R by taking

$$a_0 = a'_0 = e,$$

$$a_1 = v, \qquad a'_1 = v^7,$$

$$a_2 = v^2, \qquad a'_2 = v^6,$$

$$a_3 = v^3, \qquad a'_3 = v^5.$$

For the computation of the $\mathscr{R}$-representation of M relatively to e, we proceed as follows: if $H \cdot m = H'$, then the permutation $H * m$ on S is not computed by computing the matrix product $H * m = l_H m c_{H'}$ of formula (3.7), but, noting that $H * m$ is the restriction to S of $ea_H m a'_H e$, by evaluating this function on S. Thus we avoid unnecessary matrix computations when dealing with functions.

Figure 4.23 shows the $\mathscr{R}$-representation obtained.

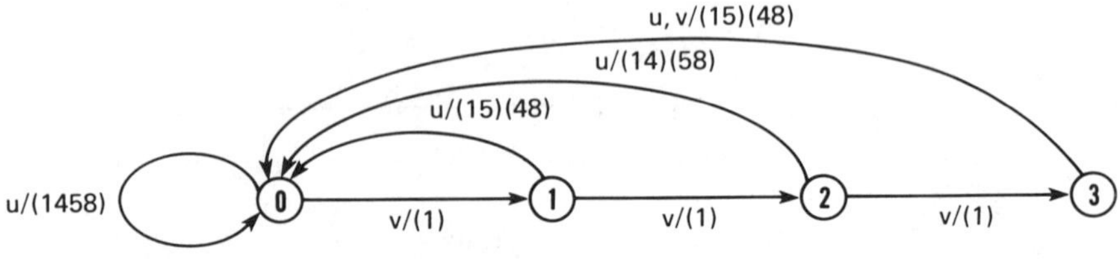

Fig. 4.23 The $\mathscr{R}$-representation.

According to Proposition 3.6, the group G_e is generated by the permutations

$$(1458), \qquad (15)(48), \qquad (14)(58).$$

It is the *dihedral* group D_4 which is the group of all symmetries of the square

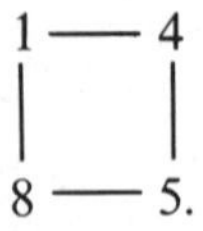

It contains 8 elements.

4. RANK AND MINIMAL IDEAL

Let m be an $\mathcal{N}$-relation between two sets P and Q. The *rank* of m is the minimum of the cardinalities of the sets R such that there exist two $\mathcal{N}$-relations $c \in \mathcal{N}^{P \times R}$ and $l \in \mathcal{N}^{R \times Q}$ with

$$m = cl. \tag{4.1}$$

It is denoted by rank(m). It is a nonnegative integer or $+\infty$. A pair (c, l) satisfying (4.1) is a *minimal decomposition* if there exists no factorization $m = c'l'$ with $c' \in \mathcal{N}^{P \times R'}$, $l' \in \mathcal{N}^{R \times Q}$ and $R' \subseteq R$. If rank(m) is finite, this is the equivalent of saying that Card(R) is minimal.

The following properties are straightforward. First

$$\operatorname{rank}(nmn') \leq \operatorname{rank}(m)$$

since each decomposition (c, l) of m induces a decomposition (mc, ln') of nmn'. Second

$$\operatorname{rank}(m) \leq \min\{\operatorname{Card}(P), \operatorname{Card}(Q)\}.$$

If (c, l) is a minimal decomposition of m, then

$$\operatorname{rank}(m) = \operatorname{rank}(c) = \operatorname{rank}(l),$$

Further

$$\operatorname{rank}(m) = 0 \quad \Leftrightarrow \quad m = 0.$$

If $P' \subset P$, $Q' \subset Q$, and if m' is the restriction of m to $P' \times Q'$, then

$$\operatorname{rank}(m') \leq \operatorname{rank}(m).$$

We get from the first inequality that two $\mathcal{J}$-equivalent elements of a monoid of $\mathcal{N}$-relations have the same rank. Thus, the rank is constant on a $\mathcal{D}$-class.

Consider two $\mathcal{N}$-relations $m \in \mathcal{N}^{P \times S}$ and $n \in \mathcal{N}^{S \times Q}$. The pair (m, n) is called *trim* if no column of m is null and no row of n is null. This is the equivalent of saying that for all $s \in S$, there exists at least one pair $(p, q) \in P \times Q$ such that $m_{ps} \neq 0$ and $n_{sq} \neq 0$.

PROPOSITION 4.1 *Let* $n \in \mathcal{N}^{P \times R}$, $m \in \mathcal{N}^{R \times R}$, $n' \in \mathcal{N}^{R \times Q}$ *be three* $\mathcal{N}$-*relations.*

1. *If* nn' *is unambiguous and* n *has no null column, then* n' *is unambiguous.*
2. *If* nn' *is unambiguous and* n' *has no null row, then* n *is unambiguous.*
3. *If* nn' *is unambiguous and* (n, n') *is trim, then* n *and* n' *are unambiguous.*
4. *If* nmn' *is unambiguous and* (n, n') *is trim, then* m *is unambiguous.*

Proof

1. Let $r \in R$, $q \in Q$. There exists $p \in P$ such that $(p, n, r) \neq 0$. Then

$$1 \geq (p, nn', q) \geq (p, n, r)(r, n', q) \geq (r, n', q).$$

Consequently $(r, n', q) \in \{0, 1\}$ and n' is unambiguous.

Claim 2 is shown symmetrically and claim 3 is a result of claims 1 and 2.

4. Since n' has no null row, nm is unambiguous by 2. Since n has no null column, m is unambiguous. ☐

PROPOSITION 4.2 *Let m be an unambiguous relation and let (c, l) be a minimal decomposition of m. Then the pair (c, l) is trim and both c and l are unambiguous.*

Proof Assume that c contains a column which is null. Then we can delete this column and the row of same index of l without changing the value of the product. But this implies that (c, l) is not a minimal decomposition. Thus no column of c is null, and symmetrically no row of l is null. Consequently (c, l) is trim. By Proposition 4.1, c and l are unambiguous. ☐

EXAMPLE 4.1 Let $m \in \{0, 1\}^{P \times Q}$ be a bijection. Then

$$\operatorname{rank}(m) = \operatorname{Card}(P) = \operatorname{Card}(Q).$$

For the proof, we first show that $\operatorname{rank}(I_Q) = \operatorname{Card}(Q)$. Indeed let $I_Q = cl$ be a minimal decomposition of I_Q, with $c \in \{0, 1\}^{Q \times R}$ and $l \in \{0, 1\}^{R \times Q}$. Note first that if $c_{qr} = 1$ then, since no row of l is null, $l_{rq'} = 1$ for some q'. This implies $q = q'$, i.e., $l_{rq} = 1$. Next, for each $q \in Q$, there exists a unique $r \in R$ such that $c_{qr} = 1$. The existence results from the equality $I_Q = cl$. Thus c is a function from Q into R. It is injective since $c_{qr} = 1$ implies $l_{rq} = 1$; thus $c_{q'r} = 1$ would imply $(cl)_{q'q} = 1$, whence $q' = q$. This shows that $\operatorname{Card}(R) \geq \operatorname{Card}(Q)$. Consequently $\operatorname{Card}(R) = \operatorname{Card}(Q)$, and $\operatorname{rank}(I_Q) = \operatorname{Card}(Q)$.

Now let n be the reciprocal bijection of m. Then

$$\operatorname{Card}(P) = \operatorname{rank}(I_P) = \operatorname{rank}(mn) \leq \operatorname{rank}(m).$$

Thus $\operatorname{rank}(m) = \operatorname{Card}(P)$.

EXAMPLE 4.2 The notion of rank that we defined in Section II.6 is a special case of the rank defined here. Let indeed $\mathscr{A} = (Q, i, T)$ be a deterministic automaton, and let $\varphi = \varphi_{\mathscr{A}}$. We shall see that for $w \in A^*$

$$\operatorname{rank}(\varphi(w)) = \operatorname{Card}(Q \cdot w) = \operatorname{rank}_{\mathscr{A}}(w).$$

Let $R = Q \cdot w$. Then

$$\varphi(w) = cl,$$

where c is the restriction of $\varphi(w)$ to $Q \times R$ and where $l \in \{0, 1\}^{R \times Q}$ is defined, for $r \in R$ and $q \in Q$, by

$$(r, l, q) = \begin{cases} 1 & \text{if } \quad q = r, \\ 0 & \text{otherwise.} \end{cases}$$

This shows that rank $(\varphi(w)) \leq \text{Card}(R)$. Next, let $T \subset Q$ be a cross section of $\varphi(w)$. Then the restriction m of $\varphi(w)$ to $T \times R$ is a bijection, whence

$$\text{Card}(R) = \text{rank}(m) \leq \text{rank}(\varphi(w)).$$

EXAMPLE 4.3 The above example shows that if an unambiguous relation m in $\{0, 1\}^{Q \times P}$ is a function, then

$$\text{rank}(m) = \text{Card}(\text{Im}(m)).$$

EXAMPLE 4.4 Let Q be a *finite* set. The rank of an $\mathbb{N}$-relation m over Q has strong connections with the usual notion of rank as defined in linear algebra. Let K be a field containing $\mathbb{N}$. The rank over K (or K-rank) is, as is well known, the maximal number of rows (or colums) which are linearly independent over K. We can observe (Exercise 4.1) that this number may be defined in a manner analoguous to the definition of the rank over $\mathcal{N}$. In particular,

$$\text{rank}_K(m) \leq \text{rank}(m).$$

It is easy to see (Exercise 4.2) that the inequality usually is strict. However, in the case of relations which are functions, the two notions coincide.

The following proposition gives an easy method for computing the rank of an idempotent relation.

PROPOSITION 4.3 *Let e be an unambiguous idempotent relation. Then*

$$\text{rank}(e) = \text{Card}(\text{Fix}(e)).$$

Proof Set $S = \text{Fix}(e)$. The column–row decomposition of e shows that $\text{rank}(e) \leq \text{Card}(S)$. Moreover, in view of Proposition 3.3, the matrix e contains the identity matrix I_S. Thus $\text{Card}(S) = \text{rank}(I_S) \leq \text{rank}(e)$. □

The notion of rank is of interest only when it is finite. In the case of unambiguous relations there exists an interesting characterization of relations of finite rank.

PROPOSITION 4.4 *For any unambiguous relation m, the following conditions are equivalent:*

(i) *m has finite rank,*
(ii) *the set of rows of m is finite,*
(iii) *the set of columns of m is finite.*

Proof (i) $\Rightarrow$ (ii) Let $m = cl$, with $c \in \mathcal{N}^{P \times R}$ and $l \in \mathcal{N}^{R \times Q}$ be a minimal decomposition of m. By Proposition 4.2, the relations c and l are unambiguous. Now, if two rows of c, say with indices p and q, are equal, then the corresponding rows m_{p*} and m_{q*} of m also are equal. Since R is finite, the matrix c has at most $2^{\mathrm{Card}(R)}$ distinct rows. Thus the set of rows of m is finite.

(ii) $\Rightarrow$ (i) Let $(m_{r.})_{r \in R}$ be a set of representatives of the rows of m. Then $m = cl$, where l is the restriction of m to $R \times Q$, and $c \in \{0, 1\}^{Q \times R}$ is defined by

$$c_{pr} = \begin{cases} 1 & \text{if} \quad m_{q*} = m_{r*}, \\ 0 & \text{otherwise.} \end{cases}$$

This shows (i) $\Leftrightarrow$ (ii). The proof of (i) $\Leftrightarrow$ (iii) is identical. $\square$

Let M be a monoid of unambiguous relations over Q. The *minimal rank* of M is the minimum of the ranks of the elements of M other than the null relation. It is denoted by $r(M)$,

$$r(M) = \min\{\mathrm{rank}(m) \mid m \in M - \{0\}\}.$$

If M does not contain the null relation over Q, this is of course the minimum of the ranks of the elements of M. We have $r(M) > 0$ and $r(M) < \infty$ iff M contains a relation of finite positive rank.

We now study the monoids having finite minimal rank and we shall see that they have a rather precise structure. We must distinguish two cases: the case where the monoid contains the null relation, and the easier case where it does not.

Note that the null relation plays the role of a zero in view of the following, more precise statement. If M is a transitive monoid of unambiguous relations over Q, then M contains a zero iff M contains the null relation.

Indeed, the null relation always is a zero. Conversely, if M has a zero z, let us prove that z is the null relation. If $\mathrm{Card}(Q) = 1$, then $z = 0$. Thus we assume $\mathrm{Card}(Q) \geq 2$, and $z \neq 0$. Let $p, q \in Q$ such that $z_{p,q} = 1$. Let $r, s \in Q$. By transitivity of M, there exist $m, n \in M$ such that

$$m_{rp} = n_{qs} = 1.$$

From $mzn = z$, it follows that $z_{rs} = 1$. Thus $z_{rs} = 1$ for all $r, s \in Q$, which contradicts the unambiguity of M.

If M is an unambiguous monoid of relations over Q, then for $q \in Q$, let

$$\mathrm{Stab}(q) = \{m \in M \mid qmq\}.$$

THEOREM 4.5 *Let M be a transitive monoid of unambiguous relations over Q, containing the relation* 0, *and having finite minimal rank.*

1. *M contains a unique* 0*-minimal ideal J, which is the union of* 0 *and of the set K of elements of rank $r(M)$.*

2. *The set K is a regular $\mathscr{D}$-class whose $\mathscr{H}$-classes are finite.*
3. *Each $q \in Q$ is a fixed point of at least one idempotent e in K i.e., $e \in K \cap \mathrm{Stab}(q)$.*
4. *For each idempotent $e \in K$, the group G_e is a transitive group of degree $r(M)$.*
5. *The groups G_e, for e idempotent in K, are equivalent.*

Before we proceed to the proof, we establish several preliminary results.

PROPOSITION 4.6 *Let M be a monoid of unambiguous relations over Q. If $m \in M$ has finite rank, then the semigroup generated by m is finite.*

Proof Let $m = cl$ be a minimal decomposition of m, with $c \in \{0,1\}^{Q \times R}$ and $l \in \{0,1\}^{R \times Q}$. Let u be the $\mathscr{N}$-relation over R defined by $u = lc$. Then for all $n \geq 0$,

$$m^{n+1} = c(lc)^n l = cu^n{}_l.$$

Since the pair (c,l) is trim, each relation u^n is unambiguous by Proposition 4.1. Since R is finite, the set of relations u^n is finite, and the semigroup $\{m^n \mid n \geq 1\}$ is finite. □

In particular it follows from this proposition that for any unambiguous relation of finite rank, a convenient power is an idempotent relation.

PROPOSITION 4.7 *Let M be a monoid of unambiguous relations over Q, and let $e \in M$ be an idempotent. If e has finite rank, then the localized monoid eMe is finite.*

Proof Let S be the set of fixed points of e. By Proposition 4.3, the set S is finite. Thus the monoid M_e, which is a monoid of unambiguous relations over S, is finite. Since the monoid eMe is isomorphic to M_e, it is finite. □

We now verify a technical lemma which is useful to "avoid" the null relation.

LEMMA 4.8 *Let M be a transitive monoid of unambiguous relations over Q.*

1. *For all $m \in M - 0$, there exist $n \in M$ and $q \in Q$ such that*

$$mn \in \mathrm{Stab}(q) \qquad (resp.\ nm \in \mathrm{Stab}(q)).$$

Thus in particular $mn \neq 0$ (resp., $nm \neq 0$).

2. *For all $m \in M - 0$ and $q \in Q$, there exist $n, n' \in M$ such that*

$$nmn' \in \mathrm{Stab}(q).$$

3. *For all $m, n \in M - 0$, there exists $u \in M$ such that*

$$mun \neq 0.$$

In other terms, the monoid M is prime.

Proof

1. Let $q, r \in Q$ be such that $(q, m, r) = 1$. Since M is transitive, there exists $n \in M$ such that $(r, n, q) = 1$. Thus $(q, mn, q) = 1$.

2. There exist $p, r \in Q$ such that $(p, m, r) = 1$. Let $n, n' \in M$ be such that $(q, n, p) = 1, (r, n'q) = 1$. Then $(q, nmn', q) = 1$.

3. There exist $p, r, s, q \in Q$ such that $(p, m, r) = (s, n, q) = 1$. Take $u \in M$ with $(r, u, s) = 1$. Then $(p, mun, q) = 1$. □

PROPOSITION 4.9 *Let M be a transitive monoid of unambiguous relations over Q, having finite minimal rank. Each right ideal $R \neq 0$ (resp., each left ideal $L \neq 0$) of M contains a nonnull idempotent.*

Proof Let $r \in R - 0$. By Lemma 4.8, there exist $n \in M$ and $q \in Q$ such that $rn \in \mathrm{Stab}(q)$. Let $m \in M$ be an element such that $\mathrm{rank}(m) = r(M)$. Again by Lemma 4.8, there exist $u, v \in M$ such that $umv \in \mathrm{Stab}(q)$. Consider the element $m' = rnumv$. Then $m' \in R$ and $m' \in \mathrm{Stab}(q)$.

Since $\mathrm{rank}(m') \leq \mathrm{rank}(m)$, the rank of m' is finite. According to Proposition 4.6, the semigroup generated by m' is finite. Thus there exists $k \geq 1$ such that $e = (m')^k$ is idempotent. Then $e \in R$ and $e \neq 0$ since $e \in \mathrm{Stab}(q)$. □

PROPOSITION 4.10 *Let M be a transitive monoid of unambiguous relations over Q, having finite minimal rank and containing the null relation. For all $m \in M$, the following conditions are equivalent:*

(i) $\mathrm{rank}(m) = r(M)$,
(ii) *the right ideal mM is 0-minimal,*
(iii) *the left ideal Mm is 0-minimal.*

Proof (i) ⇒ (ii) Let $R \neq \{0\}$ be a right ideal contained in mM. We show that $R = mM$. According to Proposition 4.9, R contains an idempotent $e \neq 0$. Since $e \in R \subset mM$, there exist $n \in M$ such that $e = mn$. Since $\mathrm{rank}(e) \leq \mathrm{rank}(m)$ and $\mathrm{rank}(m)$ is minimal, we have $\mathrm{rank}(e) = \mathrm{rank}(m)$. Let $m = cl$ be a minimal decomposition of m, with $c \in \{0,1\}^{Q \times S}$, $l \in \{0,1\}^{S \times Q}$. Then $e = (cl)n = c(ln)$. Since $\mathrm{rank}(e) = r(M) = \mathrm{Card}(S)$, the pair (c, ln) is a minimal decomposition of e. In particular, it is trim. For all $k \geq 0$,

$$e = e^{k+1} = c(lnc)^k ln.$$

By Proposition 4.1(4), the relation $(lnc)^k$ is unambiguous for each k. Thus $(lnc)^k \in \{0,1\}^{S \times S}$ and S being finite, there exists an integer $i \geq 1$ such that $(lnc)^i$ is idempotent. Since $\mathrm{rank}((lnc)^i) = \mathrm{Card}(S)$, each element in S is a fixed point of $(lnc)^i$. Consequently $(lnc)^i = I_S$. Thus

$$em = e^i m = (cln)^i m = (cln)^i cl = c(lnc)^i l = cl = m.$$

The equality $em = m$ shows that $m \in R$, whence $R = mM$. Thus mM is a 0-minimal right ideal.

(ii) $\Rightarrow$ (i) Let $n \in M$ be such that $\text{rank}(n) = r(M)$. By Lemma 4.8, there exists $u \in M$ such that $mun \neq 0$. From $munM \subset mM$, we get $munM = mM$, whence $m \in munM$. Thus $\text{rank}(m) \leq \text{rank}(n)$, showing that $\text{rank}(m) = \text{rank}(n)$.

(i) $\Leftrightarrow$ (iii) is shown in the same way. ☐

Proof of Theorem 4.5

1. By Lemma 4.8, the monoid M is prime. According to Proposition 4.10, the monoid M contains 0-minimal left and right ideals. In view of Corollary 0.5.10, the monoid M contains a unique 0-minimal ideal J which is the union of the 0-minimal right ideals (resp., left ideals). Once more by Proposition 4.10, J is the union of 0 and of the set K of elements of minimal positive rank. This proves claim 1.

2. In view of Corollary 0.5.10, the set K is a regular $\mathscr{D}$-class. All the $\mathscr{H}$-classes of K have same cardinality by Proposition 0.5.3. The finiteness of these classes will result from claim 4.

3. Let $q \in Q$ and $k \in K$. By Lemma 4.8, $nkn' \in \text{Stab}(q)$ for some $n, n' \in M$. Since the semigroup generated by $m = nkn'$ is finite (Proposition 4.6), it contains an idempotent e. Then $e \in K \cap \text{Stab}(q)$.

4. Let e be idempotent in K. Then the $\mathscr{H}$-class of e is $H \cup 0 = eM \cap Me = eMe = G(e) \cup 0$. The first equality is a result of the fact that the $\mathscr{R}$-class of e is $eM - 0$. Next $eMe \subset eM \cap Me$, and conversely, if $n \in eM \cap Me$, then $en = ne = n$ whence $n = ene \in eMe$. This shows the second equality. Finally, $G(e) = H$ since H is a group.

According to Proposition 3.4, we have $M_e = G_e \cup 0$ and M_e is transitive. Thus G_e is a transitive permutation group. Its degree is $r(M)$.

5. Is a direct consequence of Proposition 3.5. ☐

Now let M be a monoid of unambiguous relations that does not contain the null relation. Theorem 4.5 admits a formulation which is completely analogous, and which goes as follows.

THEOREM 4.11 *Let M be an transitive monoid of unambiguous relations over Q which does not contain the null relation and which has finite minimal rank.*

1. *The set K of elements of rank $r(M)$ is the minimal ideal of M.*
2. *The set K is a regular $\mathscr{D}$-class and is a union of finite groups.*
3. *Each $q \in Q$ is the fixed point of at least one idempotent e in K i.e. $e \in K \cap \text{Stab}(q)$.*
4. *For each idempotent $e \in K$, the group G_e is a transitive group of degree $r(M)$, and these groups are equivalent.*

Proof Let M_0 be the monoid of unambiguous relations

$$M_0 = M \cup 0.$$

We have $r(M) = r(M_0)$. Thus Theorem 4.5 applies to M_0. For all m in M, we have $mM_0 = mM \cup 0$. It follows easily that mM is a minimal right ideal of M iff mM_0 is a 0-minimal right ideal of M_0. The same holds for left ideals and for two-sided ideals. In particular, the 0-minimal ideal J of M_0 is the union of 0 and of the minimal ideal K of M. This proves 1. Next K is a $\mathscr{D}$-class of M_0, thus also of M. Since the product of two elements of M is never 0, each $\mathscr{H}$-class of K is a group. This proves 2. The other claims require no proof. □

Let M be a transitive monoid of unambiguous relations over Q, of finite minimal rank, and let

$$K = \{m \in M \mid \text{rank}(m) = r(M)\}.$$

The groups G_e, for each idempotent e in K, are equivalent transitive permutation groups. The *Suschkewitch group* of M is, by definition, any one of them.

5. VERY THIN CODES

A code $X \subset A^+$ is called *very thin* if there exists a word x in X^* which is not a factor of a word in X. Recall that $F(X)$ is the set of factors of words in X, and that $\bar{F}(X) = A^* - F(X)$. With these notations, X is very thin iff

$$X^* \cap \bar{F}(X) \neq \emptyset.$$

Any very thin code is thin (i.e., satisfies $\bar{F}(X) \neq \emptyset$). Conversely, a thin code is not always very thin (see Example 5.4). However, a thin complete code X is very thin. Consider indeed a word $w \in \bar{F}(X)$. Since X is complete, there exist $u, v \subset A^*$ such that $uwv \in X^*$. Then $uwv \in X^* \cap \bar{F}(X)$.

The aim of this section is to prove the following result. It shows, in particular, that a recognizable code is very thin. This is more precise than Proposition I.5.12, which only asserts that a recognizable code is thin.

THEOREM 5.1 *Let $X \subset A^+$ be a code and let $\mathscr{A} = (Q, 1, 1)$ be an unambiguous trim automaton recognizing X^*. The following conditions are equivalent.*

(i) *X is very thin.*
(ii) *The monoid $\varphi_{\mathscr{A}}(A^*)$ has finite minimal rank.*

The proof of this result is in several steps. We start with the following property used to prove the implication (i) ⇒ (ii).

PROPOSITION 5.2 *Let $X \subset A^+$ be a code and let $\mathscr{A} = (Q, 1, 1)$ be an unambiguous trim automaton recognizing X^*. For all $w \in \bar{F}(X)$, the rank of $\varphi_{\mathscr{A}}(w)$ is finite.*

Proof Let us write φ instead of $\varphi_{\mathcal{A}}$. For each $p \in Q$, let $\Phi(p)$ be the set of left factors of w which are labels of paths from p to 1:

$$\Phi(p) = \{u \in A^* \mid u \leq w \text{ and } p\varphi(u)1\}.$$

We now show that if $\Phi(p) = \Phi(p')$ for some $p, p' \in Q$, then the rows of index p and p' in $\varphi(w)$ are equal. Consider a $q \in Q$ such that

$$p\varphi(w)q.$$

Since the automaton is trim, there exist $v, v' \in A^*$ such that $1\varphi(v)p$ and $q\varphi(v')1$. Thus $1\varphi(vwv')1$ and consequently $vwv' \in X^*$. Since $w \in \bar{F}(X)$, the path $p \xrightarrow{w} q$ is not simple; therefore there exist $u, u' \in A^*$ such that $w = uu'$ and vu, $u'v' \in X^*$. Thus there is, in $\mathcal{A}$, the path

$$1 \xrightarrow{v} p \xrightarrow{u} 1 \xrightarrow{u'} q \xrightarrow{v'} 1.$$

By definition, $u \in \Phi(p)$. Thus $u \in \Phi(p')$. It follows that $p'\varphi(u)1\varphi(u')q$, and consequently $p'\varphi(w)q$. This proves the claim.

The number of sets $\Phi(p)$, for $p \in Q$, is finite. According to the claim just proved, the set of rows of $\varphi(w)$ also is finite. By Proposition 4.4, this implies that $\varphi(w)$ has finite rank. □

EXAMPLE 5.1 Let X be the code $X = \{a^nba^n \mid n \geq 0\}$. This is a very thin code since $b^2 \in X^* \cap \bar{F}(X)$. An automaton recognizing X^* is given in Fig. 4.24. The image e of b^2 in the associated monoid of relations M is idempotent of rank 1. The finiteness of the rank also results from Proposition 5.2 since b^2 is not factor of a word in X. The localized monoid eMe is reduced to e and 0 (which is the image of b^2ab^2, for example).

The monoid M has elements of infinite rank: thus the image of a. Indeed, clearly no power of this element can be idempotent; hence by Proposition 4.6, it has infinite rank. Moreover, M has elements of finite rank n for each integer $n \geq 0$: the image of ba^nba^nb has rank $n + 1$.

PROPOSITION 5.3 *Let X be a code over A, let $\mathcal{A} = (Q,1,1)$ be an unambiguous trim automaton recognizing X^*, let φ be the associated representation and $M = \varphi(A^*)$.*

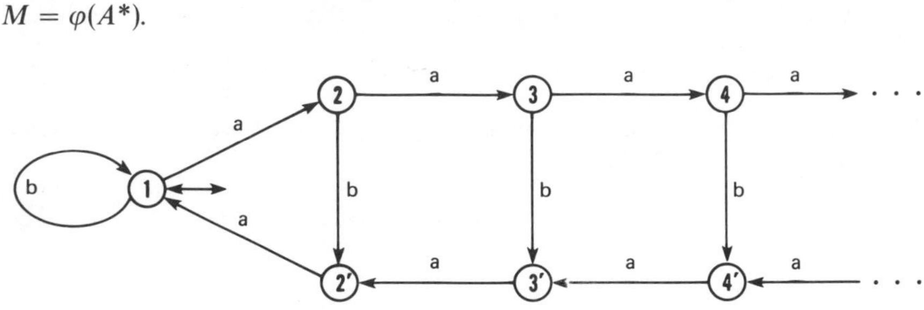

Fig. 4.24 An automaton for X^*.

Let e be an idempotent in $\varphi(X^*)$ with finite rank, and such that the group G_e is transitive.

1. *There exist $v_1, v_2, \ldots, v_{n+1} \in \varphi^{-1}(G(e))$ with the following property: for all $y, z \in A^*$ such that*

$$yv_1v_2\cdots v_i, \qquad v_{i+1}\cdots v_{n+1}z \in X^*.$$

2. *The set $\varphi^{-1}(e) \cap \bar{F}(X)$ is nonempty.*

Proof Let $e = cl$ be the column–row decomposition of e, let S be the set of its fixed points, let $G = G(e)$ be the group of invertible elements of the monoid $M(e) = eMe$. The restriction $\gamma\colon M(e) \to M_e$ is the isomorphism $m \mapsto lmc$, and its inverse is the function $n \mapsto cnl$.

The set S contains the element 1, since $e \in \varphi(X^*)$. Set $S = \{1, 2, \ldots, n\}$. We first rule out the case where $\varphi^{-1}(e) = \{1\}$. Then e is the neutral element of M. Thus $S = Q$. Further for $p, q \in Q$ there exist $g \in G(e)$ $(= G_e)$ such that pgq and $qg^{-1}p$. If $u, v \in A^*$ are such that $\varphi(u) = g$, $\varphi(v) = g^{-1}$, then $\varphi(uv) = e$ and consequently $u = v = 1$. This shows that Q has just one element; but $\varphi^{-1}(e) = A^*$, whence $A = X = \varnothing$. Thus the result holds trivially.

We now assume that $\varphi^{-1}(e) \neq \{1\}$. Choose elements $g_2, g_3, \ldots, g_n \in G_e$ such that

$$\begin{gathered} 2g_2 1 \\ 3g_2g_3 1 \\ \vdots \\ ng_2g_3\cdots g_n 1. \end{gathered}$$

These elements exist because G_e is a transitive permutation group. The permutations $g_2, g_3, \ldots, g_n$ are the restrictions to S of elements

$$h_2, h_3, \ldots, h_n$$

of $G(e)$. Each h_i is equal to $h_i = cg_il$. Let $v_1, v_2, \ldots, v_{n+1} \in A^+$ be such that

$$\varphi(v_1) = \varphi(v_{n+1}) = e, \qquad \varphi(v_2) = h_2, \ldots, \varphi(v_n) = h_n.$$

Set $w = v_1v_2\cdots v_{n+1}$. Consider words $y, z \in A^*$ such that $ywz \in X^*$. Then there exist $p, q \in Q$ such that

$$1 \xrightarrow{y} p \xrightarrow{w} q \xrightarrow{z} 1.$$

Note that

$$\varphi(w) = clh_2\cdots h_ncl = cg_2\cdots g_nl.$$

Since $p\varphi(w)q$, there exist $r, s \in S$ such that

$$pcr, \qquad rg_2 \cdots g_n s, \qquad slq.$$

Then $rg_2 \cdots g_r 1$ (with $g_2 \cdots g_r = I_S$ when $r = 1$). Since the g_i's are functions, this implies

$$1 g_{r+1} \cdots g_n s.$$

Consequently

$$rh_2 \cdots h_r 1, \qquad 1 h_{r+1} \cdots h_n s,$$

and since $pcr = per$, $slq = seq$, we have

$$peh_2 \cdots h_r 1, 1 h_{r+1} \cdots h_n eq.$$

This implies that

$$yv_1 v_2 \cdots v_r, v_{r+1} \cdots v_{n+1} z \in X^*.$$

Thus the words $v_1, \ldots, v_{n+1}$ satisfy the first statement.

To show the second part, we verify that the word $w = v_1 v_2 \cdots v_{n+1}$ is in $\bar{F}(X)$. Assume indeed that $ywz \in X$ for some $y, z \in A^*$. Then there exists an integer i $(1 \le i \le n)$ such that $yv_1 \cdots v_i, v_{i+1} \cdots v_{n+1} z \in X^*$. Since $v_1, \ldots, v_{n+1} \in A^+$, these two words are in fact in X^+, contradicting the fact that X is a code. Thus $w \in \bar{F}(X)$.

Let h' be the inverse of $h = \varphi(w)$ in $G(e)$, and let w' be such that $\varphi(w') = h'$. Then $ww' \in \varphi^{-1}(e)$, and also $ww' \in \bar{F}(X)$. This concludes the proof. □

Proof of Theorem 5.1 (i) ⇒ (ii) Let $x \in X^* \cap \bar{F}(X)$. According to Proposition 5.2, the rank of $\varphi_{\mathscr{A}}(x)$ is finite. Since $x \in X^*$, we have $(1, \varphi_{\mathscr{A}}(x), 1) = 1$ and thus $\varphi_{\mathscr{A}}(x) \neq 0$. This shows that $\varphi_{\mathscr{A}}(A^*)$ has finite minimal rank.

(ii) ⇒ (i). The monoid $M = \varphi_{\mathscr{A}}(A^*)$ is a transitive monoid of unambiguous relations having finite minimal rank $r(M)$. Let

$$K = \{m \in M \mid \text{rank}(m) = r(M)\}.$$

By Theorems 4.5 and 4.11, there exists an idempotent e in $K \cap \text{Stab}(1)$, and the group G_e is transitive of degree $r(M)$. By Proposition 5.3, the set $\varphi_{\mathscr{A}}^{-1}(e) \cap \bar{F}(X)$ is not empty. Since $\varphi_{\mathscr{A}}^{-1}(e) \subset X^*$, the code X is very thin. □

We now examine a series of consequences of Theorem 5.1.

COROLLARY 5.4 *Let X be a complete code, and let $\mathscr{A} = (Q, 1, 1)$ be an unambiguous trim automaton recognizing X^*. The following conditions are equivalent.*

(i) *X is thin.*
(ii) *The monoid $\varphi_{\mathscr{A}}(A^*)$ contains elements of finite rank.*

Proof Since X is complete, the monoid $\varphi_{\mathscr{A}}(A^*)$ does not contain the null relation (Proposition 1.8). Thus the result follows directly from Theorem 5.1. □

Another consequence of Theorem 5.1 is an algebraic proof, independent of measures, of Theorem I.5.7.

COROLLARY 5.5 *If X is a thin complete code, then X is a maximal code.*

Proof Let $\mathscr{A} = (Q, 1, 1)$ be an unambiguous trim automaton recognizing X^* and let φ be the associated representation. Let $x \in X^*$ such that $e = \varphi(x)$ is an idempotent of the minimal ideal J of the monoid $\varphi(A^*)$. (Such an idempotent exists by Theorem 4.11, claim 3).

Let $y \notin X$. Then $e\varphi(y)e = \varphi(xyx)$ is in the $\mathscr{H}$-class of e. This $\mathscr{H}$-class is a finite group. Thus there exists an integer $n \geq 1$ such that $(\varphi(xyx))^n = e$. Consequently $(xyx)^n \in X^*$. This shows that $X \cup y$ is not a code. □

Let $X \subset A^+$ be a code and let $\mathscr{A} = (Q, 1, 1)$ be an unambiguous trim automaton recognizing X^*. We have shown that X is very thin iff the monoid $M = \varphi_{\mathscr{A}}(A^*)$ has elements of finite, positive rank. Let r be the minimum of these nonzero ranks, and let K be the set of elements in M of rank r. Set $\varphi = \varphi_{\mathscr{A}}$. It is useful to keep in mind the following facts.

1. $\varphi(X^*)$ meets K. Indeed $\varphi(X^*) = \text{Stab}(1)$ and according to Theorems 4.5 and 4.11, K meets Stab(1).

2. Every $\mathscr{H}$-class H contained in K that meets $\varphi(X^*)$ is a group. Moreover, $\varphi(X^*) \cap H$ is a subgroup of H. These $\mathscr{H}$-classes are those which contain an idempotent having 1 as a fixed point.

Indeed, let H be an $\mathscr{H}$-class meeting $\varphi(X^*)$. Let $h \in H \cap \varphi(X^*)$. Then h^2 is not the null relation since $h^2 \in \text{Stab}(1)$. Thus $h^2 \in H$ and consequently H is a group (Proposition 0.5.8). Let $N = H \cap \varphi(X^*)$. Since $\varphi(X^*)$ is a stable submonoid of M, N is a stable submonoid of H, hence a subgroup (Example I.2.2.).

Figure 4.25 represents, with slashed triangles, the intersection $K \cap \varphi(X^*)$. It expresses that the $\mathscr{H}$-classes of K meeting $\varphi(X^*)$ "form a rectangle" in K (see Exercise 4.3). Collecting together these facts, we have proved.

THEOREM 5.6 *Let $X \subset A^+$ be a very thin code. Let $\mathscr{A} = (Q, 1, 1)$ be an unambiguous trim automaton recognizing X^*. Let K be the set of elements of minimal nonzero rank in the monoid $M = \varphi_{\mathscr{A}}(A^*)$.*

1. *$\varphi_{\mathscr{A}}(X^*)$ meets K.*
2. *Any $\mathscr{H}$-class H in K that meets $\varphi_{\mathscr{A}}(X^*)$ is a group. Moreover, $H \cap \varphi_{\mathscr{A}}(X^*)$ is a subgroup of H.*
3. *The $\mathscr{H}$-classes of K meeting $\varphi_{\mathscr{A}}(X^*)$ are those whose idempotent has the state 1 as a fixed point.* □

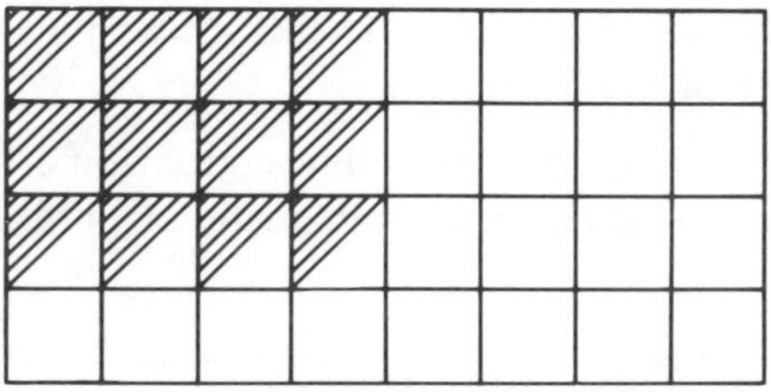

Fig. 4.25 The minimal ideal.

Another consequence of the results of this section is the proof of the following lemma which was stated without proof in Chapter I (Lemma I.6.4).

LEMMA 5.7 *Let X be a complete thin code. For any word $u \in X^*$ there exists a word $w \in X^*uX^*$ satisfying the following property: if $ywz \in X^*$, then there exists a factorization $w = fug$ such that $yf, gz \in X^*$.*

Proof Let φ be the representation associated with some unambiguous trim automaton recognizing X^*. Since X is thin, the monoid $M = \varphi(A^*)$ has a minimal ideal J, and since X is complete, M has no zero. Thus $\varphi(X^+)$ meets J. Let e be an idempotent in $\varphi(X^*) \cap J$. The group G_e is transitive and, according to Proposition 5.3, there exist words $v_1, v_2, \ldots, v_{n+1} \in \varphi^{-1}(G(e))$ such that the word $v = v_1 v_2 \cdots v_{n+1}$ has the following property: if $yvz \in X^*$ for some $y, z \in A^*$, then there exists an integer i such that $yv_1 \cdots v_i, v_{i+1} \cdots v_{n+1}z \in X^*$.

We have $e\varphi(u)e \in eMe = G(e)$, and $e\varphi(u)e \in \varphi(X^*)$. Since $G(e) \cap \varphi(X^*)$ is a subgroup of $G(e)$, there exists $h \in G(e) \cap \varphi(X^*)$ such that $e\varphi(u)eh = e$. Since $h = eh$, we have $e\varphi(u)h = e$. Consider words $r \in \varphi^{-1}(e)$, $s \in \varphi^{-1}(h)$, set $u' = rus$ and consider the word

$$w = u'v_1u'v_2 \cdots u'v_{n+1}u'.$$

Let $y, z \in A^*$ be words such that $ywz \in X^*$. Since $\varphi(u') = e$, we have

$$\varphi(w) = \varphi(v).$$

Consequently also yvz is in X^*; thus for some integer i,

$$yv_1v_2 \cdots v_i, v_{i+1} \cdots v_{n+1}z \in X^*.$$

Observe that $\varphi(v_1v_2 \cdots v_i) = \varphi(u'v_1u'v_2 \cdots u'v_i)$ and

$$\varphi(v_{i+1} \cdots v_{n+1}) = \varphi(v_{i+1}u' \cdots u'v_{n+1}u').$$

Thus also $yu'v_1u'v_2 \cdots u'v_i$ and $v_{i+1}u' \cdots v_{n+1}u'$ are in X^*.

Let

$$f = u'v_1u'v_2 \cdots u'v_ir, \qquad g = sv_{i+1}u' \cdots v_{n+1}u'.$$

Since $r, s \in X^*$, we have $yf, gz \in X^*$ and this shows that the word $w = fug$ satisfies the property of the statement. □

Finally, we note that for complete thin codes, some of the information concerning the minimal ideal are characteristic of prefix, suffix, or biprefix codes.

PROPOSITION 5.8 *Let X be a thin complete code over A, let φ be the representation associated with an unambiguous trim automaton $\mathcal{A} = (Q, 1, 1)$ recognizing X^*, let $M = \varphi(A^*)$ and J its minimal ideal. Let H_0, R_0, L_0 be an $\mathcal{H}, \mathcal{R}, \mathcal{L}$-class of J such that $H_0 = R_0 \cap L_0$ and $\varphi(X^*) \cap H_0 \neq \emptyset$.*

1. *X is prefix iff $\varphi(X^*)$ meets every $\mathcal{H}$-class in L_0.*
2. *X is suffix iff $\varphi(X^*)$ meets every $\mathcal{H}$-class in R_0.*
3. *X is biprefix iff $\varphi(X^*)$ meets all $\mathcal{H}$-classes in J.*

Proof

(1) Let H be an $\mathcal{H}$-class in L_0, let e_0 be the idempotent of H_0 and let e be the idempotent of H (each $\mathcal{H}$-class in J is a group). We have $e_0 e = e_0$ since $e \in L_0$ (for some m, we have $me = e_0$; consequently $e_0 = mee = me = e_0 e$).

If X is prefix, then $\varphi(X^*)$ is right unitary. Since $e_0 \in \varphi(X^*)$ and $e_0 = e_0 e$, it follows that $e \in \varphi(X^*)$. Thus $H \cap \varphi(X^*) \neq \emptyset$.

Conversely, let us show that $\varphi(X^*)$ is right complete. Let $m \in M$. Then $me_0 \in L_0$, thus $m_0 \in H$ for some $\mathcal{H}$-class $H \subset L_0$. If n is the inverse of me_0 in the group H, then $me_0 n \in \varphi(X^*)$. Thus $\varphi(X^*)$ is right complete and X is prefix.

The proof of (2) is symmetric, and (3) results from the preceding points. □

Let $X \subset A^*$ be a thin, maximal prefix code, and let $\mathcal{A} = (Q, 1, 1)$ be a complete, deterministic automaton recognizing X^*. The monoid $M = \varphi_{\mathcal{A}}(A^*)$ then is a monoid of (total) functions. We will write, for $m \in M$, $qm = q'$ instead of $(q, m, q') = 1$. Let $m \in M$, and $w \in A^*$ with $m = \varphi(w)$. The *image* of m is

$$\mathrm{Im}(m) = Qm = Q \cdot w,$$

and the *nuclear equivalence* of m, denoted by $\mathrm{Ker}(m)$, is defined by

$$q \equiv q' \quad (\mathrm{Ker}(m)) \qquad \Leftrightarrow \qquad qm = q'm.$$

The number of classes of the equivalence relation $\mathrm{Ker}(m)$ is equal to $\mathrm{Card}(\mathrm{Im}(m))$; both are equal to $\mathrm{rank}(m)$, in view of Example 4.3.

A *maximal nuclear equivalence* is an equivalence which is maximal among the nuclear equivalences of elements in M. It is an equivalence relation with a number of classes equal to $r(M)$. A *minimal image* is similarly an image of cardinality $r(M)$, i.e., an image which does not strictly contain any other image.

PROPOSITION 5.9 *Let $X \subset A^+$ be a thin maximal prefix code, let $\mathcal{A} = (Q, 1, 1)$ be a deterministic, complete automaton recognizing X^*, let*

$M = \varphi_{\mathscr{A}}(A^*)$ and let K be the $\mathscr{D}$-class of the elements of M of rank $r(M)$. Then

1. *there is a bijection between the minimal images and the $\mathscr{L}$-classes of K,*
2. *there is a bijection between the maximal nuclear equivalences and the $\mathscr{R}$-classes of K.*

Proof

1. Let $n, m \in M$ be two $\mathscr{L}$-equivalent elements. We prove that $\mathrm{Im}(m) = \mathrm{Im}(n)$. There exist $u, v \in M$ such that $m = un$, $n = vm$. Thus $Qm = Qun \subset Qn$, and also $Qn \subset Qm$. This shows that $\mathrm{Im}(m) = \mathrm{Im}(n)$.

Conversely let $m, n \in K$ be such that $\mathrm{Im}(m) = \mathrm{Im}(n)$. K being a regular $\mathscr{D}$-class, the $\mathscr{L}$-class of m contains an idempotent, say e, and the $\mathscr{L}$-class of n contains an idempotent f (Proposition 0.5.7). Then $\mathrm{Im}(e) = \mathrm{Im}(m)$ and $\mathrm{Im}(f) = \mathrm{Im}(n)$, in view of the first part. Thus $\mathrm{Im}(e) = \mathrm{Im}(f)$. We shall see that $ef = e$ and $fe = f$.

Let indeed $q \in Q$, and $q' = qe$. Then $q' = qe^2 = q'e$. Further $q' \in \mathrm{Im}(e) = \mathrm{Im}(f)$. Thus $q' = q'f$ since f is idempotent. Consequently $qe = qef$. Thus $e = ef$. The equality $fe = f$ is shown by interchanging e and f. These relations imply $e\mathscr{L}f$. Thus $m\mathscr{L}n$.

2. The proof is entirely analogous. □

Note also that in the situation described above, *every state appears in some minimal image.* This is indeed the translation of Theorem 4.11(4). This description of the minimal ideal of a monoid of functions, by means of minimal images and maximal equivalences, appears to be particularly convenient.

EXAMPLE 5.2 Let $X = \{aa, ba, baa\}$. We consider the automaton given in Fig. 4.26.

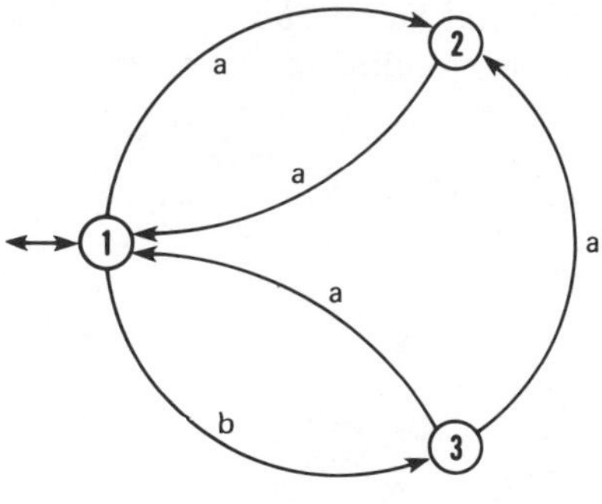

Fig. 4.26 An automaton for X^*.

The 0-minimal ideal of the corresponding monoid is the following: it is formed of elements of rank 1.

	001	110
011	* $\alpha\beta$	* $\alpha\beta\alpha$
100	β	* $\beta\alpha$
101	* $\alpha\alpha\beta$	* $\alpha\alpha\beta\alpha$

$$\alpha = \varphi(a) = \begin{bmatrix} 0 & 1 & 0 \\ 1 & 0 & 0 \\ 1 & 1 & 0 \end{bmatrix}$$

$$\beta = \varphi(b) = \begin{bmatrix} 0 & 0 & 1 \\ 0 & 0 & 0 \\ 0 & 0 & 0 \end{bmatrix}$$

For each element we indicate, on the top, its unique nonnull row, and, on its left, its unique nonnull column. The existence of an idempotent is indicated by an asterisk in the $\mathscr{H}$-class. The column–row decomposition of an idempotent is simply given by the vectors in the rows and columns of the array. For example, the column–row decomposition of $\alpha\beta$ is

$$\alpha\beta = \begin{bmatrix} 0 \\ 1 \\ 1 \end{bmatrix} [0 \quad 0 \quad 1].$$

The following array gives the fixed point of each idempotent

3	2
	1
3	1

EXAMPLE 5.3 Let $X = \{aa, ba, baa, bb, bba\}$. We consider the automaton given in Fig. 4.27. The corresponding monoid has no 0 (the code is complete).

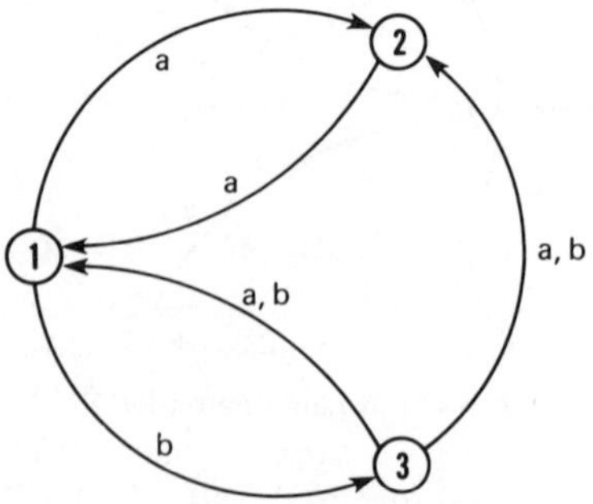

Fig. 4.27 An automaton for X^*.

The minimal ideal, formed of elements of rank 1, is represented by

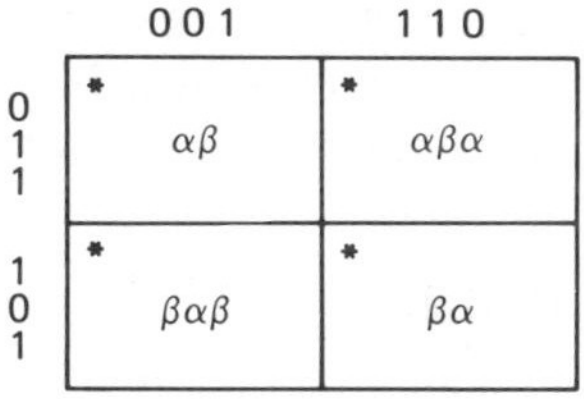

$$\alpha = \varphi(a) = \begin{bmatrix} 0 & 1 & 0 \\ 1 & 0 & 0 \\ 1 & 1 & 0 \end{bmatrix}$$

$$\beta = \varphi(b) = \begin{bmatrix} 0 & 0 & 1 \\ 0 & 0 & 0 \\ 1 & 1 & 0 \end{bmatrix}$$

The fixed points of the idempotents are:

3	2
3	1

EXAMPLE 5.4 Let $A = \{a, \bar{a}, b, \bar{b}\}$. Denote by θ the congruence on A* generated by the relations

$$a\bar{a} \sim 1, \qquad b\bar{b} \sim 1.$$

The class of 1 for the congruence θ is a biunitary submonoid. We denote by D'_2 the code generating this submonoid. The set $D'_2{}^*$ can be considered to be the set of "systems of parentheses" with two types of brackets: a, b represent left brackets, and $\bar{a}$, $\bar{b}$ the corresponding right brackets.

The code D'_2 is thin since D'_2 is not complete. Indeed, for instance,

$$a\bar{b} \notin F(D'_2{}^*).$$

However, D'_2 is not very thin, Indeed, for all $w \in D'_2{}^*$, we have

$$aw\bar{a} \in D'_2.$$

The code D'_2 is biprefix. Let $\mathscr{A}(D'_2{}^*) = (Q, 1, 1)$, let $\varphi = \varphi_{\mathscr{A}}$ and let $M = \varphi(\mathrm{A}^*)$. The monoid M is isomorphic with the syntactic monoid of $D'_2{}^*$.

We have $D'_2{}^* = \varphi^{-1}(1)$. The monoid M contains a 0 and

$$\varphi^{-1}(0) = \bar{F}(D'_2{}^*).$$

The only two sided ideals of M are M and 0. Indeed, if $m \in M - 0$ and $w \in \varphi^{-1}(m)$, then $w \in F(D'_2{}^*)$. Therefore, there exist $u, v \in A^*$ such that $uwv \in D'_2{}^*$. Hence $\varphi(u)m\,\varphi(v) = 1$ whence $1 \in MmM$ and $MmM = M$.

This shows that M itself is a 0-minimal ideal. Nonetheless, M does not contain any 0-minimal right ideal. Suppose the contrary. By Proposition 0.5.9, M would be the union of all 0-minimal right ideals. Thus any element of $M - 0$ would generate a 0-minimal right ideal. This is false as we shall see now.

For all $n \geq 1$, $\varphi(\bar{a}^n)M \supset \varphi(\bar{a}^{n+1})M$. This inclusion is strict, since if $\varphi(\bar{a}^n) = \varphi(\bar{a}^{n+1}w)$ for some $w \in A^*$, then $a^n\bar{a}^n \in D_2'^*$ would imply $a^n\bar{a}^{n+1}w \in D_2'^*$, whence $\bar{a}w \in D_2'^*$ which is clearly impossible.

This example illustrates the fact that for a code X which is not very thin, no automaton recognizing X^* has elements of finite, positive rank (Theorem 5.1).

6. GROUP AND DEGREE OF A CODE

Let $X \subset A^+$ be a very thin code, let $\mathscr{A}_D^*(X)$ be the flower automaton of X and let φ_D be the associated representation. By Theorem 5.1, the monoid $\varphi_D(A^*)$ has elements of finite, positive rank.

The *group of the code* X is, by definition, the Suschkewitch group of the monoid $\varphi_D(A^*)$ defined at the end of Section 4. It is a transitive permutation group of finite degree. Its degree is equal to the minimal rank $r(\varphi_D(A^*))$ of the monoid $\varphi_D(A^*)$.

We denote by $G(X)$ the group of X. Its degree is, by definition, the *degree of the code* X and is denoted by $d(X)$. Thus one has

$$d(X) = r(\varphi_D(A^*)).$$

We already met a notion of degree in the case of thin maximal biprefix codes. We shall see below that the present and previous notions of degree coincide.

The definition of $G(X)$ and $d(X)$ rely on the flower automaton of X. In fact, these concepts are independent of the automaton which is considered. In order to show this, we first establish a result which is interesting in its own right.

PROPOSITION 6.1 *Let* $X \subset A^+$ *be a thin code. Let* $\mathscr{A} = (P, 1, 1)$ *and* $\mathscr{B} = (Q, 1, 1)$ *be two unambiguous trim automata recognizing* X^*, *and let* φ *and* ψ *be the associated representations. Let* $M = \varphi(A^*)$, $N = \psi(A^*)$, $\Phi = \varphi(\bar{F}(X))$, $\Psi = \psi(\bar{F}(X))$, *let* E *be the set of idempotents in* Φ, and E' *the set of idempotent in* Ψ.
Let $\rho: P \to Q$ *be a reduction of* $\mathscr{A}$ *onto* $\mathscr{B}$ *and let* $\hat{\rho}: M \to N$ *be the morphism associated with* ρ. *Then*

1. $\hat{\rho}(E) = E'$.
2. *Let* $e \in E, e' = \hat{\rho}(e)$. *The restriction of* ρ *to* Fix(e) *is a bijection from* Fix(e) *onto* Fix(e'), *and the monoids* M_e *and* $N_{e'}$ *are equivalent.*

Proof Since $\mathscr{A}$ and $\mathscr{B}$ recognize the same set, we have $\rho^{-1}(1) = 1$ (Proposition 2.3). The morphism $\hat{\rho}: M \to N$ defined by ρ satisfies $\psi = \hat{\rho} \circ \varphi$.

1. Let $e \in E$. Then $\hat{\rho}(e) = \hat{\rho}(e^2) = (\hat{\rho}(e))^2$. Thus $\hat{\rho}(e)$ is an idempotent. If $e = \varphi(w)$ for some $w \in \bar{F}(X)$, then $\hat{\rho}(e) = \psi(w)$, whence $\hat{\rho}(e) \in \Psi$. This shows that $\hat{\rho}(E) \subset E'$.

Conversely, let $e' \in E'$, and let $w \in \bar{F}(X)$ with $e' = \psi(w)$. Then $\varphi(w)$ has finite rank by Proposition 5.2, and by Proposition 4.6, there is an integer $n \geq 1$ such that $(\varphi(w))^n$ is an idempotent. Set $e = (\varphi(w))^n$; then $e = \varphi(w^n)$ and $w^n \in \bar{F}(X)$. Thus $e \in E$. Next $\hat{\rho}(e) = \psi(w^n) = e'^n = e'$. This shows that $\hat{\rho}(E) = E'$.

2. Let $S = \text{Fix}(e)$, $S' = \text{Fix}(e')$. Consider $s \in S$ and let $s' = \rho(s)$. From ses, we get $s'e's'$. Thus $\rho(S) \subset S'$. Conversely, if $s'e's'$, then peq for some $p, q \in \rho^{-1}(s')$. By Proposition 3.5(2), there exists $s \in S$ such that $peseq$. This implies that $s'e'\rho(s)e's'$ and, by unambiguity, $\rho(s) = s'$. Thus $\rho(S) = S'$.

Now let $s, t \in S$ be such that $\rho(s) = \rho(t) = s'$. If $s = 1$ then $t = 1$, since $\rho^{-1}(1) = 1$. Thus we may assume that $s, t \neq 1$. Since $e \in \Phi$, there exist u, v, u', $v' \in A^+$ such that

$$\varphi(uv) = \varphi(u'v') = e$$

and

$$s \xrightarrow{u} 1 \xrightarrow{v} s, \qquad t \xrightarrow{u'} 1 \xrightarrow{v'} t.$$

This implies that

$$s' \xrightarrow{u} 1 \xrightarrow{v} s', \qquad s' \xrightarrow{u'} 1 \xrightarrow{v'} s',$$

whence in particular in $\mathscr{B}$,

$$1 \xrightarrow{vu'} 1.$$

Since $\rho^{-1}(1) = 1$, this implies that there is also a path $1 \xrightarrow{vu'} 1$ in $\mathscr{A}$; this in turn implies that

$$s \xrightarrow{u} 1 \xrightarrow{vu'} 1 \xrightarrow{v'} t$$

or, equivalently,

$$set.$$

Since e is an idempotent and $s, t \in S$, this implies that $s = t$. Thus the restriction of ρ to S is a bijection from S onto S'.

Since $\hat{\rho}(eMe) = e'Ne'$, the restriction of ρ to S induces an isomorphism from M_e onto $N_{e'}$. ▯

PROPOSITION 6.2 *Let X be a very thin code over A. Let $\mathscr{A} = (Q, 1, 1)$ be an unambiguous trim automaton recognizing X^*, and let φ be the associated representation. Then the Suschkewitch group of $\varphi(A^*)$ is equivalent to* $G(X)$.

Proof According to Proposition 2.5, there exists a reduction from $\mathscr{A}_D^*(X)$ onto $\mathscr{A}$. Let e be a nonnull idempotent in the 0-minimal ideal of $M = \varphi_D(A^*)$. The image of e by the reduction is a nonnull idempotent e' in the 0-minimal ideal of $N = \varphi(A^*)$. Since $\varphi_D(\bar{F}(X))$, $\varphi(\bar{F}(X))$ are ideals (which are nonnull because they meet $\varphi_D(X^*)$, $\varphi(X^*)$), both $e \in \varphi_D(\bar{F}(X))$, $e' \in \varphi(\bar{F}(X))$. By the preceding proposition, $M_e \simeq N_{e'}$. Thus $G(X) \simeq N_{e'} - \{0\}$ which is the Suschkewitch group of $\varphi(A^*)$. ▯

EXAMPLE 6.1 Let G be a transitive permutation group on a finite set Q, and let H be the subgroup of G stabilizing an element q of Q. Let φ be a morphism from A^* onto G, and let X be the (group) code generating $X^* = \varphi^{-1}(H)$. The group $G(X)$ then is equivalent to G and $d(X)$ is the number of elements in Q.

In particular, we have for all $n \geq 1$,

$$G(A^n) = Z/n\mathbb{Z},\ d(A^n) = n.$$

The preceding proposition shows that the group of a very thin code and consequently also its degree, are independent of the automaton chosen. Thus we may expect that the degree reflects some combinatorial property of the code. This is indeed the fact, as we will see now.

Let X be a very thin code over A. An *interpretation* of a word $w \in A^*$ (with respect to X) is a triple

$$(d, x, g)$$

with

$$d \in A^- X, \qquad x \in X^*, \qquad g \in XA^-$$

and

$$w = dxg.$$

We denote by $I(w)$ the set of interpretations of w. Two interpretations (d, x, g) and (d', x', g') of w are *adjacent* or *meet* if there exist $y, z, y', z' \in X^*$ such that

$$x = yz, \qquad x' = y'z', \qquad dy = d'y', \qquad zg = z'g'$$

(see Fig. 4.28). Two interpretations which do not meet are called *disjoint*. A set $\Delta \subset I(w)$ is *disjoint* if its elements are pairwise disjoint.

Let $w \in A^*$. The *degree* of w with respect to X is the nonnegative number

$$\delta_X(w) = \max\{\mathrm{Card}(\Delta) \mid \Delta \subset I(w),\ \Delta \text{ disjoint}\}.$$

Thus $\delta_X(w)$ is the maximal number of pairwise disjoint interpretations of w. Note that for $w \in \bar{F}(X)$,

$$\delta_X(uwv) \leq \delta_X(w).$$

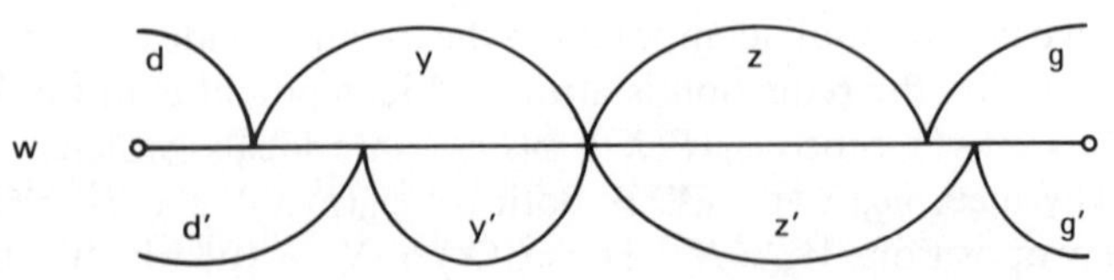

Fig. 4.28 Two adjacent interpretation.

Indeed, every interpretation of uwv gives rise to an interpretation of w, and disjoint interpretations of uwv have their restriction to w also disjoint. Observe also that this inequality does not hold in general if $w \in F(X)$. In particular, a word in $F(X)$ may have no interpretation at all, whereas $\delta_X(w)$ is always at least equal to 1, for $w \in \bar{F}(X) \cap X^*$.

PROPOSITION 6.3 *Let X be a very thin code. Then*

$$d(X) = \min\{\delta_X(w) \mid w \in X^* \cap \bar{F}(X)\}.$$

Proof Let $\mathscr{A}_D^*(X) = (P, 1, 1)$ be the flower automaton of X, with the shorthand notation 1 instead of $(1, 1)$ for the initial and final state. Let $M = \varphi_D(A^*)$, let J be the 0-minimal ideal of M, let e be an idempotent in $\varphi(X^*) \cap J$ and let $S = \mathrm{Fix}(e)$. Then by definition $d(X) = \mathrm{Card}(S)$.

According to Proposition 5.3, we have $\varphi_D^{-1}(e) \cap \bar{F}(X) \neq \varnothing$. Take a fixed word $x \in \varphi_D^{-1}(e) \cap \bar{F}(X)$. Then $x \in X^* \cap \bar{F}(X)$, since $e \in \varphi_D(X^*)$.

Let $w \in X^* \cap \bar{F}(X)$ and let us verify that $d(X) \leq \delta_X(w)$. For this, it suffices to show that $d(X) \leq \delta_X(xwx)$, because of the inequality $\delta_X(xwx) \leq \delta_X(w)$. Now $\varphi_D(xwx) \in H(e)$, and consequently its restriction to S is a permutation on S. Thus for each $s \in S$, there exists one and only one $s' \in S$ such that $(s, \varphi_D(xww), s') = 1$, or equivalently such that

$$s \xrightarrow{xwx} s'.$$

Since $w \in \bar{F}(X)$, this path is not simple. Setting $s = (u, d)$, $s' = (g, v)$ it factorizes into

$$s \xrightarrow{d} 1 \xrightarrow{y} 1 \xrightarrow{g} s'$$

and (d, y, g) is an interpretation of xwx. Thus each path from a state in S to another state in S, labeled by xwx, gives an interpretation of xwx. Two such interpretations are disjoint. Assume indeed the contrary. Then there are two interpretations (d_1, y_1, g_1) and (d_2, y_2, g_2) derived from paths $s_1 \xrightarrow{xwx} s'_1$ and $s_2 \xrightarrow{xwx} s'_2$ that are adjacent. This means that the paths factorize into

$$s_1 \xrightarrow{d_1} 1 \xrightarrow{z_1} 1 \xrightarrow{z'_1} 1 \xrightarrow{g_1} s'_1,$$

$$s_2 \xrightarrow{d_2} 1 \xrightarrow{z_2} 1 \xrightarrow{z'_2} 1 \xrightarrow{g_2} s'_2,$$

with $d_1 z_1 = d_2 z_2$, whence also $z'_1 g_1 = z'_2 g_2$. Then there is also, in $\mathscr{A}_D^*(X)$, a path

$$s_1 \xrightarrow{d_1} 1 \xrightarrow{z_1} 1 \xrightarrow{z'_2} 1 \xrightarrow{g_2} s'_2$$

labeled xwx. This implies $(s_1, \varphi_D(xwx), s'_2) = 1$; since $s'_2 \in S$, one has $s'_2 = s'_1$, whence $s_2 = s_1$.

Thus the mapping associating to each fixed point an interpretation produces a set of pairwise disjoint interpretations. Consequently $\mathrm{Card}(S) \leq \delta_X(xwx)$.

We now show that

$$\delta_X(x^3) \le d(X),$$

where x is the word in $\varphi_D^{-1}(e) \cap \bar{F}(X)$ fixed above. This will imply the proposition.

Let (d, y, g) be an interpretation of x^3. Let $p = (u, d)$, $q = (g, v) \in P$. Then there is a unique path

$$p \xrightarrow{d} 1 \xrightarrow{y} 1 \xrightarrow{g} q, \tag{6.1}$$

and moreover the paths $p \xrightarrow{d} 1$, $1 \xrightarrow{g} q$ are simple or null. Since $\varphi_D(x) = e$, there exists a unique $s \in S$ such that $p\varphi_D(x)s\varphi_D(x)s\varphi_D(x)q$ or, equivalently, the path (6.1) also factorizes into

$$p \xrightarrow{x} s \xrightarrow{x} s \xrightarrow{x} q.$$

The word d is a left factor of x since $x \in \bar{F}(X)$.

Thus there exist words $z, z' \in A^*$ such that

$$y = zx\bar{z}, \qquad dz = x = \bar{z}g.$$

Observe that the fixed point $s \in S$ associated to the interpretation is independent of the endpoints of the path (6.1): Consider indeed another path

$$p' \xrightarrow{d} 1 \xrightarrow{y} 1 \xrightarrow{g} q'$$

associated to the interpretation (d, y, g), and a fixed point $s' \in S$ such that $p' \xrightarrow{x} s' \xrightarrow{x} s' \xrightarrow{x} q'$. Since d is strictly shorter than x, the inner part of this path coincides with the corresponding segment in path (6.1), and consequently $s = s'$.

Thus we have associated, to each interpretation (d, y, g), a fixed point $s \in S$, which in turn determines two words $z, \bar{z}$ such that $y = zx\bar{z}$, and

$$1 \xrightarrow{z} s \xrightarrow{x} s \xrightarrow{\bar{z}} 1.$$

We now show that the fixed points associated to distinct interpretations are distinct. This will imply that $\delta_X(x^3) \le \mathrm{Card}(S) = d(X)$ and will complete the proof.

Let (d', y', g') be another interpretation of x^3, let $p' = (u', d')$, $q' = (g', v') \in P$, and assume that the path

$$p' \xrightarrow{d'} 1 \xrightarrow{y'} 1 \xrightarrow{g'} q'$$

decomposes into

$$p' \xrightarrow{d'} 1 \xrightarrow{z'} s \xrightarrow{x} s \xrightarrow{\bar{z}'} 1 \xrightarrow{g'} q'. \tag{6.2}$$

Since $x \in \bar{F}(X)$, the path $s \xrightarrow{x} s$ is not simple. Thus there exist $h, \bar{h} \in A^*$ such that $x = h\bar{h}$ and

$$s \xrightarrow{h} 1 \xrightarrow{\bar{h}} s.$$

The paths (6.1) and (6.2) become

$$p \xrightarrow{d} 1 \xrightarrow{z} s \xrightarrow{h} 1 \xrightarrow{\bar{h}} s \xrightarrow{\bar{z}} 1 \xrightarrow{g} q,$$
$$p' \xrightarrow{d'} 1 \xrightarrow{z'} s \xrightarrow{h} 1 \xrightarrow{\bar{h}} s \xrightarrow{\bar{z}'} 1 \xrightarrow{g'} q'.$$

This shows that $zh, \bar{h}\bar{z}, z'h, \bar{h}z' \in X^*$. Next $dz = d'z' = x$. Thus $dzh = d'z'h$, showing that the interpretations (d, y, g) and (d', y', g') are adjacent. The proof is complete. □

Now we are able to make the connection with the concept of degree of biprefix codes introduced in the previous chapter. If $X \subset A^+$ is a thin maximal biprefix code, then two adjacent interpretations of a word $w \in A^*$ are equal. Thus $\delta_X(w)$ is the number of interpretations of w. As we have seen in Chapter III, this number is constant on $\bar{H}(X)$, whence on $\bar{F}(X)$. Thus Proposition 6.3 shows that the two notions of degree we have defined are identical.

A classification of very thin codes according to their degree starts with the study of codes of degree 1. A very thin code X is called *synchronous* iff $d(X) = 1$. We will see below that this terminology is compatible with that introduced in Chapter II. The following is a characterization of synchronous codes.

PROPOSITION 6.4 *Let X be a very thin code over A. Then X is synchronous iff there exist $x, y \in X^*$ such that, for $u, v \in A^*$*

$$uxyv \in X^* \Rightarrow ux, yv \in X^*.$$

Proof Let X be a synchronous code, and let $x \in X^* \cap \bar{F}(X)$ be a word such that $\delta_X(x) = 1$. Such a word exists by Proposition 6.3. We show that the pair (x, x) satisfies the condition stated above. Let indeed $u, v \in A^*$ be such that $uxxv \in X^*$. The interpretation $(1, uxxv, 1)$ induces two interpretations of x, the first on the first occurrence, the second on the second occurrence of x in $uxxv$. Denote them by

$$(d, y, g), \qquad (d', y', g')$$

with $ud \in X^*, g'v \in X^*$, and $gd' \in 1 \cup X$. Since (d, y, g) and $(1, x, 1)$ are adjacent interpretations (degree is one), there exist $x_1, x_2, y_1, y_2 \in X^*$ such that

$$x = x_1x_2, \qquad y = y_1y_2, \qquad x_1 = dy_1, \qquad x_2 = y_2g.$$

Consequently, $ux = ux_1x_2 = (ud)y_1x_2 \in X^*$. Similarly $xv \in X^*$.

Conversely, let $x, y \in X^*$ be words satisfying the implication. Then $xy \in \bar{F}(X)$. Otherwise there would exist $u, v \in A^*$ such that $uxyv \in X$; but then $ux, yv \in X^*$, contradicting the fact that X is a code. Next consider an interpretation (d, z, g) of xy. Then $ud, gv \in X$ for convenient $u, v \in A^*$. Thus $uxyv \in X^*$, hence $ux \in X^*$ and $yv \in X^*$. This shows that the interpretations (d, z, g) and $(1, xy, 1)$ are adjacent. Thus, $\delta_X(xy) = 1$. □

A pair (x, y) of words in X^+ satisfying the condition of Proposition 6.4 is called a *synchronizing pair*.

The existence of a synchronizing pair (x, y) has the following meaning. When we try to decode a word $w \in A^*$, the occurrence of a factor xy in w implies that the factorization of w into words in X, whenever it exists, must pass between x and y: if $w = uxyv$, it suffices to decode separately ux and yv.

PROPOSITION 6.5 *Let $X \subset A^+$ be a very thin code. The X is complete and synchronous iff there exist $x, y \in X^*$ such that*

$$xA^*y \subset X^*.$$

Proof Assume first that X is complete and synchronous. Let (x, y) be a synchronizing pair. We show that $yA^*x \subset X^*$..Let $w \in A^*$. The word $xywxy$ is completable in X^*. Thus there exist $u, v \in A^*$ such that $uxywxyv \in X^*$. This implies that $ywxyv \in X^*$ and then also $ywx \in X^*$.

Conversely, assume that $xA^*y \subset X^*$. Then the code X is clearly complete. Set $z = xy$. Then (z, z) is a synchronizing pair. Suppose indeed that $uzzv \in X^+$. Then $zuz = x(yux)y \in X^+$ and also $zvz \in X^+$. Thus $z, z(uz), uz(zvz), zvz \in X^*$. By stability, this implies that $uz \in X^*$. Symmetrically, we show that $zv \in X^*$. □

Let us now discuss prefix codes. Let X be a thin maximal prefix code over A. Then X is very thin since any word in $\bar{F}(X)$ can be completed (on the right) into a word in X^*. Of course, X is complete. The condition

$$xA^*y \subset X^*$$

for $x, y \in X^*$ of the preceding proposition is equivalent, since X^* is right unitary, to the condition

$$A^*y \subset X^*$$

stated in Chapter II.

EXAMPLE 6.2 The code $X = \{aa, ba, baa, bb, bba\}$ is synchronous. Indeed, the pair (aa, ba) is an example of a synchronizing pair: assume that $uaabav \in X^*$ for some $u, v \in A^*$. Since $ab \notin F(X)$, we have $uaa, bav \in X^*$. Since

X is also a complete code, it follows by (the proof of) Proposition 6.5 that

$$baA^*aa \subset X^*.$$

We now examine the behavior of the group of a code under composition.

Let G be a transitive permutation group over a set Q. Recall (cf. Sect. 0.8) that an *imprimitivity equivalence* of G is an equivalence relation θ on Q stable with respect to the action of G, i.e., such that for all $g \in G$,

$$p \equiv q \mod \theta \quad \Rightarrow \quad pg \equiv qg \mod \theta.$$

The action of G on the classes of θ defines a transitive permutation group denoted by G_θ and called the *imprimitivity quotient* of G for θ.

For any $q \in Q$, the restriction to the class mod θ of q of the subgroup

$$K = \{k \in G \mid qk \equiv q \bmod \theta\}$$

formed of the elements globally stabilizing the class of $q \bmod \theta$ is a transitive permutation group. The groups induced by G on the equivalence classes mod θ are all equivalent. Any one of these groups is called the *group induced* by G. It is denoted by G^θ.

Let $d = \text{Card}(Q)$ be the degree of G, let e be the cardinality of a class of θ (thus e is the degree of G^θ), and let f be the number of classes of θ (i.e., the degree of G_θ). Then we have the formula

$$d = ef.$$

EXAMPLE 6.3 The permutation group over the set $\{1, 2, 3, 4, 5, 6\}$ generated by the two permutations

$$\alpha = (123456), \qquad \beta = (26)(35)$$

is the group of symmetries of the hexagon,

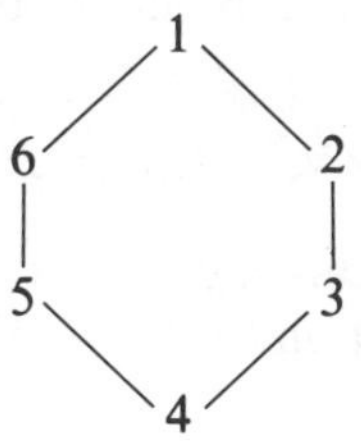

It is known under the name of *dihedral group* D_6, and has of course degree 6. It admits the imprimitivity partition

$$\{1,4\}, \quad \{2,5\}, \quad \{3,6\}$$

The groups G_θ and G^θ are, respectively, equivalent to $\mathfrak{S}_3$ and $\mathbb{Z}/2\mathbb{Z}$.

PROPOSITION 6.6 *Let X be a very thin code which decomposes into*

$$X = Y \circ Z$$

with Y a complete code. There exists an imprimitivity equivalence θ of $G = G(X)$ such that

$$G^\theta = G(Y), \quad G_\theta \simeq G(Z).$$

In particular, we have

$$d(X) = d(Y)d(Z).$$

Proof Let P and S be the sets of states of the flower automata $\mathscr{A}_D^*(X)$, $\mathscr{A}_D^*(Z)$, respectively. Let φ (resp. ψ) be the morphism associated to $\mathscr{A}_D^*(X)$ (resp., $\mathscr{A}_D^*(Z)$). In view of Proposition 2.8, and since Y is complete, there exists a reduction $\rho: P \to S$. Moreover, $\mathscr{A}_D^*(Y)$ can be identified with the restriction of $\mathscr{A}_D^*(X)$ to the states which are in $Z^* \times Z^*$. As usual, we denote by $\hat{\rho}$ the morphism from $M = \varphi(A^*)$ into $M' = \psi(A^*)$ induced by ρ. Thus $\psi = \hat{\rho} \circ \varphi$.

Let J (resp., K) be the 0-minimal ideal of M (resp., of M'). Then $J \subset \hat{\rho}^{-1}(K)$, since $\hat{\rho}^{-1}(K)$ is a nonnull ideal. Thus $\hat{\rho}(J) \subset K$. Since $\hat{\rho}(J) \neq 0$, we have

$$\hat{\rho}(J) = K.$$

Let e be an idempotent in $J \cap \varphi(X^*)$, let $R = \mathrm{Fix}(e) \subset P$ and let $G = G_e$. The nuclear equivalence of the restriction of ρ to R defines an equivalence relation θ on R which is an imprimitivity equivalence of G. It can be verified that ρ is a surjective function from R onto $\mathrm{Fix}(\hat{\rho}(e))$. The group $G_{\hat{\rho}(e)}$ is the corresponding imprimitivity quotient G_θ. This shows that $G(Z)$ is equivalent to G_θ.

Let $T = \{(u, v) \in P \mid u, v \in Z^*\}$. Then T can be identified with the states of the flower automaton of Y. Let L be the restriction to T of the submonoid $N = \varphi(Z^*)$ of M. Then

$$eNe = G(e) \cap N.$$

Since $G(e) \cap N$ is a group, this shows that e is in the minimal ideal of the monoid N and that the restriction to $R \cap T$ of $G(e) \cap N$ is the Suschkewitch group of L.

Thus the restriction to $R \cap T$ of the group $G(e) \cap L$ is equivalent to the group $G(Y)$. On the other hand, since $T = \rho^{-1}(1, 1)$, this group is also the group G^θ induced by G on the classes of θ. $\square$

EXAMPLE 6.4 Let $X = Z^n$ where Z is a very thin code and $n \geq 1$. Then

$$d(X) = nd(Z)$$

TABLE 4.1

The Next-State Function of $\mathscr{A}(X^*)$

	1	2	3	4	5	6	7	8
a	4	5	4	5	8	1	8	1
b	2	3	4	5	6	7	8	1

EXAMPLE 6.5 Consider the maximal prefix code

$$Z = (A^2 - b^2) \cup b^2 A^2$$

over $A = \{a, b\}$. Set

$$X = Z^2.$$

The automaton $\mathscr{A}(X^*)$ is given in Table 4.1. Let φ be the corresponding representation. The monoid $\varphi(A^*)$ is the monoid of functions of Example 3.4, when setting $\varphi(a) = u, \varphi(b) = v$.

The idempotent $e = \varphi(a^4)$ has minimal rank since the action of A on the $\mathscr{R}$-class of e given in Fig. 3.5 is complete. Consequently, the group $G(X)$ is the dihedral group D_4. This group admits an imprimitivity partition with a quotient and an induced group both equivalent to $\mathbb{Z}/2\mathbb{Z}$. This corresponds to the fact that

$$G(Z) = \mathbb{Z}/2\mathbb{Z},$$

since

$$Z = T \circ A^2,$$

where T is a synchronous code.

In the case of prefix codes, we can continue the study of the influence of the decompositions of the code on the structure of its group.

We first define a canonical decomposition of a prefix code called its maximal decomposition. This is used to show that only maximal prefix codes may produce nontrivial groups by composition.

Let $X \subset A^+$ be a prefix code. Let

$$D = X^*(A^*)^{-1} = \{w \in A^* \mid wA^* \cap X^* \neq \varnothing\}$$

be the set of left factors of X^*, i.e., the set of right-completable words in X^*.

Consider the set

$$U = \{u \in A^* \mid u^{-1}D = D\}.$$

Note first that $U \subset D$: Let $u \in U$. Since $1 \in D$, we have $1 \in u^{-1}D$, whence $u \in D$.

The set U is a right unitary submonoid of A^*. Let indeed $u, v \in U$. Then $(uv)^{-1}D = v^{-1}u^{-1}D = v^{-1}D = D$ showing that $uv \in U$. Assume next that $u, uv \in U$. Then $u^{-1}D = D$, and $v^{-1}D = v^{-1}u^{-1}D = (uv)^{-1}D = D$. Thus U is right unitary.

Let Z be the prefix code generating U: $U = Z^*$. We have $X^* \subset Z^* = U$. Indeed, X^* is right unitary. Thus for all $x \in X^*$, $x^{-1}X^* = X^*$. It follows that

$$\begin{aligned} x^{-1}D &= x^{-1}(X^*(A^*)^{-1}) \\ &= (x^{-1}X^*)(A^*)^{-1} \\ &= X^*(A^*)^{-1} \\ &= D. \end{aligned}$$

We now show that

$$X = Y \circ Z \tag{6.3}$$

for some maximal prefix code Y. For this, we verify that for $u \in U$, there exists $v \in U$ such that $uv \in X^*$.

Indeed, let $u \in U$. Then $u \in D$, and therefore $uv \in X^*$ for some $v \in A^*$. Since $X^* \subset U$, we have $u, uv \in U$, and consequently $v \in U$ (U is right unitary). The claim shows that X decomposes over Z. Let Y be such that $X = Y \circ Z$. Then the claim also shows that Y is right-complete, hence Y is prefix maximal.

It can be shown (Exercise 6.2) that for any other decomposition $X = Y' \circ Z'$ with Z' prefix and Y' maximal prefix, we have $Z'^* \subset Z^*$. This justifies the name of *maximal decomposition* of the prefix code X given to the decomposition (6.3).

In the case where X is a maximal prefix code, the set D defined above is A^*. Thus $U = A^*$ and $Z = A$ in (6.3). Thus the maximal decomposition, in this case, is trivial.

PROPOSITION 6.7 *Let X be a very thin prefix code, and let*

$$X = Y \circ Z$$

be its maximal decomposition. Then Z is synchronous, and thus $G(X) = G(Y)$.

Proof Let $D = X^*(A^*)^{-1}$, $U = \{u \in A^* \mid u^{-1}D = D\}$. Then $Z^* = U$. Let φ be the morphism associated with the automaton $\mathscr{A}(X^*)$. Let J be the 0-minimal ideal of the monoid $\varphi(A^*)$.

Consider $x \in X^*$ such that $\varphi(x) \in J$. First we show that

$$D = \{w \in A^* \mid \varphi(xw) \neq 0\}. \tag{6.4}$$

Indeed, if $w \in D$, then $xw \in D$ and thus $\varphi(xw) \neq 0$. Conversely, if $\varphi(xw) \neq 0$ for some $w \in A^*$, then the fact that the right ideal generated by $\varphi(x)$ is 0-

minimal implies that there exists a word $w' \in A^*$ such that $\varphi(x) = \varphi(xww')$. Thus $xww' \in X^*$. By right unitarity, we have $ww' \in X^*$, whence $w \in D$. This proves (6.4).

Next $Dx^{-1} = Ux^{-1}$. Indeed $D \supset U$ implies $Dx^{-1} \supset Ux^{-1}$. Conversely, consider $w \in Dx^{-1}$. Then $wx \in D$. By (6.4), $\varphi(xwx) \neq 0$. Using now the 0-minimality of the *left* ideal generated by $\varphi(x)$, there exists a word $w' \in A^*$ such that $\varphi(w'xwx) = \varphi(x)$. Using again (6.4), we have, for all $w'' \in D$, $\varphi(xw'') = \varphi(w'xwxw'') \neq 0$. Then also $\varphi(xwxw'') \neq 0$ and, again by (6.4), $wxw'' \in D$. This shows that $D \subset (wx)^{-1}D$. For the converse inclusion, let $w'' \in (wx)^{-1}D$. Then $wxw'' \in D$. Thus $\varphi(xwxw'') \neq 0$. This implies that $\varphi(xw'') \neq 0$, whence $w'' \in D$. Thus $D = (wx)^{-1}D$, showing that $w \in Ux^{-1}$.

Now we prove that (x, x) is a synchronizing pair for Z. Let $w, w' \in A^*$ be such that $wxxw' \in Z^* = U$. Since $U \subset D$, we have $wx \in D$. By the preceding equation $Dx^{-1} = Ux^{-1}$, this implies $wx \in U$. Since U is right unitary, xw' also is in U. Thus Z is synchronous. In view of Proposition 6.6, this concludes the proof. ▯

We now prove a converse of Proposition 6.6 in the case of prefix codes.

PROPOSITION 6.8 *Let X be a thin maximal prefix code. If the group $G = G(X)$ admits an imprimitivity equivalence θ, then there exists a decomposition of X into*

$$X = Y \circ Z$$

such that $G(Y) = G^\theta$ and $G(Z) = G_\theta$.

Proof Let φ be the representation associated to the minimal automaton $\mathscr{A}(X^*) = (Q, 1, 1)$, and set $M = \varphi(A^*)$. Let J be the minimal ideal of M, let $e \in J \cap \varphi(X^*)$ be an idempotent, let L be the $\mathscr{L}$-class of e and Γ be the set of $\mathscr{H}$-classes of L. Let $S = \mathrm{Fix}(e)$. We have $G(X) = G_e$.

Since X is complete, each $H \in \Gamma$ is a group and therefore has an idempotent e_H with $\mathrm{Fix}(e_H) = \mathrm{Fix}(e)$. The code X being prefix, e_H is in $\varphi(X^*)$ for all $H \in \Gamma$, by Proposition 5.8.

By assumption, there exists an equivalence relation θ on S that is an imprimitivity equivalence of the group G_e. Consider the equivalence relation $\hat{\theta}$ on the set Q of states of $\mathscr{A}(X^*)$ defined by

$$p \equiv q \mod \hat{\theta} \qquad \text{iff} \quad \forall H \in \Gamma, \quad pe_H \equiv qe_H \mod \theta.$$

Let us verify that $\hat{\theta}$ is stable, i.e., that

$$p \equiv q \mod \hat{\theta} \quad \Rightarrow \quad p \cdot w \equiv q \cdot w \mod \hat{\theta}$$

for $w \in A^*$. Indeed, let $m = \varphi(w)$. Note that for $H \in \Gamma$,

$$me_H = e_{mH}me_H = e_{mH}eme_H \tag{6.5}$$

since $e_{mH}e = e_{mH}$. Observe also that $eme_H \in G(e)$ since $en \in G(e)$ for all $n \in L$. Assume now that $p \equiv q \bmod \hat{\theta}$. Then by definition $pe_{mH} \equiv qe_{mH} \bmod \theta$ and θ being an imprimitivity equivalence, this implies

$$pe_{mH}eme_H \equiv qe_{mH}eme_H \mod \theta$$

By (6.5), it follows that $pme_H \equiv qme_H \bmod \theta$ for all $H \in \Gamma$. Thus $p \cdot w \equiv q \cdot w \bmod \hat{\theta}$.

Moreover, the restriction of $\hat{\theta}$ to the set $S = \mathrm{Fix}(e)$ is equal to θ. Assume indeed that $p \equiv q \bmod \hat{\theta}$ for some $p, q \in S$. Then $pe \equiv qe \bmod \theta$. Since $p = pe$ and $q = qe$, it follows that $p \equiv q \bmod \theta$. Conversely, if $p \equiv q \bmod \theta$, then for all $H \in \Gamma$, $pe_H = p$ and $qe_H = q$, because of the equality $\mathrm{Fix}(e_H) = S$. Consequently $p \equiv q \bmod \hat{\theta}$.

Consider the prefix code Z defined by the right-unitary submonoid

$$Z^* = \{z \in A^* \mid 1 \cdot z \equiv 1 \bmod \hat{\theta}\}.$$

Then clearly $X \subset Z^*$, and the automaton $\mathscr{A}(X^*)$ being trim, X decomposes over Z: $X = Y \circ Z$. The automaton defined by the action of A^* on the classes of $\hat{\theta}$ is easily seen to recognize Z^*. The group $G(Z)$ is the group G_θ. The automaton obtained by considering the action of Z on the class of $1 \bmod \hat{\theta}$ can by identified with an automaton recognizing Y^*, and its group is G^θ. □

Corollary 6.9 *Let X be a thin maximal prefix code. If X is indecomposable, then the group $G(X)$ is primitive.* □

Example 6.6 We consider once more the finite maximal biprefix code $X = ((A^2 - b^2) \cup b^2A^2)^2$ of Example 6.5, with the minimal automaton of X^* given in Fig. 4.29. Let φ be the associated representation. We have seen that $e = \varphi(a^4)$ is an idempotent of minimal rank. The group $G_e = G(X)$ is the

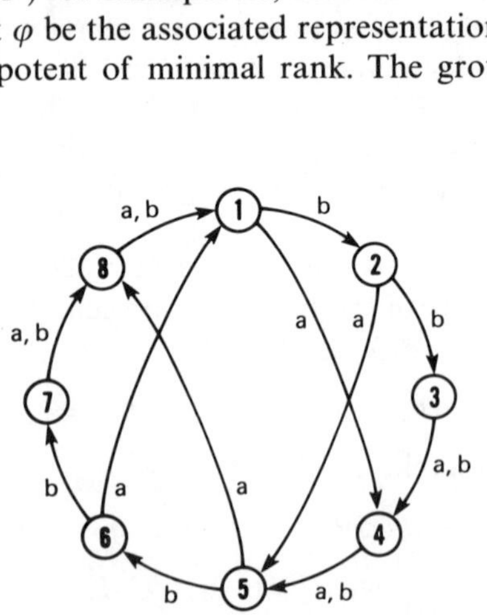

Fig. 4.29 The minimal automaton of X^*.

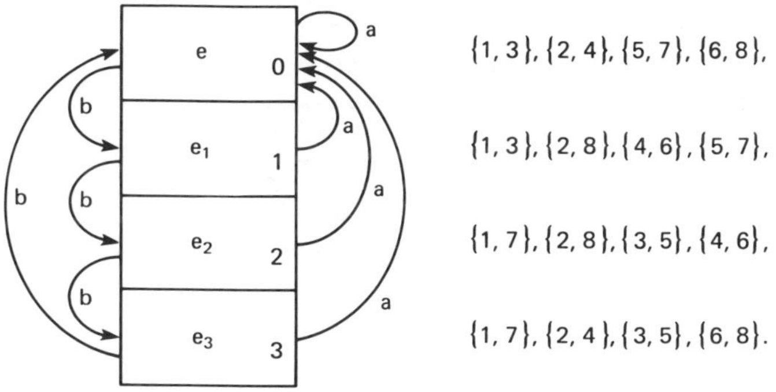

Fig. 4.30 The $\mathscr{L}$-class of $e = \varphi(a^4)$.

dihedral group D_4 generated by the permutations

$$(1458), \qquad (15)(48).$$

The partition $\theta = \{\{1,5\}, \{4,8\}\}$ is an imprimitivity partition of G_e.

The $\mathscr{L}$-class of e is composed of four $\mathscr{H}$-classes. They are represented in Fig. 4.30 together with the associated nuclear equivalences.

The equivalence $\hat{\theta}$ is

$$\hat{\theta} = \{\{1,3,5,7\}, \{2,4,6,8\}\}$$

The stabilizer of the class of 1 mod $\hat{\theta}$ is the uniform code $Z = A^2$ with group $\mathbb{Z}/2\mathbb{Z}$. We have already seen that

$$X = (T \circ A^2)^2 = T^2 \circ A^2$$

for some synchronous code T. The decomposition of X into $X = T^2 \circ Z$ is that obtained by applying to X the method used in the proof of Proposition 6.8.

EXAMPLE 6.7 Let Z be the finite complete prefix code over $A = \{a, b\}$,

$$Z = a \cup bA^2,$$

and consider

$$X = Z^4.$$

The automaton $\mathscr{A}(X^*)$ is given in Table 4.2. Let φ be the representation associated with $\mathscr{A}(X^*)$. The element $e = \varphi(a^4)$ is easily seen to be an idempotent of minimal rank 4, with $\text{Fix}(e) = \{1,4,7,10\}$. It is given in Table 4.3. The minimal ideal of $\varphi(A^*)$ reduces to the $\mathscr{R}$-class of e, and we have $G(X) = \mathbb{Z}/4\mathbb{Z}$, as a result of computing the $\mathscr{L}$-representation with respect to e given in Fig. 4.31. The partition $\theta = \{\{1,7\}, \{4,10\}\}$ is an imprimitivity

TABLE 4.2

The Automaton of $((a \cup bA^2)^4)^*$

	1	2	3	4	5	6	7	8	9	10	11	12
a	4	3	4	7	6	7	10	9	10	1	12	1
b	2	3	4	5	6	7	8	9	10	11	12	1

TABLE 4.3

The Idempotent $e = \varphi(a^4)$

	1	2	3	4	5	6	7	8	9	10	11	12
a^4	7	4	7	10	7	10	1	10	1	4	1	4

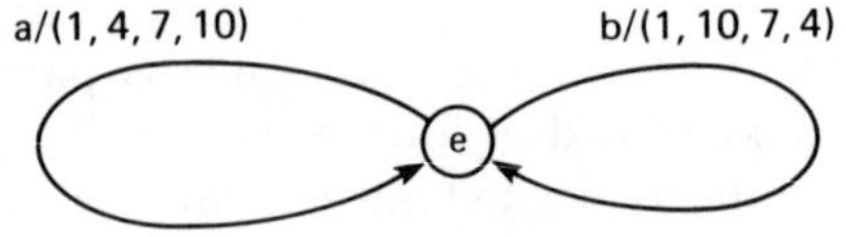

Fig. 4.31 The $\mathscr{L}$-representation with respect to e.

partition of G_e. The corresponding equivalence $\hat{\theta}$ is

$$\hat{\theta} = \{\{1, 3, 5, 7, 9, 11\}, \{2, 4, 6, 8, 10, 12\}\}.$$

The stabilizer of the class of 1 mod $\hat{\theta}$ is the uniform code A^2, and we have

$$X \subset (A^2)^*.$$

Observe that we started with $X = Z^4$. In fact, the words in Z all have odd length, and consequently

$$Z^2 = Y \circ A^2$$

for some Y. Thus X has the two decompositions

$$X = Z^4 = Y^2 \circ A^2.$$

7. SYNCHRONIZATION OF SEMAPHORES

In this section, we prove the result announced in Chapter II, namely,

THEOREM 7.1 *Let X be a semaphore code. There exist a synchronous semaphore code Z and an integer $d \geq 1$ such that*

$$X = Z^d.$$

In view of Proposition 6.6, the integer d is of course the degree $d(X)$ of the code X.

The proof of the theorem is in several parts. We first examine the group of a semaphore code. However, the following proposition is just an intermediate step, since the theorem implies a stronger property.

We recall that a transitive permutation group over a set is called *regular* if its elements, with the exception of the identity, fix no point (See Sect. 0.8).

LEMMA 7.2 *The group of a semaphore code is regular.*

Proof Let $X \subset A^+$ be a semaphore code, let $P = XA^-$ be the set of proper left factors of words in X, and let $\mathscr{A} = (P, 1, 1)$ be the literal automaton of X^*. Let φ be the representation associated with $\mathscr{A}$, and set $M = \varphi(A^*)$.

A semaphore code is thin and complete; thus $0 \notin M$ and the ideal $\varphi(\bar{F}(X))$ of images of words which are not factors of words in X contains the minimal ideal, say K, of M.

Let e be an idempotent in $\varphi(X^*) \cap K$, and let $R = \text{Fix}(e)$. These fixed points are words in P. They are totally ordered by their length. Indeed let w be in $\varphi^{-1}(e) \cap \bar{F}(X)$. Then we have $r \cdot w = r$ for all $r \in R$. Since w is not a factor of a word in X, no rw is in P. Thus each word $r \in R$ is a right factor of w. Thus, for two fixed points of e, one is a right factor of the other.

Next, we recall that, by Corollary II.5.4,

$$PX \subset X(P \cup X).$$

By induction, this implies that for $n \geq 1$,

$$PX^n \subset X^n(P \cup X). \tag{7.1}$$

To show that G_e is regular, we verify that each $g \in H(e) \cap \varphi(X^*)$ is an "increasing" permutation on R, i.e., for $r, s \in R$,

$$|r| < |s| \quad \Rightarrow \quad |rg| < |sg|. \tag{7.2}$$

This property clearly implies that g is the identity on R. Since $H(e) \cap \varphi(X^*)$ is composed of the elements of $H(e)$ fixing 1, this means that only the identity of G_e fixes 1. Since G_e is transitive, this implies that G_e is regular.

For the proof of (7.2), let $g \in H(e) \cap \varphi(X^*)$, and let $x \in \varphi^{-1}(g)$. Then $x \in X^n$ for some $n \geq 0$. Let $r, s \in R$ with $|r| < |s|$. Then by (7.1),

$$rx = yu, \qquad sx = zv \qquad \text{with} \quad y, z \in X^n, \quad u, v \in P \cup X.$$

The word u is a right factor cf v (see Fig. 4.32) since otherwise $z \in A^*yA^+$ contradicting the fact that X^n is semaphore. Further, we have in M

$$rg = u \text{ or } 1 \quad \text{according to} \quad u \in P \quad \text{or} \quad u \in X,$$

$$sg = v \text{ or } 1 \quad \text{according to} \quad v \in P \quad \text{or} \quad v \in X.$$

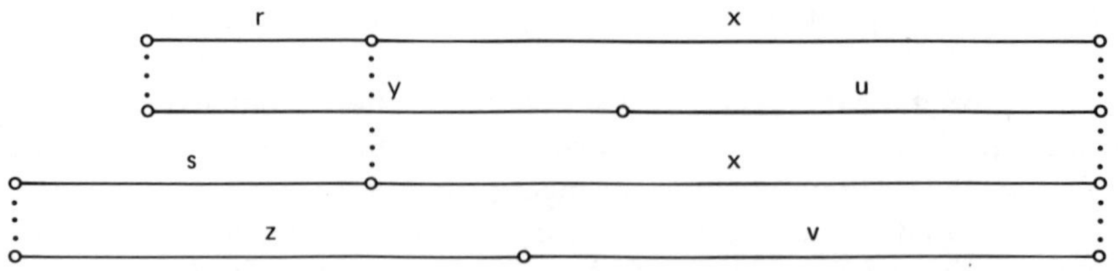

Fig. 4.32 Comparison of rx and sx.

Since g is a permutation on R and $1g = 1$ and $s \neq 1$, we have $sg \neq 1$. Thus $sg = v$. Since $r \neq s$, we have $rg \neq sg$. Since u is a right factor of v, we have $|rg| < |sg|$ both in the two cases $rg = u$ and $rg = 1$. □

Now let $X \subset A^+$ be a group code. Then by definition,

$$X^* = \alpha^{-1}(H),$$

where $\alpha: A^* \to G$ is a surjective morphism onto a group G and H is a subgroup of G. The code X is called a *regular group code* if

$$H = \{1\}.$$

Then the permutation group $G(X)$ is the representation of G by multiplication on the right over itself. It is a regular group.

The following proposition is useful for the proof of Theorem 7.1. However, it is interesting in itself, because it describes the prefix codes having a regular group.

PROPOSITION 7.3 *Let X be a thin maximal prefix code. Then the group $G(X)$ is regular iff*

$$X = U \circ V \circ W,$$

where V is a regular group code and U, W are synchronous codes.

Proof The condition is sufficient. Indeed, if $X = U \circ V \circ W$, then by Proposition 6.6, we have $G(X) = G(V)$.

Conversely, let $\mathscr{A} = (Q, 1, 1)$ be an unambiguous trim automaton recognizing X^*, let φ be the associated representation and $M = \varphi(A^*)$. Since X is thin and complete, the minimal ideal J of M is a union of groups.

Consider an idempotent $e \in \varphi(X^*) \cap J$, let $G = G(e)$ be its $\mathscr{H}$-class, L its $\mathscr{L}$-class and let Γ be the set of $\mathscr{H}$-classes contained in L. Each of them is a group, and the idempotent of H will be denoted by e_H. The set of pairs.

$$\{(e_H, e) \mid H \in \Gamma\}$$

is a system of coordinates of L relative to e since

$$e_H e \in H, \qquad e e_H e = e.$$

Let us consider the corresponding $\mathscr{L}$-representation of M. For this choice of coordinates we have for $m \in M$ and $H \in \Gamma$,

$$m * H = lme_Hc, \tag{7.3}$$

where $e = cl$ is the column–row decomposition of e.

Set

$$N = \{n \in M \mid \forall H \in \Gamma, n * H = n * G\}.$$

The set N is composed of those elements $n \in M$ for which the mapping

$$H \in \Gamma \mapsto n * H \in G_e$$

is constant. It is a right-unitary submonoid of M. Indeed, first $1 \in N$ and if n, $n' \in N$, then

$$\begin{aligned} nn' * H &= (n * n'H)(n' * H) \\ &= (n * G)(n' * G) \end{aligned} \tag{7.4}$$

which is independent of H. Thus $nn' \in N$. Assume now that $n, nn' \in N$. Then by (7.4),

$$n' * H = (n * n'H)^{-1}(nn' * H) = (n * G)^{-1}(nn' * G)$$

which is independent of H, showing that $n' \in N$. Thus

$$\varphi^{-1}(N) = W^*$$

for some prefix code W.

The hypothesis that $G(X)$ is regular implies that $X^* \subset W^*$. Indeed, let $m \in \varphi(X^*)$. Then by (7.3) we have for $H \in \Gamma$,

$$m * H = lme_Hc.$$

Since X is prefix, $e_H \in \varphi(X^*)$ by Proposition 5.8. Consequently $m * H$ fixes the state $1 \in Q$ (since l, m, e_H and c do). Since $G(X)$ is regular, $m * H$ is the identity for all $H \in \Gamma$. This shows that $m \in N$.

We now consider the function

$$\theta: \quad W^* \to G_e$$

which associates to each $w \in W^*$ the permutation $\varphi(w) * G$. By (7.4), θ is a morphism. Moreover, θ is surjective: if $g \in G$, then

$$g * G = lgec = lgc$$

which is the element of G_e associated to g. From $g * H = lge_Hc = l(ge)e_H(ec) = lgec = lgc$, it follows that $g \in N$.

The preceding argument shows that for all $x \in X^*$, $\theta(x) = 1$.

Since $X^* \subset W^*$ and X is a maximal code, we have

$$X = Y \circ_\beta W,$$

where $\beta: B^* \to A^*$ is some injective morphism, $\beta(B) = W$ and $\beta(Y) = X$. Set

$$\alpha = \theta \circ \beta.$$

Then $\alpha: B^* \to G_e$ is a morphism and $Y^* \subset \alpha^{-1}(1)$ since for all $x \in X^*$, we have $\theta(x) = 1$. Let V be the regular group code defined by

$$V^* = \alpha^{-1}(1).$$

Then $Y = U \circ V$ and consequently

$$X = U \circ V \circ W.$$

By construction, $G(V) = G_e$. Thus $G(X) = G(V)$. The codes U and W are synchronous since $d(X) = d(V)$ and $d(X) = d(U)d(V)d(W)$, whence $d(U) = d(W) = 1$. This concludes the proof. □

The following result is the final lemma needed for the proof of Theorem 7.1.

LEMMA 7.4 *Let $Y \subset B^+$ be a semaphore code, and let $V \neq B$ be a regular group code. If*

$$Y^* \subset V^*,$$

then

$$Y = (C^*D)^d$$

for some integer d, where $C = B \cap V$ and $D = B - C$. Moreover, C^*D is synchronous.

Proof Let $\alpha: B^* \to G$ be a morphism onto a group G such that $V^* = \alpha^{-1}(1)$. Since $V \neq B$, we have $G \neq \{1\}$. We have

$$C = \{b \in B \mid \alpha(b) = 1\} \qquad \text{and} \qquad D = \{b \in B \mid \alpha(b) \neq 1\}.$$

The set D is nonempty. We claim that for $y \in Y, |y|_D > 0$. Assume the contrary, and let $y \in Y$ such that $|y|_D = 0$. Let $b \in D$. Then $\alpha(bu) \neq 1$ for each left factor u of y since $\alpha(u) = 1$. Thus no left factor of by is in V, whence in Y. On the other hand, $B^*Y \subset YB^*$ because Y is semaphore (Proposition II.5.2). This gives the contradiction and proves the claim.

Set $T = C^*D$. Consider a word $y \in Y$ such that $|y|_D$ is minimal and let $d = |y|_D$. Next consider a word

$$t = t_1 t_2 \cdots t_d, \qquad t_i \in T.$$

Since Y is a semaphore code, $t_d y \in YB^*$. Thus

$$t_d y = y_1 w_1$$

for some $y_1 \in Y$, $w_1 \in B^*$. Then $|y_1|_D = d$. Indeed, otherwise $|y_1|_D = d + 1$ by the minimality of $d = |y|_D$, and

$$\alpha(y_1) = \alpha(y_1 w_1) = \alpha(t_d) \neq 1,$$

a contradiction. Thus, $|y_1|_D = d$, $|w_1|_D = 1$. In the same way, we get

$$t_{d-1} y_1 = y_2 w_2, \ldots, t_1 y_{d-1} = y_d w_d,$$

where each of the $y_2, \ldots, y_d$ satisfies $|y_i|_D = d$, and each $w_2, \ldots, w_d \in C^*DC^*$. Composing these equalities, we obtain (see Fig. 4.33)

$$ty = t_1 t_2 \cdots t_d y = y_d w_d w_{d-1} \cdots w_1. \tag{7.5}$$

Since $y_d \in (C^*D)^d C^*$ and $t \in (C^*D)^d$, we have

$$y_d = t_1 t_2 \cdots t_d v \in Y \tag{7.6}$$

for some $v \in C^*$ which is also a left factor of y. This construction applies in particular if $t_1 \in D$, showing that Y contains a word $x\,(= y_d)$ with d letters in D and starting with a letter in D, i.e., $x \in (DC^*)^d$. Thus x is one of the words in Y for which $|x|_D$ is minimal. Substitute x for y in (7.5). Then starting with any word $t = t_1 t_2 \cdots t_d \in T^d$, we obtain (7.6), with $v = 1$, since $v \in C^*$ and is a left factor of x. This shows that $t \in Y$. Thus $T^d \subset Y$. Since T^d is a maximal code, we have $T^d = Y$. Since $B^*b \subset T^*$ for $b \in D$, the code T is synchronous. □

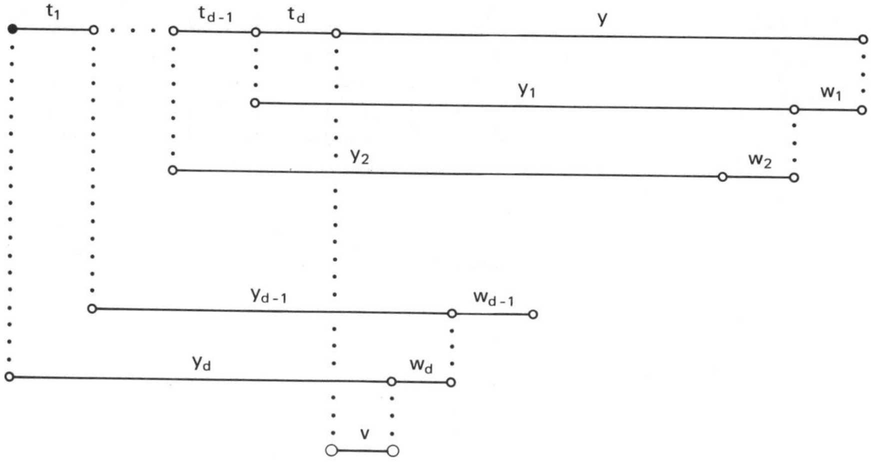

Fig. 4.33

Proof of Theorem 7.1 Let X be a semaphore code. By Lemma 7.2, the group $G(X)$ is regular. In view of Proposition 7.3, we have

$$X = U \circ V \circ W,$$

where V is a regular group code and U and W are synchronous. Set $Y = U \circ V$. If $d(V) = 1$, then X is synchronous and there is nothing to prove. Otherwise, according to Lemma 7.4, there exists a synchronous code T such that $Y = T^d$. Thus

$$X = T^d \circ W = (T \circ W)^d.$$

The code $Z = T \circ W$ is synchronous because T and W are. Finally, since $X = Z^d$ is semaphore, Z is semaphore by Corollary II.5.9. This proves the theorem. □

Example 7.1 Let Z be the semaphore code $Z = \{a, ba, bb\}$ over $A = \{a, b\}$. This code is synchronous since $A^*a \subset Z^*$. Set

$$X = Z^2.$$

The minimal automaton $\mathscr{A}(X^*)$ is given by Fig. 4.34. Let φ be the associated representation and $M = \varphi(A^*)$. The element $e = \varphi(a^2)$ is an idempotent of minimal rank $2 = d(X)$. Its $\mathscr{L}$-class is composed of two groups $G_1 = G(e)$ and G_2. The $\mathscr{L}$-representation of M with respect to e is given in Fig. 4.35, with the

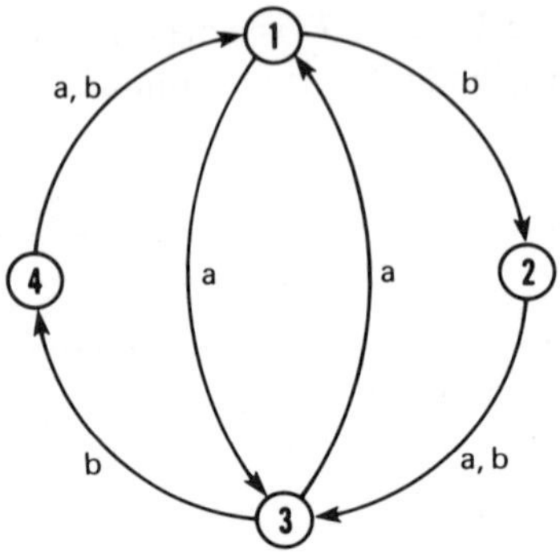

	1	2	3	4
a	3	3	1	1
b	2	3	4	1

Fig. 4.34 The automaton $\mathscr{A}(X^*)$ and its table.

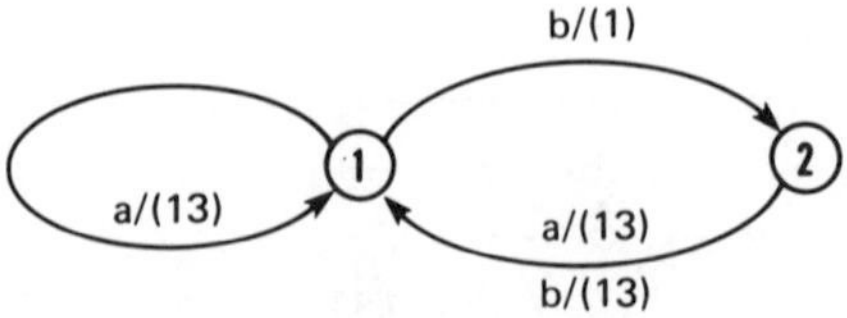

Fig. 4.35 The $\mathscr{L}$-representation of M.

notation a instead of $\varphi(a)$. The prefix code W of Proposition 7.3 is $W = Z$. Indeed, we have $a * 1 = a * 2 = (13)$; $ba * 1 = ba * 2 = (13)$; $bb * 1 = bb * 2 = (13)$. In this case, the code U is trivial.

EXAMPLE 7.2 Consider, over $A = \{a, b\}$, the synchronous semaphore code $Z = a^*b$. Let $X = Z^2$. The automaton $\mathscr{A}(X^*)$ is given in Fig. 4.36.

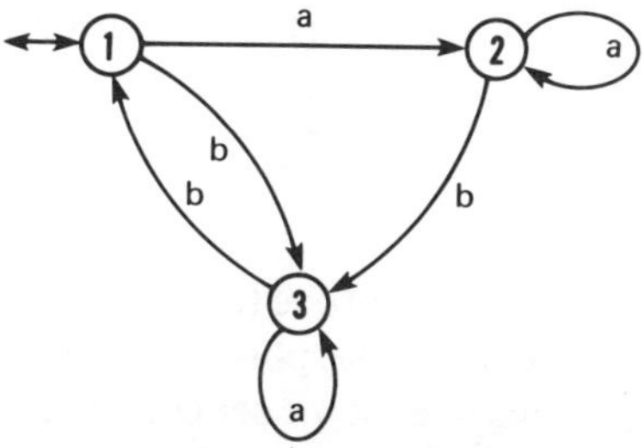

Fig. 4.36 The automaton of $X^* = [(a^*b)^2]^*$.

Let φ be the associated representation. The element $e = \varphi(b^2)$ is an idempotent. Its set of fixed points is $\{1, 3\}$. The $\mathscr{L}$-class of e is reduced to the group $G(e)$, and the monoid N of the proof of Proposition 7.3 therefore is the whole monoid $\varphi(A^*)$. Thus $W = A$. The morphism α from A^* into G_e is given by

$$\alpha(a) = I_{\{1,3\}}, \qquad \alpha(b) = (13).$$

We have

$$X = U \circ V$$

with

$$V = a \cup ba^*b.$$

This example shows that the decomposition given in the proof of Proposition 7.3 is not always that one looked for. Lemma 7.4 must be used in this case to find the desired decomposition $X = Z^2$.

EXERCISES

SECTION 1

1.1. Show that a submonoid M of A^* is recognizable and free iff there exists an unambiguous trim finite automaton $\mathscr{A} = (Q, 1, 1)$ that recognizes M.

SECTION 2

2.1. Let X be a subset of A^+ and let $\mathscr{A}_D^*(X) = (P, (1, 1), (1, 1))$ be the flower automaton of X. Let φ be the associated representation. Show that for all

$$(p,q),(r,s) \in P \qquad \text{and} \qquad w \in A^*$$

we have

$$((p,q),\varphi(w),(r,s)) = (q(\underline{X})^*r, w) + (pw, r)(q, ws).$$

2.2. Let $\mathscr{A} = (P, i, T)$ and $\mathscr{B} = (Q, j, S)$ be two automata, and let $\rho: P \to Q$ be a reduction from $\mathscr{A}$ on $\mathscr{B}$ such that $i = \rho^{-1}(j)$. Show that if $\mathscr{A}$ is deterministic, then so is $\mathscr{B}$.

SECTION 3

***3.1.** The aim of this problem is to prove that for any stable submonoid N of a monoid M, there exists a morphism φ from M onto a monoid of unambiguous relations over some set Q and an element $1 \in Q$ such that

$$N = \{m \in M \mid 1\,\varphi(m)\,1\}.$$

For this let

$$D = \{(u,v) \in M \times M \mid uv \in N\}.$$

Let ρ be the relation over D defined by

$$(u,v)\,\rho(u',v') \qquad \text{iff} \quad Nu \cap Nu' \neq \varnothing \quad \text{and} \quad vN \cap v'N \neq \varnothing.$$

Show that the equivalence classes of the transitive closure ρ^* of ρ are cartesian products of subsets of M.

Show that $N \times N$ is a class of ρ^*.

Let Q be the set of classes of ρ^* and let 1 denote the class $N \times N$. Let φ be the function from M into $\{0,1\}^{Q \times Q}$ defined by

$$(U \times V)\varphi(m)(U' \times V') \Leftrightarrow Um \subset U' \quad \text{and} \quad mV' \subset V.$$

Show that φ is a morphism and that

$$N = \{m \in M \mid 1\,\varphi(m)\,1\}.$$

Show that in the case where $M = A^*$, the construction above coincides with the construction of the flower automaton.

3.2. Let K be a field and let m be an $n \times n$ matrix with elements in K. Show that $m = m^2$ iff there exist $c \in K^{n \times p}$ and $l \in K^{p \times n}$ such that

$$m = cl \qquad \text{and} \qquad lc = I_p,$$

where I_p denotes the identity matrix.

3.3. Let M be a monoid of unambiguous relations over a set Q. Let D be a $\mathscr{D}$-class of M containing an idempotent e. Let R (resp. L) be the $\mathscr{R}$-class (resp. the $\mathscr{L}$-class) of e and let Λ (resp. Γ) be the set of its $\mathscr{H}$-classes. Let $(a_H, a'_H)_{H\in\Lambda}$ be a system of coordinates of R, and let $(b_K, b'_K)_{K\in\Gamma}$ be a system of coordinates of L. Let $e = cl$ be the column-row decomposition of e and set $l_H = la_H$, $c_H = b_H c$.

The *sandwich matrix* of D (with respect to these systems of coordinates) is defined as the $\Lambda \times \Gamma$ matrix with elements in $G_e \cup 0$ given by

$$S_{HK} = \begin{cases} l_H c_K & \text{if} \quad ea_H b_K e \in G(e), \\ 0 & \text{otherwise.} \end{cases}$$

Show that for all $m \in M$, $H \in \Lambda$, $K \in \Gamma$,

$$(H * m)S_{H'K} = S_{HK'}(m * K)$$

with $H' = H \cdot m$, $K' = m \cdot K$.

Section 4

4.1. Let K be a semiring and let m be a K-relation between P and Q. The *rank over* K of m is the minimum of the cardinalities of the sets R such that

$$m = cl$$

for some K-relations $c \in K^{P\times R}$, $1 \in K^{R\times Q}$. Denote it by $\text{rank}_K(m)$. For $K = \mathscr{N}$ this gives the notion introduced in Section 4.

Show that if K is a field and Q is finite, the rank over K coincides with the usual notion of rank in linear algebra.

4.2. Let

$$m = \begin{bmatrix} 1 & 0 & 0 & 1 \\ 1 & 1 & 0 & 0 \\ 0 & 1 & 1 & 0 \\ 0 & 0 & 1 & 1 \end{bmatrix}.$$

Show that $\text{rank}_{\mathbb{N}}(m) = 4$, but that $\text{rank}_{\mathbb{Z}}(m) = 3$.

4.3. Let M be a monoid of unambiguous relations over Q, that is transitive and has finite minimal rank. Let $1 \in Q$ and $N = \text{Stab}(1)$.

Let Λ (resp. Γ) be the set of 0-minimal or minimal left (resp. right) ideals of M, according to M contains or does not contain a zero.

Let $R, R' \in \Gamma$, $L, L' \in \Lambda$. Show that if

$$R \cap L \cap N \neq \varnothing \qquad \text{and} \qquad R' \cap L' \cap N \neq \varnothing,$$

then also

$$R \cap L' \cap N \neq \varnothing \qquad \text{and} \qquad R' \cap L \cap N \neq \varnothing.$$

In other words, the set of pairs $(R, L) \in \Gamma \times \Lambda$ such that $R \cap L \cap N \neq \emptyset$ is a Cartesian product.

SECTION 5

5.1. Let $X \subset A^+$ be a very thin code. Let M be the syntactic monoid of X^* and let φ be the canonical morphism from A^* onto M. Show that M has a unique 0-minimal or minimal ideal J, according to M contains a zero or not. Show that $\varphi(X^*)$ meets J, that J is a $\mathscr{D}$-class, and that each $\mathscr{H}$-class contained in $\mathscr{D}$ and which meets $\varphi(X^*)$ is a finite group.

5.2. Let $X \subset A^+$ be a very thin code, let $\mathscr{A} = (Q, 1, 1)$ be an unambiguous trim automaton recognizing X^*. Let φ be the associated morphism and $M = \varphi(A^*)$. Let J be the minimal or 0-minimal ideal of M and $K = J - 0$. Let $e \in M$ be an idempotent of minimal rank, let R be its $\mathscr{R}$-class and L be its $\mathscr{L}$-class. Let Λ (resp. Γ) be the set of $\mathscr{H}$-classes contained in R (resp. L), and choose two systems of coordinates

$$(a_H, a'_H)_{H \in \Lambda}, \qquad (b_K, b'_K)_{K \in \Gamma}$$

of R and L, respectively. Let

$$\mu: \quad M \to (G_e \cup 0)^{\Lambda \times \Lambda}$$

be the morphism of M into the monoid of row-monomial $\Lambda \times \Lambda$-matrices with elements in $G_e \cup 0$ defined by the $\mathscr{R}$-representation with respect to e. Similarly, let

$$\nu: \quad M \to (G_e \cup 0)^{\Gamma \times \Gamma}$$

be the morphism associated with the $\mathscr{L}$-representation with respect to e. Let S be the sandwich matrix of J relative to the systems of coordinates introduced (see Exercise 3.3). Show that for all $m \in M$,

$$\mu(m)S = S\nu(m)$$

Show that for all $m, n \in M$,

$$\mu(m) = \mu(n) \quad \Leftrightarrow \quad (\forall H \in \Lambda,\ l_H m = l_H n),$$

$$\nu(m) = \nu(n) \quad \Leftrightarrow \quad (\forall K \in \Gamma,\ m c_K = n c_K),$$

where $l_H = l a_H$, $c_K = b_K c$ and cl is the column–row decomposition of e.

Show, using these relations, that the function

$$m \mapsto (\mu(m), \nu(m))$$

is injective.

SECTION 6

6.1. Let X be a very thin code. Let M be the syntactic monoid of X^*, and let J be the 0-minimal or minimal ideal of M (see Exercise 5.1). Let G be an $\mathscr{H}$-class in J that meets $\varphi(X^*)$, and let $H = G \cap \varphi(X^*)$.

Show that the representation of G over the right cosets of H is injective, and that the permutation group obtained is equivalent to $G(X)$.

6.2. Let $X \subset A^+$ be a prefix code and let $X = Y \circ Z$ be its maximal decomposition. Show that if $X = Y' \circ Z'$ with Z' prefix and Y' maximal prefix, then

$$Z'^* \subset Z^*.$$

6.3. Let $X \subset A^+$ be a maximal prefix code. Let

$$R = \{r \in A^* \mid \forall x \in X^*, \exists y \in X^*: rxy \in X^*\}.$$

(a) Show that R is a right unitary submonoid containing X^*.

(b) Let Z be the maximal prefix code such that $R = Z^*$ and set

$$X = Y \circ Z.$$

Show that if X is thin, then Y is synchronous.

(c) Show that if $X = Y' \circ Z'$ with Y' synchronous, then

$$Z'^* \subset Z^*.$$

(d) Suppose that X is thin. Let $\mathscr{A} = (Q, 1, 1)$ be a deterministic trim automaton recognizing X^* and let φ be the associated representation. Show that a word $r \in A^*$ is in R iff for all $m \in \varphi(A^*)$ with minimal rank,

$$1 \cdot r \equiv 1 \mod \operatorname{Ker}(m).$$

6.4. Let X and Y be complete thin codes. Let Z be the code for which

$$Z^* = X^* \cap Y^*.$$

(a) Show that Z is thin. (Hint: use the direct product of automata.)

(b) Show that if X is biprefix, then Z is complete. (Hint: Proposition III.2.2.)

SECTION 7

7.1. Let $X \subset A^+$ be a semaphore code, let $\mathscr{A} = (Q, 1, 1)$ be a deterministic trim automaton recognizing X^* and let φ be the associated representation. Show that any group $G \subset \mathscr{S}(A^*)$ which meets $\varphi(\bar{F}(X))$ is cyclic (use Proposition 7.1).

NOTES

Unambiguous automata and their relation to codes appear in Schützenberger (1965b). Unambiguous automata are a special case of automata with multiplicities. The latter are the K-automata which are extensively studied in Eilenberg (1974) and Berstel and Reutenauer (1984). Kleene's theory for these automata goes back to Schützenberger (1961a). A significant step in the study of monoids of unambiguous relations using such tools as the column–row decomposition appears in Césari (1974).

An automaton with output labels such as the decoding automaton of Section 2 is called a *transducer* (see Eilenberg, 1974). For a finite code, this transducer is finite and unambiguous. This is a particular case of a more general result from the theory of transducers: any function realizable by a finite transducer can also be realized by a finite unambiguous transducer (Elgot and Mezei, 1965). For another proof of this result, see Arnold and Latteux (1979). On this subject, see Eilenberg (1974), Berstel (1979), and Pin and Sakarovitch (1983).

The study of the structure of the $\mathscr{D}$-classes in monoids of unambiguous relations is very close to the classical development for abstract semigroups presented in the usual textbooks. In particular, the $\mathscr{R}$-and $\mathscr{L}$-representations are the right and left Schützenberger representations of Clifford and Preston (1961) and Lallement (1979). The generalization of the results of Section 3 to monoids of (Boolean) relations is partly possible. See, for instance, Lerest and Lerest (1980). The notion of rank and the corresponding results appear in Lallement (1979) for the particular case of monoids of functions.

Theorem 5.1 is due to Schützenberger. An extension to sets which are not codes appears in Schützenberger (1979). The maximal decomposition of prefix codes and Propositions 6.7, 6.8 are due to Perrot (1972). The theorem of the synchronization of semaphore codes (Theorem 7.1) is in Schützenberger (1964). This paper contains also a difficult combinatorial proof of this result. Problem 3.1 is a theorem due to Boë *et al.* (1979). Extensions may be found in Boë (1976). The notion of sandwich matrix (Exercise 3.3) is a classical one. Exercise 7.1 is from Schützenberger (1964).

CHAPTER **V**

Groups of Biprefix Codes

0. INTRODUCTION

We have seen in Chapter IV that there is a permutation group $G(X)$ of degree $d(X)$ associated with every thin maximal code X which we called the group and the degree of the code. We have already established several relations between a code and its group. Thus the fact that a code X is synchronous, i.e., has a trivial group, has been shown equivalent to the existence of synchronizing pairs. Another example is the fact that an indecomposable prefix code X has a permutation group $G(X)$ that is primitive (Proposition IV.6.8). We have also seen that a thin maximal prefix code X has a regular group iff $X = U \circ V \circ W$ with U, W synchronous and V a regular group code (Proposition IV.7.3).

In this chapter we study the groups of biprefix codes. We start with the simplest class, namely the group codes in Section 1. We show in particular (Theorem 1.1) that a finite group code is uniform.

In the second and the third sections, we again examine the techniques introduced in Chapter IV and particularize them to biprefix codes. Specifically, we shall see that biprefix codes are characterized by the algebraic property of their syntactic monoids being nil-simple (Theorem 3.3). The proof makes use of Theorem II.8.4 concerning codes with bounded deciphering delay. Section 4 is devoted to groups of finite biprefix codes. The main result is

Theorem 4.6 stating that the group of a finite, indecomposable, nonuniform maximal biprefix code is doubly transitive. For the proof of this theorem, we use difficult results from the theory of permutation groups without proof. This is the only place in the book where nonelementary knowledge is required.

The fifth section contains a series of examples of finite biprefix codes with special groups.

1. GROUP CODES

Let us first recall the definition of a group code. Let G be a group, H a subgroup of G. Let $\varphi: A^* \to G$ be a surjective morphism. Then the submonoid $\varphi^{-1}(H)$ *is biunitary. It is generated by a biprefix code called a group code.*

A group code is a maximal code (see Section I.2). It is thin iff it is recognizable (Example I.5.11), or equivalently, if the index of H in G is finite.

Rather than define a group code by an "abstract" group, it is frequently convenient to use a permutation group. This is always possible for a group code X by considering the minimal automaton of X^*. We give here the detailed description of the relation between the initial pair (G, H) and the minimal automaton of X^* (see also Sect. 0.8).

Let G be a group and H a subgroup of G. Let Q be the set of the right cosets of H in G, i.e., the set of subsets of the form Hg, for $g \in G$. To each element g in G, we associate a permutation $\pi(g)$ of Q as follows: for $p = Hk$, we define

$$p\pi(g) = H(kg).$$

It is easily verified that π is well defined and that it is a morphism from the group G into the symmetric group over Q. The subgroup H is composed of the elements of G whose image by π fixes the coset H. The index of H in G is equal to $\mathrm{Card}(Q)$. In particular H has finite index in G iff $\pi(G)$ is a finite group.

Now let $\varphi: A^* \to G$ be a surjective morphism. Let X be the code generating $X^* = \varphi^{-1}(H)$. For all $u, v \in A^*$,

$$H\varphi(u) = H\varphi(v) \quad \Leftrightarrow \quad u^{-1}X^* = v^{-1}X^*.$$

Indeed, set $g = \varphi(u)$, $k = \varphi(v)$. Then $Hg = Hk$ iff $g^{-1}H = k^{-1}H$ (since $(Hg)^{-1} = g^{-1}H$). Further $u^{-1}X^* = \varphi^{-1}(g^{-1}H)$, $v^{-1}X = \varphi^{-1}(k^{-1}H)$. This proves the formula.

According to Example III.3.1, we have the equality

$$\mathrm{Card}(Q) = d(X). \tag{1.1}$$

THEOREM 1.1 *Let $X \subset A^+$ be a group code. If X is finite, then $X = A^d$ for some integer d.*

Proof Let $\mathscr{A} = (Q, 1, 1)$ be the minimal automaton of X^*, and let φ be the associated representation. Let d be the degree of X. Then $d = \mathrm{Card}(Q)$ by (1.1).

Consider the relation on Q defined as follows: for $p, q \in Q$, we have $p \leq q$ iff $p = q$ or $q \neq 1$ and there exists a simple path from p to q in $\mathscr{A}$. Thus $p \leq q$ iff $p = q$, or there exists a word $w \in A^*$ such that both $p \cdot w = q$ and $p \cdot u \neq 1$ for each left factor $u \neq 1$ of w. This relation is reflexive and transitive.

If X is finite, then the relation $\leq$ is an order on Q. Assume indeed that $p \leq q$ and $q \leq p$. Then either $p = 1$ and $q = 1$ or both $p \neq 1$, $q \neq 1$. In the second case, there exist simple paths $p \xrightarrow{w} q$ and $q \xrightarrow{w'} p$. There are also simple paths

$$1 \xrightarrow{u} p, \qquad p \xrightarrow{v} 1.$$

Thus for all $i \geq 0$, the paths

$$1 \xrightarrow{u} p \xrightarrow{(ww')^i} p \xrightarrow{v} 1$$

are simple, showing that $u(ww')^* v \subset X$. Since X is finite, this implies $ww' = 1$, whence $p = q$. Thus $\leq$ is an order.

Now let $a, b \in A$ be two letters. According to Proposition III.5.1, we have

$$a^d, b^d \in X.$$

Thus none of the states $1 \cdot a^i$, $1 \cdot b^i$ for $1 < i < d$ is equal to 1. Consequently,

$$1 < 1 \cdot a < 1 \cdot a^2 < \cdots < 1 \cdot a^i < \cdots < 1 \cdot a^{d-1}$$

and

$$1 < 1 \cdot b < 1 \cdot b^2 < \cdots < 1 \cdot b^i < \cdots < 1 \cdot b^{d-1}.$$

Since Q has d states, this implies that $1 \cdot a^i = 1 \cdot b^i$ for all $i \geq 0$. Thus $\varphi(a) = \varphi(b)$ for all $a, b \in A$. We get that for all $w \in A^*$ of length n, we have $w \in X^*$ iff $a^n \in X^*$, i.e., iff n is a multiple of d. This shows that $X = A^d$. ▯

The following theorem gives a sufficient condition, concerning the group $G(X)$, for a biprefix code to be a group code. It will be useful later, in Section 4.

THEOREM 1.2 *Let X be a thin maximal biprefix code. If the group $G(X)$ is regular, then X is a group code.*

Proof According to Proposition IV.7.3, there exist two synchronous codes U, W and a group code V such that

$$X = U \circ V \circ W.$$

Since X is thin maximal biprefix, so are U and W (Proposition I.6.9). Since U and W are synchronous, they are reduced to their alphabets (Example II.6.2). Thus, $X = V$ and this gives the result. ▯

THEOREM 1.3 *Let $X \subset A^+$ be a code with $A = \text{alph}(X)$. The two following conditions are equivalent.*

(i) *X is a regular group code,*
(ii) *X^* is closed under conjugacy, i.e., $uv \in X^* \Rightarrow vu \in X^*$.*

Proof If X is a regular group code, the syntactic monoid of X^* is a group $G = \varphi(A^*)$ and $X^* = \varphi^{-1}(1)$. If $uv \in X^*$, then $\varphi(u)\varphi(v) = 1$, hence also $\varphi(v)\varphi(u) = 1$, showing that vu is in X^*.

To show the other implication, let us first show that X is biprefix. Let $u, v \in A^*$ be such that u, $uv \in X^*$. Then also $vu \in X^*$. Since X^* is stable, it follows that $v \in X^*$. Thus, X^* is right unitary. The proof for left unitarity is analogous. Now let $M = \varphi(A^*)$ be the syntactic monoid of X^*. We verify that $\varphi(X^*) = 1$. For $x \in X^*$, we have the equivalences

$$uxv \in X^* \quad \Leftrightarrow \quad xvu \in X^* \quad \Leftrightarrow \quad vu \in X^* \quad \Leftrightarrow \quad uv \in X^*.$$

Thus, $\varphi(x) = \varphi(1)$. Since $\varphi(1) = 1$, it follows that $\varphi(X^*) = 1$.

Finally, we show that M is a group. From $A = \text{alph}(X)$, for each letter $a \in A$, there exists $x \in X$ of the form $x = uav$. Then $avu \in X^*$, whence $\varphi(a)\varphi(vu) = 1$. This shows that all elements $\varphi(a)$, for $a \in A$, are invertible. This implies that M is a group. □

COROLLARY 1.4 *Let $X \subset A^+$ be a finite code with $A = \text{alph}(X)$. If X^* is closed under conjugacy, then $X = A^d$ for some $d \geq 1$.* □

2. AUTOMATA OF BIPREFIX CODES

The general theory of unambiguous monoids of relations takes a nice form in the case of biprefix codes, since the automata satisfy some additional properties. Thus, the property to be biprefix can be "read" on the automaton.

PROPOSITION 2.1 *Let X be a thin maximal prefix code over A, and let $\mathscr{A} = (Q, 1, 1)$ be a deterministic trim automaton recognizing X^*. The following conditions are equivalent.*

(i) *X is maximal biprefix,*
(ii) *for all $w \in A^*$, we have $1 \in Q \cdot w$,*
(iii) *for all $w \in A^*$, $q \cdot w = 1 \cdot w$ implies $q = 1$.*

Proof In a first step, we show that

$$\text{(ii)} \quad \Leftrightarrow \quad X \text{ is left complete.} \tag{2.1}$$

If (ii) is satisfied, consider a word w, and let $q \in Q$ be a state such that $q \cdot w = 1$. Choose $u \in A^*$ satisfying $1 \cdot u = q$. Then $1 \cdot uw = 1$, whence $uw \in X^*$. This shows that X is left complete. Conversely, assume X left complete. Let $w \in A^*$. Then there exists $u \in A^*$ such that $uw \in X^*$. Thus, $1 = 1 \cdot uw = (1 \cdot u) \cdot w$ shows that $1 \in Q \cdot w$.

Next, we prove that

$$\text{(iii)} \quad \Leftrightarrow \quad X^* \text{ is left unitary.} \tag{2.2}$$

Assume that (iii) holds and let $u, v \in A^+$ be such that $u, vu \in X^*$. Set $q = 1 \cdot v$. Then $1 \cdot u = 1$ and $q \cdot u = (1 \cdot v) \cdot u = 1 \cdot vu = 1$. Thus, $q \cdot u = 1 \cdot u$, whence $q = 1$. This shows that $1 \cdot v = 1$ and consequently $v \in X^*$.

Assume conversely that X^* is left unitary and let w be such that $q \cdot w = 1 \cdot w = p$ for some $p, q \in Q$. Let $u, v \in A^*$ be such that $1 \cdot u = q$, $p \cdot v = 1$. Then

$$1 \cdot uwv = 1 = 1 \cdot wv.$$

Thus, $uwv, wv \in X^*$ and by unitarity, $u \in X^*$. Consequently, $1 \cdot u = 1 = q$, proving the equivalence (2.2).

In view of (2.1) and (2.2), the proposition is a direct consequence of Proposition III.2.1. □

Let X be a thin maximal biprefix code, and let $\mathscr{A} = (Q, 1, 1)$ be a trim deterministic automaton recognizing X^*. Then the automaton $\mathscr{A}$ is complete, and the monoid $M = \varphi_{\mathscr{A}}(A^*)$ is a monoid of (total) functions. The minimal ideal J is composed of the functions m such that $\mathrm{Card}(\mathrm{Im}(m)) = \mathrm{rank}(m)$ equals the minimal rank $r(M)$ of M. The $\mathscr{H}$-classes of J are indexed by the minimal images and by the maximal nuclear equivalences (Proposition IV.5.9). Each state appears in at least one minimal image and the state 1 is in all minimal images. Each $\mathscr{H}$-class H meets $\varphi(X^*)$ and the intersection is a subgroup of H.

Note the following important fact: If S is a minimal image and w is any word, then $T = S \cdot w$ is again a minimal image. Thus, $\mathrm{Card}(S) = \mathrm{Card}(T)$ and consequently w realizes a *bijection* from S onto T.

In the sequel, we will be interested in the *minimal* automaton $\mathscr{A}(X^*)$ of X^*. According to Proposition II.3.9, this automaton is complete and has a unique final state coinciding with the initial state. Thus, $\mathscr{A}(X^*)$ is of the form considered above.

Let φ be the representation associated with the minimal automaton $\mathscr{A}(X^*) = (Q, 1, 1)$, and let $M = \varphi(A^*)$. Let J be the minimal ideal of M. We define

$$E(X) = \varphi^{-1}(J).$$

This is an ideal in A^*. Moreover, we have

$$w \in E(X) \quad \Leftrightarrow \quad \begin{cases} \text{for all minimal images } A \text{ and} \\ T \text{ of } \mathscr{A} \text{ we have } S \cdot w = T \cdot w. \end{cases} \tag{2.3}$$

Indeed, let $w \in E(X)$. Then $U = Q \cdot w$ is a minimal image. For any minimal image T, we have $T \cdot w \subset Q \cdot w = U$, hence $T \cdot w = U$ since $T \cdot w$ is minimal. Thus, $T \cdot w = S \cdot w = Q \cdot w$. Conversely, assume that for $w \in A^*$, we have $S \cdot w = T \cdot w$ for all minimal images S, T. Set U equal to this common image. Since every state in Q appears in at least one minimal image, we have

$$Q \cdot w = \left(\bigcup_S S \right) \cdot w = \bigcup_S S \cdot w = U,$$

where the union is over the minimal images. This shows that $\varphi(w)$ has minimal rank, and consequently $w \in E(X)$. Thus, the equivalence (2.3) is proved.

PROPOSITION 2.2 *Let X be a thin maximal biprefix code and let $\mathscr{A}(X^*) = (Q, 1, 1)$ be the minimal automaton of X^*. Let $p, q \in Q$ be two states. If $p \cdot h = q \cdot h$ for all $h \in E(X)$, then $p = q$.*

Proof It suffices to prove that for all $w \in A^*$, $p \cdot w = 1$ iff $q \cdot w = 1$. The conclusion, namely that $p = q$, follows then by the definition of $\mathscr{A}(X^*)$.

Let $h \in E(X) \cap X^*$. Let $w \in A^*$ be such that $p \cdot w = 1$. We must show that $q \cdot w = 1$. We have $p \cdot wh = (p \cdot w) \cdot h = 1 \cdot h = 1$, since $h \in X^*$. Now $wh \in E(X)$, hence by assumption $q \cdot wh = p \cdot wh = 1$. Thus, $(q \cdot w) \cdot h = 1$. By Proposition 2.1(iii), it follows that $q \cdot w = 1$. This proves the proposition. □

For a transitive permutation group G of degree d it is customary to consider the number $k(G)$ which is the maximum number of fixed points of an element of G distinct from the identity. We call *minimal degree* of G the number $\delta = d - k(G)$. The group is regular iff $k(G) = 0$, it is a *Frobenius group* if $k(G) = 1$.

If X is a code of degree d and with group $G(X)$, we denote by $k(X)$ the integer $k(G(X))$. We will prove

THEOREM 2.3 *Let $X \subset A^+$ be a thin maximal biprefix code of degree d, and let $k = k(X)$. Then*

$$A^k - A^*XA^* \subset E(X).$$

LEMMA 2.4 *With the above notation, let $\mathscr{A} = (Q, 1, 1)$ be the minimal automaton recognizing X^*. For any two distinct minimal images S and T of $\mathscr{A}$, we have*

$$\text{Card}(S \cap T) \leq k.$$

Proof Let $M = \varphi_{\mathscr{A}}(A^*)$, and consider an idempotent $e \in M$ having image S, i.e., such that $Qe = S$. Consider an element $t \in T - S$, and set $s = te$. Then

$s \in S$, and therefore, $s \neq t$. We will prove that there is an idempotent f separating s and t, i.e., such that $sf \neq tf$.

According to Proposition 2.2, there exists $h \in E(X)$ such that $s \cdot h \neq t \cdot h$. Let $m = \varphi(h) \in J$, where J is the minimal ideal of M. Multiplying on the right by a convenient element $n \in M$, the element $mn \in J$ will be in the $\mathscr{L}$-class characterized by the minimal image T. Since n realizes a bijection from $\mathrm{Im}(m)$ onto $\mathrm{Im}(mn) = T$ we have $smn \neq tmn$. Let f be the idempotent of the $\mathscr{H}$-class of mn. Then f and mn have the same nuclear equivalence. Consequently $sf \neq tf$. Since $t \in T = \mathrm{Im}(mn) = \mathrm{Im}(f) = \mathrm{Fix}(f)$, we have $tf = t$.

Consider now the restriction to T of the mapping ef. For all $p \in S \cap T$, we obtain $pef = pf = p$. Thus ef fixes the states in $S \cap T$. Further $t(ef) = sf \neq t$, showing that ef is not the identity on T. Thus, by definition of k, we have $\mathrm{Card}(S \cap T) \leq k$. □

Proof of Theorem 2.3 Let $\mathscr{A} = (Q, 1, 1)$ be the minimal automaton of X^*. Let $w \in A^* - A^*XA^*$ and set $w = a_1 a_2 \cdots a_k$ with $a_i \in A$. Let S be a minimal image. For each $i \in \{1, \ldots, k\}$, the word $a_1 a_2 \cdots a_i$ defines a bijection from S onto $S_i = S \cdot a_1 a_2 \cdots a_i$. Since S_i is a minimal image, it contains the state 1. Thus S_k contains all the $k + 1$ states

$$1 \cdot a_1 a_2 \cdots a_k, \qquad 1 \cdot a_2 \cdots a_k, \ldots, \qquad 1 \cdot a_k, \qquad 1.$$

These states are distinct. Indeed, assume that

$$1 \cdot a_i a_{i+1} \cdots a_k = 1 \cdot a_j \cdots a_k$$

for some $i < j$. Then setting $q = 1 \cdot a_i a_{i+1} \cdots a_{j-1}$, we get $q \cdot a_j \cdots a_k = 1 \cdot a_j \cdots a_k$. By Proposition 2.1, this implies $q = 1$. But then $w \in A^*XA^*$, contrary to the assumption.

Thus $S \cdot w$ contains $k + 1$ states which are determined in a way independent from S. In other words, if T is another minimal image, then $T \cdot w$ contains these same $k + 1$ states. This means that $\mathrm{Card}(T \cdot w \cap S \cdot w) \geq k$, and by Lemma 2.4, we have $S \cdot w = T \cdot w$. Thus two arbitrary minimal images have the same image by w. This shows by (2.3) that w is in $E(X)$. □

Remark Consider, in Theorem 2.3, the special case where $k = 0$, i.e., where the group $G(X)$ is regular. Then $1 \in E(X)$. Now

$$1 \in E(X) \quad \Leftrightarrow \quad X \text{ is a group code.} \tag{2.4}$$

Indeed, if $1 \in E(X)$, then the syntactic monoid $M = \varphi_{\mathscr{A}(X^*)}(A^*)$ coincides with its minimal ideal.

This minimal ideal is a single group since it contains the neutral element of M. The converse is clear. Thus we obtain, in another way, Theorem 1.2.

TABLE 5.1

The Automaton $\mathscr{A}(X^*)$

	1	2	3	4	5
a	1	4	5	2	3
b	2	3	1	1	3

EXAMPLE 2.1 If X is a thin maximal biprefix code over A with degree $d(X) = 3$, then $k = 0$ (if $G(X) = \mathbb{Z}/3\mathbb{Z}$) or $k = 1$ (if $G(X) = \mathfrak{S}_3$). In the second case by Theorem 2.3, we have

$$A - X \subset E(X).$$

The following example shows that the inclusion $A \subset E(X)$ does not always hold. Let X be the maximal prefix code over $A = \{a, b\}$ defined by the automaton $\mathscr{A}(X^*) = (Q, 1, 1)$ with $Q = \{1, 2, 3, 4, 5\}$ and transition function given in Table 5.1.

The set of images, together with the actions by a and b, is given in Fig. 5.1. Each of the images contains the state 1. Consequently X is a biprefix code. We have $d(X) = 3$ (which is the number of elements of the minimal images). We have $Q \cdot b = \{1, 2, 3\}$. Thus $\varphi_{\mathscr{A}}(b)$ has minimal rank; consequently $b \in E(X)$. However, $a \notin E(X)$ since $Q \cdot a = Q$. In fact $a \in X$, in agreement with Theorem 2.3.

THEOREM 2.5 *Let X be a thin maximal biprefix code. Then the code X is indecomposable iff $G(X)$ is a primitive group.*

Proof If $X = Y \circ Z$, then Y and Z are thin maximal biprefix codes by Proposition I.6.9. According to Proposition IV.6.6, there exists an imprimitivity partition θ of $G(X)$ such that $G^\theta = G(Y)$ and $G_\theta = G(Z)$. If $G(X)$ is primitive, then $G_\theta = 1$ or $G^\theta = 1$. In the first case, $d(Y) = 1$, implying $X = Z$. In the second case, $d(Z) = 1$, whence $Z = A$. Thus, the code X is indecomposable.

The converse implication follows directly from Corollary IV.6.9. □

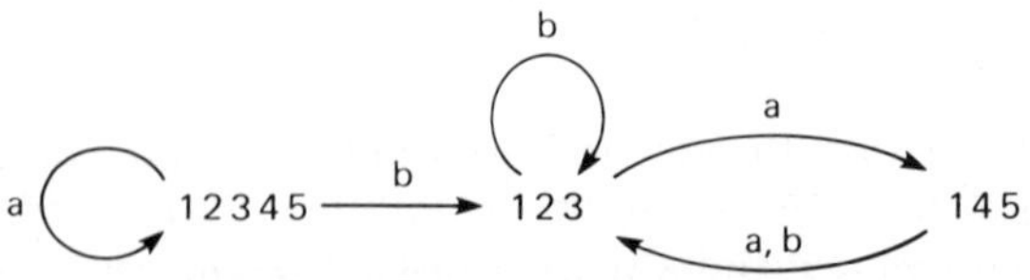

Fig. 5.1 The diagram of images.

3. DEPTH

Let S be a finite semigroup, and let J be its minimal (two-sided) ideal. We say that S is *nil-simple* if there exists an integer $n \geq 1$ such that

$$S^n \subset J. \tag{3.1}$$

The smallest integer $n \geq 1$ satisfying (3.1) is called the *depth* of S. Since S^n is, for all n, a two-sided ideal, (3.1) is equivalent to $S^n = J$, which in turn implies $S^n = S^{n+1}$.

PROPOSITION 3.1 *Let S be a finite semigroup. The following conditions are equivalent.*

(i) *S is nil-simple.*
(ii) *All idempotents of S are in the minimal ideal J of S.*

Proof (i) $\Rightarrow$ (ii) Let n be the depth of S. For any idempotent e in S, we have $e = e^n \in J$.

(ii) $\Rightarrow$ (i) Set $n = 1 + \mathrm{Card}(S)$. We show the inclusion $S^n \subset J$. Indeed let $s \in S^n$. Then $s = s_1 s_2 \cdots s_n$, with $s_i \in S$. Let $t_i = s_1 s_2 \cdots s_i$, for $1 \leq i \leq n$. Then there exist indices i, j with $1 \leq i < j \leq n$ and $t_i = t_j$. Setting $r = s_{i+1} \cdots s_j$, we have

$$t_i r = t_i,$$

hence also $t_i r^k = t_i$ for all $k \geq 1$. Since S is finite, there exists an integer k such that $e = r^k$ is an idempotent. Then $e \in J$, and consequently

$$s = t_i s_{i+1} \cdots s_n = t_i e s_{i+1} \cdots s_n \in J.$$

This proves that S is nil-simple. □

We shall use nil-simple semigroups for a characterization of biprefix codes. Before stating this result, we have to establish a property which is interesting in itself.

PROPOSITION 3.2 *Let $X \subset A^+$ be a thin maximal biprefix code, and let φ be the representation associated to an unambiguous trim automaton recognizing X^*. Let J be the minimal ideal of $\varphi(A^*)$. Then*

$$\varphi(\bar{H}(X)) \subset J.$$

Recall that $H(X) = A^- X A^-$ is the set of internal factors of X, and $\bar{H}(X) = A^* - H(X)$.

Proof Let φ_D be the representation associated with the flower automaton of X, set $M_D = \varphi_D(A^*)$ and let J_D be the minimal ideal of M_D. It suffices to prove the result for φ_D. Indeed, there exists by Proposition IV.2.4, a surjective morphism $\hat{\rho}\colon M_D \to \varphi(A^*)$ such that $\varphi = \hat{\rho} \circ \varphi_D$. Moreover, we have $\hat{\rho}(J_D) = J$.

Thus the inclusion $\varphi_D(\bar{H}(X)) \subset J_D$ implies $\varphi(\bar{H}(X)) \subset \hat{\rho}(J_D) = J$. Thus it remains to prove the inclusion $\varphi_D(\bar{H}(X)) \subset J_D$.

Let $\mathscr{A}_D = (Q, (1,1), (1,1))$ be the flower automaton of X. Let $w \in \bar{H}(X)$. Then w has $d = d(X)$ interpretations. We prove that rank $(\varphi_D(w)) = d$. Since this is the minimal rank, it implies that $\varphi_D(w)$ is in J_D.

Clearly rank $(\varphi_D(w)) \geq d$. To prove the converse inequality, let I be the set of the d interpretations of w. We define two relations

$$\alpha \in \{0,1\}^{Q \times I}, \qquad \beta \in \{0,1\}^{I \times Q}$$

as follows: if $(u, v) \in Q$, and $(s, x, p) \in I$, with $s \in A^- X$, $x \in X^*$, $p \in XA^-$, then

$$((u,v), \alpha, (s,x,p)) = \delta_{v,s},$$

$$((s,x,p), \beta, (u,v)) = \delta_{p,u},$$

where δ is the Kronecker symbol. We claim that

$$\varphi_D(w) = \alpha\beta. \tag{3.2}$$

Assume first that $(u,v)\alpha\beta(u',v')$. Then there exists an interpretation $i = (v, x, u') \in I$ such that $(u,v)\alpha i\beta(u',v')$. Note that i is uniquely determined by v or by u', because X is biprefix. Next $w \in vX^*u'$, showing that $((u,v), \varphi_D(w), (u',v')) = 1$.

Conversely, assume that $((u,v), \varphi_D(w), (u',v')) = 1$. Then either $uw = u'$ and $v = wv'$, or $w \in vX^*u'$. The first possibility implies the second one: Indeed, if $uw = u'$ and $v = wv'$, then $uwv' \in X$. Since $w \in \bar{H}(X)$ this implies $u = v' = 1 = u' = v$. It follows that $w \in vX^*u'$. Thus, $w = vxu'$ for some $x \in X^*$, showing that $i = (v, x, u')$ is an interpretation of w. Thus, $(u,v)\alpha i$ and $i\beta(u',v')$. This proves (3.2).

By (3.2), we have rank $\varphi_D(w) \leq \text{Card}(I) = d(X)$. □

The following result gives an algebraic characterization of finite maximal biprefix codes. The proof uses Theorem II.8.4 on codes with finite deciphering delay.

THEOREM 3.3 *Let $X \subset A^+$ be a finite maximal code, and let $\mathscr{A}$ be an unambiguous trim automaton recognizing X^*. The two following conditions are equivalent.*

(i) *X is biprefix,*
(ii) *the semigroup $\varphi_{\mathscr{A}}(A^+)$ is nil-simple.*

Proof Set $\varphi = \varphi_{\mathscr{A}}$, and set $S = \varphi(A^+)$. Let J be the minimal ideal of S.

(i) ⇒ (ii) Let n be the maximum of the lengths of words in X. A word in X of length n cannot be an internal factor of X. Thus $A^nA^* \subset \bar{H}(X)$. Observe that $A^nA^* = (A^+)^n$. Thus, $S^n = \varphi((A^+)^n) \subset \varphi(\bar{H}(X))$. By Proposition 3.2, we obtain $S^n \subset J$, showing that S is nil-simple.

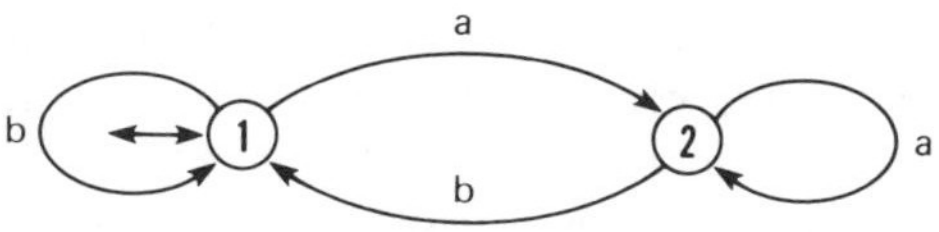

Fig. 5.2 The minimal automaton of $(a^*b)^*$.

(ii) $\Rightarrow$ (i) Let n be the depth of S. Then for all $y \in X^n \subset A^nA^* = (A^+)^n$, we have $\varphi(y) \in J$. We prove that for any $y \in X^n$, and for all $x \in X$, $u \in A^*$,

$$xyu \in X^* \quad \Rightarrow \quad yu \in X^*. \tag{3.3}$$

The semigroup S contains no zero. Further, the elements $\varphi(y)$ and $\varphi(yxy)$ of $\varphi(X^*)$ are in the same group, say G, of the minimal ideal, because $\varphi(yxy) = \varphi(yx)\varphi(y)$ and $\varphi(y) = [\varphi(yx)]^{-1}\varphi(yxy)$, showing that $\varphi(y)\mathscr{L}\varphi(yxy)$. The same argument holds for the other side. In fact, both $\varphi(yx)$ and $\varphi(yx)^{-1}$ are in the subgroup $G \cap \varphi(X^*)$. Thus there exists some $r \in X^*$ such that $[\varphi(yx)]^{-1} = \varphi(r)$, or also $\varphi(y) = \varphi(r)\varphi(yxy)$.

This gives

$$\varphi(yu) = \varphi(r)\varphi(y)\varphi(xyu) \in \varphi(X^*),$$

showing that $yu \in X^*$. This proves (3.3).

Formula (3.3) shows that the code X has finite deciphering delay (from left to right) at most n. According to Theorem II.8.4, X is a prefix code. Symmetrically, X is suffix. Thus X is a biprefix code. □

EXAMPLE 3.1 Consider again the maximal biprefix code X of Example 2.1. The semigroup $\varphi_{\mathscr{A}(X^*)}(A^+)$ is not nil-simple. Indeed, $\varphi(a)$ is a permutation of Q and thus $\varphi(a^n) \notin J$ of for all $n \geq 1$. This shows that the implication (i) $\Rightarrow$ (ii) of Theorem 3.3 is, in general, false, without the assumption of finiteness on the code.

EXAMPLE 3.2 Let $A = \{a, b\}$ and $X = a^*b$. The code X is maximal prefix, but is not suffix. The automaton $\mathscr{A}(X^*)$ is given in Fig. 5.2.

The semigroup $\varphi(A^+)$ is nil-simple: it is composed of the two constant functions $\varphi(a)$ and $\varphi(b)$. This example shows in addition that the implication (ii) $\Rightarrow$ (i) of Theorem 3.3 may become false if the code is infinite.

4. GROUPS OF FINITE BIPREFIX CODES

In the case of a thin maximal biprefix code X, the $\mathscr{L}$-representation, introduced in Chapter IV (Section IV.3), of the minimal automaton of X^* takes a particular form which makes it easy to manipulate.

Consider a thin maximal biprefix code $X \subset A^+$ of degree d, let $\mathscr{A}(X^*) = (Q, 1, 1)$ be the minimal (deterministic) automaton of X^* and let $\varphi = \varphi_{\mathscr{A}(X^*)}$ be the associated representation. Finally, let $M = \varphi(A^*)$ and let J be the minimal ideal of M. Each $\mathscr{H}$-class of J is a group.

Fix an idempotent $e \in J$, let $S = \mathrm{Im}(e) = \mathrm{Fix}(e)$, and let Γ be the set of $\mathscr{H}$-classes of the $\mathscr{L}$-class of e. Denote by e_H the idempotent of the $\mathscr{H}$-class $H \in \Gamma$. The set of pairs $(e_H, e)_{H \in \Gamma}$ constitutes a system of coordinates. Indeed, for $H \in \Gamma$,

$$e_H e = e_H, \qquad e e_H = e.$$

If $e = cl$ is the column–row decomposition of e, then for $H \in \Gamma$ $e_H = c_H l$, with $c_H = e_H c$, is the column–row decomposition of e_H. The notations of Section IV.3 then simplify considerably. In particular, for $m \in M$ and $H \in \Gamma$,

$$m * H = lmc_H = l(eme_H)c.$$

Of course, $m * H \in G_e$. This can be used to define a function

$$A^* \times E(X) \to G_e,$$

where $E(X) = \varphi^{-1}(J)$ as in the previous section. Let $u \in A^*$ and let $k \in E(X)$. Then $\varphi(k) \in J$, and corresponding to this element, there is an $\mathscr{H}$-class denoted $H^{(k)}$ in Γ which by definition is the intersection of the $\mathscr{R}$-class of $\varphi(k)$ and of the $\mathscr{L}$-class of e. In other words, $H^{(k)} = Me \cap \varphi(k)M$.

The function from $A^* \times E(X)$ into G_e is then defined by $u * k = \varphi(u) * H^{(k)}$. Thus

$$u * k = l\varphi(u)c_{H^{(k)}} = l(e\varphi(u)e_{H^{(k)}})c.$$

Thus $u * k \in G_e$. It is a permutation on the set $S = \mathrm{Fix}(e)$ obtained by restriction to S of the relation $e\varphi(u)e_{H^{(k)}}$.

The following explicit characterization of $u * k$ is the basic formula for the computations. For $u \in A^*$, $k \in E(X)$, we have for $s, t \in S$,

$$\boxed{s(u * k) = t \quad \Leftrightarrow \quad s \cdot uk = t \cdot k.} \tag{4.1}$$

In this formula, the computation of $s \cdot uk$ and $t \cdot k$ is of course done in the automaton $\mathscr{A}(X^*)$. Let us verify (4.1). If $s(u * k) = t$, then $se\varphi(u)e_{H^{(k)}} = t$. From $se = s$, it follows that $s\varphi(u)e_{H^{(k)}} = t$. Taking the image by $\varphi(k)$, we obtain

$$s\varphi(u)e_{H^{(k)}}\varphi(k) = t\varphi(k).$$

Since $e_{H^{(k)}}\varphi(k) = \varphi(k)$, we get that $s\varphi(uk) = t\varphi(k)$, or in other words, $s \cdot uk = t \cdot k$.

Conversely, assume that $s\varphi(uk) = t\varphi(k)$. Let $m \in M$ such that $\varphi(k)m = e_{H^{(k)}}$. Then $s\varphi(u)\varphi(k)m = t\varphi(k)m$ implies $s\varphi(u)e_{H^{(k)}} = te_{H^{(k)}}$. Since $se = s$ and $te = t$, we get

$$se\varphi(u)e_{H(k)} = tee_{H(k)} = te = t,$$

showing that $s(u * k) = t$. This proves (4.1).

The function from $A^* \times E(X)$ into G_e defined above is called the *ergodic representation* of X (relative to e).

We will manipulate it via the relation (4.1). Note the following formulas which are the translation of the corresponding relations given in Section IV.3, and which also can be simply proved directly using formula (4.1).

For $u \in A^*$, $k \in E(X)$, and $v \in A^*$,

$$u * kv = u * k, \tag{4.2}$$

$$uv * k = (u * vk)(v * k). \tag{4.3}$$

PROPOSITION 4.1 *Let $X \subset A^+$ be a thin maximal biprefix code, and let $R = E(X) - E(X)A^+$ be the basis of the right ideal $E(X)$. Let e be an idempotent in the minimal ideal of $\varphi_{\mathscr{A}(X^*)}(A^*)$ and let $S = \text{Fix}(e)$. The group $G(X)$ is equivalent to the permutation group over S generated by the permutations $a * r$, with $a \in A$, $r \in R$.*

Proof It suffices to show that the permutations $a * r$ generate G_e, since G_e is equivalent to $G(X)$. Set $\varphi = \varphi_{\mathscr{A}(X^*)}$. Every permutation $u * k$, for $u \in A^*$ and $k \in E(X)$, clearly is in G_e. Conversely, consider a permutation $\sigma \in G_e$. Let $g \in G(e)$ be the element giving σ by restriction to S, and let $u \in \varphi^{-1}(g)$, $k \in \varphi^{-1}(e)$. Then $u * k$ is the restriction to S of $e\varphi(u)e_{H(k)} = e\varphi(u)e = g$. Thus $u * k = \sigma$.

Thus $G_e = \{u * k \mid u \in A^*,\ k \in E(X)\}$. For $u = a_1a_2 \cdots a_n$ with $a_i \in A$, and $k \in E(X)$, we get, by (4.3),

$$u * k = (a_1 * a_2a_3 \cdots a_nk)(a_2 * a_3 \cdots a_nk) \cdots (a_n * k).$$

Thus G_e is generated by the permutation $a * k$, for a in A and k in $E(X)$. Now for each k in $E(X)$, there exists $r \in R$ such that $k \in rA^*$. By (4.2), we have $a * k = a * r$. This completes the proof. □

Note that Proposition 4.1 can also be derived from Proposition IV.3.6.

PROPOSITION 4.2 *Let X be a finite maximal biprefix code over A of degree d and let $\varphi = \varphi_{\mathscr{A}(X^*)}$. For each letter $a \in A$, we have $a^d \in E(X) \cap X$ and $\varphi(a^d)$ is an idempotent.*

Proof Let $\mathscr{A}(X^*) = (Q, 1, 1)$. By Proposition III.5.1, we have $a^d \in X$ for $a \in A$. The states

$$1, \qquad 1 \cdot a, \ldots, \qquad 1 \cdot a^{d-1}$$

are distinct. Indeed, if $1 \cdot a^i = 1 \cdot a^j$ for some $0 \le i < j \le d - 1$, then setting $p = j - i$, we would have $1 \cdot a^i = (1 \cdot a^p) \cdot a^i$, and in view of Proposition 2.1, this would imply $1 \cdot a^p = 1$, whence $a^p \in X^*$ with $0 < p < d$, contradicting the fact that $a^d \in X$ and X is prefix. Moreover, we have

$$\mathrm{Im}(a^d) = Q \cdot a^d = \{1, 1 \cdot a, \ldots, 1 \cdot a^{d-1}\}.$$

Indeed, let $q \in Q$, $q \neq 1$, Let $w \in XA^-$ be a word such that $1 \cdot w = q$. Since X is right complete and finite there exists a power of a, say a^j, such that $wa^j \in X$. Then $j < d$ since X is suffix, and $j > 0$ since $w \notin X$. Thus $q \cdot a^j = 1$ and $q \cdot a^d = 1 \cdot a^{d-j} \in \{1, 1 \cdot a, \ldots, 1 \cdot a^{d-1}\}$. This proves that $\mathrm{Im}(a^d) \subset \{1, 1 \cdot a, \ldots, 1 \cdot a^{d-1}\}$. The converse inclusion is a consequence of $(1 \cdot a^i) \cdot a^d = 1 \cdot a^{d+i} = 1 \cdot a^i$, for $i = 0, \ldots, d - 1$.

Thus $\varphi(a^d)$ has rank d, showing that $\varphi(a^d)$ is in the minimal ideal of $\varphi(A^*)$, which in turn implies that $a^d \in E(X)$. Next $(1 \cdot a^j) \cdot a^d = 1 \cdot a^j$ for $j = 0, \ldots, d - 1$; thus $\varphi(a^d)$ is the identity on its image. This proves that $\varphi(a^d)$ is an idempotent. □

Proposition 4.2 shows that in the case of a finite maximal biprefix code X, a particular ergodic representation can be chosen by taking, as basic idempotent for the system of coordinates, the $d(X)$th power of any of the letters a of the alphabet. More precisely, let

$$\mathscr{A}(X^*) = (Q, 1, 1)$$

and let φ be the associated morphism, set $e = \varphi(a^d)$ with the convention that for $1 \le i \le d$,

$$i = 1 \cdot a^{i-1}.$$

The ergodic representation relative to the idempotent $\varphi(a^d)$ is denoted by $*_a$. It is defined, for $u \in A^*$, $k \in E(X)$, and for $1 \le i, j \le d$, by

$$\begin{aligned} i(u *_a k) = j \quad &\Leftrightarrow \quad i \cdot uk = j \cdot k \\ &\Leftrightarrow \quad 1 \cdot a^{i-1}uk = 1 \cdot a^{j-1}k. \end{aligned} \tag{4.4}$$

Observe that for $u = a$ and for any $k \in E(X)$,

$$a *_a k = \alpha \tag{4.5}$$

with $\alpha = (1, 2 \cdots d)$. Indeed, by (4.4) $i(a *_a k) = j$ iff $i \cdot ak = j \cdot k$, thus iff $(i + 1) \cdot k = j \cdot k$. Since k induces a bijection from S onto $S \cdot k$, this implies $j = i + 1$, which is the claim.

Example 4.1 Let $A = \{a, b\}$, and consider the finite maximal biprefix code $X \subset A^+$ of degree 3 with kernel $K(X) = \{ab\}$. The transitions of the minimal automaton of X^*, with states $\{1, 2, 3, 4, 5\}$, are given in Fig. 5.3.

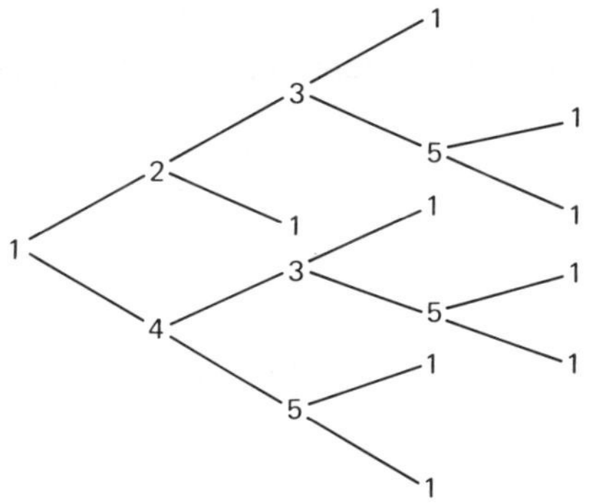

Fig. 5.3 Transitions for a biprefix code.

The letters a and b define mappings $\varphi(a)$ and $\varphi(b)$ of rank 3. Thus a, $b \in E(X)$. We consider the ergodic representation $*_a$, i.e., relative to the idempotent $e = \varphi(a^3)$. To compute it, it is sufficient (according to Proposition 4.1) to compute the four permutations $a *_a a, a *_a b, b *_a a, b *_a b$ by using (4.4). For instance, we have $i(a *_a a) = j \Leftrightarrow i \cdot a^2 = j \cdot a \Leftrightarrow i + 1 = j \bmod 3$. The permutations are easily seen to be

$$a *_a a = a *_a b = (123), \qquad b *_a a = (12), \qquad b *_a b = (132).$$

The group $G(X)$ therefore is the symmetric group over S.

PROPOSITION 4.3 *Let $X \subset A^+$ be a finite maximal biprefix code of degree d, and let $a \in A$. Then $a *_a a^d$ is a cycle of length d.*

Proof By (4.4),

$$i(a *_a a^d) = j \Leftrightarrow i \cdot a^{d+1} = j \cdot a^d.$$

This is equivalent to $i \cdot a = j$, or $i + 1 = j \bmod d$. Thus $i(a *_a a^d) \equiv i + 1 \bmod d$, proving the statement. □

We are now ready to study the groups of finite biprefix codes. We recall that a transitive permutation group G of degree $d \geq 2$ is called a *Frobenius group* if $k(G) = 1$.

THEOREM 4.4 *Let X be a finite maximal biprefix code of degree $d \geq 4$. Then $G(X)$ is not a Frobenius group.*

Proof Let $\mathscr{A} = (Q, 1, 1)$ be the minimal automaton of X^*. Since $d \geq 4$, no letter is in X. Arguing by contradiction, we suppose that $G(X)$ is a Frobenius group. Thus $k(G(X)) = 1$. By Theorem 2.3, we have $A \subset E(X)$. This means that for all $a \in A$, $\mathrm{Im}(a)$ has d elements.

Let $a \in A$ be a letter, and set $S = \mathrm{Im}(a^d) = \{1, 2, \ldots, d\}$, where, for $1 \le i \le d$, $i = 1 \cdot a^{i-1}$. Consider the ergodic representation $*_a$, and set

$$\alpha = a *_a a, \qquad \beta = b *_a a,$$

where $b \in A$ is an arbitrary letter. We want to prove that

$$\beta = \alpha. \tag{4.6}$$

Note that, by (4.4) and (4.5) we have for $i \in S$,

$$i \cdot ba = i\beta \cdot a,$$

$$i \cdot \alpha = \begin{cases} i + 1 & \text{if} \quad i < d \\ 1 & \text{if} \quad i = d. \end{cases}$$

Since $S \cdot b$ is a minimal image, it contains the state 1. Thus there exists a (unique) state $q' \in S$ such that $q' \cdot b = 1$. For the same reason, there exists a unique state $q'' \in S$ such that $q'' \cdot ba = 1$. We claim that $q'\beta = 1$, $q''\beta = d$. Indeed, we have $1 \cdot a = q' \cdot ba = q'\beta \cdot a$. Next $q'' \cdot ba = q''\beta \cdot a = 1 = d \cdot a$.

Since a defines a bijection from S onto itself, it follows that $1 = q'\beta$ and $q''\beta = d$. This proves the claim.

Now we verify that

$$q\beta \ge q \qquad \text{for} \quad q \in S, \quad q \ne q'. \tag{4.7}$$

First, we observe that the inequality holds for q'', since $q''\beta = d$. Thus, arguing by contradiction, suppose that $q\beta = p < q$ for some $q \in S$, $q \ne q', q''$. Then

$$q\beta \cdot a = q \cdot ba = p \cdot a = p + 1 \le q.$$

Setting $n = q - (p + 1)$, it follows that $q \cdot ba^{n+1} = q$. Consider the path

$$q \xrightarrow{ba^{n+1}} q.$$

Since $q \ne q', q''$, we have $q \cdot b \ne 1$, $q \cdot ba \ne 1$. Also $q \cdot ba^i = p + i \ne 1$ for $i = 1, \ldots, n + 1$. Thus this path is simple. Consequently,

$$a^{q-1}(ba^{n+1})^* a^{d-q+1} \subset X,$$

contradicting the finiteness of X. This proves (4.7).

It follows from (4.7) that there exists at most one state $q \in S$ such that $q\beta < q$, namely the state q'. This implies that the permutation β is composed of at most one cycle (of length > 1) and the rest are fixed points. Further, β cannot be the identity on S, since otherwise the relation $q'\beta = 1$ would imply $q' = 1$, hence $1 \cdot b = 1$ and $b \in X$ which is not true. Now by assumption, $G(X)$ is a Frobenius group. Thus β has at most one fixed point. If β has no fixed point, then the inequalities in (4.7) are strict and this implies that

$$\beta = (1\,2\,3 \cdots d) = \alpha.$$

Assume now that β has just one fixed point i. Then $\beta = (1\,2\,3 \cdots i-1 \;\; i+1 \cdots d)\,(i)$. This implies that

$$\beta^{-1}\alpha = (i, i+1) \qquad \text{if} \quad i \neq d,$$

$$\beta^{-1}\alpha = (d\,1) \qquad \text{if} \quad i = d.$$

Since $\beta^{-1}\alpha \in G(X)$ and $\beta^{-1}\alpha$ has $d-2$ fixed points, $G(X)$ can be a Frobenius group only if $d \leq 3$. This yields a contradiction and proves formula (4.6).

It follows from (4.4) and (4.6) that $i \cdot ba = i \cdot a^2$ for $i \in S$. This shows that for $m \geq 0$,

$$1 \cdot a^m ba = 1 \cdot a^{m+2}. \tag{4.8}$$

Observe that this formula holds for arbitrary letters $a, b \in A$. This leads to another formula, namely, for $i \geq 0$ and $a, b \in A$,

$$1 \cdot a^i b = 1 \cdot b^{i+1}. \tag{4.9}$$

This formula holds indeed for $a, b \in A$ and $i = 0$. Arguing by induction, we suppose that (4.9) holds for some $i \geq 0$, and for all $a, b \in A$. Then we have, for $a, b \in A$, also $1 \cdot b^i a = 1 \cdot a^{i+1}$, whence $1 \cdot b^i ab = 1 \cdot a^{i+1}b$. Apply (4.8). We get

$$1 \cdot a^{i+1}b = 1 \cdot b^i ab = 1 \cdot b^{i+2}.$$

This proves (4.9).

Finally we show, by a descending induction on $i \in \{0, 1, \ldots, d\}$, that for all $a \in A$,

$$1 \cdot a^i A^{d-i} = \{1\}.$$

This holds for $i = d$, and for $i < d$ we have

$$1 \cdot a^i A^{d-i} = \bigcup_{b \in A} 1 \cdot a^i b A^{d-i-1} = \bigcup_{b \in A} 1 \cdot b^{i+1} A^{d-i-1} = \{1\}$$

by using (4.9). This proves the formula. For $i = 0$, it becomes $1 \cdot A^d = \{1\}$, showing that $A^d \subset X$. This implies that $A^d = X$. Since $G(A^d)$ is a cyclic group, it is not a Frobenius group. This yields the contradiction and concludes the proof. $\square$

Remark Consider a finite maximal biprefix code X of degree at most 3. If the degree is 1 or 2, then the code is uniform, and the group is a cyclic group. If $d(X) = 3$, then $G(X)$ is either the symmetric group $\mathfrak{S}_3$ or the cyclic group over 3 elements. The latter group is regular, and according to Theorems 1.2 and 1.1, the code X is uniform. Thus except for the uniform code, all finite maximal biprefix codes of degree 3 have as a group $\mathfrak{S}_3$ which is a Frobenius group.

We now establish an interesting property of the groups of biprefix codes. For this, we use a result from the theory of permutation groups which we formulate for convenience as stated in Theorem 4.5 (proofs can be found in the classical literature and references are given in Section 7). Recall that a permutation group G over a set Q is *k-transitive* if for all $(p_1, \ldots, p_k) \in Q^k$ and $(q_1, \ldots, q_k) \in Q^k$ composed of distinct elements, there exists $g \in G$ such that $p_1 g = q_1, \ldots, p_k g = q_k$. Thus 1-transitive groups are precisely the transitive groups. A 2-transitive group is usually called *doubly transitive.*

THEOREM 4.5 *Let G be a primitive permutation group of degree d containing a d-cycle. Then either G is a regular group or a Frobenius group or is doubly transitive.*

THEOREM 4.6 *Let X be a finite maximal biprefix code over A. If X is indecomposable and not uniform, then $G(X)$ is doubly transitive.*

Proof According to Theorem 2.5, the group $G(X)$ is primitive. Let d be its degree. In view of Proposition 4.3, $G(X)$ contains a d-cycle. By Theorem 4.5, three cases may arise. Either $G(X)$ is regular and then, by Theorem 1.2, X is a group code and by Theorem 1.1, the code X is uniform. Or $G(X)$ is a Frobenius group. By Theorem 4.4, we have $d \leq 3$. The only group of a nonuniform code then is $\mathfrak{S}_3$, as shown in the remark. This group is both a Frobenius group and doubly transitive. Thus in any case, the group is doubly transitive. □

In Theorem 4.6, the condition on X to be indecomposable is necessary. Indeed, otherwise by Theorem 2.5, the group $G(X)$ would be imprimitive. But it is known that a doubly transitive group is primitive (Proposition 0.8.6).

There is an interesting combinatorial interpretation of the fact that the group of a biprefix code is doubly transitive.

PROPOSITION 4.7 *Let X be a thin maximal biprefix code over A, and let $P = XA^-$. The group $G(X)$ is doubly transitive iff for all $p, q \in P - \{1\}$, there exist $x, y \in X^*$ such that*

$$px = yq.$$

Proof Let φ be the representation associated with the literal automaton $\mathscr{A} = (P, 1, 1)$ of X^*. Let $d = d(X)$, and let e by an idempotent of rank d in $\varphi(X^*)$. Let $S = \text{Fix}(e)$. We have $1 \in S$, since $S = \text{Im}(e)$.

Let $p, q \in S - \{1\}$, and assume that there exist $x, y \in X^*$ such that $px = yq$. We have $1 \cdot p = p$ and $1 \cdot q = q$, whence

$$p \cdot x = 1 \cdot px = 1 \cdot yq = 1 \cdot q = q.$$

This shows that for the element $e\varphi(x)e \in G(e)$, we have $pe\varphi(x)e = q$. Since $1e\varphi(x)e = 1$, this shows that the restriction to S of $e\varphi(x)e$, which is in the stabilizer of 1, maps p on q. Thus this stabilizer is transitive, and consequently the group $G_e = G(X)$ is doubly transitive.

Assume now conversely that $G(X)$ is doubly transitive, and let $p, q \in P - \{1\}$. Let $i, j \in S$ be such that $pe = i, qe = j$. Then $i, j \neq 1$. Consider indeed a word $w \in \varphi^{-1}(e)$. Then $1 \cdot w = 1$; thus the assumption $i = 1$ would imply that $p \cdot w = pe = i = 1$, and since $1 \cdot w = 1$, Proposition 2.1 gives $p = 1$, a contradiction. Since $G(X)$ is doubly transitive, and $G(X)$ is equivalent to G_e, there exists $g \in G(e)$ such that

$$ig = j \qquad \text{and} \qquad 1g = 1.$$

Let $m \in \varphi(A^*)$ be such that $jm = q$, and let f be the idempotent of the group $G(em)$. Since e and f are in the same $\mathscr{R}$-class, they have the same nuclear equivalence. Thus the equalities $qe = j = je$ imply $qf = jf$. Further $\mathrm{Im}(f) = \mathrm{Im}(em)$. Since $qem = jm = q$, we have $q \in \mathrm{Im}(f)$. Thus q is a fixed point of f, and $jf = qf = q$. Consider the function egf. Then

$$1egf = 1gf = 1f = 1,$$

$$pegf = igf = jf = q.$$

Let x be in $\varphi^{-1}(egf)$. Then $x \in X^*$ and $p \cdot x = q$. This holds in the literal automaton. Thus there exists $y \in X^*$ such that $px = yq$. □

5. EXAMPLES

The results of Section 4 show that the groups of finite maximal biprefix codes are particular ones. This of course holds only for finite codes since every transitive group appears as the group of some group code. We describe, in this section, examples of finite maximal biprefix codes with particular groups.

Call a permutation group G *realizable* if there exists a finite maximal biprefix code X such that $G(X) = G$.

We start with an elementary property of permutation groups.

LEMMA 5.1 *For any integer $d \geq 1$, the group generated by $\alpha = (1\,2 \cdots d)$ and one transposition of adjacent elements modulo d is the whole symmetric group $\mathfrak{S}_d$.*

Proof Let $\beta = (1\,d)$. Then for $j \in \{1, 2, \ldots, d-1\}$,

$$\alpha^{-j}\beta\alpha^{j} = (j, j+1). \tag{5.1}$$

Next for $1 \leq i < j \leq d$,

$$(i, j) = \tau(j-1, j)\tau^{-1},$$

where

$$\tau = (i, i+1)(i+1, i+2)\cdots(j-2, j-1).$$

This shows that the group generated by α and β contains all transpositions. Thus it is the symmetric group $\mathfrak{S}_d$. Formula (5.1) shows that the same conclusion holds if β is replaced by any transposition of adjacent elements. □

PROPOSITION 5.2 *For all $d \geq 1$, the symmetric group $\mathfrak{S}_d$ is realizable by a finite maximal biprefix code.*

Proof Let $A = \{a, b\}$. For $d = 1$ or 2, the code $X = A^d$ can be used. Assume $d \geq 3$. By Theorems III.4.2 and III.4.3., there exists a unique maximal biprefix code X of degree d with kernel

$$K = \{ba\}.$$

Indeed, $\mu(K) = (L_K, ba) = 2$. No word has more than one K-interpretation. Consequently K is insufficient and by Proposition III.5.4, the code X is finite. Let us verify that

$$X \cap a^*ba^* = ba \cup \{a^iba^{d-i} \mid 1 \leq i \leq d-2\} \cup a^{d-1}b. \tag{5.2}$$

For each integer $j \in \{0, 1, \ldots. d-1\}$, there is a unique integer $i \in \{0, 1, \ldots, d-1\}$ such that $a^iba^j \in X$. It suffices to verify that the integer i is determined by formula (5.2).

Let $i, j \in \{0, 1, \ldots, d-1\}$ be such that $a^iba^j \in X$. By formula (1.5) in Chapter III, the number of X-interpretations of a^iba^j is

$$\begin{aligned}(L_X, a^iba^j) &= 1 + |a^iba^j| - (\underline{A}^*\underline{X}\underline{A}^*, a^iba^j)\\ &= i + j + 2 - (\underline{A}^*\underline{X}\underline{A}^*, a^iba^j).\end{aligned}$$

The number $(\underline{A}^*\underline{X}\underline{A}^*, a^iba^j)$ of occurrences of words of X in a^iba^j is equal to 1 plus the number of occurrences of words of K in a^iba^j, except when $j = 1$ which implies $i = 0$ since $ba \in X$. Thus

$$(L_X, a^iba^j) = \begin{cases} i + j & \text{if} \quad i \in \{1, 2, \ldots, d-1\}, \\ i + j + 1 & \text{if} \quad i = 0. \end{cases}$$

On the other hand, the word a^iba^j must have d interpretations since it is not in $K = K(X)$. This proves formula (5.2).

Now we consider the automaton $\mathscr{A}(X^*) = (Q, 1, 1)$ and consider the ergodic representation $*_a$ associated to the idempotent $\varphi(a^d)$ defined in Section 4. Setting $i = 1 \cdot a^{i-1}$ for $i \in \{1, 2, \ldots, d\}$ we have

$$a *_a a^d = (1\,2 \cdots d).$$

Set $\beta = b *_a a^d$ and observe that $\beta = (1\ d)$. Indeed by formula (4.4),

$$i\beta = j \quad \Leftrightarrow \quad 1 \cdot a^{i-1}ba^d = 1 \cdot a^{j-1}a^d$$
$$\Leftrightarrow \quad 1 \cdot a^{i-1}ba^d = 1 \cdot a^{j-1}.$$

Thus $i\beta = 1 \cdot a^{i-1}ba^d$. For $i = 1$, this gives $1\beta = 1 \cdot baa^{d-1}$, whence $1\beta = 1 \cdot a^{d-1} = d$. Next for $i = d$, we have $d\beta = (1 \cdot a^{d-1}) \cdot a^d = 1$. Finally, if $1 < i < d$, then $i\beta = 1 \cdot a^{i-1}ba^{d-(i-1)}a^{i-1} = 1 \cdot a^{i-1} = i$. This shows that the group $G(X)$ contains the cycle

$$\alpha = (1\,2 \cdots d)$$

and the transposition $\beta = (1d)$. In view of Lemma 5.1, $G(X) = \mathfrak{S}_d$. □

For the next result, we prove again an elementary property of permutations.

LEMMA 5.3 *Let d be an odd integer. The group generated by the two permutations*

$$\alpha = (1, 2, \ldots, d) \qquad \textit{and} \qquad \gamma = \delta\alpha\delta,$$

where δ is a transposition of adjacent elements modulo d, is the whole alternating group $\mathfrak{A}_d$.

Proof The group $\mathfrak{A}_d$ consists of all permutations $\sigma \in \mathfrak{S}_d$ which are a product of an even number of transpositions. A cycle of length k is in $\mathfrak{A}_d$ iff k is odd. Since d is odd, $\alpha, \gamma \in \mathfrak{A}_d$.

By Lemma 5.1, the symmetric group is generated by α and δ. Each permutation $\sigma \in \mathfrak{S}_d$ can be written as

$$\sigma = \alpha^{k_1}\delta\alpha^{k_2}\delta \cdots \alpha^{k_{n-1}}\delta\alpha^{k_n}$$

and $\sigma \in \mathfrak{A}_d$ if n is odd. In this case, setting $n = 2m + 1$,

$$\sigma = \alpha^{k_1}\beta_2\alpha^{k_3}\beta_4 \cdots \beta_{2m}\alpha^{k_{2m+1}}$$

with $\beta_{2i} = \delta\alpha^{k_{2i}}\delta$. Since $\beta_{2i} = (\delta\alpha\delta)^{k_{2i}}$, this formula shows that $\mathfrak{A}_d$ is generated by α and $\delta\alpha\delta = \gamma$. □

PROPOSITION 5.4 *For each odd integer d, the alternating group $\mathfrak{A}_d$ is realizable by a finite maximal biprefix code.*

Proof Let $A = \{a, b\}$. For $d = 1$ or 3, the code $X = A^d$ can be used. Assume $d \geq 5$. Let

$$I = \{1, 2, \ldots, d\}, \qquad J = \{1, \bar{2}, \bar{3}, \ldots, \bar{d}\},$$

and

$$Q = I \cup J.$$

Consider the deterministic automaton $\mathscr{A} = (Q, 1, 1)$ with transitions given by

$$
\begin{aligned}
i \cdot a &= i + 1 \qquad (1 \le i \le d - 1),\\
d \cdot a &= 1,\\
\bar{\imath} \cdot a &= i + 1 \qquad (1 \le i \le d - 2),\\
\overline{d - 1} \cdot a &= 1,\\
\bar{d} \cdot a &= d,
\end{aligned}
$$

and

$$
\begin{aligned}
i \cdot b &= \overline{i + 1} \qquad (1 \le i \le d - 3),\\
(d - 2) \cdot b &= \bar{d},\\
(d - 1) \cdot b &= \overline{d - 1},\\
d \cdot b &= 1,\\
\bar{\imath} \cdot b &= \overline{i + 1} \qquad (2 \le i \le d - 1),\\
\bar{d} \cdot b &= 1.
\end{aligned}
$$

It is easily verified that this automaton is minimal. Let X be the prefix code such that $|\mathscr{A}| = X^*$. Since

$$
I \cdot a = I, \qquad J \cdot a = I,
$$
$$
I \cdot b = J, \qquad J \cdot b = J,
$$

the functions $\varphi(a)$ and $\varphi(b)$, of rank d, have minimal rank. Since I and J are the only minimal images, and since they contain the state 1, Proposition 2.1(ii) shows that X is a maximal biprefix code. It has degree d.

Let us show that X is finite. For this, consider the following order on Q:

$$
1 < 2 < \bar{2} < 3 < \bar{3} < \cdots < d - 1 < \overline{d - 1} \qquad \text{and} \qquad \overline{d - 1} < \bar{d} < d.
$$

For all $c \in \{a, b\}$ and $q \in Q$, either $q \cdot c = 1$ or $q \cdot c > q$. Thus, there are only finitely many simple paths in $\mathscr{A}$. Consequently, X is finite.

Now let us compute $G(X)$. Since $\varphi(a)$, $\varphi(b)$ have minimal rank, both $a, b \in E(X)$. According to Proposition 4.1, the group $G(X)$ is equivalent to the group generated by the four permutations

$$
a *_a a, \qquad a *_a b, \qquad b *_a a, \qquad b *_a b.
$$

By formula (4.5) we have $a *_a a = a *_a b = \alpha$, with $\alpha = (1, 2, \ldots, d)$. Next, by formula (4.4),

$$
b *_a a = \alpha, \qquad b *_a b = \gamma
$$

with $\gamma = (1, 2, \ldots, d-3, d-1, d-2, d)$. In view of Lemma 5.3, $G(X) = \mathfrak{A}_d$. $\square$

Observe that for an even d, the group $\mathfrak{A}_d$ is not realizable. More generally, no subgroup of $\mathfrak{A}_d$ is realizable when d is even. Indeed, by Proposition 4.3, the group $G(X)$ of a finite maximal biprefix code X contains a cycle of length d, which is not in $\mathfrak{A}_d$ since d is even.

EXAMPLE 5.1 We give, for $d = 5$, the figures of the automaton and of the code of the previous proof, Figs. 5.4 and 5.5.

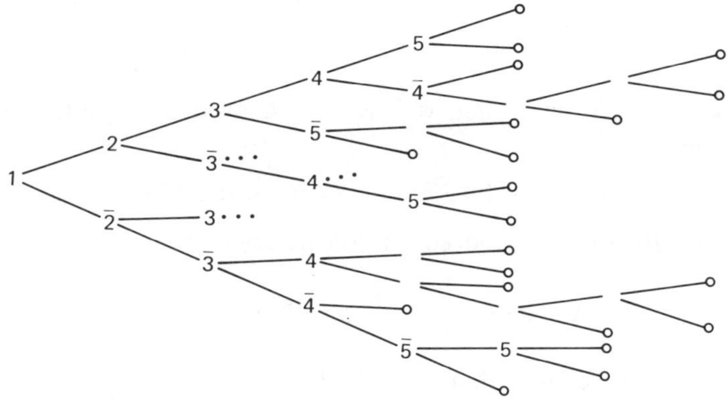

Fig. 5.4 A finite maximal biprefix code X with $G(X) = \mathfrak{A}_5$.

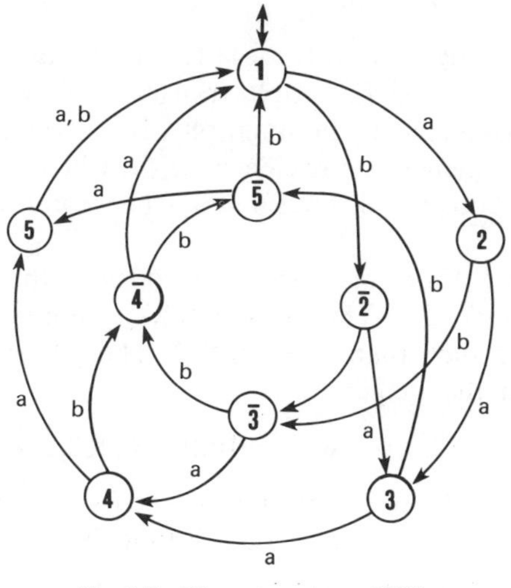

Fig. 5.5 The automaton $\mathscr{A}(X^*)$.

EXAMPLE 5.2 For degree 5, the only realizable groups are $\mathbb{Z}/5\mathbb{Z}$, $\mathfrak{S}_5$ and $\mathfrak{A}_5$. It is known indeed that with the exception of these three groups, all transitive permutations groups of degree 5 are Frobenius groups. By Theorem 4.4, they are not realizable.

EXAMPLE 5.3 For degree 6, we already know, by the preceding propositions, that $\mathbb{Z}/6\mathbb{Z}$ and $\mathfrak{S}_6$ are realizable. We also know that no subgroup of $\mathfrak{A}_6$ is realizable.

There exists, in addition to these two groups, another primitive group which is realizable. This group is denoted by $PGL_2(5)$ and is defined as follows. Let $P = \mathbb{Z}/5\mathbb{Z} \cup \{\infty\}$. The group $PGL(2, 5)$ is the group of all homographies from P into P

$$p \mapsto \frac{xp + y}{zp + t}$$

for $x, y, z, t \in \mathbb{Z}/5\mathbb{Z}$ satisfying $xt - yz \neq 0$. Consider, for later use, the permutations

$$\alpha = (\infty\ 0\ 1\ 4\ 2\ 3), \qquad \beta = (\infty\ 1\ 0\ 2\ 4\ 3).$$

We have $\alpha, \beta \in PGL_2(5)$. Indeed α and β are the homographies

$$\alpha\colon\ p \mapsto \frac{2}{p + 2}, \qquad \beta\colon\ P \mapsto \frac{p - 1}{p + 2},$$

respectively. We verify now that α and β generate all $PGL_2(5)$. A straightforward computation gives

$$\beta^2\alpha\beta = (\infty\ 0\ 4\ 2\ 1)(3), \qquad \beta^2\alpha\beta\alpha^{-1} = (\infty)(4)(0\ 1\ 3\ 2).$$

The permutation α together with these two permutations show that the group G generated by α and β is triply transitive. Now each element σ in $PGL_2(5)$ is characterized, as any homography, by its values on three points. Since G is 3-transitive, there exists an element $g \in G$ which takes the same three values on the points considered. Thus $\sigma = g$, whence $\sigma \in G$. This proves that $G = PGL_2(5)$.

To show that $PGL_2(5)$ is realizable, we consider the automaton $\mathscr{A} = (Q, 1, 1)$ given in Table 5.2. This automaton is minimal. Let X be the maximal prefix code such that $\mathscr{A} = \mathscr{A}(X^*)$. Then X is a finite maximal biprefix code. Indeed, the images

$$\mathrm{Im}(a) = \{1, 2, 3, 4, 5, 6\}, \qquad \mathrm{Im}(b) = \{1, \bar{2}, \bar{3}, \bar{4}, \bar{5}, \bar{6}\}$$

are minimal images, containing both the state 1. By Proposition 2.1(ii), X is maximal biprefix with degree 6. The code X is finite because if Q is ordered by

$$1 < 2 < \bar{2} < 3 < \bar{3} < \bar{4} < 4 < 5 < \bar{5} < \bar{6} < 6,$$

TABLE 5.2

The Transitions of the Automaton $\mathscr{A}$

	1	2	3	4	5	6	$\bar{2}$	$\bar{3}$	$\bar{4}$	$\bar{5}$	$\bar{6}$
a	2	3	4	5	6	1	3	5	4	1	6
b	$\bar{2}$	$\bar{4}$	$\bar{3}$	$\bar{6}$	$\bar{5}$	1	3	4	$\bar{5}$	$\bar{6}$	1

then the vertices on simple paths from 1 to 1 are met in strictly increasing order, with the exception of the last one.

Next $a, b \in E(X)$, because of the minimality of the images $\mathrm{Im}(a)$, $\mathrm{Im}(b)$. Thus the group $G(X)$ is generated by the permutations

$$\alpha = a *_a a = a *_a b = (1\ 2\ 3\ 4\ 5\ 6),$$

$$\gamma = b *_a a, \qquad \beta = b *_a b.$$

Formula (4.4) shows that

$$\gamma = \alpha, \qquad \beta = (1\ 3\ 2\ 5\ 4\ 6)$$

Thus $G(X)$ is generated by α and β. Let ρ be the bijection from 1, 2, 3, 4, 5, 6 onto $P = \mathbb{Z}/5\mathbb{Z} \cup \{\infty\}$ given by

1	2	3	4	5	6
∞	0	1	4	2	3

Then $\alpha = \rho^{-1}\alpha\rho$, $\beta = \rho^{-1}\beta\rho$. Consequently, the groups $G(X)$ and $PGL_2(5)$ are equivalent.

EXERCISES

SECTION 1

1.1. Let $X \subset A^+$ be a finite code and let $\mathscr{A} = (Q, 1, 1)$ be an unambiguous trim automaton recognizing X^*. Show that the group of invertible elements of the monoid $\varphi_{\mathscr{A}}(A^*)$ is a cyclic group.

****1.2.** Let G be a transitive permutation group over a finite set Q. Let $1 \in Q$, and $H = \{g \in G \mid 1g = 1\}$. Let ψ: $A^* \to G$ be a surjective morphism and let Z be the group code defined by $Z^* = \psi^{-1}(H)$.

Let X be a finite subset of Z. Let φ be the representation associated with the minimal automaton $\mathscr{A}(X^*)$ and set $M = \varphi(A^*)$.

Show that M contains an idempotent e such that the group G_e is equivalent to G iff there exists a finite subset Y of A^+ such that

(i) $Z \cap A^*YA^*$ is finite,

(ii) $Z \cap F(Y^*) \subset X$,

(iii) $\psi(Y^*) = G$.

Use this to show that for every finite transitive permutation group G, there exists a *finite* biprefix code X such that G is equivalent to G_e for some idempotent e in the transition monoid of the minimal automaton of X^*.

SECTION 2

2.1. Let $X \subset A^+$ be a biprefix code and let $\mathscr{A}(X^*) = (Q, 1, 1)$ be the minimal automaton of X^*. Let $\varphi = \varphi_{\mathscr{A}}$ be the associated representation and $M = \varphi(A^*)$. Show that for any idempotent $e \in \varphi(\bar{F}(X))$, the monoid of partial function M_e is composed of injective partial functions.

SECTION 3

3.1. Let $X \subset A^+$ be a thin maximal biprefix code, and let J_D be the minimal ideal of $\varphi_D(A^*)$. Show that for $\text{Card}(A) \geq 2$,

$$\bar{H}(X) = \varphi_D^{-1}(J_D).$$

3.2. Let $X \subset A^+$ be a finite maximal prefix code, let $\mathscr{A}(X^*) = (Q, 1, 1)$ be the minimal automaton of X^*, set $\varphi = \varphi_{\mathscr{A}(X^*)}$. Let $a \in A$ and let n be the order of a in X ($a^n \in X$).

(a) Show that the idempotent in $\varphi(a^+)$ has rank n.

(b) Show, without using Theorem 3.3, that $\varphi(A^+)$ is not nil-simple when $n \geq 1 + d(X)$.

3.3. Let $X \subset A^+$ be a thin complete code. Then X is called *elementary* if there exist an unambiguous trim automaton $\mathscr{A} = (Q, 1, 1)$ recognizing X^* such that the semigroup $S = \varphi_{\mathscr{A}}(A^+)$ has depth 1. Show that if X is elementary, then

$$X = Y \circ Z,$$

where Y is an elementary biprefix code and $G(X) = G(Y)$.

3.4. Let $\mathscr{A} = (Q, 1, 1)$ be a complete, deterministic trim automaton and let φ be the associated representation. Suppose that $\varphi(A^+)$ has finite depth, and that $\varphi(A^+)$ has minimal rank 1. Show that the depth of $\varphi(A^+)$ is at most $\text{Card}(Q) - 1$. (Hint: Consider the sequence θ_i of equivalence relations over Q defined by

$$p \equiv q \mod \theta_i \qquad \text{iff} \quad \forall w \in A^i, \quad p \cdot w = q \cdot w.)$$

3.5. Let $X \subset A^+$ be a finite biprefix code. Let φ be the representation associated with $\mathscr{A}(X^*)$ and $M = \varphi(A^*)$. Let J be the minimal ideal of M and let Λ be the set of its $\mathscr{L}$-classes. Let L_0 be a distinguished $\mathscr{L}$-class in Λ. Define a deterministic automaton

$$\mathscr{B} = (\Lambda, L_0, L_0)$$

by setting

$$L \cdot w = L\varphi(w).$$

Let ψ be the representation associated with $\mathscr{B}$, and let I be the minimal ideal of $\psi(A^*)$.

(a) Show that $\psi(A^*)$ has minimal rank 1, and that $\psi^{-1}(I) = \varphi^{-1}(J)$.

(b) Use Exercise 3.4 to show that $\varphi(A^+)$ has depth at most $\text{Card}(\Lambda) - 1$.

SECTION 4

4.1. Let X be a finite maximal biprefix code of degree d. Let $a \in A$ and $k \geq 0$ such that $a^k \in E(X)$. Show that for each integer $n \leq d - k$ and each word $u \in A^n$, there exist at least $d - k - n$ integers i, $1 \leq i \leq d$ such that

$$i(u *_a a^k) \geq i - k + 1.$$

4.2. Derive directly Theorem 1.1 from Exercise 4.1 (take $k = 0$).

4.3. Derive the inequalities (4.7) from Exercise 4.1 (take $k = 1$, $u = b$).

****4.4.** Let G be a permutation group of degree d, let $k = k(G)$ and suppose that G contains the cycle $\alpha = (1\ 2 \cdots d)$. Show that if $d \geq 4k^2 + 8k + 2$, then for every $\pi \in G$ which is not a power of α, there exist at least $2k + 2$ integers i, $1 \leq i \leq d$, such that $i\pi \leq i$.

****4.5.** Derive from Exercises 4.1 and 4.4 that a finite maximal nonuniform biprefix code X of degree d satisfies

$$k(G(X)) \geq (\sqrt{d}/2) - 1.$$

SECTION 5

****5.1.** Show that for $A = \{a, b\}$, there are exactly six elementary finite maximal biprefix codes over A (see Exercise 3.3) with group equivalent to $PGL_2(5)$.

***5.2.** Show that the automaton in Table 5.3 defines a finite maximal biprefix code X of degree 7. Show that $G(X)$ is equivalent to the group $GL_3(2)$ of invertible 3×3 matrices with elements in $\mathbb{Z}/2\mathbb{Z}$, considered as a permutation group acting on $(\mathbb{Z}/2\mathbb{Z})^3 - \{0\}$.

5.3. Show that the automaton in Table 5.4 defines a finite maximal biprefix code X of degree 11. Show that $G(X)$ is equivalent to the Mathieu group M_{11}.

TABLE 5.3

A Finite Code with Group $GL_3(2)$

	1	2	3	4	5	6	7	8	9	10	11	12	13	14	15
a	2	3	4	5	6	7	1	9	4	14	15	13	1	6	7
b	8	9	12	11	10	1	13	9	10	11	12	13	1	12	13

TABLE 5.4

A Finite Code with Group M_{11}

	1	2	3	4	5	6	7	8	9	10	11	12	13	14
a	2	3	4	5	6	7	8	9	10	11	1	22	23	24
b	12	13	16	17	14	15	20	19	18	1	21	13	14	15

15	16	17	18	19	20	21	22	23	24	25	26	27	28	29
25	26	27	28	29	21	1	4	5	6	7	8	9	10	11
16	17	18	19	20	21	1	14	15	16	17	18	19	20	21

NOTES

Theorem 1.1 already appears in Schützenberger (1956). Theorem 1.3 and Corollary 1.4 are from Reis and Thierrin (1979). The ergodic representation of Section 4 is described in Perrin (1979). It is used in Lallement and Perrin (1981) to describe a construction of finite maximal biprefix codes.

Theorem 4.5 is a combination of a theorem of Schur and of a theorem of Burnside. Schur's theorem is the following: "Let G be a primitive permutation group of degree d. If G contains a d-cycle and if d is not a prime number, then G is doubly transitive." This result is proved in Wielandt (1964, pp. 52–66). It is the final development of what H. Wielandt calls the "Method of Schur." Burnside's theorem is the following: "A transitive permutation group of prime degree is either doubly transitive or a Frobenius group." Burnside's proof uses the theory of characters. It is reproduced in Huppert (1967, p. 609). An elementary proof (i.e., without characters) is in Huppert and Blackburn (1982, Vol. III, pp. 425–434).

The other results of this chapter are from Perrin (1975, 1977b, 1978). Perrin (1975) gives a more exhaustive catalogue of examples than the list of Section 5.

Exercise 1.2 is from Rindone (1983). Exercise 2.1 is due to Margolis (1982). Exercise 3.4 is a well-known property of "definite" automata (Perles *et al.*, 1969).

The exercises of Section 4 are from Perrin (1978) and those of Section 5 are from Perrin (1975).

CHAPTER **VI**

Densities

0. INTRODUCTION

We have used measures for studying codes as early as in the first chapter. In particular we have seen that for any code X over an alphabet A and for any Bernoulli distribution π over A^*, we have $\pi(X) \le 1$. We also have seen that a thin code X is a maximal code iff $\pi(X) = 1$. We thus have obtained an astonishingly simple method for testing the maximality of a code. This is a mark of the importance of the role played by probability measures in the theory of codes.

In this chapter we again use measures. We will study asymptotic properties of certain sets related to a code. For this the notion of *density* of a subset L of A^* is introduced. It is the limit in mean, provided it exists, of the probability that a word of length n is in L. We shall prove a fundamental formula (Theorem 3.1) that relates the density of the submonoid generated by a thin complete code to that of its sets of left factors and right factors. For this, and as a preparation, we shall see how one can compute the density of a set of words by transfering the problem to a study of probabilities in abstract monoids.

1. DENSITIES

Let π be a positive Bernoulli distribution on A^*. It is a morphism

$$\pi: \quad A^* \to]0, 1]$$

such that

$$\sum_{a \in A} \pi(a) = 1.$$

In the sequel, we use the notation

$$A^{(n)} = \{1\} \cup A \cup \cdots \cup A^{n-1}.$$

In particular $A^{(0)} = \varnothing$, $A^{(1)} = \{1\}$.

Let L be a subset of A^*. The set L is said to *have a density* with respect to π if the sequence of the $\pi(L \cap A^n)$ converges in mean, i.e., if

$$\lim_{n \to \infty} \frac{1}{n} \sum_{k=0}^{n-1} \pi(L \cap A^k)$$

exists. If this is the case, the *density* of L (relative to π) denoted by $\delta(L)$, is this limit, which can also be written as

$$\delta(L) = \lim_{n \to \infty} (1/n)\, \pi(L \cap A^{(n)}).$$

An elementary result from analysis shows that if the sequence $\pi(L \cap A^n)$ has a limit, then its limit in mean also exists, and both are equal. This remark may sometimes simplify computations. Observe that

$$\delta(A^*) = 1$$

and

$$0 \leq \delta(L) \leq 1$$

for any subset L of A^* having a density. If L and M are subsets of A^* having a density, then so has $L \cup M$, and

$$\delta(L \cup M) \leq \delta(L) + \delta(M).$$

If $L \cap M \neq \varnothing$, and if two of the three sets L, M and $L \cup M$ have a density, then the third one also has a density and

$$\delta(L \cup M) = \delta(L) + \delta(M).$$

The function δ is a partial function from $\mathfrak{P}(A^*)$ into $[0, 1]$. Of course, $\delta(\{w\}) = 0$ for all $w \in A^*$. This shows that in general

$$\delta(L) \neq \sum_{w \in L} \delta(\{w\}).$$

Observe that if $\pi(L) < \infty$, then $\delta(L) = 0$ since

$$\pi(L \cap A^{(n)}) \leq \pi(L),$$

whence

$$\frac{1}{n}\pi(L \cap A^{(n)}) \to 0.$$

EXAMPLE 1.1 Let $L = (A^2)^*$ be the set of words of even length. Then

$$\pi(L \cap A^{(2k)}) = \pi(L \cap A^{(2k-1)}) = k.$$

Thus

$$\delta(L) = \tfrac{1}{2}.$$

EXAMPLE 1.2 Let $D^* = \{w \in A^* \mid |w|_a = |w|_b\}$ over $A = \{a, b\}$, and set $p = \pi(a)$, $q = \pi(b)$. Then (see Example I.4.5)

$$\pi(D^* \cap A^{2n}) = \binom{2n}{n} p^n q^n, \qquad \pi(D^* \cap A^{2n+1}) = 0.$$

Using Stirling's formula, we get

$$\pi(D^* \cap A^{2n}) \sim \frac{1}{\sqrt{\pi n}} 4^n (pq)^n$$

showing that for all values of p and q,

$$\lim_{n \to \infty} \pi(D^* \cap A^{2n}) = 0.$$

Thus $\delta(D^*) = 0$.

The definition of density clearly depends only on the values of the numbers $\pi(L \cap A^n)$. It appears to be useful to consider an analogous definition for formal power series: we restrict ourselves to formal power series in one variable with coefficients in $\mathbb{R}_+$. Let

$$f = \sum_{n \geq 0} f_n t^n \in \mathbb{R}_+[[t]]$$

be a formal series. The *density* of f, denoted by $\delta(f)$ is the limit in mean, provided it exists, of the sequence f_n,

$$\delta(f) = \lim_{n \to \infty} \frac{1}{n} \sum_{i=0}^{n-1} f_i.$$

To each set $L \subset A^*$ we associate a series $f_L \in \mathbb{R}_+[[t]]$ by

$$f_L = \sum_{n=0}^{\infty} \pi(L \cap A^n) t^n. \tag{1.1}$$

Clearly f_L has a density iff L has a density, and

$$\delta(L) = \delta(f_L).$$

Let f_L be given by (1.1). We denote by ρ_L the *radius of convergence* of the series f_L. It is the unique real number $\rho \in \mathbb{R}_+$ such that

$$\sum_{n \geq 0} \pi(L \cap A^n) z^n$$

converges for $|z| < \rho$ and diverges for $|z| > \rho$. For any set L, we have $\rho_L \geq 1$ since

$$\pi(L \cap A^n) \leq 1$$

for all $n \geq 0$.

The following proposition is a more precise formulation of Proposition I.5.6.

PROPOSITION 1.1 *Let L be a subset of A^* and let π be a positive Bernoulli distribution. If L is thin, then $\rho_L > 1$ and $\delta(L) = 0$.*

Proof Let w be a word in $\bar{F}(L)$, and set $n = |w|$. Then we have, for $0 \leq i \leq n$ and $k \geq 0$,

$$L \cap A^i (A^n)^k \subset A^i (A^n - \{w\})^k.$$

Hence

$$\pi(L \cap A^i (A^n)^k) \leq (1 - \pi(w))^k.$$

Thus for any $\rho \in \mathbb{R}_+$ satisfying $(1 - \pi(w))\rho^n < 1$, we have

$$f_L(\rho) \leq \sum_{i=0}^{n-1} \sum_{k=0}^{\infty} (1 - \pi(w))^k \rho^{i+kn}$$

$$= \sum_{i=0}^{n-1} \rho^i \left[\sum_{k=0}^{\infty} ((1 - \pi(w))\rho^n)^k \right]$$

This proves that

$$\rho_L \geq \left(\frac{1}{1 - \pi(w)} \right)^{1/n} > 1. \quad \square$$

For later use, we need an elementary result concerning the convergence of certain series. For the sake of completeness we include the proof.

PROPOSITION 1.2 *Let $f = \sum_{n \geq 0} f_n t^n$, $g = \sum_{n \geq 0} g_n t^n \in \mathbb{R}_+[[t]]$ be two power series satisfying*

(i) $0 < \sigma = \sum_{n \geq 0} g_n < \infty$;
(ii) *for all $n \geq 0$, $0 \leq f_n \leq 1$.*

Then $\delta(f)$ exists iff $\delta(fg)$ exists and in this case,

$$\delta(fg) = \delta(f)\sigma. \tag{1.2}$$

Proof Set

$$h = fg = \sum_{n=0}^{\infty} h_n t^n.$$

Then for $n \geq 1$,

$$\begin{aligned}\left(\sum_{i=0}^{n-1} f_i\right)\sigma &= \left(\sum_{i=0}^{n-1} f_i\right)\left(\sum_{j=0}^{\infty} g_j\right)\\ &= \sum_{0 \leq i+j \leq n-1} f_i g_j + \sum_{i=0}^{n-1} f_i\left(\sum_{j=n-i}^{\infty} g_j\right)\\ &= \sum_{k=0}^{n-1} h_k + \sum_{i=0}^{n-1} f_i r_{n-i},\end{aligned}$$

where $r_i = \sum_{j=i}^{\infty} g_j$. Let $s_n = \sum_{i=0}^{n-1} f_i r_{n-i}$. Then for $n \geq 1$,

$$\left(\frac{1}{n}\sum_{i=0}^{n-i} f_i\right)\sigma = \left(\frac{1}{n}\sum_{k=0}^{n-1} h_k\right) + \frac{1}{n} s_n. \tag{1.3}$$

Furthermore

$$s_n = \sum_{i=0}^{n-1} f_i r_{n-i} \leq \sum_{i=0}^{n-1} r_{n-i} = \sum_{i=1}^{n} r_i. \tag{1.4}$$

Since $\sum g_n$ converges, we have $\lim_{i\to\infty} r_i = 0$, showing that also

$$\lim_{n\to\infty} \frac{1}{n}\sum_{i=0}^{n-1} r_i = 0,$$

and in view of (1.4),

$$\lim_{n\to\infty} \frac{1}{n} s_n = 0.$$

Since $\sigma \neq 0$ Eq. (1.3) shows that $\delta(f)$ exists iff $\delta(h)$ exists and that $\delta(f)\sigma = \delta(h)$. This proves (1.2) and the proposition. □

PROPOSITION 1.3 *Let π be a positive Bernoulli distribution on A^*. Let L, M be subsets of A^* such that*

(i) $0 < \pi(M) < \infty$.
(ii) *The product LM is unambiguous.*

Then LM has a density iff L has a density, and if this is the case,

$$\delta(LM) = \delta(L)\pi(M). \tag{1.5}$$

Proof Since the product LM is unambiguous, we have

$$f_{LM} = f_L f_M.$$

In view of the preceding proposition

$$\delta(LM) = \delta(f_{LM}) = \delta(f_L)\sigma,$$

where $\sigma = \sum_{n\geq 0} \pi(M \cap A^n) = \pi(M)$. □

This proposition will be useful in the sequel. As a first illustration of its use, note

COROLLARY 1.4 *Each right (left) ideal I of A^* has a nonnull density. Each prefix-closed set has a density. More precisely*

$$\delta(I) = \pi(X), \qquad \text{where } X = I - IA^+.$$

Proof Let I be a right ideal and let $X = I - IA^+$. By Proposition II.1.2, the set X is prefix and

$$I = XA^*.$$

The product XA^* is unambiguous because X is prefix. Further $\pi(X) \leq 1$ since X is a code, and $\pi(X) > 0$ since $I \neq \varnothing$ and consequently also $X \neq \varnothing$. Thus, applying the (symmetrical version of the) preceding proposition, we obtain

$$\delta(I) = \delta(XA^*) = \pi(X)\delta(A^*) = \pi(X) \neq 0.$$

Finally, the complement of a prefix-closed set is a right ideal. □

Let X be a code over A. Then $\pi(X) \leq 1$ and $\pi(X) = 1$ if X is thin and complete. For a code X such that $\pi(X) = 1$ we define the *average length* of X (relatively to π) as the finite or infinite number

$$\lambda(X) = \sum_{x\in X} |x|\pi(x) = \sum_{n\geq 0} n\pi(X \cap A^n). \tag{1.6}$$

The following fundamental theorem gives a link between the density and the average length.

THEOREM 1.5 *Let $X \subset A^+$ be a code and let π be a positive Bernoulli distribution. If*

(i) $\pi(X) = 1$,
(ii) $\lambda(X) < \infty$,

then X^* has a density and $\delta(X^*) = 1/\lambda(X)$.

Proof Set $f_n = \pi(X \cap A^n)$. Then $f_X = \sum_{n=0}^{\infty} f_n t^n$. Since X is a code, we have as a consequence of Proposition I.1.6,

$$f_{X^*} = (1 - f_X)^{-1}. \tag{1.7}$$

Let $g = \sum_{n=0}^{\infty} g_n t^n$ be defined by

$$g = (1 - f_X)t^* = \frac{1 - f_X}{1 - t}. \tag{1.8}$$

Identifying terms, we have for $n \geq 0$,

$$g_n = 1 - \sum_{i=0}^{n} f_i.$$

From $\pi(X) = \sum_{i=0}^{\infty} f_i = 1$ we get that

$$g_n = \sum_{i=n+1}^{\infty} f_i. \tag{1.9}$$

Note that by (1.9), $g_n \geq 0$ for $n \geq 0$. Moreover, by (1.6) and (1.9),

$$\sum_{n=0}^{\infty} g_n = \sum_{n=0}^{\infty} \sum_{i=n+1}^{\infty} f_i = \sum_{i=0}^{\infty} if_i = \lambda(X). \tag{1.10}$$

We see that (1.8) and (1.7) give

$$t^* = f_{X^*} g. \tag{1.11}$$

Since $\lambda(X)$ is finite and not zero (indeed $\pi(X) = 1$ shows that $X \neq \varnothing$), we can apply Proposition 1.2 to (1.11). Since $\delta(t^*) = 1$, $\delta(f_{X^*})$ exists and

$$1 = \delta(f_{X^*})\left(\sum_{n=0}^{\infty} g_n\right) = \delta(f_{X^*})\lambda(X). \quad \square$$

Note the following important special case of Theorem 1.5.

THEOREM 1.6 *Let X be a thin complete code over A, and let π be a positive Bernoulli distribution. Then X^* has a density. Further $\delta(X^*) > 0$, $\lambda(X) < \infty$, and $\delta(X^*) = 1/\lambda(X)$.*

Proof Since X is a thin and complete code, $\pi(X) = 1$. Next, since X is thin, $\rho_X > 1$ by Proposition 1.1. Thus the derivative of f_X, which is the series

$$f'_X = \sum_{n \geq 1} n\pi(X \cap A^n)t^{n-1},$$

also has a radius of convergence strictly greater than 1. Hence $f'_X(1)$ is finite. Now

$$f'_X(1) = \sum_{n \geq 1} n\pi(X \cap A^n) = \lambda(X).$$

Thus $\lambda(X) < \infty$ and the hypotheses of Theorem 1.5 are satisfied. $\square$

2. PROBABILITIES OVER A MONOID

A detailed study of the density of a code, in relation to some of the fundamental parameters, will be presented in the next section. The aim of the present section is to prepare this investigation by the proof of some rather delicate results. We will show how certain monoids can be equipped with idempotent measures. This in turn allows us to determine the sets having a density, and to compute it.

We need the following lemma which constitutes a generalization of Proposition 1.2.

LEMMA 2.1 *Let I be a set, and for each $i \in I$, let*

$$f^{(i)} = \sum_{n=0}^{\infty} f_n^{(i)} t^n, \qquad g^{(i)} = \sum_{n=0}^{\infty} g_n^{(i)} t^n \in \mathbb{R}_+[[t]]$$

be formal power series satisfying

(i) $\sigma = \sum_{i \in I} \sum_{n \geq 0} g_n^{(i)} < \infty$,

(ii) $0 \leq f_n^{(i)} \leq 1$ *for all* $i \in I$, $n \geq 0$,

(iii) $\delta(f^{(i)})$ *exists for all* $i \in I$.

Set $\sigma^{(i)} = \sum_{n=0}^{\infty} g_n^{(i)}$ *for* $i \in I$. *Then* $\sum_{i \in I} f^{(i)} g^{(i)}$ *admits a density and*

$$\delta\left(\sum_{i \in I} f^{(i)} g^{(i)}\right) = \sum_{i \in I} \delta(f^{(i)}) \sigma^{(i)}.$$

Proof Set

$$h^{(i)} = f^{(i)} g^{(i)} = \sum_{n=0}^{\infty} h_n^{(i)} t^n, \qquad h = \sum_{i \in I} h^{(i)} = \sum_{n=0}^{\infty} h_n t^n.$$

Set also

$$r_l^{(i)} = \sum_{j=l}^{\infty} g_j^{(i)}, \qquad s_n^{(i)} = \sum_{l=0}^{n-1} f_l^{(i)} r_{n-l}^{(i)}, \qquad s_n = \sum_{i \in I} s_n^{(i)}.$$

We have, for $n \geq 1$ and $i \in I$,

$$\left(\sum_{l=0}^{n-1} f_l^{(i)}\right) \sigma^{(i)} = \sum_{k=0}^{n-1} h_k^{(i)} + s_n^{(i)}.$$

Dividing by n and summing over I, one obtains

$$\sum_{i \in I} \left(\frac{1}{n} \sum_{l=0}^{n-1} f_l^{(i)}\right) \sigma^{(i)} = \frac{1}{n} \sum_{k=0}^{n-1} h_k + \frac{s_n}{n}. \tag{2.1}$$

Set

$$d = \sum_{i \in I} \delta(f^{(i)}) \sigma^{(i)}.$$

Since $\delta(f^{(i)}) \leq 1$ for all $i \in I$, we have $d \leq \sum_{i \in I} \sigma^{(i)} = \sigma$. This shows that $d < \infty$.

Let now $\varepsilon > 0$ be a real number. Then there exists a finite subset F of I such that

$$\sigma \geq \sum_{i\in F} \sigma^{(i)} \geq \sigma - \varepsilon.$$

This is equivalent to

$$\sum_{i\in I-F} \sigma^{(i)} \leq \varepsilon.$$

Observing that $\delta(f^{(i)}) \leq 1$ for $i \in I$ and $(1/n)\sum_{l=0}^{n-1} f_l^{(i)} \leq 1$, we get that both

$$\sum_{i\in I-F} \delta(f^{(i)})\sigma^{(i)} \leq \varepsilon, \qquad \sum_{i\in I-F} \left(\frac{1}{n}\sum_{l=0}^{n-1} f_l^{(i)}\right)\sigma^{(i)} \leq \varepsilon.$$

This leads to the evaluation

$$\begin{aligned}
\left|d - \frac{1}{n}\sum_{k=0}^{n-1} h_k\right|
&= \Bigg|\sum_{i\in F} \delta(f^{(i)})\sigma^{(i)} + \sum_{i\in I-F} \delta(f^{(i)})\sigma^{(i)} \\
&\qquad - \sum_{i\in F}\left(\frac{1}{n}\sum_{l=0}^{n-1} f_l^{(i)}\right)\sigma^{(i)} \\
&\qquad - \sum_{i\in I-F}\left(\frac{1}{n}\sum_{l=0}^{n-1} f_l^{(i)}\right)\sigma^{(i)} + \frac{s_n}{n}\Bigg| \\
&\leq \left|\sum_{i\in F} \delta(f^{(i)})\sigma^{(i)} - \sum_{i\in F}\left(\frac{1}{n}\sum_{l=0}^{n-1} f_l^{(i)}\right)\sigma^{(i)}\right| + 2\varepsilon + \frac{s_n}{n} \\
&\leq \sum_{i\in F} \sigma^{(i)}\left|\delta(f^{(i)}) - \left(\frac{1}{n}\sum_{l=0}^{n-1} f_l^{(i)}\right)\right| + 2\varepsilon + \frac{s_n}{n}. \qquad (2.2)
\end{aligned}$$

Let us estimate the s_n. Since $f_l^{(i)} \leq 1$, we have

$$s_n = \sum_{i\in I} s_n^{(i)} \leq \sum_{i\in I}\sum_{l=0}^{n-1} r_{n-l}^{(i)} = \sum_{i\in I}\sum_{l=1}^{n} r_l^{(i)}.$$

Now

$$\sum_{i\in I-F}\sum_{l=1}^{n} r_l^{(i)} \leq \sum_{i\in I-F}\sum_{l=1}^{n} \sigma^{(i)} = \sum_{l=1}^{n}\sum_{i\in I-F} \sigma^{(i)} \leq n\varepsilon.$$

Thus $s_n/n \leq (\sum_{i\in F}(1/n)\sum_{l=1}^{n} r_l^{(i)}) + \varepsilon$. Next for each $i \in I$, we have $\lim_{l\to\infty} r_l^{(i)} = 0$, whence also $\lim_{n\to\infty}(1/n)\sum_{l=1}^{n} r_l^{(i)} = 0$. Consequently, by choosing a sufficiently large integer n, we have for each index i in the finite set F the inequality

$$\frac{1}{n}\sum_{l=1}^{n} r_l^{(i)} \le \frac{\varepsilon}{\operatorname{Card} F}.$$

Thus for sufficiently large n, $s_n/n \le 2\varepsilon$. Substituting in (2.2), we get for sufficiently large n,

$$\left| d - \frac{1}{n}\sum_{k=0}^{n-1} h_k \right| \le \sum_{i \in F} \sigma^{(i)} \left| \delta(f^{(i)}) - \left(\frac{1}{n}\sum_{l=0}^{n-1} f_l^{(i)} \right) \right| + 4\varepsilon.$$

Now, if n is large enough, we also have

$$\left| \delta(f^{(i)}) - \left(\frac{1}{n}\sum_{l=0}^{n-1} f_l^{(i)} \right) \right| \le \varepsilon,$$

and this holds for each index i in F. Thus

$$\left| d - \frac{1}{n}\sum_{k=0}^{n-1} h_k \right| \le \left(\sum_{i \in F} \sigma^{(i)} \right)\varepsilon + 4\varepsilon \le (\sigma + 4)\varepsilon.$$

This proves that $d = \lim_{n\to\infty} (1/n)\sum_{k=0}^{n-1} h_k$. □

Lemma 2.1 leads to the following proposition which extends Proposition 1.3.

PROPOSITION 2.2 *Let I be a set and for each $i \in I$, let L_i and M_i be subsets of A^*. Let π be a Bernoulli distribution on A^* and suppose that*

(i) $\sum_{i\in I} \pi(M_i) < \infty$,
(ii) *The products L_iM_i are unambiguous and the sets L_iM_i are pairwise disjoint,*
(iii) *Each L_i has a density $\delta(L_i)$.*

Then $\bigcup_{i\in I} L_iM_i$ has a density, and

$$\delta\left(\bigcup_{i\in I} L_iM_i \right) = \sum_{i\in I} \delta(L_i)\pi(M_i).$$

Proof Set in Lemma 2.1,

$$f_n^{(i)} = \pi(L_i \cap A^n), \qquad g_n^{(i)} = \pi(M_i \cap A^n).$$

Then $f^{(i)} = f_{L_i}$, $g^{(i)} = f_{M_i}$; furthermore $\delta(f^{(i)}) = \delta(L_i)$, $\sigma^{(i)} = \pi(M_i)$, and in particular $\sigma = \sum \pi(M_i) < \infty$. According to the lemma, we have

$$\delta\left(\sum_{i\in I} f^{(i)} g^{(i)} \right) = \sum_{i\in I} \delta(L_i)\pi(M_i).$$

Since condition (ii) of the statement implies that

$$\sum_{i\in I} f^{(i)}g^{(i)} = \sum_{i\in I} f_{L_i}f_{M_i} = \sum_{i\in I} f_{L_iM_i} = f_{\bigcup_{i\in I} L_iM_i},$$

the proposition follows. □

Let φ be a morphism from A^* onto a monoid M, and let π be a positive Bernoulli distribution on A^*. Provided M possesses certain properties which will be described below, each subset of A^* of the form $\varphi^{-1}(P)$, where $P \subset M$, has a density. The study of this phenomenon will lead us to give an explicit expression of the value of the densities of the sets $\varphi^{-1}(m)$ for $m \in M$, as a function of parameters related to M.

A monoid M is called *well founded* if it has a unique minimal ideal, if moreover this ideal is the union of the minimal left ideals of M, and also of the minimal right ideals, and if the intersection of a minimal right ideal and of a minimal left ideal is a finite group.

Any unambiguous monoid of relations of finite minimal rank is well founded by Proposition IV.4.10 and Theorem IV.4.11. It appears that the development given now does not depend on the fact that the elements of the monoid under concern are relations; therefore we present it in the more abstract frame of well-founded monoids.

Let $\varphi: A^* \to M$ be a morphism onto an arbitrary monoid, and let $m, n \in M$. We define

$$C_{m,n} = \{w \in A^* \mid m\varphi(w) = n\} = \varphi^{-1}(m^{-1}n).$$

The set $C_{n,n}$ is a right-unitary submonoid of A^*: for $u, uv \in C_{n,n}$, we have $n\varphi(u) = n = n\varphi(uv) = n\varphi(u)\varphi(v) = n\varphi(v)$. Thus $C_{n,n}$ is free. Let X_n be its base; it is a prefix code. Let

$$Z_{m,n} = C_{m,n} - C_{m,n}A^+$$

be the initial part of $C_{m,n}$. Then

$$C_{m,n} = Z_{m,n}X_n^*$$

and this product is unambiguous. Note also that

$$C_{1,n} = \varphi^{-1}(n)$$

PROPOSITION 2.3 *Let $\varphi: A^* \to M$ be a morphism onto a well-founded monoid M, and let π be a positive Bernoulli distribution on A^*. Let K be the minimal ideal of M.*

1. *For all $m, n \in M$, the set $C_{m,n} = \varphi^{-1}(m^{-1}n)$ has a density.*
2. *We have*

$$\delta(C_{m,n}) = \begin{cases} \pi(Z_{m,n})\delta(X_n^*) & \text{if } n \in K \text{ and } m^{-1}n \neq \varnothing, \\ 0 & \text{otherwise.} \end{cases}$$

3. *For* $m, n \in K$ such that $nM = mM$, $\pi(Z_{m,n}) = 1$ and consequently

$$\delta(C_{m,n}) = \delta(C_{n,n}) = \delta(X_n^*).$$

Proof Let $n \in M$, with $n \notin K$. Then $m^{-1}n \cap K = \emptyset$. Indeed, assume that $p \in m^{-1}n \cap K$. Then $mp = n$ and since K is an ideal, $p \in K$ implies $n \in K$. Thus for an element $n \notin K$, the set $C_{m,n}$ does not meet the ideal $\varphi^{-1}(K)$. Consequently $C_{m,n}$ is thin, and by Proposition 1.1, $\delta(C_{m,n}) = 0$.

Consider now the case where $n \in K$. Let $R = nM$ be the minimal right ideal containing n. Consider the deterministic automaton over A, $\mathscr{A} = (R, n, n)$ with transition function defined by $r \cdot a = r\varphi(a)$ for $r \in R$, $a \in A$. We have $|\mathscr{A}| = X_n^*$. Since R is a minimal right ideal, the automaton is complete and trim, and every state is recurrent. In particular, X_n is a complete code (Proposition II.3.9).

Let us verify that the monoid $\varphi_{\mathscr{A}}(A^*)$ has finite minimal rank. For this, let $u \in A^*$ be a word such that $\varphi(u) = n$. Since $\mathscr{A}$ is deterministic, it suffices to compute $\text{rank}_{\mathscr{A}}(u)$. Now $\text{rank}(\varphi_{\mathscr{A}}(u)) = \text{rank}_{\mathscr{A}}(u) = \text{Card}(R \cdot u) = \text{Card}(Rn) = \text{Card}(nMn)$.

By assumption, $nMn = nM \cap Mn$ is a finite group. Thus $\text{rank}(\varphi_{\mathscr{A}}(u))$ is finite and the monoid $\varphi_{\mathscr{A}}(A^*)$ has finite minimal rank. By Corollary IV.5.4, the code X_n is complete and thin and according to Theorem 1.6, X_n^* has a positive density. Since $Z_{m,n}$ is a prefix set, we have $\pi(Z_{m,n}) \leq 1$. In view of Proposition 1.3, the set $C_{m,n}$ has a density and

$$\delta(C_{m,n}) = \pi(Z_{m,n})\delta(X_n^*).$$

Clearly

$$C_{m,n} = \emptyset \quad \Leftrightarrow \quad m^{-1}n = \emptyset \quad \Leftrightarrow \quad Z_{m,n} = \emptyset;$$

moreover, π being positive, $\pi(Z_{m,n}) > 0$ iff $Z_{m,n} \neq \emptyset$; this shows that $\delta(C_{m,n}) \neq 0$ if $m^{-1}n \neq \emptyset$. This proves (2) and (1).

3. Let $u \in A^*$ be a word such that $n\varphi(u) = m$ and $n\varphi(u') \neq n$ for each proper nonempty left factor u' of u. Then

$$uZ_{m,n} \subset X_n.$$

Thus $Z_{m,n}$ is formed of right factors of words in X_n, and in particular $Z_{m,n}$ is thin. To show that $Z_{m,n}$ is right complete, let $w \in A^*$ and let $n' = m\varphi(w)$. Then $n' \in R = nM$, and since R is right-minimal, there exists $n'' \in M$ such that $n'n'' = n$. Let $v \in A^*$ be such that $\varphi(v) = n''$. Then $m\varphi(wv) = n$, and consequently $wv \in C_{m,n}$. This shows that $Z_{m,n} = \{1\}$ or $Z_{m,n}$ is a thin right complete prefix code, thus a maximal code. Thus $\pi(Z_{m,n}) = 1$. Consequently $\delta(C_{m,n}) = \delta(X_n^*)$. □

THEOREM 2.4 *Let $\varphi: A^* \to M$ be a morphism onto a well-founded monoid, and let π be a positive Bernoulli distribution on A^*. Let K be the minimal ideal of M.*

1. *For all $n \in M$, the set $\varphi^{-1}(n)$ has a density.*
2. *We have*

$$\delta(\varphi^{-1}(n)) = 0 \qquad \textit{iff} \quad n \notin K;$$

for all $\mathscr{R}$-equivalent $m, n \in K$,

$$\delta(\varphi^{-1}(n)) = \delta(\varphi^{-1}(m^{-1}n))\delta(\varphi^{-1}(nM)).$$

3. *For all $n \in K$,*

$$\delta(\varphi^{-1}(n)) = \frac{\delta(\varphi^{-1}(nM)) \cdot \delta(\varphi^{-1}(Mn))}{\operatorname{Card}(nM \cap Mn)}.$$

Note that according to Corollary 1.4, every one-sided ideal has a positive density; thus $\delta(\varphi^{-1}(nM))$ and $\delta(\varphi^{-1}(Mn))$ exist.

Proof

1. Since $\varphi^{-1}(n) = C_{1,n}$ the claim results from Proposition 2.3.
2. By Proposition 2.3, $\delta(C_{1n}) \neq 0$ iff $n \in K$, since $C_{1,n}$ is never empty. Let us prove the second formula.

For this, let $Y = \varphi^{-1}(K) - \varphi^{-1}(K)A^+$ be the initial part of the ideal $\varphi^{-1}(K)$. We have $\varphi^{-1}(K) = YA^*$. Since the set $A^* - \varphi^{-1}(K)$ is thin, we have $\delta(\varphi^{-1}(K)) = 1$. Consequently $\pi(Y) = 1$.

For each $\mathscr{R}$-class R of K, consider $Y_R = Y \cap \varphi^{-1}(R)$. Then $\varphi^{-1}(R) = Y_R A^*$, and hence, $\delta(\varphi^{-1}(R)) = \pi(Y_R)$.

Let now $R = nM$. Then

$$\varphi^{-1}(n) = \bigcup_{r \in R} (Y_R \cap \varphi^{-1}(r))C_{r,n}. \tag{2.3}$$

Indeed, each word $w \in \varphi^{-1}(n)$ factorizes uniquely into $w = uv$, where u is the shortest left factor of w such that $\varphi(u) \in R$. Then $u \in Y_R \cap \varphi^{-1}(r)$ for some $r \in R$, and $v \in C_{r,n}$. The converse inclusion is clear. The union in (2.3) is disjoint, and the products are unambiguous because the sets $Y_R \cap \varphi^{-1}(r)$ are prefix. Each $C_{r,n}$ has a density, and moreover

$$\sum_{r \in R} \pi(Y_R \cap \varphi^{-1}(r)) = \pi(Y_R) \leq 1.$$

Thus we can apply Proposition 2.2, which yields

$$\delta(\varphi^{-1}(n)) = \sum_{r \in R} \pi(Y_R \cap \varphi^{-1}(r))\delta(C_{r,n}).$$

According to Proposition 2.3, all the $\delta(C_{r,n})$ for $r \in R$ are equal. Thus, for any $m \in R$,

$$\begin{aligned}\delta(\varphi^{-1}(n)) &= \delta(C_{m,n})\pi(Y_R) = \delta(\varphi^{-1}(m^{-1}n))\pi(Y_R)\\ &= \delta(\varphi^{-1}(m^{-1}n))\delta(\varphi^{-1}(R)).\end{aligned}$$

3. Set $R = nM$, $L = Mn$, and $H = R \cap L$. Then we claim that

$$L = \bigcup_{m \in H} m^{-1}n \cap K$$

and furthermore that the union is disjoint.

First consider an element $k \in m^{-1}n \cap K$ for some $m \in H$. Then $mk = n$. Thus $n \in Mk$, and since n is in the minimal ideal, $Mn = Mk$. Therefore, $k \in Mn = L$. This proves the first inclusion.

For the converse, let $k \in L = Mn$. The right multiplication by k,

$$m \mapsto mk$$

is a bijection which exchanges the $\mathscr{L}$-classes in K and preserves $\mathscr{R}$-classes (Proposition 0.5.2). In particular, this function maps the $\mathscr{L}$-class L onto $Lk = L$, thus onto itself. It follows that there exists $m \in L$ such that $mk = n$. This element is $\mathscr{R}$-equivalent with n. Consequently $m \in H$ and $k \in m^{-1}n$ for some $m \in H$. Since the function $m \mapsto mk$ is a bijection, the sets $m^{-1}n$ are pairwise disjoint. This proves the formula.

For all $m, n \in K$,

$$\delta(\varphi^{-1}(m^{-1}n \cap K)) = \delta(\varphi^{-1}(m^{-1}n))$$

since the set $\varphi^{-1}(m^{-1}n \cap (M - K))$ is thin and therefore has density 0. The set H being finite, we have

$$\delta(\varphi^{-1}(L)) = \sum_{m \in H} \delta(\varphi^{-1}(m^{-1}n)).$$

Using the expression for $\delta(\varphi^{-1}(n))$ proved above, we obtain

$$\delta(\varphi^{-1}(L)) = \sum_{m \in H} \frac{\delta(\varphi^{-1}(n))}{\delta(\varphi^{-1}(R))} = \mathrm{Card}(H)\,\frac{\delta(\varphi^{-1}(n))}{\delta(\varphi^{-1}(R))}.$$

This proves the last claim of the theorem. □

Let E be a denumerable set. A *probability measure over* E is a function

$$\mu\colon\ \mathfrak{P}(E) \to [0, 1]$$

that satisfies the following two conditions: for any subset F of E,

$$\mu(F) = \sum_{e \in F} \mu(e) \tag{2.4}$$

and

$$\mu(E) = 1. \tag{2.5}$$

The *support* of a probability measure μ is the set

$$S = \{e \in E \mid \mu(e) \neq 0\}.$$

A probability measure over E is completely determined by a function

$$\mu: \quad E \to [0, 1]$$

such that

$$\sum_{e \in E} \mu(e) = 1.$$

Indeed, in this case, any family $(\mu(e))_{e \in F}$, where F is a subset of E, is summable, and μ is extended to $\mathfrak{P}(E)$ by (2.4).

Note once more that the density δ defined by a Benoulli distribution on A^* is *not* a probability measure over A^* since it does not satisfy (2.4).

We consider, for probability measures over E, the following notion of convergence: if $(\mu_n)_{n \geq 0}$ and μ are probability measures over E, then we set

$$\mu = \lim_{n \to \infty} \mu_n$$

iff for all elements $e \in E$, we have

$$\mu(e) = \lim_{n \to \infty} \mu_n(e).$$

The following proposition is useful.

PROPOSITION 2.5. *Let $(\mu_n)_{n \geq 0}$ and μ be probability measures over E, such that $\mu = \lim_{n \to \infty} \mu_n$. Then for all subsets F of E,*

$$\mu(F) = \lim_{n \to \infty} \mu_n(F).$$

Proof The conclusion clearly holds when F is finite. In the general case, set

$$\sigma = \liminf \mu_n(F), \qquad \tau = \limsup \mu_n(F),$$

and let $\bar{F} = E - F$. Of course, $\sigma \leq \tau$ and

$$1 - \tau = \liminf \mu_n(\bar{F}).$$

Let F' be a finite subset of F. Then $\mu_n(F') \leq \mu_n(F)$ for all n, and taking the inferior limit, $\mu(F') \leq \sigma$. It follows that

$$\mu(F) = \sup_{\substack{F' \subset F \\ F' \text{finite}}} \mu(F') \leq \sigma.$$

Similarly, $\mu(\bar{F}) \leq 1 - \tau$. Since $\mu(\bar{F}) + \mu(F) = \mu(E) = 1$, we obtain $1 \leq \sigma + (1 - \tau)$, whence $\sigma \geq \tau$. Thus $\sigma = \tau$. Since $\mu(F) \leq \sigma$ and $\mu(\bar{F}) \leq 1 - \sigma$, one has both $\mu(F) \leq \sigma$ and $\mu(F) \geq \sigma$, showing that $\mu(F) = \sigma$. □

THEOREM 2.6 *Let $\varphi: A^* \to M$ be a morphism onto a well-founded monoid, and let π be a positive Bernoulli distribution on A^*. For any subset F of M, the set*

$\varphi^{-1}(F) \subset A^*$ has a density and

$$\delta(\varphi^{-1}(F)) = \sum_{m \in F} \delta(\varphi^{-1}(m)).$$

Proof It is convenient to introduce the shorthand $\nu(F) = \delta(\varphi^{-1}(F))$. Let K be the minimal ideal of M, let Γ be the set of its $\mathscr{R}$-classes and Λ the set of its $\mathscr{L}$-classes. We have verified, during the proof of Theorem 2.4., that

$$\nu(K) = \pi(Y) = 1, \qquad \nu(R) = \pi(Y_R)$$

where Y (resp., Y_R) is the initial part of $\varphi^{-1}(K)$, (resp., of $\varphi^{-1}(R)$, with $R \in \Gamma$). Since K is the disjoint union of its $\mathscr{R}$-classes, we have

$$\pi(Y) = \sum_{R \in \Gamma} \pi(Y_R),$$

hence

$$\nu(K) = \sum_{R \in \Gamma} \nu(R) = \sum_{L \in \Lambda} \nu(L) = 1,$$

where the intermediate assertion follows by symmetry.

Now consider a fixed $\mathscr{R}$-class $R \in \Gamma$. Then by Theorem 2.4,

$$\begin{aligned}\sum_{n \in R} \nu(n) &= \sum_{n \in R} \frac{\nu(R)\nu(Mn)}{\operatorname{Card}(R \cap Mn)} = \nu(R) \sum_{L \in \Lambda} \sum_{n \in R \cap L} \frac{\nu(L)}{\operatorname{Card}(R \cap L)} \\ &= \nu(R) \sum_{L \in \Lambda} \nu(L) = \nu(R)\end{aligned}$$

and also

$$\sum_{n \in K} \nu(n) = \sum_{R \in \Gamma} \left(\sum_{n \in R} \nu(n) \right) = \sum_{R \in \Gamma} \nu(R) = 1.$$

Since $\nu(n) = 0$ for $n \notin K$, it follows that

$$\sum_{n \in M} \delta(\varphi^{-1}(n)) = 1.$$

Consider the family $\mathscr{F}$ of subsets of A^*,

$$\mathscr{F} = \{\varphi^{-1}(m) \mid m \in M\}.$$

The preceding formula gives

$$\sum_{T \in \mathscr{F}} \delta(T) = 1.$$

This shows that there exists a probability measure $\hat{\delta}$ over $\mathscr{F}$, defined for a subset $\mathscr{K} \subset \mathscr{F}$ by

$$\hat{\delta}(\mathscr{K}) = \sum_{T \in \mathscr{K}} \delta(T).$$

For any positive integer n, define $\mu_n: \mathscr{F} \to [0, 1]$ by

$$\mu_n(T) = \frac{1}{n} \pi(T \cap A^{(n)}),$$

where $A^{(n)} = \{w \in A^* \mid |w| < n\}$. The morphism φ being surjective, the sets $T \in \mathscr{F}$ form a partition of A^*. Thus

$$\sum_{T \in \mathscr{F}} \mu_n(T) = 1,$$

showing that μ_n $(n \geq 1)$ is a probability measure over $\mathscr{F}$. Moreover, we have

$$\hat{\delta}(T) = \delta(T) = \lim_{n \to \infty} \mu_n(T)$$

by the definition of a density. Thus $\hat{\delta} = \lim_{n \to \infty} \mu_n$. Proposition 2.5 shows that for any subset $\mathscr{K}$ of $\mathscr{F}$,

$$\hat{\delta}(\mathscr{K}) = \lim_{n \to \infty} \mu_n(\mathscr{K}).$$

Now $\mathscr{K} = \{\varphi^{-1}(m) \mid m \in P\}$ for some subset P of M. Thus

$$\hat{\delta}(\mathscr{K}) = \sum_{T \in \mathscr{K}} \delta(T) = \sum_{m \in P} \delta(\varphi^{-1}(m)) = \sum_{m \in P} v(m),$$

but also

$$\mu_n(\mathscr{K}) = \sum_{m \in P} \mu_n(\varphi^{-1}(m)) = \sum_{m \in P} \frac{1}{n} \pi(\varphi^{-1}(m) \cap A^{(n)}).$$

Consequently $\mu_n(\mathscr{K}) = (1/n)\pi(\varphi^{-1}(P) \cap A^{(n)})$, and thus

$$\lim_{n \to \infty} \frac{1}{n} \pi(\varphi^{-1}(P) \cap A^{(n)}) = \sum_{m \in P} v(m).$$

The left side of the formula is $\delta(\varphi^{-1}(P))$ and the right side is $\hat{\delta}(\mathscr{K})$. Thus $\delta(\varphi^{-1}(P))$ exists and has the announced value. $\square$

PROPOSITION 2.7 *Let $\varphi: A^* \to M$ be a morphism onto a well-founded monoid and let π be a positive Bernoulli distribution on A^*. The function $v: M \to [0, 1]$ defined by $v(m) = \delta(\varphi^{-1}(m))$ is a probability measure over M. Let K be the minimal ideal of M. Then the following formulas hold*:

$$\begin{aligned}
v(m) &\neq 0 && \textit{iff} \quad m \in K, \\
v(m) &= v(n^{-1}m)v(mM) && \textit{if} \quad m, n \in K \textit{ and } n\mathscr{R}m, \\
v(m) &= \frac{v(mM)v(Mm)}{\operatorname{Card}(mM \cap Mm)} && \textit{if} \quad m \in K, \\
v(M') &= v(M' \cap K) && \textit{for} \quad M' \subset M.
\end{aligned} \tag{2.6}$$

For each $\mathscr{H}$-class $H \subset K$, and $h \in H$,

$$\nu(h) = \frac{\nu(H)}{\mathrm{Card}(H)}. \tag{2.7}$$

Proof All these formulas with the exception of (2.7), are immediate consequences of the relations given in Theorem 2.4. For (2.7) observe that the value of ν is the same for all $h \in H$ by formula (2.6). Next $\nu(H) = \sum_{h \in H} \nu(h)$. This proves (2.7). □

EXAMPLE 2.1 Let $\varphi: A^* \to G$ be a morphism onto a finite group. Let π be a positive Bernoulli distribution. For $g \in G$,

$$\delta(\varphi^{-1}(g)) = \frac{1}{\mathrm{Card}(G)} \tag{2.8}$$

in view of formula (2.7) and observing that $H = K = G$. This gives another method for computing the density in Example 1.1. To that example corresponds a morphism $\varphi: A^* \to \mathbb{Z}/2\mathbb{Z}$ onto the additive group $\mathbb{Z}/2\mathbb{Z}$ with $\varphi(a) = 1$ for any letter a in A.

EXAMPLE 2.2 Let $\varphi: A^* \to M$ be the morphism from A^* onto the unambiguous monoid of relations M over $Q = \{1, 2, 3\}$ defined by $\alpha = \varphi(a)$, $\beta = \varphi(b)$, with

$$\alpha = \begin{bmatrix} 0 & 1 & 0 \\ 1 & 0 & 0 \\ 1 & 1 & 0 \end{bmatrix}, \qquad \beta = \begin{bmatrix} 0 & 0 & 1 \\ 0 & 0 & 0 \\ 1 & 1 & 0 \end{bmatrix}.$$

This monoid has already been considered in Example IV.5.3. Its minimal ideal J is composed of elements of rank 1 and is represented in Fig. 6.1. Let π be the Bernoulli distribution defined by $\pi(a) = p$, $\pi(b) = q$, with $p + q = 1$, $p, q > 0$. Let us compute the probability measure $\nu = \delta\varphi^{-1}$ over M. With the notations

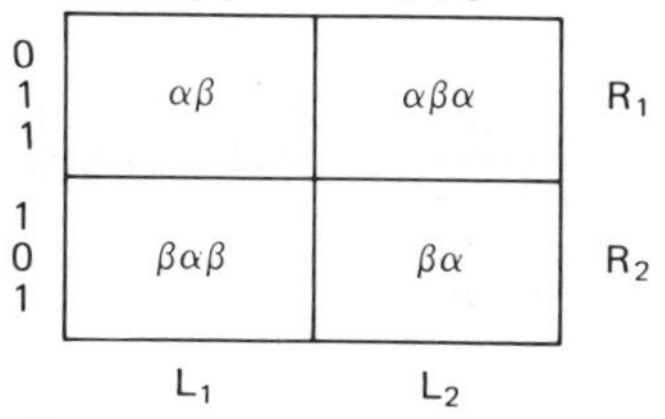

Fig. 6.1 The minimal ideal of the monoid M.

of Fig. 6.1, we have the equalities

$$L_1\alpha = L_2, \qquad L_1\beta = L_2,$$
$$L_2\alpha = L_2, \qquad L_2\beta = L_1. \tag{2.9}$$

Set $X_1 = \varphi^{-1}(L_1)$, $X_2 = \varphi^{-1}(L_2)$. By (2.9),

$$X_1a^{-1} \cap \varphi^{-1}(J) = \varnothing, \qquad X_1b^{-1} \cap \varphi^{-1}(J) = X_2,$$
$$X_2a^{-1} \cap \varphi^{-1}(J) = X_1 \cup X_2, \qquad X_2b^{-1} \cap \varphi^{-1}(J) = X_1. \tag{2.10}$$

Indeed consider, for instance, the last equation: if $w \in X_1$, then $\varphi(w) \in L_1$, hence $\varphi(wb) \in L_2$ by the fact that $L_1\beta = L_2$. Thus $wb \in X_2$, and $w \in X_2b^{-1} \cap \varphi^{-1}(J)$. Conversely, let $w \in X_2b^{-1} \cap \varphi^{-1}(J)$. Since $w \in \varphi^{-1}(J)$, $w \in X_1 \cup X_2$. But if $w \in X_2$, then $\varphi(wb) \in L_1$, showing that $wb \in X_1$, whence $w \notin X_2b^{-1}$. Thus $w \in X_1$.

In view of (2.10),

$$X_1a^{-1} = T_1, \qquad X_1b^{-1} = X_2 \cup T'_1,$$
$$X_2a^{-1} = X_1 \cup X_2 \cup T_2, \qquad X_2b^{-1} = X_1 \cup T'_2,$$

where $T_1, T'_1 T_2, T'_2$ are disjoint from $\varphi^{-1}(J)$. Multiplication by a and b on the right gives

$$X_1 = X_2b \cup (T_1a \cup T'_1b),$$
$$X_2 = X_1a \cup X_2a \cup X_1b \cup (T_2a \cup T'_2b).$$

Since T_1 is thin, $\delta(T_1a) = \delta(T_1)\pi(a) = 0$, and similarly for the other T's. Thus

$$\delta(X_1) = \delta(X_2)q, \qquad \delta(X_2) = \delta(X_1) + \delta(X_2)p$$

which together with

$$\delta(X_1) + \delta(X_2) = 1$$

gives

$$\delta(X_1) = \frac{q}{1+q}, \qquad \delta(X_2) = \frac{1}{1+q}.$$

Thus

$$\nu(L_1) = \frac{q}{1+q}, \qquad \nu(L_2) = \frac{1}{1+q}.$$

An analogous computation yields

$$\nu(R_1) = \frac{p}{1+p}, \qquad \nu(R_2) = \frac{1}{1+p}.$$

In particular, since $R_2 \cap L_2 = \{\beta\alpha\}$, we obtain

$$v(\beta\alpha) = \frac{1}{(1+p)(1+q)}.$$

3. CONTEXTS

Let $X \subset A^+$ be a thin complete code. We have seen that the *degree* $d(X)$ of X is the integer which is the minimal rank of the monoid of relations associated with any unambiguous trim automaton recognizing X^*. It is also the degree of the permutation group $G(X)$, and it is also the minimum of the number of disjoint interpretations in X (see Section IV.6). In this section, we shall see that $d(X)$ is related in a quite remarkable manner to the density $\delta(X^*)$. The set G_X of *left completable* words is

$$G_X = \{w \in A^* \mid A^*w \cap X^* \neq \varnothing\} = (A^*)^{-1}X^* = A^- X^*;$$

symmetrically, the set D_X of *right-completable* words is

$$D_X = \{w \in A^* \mid wA^* \cap X^* \neq \varnothing\} = X^*(A^*)^{-1} = X^*A^-.$$

THEOREM 3.1 Let $X \subset A^*$ *be a thin complete code, and let* π *be a positive Bernoulli distribution on* A^*. *Then*

$$\delta(X^*) = \frac{1}{d(X)}\,\delta(G_X)\delta(D_X). \tag{3.1}$$

Proof Let $\mathscr{A} = (Q, 1, 1)$ be an unambiguous trim automaton recognizing X^*, let φ be the associated morphism and $M = \varphi(A^*)$. In view of Corollary IV.5.4., the monoid M is well founded. Set $v = \delta\varphi^{-1}$. By Proposition 2.7, v is a probability measure over M, and the values of v may be computed by the formulas of this proposition.

Let K be the minimal ideal of M. Since v vanishes outside of K, we have

$$\delta(X^*) = v(\varphi(X^*) \cap K).$$

Let $\hat{R}$ be the union of the $\mathscr{R}$-classes in K meeting $\varphi(X^*)$, and similarly let $\hat{L}$ be the union of those $\mathscr{L}$-classes in K that meet $\varphi(X^*)$. Then

$$\begin{aligned} v(\varphi(X^*) \cap K) &= v(\varphi(X^*) \cap \hat{R} \cap \hat{L}) \\ &= \sum_H v(\varphi(X^*) \cap H), \end{aligned}$$

where the sum is over all $\mathscr{H}$-classes H contained in $\hat{R} \cap \hat{L}$. For such an $\mathscr{H}$-class H, we have

$$v(\varphi(X^*) \cap H) = \sum_{m \in \varphi(X^*) \cap H} v(m) = \sum_{m \in \varphi(X^*) \cap H} \frac{v(R)v(L)}{\operatorname{Card}(H)},$$

where R and L are the $\mathscr{R}$-class and $\mathscr{L}$-class containing H. Thus

$$\nu(\varphi(X^*) \cap H) = \frac{\mathrm{Card}(\varphi(X^*) \cap H)}{\mathrm{Card}(H)} \nu(R)\nu(L).$$

Now observe that for any $\mathscr{H}$-class $H \subset \hat{R} \cap \hat{L}$,

$$\frac{\mathrm{Card}(\varphi(X^*) \cap H)}{\mathrm{Card}(H)} = \frac{1}{d(X)}.$$

Thus the formula becomes

$$\delta(X^*) = \sum_H \frac{1}{d(X)} \nu(R)\nu(L) = \frac{1}{d(X)} \nu(\hat{R})\nu(\hat{L}).$$

Now

$$\varphi^{-1}(\hat{R}) = D_X \cap \varphi^{-1}(K). \tag{3.2}$$

Indeed, let $w \in D_X \cap \varphi^{-1}(K)$. Then $wu \in X^*$ for some word u. Consequently, $\varphi(wu) = \varphi(w)\varphi(u) \in \varphi(X^*) \cap K$, showing that the $\mathscr{R}$-class of $\varphi(w)$, which is the same as the $\mathscr{R}$-class of $\varphi(wu)$, meets $\varphi(X^*)$. Thus $\varphi(w) \in \hat{R}$. Conversely, let $w \in \varphi^{-1}(\hat{R})$. Then $\varphi(w) \in \hat{R}$ and there is some $m \in M$ such that $\varphi(w)m \in \varphi(X^*) \cap K$. Thus $w\varphi^{-1}(m) \cap X^* \neq \emptyset$ and we derive that $w \in D_X$.

It follows from (3.2) that

$$\nu(\hat{R}) = \delta(\varphi^{-1}(\hat{R})) = \delta(D_X \cap \varphi^{-1}(K)).$$

Since $A^* - \varphi^{-1}(K)$ is thin, we have

$$\delta(D_X) = \delta(D_X \cap \varphi^{-1}(K)).$$

Thus $\delta(D_X) = \nu(\hat{R})$ and similarly $\nu(\hat{L}) = \delta(G_X)$. This concludes the proof. □

The following corollary is a consequence of Theorem 1.6.

COROLLARY 3.2 *Let $X \subset A^+$ be a thin complete code, and let π be a positive Bernoulli distribution on A^*. Then*

$$\lambda(X) = \frac{d(X)}{\delta(G_X)\delta(D_X)}. \quad \square \tag{3.3}$$

We observe that for a thin maximal biprefix code $X \subset A^+$, we have $G_X = D_X = A^*$. Thus in this case, (3.3) becomes $\lambda(X) = d(X)$. This gives another proof of Corollary III.3.9.

EXAMPLE 3.1 Let $A = \{a, b\}$ and consider our old friend $X = \{aa, ba, baa, bb, bba\}$ which is a finite complete code. In Fig. 6.2 an automaton $\mathscr{A} = (Q, 1, 1)$ recognizing X^* is represented.

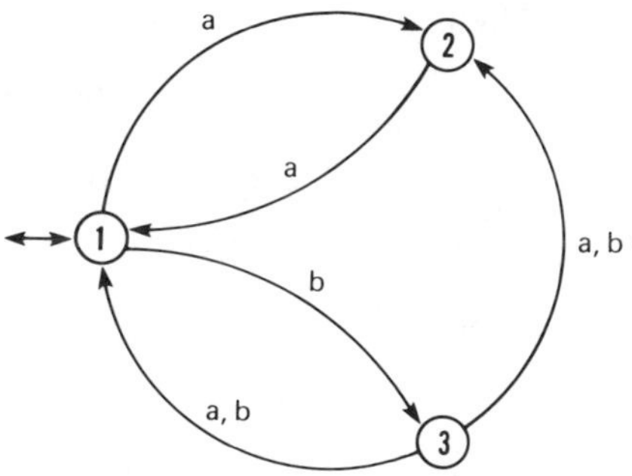

Fig. 6.2 An unambiguous trim automaton recognizing X^*.

We have $\varphi_{\mathscr{A}}(a) = \alpha$, $\varphi_{\mathscr{A}}(b) = \beta$, where α, β are the relations considered in Example 2.2. To obtain the set D_X, we can compute the deterministic automaton having as a set of states, the set of row vectors $\{0, 1\}^Q$. The transition function is determined by multiplication on the right, with the elements in $\varphi_{\mathscr{A}}(A^*)$ considered as matrices. The part of this automaton that is accessible from the vector 100 is drawn in Fig. 6.3. (Note that this automaton can also be considered as the deterministic automaton associated with $\mathscr{A}$ by the subset construction, as given in Proposition 0.4.1 with sets of states represented by vectors.) The elements of D_X are the words which are labels of paths from 100 to a state distinct from 000. We obtain

$$D_X = a^* \cup (a^2)^* bA^*.$$

A similar computation on column vectors gives

$$G_X = b^* \cup A^* a(b^2)^*.$$

Let π be the positive Bernoulli distribution given by

$$\pi(a) = p, \qquad \pi(b) = q,$$

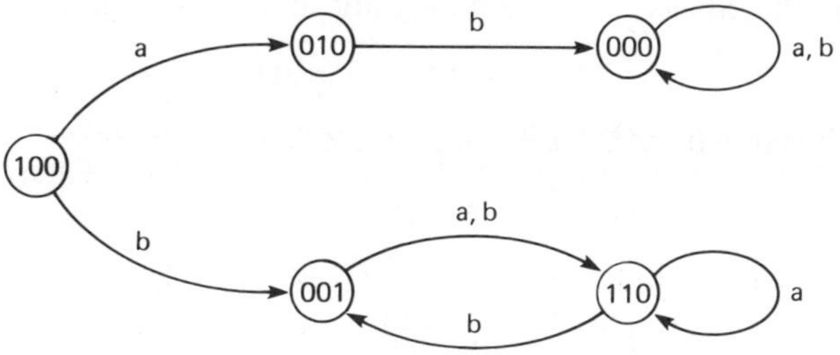

Fig. 6.3 A deterministic automaton for D_X.

with $p, q > 0$, $p + q = 1$. Then

$$\delta(D_X) = \delta(a^*) + \delta((a^2)^*bA^*) = \delta((a^2)^*bA^*)$$

since $\delta(a^*) = 0$. Since $(a^2)^*b$ is a prefix code, we have

$$\delta(D_X) = \pi((a^2)^*b).$$

Thus

$$\delta(D_X) = \frac{q}{1 - p^2} = \frac{1}{1 + p}.$$

In a similar fashion, we obtain

$$\delta(G_X) = \frac{1}{1 + q}.$$

On the other hand, $d(X) = 1$ since the monoid $\varphi_{\mathscr{A}}(A^*)$ has minimal rank 1. Thus by formula (3.3),

$$\lambda(X) = (1 + p)(1 + q).$$

This can also be verified by a direct computation of the average length of X. The computations made in this example are of course similar to those of Example 2.2.

Let $X \subset A^+$ be a code. A *context* of $w \in A^*$ is a pair (u, v) of words such that the following two conditions hold:

$$uwv = x_1 x_2 \cdots x_n \qquad (x_i \in X)$$

and

$$|u| < |x_1|, \qquad |v| < |x_n|.$$

The set of contexts of a word $w \in A^*$ (with respect to X) is denoted by $C(w)$. The set $C(1)$ is $C(1) = \{(u, v) \in A^+ \times A^+ \mid uv \in X\} \cup \{(1, 1)\}$. The context of a word can be interpreted in terms of paths in the flower automaton $\mathscr{A}_D^*(X) = (P, (1, 1), (1, 1))$: there exists a bijection between the set $C(w)$ and the set $P(w)$ of paths labeled w in the flower automaton. Indeed let

$$c: \quad (u, u') \xrightarrow{w} (v', v)$$

be a path labeled w in $\mathscr{A}_D^*(X)$. Then $uwv \in X^*$. Thus either $uwv = 1$, or

$$uwv = x_1 x_2 \cdots x_n$$

with $x_i \in X$ and $n > 0$. In that case, $|u| < |x_1|$ and $|v| < |x_n|$. Thus in both cases, (u, v) is a context. Consider another path

$$\bar{c}: \quad (u, \bar{u}') \xrightarrow{w} (\bar{v}', v).$$

Then both paths

$$(1,1) \xrightarrow{u} (u,u') \xrightarrow{w} (v',v) \xrightarrow{v} (1,1),$$
$$(1,1) \xrightarrow{u} (u,\bar{u}') \xrightarrow{w} (\bar{v}',v) \xrightarrow{v} (1,1)$$

are labeled uwv. By unambiguity, $c = \bar{c}$. Conversely, if (u, v) is a context of w and $uwv = x_1 \cdots x_n$, define two words u', v' by

$$u' = u^{-1}x_1 \quad \text{if} \quad u \neq 1, \quad u' = 1 \quad \text{otherwise},$$
$$v' = x_n v^{-1} \quad \text{if} \quad v \neq 1, \quad v' = 1 \quad \text{otherwise}.$$

Then (u, u') and (v', v) are states in $\mathscr{A}_D^*(X)$, and there is a path $(u,u') \xrightarrow{w} (v',v)$. The following result shows a strong relationship between all sets of contexts.

THEOREM 3.3 *Let $X \subset A^+$ be a thin complete code, and let π be a positive Bernoulli distribution on A^*. For all $w \in A^*$,*

$$\lambda(X) = \sum_{(u,v) \in C(w)} \pi(uv).$$

Proof Let $\mathscr{A}_D^*(X) = (P, (1,1), (1,1))$ be the flower automaton of X, let $M = \varphi_D(A^*)$ and set $\nu = \delta\varphi_D^{-1}$. Let $w \in A^*$, $m = \varphi_D(w)$, and let

$$T(m) = \{(r,l) \in M \times M \mid rml \in \varphi_D(X^*)\}$$
$$t(m) = \sum_{(r,l) \in T(m)} \nu(r)\nu(l).$$

We compute $t(m)$ in two ways. First define, for each state $p \in P$,

$$R_p = \{r \in M \mid r_{1,p} = 1\}, \qquad L_p = \{l \in M \mid l_{p,1} = 1\}.$$

Then $rml \in \varphi_D(X^*)$ iff there exist $p, q \in P$ such that $r_{1,p} = 1, m_{p,q} = 1, l_{q,1} = 1$. Consequently,

$$T(m) = \bigcup_{\substack{(p,q) \\ m_{pq}=1}} R_p \times L_q.$$

Thus

$$t(m) = \sum_{\substack{(p,q) \\ m_{pq}=1}} \nu(R_p)\nu(L_q).$$

Set $p = (u, u')$, $q = (v', v)$. Then $m_{pq} = 1$ iff there is a path $c: p \to q$ labeled w. According to the bijection defined above, this hold iff $(u, v) \in C(w)$. Next,

$$\varphi_D^{-1}(R_p) = X^*u, \qquad \varphi_D^{-1}(L_q) = vX^*,$$

hence

$$\nu(R_p) = \delta(X^*u) = \delta(X^*)\pi(u), \qquad \nu(L_q) = \delta(vA^*) = \pi(v)\delta(X^*).$$

Consequently

$$t(m) = \sum_{(u,v)\in C(w)} \delta(X^*)\pi(u)\pi(v)\delta(X^*) = [\delta(X^*)]^2 \sum_{(u,v)\in C(w)} \pi(uv).$$

This is the first expression for $t(m)$.

Now we compute $t(m)$ in the monoid M. Let K be the minimal ideal of M. Since ν vanishes for elements not in K, we have

$$t(m) = \sum_{\substack{(r,l)\in K\times K \\ rml\in\varphi_D(X^*)}} \nu(r)\nu(l).$$

Let $N = \varphi_D(X^*) \cap K$. Then

$$t(m) = \sum_{n\in N} \sum_{\substack{(r,l)\in K\times K \\ rml=n}} \nu(r)\nu(l) = \sum_{n\in N}\sum_{r\in K} \nu(r)\nu((rm)^{-1}n).$$

Let $r \in K$. Since $(rm)^{-1}n \neq \varnothing$ iff $rm\mathscr{R}n$, and since $r\mathscr{R}rm$, we have $(rm)^{-1}n \neq \varnothing$ iff $r\mathscr{R}n$ and

$$t(m) = \sum_{n\in N}\sum_{r\in nM} \nu(r)\nu((rm)^{-1}n) = \sum_{n\in N}\sum_{r\in nM} \nu(r)\frac{\nu(n)}{\nu(nM)}$$

by Proposition 2.6. Further

$$t(m) = \sum_{n\in N} \nu(n) \sum_{r\in nM} \frac{\nu(r)}{\nu(nM)} = \sum_{n\in N} \nu(n) = \nu(N) = \delta(X^*).$$

Comparing both expressions for $t(m)$, we get

$$1 = \delta(X^*) \sum_{(u,v)\in C(w)} \pi(uv). \quad \square$$

There is an interesting interpretation of the preceding result. With the notations of the theorem, set for any word $w \in A^*$,

$$\gamma(w) = \frac{1}{\lambda(X)} \sum_{(u,v)\in C(w)} \pi(uwv).$$

Call $\gamma(w)$ the *contextual probability* of w. Then the theorem claims that if π is a Bernoulli distribution we have identically

$$\gamma(w) = \pi(w).$$

The fact that γ and π coincide is particular to Bernoulli distributions (see Exercise 3.3.) We now study one-sided contexts. Let $X \subset A^+$ be a code, and let $w \in A^*$. The set of *right contexts* of w is

$$C_r(w) = \{v \in A^* | (1, v) \in C(w)\}.$$

Thus $v \in C_r(w)$ iff $wv = x_1x_2\cdots x_n$ $(x_i \in X)$ with $|v| < |x_n|$.

Symmetrically, the set of *left contexts* of w is

$$C_l(w) = \{u \in A^* \mid (u, 1) \in C(w)\}.$$

We observe that

$$C_r(w)X^* = w^{-1}X^*. \tag{3.4}$$

The product $C_r(w)X^*$ is unambiguous, because X is a code.

PROPOSITION 3.4 *Let $X \subset A^+$ be a thin complete code and let $\mathscr{A} = (Q, 1, 1)$ be an unambiguous trim automaton recognizing X^*. Let K be the minimal ideal of the monoid $M = \varphi_{\mathscr{A}}(A^*)$. Let π be a positive Bernoulli distribution.*
For all $w \in \varphi_{\mathscr{A}}^{-1}(K) \cap D_X$, we have

$$\pi(C_r(w))\delta(D_X) = 1. \tag{3.5}$$

For all $w \in \varphi_{\mathscr{A}}^{-1}(K) \cap G_X$, we have

$$\pi(C_l(w))\delta(G_X) = 1. \tag{3.6}$$

Proof Set $\varphi = \varphi_{\mathscr{A}}$, $v = \delta\varphi^{-1}$, and let $\hat{R}$ (resp., $\hat{L}$) be the union of the $\mathscr{R}$-classes (resp., $\mathscr{L}$-classes) in K that meet $\varphi(X^*)$. We have seen, in the proof of Theorem 3.1, that $\delta(D_X) = v(\hat{R})$ and $\delta(G_X) = v(\hat{L})$. According to formula (3.4),

$$\delta(w^{-1}X^*) = \pi(C_r(w))\delta(X^*).$$

Set $n = \varphi(w)$ and $T = \{k \in K \mid nk \in \varphi(X^*)\}$. Then $T \subset \hat{L}$ since for $k \in T$, we have $nk \in Mk \cap \varphi(X^*)$, showing that the left ideal Mk meets $\varphi(X^*)$. Let H be an $\mathscr{H}$-class contained in $\hat{L}$. The function $h \mapsto nh$ is a bijection from H onto the $\mathscr{H}$-class nH. Since $n \in \hat{R}$, we have $nH \subset \hat{R}$; since $H \in \hat{L}$ we have $nH \subset \hat{L}$. Thus $nH \subset \hat{R} \cap \hat{L}$. This implies that $nH \cap \varphi(X^*) \neq \varnothing$. Indeed let R and L denote the $\mathscr{R}$-class and $\mathscr{L}$-class containing nH, and take $m \in R \cap \varphi(X^*)$, $m' \in L \cap \varphi(X^*)$. Then $mm' \in R \cap L \cap \varphi(X^*) = nH \cap \varphi(X^*)$.

Setting $d = d(X)$, it follows that

$$\frac{\mathrm{Card}(nH \cap \varphi(X^*))}{\mathrm{Card}(nH)} = \frac{1}{d}.$$

Since $H \cap T = \{k \in H \mid nk \in \varphi(X^*)\}$ is in bijection with $nH \cap \varphi(X^*)$, we have

$$\mathrm{Card}(H \cap T) = \mathrm{Card}(nH \cap \varphi(X^*)) = \frac{1}{d}\mathrm{Card}(H).$$

Therefore

$$v(T) = \sum_{H \subset \hat{L}} v(H \cap T) = \sum_{H \subset \hat{L}} \frac{v(H)}{\mathrm{Card}(H)} \mathrm{Card}(H \cap T)$$
$$= \sum_{H \subset \hat{L}} \frac{v(H)}{d} = \frac{1}{d} v(\hat{L}).$$

We observe that $\varphi^{-1}(T) = w^{-1}X^* \cap \varphi^{-1}(K)$. Consequently $\delta(w^{-1}X^*) = \nu(T) = (1/d)\nu(\hat{L})$. Since also $\nu(\hat{L}) = \delta(G_X)$, we obtain

$$\pi(C_r(w))\delta(D_X) = \frac{\delta(w^{-1}X^*)}{\delta(X^*)}\delta(D_X) = \frac{1}{d}\frac{\delta(G_X)\delta(D_X)}{\delta(X^*)}. \tag{3.7}$$

By Theorem 3.1, the last expression is equal to 1. □

PROPOSITION 3.5 *Let $X \subset A^+$ be a thin complete code. Let π be a positive Bernoulli distribution on A^*. For all $w \in A^*$ the following conditions are equivalent.*

(i) *The set $C_r(w)$ is maximal among the sets $C_r(u)$, for $u \in A^*$.*
(ii) $\pi(C_r(w))\delta(D_X) = 1$.

Proof With the notations of Proposition 3.4, consider a word $x \in \varphi^{-1}(K) \cap X^*$. Then $C_r(w) \subset C_r(xw)$, hence also $\pi(C_r(w)) \le \pi(C_r(xw))$. On the other hand $xw \in \varphi^{-1}(K) \cap D_X$. Indeed the right ideal generated by x is minimal, and therefore there exists $v \in A^*$ such that $\varphi(xwv) = \varphi(x)$. Thus $xwv \in X^*$. By Proposition 3.4, we have $\pi(C_r(xw))\delta(D_X) = 1$ showing that

$$\pi(C_r(w)) \le 1/\delta(D_X). \tag{3.8}$$

Now assume $C_r(w)$ maximal. Then $C_r(w) = C_r(xw)$, implying the equality sign in the formula. This proves (i) $\Rightarrow$ (ii). Conversely formula (3.8) shows the implication (ii) $\Rightarrow$ (i). □

In fact, the set of words $w \in A^*$ such that the set of right contexts is maximal is an old friend; in Chapter II, Section 8, we defined the sets of extendable and simplifying words by

$$\mathrm{E} = \{u \in A^* \mid \forall v \in A^*, \exists w \in A^*: uvw \in X^*\},$$

$$\mathrm{S} = \{u \in A^* \mid \forall x \in X^*, \forall v \in A^*: xuv \in X^* \Rightarrow uv \in X^*\}.$$

We have seen that these sets are equal provided they are both nonempty (Proposition II.8.5). It can be shown (Exercise 3.1) that, for a thin complete code X, the following three conditions are equivalent for all words $w \in A^*$:

(i) $w \in \mathrm{E}$,
(ii) $w \in \mathrm{S}$,
(iii) $C_r(w)$ is maximal.

This leads to a natural interpretation of formula (3.5) (see Exercise 3.1).

We now establish, as a corollary of formula (3.5) a property of finite maximal codes which generalizes the property for prefix codes shown in Chapter II (Theorem II.6.4).

THEOREM 3.6 *Let $X \subset A^+$ be a finite maximal code. For any letter $a \in A$, the order of a is a multiple of $d(X)$.*

Recall that the order of a is the integer n such that $a^n \in X$.

Proof Let π be a positive Bernoulli distribution on A^*. Let $\mathscr{A} = (Q, 1, 1)$ be a trim unambiguous automaton recognizing X^*. Let K be the minimal ideal of the monoid $M = \varphi_{\mathscr{A}}(A)$. Let $x \in X^* \cap \varphi_{\mathscr{A}}^{-1}(K)$. According to Proposition 3.4,

$$\pi(C_r(x))\delta(D_X) = 1, \qquad \pi(C_l(x))\delta(G_X) = 1.$$

By formula (3.3) the average length of X is

$$\lambda(X) = \frac{d(X)}{\delta(G_X)\delta(D_X)}.$$

Thus

$$\lambda(X) = d(X)\pi(C_r(x))\pi(C_l(x)).$$

Let a be a fixed letter and let n be its order. Consider a sequence $(\pi_k)_{k\geq 0}$ of positive Bernoulli distributions such that

$$\lim_{k\to\infty} \pi_k(a) = 1$$

and for any $b \in A - a$, $\lim_{k\to\infty} \pi_k(b) = 0$. For any word $w \in A^*$ we have $\lim_{k\to\infty} \pi_k(w) = 1$ iff $w \in a^*$, and $= 0$ otherwise. For any $k \geq 0$, denote by $\lambda_k(X)$ the average length of X with respect to π_k. Then

$$\lambda_k(X) = d(X)\pi_k(C_r(x))\pi_k(C_l(x)).$$

But also, by definition

$$\lambda_k(X) = \sum_{x\in X} |x|\pi_k(x).$$

Since X is finite, this sum is over a finite number of terms, and going to the limit,

$$\lim_{k\to\infty} \lambda_k(X) = \sum_{x\in X} |x| \lim_{k\to\infty} \pi_k(x).$$

Since $\lim_{k\to\infty} \pi_k(x) = 0$ unless $x \in a^*$, we have

$$\lim_{k\to\infty} \lambda_k(X) = n,$$

where n is the order of a. On the other hand,

$$\pi_k(C_r(x)) = \sum_{v\in C_r(x)} \pi_k(v).$$

The words in $C_r(x)$ are right factors of words in X. Since X is finite, $C_r(x)$ is finite. Thus, going to the limit, we have

$$\lim_{k\to\infty} \pi_k(C_r(x)) = \sum_{v\in C_r(x)} \lim_{k\to\infty} \pi_k(v) = \mathrm{Card}(C_r(x) \cap a^*).$$

Similarly

$$\lim_{k\to\infty} \pi_k(C_r(x)) = \sum_{v\in C_r(x)} \lim_{k\to\infty} \pi_k(v) = \mathrm{Card}(C_r(x) \cap a^*).$$

Thus

$$n = d(X) \cdot \mathrm{Card}(C_r(x) \cap a^*)\,\mathrm{Card}(C_l(x) \cap a^*)$$

This proves that $d(X)$ divides n. □

EXERCISES

Section 1

1.1. Let X be a recognizable subset of A^* and let π be a positive Bernoulli distribution.

(a) Show that $\rho_X = \infty$ iff X is finite.

(b) Show that if X is infinite, then ρ_X is a pole of the rational function f_X.

Section 2

2.1. Show that any recognizable subset of A^* has a density.

2.2. Let M be a monoid, and let μ, ν be two probability measures over M. The *convolution* of μ and ν is defined as the probability measure given by

$$\mu * \nu(m) = \sum_{uv=m} \mu(u)\nu(v).$$

(a) Show that

$$\left(\lim_{n\to\infty} \mu_n\right) * \nu = \lim_{n\to\infty} (\mu_n * \nu).$$

(b) Let π be a positive Bernoulli distribution on A^*. For $n \geq 0$, let $\pi^{(n)}$ the probability measure defined by

$$\pi^{(n)}(L) = \pi(L \cap A^n)$$

for $L \subset A^*$. Show that

$$\pi^{(n+1)} = \pi^{(n)} * \pi^{(1)}.$$

(c) Let $\varphi: A^* \to M$ be a morphism onto a well-founded monoid. Let π be as above and let $\nu = \delta\varphi^{-1}$ be the probability measure over

M defined in Proposition 2.7. Show that v is idempotent, i.e,

$$v * v = v.$$

2.3. Let $\mathscr{A} = (Q, i, T)$ be a deterministic automaton and let π be a Bernoulli distribution on A^*. A function

$$\gamma: \quad Q \to [0, 1]$$

is a *stationary distribution* if

(i) $\sum_{q \in Q} \gamma(q) = 1$.

(ii) $\sum_{p \cdot a = q} \gamma(p)\pi(a) = \gamma(q)$ $(q \in Q)$.

(a) Let φ be the representation associated with $\mathscr{A}$ and let $M = \mathscr{S}(A^*)$. Show that if $\mathscr{A}$ has finite minimal rank, and if all states of $\mathscr{A}$ are recurrent, it admits a unique stationary distribution given for $p \in Q$ by

$$\gamma(p) = 1/\lambda(X_p),$$

where X_p is the prefix code such that $X_p^* = \mathrm{Stab}(p)$. (*Hint:* show that for a stationary distribution γ

$$\sum_{p \in Q} \gamma(p)\delta(L_{pq}) = \gamma(q) \qquad \text{for all } q \in Q,$$

where L_{pq} is the set recognized by the automaton (Q, p, q).

(b) Let d be the minimal rank of M, with the hypotheses of (a). Let $\mathscr{E}$ be the set of minimal images of $\mathscr{A}$. Let $\mathscr{B}$ be the deterministic automaton with states $\mathscr{E}$ and with the action induced by $\mathscr{A}$. Let γ be the stationary distribution of $\mathscr{A}$, and σ that of $\mathscr{B}$. Show that

$$\gamma(q) = \frac{1}{d} \sum \sigma(I).$$

Where the sum runs over the minimal images $I \in \mathscr{E}$ such that $q \in I$.

SECTION 3

3.1. Let $X \subset A^+$ be a thin complete code. Let $\mathrm{S}(X)$ and $\mathrm{E}(X)$ be the sets of simplifying and extendable words defined in II.8. Show that for $w \in A^*$, the following conditions are equivalent:

(i) $w \in \mathrm{S}(X)$;

(ii) $w \in \mathrm{E}(X)$;

(iii) $C_r(w)$ is maximal among all $C_r(u)$, $u \in A^*$.

3.2. Use Proposition II.8.6 to give another proof of formula (3.7.).

3.3. Let $\pi: A^* \to [0, 1]$ be a function. Then π is called an *invariant distribution* if

(i) $\pi(1) = 1$;

(ii) $\sum_{a \in A} \pi(wa) = \sum_{a \in A} \pi(aw) = \pi(w)$ for $w \in A^*$.

Let $X \subset A^+$ be a code and $\alpha: B^* \to A^*$ a coding morphism for X, i.e., $\alpha(B) = X$. Let π be an invariant distribution on B^*. Show that the function π^α from A^* into $[0, 1]$ defined by

$$\pi^\alpha(w) = \frac{1}{\lambda(\alpha)} \sum_{(u,v) \in C(w)} \pi(\alpha^{-1}(uvw))$$

with $\lambda(\alpha) = \sum_{x \in X} |x| \pi(\alpha^{-1}(x))$ is an invariant distribution on A^*. Compare with the definition of the contextual probability.

NOTES

Theorem 1.5 is a special case of a theorem of Feller which can be formulated as follows in our context: "Let $X \subset A^+$ be a code, and let π be a positive Bernoulli distribution such that $\pi(X) = 1$. Let p be the g.c.d. of the lengths of the words in X. Then the sequence

$$\pi(X^* \cap A^{np}) \qquad (n \geq 0)$$

has a limit, which is 0 or $p/\lambda(X)$, according to $\lambda(X) = \infty$ or not" (see Feller, 1957). Theorem 1.5 is less precise on two points: (i) we only consider the case where $\lambda(X) < \infty$ and (ii) we only consider the limit in mean of the sequence $\pi(X^* \cap A^n)$.

The results of Section 2 and related results, can be found in Greenander (1963) and Martin-Löf, (1965). Theorem 3.1 is due to Schützenberger (1965b). Theorem 3.3 is from Hansel and Perrin (1983).

Exercise 2.1 belongs to the folklore of automata theory. The notion of stationary distribution introduced in Exercise 2.3 is a classical one in the theory of Markov processes.

Further developments of the results presented in this chapter may be found in Blanchard and Perrin (1980) and Hansel and Perrin (1983). In particular these papers discuss the relationship of the concepts developped in this chapter with ergodic theory.

CHAPTER **VII**

Conjugacy

0. INTRODUCTION

In this chapter we study a particular family of codes called circular codes. The main feature of these codes is that they define a unique factorization of words written on a circle. The family of circular codes has numerous interesting properties. They appear in many problems of combinatorics on words, several of which will be mentioned here.

In Section 1 we give the definition of circular codes and we characterize the submonoid generated by a circular code. We also describe some elementary properties of circular codes. In particular we characterize maximal circular codes (Theorem 1.8).

In Section 2 we introduce successive refinements of the notion of a circular code. For this we define two notions, namely (p, q)-limitedness and sychronization delay. We study the relations between these parameters. For finite codes we show that these notions allow us to classify completely the family of circular codes (Theorem 2.6). We then proceed to a more detailed study of $(1, 0)$-limited codes. These codes are exactly the left factors of bisections studied in Sections 4 and 5. In particular, we show (Proposition 2.7) that $(1, 0)$-limited codes correspond to ordered automata. Comma-free codes are defined as circular codes satisfying the strongest possible condition.

Section 3 is concerned with length distributions of circular codes. Two important theorems are proved. The first gives a characterization of sequences of integers which are the length distribution of a circular code (Theorem 3.6). The second shows that for each odd integer n there exists a system of representatives of conjugacy classes of primitive words of length n which not only is circular but even comma-free (Theorem 3.8). The proofs of these results use similar combinatorial constructions. As a matter of fact they are based on the notion of factorization of free monoids studied in the following sections.

The main result of Section 4 (Theorem 4.1) characterizes factorizations of free monoids. It shows in particular that the codes which appear in these factorizations are circular. The proof is based on an enumeration technique. For this, we define the logarithm in a ring of formal power series in noncommutative variables. The properties necessary for the proof are derived. We illustrate the factorization theorem by considering a very general family of factorizations obtained from sets called Lazard sets.

Section 5 is devoted to the study of factorizations into finitely many submonoids. We first consider factorizations into two submonoids called bisections. The main result (Theorem 5.3) gives a method to construct all bisections. We then examine trisections or factorizations into three submonoids. We prove a difficult result (Theorem 5.4) showing that every trisection can be obtained by "pasting" together factorizations into four factors obtained by successive bisections.

1. CIRCULAR CODES

We define in this section a new family of codes which take into account, in a natural way, the operation of conjugacy.

By definition, a subset X of A^+ is a *circular code* if for all $n, m \geq 1$ and $x_1, x_2, \ldots, x_n \in X$, $y_1, y_2, \ldots, y_m \in X$, and $p \in A^*$ and $s \in A^+$, the equalities

$$sx_2x_3 \cdots x_n p = y_1 y_2 \cdots y_m, \tag{1.1}$$

$$x_1 = ps \tag{1.2}$$

imply

$$n = m, \qquad p = 1 \qquad \text{and} \qquad x_i = y_i \qquad (1 \leq i \leq n)$$

(see Fig. 7.1).

A circular code is clearly a code. The converse is false, as shown in Example 1.3. The asymmetry in the definition is only apparent, and comes from the choice of the cutting point on the circle in Fig. 7.1. Clearly, any subset of a circular code is also a circular code.

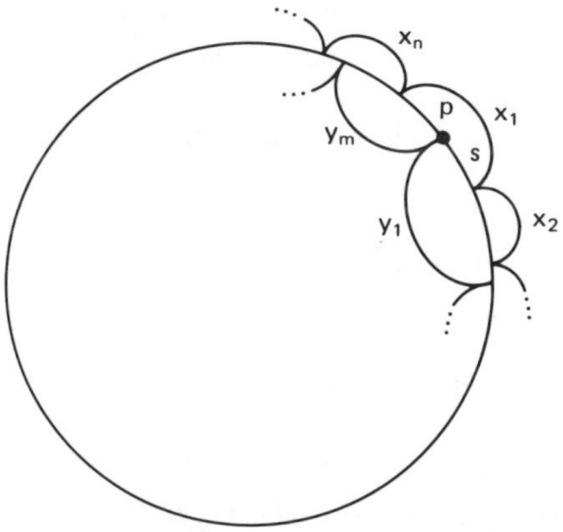

Fig. 7.1 Two circular factorizations.

Note that a circular code X cannot contain two distinct conjugate words. Indeed, if $ps, sp \in X$ with $s, p \in A^+$, then

$$s(ps)p = (sp)(sp).$$

Since X is circular, this implies $p = 1$ which yields a contradiction. Moreover, all words in X are primitive, since assuming $u^n \in X$ with $n \geq 2$, it follows that

$$u(u^n)u^{n-1} = u^n u^n.$$

This implies $u = 1$ and gives again a contradiction.

We shall now characterize in various ways the submonoids generated by circular codes. The first characterization facilitates the manipulation of circular codes.

A submonoid M of A^* is called *pure* if for all $x \in A^*$ and $n \geq 1$,

$$x^n \in M \Rightarrow x \in M \tag{1.3}$$

or equivalently

$$x \in M \Rightarrow \sqrt{x} \in M.$$

A submonoid M of A^* is *very pure* if for all $u, v \in A^*$,

$$uv, vu \in M \quad \Rightarrow \quad u, v \in M. \tag{1.4}$$

A very pure monoid is pure. The converse does not hold (see Example 1.3).

Proposition 1.1 *A submonoid M of A^* is very pure iff its minimal set of generators is a circular code.*

Proof Let M be a very pure submonoid. We show that M is stable. Let m, m', xm, $m'x \in M$. Then setting $u = x$, $v = mm'$, we have uv, $vu \in M$. This implies $x \in M$.

Thus M is stable, hence M is free. Let X be its base. Assume that (1.1) and (1.2) hold. Set $u = s$, $v = x_2x_3 \cdots x_np$. Then uv, $vu \in M$. Consequently $s \in M$. Since ps, $x_2x_3 \cdots x_np \in M$, the stability of M implies that $p \in M$. From $ps \in X$, it follows that $p = 1$. Since X is a code, this implies $n = m$ and $x_i = y_i$ for $i = 1, \ldots, n$.

Conversely, let X be a circular code and $M = X^*$. To show that M is very pure, consider u, $v \in A^*$ such that uv, $vu \in M$. Set

$$uv = x_1x_2 \cdots x_n, \qquad vu = y_1y_2 \cdots y_m,$$

with x_i, $y_j \in X$. There exists an integer i, $1 \le i \le n$ such that

$$u = x_1x_2 \cdots x_{i-1}p, \qquad v = sx_{i+i} \cdots x_n$$

with $x_i = ps$, $p \in A^*$, $s \in A^+$. Then vu may be written in two ways:

$$sx_{i+1} \cdots x_nx_1x_2 \cdots x_{i-1}p = y_1y_2 \cdots y_m.$$

Since X is a circular code, this implies $p = 1$ and $s = y_1$. Thus $u, v \in M$, showing that M is very pure. □

EXAMPLE 1.1 Let $A = \{a, b\}$ and $X = a^*b$. Then $X^* = A^*b \cup 1$. Thus if uv, $vu \in X^*$, the words u, v either are the empty word or terminate by a letter b; hence u, $v \in X^*$. Consequently X^* is very pure and X is circular.

EXAMPLE 1.2 Let $A = \{a\}$ and $X = \{a^2\}$. The submonoid X^* clearly is not pure. Thus X is not a circular code.

EXAMPLE 1.3 Let $A = \{a, b\}$ and $X = \{ab, ba\}$. The code X is not circular. However, X^* is pure (Exercise 1.1).

The following proposition characterizes the flower automaton of a circular code.

PROPOSITION 1.2 *Let $X \subset A^+$ be a code and let φ be the representation associated with the flower automaton of X. The following conditions are equivalent*:

(i) *X is a circular code.*
(ii) *For all $w \in A^+$, the relation $\varphi(w)$ has at most one fixed point.*

Proof For convenience, let 1 denote the state $(1, 1)$ of the flower automaton $\mathscr{A}_D^*(X)$.

(i) $\Rightarrow$ (ii) Let $w \in A^+$, and let $p = (u, v)$, $p' = (u', v')$ be two states of $\mathscr{A}_D^*(X)$ which are fixed points, i.e., such that $(p, \varphi(w), p) = (p', \varphi(w), p') = 1$.

Since $w \neq 1$, Proposition IV.2.2 shows that $w \in vX^*u$ and $w \in v'X^*u'$. Thus both paths $c: p \xrightarrow{w} p$ and $c': p' \xrightarrow{w} p'$ pass through the state 1.

We may assume that $v \leq v'$. Let $z, t \in A^*$ be the words such that $v' = vz$ and $w = vzt$. Then the paths c, c' factorize as

$$c: \quad p \xrightarrow{v} 1 \xrightarrow{z} r \xrightarrow{t} p, \qquad c': \quad p' \xrightarrow{v} s \xrightarrow{z} 1 \xrightarrow{t} p'.$$

Thus there are also paths

$$d: \quad 1 \xrightarrow{z} r \xrightarrow{t} p \xrightarrow{v} 1, \qquad d': \quad 1 \xrightarrow{t} p' \xrightarrow{v} s \xrightarrow{z} 1$$

showing that $ztv, tvz \in X^*$. Since X^* is very pure, it follows that $z, tv \in X^*$. Consequently, there is a path $e: 1 \xrightarrow{z} 1 \xrightarrow{tv} 1$. By unambiguity, $d = e$, whence $r = 1$. Thus $1 \xrightarrow{t} p \xrightarrow{vz} 1$ which compared to d' gives $p = p'$. This proves that $\varphi(w)$ has at most one fixed point.

(ii) $\Rightarrow$ (i) Let $u, v \in A^*$ be such that $uv, vu \in X^*$. Then there are two paths $1 \xrightarrow{u} p \xrightarrow{v} 1$ and $1 \xrightarrow{v} q \xrightarrow{u} 1$. Thus the relation $\varphi(uv)$ has two fixed points, namely 1 and q. This implies $q = 1$, and thus $u, v \in X^*$. □

COROLLARY 1.3 *A thin circular code is synchronous.*

Proof Let φ be the representation associated with the flower automaton $\mathcal{A}_D^*(X)$ of X. Let $e \in \varphi(A^+)$ be an idempotent with positive minimal rank. According to Proposition 1.2, the rank of e is 1. Thus $d(X) = 1$. □

We now give a characterization of circular codes in terms of conjugacy. For this, the following terminology is used:

Let $X \subset A^+$ be a code. Two words $w, w' \in X^*$ are called *X-conjugate* if there exist $x, y \in X^*$ such that

$$w = xy, \qquad w' = yx.$$

The word $x \in X^*$ is called *X-primitive* if $x = y^n$ with $y \in X^*$ implies $n = 1$. The *X-exponent* of $x \in X^+$ is the unique integer $p \geq 1$ such that $x = y^p$ with y an X-primitive word.

Let $\alpha: B \to A^*$ be a coding morphism for X. It is easily seen that $w, w' \in X^*$ are X-conjugate iff $\alpha^{-1}(w)$ and $\alpha^{-1}(w')$ are conjugate in B^*. Likewise, $x \in X^*$ is X-primitive iff $\alpha^{-1}(x)$ is a primitive word of B^*.

Thus, X-conjugacy is an equivalence relation on X^*. Of course, two words in X^* which are X-conjugate are conjugate. Likewise, a word in X^* which is primitive is also X-primitive.

When $X = A$, we get the usual notions of conjugacy and primitivity.

PROPOSITION 1.4 *Let $X \subset A^+$ be a code. The following conditions are equivalent.*

(i) *X is a circular code;*

(ii) *X^* is pure, and any two words in X^* which are conjugate are also X-conjugate.*

Proof (i) $\Rightarrow$ (ii) Since X^* is very pure, it is pure. Next let $w, w' \in X^*$ be conjugate words. Then $w = uv$, $w' = vu$ for some $u, v \in A^*$. By (1.4), $u, v \in X^*$, showing that w and w' are X-conjugate.

(ii) $\Rightarrow$ (i) Let $u, v \in A^*$ be such that $uv, vu \in X^*$. If $u = 1$ or $v = 1$, then $u, v \in X^*$. Otherwise, let x, y be the primitive words which are the roots of uv and vu: then $uv = x^n$, $vu = y^n$ for some $n \geq 1$. Since X^* is pure, we have $x, y \in X^*$. Next $uv = x^n$ gives a decomposition $x = rs$, $u = x^p r$, $v = sx^q$ for some $r \in A^*$, $s \in A^+$, and $p + q + 1 = n$. Reporting this in the equation $vu = y^n$, yields $y = sr$. Since x, y are conjugate, they are X-conjugate. But for primitive words x, y, there exists a unique pair $(r', s') \in A^* \times A^+$ such that $x = r's'$, $y = s'r'$. Consequently $r, s \in X^*$. Thus $u, v \in X^*$, showing that X^* is very pure. □

PROPOSITION 1.5 *Let $X \subset A^+$ be a code and let $C \subset A^n$ be a conjugacy class that meets X^*. Then*

$$\sum_{m \geq 1} \frac{1}{m} \mathrm{Card}(X^m \cap C) \geq \frac{1}{n} \mathrm{Card}(C). \tag{1.5}$$

Further, the equality holds iff the following two conditions are satisfied:

(i) *The exponent of the words in $C \cap X^*$ is equal to their X-exponent.*
(ii) *$C \cap X^*$ is a class of X-conjugacy.*

Proof Let p be the exponent of the words in C. Then $\mathrm{Card}(C) = n/p$. The set $C \cap X^*$ is a union of X-conjugacy classes. Let D be such a class, and set $C' = C - D$. The words in D all belong to X^k for the same k, and all have the same X-exponent, say q. Then $\mathrm{Card}(D) = k/q$. Since $C = C' \cup D$, the left side of (1.5) is

$$\sum_{m=1}^{n} \frac{1}{m} \mathrm{Card}(X^m \cap C') + \sum_{m=1}^{n} \frac{1}{m} \mathrm{Card}(X^m \cap D).$$

In the second sum, all terms vanish except for $m = k$. Thus this sum equals $(1/k)\,\mathrm{Card}(X^k \cap D) = 1/q$. Thus

$$\sum_{m=1}^{n} \frac{1}{m} \mathrm{Card}(X^m \cap C) = \frac{1}{q} + \sum_{m=1}^{n} \frac{1}{m} \mathrm{Card}(X^m \cap C'). \tag{1.6}$$

Since $q \leq p$, we have $1/q \geq 1/p = (1/n)\,\mathrm{Card}(C)$. This proves formula (1.5).

Assume now that (i) and (ii) hold. Then $p = q$, and $D = C \cap X^*$. Thus $C' \cap X^* = \varnothing$. Thus the right side of (1.6) is equal to $1/p$, which shows that equality holds in (1.5). Conversely, assuming the equality sign in (1.5), it follows from (1.6) that

$$\frac{1}{p} = \frac{1}{q} + \sum_{m=1}^{n} \frac{1}{m} \operatorname{Card}(X^m \cap C') \geq \frac{1}{q} \geq \frac{1}{p},$$

which implies $p = q$ and $C' \cap X^* = \emptyset$. □

The proposition has the following consequence:

PROPOSITION 1.6 *Let $X \subset A^+$ be a code. The following conditions are equivalent*:

(i) *X is a circular code.*
(ii) *For any integer $n \geq 1$ and for any conjugacy class $C \subset A^n$ that meets X^*, we have*

$$\sum_{m \geq 1} \frac{1}{m} \operatorname{Card}(X^m \cap C) = \frac{1}{n} \operatorname{Card}(C). \tag{1.7}$$

Proof By Proposition 1.4, the code X is circular iff we have

(iii) X^* is pure.
(iv) Two conjugate words in X^* are X-conjugate.

Condition (iii) is equivalent to: the X-exponent of any word in X^* is equal to its exponent. Thus X is circular iff for any conjugacy class C meeting X^*, we have

(v) The exponent of words in $C \cap X^*$ equals their X-exponent.
(vi) $C \cap X^*$ is a class of X-conjugacy.

In view of Proposition 1.5, conditions (v) and (vi) are satisfied iff the conjugacy class $C \cap A^n$ satisfies the equality (1.7). This proves the proposition. □.

We now prove a result which is an analogue of Theorem I.5.1.

PROPOSITION 1.7 *Let $X \subset A^+$ be a circular code. If X is maximal as a circular code, then X is complete.*

Proof If $A = \{a\}$, then $X = \{a\}$. Therefore, we assume $\operatorname{Card}(A) \geq 2$. Suppose that X is not complete. Then there is a word, say w, which is not a factor of a word in X^*. By Proposition 0.3.6, there is a word $v \in A^*$ such that $y = wv$ is unbordered.

Set $Y = X \cup y$. We prove that Y is a circular code. For this, let x_i $(1 \leq i \leq n)$ and y_i $(1 \leq i \leq m)$ be words in Y, let $p \in A^*$, $s \in A^+$ such that

$$sx_2x_3 \cdots x_n p = y_1 y_2 \cdots y_m$$

$$x_1 = ps.$$

If all x_i $(1 \le i \le n)$ are in X, then also all y_j are in X, because y is not a factor of a word in X^*. Since X is circular, this then implies that

$$n = m, \qquad p = 1, \qquad x_i = y_i \qquad (1 \le i \le n). \tag{1.8}$$

Suppose now that $x_i = y$ for some $i \in \{1, \ldots, n\}$ and suppose first that $i \ne 1$. Then x_i is a factor of $y_1 y_2 \cdots y_m$. Since $y \notin F(X^*)$, and since y is unbordered, this implies that there is a $j \in \{1, 2, \ldots, m\}$ such that $y_j = y$, and

$$sx_2 \cdots x_{i-1} = y_1 y_2 \cdots y_{j-1}, \qquad x_{i+1} \cdots x_n p = y_{j+1} \cdots y_m.$$

This in turn implies

$$sx_2 \cdots x_{i-1} x_{i+1} \cdots x_n p = y_1 y_2 \cdots y_{j-1} y_{j+1} \cdots y_m,$$

and (1.8) follows by induction on the length of the words.

Consider finally the case where $i = 1$, i.e., $x_1 = y$. Since

$$x_1 x_2 \cdots x_n p = p y_1 y_2 \cdots y_m,$$

we have $yx_2 \cdots x_n p = py_1 y_2 \cdots y_m$. Now p is a right factor of a word in Y^*; further $y \notin F(X^*)$ and y is unbordered. Thus $p = 1$ and $y_1 = y$. This again gives (1.8) by induction on the length of the words. Thus if X is not complete, then $Y = X \cup y$ is a circular code. Since $y \notin X$, X is not maximal as a circular code. □

The preceding proposition and Theorem I.5.7 imply

THEOREM 1.8 *Let X be a thin circular code. The three following conditions are equivalent.*

(i) *X is complete.*
(ii) *X is a maximal code.*
(iii) *X is maximal as a circular code.* □

Observe that a maximal circular code $X \subset A^+$ is necessarily infinite, except when $X = A$. Indeed, assume that X is a finite maximal circular code. Then by Theorem 1.8, it is a maximal code. According to Proposition I.5.9, there is, for each letter $a \in A$, an integer $n \ge 1$ such that $a^n \in X$. Since X is circular, we must have $n = 1$, and consequently $a \in X$ for all $a \in A$. Thus $X = A$.

We shall need the following property which allows us to construct circular codes.

PROPOSITION 1.9 *Let Y, Z be two composable codes, and let $X = Y \circ Z$. If Y and Z are circular, then X is circular.*

Proof Let $\alpha: B^* \to A^*$ be a morphism such that $X = Y \circ_\alpha Z$. Let $u, v \in A^*$ be such that $uv, vu \in X^*$. Then $uv, vu \in Z^*$, whence $u, v \in Z^*$ because Z^* is very pure. Let $s = \alpha^{-1}(u)$, $t = \alpha^{-1}(v)$. Then $st, ts \in Y^*$. Since Y^* is very pure, $s, t \in Y^*$, showing that $u, v \in X^*$. Thus X^* is very pure. □

2. LIMITED CODES

We introduce special families of circular codes which are defined by increasingly restrictive conditions concerning overlapping between words. The most special family is that of comma-free codes which is the object of an important theorem proved in the next section.

Let $p, q \geq 0$ be two integers. A submonoid M of A^* is said to satisfy *condition* $C(p, q)$ if for any sequence

$$u_0, u_1, \ldots, u_{p+q}$$

of words in A^*, the assumptions

$$u_{i-1}u_i \in M \qquad (1 \leq i \leq p + q) \tag{2.1}$$

imply

$$u_p \in M$$

(see Fig. 7.2).

For example, the condition $C(1, 0)$ simply gives

$$uv \in M \Rightarrow v \in M,$$

i.e., M is suffix-closed, and condition $C(1, 1)$ is

$$uv,\ vw \in M \Rightarrow v \in M.$$

It is easily verified that a submonoid M satisfying $C(p, q)$ also satisfies conditions $C(p', q')$ for $p' \geq p$, $q' \geq q$.

PROPOSITION 2.1 *Let $p, q \geq 0$ and let M be a submonoid of A^*. If M satisfies condition $C(p, q)$, then M is very pure.*

Proof Let $u, v \in A^*$ be such that $uv, vu \in M$. Define words u_i ($0 \leq i \leq p + q$) to be alternatingly u and v. Then assumption (2.1) is satisfied and

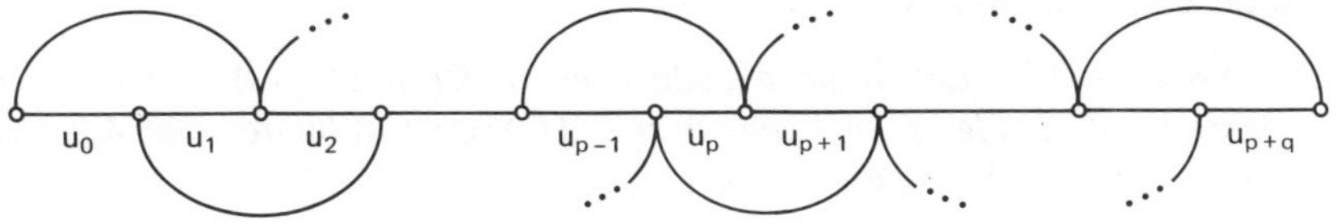

Fig. 7.2 The condition $C(p, q)$ (for p odd and q even).

consequently either u or v is in M. Interchanging the roles of u and v, we get that both u and v are in M. □

Let M be a submonoid satisfying a condition $C(p, q)$. By the preceding proposition, M is very pure. Thus M is free. Let X be its base. By definition, X is called a (p, q)-*limited* code.

A code X is *limited* if there exist integers $p, q \geq 0$ such that X is (p, q)-limited.

PROPOSITION 2.2 *Any limited code is circular.* □

EXAMPLE 2.1 The only $(0, 0)$-limited code over A is $X = A$.

EXAMPLE 2.2 A $(p, 0)$-limited code X is prefix. Assume indeed X is $(p, 0)$-limited. If $p = 0$ then $X = A$. Take $u_0 = \cdots = u_{p-2} = 1$. Then for any u_{p-1}, u_p, we have

$$u_{p-1}, u_{p-1}u_p \in X^* \quad \Rightarrow \quad u_p \in X^*$$

showing that X^* is right unitary. Likewise, a $(0, q)$-limited code is suffix.

However, a prefix code is not always limited, since it is not necessarily circular.

EXAMPLE 2.3 The code $X = a^*b$ is $(1, 0)$-limited. It satisfies even the stronger condition

$$uv \in X \quad \Rightarrow \quad v \in X \cup 1.$$

EXAMPLE 2.4 Let $A = \{a, b, c\}$ and $X = ab^*c \cup b$. The set X is a biprefix code. It is neither $(1, 0)$-limited nor $(0, 1)$-limited. However, it is $(2, 0)$- and $(0, 2)$-limited.

EXAMPLE 2.5 Let $A = \{a_i \mid i \geq 0\}$ and $X = \{a_i a_{i+1} \mid i \geq 0\}$. The code X is circular, as it is easily verified. However, it is not limited. Indeed, set $u_i = a_i$ for $0 \leq i \leq n$. Then $u_{i-1}u_i \in X$ for $i \in \{1, 2, \ldots, n\}$, but none of the u_i is in X^*.

This example shows that the converse of Proposition 2.2 does not hold in general. However it holds for finite codes, as we shall see below (Theorem 2.6). It also holds for recognizable codes (Exercise 2.5).

One of the reasons which makes the use of (p, q)-limited codes convenient, is that they behave well with respect to composition. In the following statement, we do not use the notation $X = Y \circ Z$ because we do not assume that every word of Z appears in a word in X.

PROPOSITION 2.3 *Let Z be a code over A, let $\beta: B^* \to A^*$ be a coding morphism for Z, and let Y be a code over B. If Y is (p, q)-limited and Z is (r, t)-limited, then $X = \beta(Y)$ is $(p + r, q + t)$-limited.*

Proof Let $u_0, u_1, \ldots, u_{p+r+q+t} \in A^*$ be such that

$$u_{i-1}u_i \in X^* \quad (1 \leq i \leq p + r + q + t) \tag{2.2}$$

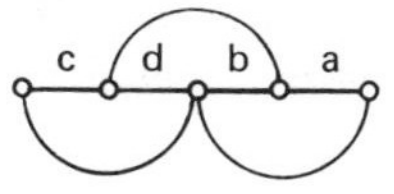

Fig. 7.3 X is not (p, q)-limited for $p + q \leq 3$.

Since $X \subset Z^*$ and Z is (r, t)-limited, it follows from (2.2) that

$$u_r, u_{r+1}, \ldots, u_{r+p+q} \in Z^* \tag{2.3}$$

Since Y is (p, q)-limited, (2.3) and (2.2) for $r + 1 \leq i \leq p + q + r$ show that $u_{r+p} \in X^*$. Thus X is $(p + r, q + t)$-limited. □

EXAMPLE 2.6 Let $A = \{a, b, c, d\}$ and $X = \{ba, cd, db, cdb, dba\}$. Then

$$X = Z_1 \circ Z_2 \circ Z_3 \circ Z_4,$$

with

$$Z_4 = \{b, c, d, ba\},$$

$$Z_3 \circ Z_4 = \{c, d, ba, db\},$$

$$Z_2 \circ Z_3 \circ Z_4 = \{d, ba, db, cd, cdb\}.$$

The codes Z_3 and Z_4 are $(0, 1)$-limited. The code $Z_3 \circ Z_4$ is not $(0, 1)$-limited, but it is $(0, 2)$-limited, in agreement with Proposition 2.3. The codes Z_1 and Z_2 are $(0, 1)$-limited. Thus X is $(2, 2)$-limited. It is not (p, q)-limited for any (p, q) such that $p + q \leq 3$, as shown by Fig. 7.3.

Let $X \subset A^+$ be a code. Then X is called *uniformly synchronous* if there is an integer $s \geq 0$ such that

$$x \in X^s, \quad u, v \in A^*, \quad uxv \in X^* \quad \Rightarrow \quad ux, xv \in X^* \tag{2.4}$$

If (2.4) holds for an integer s, it also holds for $s' \geq s$. The smallest integer s such that (2.4) holds is called the *synchronization delay* of X. It is denoted by $\sigma(X)$.

Observe that the synchronization delay is greater than or equal to the deciphering delay. Indeed, assume that $\sigma(X) = s$. Then for all $y \in X$, $x \in X^s$, and $v \in A^*$

$$yxv \in X^* \Rightarrow xv \in X^*$$

showing that the deciphering delay of X is at most s.

The term "uniformly synchronous" is justified by

PROPOSITION 2.4 *A code X is uniformly synchronous iff there exists an integer $s \geq 0$ such that any pair $(x, y) \in X^s \times X^s$ is a synchronizing pair.*

Proof Let $s = \sigma(X)$, and consider a pair $(x, y) \in X^s \times X^s$. To show that (x, y) is synchronizing, let $u, v \in A^*$ be such that $uxyv \in X^*$. Then indeed, by (2.4), $ux, yv \in X^*$.

Conversely, assume that any pair in $X^s \times X^s$ is synchronizing and set $t = 2s$. Let $x \in X^t$, and $u, v \in A^*$ such that $uxv \in X^*$. Set $x = x'x''$ with $x', x'' \in X^s$. Since the pair (x', x'') is synchronizing, $ux'x''v \in X^*$ implies $ux', x''v \in X^*$. Consequently $ux, xv \in X^*$. Thus $\sigma(X) \leq t$. □

EXAMPLE 2.7 Let $A = \{a, b\}$ and $X = a^*b$. Then X has synchronizing delay 1. Indeed $X^+ = A^*b$; if $x \in X$ and $uxv \in X^*$, then ux and xv are in A^*b.

To verify that a code X is uniformly synchronous, we may use the following formulation: Call a word $x \in X^*$ a *constant* for X if the set of its contexts is the direct product of the sets of its left contexts and of its right contexts, i.e.,

$$C(x) = C_l(x) \times C_r(x).$$

Then a word $x \in X^s$ satisfies condition (2.4) iff x is a constant. Thus $\sigma(X) \leq s$ iff the set X^s is composed of constants.

PROPOSITION 2.5 *Any uniformly synchronous code is limited.*

Proof Let $X \subset A^+$ be a uniformly synchronous code, and let $s = \sigma(X)$ be its synchronization delay. We show that X is $(2s, 2s)$-limited. (see Fig. 7.4). Consider indeed words

$$u_0, u_1, \ldots, u_{4s} \in A^*,$$

and assume that for $1 \leq i \leq 4s$,

$$u_{i-1}u_i \in X^*.$$

Set, for $1 \leq i \leq 2s$,

$$x_i = u_{2i-2}u_{2i-1}, \quad y_i = u_{2i-1}u_{2i}$$

Let $y = y_1 y_2 \cdots y_s$ and $x = x_1 x_2 \cdots x_s$.

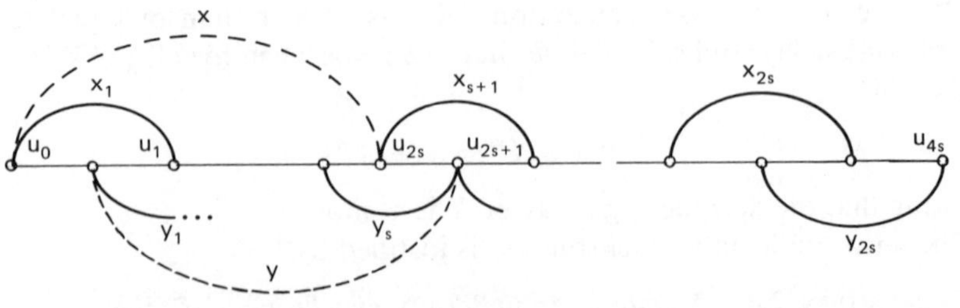

Fig. 7.4 An X-factorization with $s = \sigma(X)$.

Assume first that $y_i \neq 1$ for all $i = 1, \ldots, s$. Then $y \in X^s X^*$.

Since $u_0 y u_{2s+1} \in X^*$, the uniform synchronization shows that $u_0 y \in X^*$. Since $u_0 y = x u_{2s}$, this is equivalent to

$$x u_{2s} \in X^*. \tag{2.5}$$

Next, consider the case that $y_i = 1$ for some $i \in \{1, 2, \ldots, s\}$. Then $u_{2i-1} = u_{2i} = 1$. It follows that

$$y_{i+1} \cdots y_s = u_{2i+1} \cdots u_{2s} = u_{2i} \cdots u_{2s} = x_{i+1} \cdots x_s u_{2s}.$$

Thus, in this case also $x u_{2s}$ is in X^*.

Setting $y' = y_{s+1} \cdots y_{2s}$, we prove in the same manner that

$$u_{2s} y' \in X^*. \tag{2.6}$$

Since X^* is stable, (2.5) and (2.6) imply that $u_{2s} \in X^*$. This shows that X is $(2s, 2s)$-limited. □

EXAMPLE 2.8 Consider the (2, 2)-limited code $X = \{ba, cd, db, cdb, dba\}$ of Example 2.5. We have $\sigma(X) = 1$. Indeed, the contexts of words in X are

$$C(ba) = \{(1,1), (d,1)\}, \qquad C(cd) = \{(1,1), (1,b)\}$$
$$C(db) = \{(1,1), (1,a), (c,1), (c,a)\}$$
$$C(cdb) = \{(1,1), (1,a)\}$$
$$C(dba) = \{(1,1), (c,1)\}$$

Thus each $x \in X$ is a constant, and therefore $\sigma(X) = 1$.

EXAMPLE 2.9 Let $X = ab^*c \cup b$ be the limited code of Example 2.4. It is not uniformly synchronous. Indeed, for all $s \geq 0$, one has $b^s \in X^s$ and $ab^s c \in X$. However ab^s, $b^s c \notin X$. This example shows that the converse of Proposition 2.5 does not hold.

We now prove that in the case of finite codes, the concepts introduced coincide.

THEOREM 2.6 *Let X be a finite code. The following conditions are equivalent.*

(i) *X is circular.*
(ii) *X is limited.*
(iii) *X is uniformly synchronous.*

Proof We have already established the implications (iii) ⇒ (ii) ⇒ (i) without the finiteness assumption. Thus it remains to prove (i) ⇒ (iii).

Let $X \subset A^+$ be a finite circular code, and let $\mathscr{A}_D^*(X) = (P, 1, 1)$ be the flower automaton of X with the shorthand notation 1 for the state $(1, 1)$. By Proposition 1.2, each element in $\varphi_D(A^+)$ has at most one fixed point. In particular, every nonzero idempotent in $\varphi_D(A^+)$ has rank 1. Let $M = \varphi_D(A^*)$, and let J be its 0-minimal ideal. Since X is finite, the monoid M is finite. Let $s = \text{Card}(M - J)$. We show that $\varphi_D(w) \in J$ for every word w of length s. Indeed, set $w = a_1 a_2 \cdots a_s$, with $a_i \in A$, and set $m_i = \varphi_D(a_1 a_2 \cdots a_i)$ for $i = 0, \ldots, s$. If the m_i are pairwise distinct, then at least one of them is in J, and consequently $\varphi_D(w) \in J$. On the contrary, there are indices i, j, with $0 \leq i < j \leq s$, such that $m_i = m_j$. Set $u = \varphi_D(a_{i+i} \cdots a_j)$. Then $m_i u = m_j$. Let e be the idempotent which is a positive power of u. (Recall that M is finite). Then $m_i e = m_j$. Further, e has minimal rank; thus $e \in J$. Consequently, $m_j \in J$ and also $\varphi_D(w) \in J$. This proves the claim.

We now show that $\sigma(X) \leq s$. Indeed, let $x \in X^s$ and let $u, v \in A^*$ be such that $uxv \in X^*$. Since $|x| \geq s$, one has $\varphi_D(x) \in J$. Thus $\varphi_D(x)$ has rank 1. Consequently, there are two matrices $\alpha \in \{0, 1\}^{P \times t}$ and $\beta \in \{0, 1\}^{t \times P}$ such that $\varphi_D(x) = \alpha\beta$. Since $uxv \in X^*$, there is a path $1 \xrightarrow{u} p \xrightarrow{x} q \xrightarrow{v} 1$. Hence $p\alpha t\beta q$. From $x \in X^*$, one gets $1\alpha t\beta 1$. It follows that $p\alpha t\beta 1$ and $1\alpha t\beta q$. Therefore $p \xrightarrow{x} 1$ and $1 \xrightarrow{x} q$, showing that $ux, xv \in X^*$. This shows that X is uniformly synchronous. □

EXAMPLE 2.10 Let $A = \{a_1, a_2, \ldots, a_{2k}\}$ and

$$X = \{a_i a_j \mid 1 \leq i < j \leq 2k\}.$$

We show that X is uniformly synchronous and $\sigma(X) = k$. First, $\sigma(X) \geq k$ since $(a_2 a_3)(a_4 a_5) \cdots (a_{2k-2} a_{2k-1}) \in X^{k-1}$ and also $(a_1 a_2) \cdots (a_{2k-1} a_{2k}) \in X^*$ and however $a_1 a_2 \cdots a_{2k-1} \notin X^*$. Next, assume that $x \in X^k$, and $uxv \in X^*$. If u and v have even length, then they are in X^*. Therefore we assume the contrary. Then $u = u' a_j$, $v = a_l v'$ with $a_j, a_l \in A$ and $u', v' \in X^*$. Moreover $a_j x a_l \in X^*$. Set $x = a_{i_1} \cdots a_{i_{2k}}$. Since $x \in X^*$, we have $i_1 < i_2, i_3 < i_4, \ldots, i_{2k-1} < i_{2k}$; since $a_j x a_l \in X^*$, we have $j < i_1$, $i_2 < i_3, \ldots, i_{2k} < l$. Thus $1 \leq j < i_1 < i_2 < \cdots < i_{2k-1} < i_{2k} < l \leq 2k$, which is clearly impossible. Thus u and v have even length, showing that $\sigma(X) \leq k$. This proves the equality.

Compare this example with Example 2.5, which is merely Example 2.10 with $k = \infty$. The infinite code was circular but not limited, hence not uniformly synchronous.

We now give a characterization of $(1, 0)$-limited codes by means of automata. These codes intervene in Section 5. For that, say that a deterministic automaton $\mathscr{A} = (Q, 1, 1)$ is an *ordered automaton* if Q is a partially ordered set, and if the two following conditions hold:

(i) For all $q \in Q$, $q \leq 1$.

(ii) For all $p, q \in Q$, and $a \in A$,

$$p \leq q \quad \Rightarrow \quad p \cdot a \leq q \cdot a.$$

PROPOSITION 2.7 *Let $X \subset A^+$ be a prefix code. The following conditions are equivalent*:

(i) *X is (1, 0)-limited, i.e., $uv \in X^* \Rightarrow v \in X^*$.*
(ii) *X^* is recognized by some ordered automaton.*

Proof (i) ⇒ (ii) Let $\mathscr{A}(X^*) = (Q, 1, 1)$ be the minimal automaton of X^*. Define a partial order on Q by

$$p \leq q \qquad \text{iff} \quad L_p \subset L_q,$$

where for each state p, $L_p = \{u \in A^* \mid p \cdot u = 1\}$. This defines an order on Q, since by the definition of a minimal automaton, $L_p = L_q \Rightarrow p = q$. Next let $q \in Q$, and let $u \in A^*$ be such that $1 \cdot u = q$. Then $v \in L_q$ iff $uv \in X^*$. Since X is (1, 0)-limited, $uv \in X^*$ implies $v \in X^*$, or also $v \in L_1$. Thus $L_q \subset L_1$, and therefore $q \leq 1$. Further, if $p, q \in Q$ with $p \leq q$, and $a \in A$, let $v \in L_{p \cdot a}$. Then $av \in L_p$, hence $av \in L_q$, and thus $v \in L_{q \cdot a}$. This proves that $\mathscr{A}(X^*)$ is indeed an ordered automaton for this order.

(ii) ⇒ (i) Let $\mathscr{A} = (Q, 1, 1)$ be an ordered automaton recognizing X^*. Assume that $uv \in X^*$, for some $u, v \in A^*$. Then $1 \cdot uv = 1$. Since $1 \cdot u \leq 1$, we have $1 \cdot uv \leq 1 \cdot v$. Thus $1 \leq 1 \cdot v \leq 1$, whence $1 \cdot v = 1$. Consequently $v \in X^*$. □

EXAMPLE 2.11 Consider the automaton $(Q, 1, 1)$ given in Fig. 7.5. The set $Q = \{1, 2, 3, 4\}$ is equipped with the partial order given by $3 < 2 < 1$ and $4 < 1$. For this order, the automaton $(Q, 1, 1)$ is ordered. It recognizes the submonoid X^* generated by

$$X = (b^2 b^* a)^* \{a, ba\}.$$

Consequently, this is a (1, 0)-limited code. □

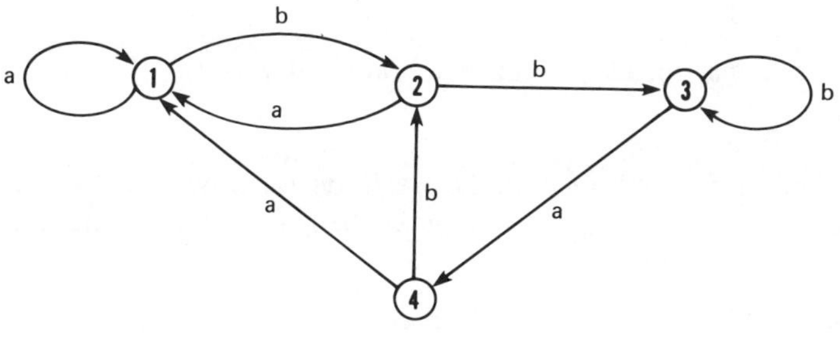

Fig. 7.5 An ordered automaton.

The following proposition gives another characterization of (1, 0)-limited codes.

PROPOSITION 2.8 *A prefix code* $X \subset A^+$ *is* (1, 0)*-limited iff the set*

$$R = A^* - XA^*$$

of words having no left factor in X *is a submonoid.*

Proof By Theorem II.1.4, $\underline{A}^* = \underline{X}^*\underline{R}$. Suppose first that X is (1, 0)-limited. Let $u, u' \in R$, and set

$$uu' = xr$$

with $x \in X^*$, $r \in R$. Arguing by contradiction, suppose that $x \neq 1$. Then x is not a left factor of u. Consequently $x = uv$, $vr = u'$ for some $v \in A^*$. Since X is (1, 0)-limited, one has $v \in X^*$; this implies that $v = 1$, since v is a left factor of u'. Thus $x = u$, a contradiction. Consequently $x = 1$ and $uu' \in R$.

Conversely, suppose that R is a submonoid. Then, being prefix-closed, R is a left unitary submonoid. Thus $R = Y^*$ for some suffix code Y. From the power series equation, we get

$$\underline{A}^* = \underline{X}^*\underline{Y}^*.$$

Multiplication with $1 - \underline{Y}$ on the right gives $\underline{X}^* = \underline{A}^* - \underline{A}^*\underline{Y}$. Thus X^* is the complement of a left ideal. Consequently X^* is suffix-closed. Thus X is (1, 0)-limited. □

EXAMPLE 2.12 The code $X = (b^2b^*a)^*\{a, ba\}$ of Example 2.11 gives, for $R = A^* - XA^*$, the submonoid

$$R = \{b, b^2a\}^*.$$

We end this section with the definition of a family of codes which is the most restrictive of the families we have examined: a code $X \subset A^+$ is called *comma-free* if:

(i) X is biprefix;
(ii) $\sigma(X) = 1$.

Thus X is comma-free iff for all $x \in X^+$, $u, v \in A^*$,

$$uxv \in X^* \quad \Rightarrow \quad u, v \in X^*. \tag{2.7}$$

Comma-free codes are those with the easiest deciphering: if in a word $w \in X^*$, some factor can be identified to be in X, then this factor is one term of the unique X-factorization of w.

PROPOSITION 2.9 *A code* $X \subset A^+$ *is comma-free iff it is* (p, q)*-limited for all* p, q *with* $p + q = 3$, *and if* $A^+XA^+ \cap X = \varnothing$.

Proof First suppose that X is comma-free. Let $u_0, u_1, u_2, u_3 \in A^*$ be such that u_0u_1, u_1u_2, $u_2u_3 \in X^*$. If $u_1 = u_2 = 1$, then u_0, $u_3 \in X^*$. Otherwise $u_1u_2 \in X^+$ and $u_0u_1u_2u_3 \in X^+$. Thus by (2.7) $u_0, u_3 \in X^*$. Since X is prefix, u_0, $u_0u_1 \in X^*$ implies that $u_1 \in X^*$, and X being suffix, u_2u_3, $u_3 \in X$ implies that u_2 is in X^*. Thus $u_0, u_1, u_2, u_3 \in X^*$. Consequently, X is (p, q)-limited for all p, $q \geq 0$ with $p + q = 3$. Furthermore $A^+XA^+ \cap X = \varnothing$. Indeed assume that uxv, $x \in X$. Then by (2.7) $u, v \in X^*$, whence $u = v = 1$.

Conversely, let $u, v \in A^*$ and $x \in X^+$ be such that $uxv \in X^*$. Since $A^+xA^+ \cap X = \varnothing$, there exists a factorization $x = ps$, with $p, s \in A^*$, such that $up, sv \in X^*$. From $up, ps, sv \in X^*$ it follows, by the limitedness of X, that u, p, s, $v \in X^*$. Thus (2.7) holds. □

PROPOSITION 2.10 *Let X, Z be two composable codes and let*

$$X = Y \circ Z.$$

If Y and Z are comma-free, then X is comma-free.

Proof Let $u, v \in A^*$ and $x \in X^+$ be such that $uxv \in X^*$. Since $X \subset Z^*$, we have $uxv \in Z^*$, $x \subset Z^+$. Since Z is comma-free, it follows that $u, v \in Z^*$. Since Y is comma-free, this implies that u, v are in X^*. Thus X is comma-free by (2.7). □

EXAMPLE 2.13 Let $A = \{a, b\}$ and $X = \{aab, bab\}$. The code X is biprefix. Next $C(aab) = C(bab) = \{(1, 1)\}$. Thus $\sigma(X) = 1$. This shows that X is comma-free.

3. LENGTH DISTRIBUTIONS

In this section, A is supposed to be a finite alphabet. Let X be a subset of A^+. For $n \geq 1$, let

$$\alpha_n = \text{Card}(X \cap A^n). \tag{3.1}$$

The sequence $\alpha = (\alpha_n)_{n \geq 1}$ is called the *length distribution* of X. We shall determine, in this paragraph, the length distributions of various families of codes.

If X is a code, then by Corollary I.4.3, the inequality

$$\sum_{n \geq 1} \alpha_n k^{-n} \leq 1 \tag{3.2}$$

holds, where $k = \text{Card}(A)$. We begin with the following result which could, of course, have been proved much earlier since its proof is quite elementary.

PROPOSITION 3.1 *For each sequence of integers $\alpha = (\alpha_n)_{n \geq 1}$ such that $\sum_{n \geq 1} \alpha_n k^{-n} \leq 1$, there exists a prefix code X over a k letter alphabet having length distribution α.*

Proof Take A a k letter alphabet. We define a sequence $(X_n)_{n \geq 1}$ such that

(i) $X_n \subset A^n$,
(ii) $\text{Card}(X_n) = \alpha_n$,
(iii) the union of the X_n is prefix.

First choose $X_1 \subset A$ such that $\text{Card}(X_1) = \alpha_1$. This is possible because $\alpha_1 \leq k$. Next suppose that X_m is constructed for $1 \leq m \leq n-1$. Set

$$Y^{(n)} = X_1 \cup X_2 \cup \cdots \cup X_{n-1}$$

and

$$R^{(n)} = A^* - Y^{(n)}A^*.$$

We have

$$\text{Card}(R^{(n)} \cap A^n) = k^n - \sum_{m=1}^{n-1} \alpha_m k^{n-m} = k^n\left(1 - \sum_{m=1}^{n-1} \alpha_m k^{-m}\right).$$

Since $\sum_{m=1}^{n} \alpha_m k^{-m} \leq 1$, we have $1 - \sum_{m=1}^{n-1} \alpha_m k^{-m} \geq \alpha_n k^{-n}$. Thus

$$\text{Card}(R^{(n)} \cap A^n) \geq \alpha_n.$$

Thus we may choose α_n elements in $R^{(n)} \cap A^n$ to form the set X_n. By construction, $X_n \cup Y^{(n)}$ is prefix. □

Having proved that a sequence α is the length distribution of a code if it satisfies (3.2), we now determine a stronger inequality for the length distribution of a circular code. The enumeration of classes of X-conjugacy plays a central role in this discussion.

Given a code $X \subset A^+$, we denote by $L_n(X)$ the number of X-conjugacy classes of X-primitive words in $X^* \cap A^n$.

PROPOSITION 3.2 *Let $X \subset A^+$ be a circular code. Then for all $n \geq 1$,*

$$L_n(X) \leq L_n(A) \tag{3.3}$$

and the equality holds iff each primitive conjugacy class in A^n meets X^*.

Proof Let $\mathscr{X}$ be the set of X-primitive X-conjugacy classes in $X^* \cap A^n$, and let $\mathscr{A}$ be the set of primitive conjugacy classes in A^n. Then by definition

$$L_n(X) = \text{Card}(\mathscr{X}), \qquad L_n(A) = \text{Card}(\mathscr{A}).$$

Let $C \in \mathscr{X}$. Since the words in C are X-conjugate, they are conjugate, and since X is circular, they are primitive. Thus each class in $\mathscr{X}$ is a subset of a class in $\mathscr{A}$. This defines a function $\varphi: \mathscr{X} \to \mathscr{A}$ which associates, with $C \in \mathscr{X}$, the class $C' \in \mathscr{A}$ containing C. This function is injective since two words in X^* which are conjugate are also X-conjugate. This proves (3.3). The function φ is surjective iff each element in $\mathscr{A}$ contains an element in $\mathscr{X}$. This proves the second claim. □

We now compute the numbers $L_n(X)$, starting with the length distribution α of X. This will yield an inequality analogous to (3.3) but depending only upon α.

Let $\alpha = (\alpha_n)_{n\geq 1}$ be a sequence of numbers. Define for $i \geq 1$

$$\alpha_n^{(i)} = \sum_{m_1+m_2+\cdots+m_i=n} \alpha_{m_1}\alpha_{m_2}\cdots\alpha_{m_i}.$$

Of course, the indices m_k satisfy $0 < m_k \leq n$, and clearly $\alpha_n^{(i)} = 0$ for $i \geq n+1$. If α is the length distribution of a code $X \subset A^+$, then

$$\alpha_n^{(i)} = \mathrm{Card}(X^i \cap A^n) \tag{3.4}$$

since $\underline{X}^i = (\underline{X})^i$ and since $\alpha_n^{(i)}$ is the coefficient of t^n in the series $(\sum_{n\geq 1} \alpha_n t^n)^i$. Set further

$$s_n(\alpha) = \sum_{i=1}^{n} \frac{n}{i}\alpha_n^{(i)} \tag{3.5}$$

and

$$l_n(\alpha) = \frac{1}{n}\sum_{d|n} \mu\left(\frac{n}{d}\right) s_d(\alpha) \tag{3.6}$$

where μ denotes the Möbius function (see Section 0.3).

PROPOSITION 3.3 *Let $X \subset A^+$ be a code and let α be its length distribution. The number $L_n(X)$ of X-conjugacy classes of X-primitive words in $X^* \cap A^n$ is given by*

$$L_n(X) = l_n(\alpha).$$

Proof Set for $n \geq 1$

$$S_n(X) = \sum_{d|n} d L_d(X)$$

We shall prove that $S_n(X) = s_n(\alpha)$ by evaluating in two different ways the sum

$$p_n = \sum_{i=1}^{n} \frac{n}{i}\mathrm{Card}(X^i \cap A^n).$$

First, by (3.4), we have $p_n = \sum_{i=1}^{n} (n/i)\,\alpha_n^{(i)}$. Hence $p_n = s_n(\alpha)$ by (3.5). To show that $p_n = S_n(X)$, we introduce two notations: for $x \in X^*$, we define $\|x\|$ to be the unique integer i such that $x \in X^i$. Next, we denote by $\hat{X}$ the set of X-

primitive words in X^*. With this notation, we may express p_n as

$$p_n = \sum_{w \in X^* \cap A^n} \frac{|w|}{||w||}$$

Since each word w in $X^* \cap A^n$ is the power of a unique word x in $\hat{X}$, and conversely, one has

$$p_n = \sum_{d|n} \sum_{x \in \hat{X} \cap A^d} \frac{|x^{n/d}|}{||x^{n/d}||}$$

$$= \sum_{d|n} \sum_{x \in \hat{X} \cap A^d} \frac{d}{||x||}.$$

Next we observe that

$$L_d(X) = \sum_{x \in \hat{X} \cap A^d} \frac{1}{||x||},$$

since the X-conjugacy class of a word $x \in \hat{X}$ has exactly $||x||$ elements. Consequently

$$p_n = \sum_{d|n} dL_d(X) = S_n(X).$$

Thus, we have shown that $s_n(\alpha) = S_n(X)$. In other words, we have for $n \geq 1$, $\sum_{d|n} dL_d(X) = s_n(\alpha)$. In view of Möbius' inversion formula (Proposition 0.3.4), this is equivalent to

$$L_n(X) = \frac{1}{n} \sum_{d|n} \mu\left(\frac{n}{d}\right) s_d(\alpha).$$

According to (3.6), this yields $L_n(X) = l_n(\alpha)$. □

Observe that in the case where $X = A$, the length distribution of X is $\alpha = (k, 0, 0, \ldots)$ with $k = \text{Card } A$. In this case also $s_d(\alpha) = k^d$; thus formula (3.6) becomes

$$l_n(k) = \frac{1}{n} \sum_{d|n} \mu\left(\frac{n}{d}\right) k^d$$

with the convenient notation $l_n(k) = l_n(\alpha)$. Proposition 3.3 thus gives as a special case, Proposition 0.3.5.

Proposition 3.3 shows that the numbers $L_n(X)$ depend only on the length distribution of X. The expression of $l_n(\alpha)$ allows us to give an explicit form for the inequalities of Proposition 3.2. If α is the length distribution of a circular code over a k letter alphabet, then for all $n \geq 1$

$$l_n(\alpha) \leq l_n(k). \tag{3.7}$$

TABLE 7.1

Length Distributions of Circular Codes
($k = 2$)

α_1	2	1	1	1	1	1	0
α_2	0	1	1	0	0	0	1
α_3	0	1	0	2	1	0	2
α_4	0	1	2	1	2	3	3

For $n = 1, 2, 3, 4$, we obtain

$$s_1(\alpha) = \alpha_1,$$
$$s_2(\alpha) = 2\alpha_2 + \alpha_1^2,$$
$$s_3(\alpha) = 3\alpha_3 + 3\alpha_1\alpha_2 + \alpha_1^3,$$
$$s_4(\alpha) = 4\alpha_4 + 2(\alpha_2^2 + 2\alpha_1\alpha_3) + 4\alpha_1^2\alpha_2 + \alpha_1^4.$$

The inequalities (3.7) become

$$\alpha_1 \le k$$
$$2\alpha_2 + \alpha_1^2 - \alpha_1 \le k^2 - k$$
$$3\alpha_3 + 2\alpha_1\alpha_2 + \alpha_1^3 - \alpha_1 \le k^3 - k,$$
$$4\alpha_4 + 2(\alpha^2 + 2\alpha_1\alpha_3) + 4\alpha_1^2\alpha_2 + \alpha_1^4 - 2\alpha_2 - \alpha_1^2 \le k^4 - k^2.$$

Table 7.1 gives, for $k = 2$, the sequences $(\alpha_n)_{1 \le n \le 4}$ such that the inequalities above are satisfied. We have only reported maximal sequences in the sense that if $\alpha'_n \le \alpha_n$ $(1 \le n \le 4)$, then only (α_n) is represented since (α'_n) satisfies the inequalities a fortiori.

We shall need in the sequel several arithmetic properties of the functions l_n. They are gathered together in

PROPOSITION 3.4 *Let $\alpha = (\alpha_n)_{n \ge 1}$ and $\beta = (\beta_n)_{n \ge 1}$ be two sequences of numbers.*

1. *If $\alpha_m = \beta_m$ for $1 \le m \le n - 1$, then*

$$l_n(\alpha) - l_n(\beta) = \alpha_n - \beta_n.$$

2. *If $\alpha_m = 0$ for $1 \le m \le n - 1$, then*

$$l_n(\alpha) = \alpha_n.$$

3. *Let $n \ge 1$ be an odd integer. If $\alpha_m = 0$ for all odd integers m with $1 \le m \le n - 2$, then*

$$l_n(\alpha) = \alpha_n.$$

Proof 1. By definition, $l_n(\alpha) = (1/n)\sum_{d|n}\mu(n/d)s_d(\alpha)$. Let d be a divisor of n. Then

$$s_d(\alpha) = \sum_{i=1}^{d}\frac{d}{i}\sum_{m_1+\cdots+m_i=d}\alpha_{m_1}\alpha_{m_2}\cdots\alpha_{m_i}. \tag{3.8}$$

In each monomial $\alpha_{m_1}\alpha_{m_2}\cdots\alpha_{m_i}$, all indices m_j satisfy $m_j \le n-1$ except if $d = n$ and $i = 1$. By the hypothesis, we have $\alpha_{m_1}\alpha_{m_2}\cdots\alpha_{m_i} = \beta_{m_1}\beta_{m_2}\cdots\beta_{m_i}$ for each of these monomials except for $d = n$ and $i = 1$. Hence $s_d(\alpha) = s_d(\beta)$ for $d\,|\,n$ and $d \neq n$, and $s_n(\alpha) - s_n(\beta) = \alpha_n - \beta_n$. Hence $l_n(\alpha) - l_n(\beta) = \alpha_n - \beta_n$.

Claim 2 is a consequence of 1 for $\beta = 0$.

3. Let d be a divisor of n. Since n is odd, d is odd. All the monomials in the sum (3.8) vanish except for $d = n$ and $i = 1$. In fact, in the other cases, all the indices m_j satisfy $m_j \le n-1$ and at least one of them has to be odd since their sum is d. Hence $l_n(\alpha) = s_n(\alpha) = \alpha_n$. □

We shall now prove that the inequalities (3.7) characterize the length distributions of circular codes.

For this, we say that a finite or infinite sequence $(x_i)_{i\ge1}$ of words in A^+ is a *Hall sequence* over A if it is obtained in the following way:

Let $X_1 = A$. Then x_1 is an arbitrary word in X_1. If x_i and X_i are defined, then set

$$X_{i+1} = x_i^*(X_i - x_i),$$

and x_{i+1} is an arbitrary chosen element in X_{i+1} satisfying

$$|x_{i+1}| \ge |x_i|.$$

The sequence $(X_i)_{i\ge1}$ is the sequence of codes *associated* with the sequence $(x_i)_{i\ge1}$.

PROPOSITION 3.5 *Let $(x_i)_{i\ge1}$ be a Hall sequence over A and let $(X_i)_{i\ge1}$ be the associated sequence of codes.*

1. *For all $i \ge 1$, the set X_i is a $(i-1, 0)$-limited code.*
2. *For all $n \ge 1$, each primitive word $w \in A^+$ such that*

$$|w| > |x_i|$$

has a conjugate in X_{i+1}^*

3. *For all $n > |x_i|$,*

$$L_n(X_{i+1}) = L_n(A) \tag{3.9}$$

Proof 1. $X_1 = A$ is $(0,0)$-limited. Next

$$X_{i+1} = T \circ X_i,$$

where T is a code of the form $b^*(B - b)$. Clearly T is $(1,0)$-limited. Assuming by induction that X_i is $(i-1,0)$-limited, the conclusion follows from Proposition 2.3.

2. Define $x_0 = 1$. We prove that the claim holds for all $i \geq 0$ by induction on i. For $i = 0$, the claim just states that any primitive word is in A^*. Thus assume $i \geq 1$, and let $w \in A^+$ be a primitive word of length $|w| > |x_i|$. Since $|x_i| \geq |x_{i-1}|$, one has $|w| > |x_{i-1}|$. By the induction hypothesis, there is a conjugate word w' of w which is in X_i^*. The word w' is not in x_i^* since w' is primitive and $|w'| > |x_i|$. Thus w' factorizes into

$$w' = uxv$$

for some $u, v \in X_i^*$ and $x \in X_i - x_i$. Then the conjugate

$$w'' = vux$$

of w' is in $X_i^*(X_i - x_i) \subset X_{i+1}^*$. Thus a conjugate of w is in X_{i+1}^*.

Claim 3 Follows from claim 2 and Proposition 3.2. □

Theorem 3.6 *Let A be an alphabet with $k \geq 1$ letters. For any sequence $\alpha = (\alpha_n)_{n \geq 1}$ of integers such that*

$$l_n(\alpha) \leq l_n(k) \qquad (n \geq 1), \tag{3.10}$$

there exists a circular code X over A with length distribution α.

Proof Set for $n, m \geq 1$

$$\varepsilon_n = l_n(k) - l_n(\alpha) \tag{3.11}$$

and

$$\sigma_m = \sum_{n=1}^{m} \varepsilon_n. \tag{3.12}$$

Define inductively a Hall sequence

$$x_1, x_2, \ldots, x_n, \ldots$$

as follows. Assume that a Hall sequence

$$(x_1, x_2, \ldots, x_{\sigma_m})$$

of words of length at most m is already constructed, in such a way that the length distribution β of $Y_m = X_{\sigma_m + 1}$ satisfies

$$\beta_n = \alpha_n \qquad (1 \leq n \leq m). \tag{3.13}$$

According to Proposition 3.5(3), we have

$$L_{m+1}(Y_m) = l_{m+1}(k), \tag{3.14}$$

since $m + 1 \geq |x_{\sigma_m}|$. In view of Proposition 3.4(1), and using (3.13), we obtain

$$\begin{aligned}\beta_{m+1} - \alpha_{m+1} &= l_{m+1}(\beta) - l_{m+1}(\alpha)\\ &= L_{m+1}(Y_m) - l_{m+1}(\alpha)\\ &= l_{m+1}(k) - l_{m+1}(\alpha)\\ &= \varepsilon_{m+1}.\end{aligned}$$

This implies that the code Y_m contains at least ε_{m+1} words of length $m + 1$.

Extend the Hall sequence already obtained by choosing a sequence of ε_{m+1} words of length $m + 1$ in Y_m, denoted by

$$(x_{\sigma_m+1}, x_{\sigma_m+2}, \ldots, x_{\sigma_{m+1}}).$$

Let γ be the length distribution of the associated code $Y_{m+1} = X_{1+\sigma_{m+1}}$. Then

$$\gamma_n = \beta_n \qquad (1 \leq n \leq m).$$

Indeed, since the sequence of lengths $|x_i|$ is nondecreasing, the codes X_i and X_{i+1} coincide on all words of length less than $|x_i|$. Consequently, the codes $X_{1+\sigma_m}, \ldots, X_{1+\sigma_{m+1}}$ possess the same words of length at most m.

Furthermore, one has $\gamma_{m+1} = \alpha_{m+1}$, since in the process of constructing Y_{m+1}, one has suppressed, in Y_m, ε_{m+1} words of length $m + 1$, implying that

$$\gamma_{m+1} = \beta_{m+1} - \varepsilon_{m+1} = \alpha_{m+1}.$$

This shows that

$$\gamma_n = \alpha_n, \qquad 1 \leq n \leq m + 1.$$

Starting with the empty Hall sequence, we have thus constructed a sequence

$$(Y_0, Y_1, \ldots, Y_m, \ldots)$$

of circular codes such that Y_m and Y_{m+1} have the same words of length at most m, and such that

$$\mathrm{Card}(Y_m \cap A^m) = \alpha_m.$$

Define Y by

$$Y \cap A^m = Y_m \cap A^m.$$

Then Y is a circular code with length distribution α. □

Example 3.1 Table 7.2 gives circular codes with length distributions agreeing with those of Table 7.1. They are constructed by the method of Theorem 3.6.

TABLE 7.2

Circular Codes with Prescribed Length Distribution

a, b	b	b	b	b	b	
	ab	ab				ab
	a^2b		a^2b, ab^2	a^2b		a^2b, bab
	a^3b	a^3b, a^2b^2	a^3b	a^3b, ab^3	a^3b, ab^3	a^3b, ba^2b
					a^2b^2	b^2ab

COROLLARY 3.7 *Let A be an alphabet with $k \geq 1$ letters. For all $m \geq 1$, there exists a circular code $X \subset A^m$ such that*

$$\mathrm{Card}(X) = l_m(k).$$

Proof Let $\alpha = (\alpha_n)_{n \geq 1}$ be the sequence with all terms zero except for α_m which is equal to $l_m(k)$. By Proposition 3.4(2), one has $l_n(\alpha) = 0$ for $1 \leq n \leq m-1$ and $l_m(\alpha) = \alpha_m$. Thus $l_n(\alpha) \leq l_n(k)$ for $1 \leq n \leq m$. According to the proof of Theorem 3.6, this suffices to ensure the existence of a circular code X having α_m words of length m. Thus $X \cap A^m$ satisfies the claim. □

Corollary 3.7 can be formulated in the following way: It is possible to choose a system X of representatives of the primitive conjugacy classes of words of length m in such a manner that X is a circular code. The following example shows that this does not hold for an arbitrary set of representatives of the primitive conjugacy classes within the words of the same length.

EXAMPLE 3.2 Let X be a subset of $A^2 - \{a^2 \mid a \in A\}$ and let θ be the relation over A defined by

$$a\theta b \quad \text{iff} \quad ab \in X.$$

Then X is a circular code iff the reflexive and transitive closure θ^* of θ is an order relation.

Indeed, assume first that θ is not an order. Then

$$a_1a_2, a_2a_3, \ldots, a_{n-1}a_n, a_na_1 \in X$$

for some $n \geq 1$, and $a_1, \ldots, a_n \in A$. If n is even, then setting $u = a_1$, $v = a_2 \cdots a_n$, one has $uv, vu \in X^*$ and $u \notin X^*$. If n is odd, then $(a_1a_2 \cdots a_n)^2 \in X^*$ but not $a_1a_2 \cdots a_n$. Thus X is not circular.

Assume conversely that θ is an order. Then A can be ordered in such a way that $A = \{a_1, a_2, \ldots, a_k\}$ and $a_i\theta a_j \Rightarrow i < j$. Then $X \subset \{a_ia_j \mid i < j\}$, and in view of Example 2.10, the set X is a circular code.

This statement shows that codes like $\{ab, bc, ca\}$ are not circular codes, despite the fact that they are composed of representatives of primitive conjugacy classes of words of the same length.

Not only are the codes $X \subset A^m$ in Corollary 3.7 circular, but they also are uniformly synchronous by Theorem 2.6. We may want to determine the synchronization delay of these codes. More precisely, we may look for the minimum delay which is realizable. The following result shows that for odd integers m, delay 1 is realizable.

THEOREM 3.8 *For any alphabet A with k letters and for any odd integer $m \geq 1$, there exists a comma-free code $X \subset A^m$ such that*

$$\mathrm{Card}(X) = l_m(k).$$

It follows from Example 3.2 that a circular code $X \subset A^2$ having $l_2(k)$ elements has the form $X = \{a_i a_j \mid i < j\}$ for some numbering of the alphabet. If k is even, then according to Example 2.10, the code X has synchronization delay $k/2$. Consequently, a result like Theorem 3.8 does not hold for even integers m.

To prove Theorem 3.8, we construct a Hall sequence $(x_i)_{i \geq 1}$ and the sequence $(X_i)_{i \geq 1}$ of associated codes by setting

$$X_1 = A, \qquad X_{i+1} = x_i^*(X_i - x_i), \qquad i \geq 1, \tag{3.15}$$

where x_i is an element of X_i of minimal *odd* length. By construction, $(x_i)_{i \geq 1}$ is indeed a Hall sequence. Set

$$U = \bigcup_{i \geq 1} X_i, \qquad Y = U \cap (A^2)^*, \qquad Z = U \cap A(A^2)^*.$$

Thus Y is the set of words of even length in U, and

$$Z = \{x_i \mid i \geq 1\}.$$

For any word $u \in U$, we define

$$v(u) = \min\{i \in \mathbb{N} \mid u \in X_i\} - 1,$$
$$\delta(u) = \sup\{i \in \mathbb{N} \mid u \in X_i\}.$$

Thus $v(u)$ denotes the last time before u appears in some X_i and $\delta(u)$ is the last time u appears in a X_i. Observe that $Y = \{u \in U \mid \delta(u) = +\infty\}$. Next, note that $\delta(x_i) = i$, and if $v(u) = q$ for some $u \in U - A$, then $u \in X_{1+q}$ and $u \notin X_q$. Consequently $u = x_q v$ for some $v \in X_{q+1}$. Further, for all $u \in U$ and $n \geq 1$, we have

$$v(u) \leq n < \delta(u) \quad \Rightarrow \quad x_n u \in U. \tag{3.16}$$

We shall prove by a series of lemmas that for any odd integer m, the code $Z \cap A^m$ satisfies the conclusion of Theorem 3.8.

LEMMA 3.9 *For all odd integers m, we have*

$$\mathrm{Card}(Z \cap A^m) = l_m(k).$$

Proof Let n be the smallest integer such that $|x_n| = m$. Then by construction of the Hall sequence (x_i), we have

$$Z \cap A^m = \{x_n, x_{n+1}, \ldots, x_{n+p}\}$$

for some integer p. Then $Z \cap A^m = X_n \cap A^m$, since for all $k \geq 1$, words in X_{n+k} which are not in X_n have length strictly greater than $|x_n|$. Next, by the definition of n, we have $m > |x_{n-1}|$. According to Proposition 3.5(3), we have $L_m(X_n) = L_m(A)$.

By Proposition 3.3, $L_m(A) = l_m(k)$, and $L_m(X_n) = l_n(\alpha)$, where α is the length distribution of X_n. By Proposition 3.4(3), $l_m(\alpha) = \mathrm{Card}(X_n \cap A^m)$, because $\alpha_i = 0$ for all odd integers $i \leq m - 2$. □

LEMMA 3.10 *Each word $w \in A^*$ admits a unique factorization*

$$w = yz_1z_2 \cdots z_n \tag{3.17}$$

with $y \in Y^*$, $z_1 \in Z$, $n \geq 0$, and

$$\delta(z_1) \geq \delta(z_2) \geq \cdots \geq \delta(z_n)$$

Proof First we show that for $n \geq 1$

$$\underline{X}_n^* = \underline{X}_{n+1}^* \underline{x}_n^*.$$

Indeed, by definition $X_{n+1} = x_n^*(X_n - x_n)$. The product of x_n^* with $X_n - x_n$ is unambiguous since X_n is a code. Thus one has in terms of formal power series

$$\underline{X}_{n+1} = \underline{x}_n^*(\underline{X}_n - \underline{x}_n). \tag{3.18}$$

Consequently, $\underline{X}_{n+1} = x_n^* \underline{X}_n - \underline{x}_n^+$, and

$$\underline{X}_{n+1} - 1 = x_n^* \underline{X}_n - \underline{x}_n^* = \underline{x}_n^*(X_n - 1).$$

Formula (3.18) follows by inversion.

By successive substitutions in (3.18), starting with $A^* = X_1^*$, one gets for all $n \geq 1$

$$\underline{A}^* = \underline{X}_{n+1}^* x_n^* x_{n-1}^* \cdots x_1^* \tag{3.19}$$

Now let $w \in A^*$ and set $p = |w|$. Let n be an integer such that X_{n+1} contains no word of odd length $\leq p$.

By (3.19) there exists a factorization of w as

$$w = yz_1z_2 \cdots z_k$$

with $\delta(z_1) \geq \delta(z_2) \geq \cdots \geq \delta(z_k)$, $z_i \in Z$ and $y \in X_{n+1}^*$. Since $|y| \leq p$, the choice of n implies that y is a product of words in X_{n+1} of even length. Consequently $y \in Y^*$. This proves the existence of one factorization (3.17). Assume that there is second factorization of the same type, say,

$$w = y'z'_1 z'_2 \cdots z'_k.$$

Let m be an integer greater than $\delta(z_1)$ and $\delta(z'_1)$, and large enough to ensure $y, y' \in X^*_{m+1}$. Such a choice is possible since all even words of some code X_l are also in the codes $X_{l'}$ for $l' \geq l$. Then according to (3.19), both factorizations of w are the same. □

Now, we characterize successively the form of the factorization (3.17), for words which are left factors and for words which are right factors of words in U.

LEMMA 3.11 *Each proper left factor w of a word in U admits a factorization (3.17) with $y = 1$.*

Proof Each of the codes X_n is a maximal prefix code. This follows by iterated application of Proposition II.4.10. Consequently for $n \geq 0$,

$$\underline{A}^* = \underline{X}^*_{n+1} \underline{P}_{n+1},$$

where $P_{n+1} = X_{n+1}A^-$ is the set of proper left factors of words of X_{n+1}. Comparing this equation with (3.19), we get

$$\underline{P}_{n+1} = \underline{x}^*_n \underline{x}^*_{n-1} \cdots \underline{x}^*_1. \tag{3.20}$$

Let now w be a proper left factor of some word u in U. Then $u \in X_{n+1}$ for some $n \geq 0$ and consequently $w \in P_{n+1}$. By Eq. (3.20), w admits a factorization of the desired form. □

LEMMA 3.12 *For all $n, p \geq 1$, we have $x_n x_{n+p} \in Y^*$. Further for $z \in Z$ and $y \in Y$, we have $zy \in Y^*Z$.*

Proof The first formula is shown by induction on p. For $p = 1$, we have $\nu(x_{n+1}) \leq n$ since $x_{n+1} \in X_{n+1}$. Thus according to formula (3.16), we have $x_n x_{n+1} \in U$. Since $x_n x_{n+1}$ has even length, $x_n x_{n+1} \in Y$.

Assume that the property holds up to $p - 1$, and set $q = \nu(x_{n+p})$. We distinguish two cases. First assume $q \leq n$. Then by (3.16), with x_{n+p} playing the role of u, we have $x_n x_{n+p} \in U$. This word has even length. Thus $x_n x_{n+p} \in Y$.

Next suppose that $n < q$. Then $x_{n+p} \in U - A$. Consequently $x_{n+p} = x_q u$ for some $u \in U$. Since $q < n + p\ (= \delta(x_{n+p}))$, we have $x_n x_q \in Y^*$ by the induction hypothesis. Next u has even length (because $|x_n|, |x_q|$ are both odd). Thus $u \in Y$, whence $x_n x_{n+p} \in Y^*$.

Let us prove the second formula. Set $n = \delta(z)$ and $q = \nu(y)$. Then $z = x_n$ and $y = x_q x_t$ for some t. If $n < q$, then $x_n x_q \in Y^*$ by the preceding argument, and consequently $zy \in Y^*Z$. On the contrary, assume $q < n$. Then by (3.16), $x_n x_q x_t = x_n y \in U$. Since it has odd length this word is in Z. □

LEMMA 3.13 *Any right factor w of a word in U admits a factorization* (3.17) *with $n = 0$ or $n = 1$.*

Proof Given a word $u \in U$, we prove that all its right factors are in $Y^*Z \cup Y^*$, by induction on $|u|$. The case $|u| = 1$ is clear, and clearly it suffices to prove the claim for proper right factors of words in U.

Assume $|u| \geq 2$. Set $n = \nu(u)$. Since $u \in U - A$, we have $u = x_n u'$ for some $u' \in U$.

Let w be a proper right factor of u. If w is a right factor of u', then by the induction hypothesis, w is in $Y^*Z \cup Y^*$. Thus we assume that $w = w'u'$, with w' a proper right factor of x_n. By induction, w' is in $Y^*Z \cup Y^*$. If $w' \in Y^*$, then $w'u' \in Y^*(Y \cup Z)$ and the claim is proved. Thus it remains the case where $w' \in Y^*Z$. In this case, set $w' = yx_k$ with $y \in Y^*$, $k \geq 1$. Observe that $k \leq n$ since $|x_k| \leq |w'| \leq |x_n|$ (see Fig. 7.6).

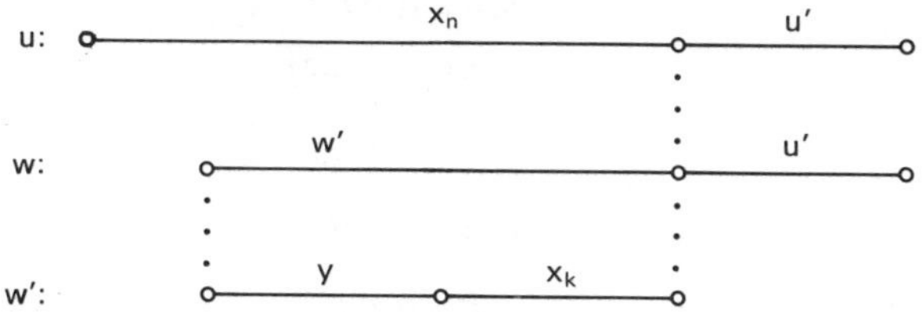

Fig. 7.6

We now distinguish two cases: First, assume $u' \in Y$. Then by Lemma 3.12, $x_k u' \in Y^*Z$. Consequently, $w = yx_k u' \in Y^*Z$. Second, suppose that $u' \in Z$. Then $u' = x_m$ for some m. We have $x_m \in X_{n+1}$, implying that $m > n$. Since $k \leq n$, we have $k < m$ and by Lemma 3.12, $x_k x_m \in Y^*$. Thus $w = yx_k x_m \in Y^*$. This concludes the proof. □

Proof of Theorem 3.8 Let m be an odd integer and let $X = Z \cap A^m$. Let x, x', $x'' \in X$. Assume that for some $u, v \in A^+$,

$$xx' = ux''v \tag{3.21}$$

Then for some $w, t \in A^+$, we have $x = uw$, $x'' = wt$, $x' = tv$. Since x'' has odd length, one of the words w and t must have even length. Assume that the length of w is even (see Fig. 7.7). Since w is a proper left factor of $x'' \in Z$, we have by Lemma 3.11, a factorization $w = z_1 z_2 \cdots z_n$ with $z_1, z_2, \ldots, z_n \in Z$ and $\delta(z_1) \geq \cdots \geq \delta(z_n)$. On the other hand, the word w is a right factor of $x \in Z$, and according to Lemma 3.13, we have $w \in Y^*Z \cup Y^*$. Since w has even length, $w \in Y^*$. Thus $n = 0$ and $w = 1$, a contradiction. □

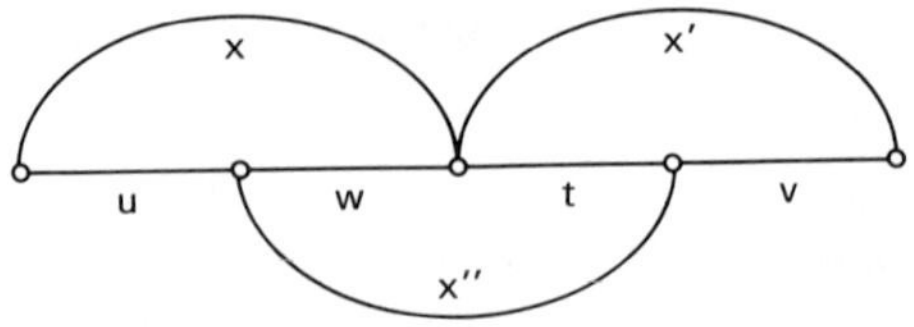

Fig. 7.7

EXAMPLE 3.3 Let $A = \{a, b\}$. A sequence $(X_n)_{n \geq 1}$ satisfying the conditions of the construction given above is

$$
\begin{aligned}
X_1 &= \{a,\ b\},\\
X_2 &= \{b,\ ab,\ a^2b,\ a^3b, a^4b, \ldots\},\\
X_3 &= \{ab, a^2b, a^3b,\ a^4b, \ldots\\
&\qquad bab, ba^2b, ba^3b, \ldots\\
&\qquad\quad b^2ab, b^2a^2b, \ldots\\
&\qquad\qquad b^3ab, \ldots\},\\
X_4 &= \{ab, bab, a^3b,\ a^4b, \ldots\\
&\qquad ba^2b, ba^3b, \ldots\\
&\qquad b^2ab, b^2a^2b, \ldots\\
&\qquad\quad b^3ab, \ldots\\
&\qquad\quad a^2bab, \ldots\},\\
X_5 &= \{ab,\qquad a^3b,\ a^4b, \ldots\\
&\qquad ba^2b, ba^3b, \ldots\\
&\qquad b^2ab, b^2a^2b, \ldots\\
&\qquad\quad b^3ab, \ldots\\
&\qquad\quad a^2bab, \ldots\\
&\qquad\quad babab, \ldots\}.
\end{aligned}
$$

We have represented only words of length at most five. Words of the same length are written in a column. Taking the words of length five in X_5, we obtain all words of length five in the code Z. Thus the following is a comma-free code $X \subset A^5$:

$$X = \{a^4b, ba^3b, b^2a^2b, b^3ab, a^2bab, babab\}.$$

It has $\mathrm{Card}(X) = l_2(5) = 6$ elements. The words of length three in X_3 give the comma-free code of Example 2.13.

4. FACTORIZATIONS OF FREE MONOIDS

Several times in the previous sections, we have used special cases of the notion of factorization which will be defined here. We shall see in this section that these factorizations are closely related to circular codes.

Let I be a totally ordered set and let $(X_i)_{i \in I}$ be a family of subsets of A^+ indexed by I. An *ordered factorization* of a word $w \in A^*$ is a factorization

$$w = x_1 x_2 \cdots x_n, \tag{4.1}$$

with $n \geq 0$, $x_i \in X_{j_i}$ such that $j_1 \geq j_2 \geq \cdots j_n$.

A family $(X_i)_{i \in I}$ is a *factorization* of the free monoid A^* if each word $w \in A^*$ has exactly one ordered factorization.

If $(X_i)_{i \in I}$ is a factorization, then each X_i is a code, since otherwise the unique factorization would not hold for words in X_i^*. We shall see later (Theorem 4.1) that each X_i is in fact a circular code.

Let us give a formulation in formal power series. Consider a family $(\sigma_i)_{i \in I}$ of formal power series over an alphabet A with coefficients in a semiring K, indexed by a totally ordered set I. Assume furthermore that the family $(\sigma_i)_{i \in I}$ is locally finite. Let $J = \{j_1, j_2, \ldots, j_n\}$ be a finite subset of I, with $j_1 \geq j_2 \geq \cdots \geq j_n$. Set

$$\tau_J = \sigma_{j_1} \sigma_{j_2} \cdots \sigma_{j_n}.$$

Then for all $w \in A^*$,

$$(\tau_J, w) = \sum_{x_1 x_2 \cdots x_n = w} (\sigma_{j_1}, x_1)(\sigma_{j_2}, x_2) \cdots (\sigma_{j_n}, x_n). \tag{4.2}$$

Let $\mathscr{A}$ be the set of all finite subsets of I. Then the family $(\tau_J)_{J \in \mathscr{A}}$ is locally finite. Indeed, for each word $w \in A^*$, the set $F(w)$ of factors of w is finite. For each $x \in F(w)$, the set I_x of indices $i \in I$ such that $(\sigma_i, x) \neq 0$ is finite. From (4.2), it follows that if $(\tau_J, w) \neq 0$, then $J \subset \bigcup_{x \in F(w)} I_x$. Consequently there are only finitely many sets J such that $(\tau_J, w) \neq 0$.

These considerations allow us to define the product

$$\sigma = \prod_{i \in I} (1 + \sigma_i)$$

by the formula

$$\sigma = \sum_{J \in \mathscr{A}} \tau_J.$$

If I is finite, we obtain the usual notion of a product of a sequence of formal power series, and the latter expression is just the expanded form obtained by distributivity.

Consider a family $(X_i)_{i \in I}$ of subsets of A^+ indexed by a totally ordered set I. If the family is a factorization of A^*, then

$$\underline{A}^* = \prod_{i \in I} \underline{X}_i^*. \tag{4.3}$$

Conversely, if the sets X_i are codes and if the semigroups X_i^+ are pairwise disjoint, then the product $\prod_{i \in I} \underline{X}_i^*$ is defined and (4.3) implies that the family $(X_i)_{i \in I}$ is a factorization of A^*.

EXAMPLE 4.1 Formula (3.19) states that the family $(X_{n+1}, x_n, \ldots, x_1)$ is a factorization of A^* for all $n \geq 1$. Lemma 3.10 says that the family $(Y, \ldots, x_n, x_{n-1}, \ldots, x_1)$ is a factorization of A^*.

The main result of this section is the following theorem.

THEOREM 4.1 *Let $(X_i)_{i \in I}$ be a family of subsets of A^+ indexed by a totally ordered set I. Two of the three following conditions imply the third.*

(i) *Each word $w \in A^*$ has at least one ordered factorization.*
(ii) *Each word $w \in A^*$ has at most one ordered factorization.*
(iii) *Each of the X_i $(i \in I)$ is a circular code and each conjugacy class of nonempty words meets exactly one among the submonoids X_i^*.*

The proof is based on an enumeration technique. Before we give the proof, we need some results concerning the logarithm of a formal power series in commuting or noncommuting variables.

We shall consider a slightly more general situation, namely, the formal power series defined over monoids which are direct products of a finite number of free monoids.

Let M be a monoid which is a direct product of finitely many free monoids. The set

$$S = \mathbb{Q}^M$$

of functions from M into the field $\mathbb{Q}$ of rational numbers is equipped with the structure of an algebra as it was done for formal series over a free monoid. In particular if $\sigma, \tau \in S$, the product $\sigma\tau$ given by

$$(\sigma\tau, m) = \sum_{uv=m} (\sigma, u)(\tau, v)$$

is well defined since the set of pairs (u, v) with $uv = m$ is finite. As in the case of formal power series over a free monoid, a family $(\sigma_i)_{i \in I}$ of elements of S is locally finite if for all $m \in M$, the set $\{i \in I \mid (\sigma_i, m) \neq 0\}$ is finite. Define

$$S^{(1)} = \{\sigma \in S \mid (\sigma, 1) = 0\}.$$

For $\sigma \in S^{(1)}$, the family $(\sigma^n)_{n \geq 0}$ of powers of σ is locally finite. Indeed, for each $m \in M$, $(\sigma^n, m) = 0$ for all n greater than the sum of the lengths of the components of m. This allows us to define for all $\sigma \in S^{(1)}$.

$$\log(1 + \sigma) = \sigma - \sigma^2/2 + \sigma^3/3 - \cdots + (-1)^{n+1}\sigma^n/n + \cdots \tag{4.4}$$

$$\exp(\sigma) = 1 + \sigma + \frac{\sigma^2}{2!} + \cdots + \frac{\sigma^n}{n!} + \cdots \tag{4.5}$$

Let M and N be monoids which are finite direct products of free monoids. Let $S = \mathbb{Q}^M$ and $T = \mathbb{Q}^N$. A morphism

$$\alpha\colon \quad M \to T$$

from the monoid M into the multiplicative monoid T is called *continuous* iff the family $(\alpha(m))_{m \in M}$ is locally finite. In this case, the morphism α can be extended into a morphism, still denoted by α, from the algebra S into the algebra T by the formula

$$\alpha(\sigma) = \sum_{m \in M} (\sigma, m)\alpha(m). \tag{4.6}$$

This sum is well defined since the family $(\alpha(m))_{m \in M}$ is locally finite. The extended morphism α is also called a continuous morphism from S into T. For any locally finite family $(\sigma_i)_{i \in I}$ of elements of S, the family $(\alpha(\sigma_i))_{i \in I}$ also is locally finite and

$$\sum_{i \in I} \alpha(\sigma_i) = \alpha\left(\sum_{i \in I} \sigma_i\right). \tag{4.7}$$

According to formula 4.7, a continuous morphism $\alpha\colon S \to T$ is entirely determined by its definition on M, thus on a set X of generators for M. Furthermore, α is continuous iff $\alpha(X - \{1\}) \subset T^{(1)}$ and the family $(\alpha(x))_{x \in X}$ is locally finite. This is due to the fact that each $m \in M$ has only finitely many factorizations $m = x_1 x_2 \cdots x_k$ with $x_1, x_2, \ldots, x_k \in X - 1$.

It follows from (4.6) that if $\sigma \in S^{(1)}$, then $\alpha(\sigma) \in T^{(1)}$. From (4.7), we obtain

$$\log(1 + \alpha(\sigma)) = \alpha(\log(1 + \sigma)), \tag{4.8}$$

$$\exp(\alpha(\sigma)) = \alpha(\exp(\sigma)). \tag{4.9}$$

According to classical results from elementary analysis, we have the following formulas in the algebra $\mathbb{Q}[[s]]$ of formal power series in one variable s:

$$\exp(\log(1 + s)) = 1 + s, \qquad \log(\exp(s)) = s. \tag{4.10}$$

Furthermore, in the algebra $\mathbb{Q}[[s,t]]$ of formal power series in two commuting variables s, t, we have

$$\exp(s + t) = \exp(s)\exp(t), \qquad \log((1 + s)(1 + t)) = \log(1 + s) + \log(1 + t). \tag{4.11}$$

Let M be a monoid which is a finite direct product of free monoids and let $S = \mathbb{Q}^M$. Let $\sigma \in S^{(1)}$ and let α be the continuous morphism from the algebra $\mathbb{Q}[[s]]$ into S defined by $\alpha(s) = \sigma$. Then by formulas (4.8)–(4.10), we have

$$\exp(\log(1 + \sigma)) = 1 + \sigma, \qquad \log(\exp(\sigma)) = \sigma \tag{4.12}$$

showing that exp and log are inverse bijections of each other from the set $S^{(1)}$ onto the set

$$1 + S^{(1)} = \{1 + \tau \mid \tau \in S^{(1)}\}.$$

Now consider two series $\sigma, \tau \in S^{(1)}$ which commute, i.e., such that $\sigma\tau = \tau\sigma$. Since the submonoid of S generated by σ and τ is commutative, the function α from $s^* \times t^*$ into S defined by $\alpha(s^p t^q) = \sigma^p \tau^q$ is a continuous morphism from $\mathbb{Q}[[s,t]]$ into S and by (4.11),

$$\begin{aligned} \exp(\sigma + \tau) &= \exp(\sigma)\exp(\tau), \\ \log((1 + \sigma)(1 + \tau)) &= \log(1 + \sigma) + \log(1 + \tau). \end{aligned} \tag{4.13}$$

These formulas do not hold when σ and τ do not commute. We shall give a property of the difference of the two sides of (4.13) in the general case.

A series $\sigma \in \mathbb{Q}^{A^*} = \mathbb{Q}\langle\langle A \rangle\rangle$ is called *cyclically null* if for each conjugacy class $C \subset A^*$ one has

$$(\sigma, \underline{C}) = \sum_{w \in C} (\sigma, w) = 0.$$

Clearly any sum of cyclically null series still is cyclically null.

PROPOSITION 4.2 *Let A be an alphabet and let $S = \mathbb{Q}\langle\langle A \rangle\rangle$. Let $\alpha: S \to S$ be a continuous morphism. For each cyclically null series $\sigma \in S$, the series $\alpha(\sigma)$ is cyclically null.*

Proof Let $T \subset A^*$ be a set of representatives of the conjugacy classes of A^*. Denote by $C(t)$ the conjugacy class of $t \in T$. Let

$$\tau = \sum_{t \in T} \left(\sum_{w \in C(t)} (\sigma, w)(w - t) \right)$$

The family of polynomials $(\sum_{w \in C(t)} (\sigma, w)(w - t))_{t \in T}$ is locally finite. Thus the sum is well defined. Next

$$\tau = \sum_{t \in T} \sum_{w \in C(t)} (\sigma, w)w - \sum_{t \in T} \sum_{w \in C(t)} (\sigma, w)t$$

$$= \sigma - \sum_{t \in T} (\sigma, \underline{C}(t))t.$$

Since σ is cyclically null, the second series vanishes and consequently $\tau = \sigma$. It follows that

$$\alpha(\sigma) = \sum_{t \in T} \left(\sum_{w \in C(t)} (\sigma, w)(\alpha(w) - \alpha(t) \right).$$

In order to prove the claim, it suffices to show that each series $\alpha(w) - \alpha(t)$ for $w \in C(t)$ is cyclically null. For this, consider $w \in C(t)$. Then $t = uv$, $w = vu$ for some $u, v \in A^*$. Setting $\mu = \alpha(u)$, $\nu = \alpha(v)$, one has

$$\alpha(w) - \alpha(t) = \nu\mu - \mu\nu.$$

Next

$$\nu\mu = \sum_{x, y \in A^*} (\nu, x)(\mu, y)xy.$$

Thus,

$$\nu\mu - \mu\nu = \sum_{x, y \in A^+} (\nu, x)(\mu, y)(xy - yx).$$

Since each polynomial $xy - yx$ clearly is cyclically null, the series $\nu\mu - \mu\nu$ and hence $\alpha(\sigma)$ is cyclically null. □

PROPOSITION 4.3 *Let $A = \{a, b\}$, and let C be a conjugacy class of A^*. Then*

$$(\log((1 + a)(1 + b)), \underline{C}) = (\log(1 + a), \underline{C}) + \log(1 + b), \underline{C}) \qquad (4.14)$$

In other words, the series $\log((1 + a)(1 + b)) - \log(1 + a) - \log(1 + b)$ *is cyclically null.*

Proof One has $(1 + a)(1 + b) = 1 + a + b + ab$ and

$$\log((1 + a)(1 + b)) = \sum_{m \geq 1} \frac{(-1)^{m+1}}{m}(a + b + ab)^m.$$

Let $w \in A^n$, and let d be the number of times ab occurs as a factor in w. Let us verify that

$$((a + b + ab)^m, w) = \binom{d}{n - m}. \qquad (4.15)$$

Indeed, $((a + b + ab)^m, w)$ is the number of factorizations

$$w = x_1 x_2 \cdots x_m$$

of w in m words, with $x_i \in \{a, b, ab\}$. Since w has length n and the x_i's have length 1 or 2, there are exactly $n - m$ x_i's which are equal to ab. Each factorization of w thus corresponds to a choice of $n - m$ factors of w equal to ab among the d occurrences of ab. Thus there are exactly $\binom{d}{n-m}$ factorizations. This proves (4.15).

Now let C be a conjugacy class, let n be the length of the words in C and let p be their exponent. Then $\text{Card}(C) = n/p$. If $C \subset a^*$, then $C = \{a^n\}$. Then formula 4.15 shows that $((a + b + ab)^m, a^n)$ equals 1 or 0 according to $n = m$ or not. Thus both sides of (4.14) in this case are equal to $(-1)^n/n$. The same holds if $C \subset b^*$. Thus we may assume that C is not contained in $a^* \cup b^*$. Then the right-hand side of (4.14) equals 0. Consider the left-hand side. Since each word in C contains at least one a, there is a word w in C whose first letter is a. Let d be the number of occurrences of ab as a factor in w. Among the n/p conjugates of w, there are d/p which start with the letter b and end with the letter a. Indeed, set $w = v^p$. Then the word v has d/p occurrences of the factor ab. Each of the d/p conjugates of w in bA^*a is obtained by "cutting" v in the middle of one occurrence of ab. Each of these d/p conjugates has only $d - 1$ occurrences of ab as a factor. The $(n - d)/p$ other conjugates of w have all d occurrences of the factor ab.

According to formula 4.15, we have for each conjugate u of w,

$$((a + b + ab)^m, u) = \begin{cases} \dbinom{d-1}{n-m} & \text{if } u \in bA^*a, \\ \dbinom{d}{n-m} & \text{otherwise.} \end{cases}$$

Summation over the elements of C gives

$$((a + b + ab)^m, \underline{C}) = \frac{d}{p}\binom{d-1}{n-m} + \frac{n-d}{p}\binom{d}{n-m}.$$

Since $\binom{d-1}{n-m} = ((d - n + m)/d)\binom{d}{n-m}$, we obtain $((a + b + ab)^m, \underline{C}) = (m/p)\binom{d}{n-m}$. Consequently

$$(\log(1 + a)(1 + b), \underline{C}) = \frac{1}{p}\sum_{m \geq 1}(-1)^{m+1}\binom{d}{n-m} \tag{4.16}$$

Since $n > d$ and $d \neq 0$, this alternating sum of binomial coefficients equals 0. □

The following proposition is an extension of Proposition 4.3.

PROPOSITION 4.4 *Let $(\sigma_i)_{i \in I}$ be a locally finite family of elements of $\mathbb{Q}\langle\langle A \rangle\rangle$ indexed by a totally ordered set I, such that $(\sigma_i, 1) = 0$ for all $i \in I$. The* *series*

$$\log \prod_{i \in I} (1 + \sigma_i)) - \sum_{i \in I} \log(1 + \sigma_i) \tag{4.17}$$

is cyclically null.

Proof Set $S = \mathbb{Q}^{A^*} = \mathbb{Q}\langle\langle A \rangle\rangle$ and $S^{(1)} = \{\sigma \in S \mid (\sigma, 1) = 0\}$. Let $\sigma, \tau \in S^{(1)}$. The series

$$\delta = \log((1 + \sigma)(1 + \tau)) - \log(1 + \sigma) - \log(1 + \tau)$$

is cyclically null. Indeed, either σ and τ commute and δ is null by (4.13), or the alphabet A has at least two letters a, b. Consider a continuous morphism α such that $\alpha(a) = \sigma$, $\alpha(b) = \tau$. The series

$$d = (\log((1 + a)(1 + b)) - \log(1 + a) - \log(1 + b)$$

is cyclically null by Proposition 4.3. Since $\delta = \alpha(d)$, Proposition 4.2 shows that δ is cyclically null.

Now let $\tau_1, \tau_2, \ldots, \tau_n \in 1 + S^{(1)}$. Arguing by induction, assume that

$$\varepsilon = \log(\tau_n \cdots \tau_2) - \sum_{i=2}^{n} \log \tau_i$$

is cyclically null. In view of the preceding discussion, the series

$$\varepsilon' = \log(\tau_n \cdots \tau_2 \tau_1) - \log(\tau_n \cdots \tau_2) - \log \tau_1$$

is cyclically null. Consequently

$$\varepsilon + \varepsilon' = \log(\tau_n \cdots \tau_1) - \sum_{i=1}^{n} \log \tau_i$$

is cyclically null. This proves (4.17) for finite sets I.

For the general case, we consider a fixed conjugacy class C. Let n be the length of words in C and let $B = \mathrm{alph}(C)$. Then B is finite and $C \subset B^n$.

Define an equivalence relation on S by

$$\sigma \sim \tau \qquad \text{iff} \quad (\sigma, w) = (\tau, w) \quad \text{for all } w \in B^{[n]}.$$

(Recall that $B^{[n]} = \{w \in B^* \mid |w| \leq n\}$.) Observe first that $\sigma \sim \tau$ implies $\sigma^k \sim \tau^k$ for all $k \geq 1$. Consequently $\sigma \sim \tau$ and $\sigma, \tau \in S^{(1)}$ imply $\log(1 + \sigma) \sim \log(1 + \tau)$.

Consider the family $(\sigma_i)_{i \in I}$ of the statement. Let

$$I_0 = \{i \in I \mid \sigma_i \sim 0\}, \qquad I' = I - I_0.$$

Then I' is finite. Indeed, for each $w \in B^{[n]}$ there are only finitely many indices i such that $(\sigma_i, w) \neq 0$. Since B is finite, the set $B^{[n]}$ is finite and therefore I' is finite.

Next observe that

$$\prod_{i\in I}(1+\sigma_i) \sim \prod_{i\in I'}(1+\sigma_i), \tag{4.18}$$

since in view of (4.2), we have $(\tau_J, w) = 0$ for $w \in B^{[n]}$ except when $J \subset I'$. It follows from (4.18) that

$$\log\left(\prod_{i\in I}(1+\sigma_i)\right) \sim \log\left(\prod_{i\in I'}(1+\sigma_i)\right).$$

Consequently

$$\left(\log\left(\prod_{i\in I}(1+\sigma_i)\right), \underline{C}\right) = \left(\log\left(\prod_{i\in I'}(1+\sigma_i)\right), \underline{C}\right).$$

Next, since $\sigma_i \sim 0$ for $i \in I_0$, we have $\log(1+\sigma_i) \sim 0$ for $i \in I_0$. Thus

$$\left(\sum_{i\in I}\log(1+\sigma_i), \underline{C}\right) = \left(\sum_{i\in I'}\log(1+\sigma_i), \underline{C}\right).$$

From the finite case, one obtains

$$\left(\left(\log\prod_{i\in I'}(1+\sigma_i)\right), \underline{C}\right) = \left(\left(\sum_{i\in I'}\log(1+\sigma_i)\right), \underline{C}\right).$$

Putting all this together, we obtain

$$\left(\log\prod_{i\in I}(1+\sigma_i), \underline{C}\right) = \left(\sum_{i\in I'}\log(1+\sigma_i), \underline{C}\right) = \left(\sum_{i\in I}\log(1+\sigma_i), \underline{C}\right).$$

Thus the proof is complete. □

To prove Theorem 4.1, we need a final lemma which is a reformulation of Propositions 1.5 and 1.6.

PROPOSITION 4.5 *Let $X \subset A^+$ be a code.*

1. *For each conjugacy class C meeting X^*, we have*

$$(\log \underline{X}^*, \underline{C}) \geq (\log \underline{A}^*, \underline{C}),$$

and the equality holds if X is a circular code.

2. *Conversely if $(\log \underline{X}^*, \underline{C}) = (\log \underline{A}^*, \underline{C})$ for all conjugacy classes that meet* X*, *then* X *is a circular code.*

Proof We have $\underline{X}^* = (1-\underline{X})^{-1}$. Thus $\log(\underline{X}^*(1-\underline{X})) = 0$. Since the series $\underline{X}^*$ and $1-\underline{X}$ commute, we have $0 = \log \underline{X}^* + \log(1-\underline{X})$, showing that $\log \underline{X}^* = -\log(1-\underline{X})$. Thus

$$\log \underline{X}^* = \sum_{m\geq 1}\frac{1}{m}\underline{X}^m.$$

In particular, if $C \subset A^m$ is a conjugacy class, then

$$(\log \underline{X}^*, \underline{C}) = \sum_{m \geq 1} \frac{1}{m} \operatorname{Card}(X^m \cap C).$$

For $X = A$, the formula becomes

$$(\log \underline{A}^*, \underline{C}) = \frac{1}{n} \operatorname{Card}(C).$$

With these computations, the proposition is a direct consequence of Propositions 1.4 and 1.5. □

Proof of Theorem 4.1 Assume first that conditions (i) and (ii) are satisfied, i.e., that the family $(X)_{i \in I}$ is a factorization of A^*. Then the sets X_i are codes and by formula 4.3, we have

$$\underline{A}^* = \prod_{i \in I} \underline{X}_i^*. \tag{4.19}$$

Taking the logarithm on both sides, we obtain

$$\log \underline{A}^* = \log\left(\prod_{i \in I} \underline{X}_i^* \right). \tag{4.20}$$

By Proposition 4.4, the series

$$\delta = \log \underline{A}^* - \sum_{i \in I} \log \underline{X}_i^* \tag{4.21}$$

is cyclically null. Thus for each conjugacy class C

$$(\log \underline{A}^*, \underline{C}) = \sum_{i \in I} (\log \underline{X}_i^*, \underline{C}). \tag{4.22}$$

In view of Proposition 4.5, we have for each $i \in I$ and for each C that meets X_i^* the inequality

$$(\log \underline{A}^*, \underline{C}) \leq (\log \underline{X}_i^*, \underline{C}) \tag{4.23}$$

Formulas (4.22) and (4.23) show that for each conjugacy class C, there exists a unique $j \in I$ such that C meets X_j^*. For this index j, we have

$$(\log \underline{A}^*, \underline{C}) = (\log \underline{X}_j^*, \underline{C}). \tag{4.24}$$

Thus if some X_j^* meets a conjugacy class, no other X_i^* $(i \in I - j)$ meets this conjugacy class. Since (4.24) holds, each of the codes X_i is a circular code by Proposition 4.5. This proves condition (iii).

Now assume that condition (iii) holds. Let C be a conjugacy class and let $i \in I$ be the unique index such that X_i^* meets C. Since X_i is circular, (4.24) holds by Proposition 4.5 and furthermore $(\log \underline{X}_j^*, \underline{C}) = 0$ for all $j \neq i$. Summing up all equalities (4.24), we obtain Eq. (4.22). This proves that the series δ defined by (4.21) is cyclically null.

Let α be the canonical morphism from $\mathbb{Q}\langle\langle A\rangle\rangle$ onto the algebra $\mathbb{Q}[[A]]$ of formal power series in commutative variables in A. The set of words in A^* having the same image by α is union of conjugacy classes, since $\alpha(uv) = \alpha(vu)$. Since the series δ is cyclically null, the series $\alpha(\delta)$ is null.

Since α is a continuous morphism, we obtain by applying α to both sides of (4.21)

$$0 = \log \alpha(\underline{A}^*) - \sum_{i \in I} \log \alpha(\underline{X}_i^*)$$

Hence

$$\log \alpha(\underline{A}^*) = \sum_{i \in I} \log \alpha(\underline{X}_i^*) \tag{4.25}$$

Next, condition (iii) ensures that the product $\prod_{i \in I} \underline{X}_i^*$ exists. By Proposition 4.4, the series

$$\log\left(\prod_{i \in I} \underline{X}_i^*\right) - \sum_{i \in I} \log \underline{X}_i^*$$

is cyclically null. Thus its image by α is null, whence

$$\log \alpha\left(\prod \underline{X}_i^*\right) = \sum_{i \in I} \log \alpha(\underline{X}_i^*).$$

This together with (4.25) shows that

$$\log \alpha(\underline{A}^*) = \log \alpha\left(\prod_{i \in I} \underline{X}_i^*\right).$$

Since log is a bijection, this implies

$$\alpha(\underline{A}^*) = \alpha\left(\prod_{i \in I} \underline{X}_i^*\right).$$

This means that $\alpha(\varepsilon) = 0$, where

$$\varepsilon = \underline{A}^* - \prod_{i \in I} \underline{X}_i^*.$$

Observe that condition (i) means that all the coefficients of ε are negative or zero. Condition (ii) says that all coefficients of ε are positive or zero. Thus in both cases, all the coefficients of ε have the same sign. This together with the condition $\alpha(\varepsilon) = 0$ implies that $\varepsilon = 0$. Thus if condition (iii) and either (i) or (ii) hold, then the other one of conditions (i) and (ii) also holds. □

A factorization $(X_i)_{i \in I}$ is called *complete* if each X_i is reduced to a singleton x_i. The following result is a consequence of Theorem 4.1.

COROLLARY 4.6 *Let $(x_i)_{i \in I}$ be a complete factorization of A^*. Then the set*

$X = \{x_i \mid i \in I\}$ is a set of representatives of the primitive conjugacy classes. In particular, for all $n \geq 1$,

$$\mathrm{Card}(X \cap A^n) = l_n(k) \tag{4.26}$$

with $k = \mathrm{Card}(A)$.

Proof According to condition (iii) of Theorem 4.1, each conjugacy class intersects exactly one of the submonoids x_i^*. In view of the same condition, each code $\{x_i\}$ is circular and consequently each word x_i is primitive. This shows that X is a system of representatives of the primitive conjugacy classes. Formula (4.26) is an immediate consequence. □

Now we describe a systematic procedure to obtain a large class of complete factorizations of free monoids. These include the construction used in Section 3.

A *Lazard set* is a totally ordered subset Z of A^+ satisfying the following property:

For each $n \geq 1$, the set $Z \cap A^{[n]} = \{z_1, z_2, \ldots, z_k\}$ with $z_1 < z_2 < \cdots < z_k$ satisfies

$$z_i \in Z_i \quad \text{for} \quad 1 \leq i \leq k, \qquad \text{and} \qquad Z_{k+1} \cap A^{[n]} = \varnothing,$$

where the sets $Z_1, \ldots, Z_{k+1}$ are defined by

$$Z_1 = A, \qquad Z_{i+1} = z_i^*(Z_i - z_i) \qquad (1 \leq i \leq k).$$

(Recall that $A^{[n]} = \{w \in A^* \mid |w| \leq n\}$.)

EXAMPLE 4.2 Let $(x_n)_{n \geq 1}$ be a Hall sequence over A and let $Z = \{x_n \mid n \geq 1\}$ be the subset of A^+ ordered by the indices. Then Z is a Lazard set.

EXAMPLE 4.3 Let $(x_n)_{n \geq 1}$ be the sequence used in the proof of Theorem 3.7. Recall that we start with $X_1 = A$ and

$$X_{i+1} = x_i^*(X_i - x_i) \qquad i \geq 1,$$

where x_i is a word in X_i of minimal odd length. Denote by Y the set of even words in $\bigcup_{i \geq 1} X_i$.

Now set $Y_1 = Y$ and for $i \geq 1$,

$$Y_{i+1} = y_i^*(Y_i - y_i),$$

where $y_i \in Y_i$ is chosen with minimal length. Let

$$T = \{x_i, y_i \mid i \geq 1\}$$

ordered by

$$x_1 < x_2 < \cdots < x_n < \cdots < y_1 < y_2 < \cdots.$$

The ordered set T is a Lazard set. Indeed, let $n \geq 1$ and

$$T \cap A^{[n]} = \{x_1, x_2, \ldots, x_r, y_1, y_2, \ldots, y_s\}.$$

Set

$$Z_i = X_i, \qquad 1 \leq i \leq r+1,$$
$$Z_{r+i+1} = y_i^*(Z_{r+i} - y_i), \qquad 1 \leq i \leq s.$$

We show by induction on i that

$$Z_{r+i} \cap A^{[n]} = Y_i \cap A^{[n]} \qquad (1 \leq i \leq s+1). \tag{4.27}$$

Indeed, words in $X_{r+1} = Z_{r+1}$ of length at most n all have even length (since the words with odd length are $x_1, x_2, \ldots, x_r$). Thus all these words are in $Y = Y_1$. Conversely, any word of even length $\leq n$ is already in X_{r+1}, since $|x_{r+1}| > n$.

Next, consider $y \in Y_{i+1} \cap A^{[n]}$. Then $y = y_i^p y'$ for some $y' \in Y_i - y_i$. Since $|y'| \leq n$, we have by the induction hypothesis $y' \in Z_{r+i}$, whence $y \in Z_{r+i+1}$. The converse is proved in the same way.

Equation (4.27) shows that $y_i \in Z_{r+i}$ for $1 \leq i \leq s$ and that $Z_{r+s+1} \cap A^{[n]} = \emptyset$. Thus T is a Lazard set.

PROPOSITION 4.7 *Let $Z \subset A^+$ be a Lazard set. Then the family $(z)_{z \in Z}$ is a complete factorization of A^*.*

Proof Let $w \in A^*$ and $n = |w|$. Set $Z \cap A^{[n]} = \{z_1, z_2, \ldots, z_k\}$ with $z_1 < z_2 < \cdots < z_k$. Let $Z_1 = A$ and $Z_{i+1} = z_i^*(Z_i - z_i)$ for $i = 1, 2, \ldots, k$. Then $z_i \in Z_i$ for $i = 1, 2, \ldots, k$ and $Z_{k+1} \cap A^{[n]} = \emptyset$. As in the proof of Lemma 3.10, we have for $1 \leq i \leq k$,

$$\underline{Z}_i^* = \underline{Z}_{i+1}^* z_i^*,$$

whence by successive substitutions

$$\underline{A}^* = \underline{Z}_{k+1}^* z_k^* \cdots z_1^*. \tag{4.28}$$

Thus there is a factorization $w = y z_{i_1} z_{i_2} \cdots z_{i_n}$ with $y \in Z_{k+1}$ and $i_1 \geq i_2 \geq \cdots \geq i_n$. Since $Z_{k+1} \cap A^{[n]} = \emptyset$, we have $y = 1$. This proves the existence of an ordered factorization. Assume there is another factorization, say $w = t_1 t_2 \cdots t_m$, with $t_i \in Z$, $t_1 \geq t_2 \geq \cdots \geq t_m$. Then $t_i \in Z \cap A^{[n]}$ for each i. Thus by (4.28) both factorizations coincide. □

We conclude this section with an additional example of a complete factorization.

Consider a totally ordered alphabet A. Define a relation called *alphabetic ordering* on A^* by setting $u \prec v$ if u is a proper left factor of v, or if $u = ras$,

$v = rbt$, $a < b$ for $a, b \in A$ and $r, s, t \in A^*$. The alphabetic ordering has the property

$$u \prec v \quad \Rightarrow \quad wu \prec wv.$$

By definition, a *Lyndon word* is a primitive word which is minimal in its conjugacy class. In an equivalent way, a word $w \in A^+$ is a Lyndon word iff $w = uv$ with $u, v \in A^+$ implies $w \prec vu$.

Let L denote the set of Lyndon words. We shall show that $(l)_{l \in L}$ is a complete factorization of A^*. For this we establish lemmas which are interesting on their own.

PROPOSITION 4.8 *A word is a Lyndon word iff it is smaller than all its proper nonempty right factors.*

Proof The condition is sufficient. Let $w = uv$, with $u, v \in A^+$. Since $w \prec v$ and $v \prec vu$, we have $w \prec vu$. Consequently $w \in L$.

Conversely, let $w \in L$ and consider a factorization $w = uv$ with $u, v \in A^+$. First, let us show that v is not a left factor of w. Assume the contrary. Then $w = vt$ for some $t \in A^+$. Since $w \in L$, we have $w \prec tv$. But $w = uv$ implies $uv \prec tv$. This in turn implies $u \prec t$ whence, multiplying on the left by v,

$$vu \prec vt = w,$$

a contradiction.

Suppose that $v \prec uv$. Since v is not a left factor of w, this implies that $vu \prec uv$ and $w \notin L$, a contradiction. Thus $uv \prec v$, and the proof is completed. □

PROPOSITION 4.9 *Let l, m be two Lyndon words. If $l \prec m$, then lm is a Lyndon word.*

Proof First we show that $lm \prec m$. If l is a left factor of m, let $m = lm'$. Then $m \prec m'$ by Proposition 4.8. Thus $lm \prec lm' = m$. If l is not a left factor of m, then the inequality $l \prec m$ directly implies $lm \prec m$.

Let v be a nonempty proper right factor of lm. If v is a right factor of m, then by Proposition 4.8, $m \prec v$. Hence $lm \prec m \prec v$. Otherwise $v = v'm$ for some proper nonempty right factor v' of l. Then $l \prec v'$ and consequently $lm \prec v'm$. Thus in all cases $lm \prec v$. By Proposition 4.8, this shows that $lm \in L$. □

THEOREM 4.10 *The family $(l)_{l \in L}$ is a complete factorization of A^*.*

Proof We prove that conditions (i) and (iii) of Theorem 4.1 are satisfied. This is clear for condition (iii) since L is a system of representatives of primitive conjugacy classes.

For condition (i), let $w \in A^+$. Then w has at least one factorization $w = l_1 l_2 \cdots l_n$ with $l_i \in L$. Indeed each letter is already at Lyndon word. Consider a factorization

$$w = l_1 l_2 \cdots l_n$$

into Lyndon words with minimal n. Then this is an ordered factorization. Indeed, otherwise, these would be some index i such that $l_i \prec l_{i+1}$. But then $l = l_i l_{i+1} \in L$ and w would have a factorization into $n-1$ Lyndon words. Thus condition (i) is satisfied. □

It can be seen (Exercises 4.3, 4.4) that the set L is a Lazard set.

5. FINITE FACTORIZATIONS

In this section we consider factorizations $(X_i)_{i \in I}$ with I a finite set. These are families $X_n, X_{n-1}, \ldots, X_1$ of subsets of A^+ such that

$$\underline{A}^* = \underline{X}_n^* \underline{X}_{n-1}^* \cdots \underline{X}_1^*. \tag{5.1}$$

According to Theorem 4.1, each X_i is a circular code and each conjugacy class meets exactly one of the X_i^*. The aim of this section is to refine these properties. We shall see that in some special cases the codes X_i are limited. The question whether all codes appearing in finite factorizations are limited is still open.

We start with the study of *bisections*, that is, factorizations of the form (X, Y). Here X is called *left factor* and Y is called *right factor* of the bisection. Then

$$\underline{A}^* = \underline{X}^* \underline{Y}^*. \tag{5.2}$$

EXAMPLE 5.1 Let $A = \{a, b\}$. The pair (a^*b, a) is a bisection of A^*. More generally, if $A = A_0 \cup A_1$ is a partition of A, the pair $(A_0^* A_1, A_0)$ is a bisection of A^*.

Formula (5.2) can be written as

$$\underline{Y}\underline{X} + \underline{A} = \underline{X} + \underline{Y}. \tag{5.3}$$

Indeed, (5.2) is equivalent to $1 - \underline{A} = (1 - \underline{Y})(1 - \underline{X})$ by taking the inverses. This gives (5.3). Equations (5.2) and (5.3) show that a pair (X, Y) of subsets of A^+ is a bisection iff the following are satisfied:

$$A \subset X \cup Y, \tag{5.4}$$

$$X \cap Y = \varnothing, \tag{5.5}$$

$$YX \subset X \cup Y, \tag{5.6}$$

each $z \in X \cup Y$, $z \notin A$ factorizes uniquely into $z = yx$ with $x \in X$, $y \in Y$. (5.7)

We shall see later (Theorem 5.4) that a subset of these conditions is already enough to ensure that a pair (X, Y) is a bisection.

Before doing that, we show that for a bisection (X, Y) the code X is $(1,0)$-limited and the code Y is $(0,1)$-limited. Recall that a $(1,0)$-limited code is prefix and that by Proposition 2.8 a prefix code X is $(1,0)$-limited iff the set $R = A^* - XA^*$ is a submonoid. Symmetrically, a suffix code Y is $(0,1)$-limited iff the set $S = A^* - A^*Y$ is a submonoid.

PROPOSITION 5.1 *Let X, Y be two subsets of A^+. The following conditions are equivalent*:

(i) *(X, Y) is a bisection of A^*.*
(ii) *X, Y are codes, X is $(1,0)$-limited and $Y^* = A^* - XA^*$.*
(iii) *X, Y are codes, Y is $(0,1)$-limited and $X^* = A^* - A^*Y$.*

Proof (i) $\Rightarrow$ (ii) From $\underline{A}^* = \underline{X}^*\underline{Y}^*$ we obtain by multiplication on the left by $1 - X$ the equation $(1 - \underline{X})\underline{A}^* = \underline{Y}^*$, showing that $\underline{Y}^* = \underline{A}^* - \underline{X}\underline{A}^*$. The number of left factors in X of any word $w \in A^*$ is $(\underline{X}\underline{A}^*, w)$. The equation shows that this number is 0 or 1, according to $w \in Y^*$ or $w \notin Y^*$. This proves that X is a prefix code. This also gives the set relation $Y^* = A^* - XA^*$. Thus $A^* - XA^*$ is a submonoid and by Proposition 2.8, the code X is $(1,0)$-limited.

(ii) $\Rightarrow$ (i) By Theorem II.1.3, we have $\underline{A}^* = \underline{X}^*\underline{R}$ with $R = A^* - XA^*$. Since $R = Y^*$ and Y is a code, we have $\underline{R} = \underline{Y}^*$. Thus $\underline{A}^* = \underline{X}^*\underline{Y}^*$.

Consequently (i) and (ii) are equivalent. The equivalence between (i) and (iii) is shown in the same manner. □

COROLLARY 5.2 *The left factors of bisections are precisely the* $(1,0)$-*limited codes.* □.

Observe that for a bisection (X, Y), either X is maximal prefix or Y is maximal suffix. Indeed, we have $Y^* = A^* - XA^*$. If Y^* contains no right ideal, then XA^* is right dense and consequently X is maximal prefix. Otherwise, Y^* is left dense and thus Y is maximal suffix.

PROPOSITION 5.3 *Let M, N be two submonoids of A^* such that*

$$\underline{A}^* = \underline{M}\underline{N}.$$

Then M and N are free and the pair (X, Y) of their bases is a bisection of A^*.

Proof Let u, v be in A^* such that $uv \in M$. Set $v = mn$ with $m \in M$, $n \in N$. Similarly set $um = m'n'$ for some $m' \in M$, $n' \in N$ (see Fig. 7.8). Then $uv = m'(n'n)$. Since $uv \in M$, unique factorization implies $n = n' = 1$. Thus $v \in M$. This shows that M satisfies condition $C(1,0)$. Thus M is generated by a $(1,0)$-limited code X. Similarly N is generated by a $(0,1)$-limited code Y. Clearly (X, Y) is a factorization. □

EXAMPLE 5.2 Let M and N be two submonoids of A^* such that

$$M \cap N = \{1\}, \qquad M \cup N = A^*.$$

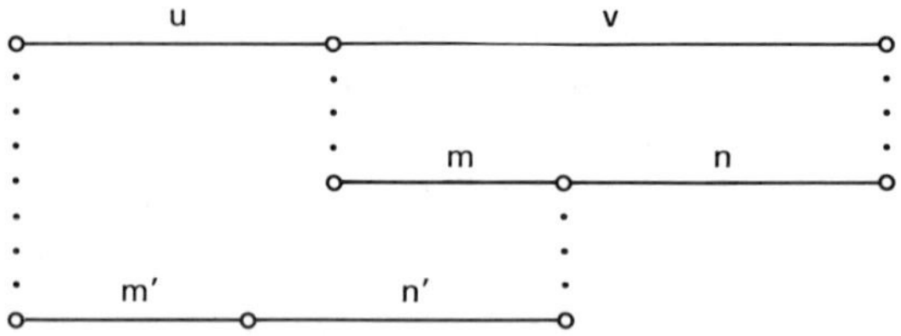

Fig. 7.8 Factorizations.

We shall associate a special bisection of A^* with the pair (M, N). For this, let

$$R = \{r \in A^* \mid r = uv \Rightarrow v \in M\}$$

be the set of words in M having all its right factors in M. Symmetrically, define

$$S = \{s \in A^* \mid s = uv \Rightarrow u \in N\}.$$

The set R is a submonoid of A^* because M is a submonoid. Moreover, R is suffix-closed. Consequently the base of R, say X, is a $(1,0)$-limited code. Similarly S is a free submonoid and its base, say Y, is a $(0,1)$-limited code. We prove that (X, Y) is a bisection. In view of Proposition 5.1, it suffices to show that $Y^* = A^* - XA^*$. First, consider a word $y \in Y^* = S$. Then all its left factors are in N. Thus no left factor of y is in X. This shows that $Y^* \subset A^* - XA^*$. Conversely, let $w \in A^* - XA^*$. We show that any left factor u of w is in N by induction on $|u|$. This holds clearly for $|u| = 0$. Next, if $|u| \geq 1$, then u cannot be in $R = X^*$ since otherwise w would have a left factor in X. Thus there exists a factorization $u = u'v'$ with $v' \notin M$. Hence $v' \in N$ and $v' \neq 1$. By the induction hypothesis, $u' \in N$. Since N is a submonoid, $u = u'v' \in N$. This proves that $w \in S = Y^*$.

A special case of this construction is obtained by considering a morphism $\varphi: A^* \to \mathbb{Z}$ into the additive monoid $\mathbb{Z}$ and by setting

$$M = \{m \in A^* \mid \varphi(m) > 0\} \cup \{1\},$$
$$N = \{n \in A^* \mid \varphi(n) \leq 0\}.$$

Given a word $w \in A^*$, we obtain a factorization $w = rs$ with $r \in R$, $s \in S$ as follows. The word r is the shortest left factor of w such that $\varphi(r)$ is maximal in the set of values of φ on the left factors of w (see Fig. 7.9).

The construction of Example 5.2 can be considered as a special case of the very general following result.

THEOREM 5.4 *Let (P, Q) be a partition of A^+. There exists a unique bisection (X, Y) of A^* such that $X \subset P$ and $Y \subset Q$. This bisection is obtained as follows.*

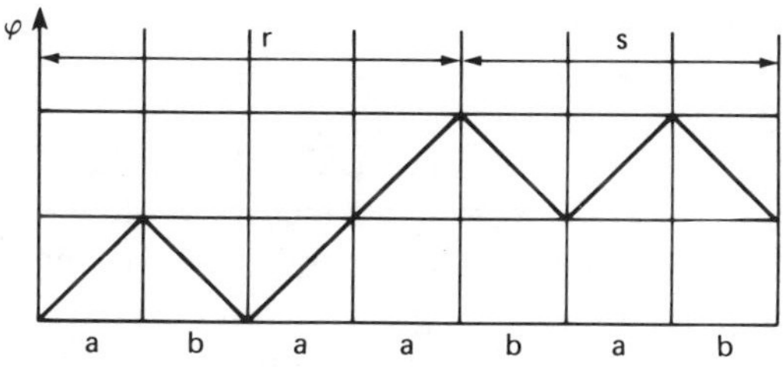

Fig. 7.9 $\varphi(a) = 1, \varphi(b) = -1, w = abaabab.$

Let

$$X_1 = P \cap A, \qquad Y_1 = Q \cap A \tag{5.8}$$

and for $n \geq 2$,

$$Z_n = \bigcup_{i=1}^{n-1} Y_i X_{n-i}, \tag{5.9}$$

$$X_n = Z_n \cap P, \qquad Y_n = Z_n \cap Q. \tag{5.10}$$

Then

$$X = \bigcup_{n \geq 1} X_n \qquad \textit{and} \qquad Y = \bigcup_{n \geq 1} Y_n. \tag{5.11}$$

Proof We first prove uniqueness. Consider a bisection (X, Y) of A^* such that $X \subset P$ and $Y \subset Q$. We show that for $n \geq 1$, we have $X \cap A^n = X_n$, $Y \cap A^n = Y_n$, with X_n and Y_n given by (5.8) and (5.10). Arguing by induction, we consider $n = 1$. Then $X \cap A \subset P \cap A = X_1$. Conversely we have $A \subset X \cup Y$ by (5.4) and $P \cap Y = \varnothing$. Consequently $P \cap A \subset X$. Thus $X \cap A = X_1$. For $n \geq 2$, we have $Z_n \subset YX \cap A^n$ by the induction hypothesis. Thus by (5.6), $Z_n \subset (X \cup Y) \cap A^n$. This implies that $Z_n \cap P \subset X \cap A^n$ and $Z_n \cap Q \subset Y \cap A^n$. Conversely, let $z \in (X \cup Y) \cap A^n$. Then by (5.7) $z = yx$ for some $y \in Y$, $x \in X$. By the induction hypothesis, $y \in Y_i$ and $x \in X_{n-i}$ for $i = |y|$. In view of (5.9), we have $z \in Z_n$. This shows that $(X \cup Y) \cap A^n \subset Z_n$. Hence $X \cap A^n \subset Z_n \cap P$ and $Y \cap A^n \subset Z_n \cap Q$.

To prove the existence of a bisection, we consider the pair (X, Y) given in (5.11). We proceed in several steps. Define $Z_1 = A$ and set $Z = \bigcup_{n \geq 1} Z_n$. In view of (5.8) and (5.10) we have $Z = X \cup Y$.

Observe first that by formula (5.9)

$$YX \cup A = X \cup Y. \tag{5.12}$$

Clearly (5.12) implies $YX \subset X \cup Y$. By induction, we obtain

$$Y^*X^* \subset X^* \cup Y^*. \tag{5.13}$$

Next, we have

$$A^* = X^*Y^*. \tag{5.14}$$

Indeed, let $w \in A^*$. Since $A \subset Z$, the word w has at least one factorization $w = z_1 z_2 \cdots z_n$ with $z_i \in Z$. Choose such a factorization with n minimal. Then we cannot have $z_i \in Y, z_{i+1} \in X$ for some $1 \le i \le n-1$, since this would imply that $z_i z_{i+1} \in Z$ by (5.12) contradicting the minimality of n. Consequently there is some $j \in \{1, \ldots, n\}$ such that $z_1, \ldots, z_j \in X$ and $z_{j+1}, \ldots, z_n \in Y$, showing that $w \in X^*Y^*$.

Now we prove that X^* is suffix-closed. For this, it suffices to show that

$$uv \in X \quad \Rightarrow \quad v \in X^*. \tag{5.15}$$

Indeed, assuming (5.15), consider a word $w = rs \in X^*$. Then $r = r'u$, $s = vs'$ for some $r', s' \in X^*$ and $uv \in X \cup 1$. By (5.15), v is in X^*, and consequently, $s \in X^*$, showing that X^* is suffix-closed.

We prove (5.15) by induction on the length of $x = uv$. Clearly the formula holds for $|x| = 1$. Assume $|x| \ge 2$. Then by (5.12) $x = y_1 x_1$ for some $y_1 \in Y$, $x_1 \in X$. If y_1 is not a letter, then again by (5.12), $y_1 = y_2 x_2$ for some $y_2 \in Y$, $x_2 \in X$. Iterating this operation, we obtain a factorization $x = y_k x_k \cdots x_2 x_1$ with $y_k \in Y \cap A$ and $x_1, \ldots, x_k \in X$.

Each proper right factor v of x has the form $v = v_p x_{p-1} \cdots x_1$ for some right factor v_p of x_p and $1 \le p \le k$. By the induction hypothesis, $v_p \in X^*$. Consequently $v \in X^*$. This proves (5.15). An analoguous proof shows that Y^* is prefix closed.

Next we claim that

$$X^* \cap Y^* = \{1\}, \tag{5.16}$$

and prove this claim by induction, showing that $X^* \cap Y^*$ contains no word of length $n \ge 1$. This holds for $n = 1$ because $X \cap Y = \varnothing$. Assume that for some $w \in A^n$, there are two factorizations $w = x_1 x_2 \cdots x_p = y_1 y_2 \cdots y_q$ with $x_i \in X$, $y_j \in Y$. Since Y^* is prefix closed, we have $x_1 \in Y^*$. Since X^* is suffix closed $y_q \in X^*$. Thus $x_1 \in X \cap Y^*$ and $y_q \in X^* \cap Y$. By the induction hypothesis this is impossible if x_1 and y_q are shorter than w. Thus we have $p = q = 1$. But then $w \in X \cap Y = \varnothing$, a contradiction. This proves (5.16).

Now we prove that X is prefix. For this, we show by induction on $n \ge 1$ that no word in X of length n has a proper left factor in X. This clearly holds for $n = 1$.

Consider $uv \in X \cap A^n$ with $n \ge 2$ and suppose that $u \in X$. In view of (5.12), we have $uv = yx$ for some $y \in Y$, $x \in X$. The word u cannot be a left factor of y, since otherwise u would be in $X \cap Y^*$ because Y^* is prefix closed and this is impossible by (5.16). Thus there is a word $u' \in A^+$ such that $u = yu'$, $u'v = x$.

By (5.15), $u' \in X^*$. Moreover $|x| < n$. By the induction hypothesis, the equation $x = u'v$ implies $v = 1$. Thus $u = uv$, showing the claim for n. Consequently X is prefix. A similar proof shows that Y is suffix.

We now are able to show that (X, Y) is a bisection. Equation (5.14) shows that any word in A^* admits a factorization. To show uniqueness, assume that $xy = x'y'$ for $x, x' \in X^*$ and $y, y' \in Y^*$. Suppose $|x| \geq |x'|$. Then $x = x'u$ and $uy = y'$ for some word u. Since X^* is suffix closed and Y^* is prefix closed, we have $u \in X^* \cap Y^*$. Thus $u = 1$ by (5.16). Consequently $x = x'$ and $y = y'$. Since X and Y are codes, this completes the proof. □

Theorem 5.4 shows that the following method allows us to construct all bisections.

1. Partition the alphabet A into two subsets X_1 and Y_1.
2. For each $n \geq 2$, partition the set $Z_n = \bigcup_{i=1}^{n-1} Y_i X_{n-i}$ into two subsets X_n and Y_n.
3. Set $X = \bigcup_{n \geq 1} X_n$ and $Y = \bigcup_{n \geq 1} Y_n$.

In other words, it is possible to construct the components of the partition (P, Q) progressively during the computation. A convenient way to represent the computations is to display the words in X and Y in two columns when they are obtained. This is illustrated by

EXAMPLE 5.3 Let $A = \{a, b\}$. We construct a bisection of A^* by distributing iteratively the products yx $(x \in X, y \in Y)$ into two columns as shown in Fig. 7.10. All the remaining products are put into the set R. This gives a defining equation for R, since from $A \cup YX = X \cup Y$ and $X = \{a, ba\} \cup R$ we obtain $R = \{b, b^2a\}R \cup b^2a\{a, ba\}$. Thus $R = \{b, b^2a\}^*b^2a\{a, ba\}$ or also $R = (b^2b^*a)^*b^2b^*a\{a, ba\}$. Consequently $X = (b^2b^*a)^*\{a, ba\}$, which is the code of Example 2.11.

	X	Y
1	a	b
2	ba	
3		bba
⩾4	R	

Fig. 7.10 A bisection of A^*.

The following convention will be used for the rest of this section. Given a code X over A, a pair (U, V) of subsets of A^* will be called a *bisection* of X^* if

$$\underline{X}^* = \underline{U}^*\underline{V}^*.$$

To fit into the ordinary definition of bisection, it suffices to consider a coding morphism for X.

A *trisection* of A^* is a triple (X, Y, Z) of subsets of A^+, which form a factorization of A^*,

$$\underline{A}^* = \underline{X}^*\underline{Y}^*\underline{Z}^*. \tag{5.17}$$

We shall prove the following result which gives a relationship between bisections and trisections.

THEOREM 5.5 *Let (X, Y, Z) be a trisection of A^*. There exist a bisection (U, V) of Y^* and a bisection (X', Z') of A^* such that (X, U) is a bisection of X'^* and (V, Z) is a bisection of Z'^*,*

$$\underline{A}^* = \underline{X}^*\underline{Y}^*\underline{Z}^* = (\underline{X}^*\underline{U}^*)(\underline{V}^*\underline{Z}^*) = \underline{X}'^*\underline{Z}'^*.$$

Before giving the proof we establish some useful formulas.

PROPOSITION 5.6 *Let (X, Y, Z) be a trisection of A^*.*

1. *The set X^*Y^* is suffix-closed and the set Y^*Z^* is prefix-closed.*
2. *One has the inclusions*

$$Y^*X^* \subset X^* \cup Y^*Z^*, \tag{5.18}$$

$$Z^*Y^* \subset Z^* \cup X^*Y^*. \tag{5.19}$$

3. *The codes X, Y, and Z are* (2, 0)-, (1, 1)-, *and* (0, 2)-*limited, respectively.*

Proof We first prove 1. Let $w \in X^*Y^*$, and let v be a right factor of w (see Fig. 7.11). Then $w = uv$ for some u. Set $v = xyz$ with $x \in X^*$, $y \in Y^*$, and $z \in Z^*$. Set also $uxy = x'y'z'$ with $x' \in X^*$, $y' \in Y^*$ and $z' \in Z^*$. Then

$$w = uv = uxyz = x'y'(z'z).$$

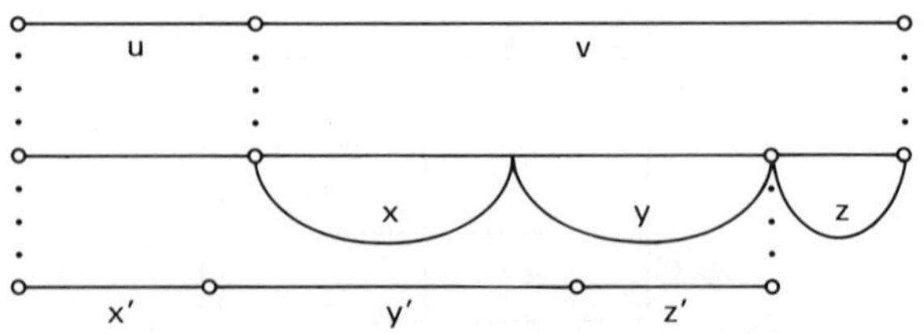

Fig. 7.11 The set X^*Y^* is suffix-closed.

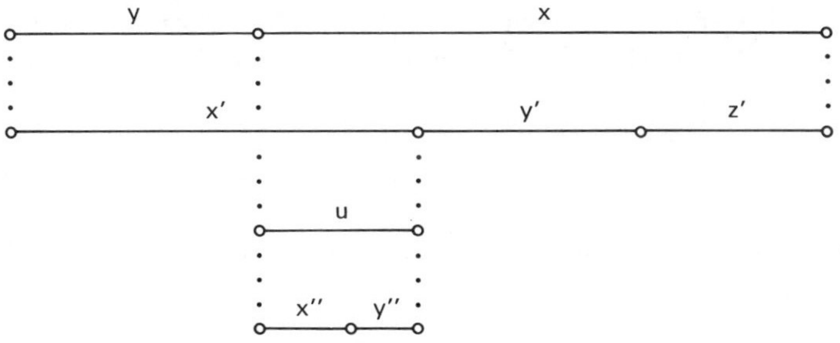

Fig. 7.12 $Y^*X^* \subset X^* \cup Y^*Z^*$

Uniqueness of factorization implies $z' = z = 1$. This shows that $v \in X^*Y^*$ and proves that X^*Y^* is suffix-closed. Likewise Y^*Z^* is prefix-closed.

We now verify (5.18). Let $x \in X^*$ and $y \in Y^*$. Set $yx = x'y'z'$ with $x' \in X^*$, $y' \in Y^*$, and $z' \in Z^*$. If $x' = 1$, then $yx \in Y^*Z^*$. Thus assume that $x' \neq 1$. The word x' cannot be a left factor of y since $y \in Y^*Z^*$ and Y^*Z^* is prefix-closed and $X^* \cap Y^*Z^* = \{1\}$. Thus there is a word u such that $x' = yu$ and $x = uy'z'$ (see Fig. 7.12). Since u is a right factor of $x' \in X^*Y^*$, it is itself in X^*Y^*. Thus $u = x''y''$ for some $x'' \in X^*$ and $y'' \in Y^*$. Thus $x = x''y''y'z'$. Uniqueness of factorization implies $y'' = y' = z' = 1$. Consequently $yx = x'y'z' = x' \in X^*$. This proves (5.18). Formula (5.19) is proved symmetrically.

The code X is $(2, 0)$-limited. Indeed, let $u, v, w \in A^+$ be words such that $uv, vw \in X^*$. Since v and w are right factors of words in X^* and since X^*Y^* is suffix closed, both v and w are in X^*Y^*. Thus

$$v = x'y', \qquad w = xy$$

for some $x, x' \in X^*$, $y, y' \in Y^*$ (see Fig. 7.13).

The word $y'x$ is a right factor of $uvx \in X^*$. Thus by the same argument, $y'x$ is in X^*Y^* and consequently $y'x = x''y''$ for some

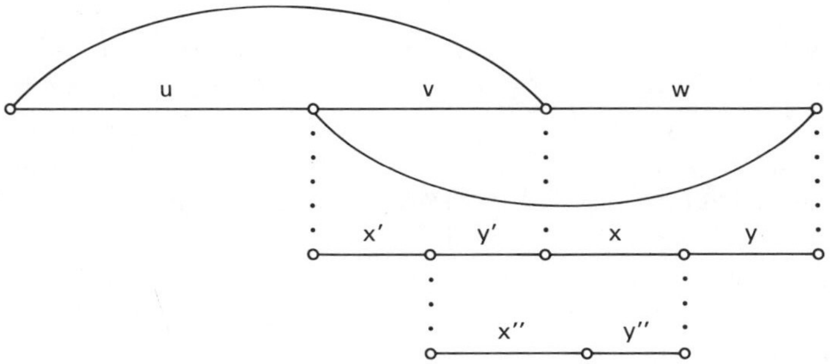

Fig. 7.13 The code X is $(2, 0)$-limited.

$x'' \in X^*$ and $y'' \in Y^*$. Thus $vw = x'x''y''y$. Since by assumption $vw \in X^*$, uniqueness of factorization implies that $y'' = y = 1$. Thus $w = x \in X^*$. This proves that X is $(2, 0)$-limited. Likewise Z is $(0, 2)$-limited.

To show that Y is $(1, 1)$-limited consider words $u, v, w \in A^*$ such that uv, $vw \in Y^*$. Then $v \in X^*Y^*$ because v is a right factor of the word uv in X^*Y^* and also $v \in Y^*Z^*$ as a left factor of the word vw in Y^*Z^*. Thus $v \in X^*Y^* \cap Y^*Z^*$. Uniqueness of factorization implies that $v \in Y^*$. This completes the proof. □

Proof of Theorem 5.5 Set $S = \{s \in Y^* \mid sX^* \subset X^*Y^*\}$. First, we observe that

$$S = \{s \in Y^* \mid sX^* \subset X^* \cup Y^*\}. \tag{5.20}$$

Indeed, consider a word $s \in Y^*$. If $sX^* \subset X^* \cup Y^*$, then clearly, $sX^* \subset X^*Y^*$. Assume conversely that $sX^* \subset X^*Y^*$. Since $s \in Y^*$ we have $sX^* \subset Y^*X^*$ and it follows by (5.18) that $sX^* \subset X^* \cup Y^*Z^*$. Thus $sX^* \subset X^*Y^* \cap (X^* \cup Y^*Z^*) = (X^*Y^* \cap X^*) \cup (X^*Y^* \cap Y^*Z^*) = X^* \cup Y^*$ by uniqueness of factorization. This proves (5.20).

Next, S is a submonoid. Indeed, $1 \in S$ and if $s, t \in S$, then $stX^* \subset sX^*Y^* \subset X^*Y^*$. We show that the monoid S, considered as a monoid on the alphabet Y satisfies condition $C(1, 0)$. In other words, $s, t \in Y^*$ and $st \in S$ imply $t \in S$. Indeed, consider $x \in X^*$. Since tx is a right factor of $stx \in X^*Y^*$ and since X^*Y^* is suffix closed, $tx \in X^*Y^*$. Thus $t \in S$. This shows that S is a free submonoid of Y^* generated by some $(1, 0)$-limited code $U \subset Y^+$. Note that U is $(1, 0)$-limited as a code over Y. According to Proposition 5.1, the code U is the left factor of some bisection (U, V) of Y^*, with $V^* = Y^* - UY^*$. We shall give another definition of V. For this, set

$$R = \{r \in Y^* \mid rX^* \cap Z^* \neq \varnothing\}.$$

Clearly $R \cap S = 1$. We prove that

$$R^* = V^*. \tag{5.21}$$

First, we show that $R \subset V^*$. Let $r \in R - \{1\}$. Set $r = st$ with $s \in Y^+, t \in Y^*$. Since $r \in R$, we have $stx \in Z^*$ for some $x \in X^*$. By (5.18), we have $tx \in X^* \cup Y^*Z^*$. If $tx \in Y^*Z^*$, then $st \in Y^+Z^*$ which is impossible since $stx \in Z^*$. Consequently $tx \in X^*$. Thus $s \in R$. Since $R \cap S = \{1\}$, it follows that $s \notin S$. Thus no left factor $s \in Y^+$ of r is in S. In other words, no left factor of r is in the code U. This proves that r is in V^*.

Second, we prove that $V^* \subset R^*$. We proceed by induction on the length of words in V, the case of the empty word being trivial. Let $v \in V^+$. Since (U, V) is a factorization, we have $U^* \cap V^* = \{1\}$. Consequently $v \notin U^* = S$. Thus by (5.20), there is some $x \in X^*$ such that $vx \notin X^* \cup Y^*$. Since $v \in Y^*$, we have by

(5.18) $vx \in Y^*Z^*$, and by a previous remark even $vx \in Y^*Z^+$. Set $vx = yz$ with $y \in Y^*, z \in Z^+$. Then z cannot be a right factor of x, since otherwise z would be in $X^*Y^* \cap Z^+$, which is impossible. Thus there is some word $w \in A^+$ such that

$$v = yw, \qquad wx = z.$$

Since w is a right factor of $v \in X^*Y^*$, we have $w \in X^*Y^*$. Similarly w is a left factor of $z \in Y^*Z^*$. Thus $w \in Y^*Z^*$. Uniqueness of factorization implies $w \in Y^*$. The word y is in V^*. Indeed, $y \in Y^*$ is a left factor of v, and since V^* is prefix closed as a subset of Y^*, $y \in V^*$. Since $|y| < |v|$, we have $y \in R^*$ by the induction hypothesis. On the other hand, $w \in Y^*$ and $wx = z \in Z^*$ imply $w \in R$. Thus $v = yw \in R^*$. This completes the proof of (5.21).

Up to now, we have proved that

$$\underline{A}^* = \underline{X}^*\underline{U}^*\underline{V}^*\underline{Z}^* \tag{5.22}$$

with $\underline{Y}^* = \underline{U}^*\underline{V}^*$, $S = U^*$ and $R^* = V^*$. To finish the proof, it suffices to show that the products $M = X^*U^*$ and $N = V^*Z^*$ are submonoids. Indeed, since the product (5.22) is unambiguous, we have $\underline{M} = \underline{X}^*\underline{U}^*$ and $\underline{N} = \underline{V}^*\underline{Z}^*$ whence $\underline{A}^* = \underline{M}\underline{N}$. By Proposition 5.3 the monoids M and N then are free and their bases constitute the desired bisection (X', Y').

To show that X^*U^* is a submonoid it suffices to show that $U^*X^* \subset X^* \cup U^*$. Thus, let us consider words $x \in X^*$ and $s \in U^* = S$. Then by (5.20) $sx \in X^* \cup Y^*$. But $sx \in Y^*$ implies $sx \in S$ because $sxX^* \subset sX^* \subset X^* \cup Y^*$. Thus $sx \subset X^* \cup S$, showing that X^*U^* is a submonoid.

Finally we show that V^*Z^* is a submonoid. For this, we show that

$$Z^*R \subset R \cup Z^*. \tag{5.23}$$

This will imply that $Z^*R^* \subset R^* \cup Z^*$ which in turn proves the claim in view of (5.21).

To show (5.23), let $z \in Z^*$ and $r \in R$. Since $r \in Y^*$, formula (5.19) implies that $zr \in Z^* \cup X^*Y^*$. Next, by definition of R, $rx \in Z^*$ for some $x \in X^*$. Thus $zrx \in Z^*$. Since Y^*Z^* is prefix-closed, we have $z \in Y^*Z^*$. Thus uniqueness of factorization shows that $zr \in Z^* \cup Y^*$. If $zr \in Y^*$, then $zr \in R$, since $zrx \in Z^*$. Thus $zr \in Z^* \cup R$ and this proves (5.23). □

Theorem 5.5 shows that all trisections can be built by "pasting" together quadrisections obtained by a sequence of bisections. The following example shows that it is false for any trisection to be obtained by two bisections.

EXAMPLE 5.4 Let $A = \{a, b\}$. The suffix code $Z' = \{b, ba, ba^2\}$ is $(0, 1)$-limited. Thus Z' is the right factor of the bisection (X', Z') of A^* with $X'^* = A^* - A^*Z'$. The equation

$$\underline{Z}'\underline{X}' + \underline{A} = \underline{Z}' + \underline{X}'$$

derived from (5.3) gives $\underline{A} - \underline{Z}' = (1 - \underline{Z}')\underline{X}'$ whence $\underline{X}' = \underline{Z}'^*(\underline{A} - \underline{Z}')$. It follows that

$$\begin{aligned}\underline{X}' &= \underline{Z}'^*(a - ba - ba^2)\\ &= (\underline{Z}'^* - \underline{Z}'^*b - \underline{Z}'^*ba)a\\ &= (1 + Z'^*(b + ba + ba^2) - Z'^*b - Z'^*ba)a\\ &= (1 + Z'^*ba^2)a.\end{aligned}$$

Thus

$$X' = Z'^*ba^3 \cup \{a\}.$$

Next define

$$U = (ba)^*ba^3, \qquad V = ba, \qquad Z = \{b, ba^2\}(ba)^*.$$

The pair (V, Z) is clearly a bisection of Z'^*. Moreover, by inspection $U \subset X'$. This inclusion shows that, over the alphabet X', the set U is the right factor of the bisection (X, U) of X'^* with $X = U^*(X' - U)$. Moreover, $U^*V^* = \{ba, ba^3\}^*$. Then setting

$$Y = \{ba, ba^3\},$$

(U, V) is a bisection of Y^*. Thus we have obtained

$$\underline{A}^* = \underline{X}'^*\underline{Z}'^* = \underline{X}^*\underline{U}^*\underline{V}^*\underline{Z}^* = \underline{X}^*\underline{Y}^*\underline{Z}^*,$$

and (X, Y, Z) is a trisection of A^*. Neither X^*Y^* nor Y^*Z^* is a submonoid. Indeed, $ba \in Y$ and $a \in X$ (since $a \in X' - U$). However, $ba^2 \in Z$ and consequently $ba^2 \notin X^*Y^*$. Similarly $b \in Z$ and $ba^3 \in Y$ but $b^2a^3 \in X$ whence $b^2a^3 \notin Y^*Z^*$. This means that the trisection (X, Y, Z) cannot be obtained by two bisections.

EXERCISES

SECTION 1

***1.1.** Let $A = \{a, b\}$. Show that $\{ab, ba\}^*$ is pure.

***1.2.** Let $X = \{x, y\}$ be a code with two elements. Show that if X^* is not pure, then the set $x^*y \cup y^*x$ contains a word which is not primitive.

1.3. Deduce from Exercise 1.2 that if $x = uv$ and $y = vu$ are conjugate primitive words, then $X^* = \{x, y\}^*$ is pure.

SECTION 2

2.1. Let $X \subset A^+$ be a finite code and let $\mathscr{A} = (Q, 1, 1)$ be an unambiguous trim automaton recognizing X^*. Let φ be the associated representation. Show that X^* is pure iff the monoid $\varphi(A^*)$ contains no nontrivial groups (Hint: Use Proposition 2.3.)

2.2. Let A be a finite alphabet and let $X \subset A^+$ be a finite code. Show that X is circular iff there exist finite subsets T, U, V, W of A^+ such that

$$X^* = T \cup (UA^* \cap A^*V) - A^*WA^*.$$

(Hint: Use Proposition 2.3.)

2.3. A set $X \subset A^+$ is called (p, q)-*constrained* for some $p, q \geq 0$ if for each sequence $u_0, u_1, \ldots, u_{p+q}$ of words the condition $u_{i-1}u_i \in X$ for $1 \leq i \leq p + q$ implies $u_p \in X^*$.

(a) Show that, for $p + q \leq 2$, a set X is (p, q)-constrained iff it is (p, q)-limited.

(b) Let $A = \{a, b\}$ and $X = \{a, ab\}$. Show that X is $(3, 0)$-constrained but not $(3, 0)$-limited.

2.4. Let $X \subset A^+$ be a maximal prefix code. Show that the following conditions are equivalent.

(i) $\sigma(X) = 1$,

(ii) $A^*X \subset X^*$,

(iii) X is a semaphore code such that $S = X - A^+X$ satisfies $SA^* \cap A^*S = S \cup SA^*S$.

2.5. Show that a recognizable code is limited iff it is circular.

SECTION 3

3.1. Show that the set L_n of Lyndon words of length n over a k letter alphabet is a circular code. Show that L_n is comma-free iff $n = 1$ or $n = 2, k \leq 3$ or ($n = 3, 4$ and $k \leq 2$).

3.2. Let A be a k letter alphabet and let $s \in A^+$ be a word of length p. Let R be the finite set

$$R = \{w \in A^* \mid sw \in A^*s, |w| < p\}.$$

Let X be the semaphore code $X = A^*s - A^*sA^+$. For all $T \subset A^*$, we denote by α_T the series

$$\alpha_T = \sum_{n \geq 0} \text{Card}(T \cap A^n)t^n.$$

Using Proposition II.7.5, show that

$$\alpha_X = \frac{t^p}{t^p + (1 - kt)\alpha_R}.$$

Now let $Z = (sA^+ \cap A^+s) - A^+sA^+$. Show that $s + \underline{A}\underline{X} = \underline{X} + \underline{Z}$. Let $U = Zs^{-1}$. Show that for all $n \geq p$, the code $U \cap A^n$ is comma-free and that the generating series of the length distribution of U is

$$\alpha_U = \frac{(kt-1)}{t^p + (1-kt)\alpha_R} + 1.$$

SECTION 4

4.1. Let $A = \{1, 2, \ldots, n\}$ and for $j \in A$, let $X_j = j\{j+1, \ldots, n\}^*$. Show that the family $(X_j)_{1 \le j \le n}$ is a factorization of A^*.

4.2. Let $\varphi: A^* \to \mathbb{R}$ be a morphism into the additive monoid. For $r \in \mathbb{R}$, let

$$C_r = \{v \in A^+ \mid \varphi(v) = r\}, \qquad B_r = C_r - \left(\bigcup_{s \ge r} C_s\right) A^+.$$

Show that if $\pi(w) = (l, m)$ and $\pi(m) = (p, q)$, then $p \preccurlyeq l \prec m$.

4.3. The *standard factorization* of a Lyndon word $w \in L - A$ is defined as the pair

$$\pi(w) = (l, m)$$

of words in A^+ such that $w = lm$ and m is the longest proper right factor of w that is in L.
Show that if $\pi(w) = (l, m)$ and $\pi(m) = (p, q)$, then $p \preccurlyeq l \prec m$.

4.4. Let L be the set of Lyndon words over A. Set $L \cap A^n = \{z_1, z_2, \ldots, z_k\}$ with $z_1 < z_2 < \cdots < z_k$ and let

$$Z_1 = A,$$
$$Z_{i+1} = z_i^*(Z_i - z_i) \qquad (1 \le i \le k).$$

(a) Show that Z_i contains all z_r such that $\pi(z_r) = (z_s, z_t)$ with $s < t \le r$.

(b) Deduce from this that L is a Lazard set.

SECTION 5

5.1. Show that if a factorization $\underline{A}^* = \underline{X}_n^* \underline{X}_{n-1}^* \cdots \underline{X}_1^*$ is obtained by a composition of bisections, then X_i is a $(i-1, n-i)$-limited code.

5.2. Let X be a $(2,0)$-limited code over A. Let $M \subset A^*$ be the submonoid generated by the right factors of words in X. Show that M is right-unitary. Let U be the prefix code generating M. Show that there exists a bisection of A^* of the form (U, Z). Show that X, considered as a code over U is $(1,0)$-limited. Derive from this a trisection (X, Y, Z) of A^*. This shows that any $(2,0)$-limited code is a left factor of some trisection.

5.3. Let $A = \{a, b, c, d, e, f, g\}$ and let $Y = \{d, eb, fa, ged, dac\}$. Show that Y is $(1,1)$-limited. Show that there is no trisection of A^* of the form (X, Y, Z).

5.4. Let $y \in A^+$ be an unbordered word. Show that there exists a trisection of A^* of the form (X, y, Z). Show that a left (resp., right) factor of y is in Z^* (resp., X^*). (Hint: First construct a bisection (X', Z) of A^* such that X'^* is the submonoid generated by the right factors of y.)

NOTES

The definition of limited codes is from Schützenberger (1965c), where limited codes are defined by some condition $\mathscr{U}_s(p, q)$ for $p < 0 < q$ which is our condition $C(-p, q)$. The notions of synchronization delay and of uniformly synchronous code have been introduced in Golomb and Gordon (1965). Theorem 1.8 is from De Luca and Restivo (1980). Theorem 2.6 is in Restivo (1975). See also Lassez (1976) where the term "circular code" is used.

The inequality (3.2) was already seen in Chapter I. This and its converse (Proposition 3.1) are due to Kraft and McMillan (McMillan, 1956). Schützenberger (1967) has proved a result which is stronger than Proposition 3.1 and gives a necessary and sufficient condition on a sequence of integers to be the length distribution of a synchronous prefix code.

The explicit computation of the sequence $L_n(X)$ as a function of the length distribution of X is given in a slightly different form in Golomb and Gordon (1965). Theorem 3.6 has been conjectured by Golomb and Gordon. It has been proved by Schützenberger (1965c) and by Scholtz (1966).

The story of comma-free codes is a pleasant one. They were introduced in Golomb *et al.* (1958). Some people thought at that time that the biological code is comma-free (Crick's hypothesis). The number of amino acids appearing in proteins is 20. They are coded by words of length three over the alphabet of bases A, C, G, U. Now, the number $l_3(4)$ which is the maximum number of elements in a comma-free (or circular) code composed of words of length three over a four-letter alphabet is precisely 20. Unfortunately for mathematics, it appeared several years later with the work of Niernberg that the biological code is not even a code in the sense of this book. Several triples of bases may encode the same acid (see Yčas, 1969 or Stryer, 1975). This disappointment does not weaken the interest of circular codes, we believe.

Theorem 3.8 has been conjectured by Golomb *et al.* and proved by Eastman (1965). A simple construction has been given by Scholtz (1969), on which the proof given here is based. Other constructions which are possible are described in Devitt and Jackson (1981). For even length, no formula is known giving the maximal number of elements of a comma-free code (See Jiggs, 1963).

The notion of a factorization has been introduced by Schützenberger (1965a) in the paper where he proves Theorem 4.1. The factorizations of free monoids are very closely related with decompositions in direct sums of free Lie algebras. This topic is not mentioned here. A complete treatment can be found in Viennot (1978) and in Lothaire (1983). Proposition 4.3 is a special case of a statement known as the Baker–Campbell–Hausdorff formula (see, e.g., Lothaire, 1983). The notion of a Lazard set is due to Viennot (1978). A series of examples of other factorizations and a bibliography on this field can be found in Lothaire (1983). Finite factorizations were studied by Schützenberger and Viennot. Theorem 5.3 is from Schützenberger (1965a). Theorem 5.4 is due to Viennot (1974). Viennot (1974) contains other results on finite factorizations. Among them, there is a necessary and sufficient condition in terms of the construction of Theorem 5.3 for the factors of a bisection to be recognizable. He also gives a construction of trisections analoguous to that of bisections given in Theorem 5.3.

Exercises 1.2 and 1.3 are from Lentin and Schützenberger (1967). Exercises 2.1 and 2.2 are from Restivo (1974) (see also Hashiguchi, Honda 1976b). These statements have a natural place within the framework of the theory of varieties of monoids (see Eilenberg, 1976 or Pin, 1984). Exercise 2.1 may be formulated in a more general way. For this a subset X of A^+ is called *aperiodic* if its syntactic monoid contains no nontrivial subgroup. Given an aperiodic code X, the monoid X^* is pure iff X^* is aperiodic (see Perrot, 1977 and Pin, 1979).

Exercise 3.2 is from Guibas and Odlyzko (1978). The codes introduced in this exercise were defined by Gilbert (1960) and named *prefix-synchronized*. Gilbert has conjectured that $U \cap A^n$ has maximal size when the word s is chosen unbordered and of length $\log_k n$. This conjecture has been settled by Guibas and Odlyzko. It holds for $k = 2, 3, 4$, but is false for $k \geq 5$.

The factorization of Example 4.2 is due to Spitzer (see Lothaire, 1983). Exercises 5.2 and 5.3 are from Viennot (1974).

CHAPTER **VIII**

Polynomial of a Code

0. INTRODUCTION

The main object of this final chapter is the study of the polynomial associated with a finite maximal code obtained using commutative variables. The main result (Theorem 1.1) links properties of the code with factorization properties of the polynomial. The proof is difficult. However, the result is just one step in the direction of analysis of the characteristic polynomial of a code. This study is far from being complete at the present time.

The main result is stated in Section 1 which also contains the notion of a factorizing code. In Section 2, it is shown that the commutative polynomial of a code is equal to the determinant of a matrix naturally associated with the code. In Section 3 a decomposition of the state space into invariant subspaces is defined. This induces a factorization of the polynomial of the code. In Section 4 the factors of the polynomial are evaluated by showing the connection with left, right, and two-sided contexts. For this, results on measures from Chapter VI are used. Section 5 contains the end of the proof and a detailed description of two examples.

The commutative polynomial of a code contains all the information concerning the commutative properties of a code, such as its length distribution. In Section 6 we consider another commutative property, namely that of being commutatively prefix. We show that this property is equivalent to the fact that the coefficients of some polynomial are nonnegative. We also give an example of a code which is not commutatively prefix.

Section 7 presents a property of biprefix codes related to the decomposition of the state space described in Section 3. It concerns a property of the syntactic representation which is the analogue of the minimal automaton in linear algebra. This representation is shown to be completely reducible iff the associated code is biprefix.

1. FACTORIZING CODES

A code X over an alphabet A is a *factorizing* code iff there exist two subsets P and Q of A^* such that each word $w \in A^*$ factorizes uniquely into

$$w = qxp \tag{1.1}$$

with $p \in P$, $q \in Q$, $x \in X^*$. In terms of formal power series, (1.1) can be expressed as

$$\underline{A}^* = \underline{Q}\underline{X}^*\underline{P}. \tag{1.2}$$

The pair (P, Q) is called a *factorization* of the code X. Observe that $1 \in P$ and $1 \in Q$.

Taking the inverses in (1.2), we obtain

$$1 - \underline{X} = \underline{P}(1 - \underline{A})\underline{Q} \tag{1.3}$$

or also

$$\underline{X} - 1 = \underline{P}\underline{A}\underline{Q} - \underline{P}\underline{Q}. \tag{1.4}$$

This equation shows that each word in X can be written in at least one way as

$$x = paq$$

with $p \in P$, $a \in A$, $q \in Q$.

If a subset $X \subset A^+$ satisfies (1.4) for some sets P, Q, then X is a code. Indeed, (1.4) implies that $\underline{A}^* = \underline{Q}(\underline{X})^*\underline{P}$, which in turn shows that $(\underline{X})^*$ has only coefficients 0 or 1.

In view of (1.2) the composition of factorizing codes is again a factorizing code.

A prefix code X is factorizing since we have $\underline{A}^* = \underline{X}^*\underline{P}$ for $P = A^* - XA^*$ being the set of word having no left factors in X. Conversely, if in a factorization (1.2), the set Q is $\{1\}$, then the code X is prefix. Indeed, if $u, uv \in X^*$, then setting $v = xp$ with $x \in X^*$ and $p \in P$, we obtain $(ux)p \in X^*$, which implies $p = 1$ by the uniqueness of factorization. Thus X^* is right unitary.

Symmetrically, for a suffix code X, $\underline{A}^* = \underline{Q}\underline{X}^*$ with $Q = A^* - A^*X$.

If X is a biprefix code, then simultaneously

$$\underline{A}^* = \underline{X}^*\underline{P} \qquad \text{and} \qquad \underline{A}^* = \underline{Q}\underline{X}^*$$

with $P = A^* - XA^*$ and $Q = A^* - A^*X$. This shows in particular that a code may have several factorizations (see also Exercise 1.5).

Recall that for a thin maximal biprefix code X, we have

$$\underline{X} - 1 = d(X)(\underline{A} - 1) + (\underline{A} - 1)T(\underline{A} - 1).$$

Hence $\underline{A}^* = \underline{X}^*\underline{P} = \underline{Q}\underline{X}^*$ with

$$\underline{P} = d(X) + (\underline{A} - 1)T, \qquad \underline{Q} = d(X) + T(\underline{A} - 1). \tag{1.5}$$

Let $X \subset A^+$ be a factorizing code and let (P, Q) be a factorization of X. If P and Q are thin, then X is a thin maximal code. Indeed, Eq. (1.4) shows that $X \subset PAQ$. Since P, A, Q are thin, the product PAQ is thin also and consequently X is thin. Furthermore, X is complete. Indeed, let $u \in \bar{F}(Q)$ and $v \in \bar{F}(P)$. For each w in A^* the word uwv is in QX^*P. By the choice of u and v, it follows that w is in $F(X^*)$. Thus X is complete.

As a special case, note that if P and Q are finite, then X is a finite maximal code. We shall see later that if, conversely X is a finite maximal code, then P and Q are finite.

There exist finite codes which are not factorizing. An example will be given in Section 6. However, no finite maximal code is known which is not factoring. Whether any finite maximal code is factorizing is still unknown. This is one of the main problems in the theory of codes. We shall prove, by passing to commutative variables a weakened version of this statement.

Given a subset $X \subset A^+$ we denote by $\underline{\underline{X}}$ the series in commutative variables which is the image of the series $\underline{X}$ under the canonical morphism

$$\alpha\colon \quad \mathbb{Q}\langle\langle A\rangle\rangle \to \mathbb{Q}[[A]].$$

Thus $\alpha(\underline{X}) = \underline{\underline{X}}$. For $a \in A$, we write indifferently a or $\underline{\underline{a}}$.

THEOREM 1.1 *Let $X \subset A^+$ be a finite maximal code. The polynomial $1 - \underline{\underline{X}}$ is divisible by $1 - \underline{\underline{A}}$. If the quotient*

$$r = (1 - \underline{\underline{X}})/(1 - \underline{\underline{A}})$$

is irreducible in $\mathbb{Q}[[A]]$, then one of the following three cases holds:

(i) *X is prefix and synchronous;*
(ii) *X is suffix and synchronous;*
(iii) *X is biprefix.*

The proof of Theorem 1.1 is given in Sections 2–4. We first discuss the relationship between Theorem 1.1 and factorizing codes.

Let X be a finite maximal factorizing code and let (P, Q) be a factorization of X,

$$1 - \underline{X} = \underline{P}(1 - \underline{A})\underline{Q}.$$

The first statement of the theorem, namely that $1 - A$ divides $1 - X$, shows that the product $r = \underline{\underline{P}}\,\underline{\underline{Q}}$ is a polynomial. Consequently P and Q are finite sets. If the polynomial r is irreducible, then $P = \{1\}$ or $Q = \{1\}$. This implies by a previous remark that X is prefix or suffix. Thus we easily obtain a weakened version of the theorem for factorizing codes. However, this gives no indication whether the code is synchronous or not.

EXAMPLE 1.1 Let $A = \{a, b\}$, and let

$$X = \{a^4, ab, aba^6, aba^3b, aba^3ba^2, aba^2ba, aba^2ba^3, aba^2b^2, aba^2b^2a^2, b, ba^2\}.$$

The set X is a factorizing code. Indeed, an easy computation gives

$$1 - \underline{X} = (1 + a + aba^2(1 + a + b))(1 - a - b)(1 + a^2).$$

Thus this is a factorization (P, Q) with

$$P = \{1, a, aba^2, aba^3, aba^2b\}, \qquad Q = \{1, a^2\}.$$

Since P and Q are finite, X is a maximal code.

We may verify that X is indecomposable. This is the smallest known example of a finite maximal indecomposable code which is neither prefix nor suffix (see Example I.6.4 and Exercise 1.4).

2. DETERMINANTS

In this section we prove two results about the determinant of a matrix which is associated in a natural way to an automaton. In the first statement, formula (2.1) gives an expression of the polynomial $1 - \underline{\underline{X}}$ for a finite code X.

PROPOSITION 2.1 *Let $X \subset A^+$ be a finite code and let $\mathscr{A} = (Q, 1, 1)$ be a finite unambiguous trim automaton recognizing X^*. Let t be the $Q \times Q$-matrix with elements in $\mathbb{Q}[A]$ given by*

$$t_{p,q} = \underline{\underline{A}}_{p,q}$$

where $A_{p,q}$ is the set of letters $a \in A$ such that $p \xrightarrow{a} q$. Then

$$1 - \underline{\underline{X}} = \det(I - t). \tag{2.1}$$

Proof There exists no path $q \xrightarrow{w} q$ with $q \neq 1$ and $w \in A^+$ that does not pass through state 1. Otherwise $uw^*v \subset X$ for words u, v such that $1 \xrightarrow{u} q \xrightarrow{v} 1$, contradicting the finiteness of X. Thus we can set $Q = \{1, 2, \ldots, n\}$ in such a way that whenever $i \xrightarrow{a} j$ for $a \in A$, $j \neq 1$, then

$i < j$. Define for $i, j \in Q$,

$$r_{ij} = \delta_{ij} - \underline{A}_{ij}, \tag{2.2}$$

where δ_{ij} is the Kronecker symbol. Let Δ be the polynomial

$$\Delta = \sum_{\sigma \in \mathfrak{S}_n} (-1)^{\varepsilon(\sigma)} r_{1,1\sigma} r_{2,2\sigma} \cdots r_{n,n\sigma},$$

where $\varepsilon(\sigma) = \pm 1$ denotes the signature of the permutation σ. According to the well-known formula for determinants we have

$$\det(I - t) = \alpha(\Delta).$$

(Recall that α maps $\mathbb{Q}\langle\langle A \rangle\rangle$ on $\mathbb{Q}[[A]]$). Thus it suffices to show that

$$\Delta = 1 - \underline{X}. \tag{2.3}$$

For this, let

$$\Delta_\sigma = r_{1,1\sigma} r_{2,2\sigma} \cdots r_{n,n\sigma},$$

so that

$$\Delta = \sum_{\sigma \in \mathfrak{S}_n} (-1)^{\varepsilon(\sigma)} \Delta_\sigma.$$

Consider a permutation $\sigma \in \mathfrak{S}_n$ such that $\Delta_\sigma \neq 0$. If $\sigma \neq 1$, then it has at least one cycle $(i_1 i_2 \cdots i_k)$ of length $k \geq 2$. Since $\Delta_\sigma \neq 0$, by (2.2) the sets $A_{i_1 i_2}$, $A_{i_2 i_3}, \ldots, A_{i_k i_1}$ are nonempty. This implies that the cycle $(i_1, \ldots, i_k)$ contains state 1. Consequently each permutation σ with $\Delta_\sigma \neq 0$ is composed of fixed points and of one cycle containing 1. If this cycle is $(i_1, i_2, \ldots, i_k)$ with $i_1 = 1$, then

$$1 < i_2 < \cdots < i_k$$

by the choice of the ordering of states in $\mathscr{A}$. Set $X_\sigma = A_{1 i_2} A_{i_2 i_3} \cdots A_{i_k, 1}$. Then $\Delta_\sigma = (-1)^k \underline{X}_\sigma$ and also $(-1)^{\varepsilon(\sigma)} = (-1)^{k+1}$.

The set X_σ is composed of words $a_1 a_2 \cdots a_k$ with $a_i \in A$ and such that

$$1 \xrightarrow{a_1} i_2 \xrightarrow{a_2} i_3 \longrightarrow \cdots \longrightarrow i_k \xrightarrow{a_k} 1.$$

These words are in X. Denote by S the set of permutations $\sigma \in \mathfrak{S} - 1$ having just one nontrivial cycle, namely, the cycle containing 1. Then $\underline{X} = \sum_{\sigma \in S} \underline{X}_\sigma$ since each word in X is the label of a unique path $(1, i_2, \ldots, i_k, 1)$ with $1 < i_2 < \cdots < i_k$. It follows that

$$\begin{aligned} \Delta &= 1 + \sum_{\sigma \in S} (-1)^{\varepsilon(\sigma)} \Delta_\sigma \\ &= 1 - \sum_{\sigma \in S} \underline{X}_\sigma \\ &= 1 - \underline{X}. \quad \square \end{aligned}$$

In the sequel, we shall need several canonical correspondences, in addition to the morphism,

$$\alpha\colon\quad \mathbb{Q}\langle\langle A\rangle\rangle \quad\to\quad \mathbb{Q}[[A]].$$

Let $n \geq 0$ be an integer. For $1 \leq i, j \leq n$, let

$$\pi_{i,j}\colon\quad \mathbb{Q}^{n\times n}\langle\langle A\rangle\rangle \quad\to\quad \mathbb{Q}\langle\langle A\rangle\rangle$$

be the $\mathbb{Q}$-linear function that associates, to a formal power series σ with coefficients in the set of $n \times n$ matrices over $\mathbb{Q}$, the series

$$\pi_{i,j}(\sigma) = \sum_{w\in A^*} (\sigma, w)_{i,j}\underline{w}.$$

Let $\theta\colon \mathbb{Q}^{n\times n}\langle\langle A\rangle\rangle \to (\mathbb{Q}\langle\langle A\rangle\rangle)^{n\times n}$ be the function defined by $\theta(\sigma)_{i,j} = \pi_{i,j}(\sigma)$. It is easily seen that θ is an isomorphism of $\mathbb{Q}$-algebras.

The morphism α is extended in the natural way to $\mathbb{Q}^{n\times n}\langle\langle A\rangle\rangle$ and to $(\mathbb{Q}\langle\langle A\rangle\rangle)^{n\times n}$. This leads to the following commutative diagram:

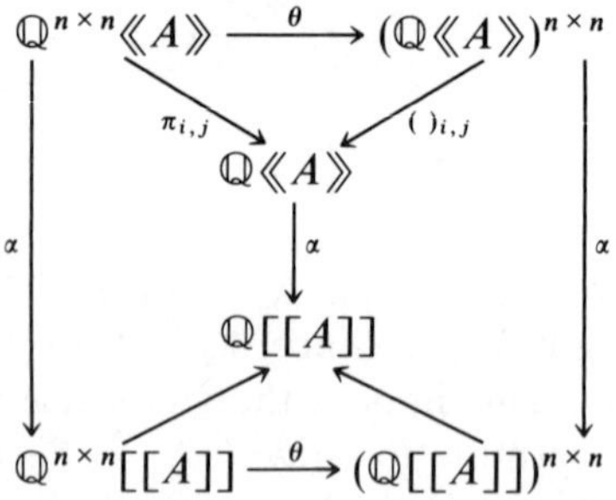

To avoid cumbersome notation, we have used the same symbol θ to denote the two horizontal bijections. Observe also that with this notation, the matrix t of Proposition 2.1 is expressed as

$$t = \theta\left(\sum_{a\in A} \varphi_{\mathcal{A}}(a)\underline{a}\right).$$

PROPOSITION 2.2 *Let*

$$\varphi\colon\quad A^* \to \mathbb{Q}^{n\times n}$$

be a morphism from A^* *into the monoid* $\mathbb{Q}^{n\times n}$. *Let* $l \in \mathbb{Q}^n$ *be a row vector, let* $c \in \mathbb{Q}^n$ *be a column vector and let* $\sigma \in \mathbb{Q}\langle\langle A\rangle\rangle$ *be the series defined by* $(\sigma, w) = l\varphi(w)c$. *Set* $t = \theta(\sum_{a\in A}\varphi(a)\underline{a})$. *Then* $\alpha(\sigma)\det(I - t)$ *is a polynomial.*

Proof Set $F = \sum_{a\in A}\varphi(a)\underline{a}$ and $E = \sum_{w\in A^*}\varphi(w)\underline{w}$. Then $E = F^*$, since φ is a morphism. Consequently

$$E(I - F) = I. \tag{2.4}$$

Applying θ to (2.4) we obtain

$$\theta(E)(I - \theta(F)) = I. \tag{2.5}$$

Let $\mu = \alpha(\theta(E))$. Since $\alpha(\theta(F)) = t$, Eq. (2.5) implies

$$\mu(I - t) = I.$$

This shows that μ is the inverse of matrix $I - t$. The usual formula from linear algebra then gives

$$\mu_{i,j} = \frac{p_{ij}}{\det(I - t)}$$

for some polynomials $p_{i,j} \in \mathbb{Q}[A]$. Thus

$$\det(I - t)\mu \in (\mathbb{Q}[A])^{n \times n}. \tag{2.7}$$

Next, for all $w \in A^*$ $(\sigma, w) = l\varphi(w)c$. Hence

$$\sigma = \sum_{w \in A^*} (\sigma, w)w = \sum_{w \in A^*} l\varphi(w)c\underline{w}.$$

An easy computation shows that $\sigma = l\theta(E)c$. Consequently

$$\alpha(\sigma) = l\mu c. \tag{2.8}$$

Multiply both sides of (2.8) by $\det(I - t)$. According to (2.7), we have

$$\alpha(\sigma)\det(I - t) \in \mathbb{Q}[A]. \quad \square$$

Remark If the series σ in Proposition 2.2 has the special form $\sigma = \underline{X}^*$, where $X \subset A^+$ is a recognizable code, then by the proposition,

$$\underline{X}^*\det(I - t) = p,$$

for some polynomial $p \in \mathbb{Q}[A]$. This implies that

$$\det(I - t) = (1 - \underline{X})p.$$

In view of Proposition 2.1, the polynomial p equals 1 for a finite code X. This can also be shown directly (Exercise 2.1).

3. STATE SPACE

In this section, we consider a fixed maximal recognizable code $X \subset A^+$. We also fix a finite unambiguous trim automaton $\mathscr{A} = (Q, 1, 1)$ recognizing X^*. Set

$$Q = \{1, 2, \ldots, n\}.$$

Let φ be the representation associated with the automaton $\mathscr{A}$ and let $M = \varphi(A^*)$. Let J be the minimal ideal of M and let Γ (resp. Λ) be the set of minimal right ideals (resp. minimal left ideals) in M. Observe that according to the assumptions, X is complete and $\varphi(X^*) \cap J \neq \varnothing$.

Let

$$E = \mathbb{Q}^{n \times 1}, \qquad E' = \mathbb{Q}^{1 \times n}.$$

The vector space E is called the *state space* of the automaton $\mathscr{A}$. A matrix $m \in M$ acts on the left on E and on the right on E'. For a subspace F of E we denote as usual by $F^\perp$ the subspace of E',

$$F^\perp = \{l \in E' \mid \forall c \in F, lc = 0\}.$$

This is the *orthogonal* of F. Symmetrically, we define the orthogonal $F'^\perp$ of a subspace F' of E'. Observe that since E has finite dimension, a classical result from linear algebra says that $(F^\perp)^\perp = F$.

A subspace F of E is called *invariant* if for all $c \in F$ and $m \in M$ we have $mc \in F$. Likewise a subspace F' of E' is invariant if $l \in F'$ and $m \in M$ imply $lm \in F'$.

Observe that F is invariant iff $F^\perp$ is invariant. Indeed, assume $F \subset E$ invariant and consider $l \in F^\perp$. Then for all $c \in F$ and $m \in M$, we have $mc \in F$ and consequently $(lm)c = l(mc) = 0$. Thus lm is in $F^\perp$.

We now define a sequence of subspaces of E and E'. For each $R \in \Gamma$, set

$$c_R = \sum_{r \in R} r_{*1}$$

Thus c_R is the sum of the first columns of the elements in R. Likewise for $L \in \Lambda$, set

$$l_L = \sum_{m \in L} m_{1*}$$

Let E_2 be the subspace of E generated by the vectors

$$c_R \qquad (R \in \Gamma)$$

and let E'_2 be the subspace of E' generated by the vectors

$$l_L \qquad (L \in \Lambda).$$

Let E_1 denote the subspace of E_2 generated by the vectors

$$c_R - c_{R'} \qquad (R, R' \in \Gamma)$$

and let $E'_1 = E_1^\perp$.

Let E'_3 denote the subspace of E'_2 generated by the vectors

$$l_L - l_{L'} \qquad (L, L' \in \Lambda)$$

and let $E_3 = E_3'^\perp$.

Finally, for convenience, set

$$E_0 = \{0\}, \qquad E'_0 = E',$$

$$E_4 = E, \qquad E'_4 = \{0\}.$$

With these wonderful notations, we have $E_i^\perp = E'_i$ for $i = 0, 1, 3, 4$. However, we do not have $E_2^\perp = E'_2$ in general (see Example 5.2).

PROPOSITION 3.1 *Let $R \in \Gamma$ and $L \in \Lambda$.*

1. *For all $m \in M$,*

$$mc_R = c_{mR}, \qquad l_L m = l_{Lm}, \tag{3.1}$$

$$m_{1*}c_R = \mathrm{Card}(mR \cap \varphi(X^*)), \tag{3.2}$$

$$l_L m_{*1} = \mathrm{Card}(Lm \cap \varphi(X^*)). \tag{3.3}$$

2. *For all $m \in J$,*

$$m_{1*} \in E'_1, m_{*1} \in E_3. \tag{3.4}$$

3. *We have*

$$l_L c_R \neq 0. \tag{3.5}$$

Proof The function $r \mapsto mr$ is a bijection of R onto the right minimal ideal $mR \in \Gamma$. Thus

$$\begin{aligned} mc_R &= m\left(\sum_{r \in R} r_{*1}\right) \\ &= \sum_{r \in R} (mr)_{*1} \\ &= c_{mR}. \end{aligned}$$

The relation $l_L m = l_{Lm}$ is shown in the same way. Next

$$\begin{aligned} m_{1*}c_R &= (mc_R)_{1*} \\ &= (c_{mR})_{1*} \\ &= \sum_{r \in mR} r_{11} \\ &= \mathrm{Card}(mR \cap \varphi(X^*)). \end{aligned}$$

This proves (3.2), formula (3.3) is shown in the same way.

Now, let $m \in J$. Then $mR = mM$, showing that $m_{1*}c_R$ is independent of R. Consequently

$$m_{1*}(c_R - c_{R'}) = 0 \tag{3.6}$$

for $R, R' \in \Gamma$. Thus m_{1*} is orthogonal to the generators of E_1 and consequently $m_{1*} \in E'_1$. Similarly $m_{*1} \in E_3$.

To show (3.5), note that

$$l_L c_R = \sum_{m \in R} \operatorname{Card}(Lm \cap \varphi(X^*)).$$

Since X is a complete code, $\varphi(X^*) \cap J \neq \emptyset$ and therefore at least one term in the sum above does not vanish. □

PROPOSITION 3.2 *The following inclusions hold*

$$E_0 \subset E_1 \subsetneq E_2 \subset E_3 \subset E_4,$$

$$E'_4 \subset E'_3 \subseteq E'_2 \subset E'_1 \subset E'_0.$$

The subspaces E_i and E'_i are invariant.

Proof The invariance of the subspaces is a direct consequence of formulas (3.1). The inclusion $E_1 \subset E_2$ is clear. Next $E_2 \subset E_3$. Consider indeed a vector $c_R = \sum_{r \in R} r_{*1}$ for some $R \in \Gamma$. Since by formula (3.4), all r_{*1} are in E_3, we have $c_R \in E_3$. Thus all c_R $(R \in \Gamma)$ are in E_3. This proves the inclusion. The same argument holds for the E'_i.

It remains to prove that $E_1 \neq E_2$. For this, we assume that some c_R is in E_1. Then c_R is orthogonal to all elements in E'_1 hence also to all elements in E'_2. In particular $l_L c_R = 0$ for $L \in \Lambda$ contradicting (3.5). Thus no c_R, $R \in \Gamma$, is in E_1. □

Now let $B = B_1 \cup B_2 \cup B_3 \cup B_4$ be a base of E such that

$$\begin{array}{rll} B_1 & \text{is a base of} & E_1, \\ B_1 \cup B_2 & \text{is a base of} & E_2, \\ B_1 \cup B_2 \cup B_3 & \text{is a base of} & E_3. \end{array}$$

Set $n_k = \dim(E_k)$ for $0 \leq k \leq 4$ and

$$S_1 = \{1, 2, \ldots, n_1\}, \qquad S_2 = \{n_1 + 1, \ldots, n_2\},$$

$$S_3 = \{n_2 + 1, \ldots, n_3\}, \qquad S_4 = \{n_3 + 1, \ldots, n_4\}.$$

With these notations, we may assume that for $1 \leq k \leq 4$, $B_k = \{b_i \mid i \in S_k\}$.

Let K be the matrix

$$K = \begin{bmatrix} b_1 b_2 \cdots b_n \end{bmatrix}.$$

Let $\psi\colon A^* \to Q^{n \times n}$ be the morphism defined by

$$\psi(w) = K^{-1} \varphi(w) K.$$

Since the subspaces E_i are invariant, the matrix $\psi(w)$ has the form

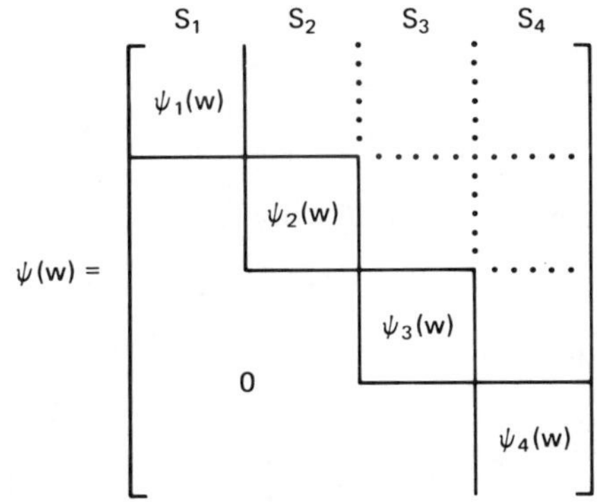

where $\psi_k(w)$ is the restriction of $\psi(w)$ to the set $S_k \times S_k$. Let $B' = \{b'_1, b'_2, \ldots, b'_n\}$ be the base of E' dual to the base B. Then

$$b'_i b_j = \delta_{ij}, \qquad 1 \leq i, j \leq n,$$

where δ is the Kronecker symbol. Set

$$\hat{B}_1 = \{b'_i \mid i \in S_1\}, \qquad \hat{B}_4 = \{b'_i \mid i \in S_4\}.$$

Since $B_1 \cup B_2 \cup B_3$ is a base of E_3 and since each $b'_i \in \hat{B}_4$ is orthogonal to the vectors in this set, $\hat{B}_4 \subset E_3^{\perp}$. Thus $\hat{B}_4 \subset E'_3$. Next $\dim(E'_3) = n - \dim(E_3) = n - n_3 = \mathrm{Card}(\hat{B}_4)$. This shows that $\hat{B}_4$ is a base of E'_3.

Similarly, since $E'_1 = E_1^{\perp}$, the set $\{b_{n_1+1}, \ldots, b'_n\}$ is a base of E'_1. This means that $\hat{B}_1$ is the base of some supplementary space of E'_1 in E'.

The base $\hat{B}_4$ of E'_3 can be completed by sets $\hat{B}_3$ and $\hat{B}_2$ in such a way that

$$\hat{B}_4 \cup \hat{B}_3 \qquad \text{is a base of} \quad E'_2,$$

$$\hat{B}_4 \cup \hat{B}_3 \cup \hat{B}_2 \qquad \text{is a base of} \quad E'_1.$$

Finally, since $\hat{B}_1$ is the base of some supplementary subspace of E'_1, the set $\hat{B} = \hat{B}_1 \cup \hat{B}_2 \cup \hat{B}_3 \cup \hat{B}_4$ is a base of E'. Set $\hat{b}_i = b'_i$ for $1 \leq i \leq n_1$ and for $n_3 + 1 \leq i \leq n$. Next let $n'_2 = \dim(E'_2)$. Set

$$\hat{S}_2 = \{n_1 + 1, \ldots, n'_2\}, \qquad \hat{S}_3 = \{n'_2 + 1, \ldots, n_3\},$$

and

$$\hat{B}_2 = \{\hat{b}_i \mid i \in \hat{S}_2\}, \qquad \hat{B}_3 = \{\hat{b}_i \mid i \in \hat{S}_3\}.$$

To have homogeneous notation, set

$$\hat{S}_1 = S_1, \qquad \hat{S}_4 = S_4.$$

Observe that $S_2 \cup S_3 = \hat{S}_2 \cup \hat{S}_3$. As before define a matrix.

$$\hat{K} = \begin{bmatrix} \hat{b}_1 \\ \hat{b}_2 \\ \vdots \\ \hat{b}_n \end{bmatrix}$$

and define a morphism $\psi'\colon A^* \to \mathbb{Q}^{n \times n}$ by setting

$$\psi'(w) = \hat{K}\varphi(w)\hat{K}^{-1}.$$

The matrices $\psi'(w)$ have the form

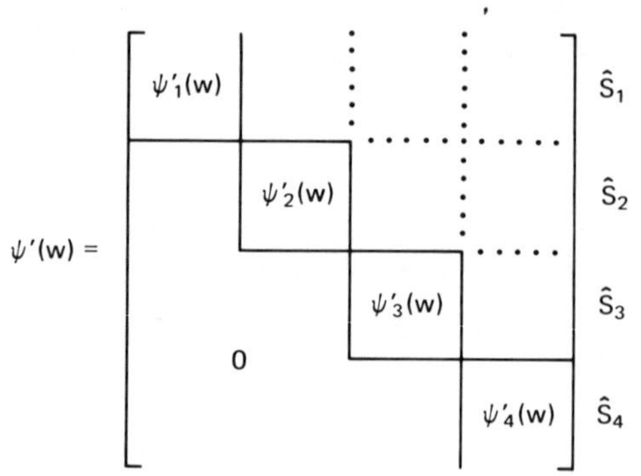

where $\psi'_i(w)$ is the restriction of $\psi'(w)$ to the set $\hat{S}_i$.

By construction, the ψ_i and ψ'_i are closely related. In fact, we have the following result.

PROPOSITION 3.3 *The following equality holds:*

$$\psi_1 = \psi'_1 \qquad \psi_4 = \psi'_4.$$

Furthermore, the matrices $\psi_2(w)$, $\psi'_2(w)$ both are the identity matrix of dimension one.

Proof By definition $K\psi(w) = \varphi(w)K$ and $\psi'(w)K = K\varphi(w)$. Thus

$$\hat{K}K\psi(w) = \psi'(w)\hat{K}K. \tag{3.7}$$

Let us compute $\hat{K}K$. We claim the $\hat{K}K$ has the form

$$\hat{K}K = \left[\begin{array}{c|c|c} I & 0 & 0 \\ \hline 0 & * & * \\ \hline 0 & 0 & I \end{array}\right] \begin{array}{l} S_1 \\ S_2 \cup S_3 \\ S_4 \end{array} \tag{3.8}$$

where the symbol $*$ denotes blocks which are not described in more detail. Indeed, first, $\hat{b}_i b_j = \delta_{ij}$ for $i \in S_1$ and $j \in \{1, \ldots, n\}$. This gives the form of the first row in (3.8). The same argument holds for the last row. Finally, we have $\hat{b}_i b_j = 0$ for $i \in S_2 \cup S_3 (= \hat{S}_2 \cup \hat{S}_3)$ and $j \in S_1$, since in this case $\hat{b}_i$ is orthogonal to E_1.

From (3.8) and from the expression of $\psi(w)$ and $\psi'(w)$, we derive the forms

$$\hat{K}K\psi(w) = \left[\begin{array}{c|c|c} \psi_1(w) & * & * \\ \hline 0 & * & * \\ \hline 0 & 0 & \psi_4(w) \end{array}\right], \qquad \psi'(w)\hat{K}K = \left[\begin{array}{c|c|c} \psi'_1(w) & * & * \\ \hline 0 & * & * \\ \hline 0 & 0 & \psi'_4(w) \end{array}\right].$$

In view of (3.7), it follows that $\psi_1(w) = \psi'_1(w)$ and also $\psi_4(w) = \psi'_4(w)$.

To prove the second claim, recall that in view of the definition of E_1 and E_2, we have $\dim(E_2) \le \dim(E_1) + 1$. Indeed, let $R_0 \in \Gamma$ be fixed. Then each $R \in \Gamma$ satisfies

$$c_R = c_{R_0} + (c_R - c_{R_0}) \in c_{R_0} + E_2.$$

Since $E_2 \ne E_1$, by Proposition 3.2, we get that $\dim(E_2) = \dim(E_1) + 1$. Thus $B_2 = \{b\}$ for some vector b in E_2. Since E_2 is generated by the c_R $(R \in \Gamma)$, we have $b = \sum_{R\in\Gamma} \alpha_R c_R$ for some $\alpha_R \in \mathbb{Q}$. Let w be a fixed word and $m = \varphi(w)$. Then

$$\varphi(w)b = \sum_{R\in\Gamma} \alpha_R c_{mR} = b + d,$$

where $d = \sum_{R\in\Gamma} \alpha_R(c_{mR} - c_R) \in E_1$. This shows that $\psi_2(w) = 1$. Similarly, we show that $\psi'_3(w) = 1$, arguing in this case on E'_3 and E'_2. □

For $1 \le i \le 4$, define

$$s_i = \theta\left(\sum_{a\in A} \psi_i(a)\underline{\underline{a}}\right), \qquad s'_i = \theta\left(\sum_{a\in A} \psi'_i(a)\underline{\underline{a}}\right),$$

where θ is the canonical isomorphism (of convenient dimension) defined in Section 2. Furthermore, set

$$p_i = \det(I - s_i), \qquad p'_i = \det(I - s'_i) \qquad \text{for} \quad i = 1, 2, 3, 4.$$

PROPOSITION 3.4 *The following equalities hold:*

$$p_1 = p'_1, \qquad p_2 = p'_3, \qquad p_3 = p'_2, \qquad p_4 = p'_4, \tag{3.9}$$

$$1 - \underline{\underline{A}} = p_2. \tag{3.10}$$

Moreover, the polynomials p_i have integral coefficients and they have constant term 1.

Proof Set

$$t = \theta\left(\sum_{a\in A} \varphi(a)\underline{\underline{a}}\right),$$

$$s = \theta\left(\sum_{a\in A} \psi(a)\underline{\underline{a}}\right).$$

Since $\psi(a) = K^{-1}\varphi(a)K$, we have $I - s = K^{-1}(I - t)K$. This shows that

$$\det(I - t) = \det(I - s). \tag{3.11}$$

Similarly, since $\psi'(a) = \hat{K}\psi(a)\hat{K}^{-1}$, we have

$$\det(I - t) = \det(I - s'). \tag{3.12}$$

The matrices $\psi(a)$ being upper triangular by blocks

$$\det(I - s) = p_1 p_2 p_3 p_4 \tag{3.13}$$

and similarly

$$\det(I - s') = p'_1 p'_2 p'_3 p'_4$$

whence $p_1 p_2 p_3 p_4 = p'_1 p'_2 p'_3 p'_4$. The polynomials p_i and p'_i as they are defined clearly have a constant term 1.

Next by Proposition 3.3, $\psi_1 = \psi'_1$ and $\psi_4 = \psi'_4$. Consequently $p_1 = p'_1$ and $p_4 = p'_4$. The same proposition shows that $s_2 = \underline{\underline{A}}$, hence $p_2 = 1 - \underline{\underline{A}}$. Likewise, $p'_3 = 1 - \underline{\underline{A}}$. Since $p_1 p_2 p_3 p_4 = p'_1 p'_2 p'_3 p'_4$ and none of these polynomials vanishes, we have $p_3 = p'_2$.

Since the p_i have a constant term equal to 1 and since the product of the p_i has integral coefficients, the lemma of Gauss shows that the p_i have integral coefficients. □

PROPOSITION 3.5 *Let $w \in \varphi^{-1}(J)$ and let*

$$U = w^{-1}X^*, \qquad U' = X^*w^{-1}.$$

Then

$$u = p'_4 p'_3 p'_2 \underline{\underline{U}}, \qquad u' = p_1 p_2 p_3 \underline{\underline{U}}'$$

are polynomials with integral coefficients.

Proof Let $z \in A^*$. Then $\varphi(zw)_{1,1} = (\underline{U}', z)$ since $zw \in X^*$ iff $z \in U'$. Using Proposition 2.2, we set $\lambda = [10\cdots 0] \in \mathbb{Q}^{1\times n}$ and $\gamma = \varphi(w)_{*1}$. Then

$$\varphi(zw)_{1,1} = \lambda\varphi(z)\gamma = \lambda K\psi(z)K^{-1}\gamma.$$

The matrix $\psi(z)$ can be partitioned as

$$\psi(z) = \left[\begin{array}{c|c} v(z) & * \\ \hline 0 & \psi_3(z) \end{array}\right] \qquad \text{where} \qquad v(z) = \left[\begin{array}{c|c|c} \psi_1(z) & * & * \\ \hline & \psi_2(z) & * \\ \hline 0 & & \psi_3(z) \end{array}\right].$$

By Proposition 3.1(ii), the vector γ is in E_3. Thus the coefficients of $K^{-1}\gamma$ with indices in S_4 vanish and

$$K^{-1}\gamma = \begin{bmatrix} c \\ 0 \end{bmatrix}.$$

Setting

$$\lambda K = [l \;\vdots\; *],$$

we obtain

$$(\underline{U}', z) = [l \quad *]\begin{bmatrix} v(z) & \vdots & * \\ \cdots & \cdots & \cdots \\ 0 & \vdots & \psi_4(z) \end{bmatrix}\begin{bmatrix} c \\ \cdots \\ 0 \end{bmatrix} = lv(z)c.$$

We now apply Proposition 3.3 to the series $\underline{U}'$ and the morphism v. Since

$$\det\left(I - \theta\left(\sum_{a \in A} v(a)\underline{a}\right)\right) = p_1 p_2 p_3,$$

Proposition 2.2 shows that $u' = p_1 p_2 p_3 \underline{U}'$ is a polynomial. It has integral coefficients since p_1, p_2, p_3, and $\underline{U}'$ have integral coefficients. The proof of the other formula is symmetric. □

PROPOSITION 3.6 *Let $D = X^*(A^*)^{-1}$, $G = (A^*)^{-1}X^*$ be the sets of words right, left completable. Let $w \in \varphi^{-1}(J) \cap D$ and let $V = Dw^{-1}$. Then*

$$v = p_1 p_2 \underline{V}$$

is a polynomial with integral coefficients. Let $w' \in \varphi^{-1}(J) \cap G$ and let $V' = w'^{-1}G$. Then

$$v' = p'_3 p'_4 \underline{V}'$$

is a polynomial with integral coefficients.

Proof The set $R = \varphi(wA^*)$ is a minimal right ideal which intersects $\varphi(X^*)$. Let

$$k = \mathrm{Card}(R \cap \varphi(X^*)).$$

For each $R' \in \Gamma$, either $\mathrm{Card}(R' \cap \varphi(X^*) = 0$ or this number is k, according to $R' \cap \varphi(X^*) = \emptyset$ or not. By Proposition 3.1. we have for $z \in A^*$,

$$(\varphi(z)c_R)_1 = \varphi(z)_{1*}c_R = \mathrm{Card}(\varphi(z)R \cap \varphi(X^*)).$$

Next $\varphi(z)R \cap \varphi(X^*) \neq \emptyset$ iff $z \in V$. Indeed, assume $z \in V$. Then $zwz' \in X^*$ for some $z' \in A^*$ and consequently $\varphi(zwz') \in \varphi(z)R \cap \varphi(X^*)$. Conversely, if $\varphi(z)R \cap \varphi(X^*) \neq \emptyset$, then there exists some $r = \varphi(wz') \in R$ such that $zwz' \in X^*$. It follows from this that $(\varphi(z)c_R)_1 = k(\underline{V}, z)$.
Set $\lambda = [1\ 0 \cdots 0] \in \mathbb{Q}^{1 \times n}$. Then

$$(\varphi(z)c_R)_1 = \lambda\varphi(z)c_R = \lambda K\varphi(z)K^{-1}c_R.$$

Set

$$\bar{v}(z) = \begin{bmatrix} \psi_1(z) & \vdots & * \\ \cdots & \cdots & \cdots \\ 0 & \vdots & \psi_2(z) \end{bmatrix}.$$

Since $c_R \in E_2$, we have

$$K^{-1}c_R = \begin{bmatrix} \bar{c} \\ \cdots \\ 0 \end{bmatrix}$$

with $\bar{c} \in \mathbb{Q}^{n_2 \times 1}$. Setting

$$\lambda K = [\bar{l} \quad *]$$

gives as before

$$\begin{aligned} k(\underline{V}, z) &= [\bar{l} \,\vdots\, *] \begin{bmatrix} \bar{v}(z) & \vdots & * \\ \cdots & & \cdots \\ 0 & \vdots & * \end{bmatrix} \begin{bmatrix} \bar{c} \\ \cdots \\ 0 \end{bmatrix} \\ &= \bar{l}\bar{v}(z)\bar{c}. \end{aligned}$$

Again we apply Proposition 2.2. In this case we get that $\bar{v} = k\underline{V}p_1p_2$ is a polynomial. This of course implies that $v = \underline{V}p_1p_2$ is a polynomial. It has integral coefficients since p_1, p_2, and $\underline{V}$ have integral coefficients. This completes the proof of the first claim. The second one is proved symmetrically. □

4. EVALUATION OF THE POLYNOMIALS

In this section we keep the notations of the preceding section and assume further that the code X is *finite*. Let A be a finite alphabet and let $\pi: A^* \to [0, 1]$ be a Bernoulli distribution. Set $A = \{a_1, \ldots, a_n\}$. For each polynomial $p = p(a_1, a_2, \ldots, a_n) \in \mathbb{Q}[A]$, we denote by $\pi(p)$ the real number

$$\pi(p) = p(\pi(a_1), \pi(a_2), \ldots, \pi(a_n)).$$

This defines a function again denoted by $\pi: \mathbb{Q}[A] \to \mathbb{R}$, which is a morphism of $\mathbb{Q}$-algebras. Moreover, if $L \subset A^*$ is a finite set, then $\pi(L) = \pi(\underline{L})$.

Now consider a series $\sigma \in \mathbb{Q}[[A]]$ and set

$$\sigma = \sum_{n \geq 0} \sigma_n,$$

where σ_n is the homogeneous component of degree n of σ (i.e., the sum of the monomials of total degree n). The density $\delta(\sigma)$ of σ with respect to π is defined as the limit in mean of the numbers $\pi(\sigma_n)$, provided it exists,

$$\delta(\sigma) = \lim_{n \to \infty} \frac{1}{n} \sum_{i=0}^{n-1} \pi(\sigma_i).$$

With this definition, it is easy to see that $\delta(\underline{L})$ exists for $L \subset A^*$ iff $\delta(L)$ exists and that $\delta(\underline{L}) = \delta(L)$.

For any $k \in \mathbb{Q}, \sigma \in \mathbb{Q}[[A]]$, we have $\delta(k\sigma) = k\delta(\sigma)$. We also have, for $w \in A^*$, the relation $\delta(w\sigma) = \pi(w)\delta(\sigma)$. It follows that for any polynomial $p \in \mathbb{Q}[A]$,

$$\delta(p\sigma) = \pi(p)\delta(\sigma). \tag{4.1}$$

The following notation is useful. Let $a \in A$ be a letter. Then

$$\zeta_a\colon \quad \mathbb{Q}[A] \quad \to \quad \mathbb{Q}[A - \{a\}]$$

is the morphism defined by

$$\zeta_a(b) = b \qquad \text{for} \quad b \in A - \{a\},$$
$$\zeta_a(a) = 1 - \sum_{b \in A - a} b.$$

The following result will be used several times in the sequel.

PROPOSITION 4.1 *Let $p \in \mathbb{Q}[A]$ be a polynomial and let $a \in A$ be a letter. The following three conditions are equivalent:*

(i) *p is divisible by the polynomial $1 - \underline{\underline{A}}$,*
(ii) $\zeta_a(p) = 0$,
(iii) *$\pi(p) = 0$ for each positive Bernoulli distribution.*

Proof The implications (i) ⇒ (ii) ⇒ (iii) are clear. To prove (iii) ⇒ (i), set $A = \{a_1, \ldots, a_n\}$. Consider p as a polynomial in the variable a_1 with coefficients in $\mathbb{Q}[a_2, \ldots, a_n]$. Likewise, consider $\underline{\underline{A}} - 1 = a_1 - k$ as a polynomial in a_1 with constant term $k = 1 - \sum_{i=2}^n a_i$. The Euclidean division of p by $a_1 - k$ gives

$$p = q(a_1 - k) + r$$

with $q \in \mathbb{Q}[A]$ and $r \in \mathbb{Q}[a_2, \ldots, a_n]$. Since $\pi(p) = 0$ and $\pi(a_1 - k) = 0$ for each positive Bernoulli distribution π, the polynomial r vanishes at all points $(z_2, \ldots, z_n) \in \mathbb{Q}^{n-1}$ such that $z_i \geq 0$ and $z_2 + \cdots + z_n \leq 1$. It follows that r vanishes and consequently $1 - \underline{\underline{A}}$ divides p. □

Remark Given a finite maximal code $X \subset A^+$, it follows from Theorem I.5.10 that $\pi(X) = 1$ for any positive Bernoulli distribution π. By Proposition 4.1, this implies that $1 - \underline{\underline{A}}$ divides $1 - \underline{\underline{X}}$. This is part of Proposition 3.4 proved in a completely different way.

We now come back to the notation of the previous sections. We shall give information about the polynomials

$$p_i = \det(I - s_i), \qquad 1 \leq i \leq 4$$

with

$$s_i = \theta\left(\sum_{a \in A} \psi_i(a)\underline{\underline{a}}\right).$$

Since X is finite, we have by Proposition 2.1 and formulas (3.11), (3.13),

$$1 - \underline{X} = p_1 p_2 p_3 p_4.$$

We have already seen that $p_2 = 1 - \underline{A}$.

We now examine the polynomial p_1. Recall that, given a word $w \in A^*$, the set $C_r(w)$ of right contexts of w (with respect to a code X) is the set of words $v \in A^*$ such that

$$wv = x_1 x_2 \cdots x_n,$$

with $x_i \in X$ and $|v| < |x_n|$.

A set of words $C \subset A^*$ is called a set of right contexts if $C = C_r(w)$ for some $w \in A^*$. In this case, we have $\underline{C}\underline{X}^* = \underline{U}$ with $U = w^{-1}X^*$. The same relations hold symmetrically for left contexts.

PROPOSITION 4.2 *Let C and C' be maximal sets of right and left contexts, respectively, with respect to X. Then there exist polynomials u and u' in $\mathbb{Z}[A]$ such that*

$$p_1 u = \underline{C}, \qquad p_4 u' = \underline{C}'.$$

Moreover, for each Bernoulli distribution π,

$$\pi(u) = \pi(u') = 1$$

and

$$\pi(p_3) = d(X).$$

Proof Set $D = X^*(A^*)^{-1}$ and $G = (A^*)^{-1}X^*$. Let $w_1 \in A^*$ be a word such that $C = C_r(w_1)$ and consider a word $x \in X^* \cap \varphi^{-1}(J)$, where J is the minimal ideal of $M = \varphi(A^*)$. Let $w = xw_1$. Since $\varphi(x)M$ is a minimal right ideal, there exists a word $v \in A^*$ such that $\varphi(xw_1v) = \varphi(x)$. Thus $xw_1v = wv \in X^*$ and consequently $w \in D \cap \varphi^{-1}(J)$. Next $C_r(w_1) \subset C_r(xw_1)$ and thus $C_r(w_1) = C_r(w)$. Thus $C = C_r(w)$ for some $w \in \varphi^{-1}(J) \cap D$. Similarly we have $C' = C_l(w')$ for some $w' \in \varphi^{-1}(J) \cap G$.

Set

$$U = w^{-1}X^*, \qquad V = Dw^{-1}.$$

According to Proposition 3.5 (and Proposition 3.4)

$$u = p_2 p_3 p_4 \underline{U} \tag{4.2}$$

is a polynomial with integral coefficients. According to Proposition 3.6,

$$v = p_1 p_2 \underline{V} \tag{4.3}$$

is a polynomial with integral coefficients. Next

$$V \cap \varphi^{-1}(J) = D \cap \varphi^{-1}(J). \tag{4.4}$$

Indeed, let $z \in V \cap \varphi^{-1}(J)$. Then $zw \in D$ and consequently $z \in D$. Thus $z \in D \cap \varphi^{-1}(J)$. Conversely, let $z \in D \cap \varphi^{-1}(J)$. Since the right ideal $\varphi(z)M$ is minimal, there exists $z' \in A^*$ such that $\varphi(zwz') = \varphi(z)$. Thus $zwz' \in D$, whence $zw \in D$. Thus $z \in V \cap \varphi^{-1}(J)$, proving (4.4).

Let π be a positive Bernoulli distribution. In view of Proposition VI.2.7, formula (4.4) implies

$$\delta(V) = \delta(D). \tag{4.5}$$

Consequently $\delta(\underline{\underline{V}}) = \delta(\underline{\underline{D}})$. Furthermore, it follows from (4.3), observing that $p_2 = 1 - A$, that $v\underline{\underline{A}}^* = p_1\underline{\underline{V}}$. Applying (4.1), we obtain $\pi(v) = \pi(p_1)\delta(\underline{\underline{V}})$ hence $\pi(v) = \pi(p_1)\delta(D)$. In view of Proposition VI.3.4, $\pi(C)\delta(D) = 1$. Thus

$$\pi(v)\pi(C) = \pi(p_1). \tag{4.6}$$

Next $\underline{\underline{U}} = \underline{\underline{C}}\underline{\underline{X}}^*$. It follows that $\underline{\underline{U}}(1 - \underline{\underline{X}}) = \underline{\underline{C}}$, which implies by (4.2), $u(1 - \underline{\underline{X}}) = p_2p_3p_4\underline{\underline{C}}$. Since $1 - \underline{\underline{X}} = p_1p_2p_3p_4$, we obtain

$$up_1 = \underline{\underline{C}}. \tag{4.7}$$

This proves the first claim. Next, substituting $\pi(\underline{\underline{C}})$ from (4.7) in formula (4.6), we obtain

$$\pi(v)\pi(u) = 1. \tag{4.8}$$

This formula holds for any positive Bernoulli distribution π. According to Proposition 4.1 $\zeta_a(vu - 1) = 0$, hence $\zeta_a(v)\zeta_a(u) = 1$. This equality holds in the ring of polynomials $\mathbb{Z}[A - \{a\}]$, because v and u have integral coefficients. It follows that $\zeta_a(v) = \zeta_a(u) = \pm 1$.

We shall see that $\zeta_a(v) = \zeta_a(u) = 1$. For this, let

$$\gamma: \quad \mathbb{Q}[A] \to \mathbb{Q}[a]$$

be the morphism defined by

$$\gamma(a) = a, \qquad \gamma(b) = 0 \qquad \text{for} \quad b \in A - \{a\}.$$

Since X is a finite maximal code, $X \cap a^* = \{a^n\}$ for some integer $n \geq 1$. For this integer n, we have $\gamma(\underline{\underline{X}}) = a^n$. Taking the image of $1 - \underline{\underline{X}} = p_1p_2p_3p_4$ by γ, we obtain

$$1 - a^n = \gamma(p_1)(1 - a)\gamma(p_3p_4).$$

Setting $q = \gamma(p_1)$, this formula becomes

$$1 + a + \cdots + a^{n-1} = q\gamma(p_3p_4). \tag{4.9}$$

The left side of (4.9) takes strictly positive values for each nonnegative value of a. Thus the polynomial $q = q(a)$ does not vanish and does not change its sign for values in $\mathbb{R}_+$. Now $q(0) = 1$, since p_1 has constant term 1. This implies in particular that $q(1) > 0$.

Observe that $q(1)$ is the value of $\zeta_a(p_1)$ at the point $(0, \ldots, 0)$. Now, by (4.7)

$$\zeta_a(u)\zeta_a(p_1) = \zeta_a(\underline{C}).$$

The polynomial on the right-hand side takes the value Card$(C \cap a^*)$ at the point $(0, \ldots, 0)$. Consequently the value of $\zeta_a(u)$ at this point is positive. Since it is a constant, it follows that $\zeta_a(u) = 1$. By Proposition 4.1, this implies that $\pi(u) = 1$. Symmetrically we can prove that $p_4 u' = \underline{C}'$ and that $\pi(u') = 1$. For the last formula, we again consider the expression $1 - \underline{X} = p_1 p_2 p_3 p_4$ and multiply it by $\underline{A}^* \underline{X}^*$. Since $\underline{X}^*(1 - \underline{X}) = 1$, we obtain $\underline{A}^* = p_1 p_3 p_4 \underline{X}^*$. According to formula (4.1) this gives

$$1 = \pi(p_1)\pi(p_3)\pi(p_4)\delta(X^*).$$

Next, by Theorem VI.3.1, $\delta(X^*) = (1/d(X))\delta(G)\delta(D)$. Since $\delta(G)\pi(C') = 1$, $\delta(D)\pi(C) = 1$ and also $\pi(p_1) = \pi(C)$, $\pi(p_4) = \pi(C')$, it follows that $d(X) = \pi(p_3)$. □

5. PROOF OF THE THEOREM

Now we are able to give a proof of Theorem 1.1. Let X be a finite maximal code over A and let

$$1 - \underline{X} = p_1(1 - \underline{A})p_3 p_4$$

be the factorization of Proposition 3.4.

PROPOSITION 5.1 *The following equivalences hold:*

1. *X is prefix* $\Leftrightarrow p_1 = 1$.
2. *X is suffix* $\Leftrightarrow p_4 = 1$.
3. *X is synchronous* $\Leftrightarrow \zeta_a(p_3) = 1$.

Proof

1. Assume that X is prefix. Then the set $C' = \{1\}$ is a maximal set of right contexts. Indeed, if $1 \in C_r(w)$, then $w \in X^*$ and any $v \in C_r(w)$ satisfies $wv \in X^*$, whence $v \in X^*$, which in turn implies $v = 1$. By Proposition 4.2, the polynomial p_1 divides the polynomial $\underline{C}' = 1$. Since the constant term of p_1 is 1, we have $p_1 = 1$.

Conversely assume $p_1 = 1$. Again by Proposition 4.2, any maximal set C of right contexts satisfies $\pi(C) = 1$ for any Bernoulli distribution π. This implies that if $1 \in C$, then $C = \{1\}$. This implication holds for any set of right contexts since any of them is contained in a maximal one. Now consider $x, y \in A^*$ with $x, xy \in X^*$. Then $1 \in C_r(x)$ and therefore $C_r(x) = \{1\}$. This implies that the X-factorization of xy passes between x and y. Thus $y \in X^*$. This shows that X^* is right unitary and hence that X is prefix.

2. The proof is analogous.

3. In view of Proposition 4.2, we have $\pi(p_3) = d(X)$ for any Bernoulli distribution. By Proposition 4.1, $\zeta_a(p_3 - d(X)) = 0$. Consequently $\zeta_a(p_3) = d(X)$. Thus the equivalence is proved. □

Proof of Theorem 1.1 The polynomial $r = (1 - \underline{X})/(1 - \underline{A})$ is a product

$$r = p_1 p_3 p_4.$$

This polynomial cannot be irreducible in $\mathbb{Z}[A]$ unless two of these three polynomials are constants. Since the constant term of these polynomials is 1, the irreducibility of r cannot be realized unless one of the three following cases holds:

(i) $p_1 = p_3 = 1$. This implies that X is prefix and synchronous.
(ii) $p_3 = p_4 = 1$. This implies that X is suffix and synchronous.
(iii) $p_1 = p_3 = 1$. This implies that X is biprefix. □

EXAMPLE 5.1 Let $A = \{a, b\}$ and let X be our friend

$$X = \{aa, ba, baa, bb, bba\}.$$

We shall illustrate on this code the computations made in the previous sections. We know already that X is a maximal code and that X^* is recognized by the automaton given in Fig. 8.1. The associated representation φ is given by

$$\varphi(a) = \begin{bmatrix} 0 & 1 & 0 \\ 1 & 0 & 0 \\ 1 & 1 & 0 \end{bmatrix}, \qquad \varphi(b) = \begin{bmatrix} 0 & 0 & 1 \\ 0 & 0 & 0 \\ 1 & 1 & 0 \end{bmatrix}.$$

We have already seen (Example IV.5.3) that the minimal ideal of the monoid $\varphi(A^*)$ is composed of elements of rank 1. They are all idempotents. The minimal ideal is represented in Fig. 8.2, with $\alpha = \varphi(a)$, $\beta = \varphi(b)$. It is formed of two minimal right ideals R_1 and R_2 and of two minimal left ideals L_1 and L_2.

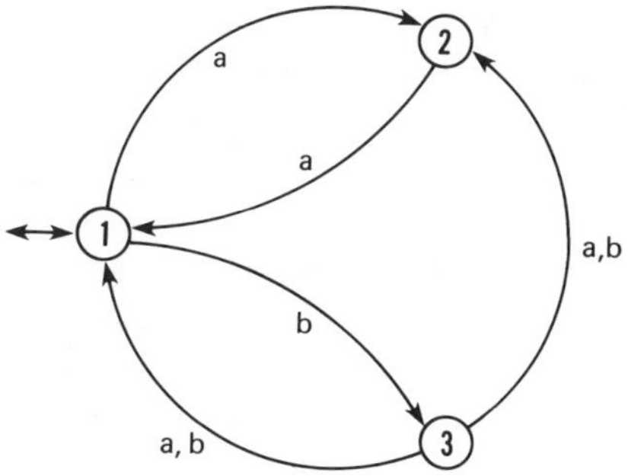

Fig. 8.1

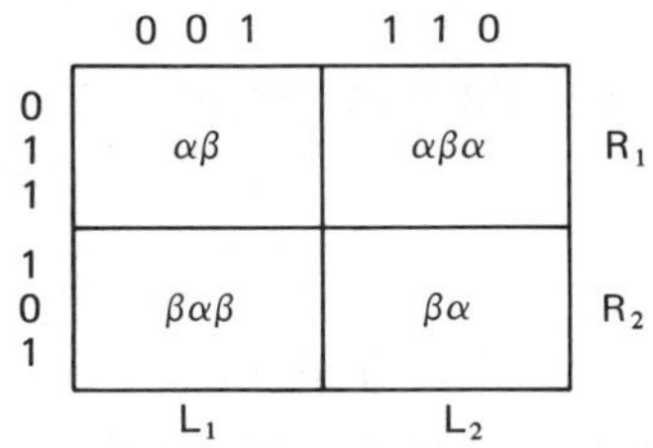

Fig. 8.2 The minimal ideal.

Set $c_1 = c_{R_1}$ and $c_2 = c_{R_2}$ and similarly for the l_L. Then

$$c_1 = \begin{bmatrix} 0 \\ 1 \\ 1 \end{bmatrix}, \qquad c_2 = \begin{bmatrix} 1 \\ 0 \\ 1 \end{bmatrix}, \qquad l_1 = [001], \qquad l_2 = [110].$$

Thus

$$E_1 = \mathbb{Q}\begin{bmatrix} 1 \\ -1 \\ 0 \end{bmatrix},$$

$$E_2 = \mathbb{Q}c_1 + \mathbb{Q}c_2,$$

$$E'_2 = \mathbb{Q}l_1 + \mathbb{Q}l_2,$$

$$E'_3 = \mathbb{Q}[1 \quad 1 \quad -1].$$

Since E'_3 has dimension 1, we have $\dim(E_3) = 2$. Since $E_2 \subset E_3$, we have $E_2 = E_3$.

Consider the base $B = \{b_1, b_2, b_3\}$ given by

$$b_1 = \begin{bmatrix} 1 \\ -1 \\ 0 \end{bmatrix}, \qquad b_2 = \begin{bmatrix} 0 \\ 1 \\ 1 \end{bmatrix}, \qquad b_3 = \begin{bmatrix} 0 \\ 1 \\ 0 \end{bmatrix}.$$

Thus b_1 is a base of E_1 and $\{b_1, b_2\}$ is a base of E_2. In this base, the matrices $\varphi(a)$ and $\varphi(b)$ become

$$\psi(a) = \begin{bmatrix} -1 & 1 & 1 \\ 0 & 1 & 1 \\ 0 & 0 & 0 \end{bmatrix}, \qquad \psi(b) = \begin{bmatrix} 0 & 1 & 0 \\ 0 & 1 & 1 \\ 0 & 0 & -1 \end{bmatrix}.$$

Thus the matrix

$$I - \theta(\underline{\underline{a}}\psi(a) + \underline{\underline{b}}\psi(b)) = \begin{bmatrix} 1 + \underline{\underline{a}} & -\underline{\underline{a}} - \underline{\underline{b}} & -\underline{\underline{a}} \\ 0 & 1 - \underline{\underline{a}} - \underline{\underline{b}} & -\underline{\underline{a}} - \underline{\underline{b}} \\ 0 & 0 & 1 + \underline{\underline{b}} \end{bmatrix}$$

gives the polynomials

$$p_1 = 1 + \underline{\underline{a}}, \qquad p_4 = 1 + \underline{\underline{b}},$$

$$1 - \underline{\underline{X}} = (1 + \underline{\underline{a}})(1 - \underline{\underline{a}} - \underline{\underline{b}})(1 + \underline{\underline{b}}). \tag{5.1}$$

This is the decomposition described in the previous sections. Of course, (5.1) may be verified by direct computation.

In fact, formula 5.1 holds in noncommuting variables because X is a factorizing code,

$$1 - \underline{X} = (1 + a)(1 - \underline{A})(1 + b).$$

To obtain this formula, we may observe that setting $Z = \{aa, ab, b\}$, we have

$$1 - \underline{Z} = (1 + a)(1 - \underline{A}), \qquad 1 - \underline{X} = (1 - \underline{Z})(1 + b),$$

which yields the desired formula. □

EXAMPLE 5.2 Let $A = \{a, b\}$ and consider the maximal prefix code $Z = a \cup bA^2$. Let $X = Z^2$. The code X is represented in Fig. 8.3 (cf. also Example IV.6.7, where the code Z^4 was considered). The minimal automaton $\mathscr{A}(X^*)$ is represented in Fig. 8.4. The matrices $\varphi(a)$ and $\varphi(b)$ are

$$\varphi(a) = \begin{bmatrix} 0 & 0 & 0 & 1 & 0 & 0 \\ 0 & 0 & 1 & 0 & 0 & 0 \\ 0 & 0 & 0 & 1 & 0 & 0 \\ 1 & 0 & 0 & 0 & 0 & 0 \\ 0 & 0 & 0 & 0 & 0 & 1 \\ 1 & 0 & 0 & 0 & 0 & 0 \end{bmatrix}, \qquad \varphi(b) = \begin{bmatrix} 0 & 1 & 0 & 0 & 0 & 0 \\ 0 & 0 & 1 & 0 & 0 & 0 \\ 0 & 0 & 0 & 1 & 0 & 0 \\ 0 & 0 & 0 & 0 & 1 & 0 \\ 0 & 0 & 0 & 0 & 0 & 1 \\ 1 & 0 & 0 & 0 & 0 & 0 \end{bmatrix}.$$

Let us compute the minimal ideal of the monoid of functions $\varphi(A^*)$. It is

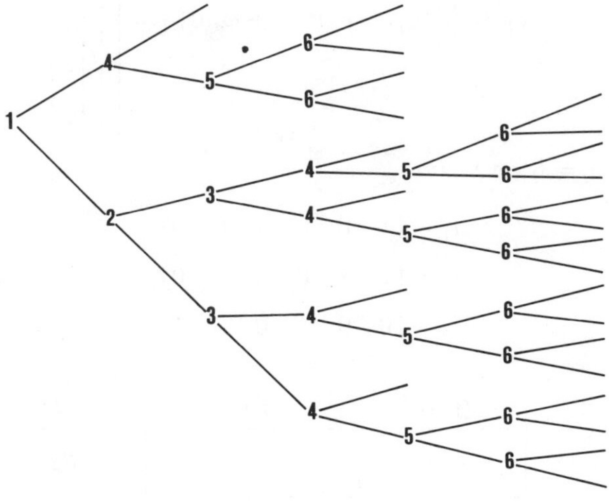

Fig. 8.3 The maximal prefix code $X = Z^2$.

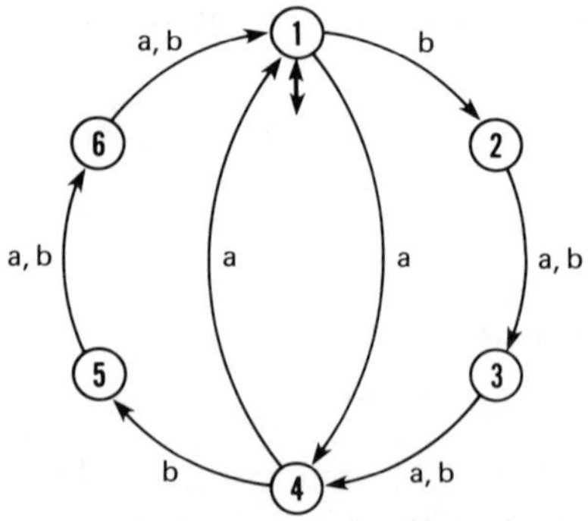

Fig. 8.4 The automaton $\mathscr{A}(X^*)$.

represented in Fig. 8.5 with the following conventions (justified by Proposition IV.5.8). Each $\mathscr{H}$-class is identified by the nuclear equivalence characterizing its $\mathscr{R}$-class and by the image characterizing its $\mathscr{L}$-class. Here $\alpha = \varphi(a)$, $\beta = \varphi(b)$. The minimal ideal is composed of a single minimal right ideal R and of three minimal left ideals. The minimal rank is 2 and the group of the code X consequently is $\mathbb{Z}/2\mathbb{Z}$.

Easy computation shows that the first column of the matrices in $L_2 \cup L_3$ vanishes. Consequently

$$c_R = \sum_{r \in R} r_{*1} = \varphi(a^2)_{*1} + \varphi(a^3)_{*1} = \begin{bmatrix} 1 \\ 1 \\ 1 \\ 1 \\ 1 \\ 1 \end{bmatrix}.$$

Next, setting $l_i = l_{L_i}$, we have

$$l_1 = [1 \quad 0 \quad 0 \quad 1 \quad 0 \quad 0],$$
$$l_2 = [0 \quad 1 \quad 0 \quad 0 \quad 1 \quad 0],$$
$$l_3 = [0 \quad 0 \quad 1 \quad 0 \quad 0 \quad 1].$$

	{1, 4}	{2, 5}	{3, 6}	
{1, 3, 5}, {2, 4, 6}	α^2, α^3	$\alpha^2\beta, \alpha^3\beta$	$\alpha^2\beta^2, \alpha^3\beta^2$	R

Fig. 8.5 The minimal ideal of $\varphi(A^*)$.

Thus $E'_2 = \mathbb{Q}l_1 + \mathbb{Q}l_2 + \mathbb{Q}l_3$ has dimension 3, whence $\dim(E'_3) = 2$. The space E'_3 is generated by

$$l_1 - l_2 = [1 \quad -1 \quad 0 \quad 1 \quad -1 \quad 0], \qquad l_1 - l_3 = [1 \quad 0 \quad -1 \quad 1 \quad 0 \quad -1].$$

Since $\dim(E_2) = 1$, we have $\dim(E_1) = 0$. Set

$$b_1 = \begin{bmatrix}1\\1\\1\\1\\1\\1\end{bmatrix}, \quad b_2 = \begin{bmatrix}0\\1\\0\\1\\0\\1\end{bmatrix}, \quad b_3 = \begin{bmatrix}1\\1\\1\\0\\0\\0\end{bmatrix}, \quad b_4 = \begin{bmatrix}0\\1\\1\\1\\0\\0\end{bmatrix}, \quad b_5 = \begin{bmatrix}1\\0\\0\\1\\0\\0\end{bmatrix}, \quad b_6 = \begin{bmatrix}0\\1\\0\\0\\0\\0\end{bmatrix}.$$

These vectors are linearly independent. Since $b_1 = c_R$, the set $\{b_1\}$ is a base for E_2. Since $\{b_1, b_2, b_3, b_4\}$ all are in $E'^{\perp}_3$ (as is easily verified), they form a base of E_3. In the new base, matrices $\varphi(a)$ and $\varphi(b)$ have the form

$$\psi(a) = \left[\begin{array}{c|ccc|cc} 1 & 1 & 0 & 0 & 1 & 0 \\ \hline & -1 & 1 & 0 & 0 & 0 \\ & 0 & 0 & 1 & 0 & 0 \\ & 0 & 0 & 0 & 0 & 0 \\ \hline & & & & 0 & 0 \\ & & & & -1 & 0 \end{array}\right],$$

$$\psi(b) = \left[\begin{array}{c|ccc|cc} 1 & 1 & 0 & 0 & 1 & 0 \\ \hline & -1 & 1 & 0 & 0 & 0 \\ & 0 & 1 & 1 & 0 & 0 \\ & 0 & -1 & 0 & 0 & 0 \\ \hline & & & & 1 & 1 \\ & & & & -1 & 0 \end{array}\right].$$

Hence we obtain the matrix

$$I - \theta(\psi(a)\underline{\underline{a}} + \psi(b)\underline{\underline{b}}) = \left[\begin{array}{c|ccc|cc} 1 - \underline{\underline{A}} & 0 & 0 & 0 & -\underline{\underline{A}} & 0 \\ \hline & 1 + \underline{\underline{A}} & -\underline{\underline{A}} & 0 & 0 & 0 \\ & 0 & 1 - \underline{\underline{b}} & -\underline{\underline{A}} & 0 & 0 \\ & 0 & \underline{\underline{b}} & 1 & 0 & 0 \\ \hline & & & & 1 + \underline{\underline{b}} & -\underline{\underline{b}} \\ & & & & \underline{\underline{A}} & 1 \end{array}\right].$$

This gives

$$p_1 = 1, \qquad p_2 = 1 - \underline{\underline{A}},$$
$$p_3 = (1 + \underline{\underline{A}})(1 - \underline{\underline{b}} + \underline{\underline{b}}\underline{\underline{A}}) = 1 + \underline{\underline{a}} + \underline{\underline{b}}\underline{\underline{A}}^2,$$
$$p_4 = 1 + \underline{\underline{b}} + \underline{\underline{b}}\underline{\underline{A}},$$

Of course $1 - \underline{\underline{X}} = p_1 p_2 p_3 p_4$. Also $\zeta_a(p_3) = 2$. Since $X = Z^2$ and $1 - \underline{Z} = (1 + b + b\underline{A})(1 - \underline{A})$, we obtain, using the formula $1 - \underline{X} = (1 + \underline{Z})(1 - \underline{Z})$,

$$1 - \underline{X} = (1 + a + b\underline{A}^2)(1 + b\underline{A})(1 - \underline{A}). \tag{5.2}$$

By passing to commutative variables in formula (5.2), the first factor gives p_3, the second one gives p_4 and the last p_2.

Observe that the code X admits a second decomposition. Indeed, all words in X have even length. Consequently $X = Y \circ A^2$ for some code Y. This leads to the factorization

$$1 - \underline{X} = (1 + ab + b\underline{A} + b\underline{A}^2 b)(1 - \underline{A}^2). \tag{5.3}$$

By passing to commutative variables in (5.3) the first factor of (5.3) is the product of p_4 with the second factor of p_3 and the second factor of (5.3) is the product of p_2 with the first factor of p_3. If we consider the invariant subspace, which is generated by b_1 and b_2, the factorization of $\det(I - \theta(\psi(a)\underline{\underline{a}} + \psi(b)\underline{\underline{b}})$ which corresponds to this decomposition of the state space, leads to expression (5.3).

6. COMMUTATIVE EQUIVALENCE

Recall that

$$\alpha: \quad \mathbb{Q}\langle\langle A\rangle\rangle \to \mathbb{Q}[[A]]$$

denotes the canonical morphism that associates to a formal power series its commutative image. By definition, for each $\sigma \in \mathbb{Q}\langle\langle A\rangle\rangle$ and $w \in A^*$,

$$(\alpha(\sigma), \underline{\underline{w}}) = (\sigma, \underline{K(w)}) = \sum_{v \in K(w)} (\sigma, v),$$

where $K(w)$ is the class of commutativity of w, $K(w) = \{v \in A^* \mid \underline{\underline{v}} = \underline{\underline{w}}\}$. Two series $\sigma, \tau \in \mathbb{Q}\langle\langle A\rangle\rangle$ are called *commutatively equivalent* if $\alpha(\sigma) = \alpha(\tau)$.

Two subsets X and Y of A^* are commutatively equivalent if their characteristics series $\underline{X}$ and $\underline{Y}$ are so, which means that $\underline{\underline{X}} = \underline{\underline{Y}}$. In an equivalent manner, X and Y are commutatively equivalent iff there exists a bijection $\gamma: X \to Y$ such that $\gamma(x) \in K(x)$ for all $x \in X$.

A subset X of A^* is called *commutatively prefix* if there exists a prefix subset Y of A^* that is commutatively equivalent to X.

EXAMPLE 6.1 Any suffix code is commutatively prefix. More generally, any code obtained by a sequence of compositions of prefix and suffix codes is commutatively prefix. In particular, our friend $X = \{aa, ba, baa, bb, bba\}$ is commutatively prefix.

EXAMPLE 6.2 Let $A = \{a, b\}$ and let

$$X = \{aa, ba, bb, abab, baab, bbab, a^3b^2, a^3ba^2, a^3b^2ab, a^3ba^3b, a^3babab\}.$$

This set is easily verified to be a code, by computing, for instance, the sets of U_i's of Section I.3,

$$U_1 = \{abb, aba^2, ab^2ab, aba^3b, (ab)^3, ab\}, \qquad U_2 = \{ab\}, \qquad U_3 = \{ab\}.$$

Further, X is maximal since for $\pi(a) = \pi(b) = \frac{1}{2}$, we obtain $\pi(X) = 1$. Finally X is commutatively prefix since

$$Y = \{aa, ba, bb, abab, abba, abbb, abaab, aba^4, aba^3b^2, aba^3ba^2, aba^3bab\}$$

is a prefix code with $\underline{\underline{Y}} = \underline{\underline{X}}$.

THEOREM 6.1 *For each subset X of A^* the following conditions are equivalent*:

(i) *X is commutatively prefix.*
(ii) *The series $(1 - \underline{\underline{X}})/(1 - \underline{\underline{A}})$ has nonnegative coefficients.*
(iii) *For each commutativity class K intersecting X, we have*

$$\operatorname{Card}(K) \geq (\underline{\underline{X}}\,\underline{\underline{A}}^*, \underline{\underline{K}}). \tag{6.1}$$

Proof (i) $\Rightarrow$ (ii). First assume that $\underline{\underline{X}} = \underline{\underline{Y}}$ for some prefix set Y. Let $P = A^* - YA^*$. Then $\underline{\underline{A}}^* = \underline{\underline{Y}}^*\underline{\underline{P}}$, hence $1 - \underline{\underline{Y}} = \underline{\underline{P}}(1 - \underline{\underline{A}})$. Thus $1 - \underline{\underline{X}} = \underline{\underline{P}}(1 - \underline{\underline{A}})$. Clearly $\underline{\underline{P}} = (1 - \underline{\underline{X}})/(1 - \underline{\underline{A}})$ has nonnegative integral coefficients.

To prove (ii) $\Rightarrow$ (iii), we show that for all $w \in A^*$,

$$(\underline{\underline{X}}\,\underline{\underline{A}}^*, \underline{\underline{w}}) = (\underline{\underline{X}}\,\underline{\underline{A}}^*, \underline{\underline{K}}), \tag{6.2}$$

where K is the commutativity class of w. Indeed

$$\begin{aligned}(\underline{\underline{X}}\,\underline{\underline{A}}^*, \underline{\underline{w}}) &= (\alpha(\underline{X})\alpha(\underline{A}^*), \underline{\underline{w}}) \\ &= (\alpha(\underline{X}\,\underline{A}^*), \underline{\underline{w}}) \\ &= (\underline{X}\,\underline{A}^*, \underline{K}).\end{aligned}$$

Next, observe that since $(1 - \underline{\underline{A}})^{-1} = \underline{\underline{A}}^*$, we have

$$(1 - \underline{\underline{X}})/(1 - \underline{\underline{A}}) = \underline{\underline{A}}^* - \underline{\underline{X}}\,\underline{\underline{A}}^*.$$

Thus the assumption for this series to have nonnegative coefficients implies that for all $w \in \underline{\underline{A}}^*$, $(\underline{\underline{A}}^*, \underline{w}) \geq (\underline{\underline{X}}\,\underline{\underline{A}}^*, \underline{w})$. Since $(\underline{\underline{A}}^*, \underline{w}) = \mathrm{Card}(K(w))$, this gives in view of (6.2),

$$\mathrm{Card}(K) \geq (\underline{\underline{X}}\,\underline{\underline{A}}^*, \underline{K}),$$

which is the desired inequality.

Finally, assume that (iii) holds. For $n \geq 1$, let

$$X_n = X \cap A^n, \qquad X_n = X \cap A^{(n)}.$$

(Recall that $A^{(n)} = 1 \cup A \cup A^2 \cup \cdots \cup A^{n-1}$). We shall define by induction on n a sequence $Y_{(n)}$ of prefix codes such that

$$\underline{\underline{Y}}_{(n)} = \underline{\underline{X}}_{(n)}.$$

For $n = 1$, set $Y_{(1)} = X_{(1)}$. Let $n \geq 2$ and assume a prefix code $Y_{(n)}$ constructed, satisfying $\underline{\underline{Y}}_{(n)} = \underline{\underline{X}}_{(n)}$. Let K be a commutativity class in A^n that meets X. Then by (6.2),

$$(\underline{\underline{X}}_{(n)}\underline{\underline{A}}^*, \underline{K}) = (\underline{\underline{Y}}_{(n)}\underline{\underline{A}}^*, \underline{K}) \tag{6.3}$$

since $\underline{\underline{X}}_{(n)} = \underline{\underline{Y}}_{(n)}$. Next (6.1) shows that

$$\mathrm{Card}(K) \geq (\underline{\underline{X}}\,\underline{\underline{A}}^*, \underline{K}) \geq (\underline{\underline{X}}_{(n+1)}\underline{\underline{A}}^*, \underline{K}) = (\underline{\underline{X}}_{(n)}\underline{\underline{A}}^*, \underline{K}) + \mathrm{Card}(K \cap X_n).$$

Using (6.3), we obtain

$$\mathrm{Card}(K) \geq (\underline{\underline{Y}}_{(n)}\underline{\underline{A}}^*, \underline{K}) + \mathrm{Card}(K \cap X_n).$$

Since $Y_{(n)}$ is prefix

$$(\underline{\underline{Y}}_{(n)}\underline{\underline{A}}^*, \underline{K}) = \mathrm{Card}(Y_{(n)}A^* \cap K).$$

Thus

$$\mathrm{Card}(K) \geq \mathrm{Card}(K \cap Y_{(n)}A^*) + \mathrm{Card}(K \cap X_n)$$

or equivalently

$$\mathrm{Card}(K \cap (A^* - Y_{(n)}A^*)) \geq \mathrm{Card}(K \cap X_n).$$

This inequality shows that we can choose, in the set K, a set Y_K of $\mathrm{Card}(K \cap X_n)$ words which have no left factor in $Y_{(n)}$. Since $Y_K \subset K$, the sets Y_K and $K \cap X_n$ are commutatively equivalent. Set $Y_n = \bigcup_K Y_K$, where K runs over the commutativity classes contained in A^n that meet X. Then

$$\underline{\underline{Y}}_n = \bigcup_K \underline{\underline{Y}}_K = \underline{\underline{\bigcup_K K \cap X_n}} = \underline{\underline{X}}_n.$$

Further, setting $Y_{(n+1)} = Y_{(n)} \cup Y_n$, this set is a prefix code. This completes the proof. □

EXAMPLE 6.3 Let $A = \{a, b\}$ and let $X \subset a^*ba^*$. Then X is commutatively prefix iff for all $n \geq 0$

$$\mathrm{Card}(X \cap A^{(n+1)}) \leq n. \tag{6.4}$$

Indeed, the only commutativity class $K \subset A^n$ that intersects X is

$$K = \{a^iba^j \mid i + j = n - 1\}.$$

Since $\mathrm{Card}(K) = n$ and since

$$(\underline{X}\underline{A}^*, \underline{K}) = (\underline{X}\underline{a}^*, \underline{K}) = \mathrm{Card}(X \cap A^{(n+1)}).$$

Formula (6.4) is a translation of formula (6.1).

COROLLARY 6.2 *A factorizing code is commutatively prefix.*

Proof Let $X \subset A^+$ be a factorizing code and let (P, Q) be a factorization of X. Then by definition $1 - \underline{X} = \underline{P}(1 - \underline{A})\underline{Q}$. Passing to commutative variables gives $1 - \underline{\underline{X}} = \underline{\underline{P}}(1 - \underline{\underline{A}})\underline{\underline{Q}}$ or also $(1 - \underline{\underline{X}})/(1 - \underline{\underline{A}}) = \underline{\underline{P}}\underline{\underline{Q}}$. Since $\underline{\underline{P}}\underline{\underline{Q}}$ has nonnegative coefficients, the conclusion follows from Theorem 6.1. □

Now we give an example of a code which is not commutatively prefix.

EXAMPLE 6.4 Let $X \subset a^*ba^*$ be the set given in Table 8.1, with the convention that $a^iba^j \in X$ iff the box (i, j) contains a dot. Clearly $X \subset A^{(16)}$ and $\mathrm{Card}(X) = 16$. Thus according to Example 6.3, X is not commutatively prefix.

To show that X is a code, assume the contrary (see Fig. 8.6). Then there are in X four words of the form

$$x = a^iba^j, \qquad y = a^ka^lba^n, \qquad z = xa^k, \qquad t = a^lba^n.$$

The dots representing x and z are in the same row in Table 8.1. Thus necessarily $k \in \{1, 2, 4, 6, 7, 12, 13, 14\}$ since these are the distances separating two dots in a same row. Next, the dots representing y and t are in rows whose difference of indices is k. Thus $k \in \{3, 5, 8, 11\}$. This gives the contradiction.

We can observe that X is a code with deciphering delay 1. Also by Corollary 6.2, the code X is not a factorizing code.

We have mentioned in Section 1 that all finite maximal codes known up to now are factorizing. A fortiori they are commutatively prefix. If this property holds for all finite maximal codes, then it follows that the code of Example 6.4 cannot be completed into a finite maximal code.

As a matter of fact, we do not know at present whether it is decidable that a finite code can be included in a finite maximal code.

TABLE 8.1

A Code X Which Is Not Commutatively Prefix

	0	1	2	3	4	5	6	7	8	9	10	11	12	13	14
0	●	●						●						●	●
1															
2															
3	●		●		●		●								
4															
5															
6															
7															
8	●		●		●		●								
9															
10															
11	●	●	●												
12															
13															
14															

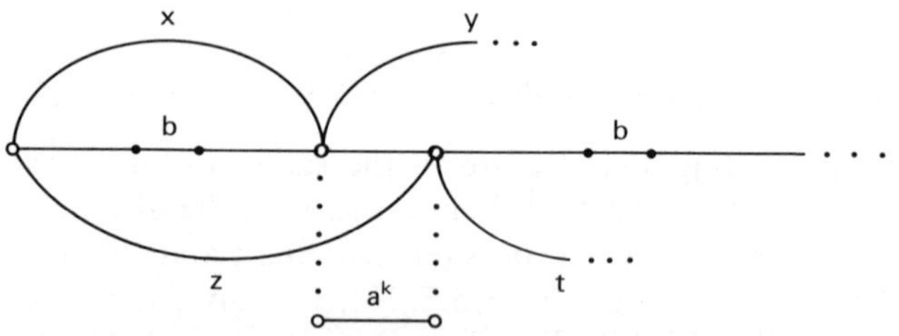

Fig. 8.6 If X were not a code.

7. COMPLETE REDUCIBILITY

Let A be an alphabet. Let $\sigma \in \mathbb{Q}\langle\langle A \rangle\rangle$ be a series and let $u \in A^*$ be a word. We define a series $\sigma \cdot u$ by $(\sigma \cdot u, v) = (\sigma, uv)$ for all $v \in A^*$. The following formulas hold:

$$\sigma \cdot 1 = \sigma, \qquad (\sigma \cdot u) \cdot v = \sigma \cdot uv.$$

Let V_σ be the subspace of the vector space $\mathbb{Q}\langle\langle A\rangle\rangle$ generated by the series $\sigma \cdot u$ for $u \in A^*$. For each word $w \in A^*$, we denote by $\psi_\sigma(w)$ the linear function from V_σ into itself (acting on the right) defined by

$$\psi_\sigma(w): \quad \rho \mapsto \rho \cdot w.$$

The formula $(\rho \cdot u)\psi_\sigma(w) = \rho \cdot uw = \rho\psi_\sigma(uw)$ is straightforward. It follows that ψ_σ is a morphism

$$\psi_\sigma: \quad A^* \to \mathrm{End}(V_\sigma)$$

from A^* into the monoid $\mathrm{End}(V_\sigma)$ of linear functions from V_σ into itself. The morphism ψ_σ is called the *syntactic representation* of σ.

PROPOSITION 7.1 *Let Y be a subset of A^* and let $\sigma = \underline{Y}$. Let φ be the canonical morphism from A^* onto the syntactic monoid of Y. Then for all $u, v \in A^*$,*

$$\varphi(u) = \varphi(v) \quad \Leftrightarrow \quad \psi_\sigma(u) = \psi_\sigma(v).$$

In particular the monoid $\psi_\sigma(A^*)$ is isomorphic to the syntactic monoid of Y.

Proof Assume first that $\psi_\sigma(u) = \psi_\sigma(v)$. Then for all $r \in A^*$,

$$\sigma \cdot ru = (\sigma \cdot r)\, \psi_\sigma(u) = (\sigma \cdot r)\, \psi_\sigma(v) = \sigma \cdot rv.$$

Thus also for all $s \in A^*$,

$$(\sigma, rus) = (\sigma \cdot ru, s) = (\sigma \cdot rv, s) = (\sigma, rvs).$$

That means that $rus \in Y$ iff $rvs \in Y$, which shows that $\varphi(u) = \varphi(v)$.

Conversely, assume $\varphi(u) = \varphi(v)$. Since the vector space V_σ is generated by the series $\sigma \cdot r$ ($r \in A^*$), it suffices to show that for $r \in A^*$,

$$(\sigma \cdot r)\psi_\sigma(u) = (\sigma \cdot r)\psi_\sigma(v).$$

Now for all $s \in A^*$,

$$((\sigma \cdot r)\psi_\sigma(u), s) = (\sigma \cdot ru, s) = (\sigma, rus)$$

$$= (\sigma, rvs) = ((\sigma \cdot r)\psi_\sigma(v), s). \quad \square$$

The preceding result gives a relationship between the syntactic representation of the characteristic series σ of a set $Y \subset A^*$ and the syntactic monoid of Y. It should be noted (see Example 7.2) that the monoid $\psi_\sigma(A^*)$ is not always equivalent to the transition monoid of the minimal automaton of Y considered as a function monoid over the vector space generated by the states. However, it can be shown that the vector space V_σ has finite dimension iff Y is recognizable (Exercise 7.2).

EXAMPLE 7.1 Let $\sigma = \underline{A}^*$. Then $\sigma \cdot u = \sigma$ for all $u \in A^*$. Consequently $V_\sigma = \mathbb{Q}\sigma$ is a vector space of dimension 1.

EXAMPLE 7.2 Let $A = \{a, b\}$ and let $X \subset A^+$ be the biprefix code of Fig. 8.7. Let $\sigma = \underline{X}^*$. We shall see that the vectors $\sigma, \sigma \cdot a, \sigma \cdot a^2$, and $\sigma \cdot b$ form

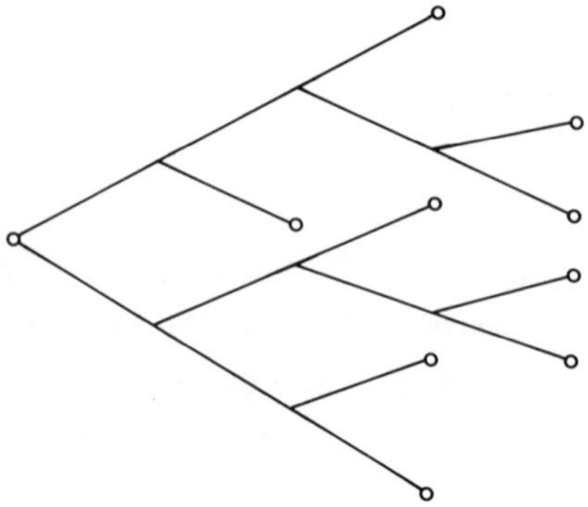

Fig. 8.7

a base of the vector space V_σ. Indeed, the formulas

$$\sigma \cdot a^3 = \sigma \cdot ab = \sigma,$$

$$\sigma \cdot ba = \sigma \cdot a^2,$$

$$\sigma \cdot b^2 = \sigma \cdot a^2 b = \sigma \cdot a + \sigma \cdot a^2 - \sigma \cdot b,$$

show that the four vectors σ, $\sigma \cdot a$, $\sigma \cdot a^2$, and $\sigma \cdot b$ generate V_σ. A direct computation shows that they are linearly independent. The matrices of the linear mappings $\psi_\sigma(a)$ and $\psi_\sigma(b)$ in this base are

$$\psi_\sigma(a) = \begin{bmatrix} 0 & 1 & 0 & 0 \\ 0 & 0 & 1 & 0 \\ 1 & 0 & 0 & 0 \\ 0 & 0 & 1 & 0 \end{bmatrix}, \qquad \psi_\sigma(b) = \begin{bmatrix} 0 & 0 & 0 & 1 \\ 1 & 0 & 0 & 0 \\ 0 & 1 & 1 & -1 \\ 0 & 1 & 1 & -1 \end{bmatrix}.$$

The relation between ψ_σ and the minimal automaton of X^* is now to be shown. The minimal automaton has five states which may be written as $1, 1 \cdot a, 1 \cdot a^2, 1 \cdot b, 1 \cdot b^2$. Let V be the $\mathbb{Q}$-vector space formed of formal linear combinations of these five states. The linear function $\alpha \colon V \to V_\sigma$ defined by $\alpha(1 \cdot u) = \sigma \cdot u$ satisfies the equality $\alpha(q \cdot u) = \alpha(q) \cdot u$ and moreover we have $\alpha(1 \cdot a + 1 \cdot a^2 - 1 \cdot b - 1 \cdot b^2) = 0$. Thus V has dimension 5 and V_σ has dimension 4.

Let V be a vector space over $\mathbb{Q}$ and let N be a submonoid of the monoid $\mathrm{End}(V)$ of linear functions from V into itself. The action of elements in $\mathrm{End}(V)$ will be written on the right.

A subspace W of V is *invariant* under N if for $\rho \in W, n \in N$, we have $\rho n \in W$. The submonoid N is called *reducible* if there exists a subspace W of V which is invariant under N and such that $W \neq \{0\}$, $W \neq V$. Otherwise, N is called *irreducible.*

The submonoid N is *completely reducible* if for all subspaces W of V which are invariant under N, there exists a subspace W' of V which is a supplementary space of W and invariant under N.

If V has finite dimension, a completely reducible submonoid N of End(V) has the following form. There exists a decomposition of V into a direct sum of invariant subspaces $W_1, W_2, \ldots, W_k$,

$$V = W_1 \oplus W_2 \oplus \cdots \oplus W_k$$

such that the restrictions of the elements of N to each of the W_i's form an irreducible submonoid of End(W_i). In a base of V composed of bases of the subspaces W_i, the matrix of an element n in N has a diagonal form by blocks,

$$n = \begin{bmatrix} n_1 & & & 0 \\ & n_2 & & \\ & & \ddots & \\ 0 & & & n_k \end{bmatrix}.$$

Let M be a monoid and let V be a vector space. A *linear representation* ψ of M over V is a morphism from M into the monoid End(V). A subspace W of V is called *invariant* under ψ if it is invariant under $\psi(M)$. Similarly ψ is called reducible, irreducible, or completely reducible if this holds for $\psi(M)$.

The syntactic representation of a series σ is an example of a linear representation of a free monoid. The aim of this section is to study cases where this representation is completely reducible. We recall that all the vector spaces considered here are over the field $\mathbb{Q}$ of rational numbers. The following result is a classical one.

THEOREM 7.2 *A linear representation of a finite group is completely reducible.*

Proof Let V be a vector space over $\mathbb{Q}$. It suffices to show that each finite subgroup of the monoid End(V) is completely reducible.

Let G be a finite subgroup of End(V) and let W be a subspace of V which is invariant under G. Let W_1 be any supplementary space of W in V. Let $\pi: V \to V$ be the linear function which associates to $\rho \in V$ the unique ρ_1 in W_1 such that $\rho = \rho_1 + \rho'$ with $\rho' \in W$. Then $\pi(\rho) = 0$ for all $\rho \in W$ and $\pi(\rho) = \rho$ for $\rho \in W_1$. Moreover, $\rho - \pi(\rho) \in W$ for all $\rho \in V$.

Let $n = \mathrm{Card}(G)$. Define a linear function $\theta: V \to V$ by setting for $\rho \in V$,

$$\theta(\rho) = \frac{1}{n} \sum_{g \in G} \pi(\rho g) g^{-1}.$$

Let $W' = \theta(V)$. We shall see that W' is an invariant subspace of V under G which is a supplementary space of W. First, for $\rho \in W$,

$$\theta(\rho) = 0. \tag{7.1}$$

Indeed, if $\rho \in W$, then $\rho g \in W$ for all $g \in G$ since W is invariant under G. Thus $\pi(\rho g) = 0$ and consequently $\theta(\rho) = 0$. Second, for $\rho \in V$,

$$\rho - \theta(\rho) \in W. \tag{7.2}$$

Indeed

$$\rho - \theta(\rho) = \rho - \frac{1}{n}\sum_{g \in G} \pi(\rho g)g^{-1} = \frac{1}{n}\sum_{g \in G} (\rho g - \pi(\rho g))g^{-1}.$$

By definition of π each $\rho g - \pi(\rho g)$ is in W for $g \in G$. Since W is invariant under G, also $(\rho g - \pi(\rho g))g^{-1} \in W$. This shows formula (7.2).

By (7.1) we have $W \subset \mathrm{Ker}(\theta)$ and by (7.2), $\mathrm{Ker}(\theta) \subset W$ since $\rho \in \mathrm{Ker}(\theta)$ implies $\rho - \theta(\rho) = \rho$. Thus

$$W = \mathrm{Ker}(\theta).$$

Formula (7.1) further shows that $\theta^2 = \theta$. Indeed, $\theta(\rho) - \theta^2(\rho) = \theta(\rho - \theta(\rho))$. By (7.2), $\rho - \theta(\rho) \in W$. Hence $\theta(\rho) - \theta^2(\rho) = 0$ by (7.1). Since $\theta^2 = \theta$, the subspaces $W = \mathrm{Ker}(\theta)$ and $W' = \mathrm{Im}(\theta)$ are supplementary. Finally, W' is invariant under G. Indeed, let $\rho \in V$ and $h \in G$. Then

$$\theta(\rho)h = \frac{1}{n}\sum_{g \in G} \pi(\rho g)g^{-1}h.$$

The function $g \mapsto k = h^{-1}g$ is a bijection from G onto G and thus

$$\theta(\rho)h = \frac{1}{n}\sum_{k \in G} \pi(\rho hk)k^{-1} = \theta(\rho h).$$

This completes the proof. □

THEOREM 7.3 *Let $X \subset A^+$ be a thin biprefix code. The syntactic representation of $\underline{X}^*$ is completely reducible.*

In the case of group codes, this theorem is a direct consequence of Theorem 7.2. For the general case, we need the following proposition in order to be able to apply Theorem 7.2.

PROPOSITION 7.4 *Let $X \subset A^+$ be a thin prefix code and let $\psi = \psi_{\underline{X}^*}$ be the syntactic representation of $\underline{X}^*$. The monoid $M = \psi(A^*)$ contains an idempotent e such that*

(i) $e \in \psi(X^*)$.

(ii) *The set eMe is the union of the finite group $G(e)$ and of the element 0, provided $0 \in M$.*

Proof Let S be the syntactic monoid of X^* and let $\varphi: A^* \to S$ be the canonical morphism. Consider also the minimal automaton $\mathscr{A}(X^*)$ of X^*. Since X is prefix, the automaton $\mathscr{A}(X^*)$ has a single final state which is the initial state (Proposition II.2.2). Let $\mu = \varphi_{\mathscr{A}(X^*)}$ be the morphism associated with $\mathscr{A}(X^*)$. We claim that for all $u, v \in A^*$,

$$\mu(u) = \mu(v) \quad \Leftrightarrow \quad \psi(u) = \psi(v). \tag{7.3}$$

Indeed, in view of Proposition 0.4.3, we have

$$\mu(u) = \mu(v) \quad \Leftrightarrow \quad \varphi(u) = \varphi(v),$$

and by Proposition 7.1,

$$\varphi(u) = \varphi(v) \quad \Leftrightarrow \quad \psi(u) = \psi(v).$$

Formula (7.3) shows that there exists an isomorphism $\beta: \mu(A^*) \to \psi(A^*) = M$ defined by $\beta \circ \mu = \psi$. In particular, $\psi(X^*) = \beta(\mu(X^*))$. Thus the monoid M shares all properties of the monoid $\mu(A^*)$. In particular by Theorem IV.5.6, the monoid M has a unique 0-minimal or minimal ideal, say J, according to whether M does or does not have a zero. There exists an idempotent e in J which is also in $\psi(X^*)$. The $\mathscr{H}$-class of this idempotent is a finite group that is isomorphic to the group of X. □

Proof of Theorem 7.3 For convenience, set $V = V_{\underline{X}^*}$ and denote by ψ the syntactic representation $\psi_{\underline{X}^*}$. Let $M = \psi(A^*)$. By Proposition 7.4, there exists an idempotent $e \in \psi(X^*)$ such that eMe is the union of 0 (if $0 \in M$) and of the group $G(e)$. Let $L = Me$ and define $S = \{\rho e \mid \rho \in V\}$. Since $e^2 = e$, we have $\tau e = \tau$ for all $\tau \in S$. Next, for all $l \in L$, we have $le = l$ since $l = me$ for some $m \in M$ and consequently $le = me^2 = me = l$. Thus for all $l \in L$,

$$Vl \subset S. \tag{7.4}$$

Let W be a subspace of V which is invariant under M. We shall see that there exists a supplementary space of W which is invariant under M. For this, set $T = W \cap S$ and $G = G(e)$.

The group G acts on S. The subspace T of S is invariant under G. Indeed, let $\tau \in T$ and let $g \in G$. Then $\tau g \in W$ since W is invariant under M and $\tau g \in S$ by (7.4) since $g = ge$. By Theorem 7.2, there exists a subspace T' of S which is supplementary of T in S and which is invariant under G. Set

$$W' = \{\rho \in V \mid \forall l \in L, \rho l \in T'\}.$$

We shall verify that W' is a supplementary space of W invariant under M. First observe that W' clearly is a subspace of V. Next it is invariant under M since for $\rho \in W'$ and $m \in M$, we have, for all $l \in L$, $(\rho m)l = \rho(ml) \in T'$ and consequently $\rho m \in W'$.

Next we show that

$$T' \subset W'. \tag{7.5}$$

Indeed, let $\tau' \in T'$. Then $\tau' \in S$ and thus $\tau' e = \tau'$. Hence $\tau' l = \tau' el$ for all $l \in L$. Since $el \in eMe$ and since T' is invariant under G, it follows that $\tau' l \in T'$. Thus $\tau' \in W'$.

Now we verify that $V = W + W'$. For this, set $\sigma = \underline{X}^*$ and first observe that

$$\sigma e = \sigma. \tag{7.6}$$

(Note that $\sigma \in V$ and e acts on V.) Indeed, let $x \in X^*$ be such that $\psi(x) = e$. Since X^* is right unitary, we have for all $u \in A^*$ the equivalence $xu \in X^* \Leftrightarrow u \in X^*$. Thus $(\sigma e, u) = (\sigma \cdot x, u) = (\sigma, xu) = (\sigma, u)$ which proves (7.6).

In view of (7.6), we have $\sigma \in S$. Since $S = T + T'$, there exists $\tau \in T$ and $\tau' \in T'$ such that $\sigma = \tau + \tau'$. Then for all $m \in M$, $\sigma m = \tau m + \tau' m$. For each $m \in M$, $\tau m \in Tm \subset Wm \subset W$, whence $\tau m \in W$. Using (7.5), also $\tau' m \in T' m \subset W' m$. Since W' is invariant under M, we obtain $\tau' m \in W'$. Thus $\sigma m \in W + W'$. Since V is generated by the vectors σm for $m \in M$, this proves that $V = W + W'$.

Finally, we claim that $W \cap W' = \{0\}$. Indeed, let $\rho \in W \cap W'$. Then for all $l \in L$,

$$\rho l = 0. \tag{7.7}$$

Indeed, let $l \in L$. Then $\rho l \in W$, since W is invariant under M and $\rho l \in S$ by Eq. (7.4). Thus $\rho l \in W \cap S = T$. Further $\rho l \in T'$ by the definition of W' and by the fact that $\rho \in W'$. Thus $\rho l \in T \cap T' = \{0\}$.

Since V is generated by the series $\sigma \cdot u$ ($u \in A^*$), there exist numbers $\alpha_u \in \mathbb{Q}$ ($u \in A^*$) with only a finite number of them nonzero such that

$$\rho = \sum_{u \in A^*} \alpha_u (\sigma \cdot u).$$

Again, let $x \in X^*$ be such that $\psi(x) = e$. Since X^* is left unitary, we have, as above, $(\sigma, w) = (\sigma, wx)$ for all $w \in A^*$. Thus for all $v \in A^*$,

$$\begin{aligned}(\rho, v) &= \sum_{u \in A^*} \alpha_u (\sigma \cdot u, v) = \sum_{u \in A^*} \alpha_u (\sigma, uv) \\ &= \sum_{u \in A^*} \alpha_u (\sigma, uvx) = \sum_{u \in A^*} \alpha_u (\sigma \cdot u, vx) \\ &= (\rho, vx) = (\rho \cdot vx, 1).\end{aligned}$$

Thus setting $m = \psi(v)$, we have $(\rho, v) = (\rho me, 1)$, and since $me \in L$, we have $\rho me = 0$ by (7.7). Consequently $(\rho, v) = 0$ for all $v \in A^*$. Thus $\rho = 0$. This shows that $W \cap W' = \{0\}$ and completes the proof. $\square$

EXAMPLE 7.2 (*continued*) The subspace W of $V = V_\sigma$ generated by the vector $\rho = \sigma + \sigma \cdot a + \sigma \cdot a^2$ is invariant under ψ_σ. Indeed, we have

$$\rho \cdot a = \rho, \qquad \rho \cdot b = \rho.$$

We shall exhibit a supplementary space of W invariant under ψ_σ. It is the subspace generated by

$$\sigma - \sigma \cdot a, \quad \sigma - \sigma \cdot a^2, \quad \sigma - \sigma \cdot b.$$

Indeed, in the base

$$\rho, \quad \sigma - \sigma \cdot a, \quad \sigma - \sigma \cdot a^2, \quad \sigma - \sigma \cdot b,$$

the linear mappings $\psi_\sigma(a)$ and $\psi_\sigma(b)$ have the form

$$\alpha = \left|\begin{array}{c:ccc} 1 & 0 & 0 & 0 \\ \hdashline 0 & -1 & 1 & 0 \\ 0 & -1 & 0 & 0 \\ 0 & -1 & 1 & 0 \end{array}\right|, \qquad \beta = \left|\begin{array}{c:ccc} 1 & 0 & 0 & 0 \\ \hdashline 0 & 0 & 0 & 1 \\ 0 & 1 & 1 & -2 \\ 0 & 1 & 1 & -2 \end{array}\right|.$$

We can observe that there are no other nontrivial invariant subspaces.

We now give a converse of Theorem 7.3 for the case of complete codes. The result does not hold in general if the code is not complete (see Example 7.3).

THEOREM 7.5 *Let $X \subset A^+$ be a thin complete code. If the syntactic representation of $\underline{X}^*$ is completely reducible, then X is biprefix.*

Proof Let $\mathscr{A} = (Q, 1, 1)$ be a trim unambiguous automaton recognizing X^*. Let φ be the associated representation and let $M = \varphi(A^*)$.

Set $\sigma = \underline{X}^*$ and also $V = V_\sigma$, $\psi = \psi_\sigma$. Let μ be the canonical morphism from A^* onto the syntactic monoid of X^*. By Proposition 0.4.3, we have for u, $v \in A^*$, $\varphi(u) = \varphi(v) \Rightarrow \mu(u) = \mu(v)$. Since by Proposition 7.1, $\mu(u) = \mu(v) \Leftrightarrow \psi(v) = \psi(v)$, it follows that $\varphi(u) = \varphi(v) \Rightarrow \psi(u) = \psi(v)$. Thus we can define a linear representation $\theta\colon M \to \mathrm{End}(V)$ by setting for $m \in M$, $\theta(m) = \psi(u)$, where $u \in A^*$ is any word such that $\varphi(u) = m$. If ψ is completely irreducible, then this holds also for θ.

For notational ease, we shall write, for $\rho \in V$ and $m \in M$, $\rho \cdot m$ instead of $\rho \cdot u$, where $u \in A^*$ is such that $\varphi(u) = m$. With this notation, we have for $m = \varphi(u)$,

$$\rho \cdot u = \rho\psi(u) = \rho\theta(m) = \rho \cdot m.$$

Observe further that with $m = \varphi(u)$,

$$(\sigma \cdot m, 1) = (\sigma \cdot u, 1) = (\sigma, u).$$

Hence

$$(\sigma \cdot m, 1) = \begin{cases} 1 & \text{if } m \in \varphi(X^*), \\ 0 & \text{otherwise.} \end{cases} \tag{7.8}$$

Finally, we have for $\rho \in V$, $m, n \in M$, $(\rho \cdot m) \cdot n = \rho \cdot mn$. For $\rho \in V$ and for a finite subset K of M, we define

$$\rho \cdot K = \sum_{k \in K} \rho \cdot k.$$

In particular, (7.8) gives

$$(\sigma \cdot K, 1) = \mathrm{Card}(K \cap \varphi(X^*)). \tag{7.9}$$

The code X being thin and complete, the monoid M has a minimal ideal J that intersects $\varphi(X^*)$. Further, J is a $\mathscr{D}$-class. Its $\mathscr{R}$-classes (resp., $\mathscr{L}$-classes) are the minimal right ideals (resp., minimal left ideals) of M (see Chap. IV, Sect. 5).

Let R be an $\mathscr{R}$-class of J and let L be $\mathscr{L}$-class of J. Set $H = R \cap L$. For each $m \in M$, the function $h \mapsto hm$ induces a bijection from H onto the $\mathscr{H}$-class $Hm = Lm \cap R$. Similarly, the function $h \mapsto mh$ induces a bijection from H onto the $\mathscr{H}$-class $mH = L \cap mR$.

To show that X is suffix, consider the subspace W of V generated by the series

$$\sigma \cdot H - \sigma \cdot K \tag{7.10}$$

for all pairs H, K of $\mathscr{H}$-classes of J contained is the same $\mathscr{R}$-class. We shall first prove that $W = \{0\}$.

The space W is invariant under M. Indeed, let H and K be two $\mathscr{H}$-classes contained in some $\mathscr{R}$-class R of J. Then for $m \in M$, $(\sigma \cdot H) \cdot m = \sigma \cdot (Hm)$ since the right multiplication by m is a bijection from H onto Hm. Thus $(\sigma \cdot H - \sigma \cdot K) \cdot m = \sigma \cdot (Hm) - \sigma \cdot (Km)$ and the right-hand side is in W since $Hm, Km \subset R$.

Next for all $\rho \in W$ and $m \in J$,

$$\rho \cdot m = 0 \tag{7.11}$$

Indeed, let H and K be two $\mathscr{H}$-classes contained in an $\mathscr{R}$-class R of J. Then for $m \in J$, Hm, $Km \subset R \cap Mm$. Since $R \cap Mm$ is an $\mathscr{H}$-class, we have $Hm = Km = R \cap Mm$. Thus

$$(\sigma \cdot H - \sigma \cdot K) \cdot m = 0.$$

Since $\rho \in W$ is a linear combination of series of the form (7.10) this proves (7.11).

Since the representation of M over V is completely reducible, there exists a supplementary space W' of W which is invariant under M. Set $\sigma = \rho + \rho'$ with $\rho \in W$, $\rho' \in W'$. Let H, K be two $\mathscr{H}$-classes of J contained in an $\mathscr{R}$-class R.

We shall prove that

$$\sigma \cdot H = \sigma \cdot K. \tag{7.12}$$

We have

$$\sigma \cdot H - \sigma \cdot K = (\rho \cdot H - \rho \cdot K) + (\rho' \cdot H - \rho' \cdot K).$$

Since $\rho \in W$ and $H, K \subset J$, it follows from (7.11) that

$$\rho \cdot H = \rho \cdot K = 0. \tag{7.13}$$

Next, there exists numbers $\alpha_m \in \mathbb{Q}$ $(m \in M)$ which almost all vanish such that $\rho' = \sum_{m \in M} \alpha_m(\sigma \cdot m)$. Since the left multiplication is a bijection on $\mathscr{H}$-classes, we have

$$(\sigma \cdot m) \cdot H - (\sigma \cdot m) \cdot K = \sigma \cdot (mH) - \sigma \cdot (mK).$$

Thus, since mH, $mK \subset mR$, the right-hand side is in W. Thus also $\rho' \cdot H - \rho' \cdot K \in W$. Since W' is invariant under M, this element is also in W'. Consequently it vanishes and

$$\rho' \cdot H = \rho' \cdot K. \tag{7.14}$$

Thus (7.12) follows from (7.13) and (7.14).

In view of (7.9), formula (7.12) shows that if $\varphi(X^*)$ intersects some $\mathscr{H}$-class H in J, then it intersects all $\mathscr{H}$-classes which are in the $\mathscr{R}$-class containing H. In view of Proposition IV.5.8, this is equivalent to X being suffix.

We conclude by showing that X is prefix. Let T be the subspace of V composed of the elements $\rho \in V$ such that $(\rho \cdot H, 1) = (\rho \cdot K, 1)$ for all pairs H, K of $\mathscr{H}$-classes of J contained in a same $\mathscr{L}$-class.

The subspace T is invariant under M. Indeed if $\rho \in T$ and $H, K \subset L$, then for all $m \in M$,

$$(\rho \cdot m) \cdot H = \rho \cdot mH, \qquad (\rho \cdot m) \cdot K = \rho \cdot mK. \tag{7.15}$$

Since mH, mK are in the $\mathscr{L}$-class L, we have by definition $((\rho \cdot m) \cdot H, 1) = ((\rho \cdot m) \cdot K, 1)$. Thus $\rho \cdot m \in T$.

Next for all $m \in J$ and $\rho \in V$,

$$\rho \cdot m \in T. \tag{7.16}$$

Indeed, let $m \in J$ and let H, K be two $\mathscr{H}$-classes contained in the $\mathscr{L}$-class $L \subset J$. Then $mH = mK$. Thus by (7.15), $((\rho \cdot m) \cdot H, 1) = ((\rho \cdot m) \cdot K, 1)$. Thus $\rho \cdot m \in T$.

Let T' be a supplementary space of T which is invariant under M. Again, set

$$\sigma = \rho + \rho'$$

this time with $\rho \in T$, $\rho' \in T'$. Let H, K be two $\mathscr{H}$-classes in J both contained in some $\mathscr{L}$-class L. Then

$$(\sigma \cdot H, 1) - (\sigma \cdot K, 1) = ((\rho \cdot H, 1) - (\rho \cdot K, 1)) + (\rho' \cdot H, 1) - (\rho' \cdot K, 1).$$

By definition of T, we have $(\rho \cdot H, 1) - (\rho \cdot K, 1) = 0$.

In view of (7.16), we have $\rho' \cdot H$, $\rho' \cdot K \in T$, whence $\rho' \cdot H - \rho' \cdot K \in T \cap T' = \{0\}$. Thus $(\sigma \cdot H, 1) = (\sigma \cdot K, 1)$. Interpreting this equality using (7.9), it is shown that if $\varphi(X^*)$ meets some $\mathscr{H}$-class of J, it intersects all $\mathscr{H}$-classes contained in the same $\mathscr{L}$-class. By Proposition IV.5.8, this shows that X is prefix. □

EXAMPLE 7.3 Let $A = \{a, b\}$ and let $X = \{a, ba\}$. The code X is prefix but not suffix. It is not complete.

Let $\sigma = \underline{X}^*$. The vectors σ and $\sigma \cdot b$ form a base of the vector space V_σ since

$$\sigma \cdot a = \sigma, \qquad \sigma \cdot ba = \sigma, \qquad \sigma \cdot bb = 0.$$

In this base, the matrices of $\psi_\sigma(a)$ and $\psi_\sigma(b)$ are

$$\psi_\sigma(a) = \begin{bmatrix} 1 & 0 \\ 1 & 0 \end{bmatrix}, \qquad \psi_\sigma(b) = \begin{bmatrix} 0 & 1 \\ 0 & 0 \end{bmatrix}.$$

The representation ψ_σ is irreducible. Indeed,

$$\psi_\sigma(ba) = \begin{bmatrix} 1 & 0 \\ 0 & 0 \end{bmatrix}, \qquad \psi_\sigma(a) - \psi_\sigma(ba) = \begin{bmatrix} 0 & 0 \\ 1 & 0 \end{bmatrix},$$

$$\psi_\sigma(b) = \begin{bmatrix} 0 & 1 \\ 0 & 0 \end{bmatrix}, \qquad \psi_\sigma(ab) - \psi_\sigma(b) = \begin{bmatrix} 0 & 0 \\ 0 & 1 \end{bmatrix}.$$

Thus the matrices $\psi_\sigma(u)$, $u \in A^*$ generate the whole algebra $\mathbb{Q}^{2 \times 2}$. Thus no nontrivial subspace of V is invariant under A^*. This example shows that Theorem 7.5 does not hold in general for codes which are not complete.

EXERCISES

SECTION 1

1.1. A code $X \subset A^+$ is called *separating* if there is a word $x \in X^*$ such that each $w \in A^*$ admits a factorization $w = uv$ with $xu, vx \in X^*$.

(a) Show that a separating code is complete and synchronous.

(b) Show that a separating code is factorizing and that its factorization is unique.

1.2. Let $b \in A$ be a letter and let $X \subset A^+$ be a finite maximal code such that for all $x \in X$, $|x|_b \leq 1$. Let $A' = A - b$. Let $X' = X' = X \cap A'^*$. Show that there is a factorization (P, Q) of X' considered as a code over A' such that

$$X = X' \cup PbQ.$$

1.3. Let $A = \{a, b\}$. Use Exercise 1.2 to show that a finite code $X \subset a^* \cup a^*ba^*$ is maximal iff $X = a^n \cup PbQ$ with $n \geq 1$ and $P, Q \subset a^*$ satisfying $\underline{P}\underline{Q} = 1 + a + \cdots + a^{n-1}$.

****1.4.** Let $X, Y \subset A^+$ be two distinct finite maximal prefix codes such that $X \cap Y \neq \emptyset$. Let $P = A^* - XA^*$, $Q = A^* - YA^*$ and let

$$R \subset (X \cap Y)^*$$

be a finite set satisfying $uv \in R, u \in (X \cap Y)^* \Rightarrow v \in R$. (This means that R is suffix-closed considered as a set on the alphabet $X \cap Y$.)

(a) Show that there is a unique finite maximal code $Z \subset A^+$ such that

$$\underline{Z} - 1 = (\underline{X \cap Y} - 1)\underline{R}.$$

(b) Show that there exists a unique finite maximal code $T \subset A^+$ such that

$$\underline{T} - 1 = (\underline{P} + w\underline{Q})(\underline{A} - 1)\underline{R},$$

where w is a word of maximal length in Z.

(c) Show that the code T is indecomposable under the following three assumptions:

(i) Z is separating.

(ii) $\operatorname{Card}(P \cup wQ)$ and $\operatorname{Card}(R)$ are prime numbers.

(iii) R is not suffix-closed (over the alphabet A).

(d) Compare with Example 1.1, by taking $P = \{1, a\}$, $Q = \{1, a, b\}$, $R = \{1, aa\}$, $w = abaa$.

1.5. Let $A = \{a, b\}$ and let

$$X = (A^2 - b^2) \cup b^2A, \qquad Y = A^2a \cup b.$$

(a) Verify that X is a maximal prefix code and that Y is maximal suffix.

(b) Show that the code Z defined by $Z^* = X^* \cap Y^*$ satisfies

$$\underline{Z} - 1 = (1 + \underline{A} + b^2)((\underline{A} - 1)a(\underline{A} - 1) + \underline{A} - 1)(1 + a + \underline{A}a).$$

[Hint: Show that $\underline{Z} - 1 = (\underline{X} - 1)\underline{P} = \underline{Q}(\underline{Y} - 1)$ for some $P \subset X^*$, $Q \subset Y^*$.]

(c) Show that Z is synchronous but not separating.

(d) Show that Z has two distinct factorizations.

SECTION 2

2.1. Let $X \subset A^+$ be a finite code. Let $\mathscr{A} = (Q, 1, 1)$ be an unambiguous trim automaton recognizing X^*.

(a) Show that $\mathscr{A}$ is finite.
(b) Let $\varphi = \varphi_{\mathscr{A}}$ and let

$$t = \theta\left(\sum_{a \in A} \varphi(a)\underline{\underline{a}}\right)$$

as in Proposition 2.2. Show that the determinant of the restriction of the matrix $I - t$ to $(Q - 1) \times (Q - 1)$ is equal to 1. Deduce from this that

$$\det(I - t) = 1 - \underline{\underline{X}}.$$

[Hint: Compute the coefficient (1, 1) of the inverse of $I - t$.]

2.2. Let $P \in Q\langle A\rangle$ be a polynomial with $(P, 1) = 0$. Show that there exists a morphism

$$\varphi: \quad A^* \to \mathbb{Q}^{n \times n}$$

such that
(i) for all $w \in A^+$, $(P, w) = \varphi(w)_{1,1}$,
(ii) $\det\left(I - \theta\left(\sum_{a \in A} \varphi(a)\underline{\underline{a}}\right)\right) = 1 - P.$

SECTION 3

The notation of Section 3 is assumed here and in the following exercise.

3.1. Let $\mathscr{A} = (Q, 1, 1)$ be a complete deterministic trim automaton and let $Q = \{1, 2, \ldots, n\}$.
(a) Show that for each $R \in \Gamma$ the vector c_R is colinear to the vector

$$\begin{bmatrix} 1 \\ 1 \\ \vdots \\ 1 \end{bmatrix}.$$

(b) Show that for each $L \in \Lambda$ the vector l_L is colinear to any vector $\sum_{q \in Q} m_{q*}$ for $m \in L$.

3.2. Let e be an idempotent in the minimal ideal J of M, let $S = \mathrm{Fix}(e)$ and let $e = cl$ be the column–row decomposition of e. Set $R = Me$, $L = eM$.
(a) Show that c_R is colinear to the vector $\sum_{s \in S} c_{*s}$.
(b) Show that l_L is colinear to the vector $\sum_{s \in S} l_{s*}$.

SECTION 4

****4.1.** Let $X \subset A^+$ be a set. A word $x \in X$ is said to be a *pure square* for X if
(i) $x = w^2$ for some $w \in A^+$,
(ii) $X \cap wA^* \cap A^*w = \{x\}$:

(a) Let $X \subset A^+$ be a finite maximal prefix code and let $x = w^2$ be a pure square for X. Set $G = Xw^{-1}$, $D = w^{-1}X$. Show that the polynomial

$$\sigma = (1 + w)(\underline{X} - 1 + (\underline{G} - 1)w(\underline{D} - 1)) + 1$$

is the characteristic series of a finite maximal prefix code denoted by $\delta_w(X)$.
[Hint: First show that σ has positive coefficients by setting $G_1 = G - w$, $D_1 = D - w$ and observing that

$$\sigma = (\underline{X} - w\underline{D}_1 - \underline{G}w) + \underline{G}w\underline{D}_1 + (\underline{X} - w\underline{D})w + \underline{G}w\underline{D}w.$$

Then show that there exists a set $P \subset A^*$ such that $\sigma - 1 = \underline{P}(\underline{A} - 1)(w + 1)$].
Show that the polynomial

$$(\underline{X} - 1 + (\underline{G} - 1)w(\underline{D} - 1))(1 + w) + 1$$

is the characteristic series of a finite maximal code denoted by $\gamma_w(X)$

(b) Let $X \subset A^+$ be a finite maximal prefix code. Show that if $x = w^2$ is a pure square for X, then x^2 is a pure square for $\gamma_w(X)$.

(c) Let $X \subset A^+$ be a finite maximal prefix code. Let $x = w^2$ be a pure square for X. Show that the codes $Y = \gamma_w(X)$ and $Z = \delta_w(X)$ have the same degree.
[Hint: Show that there is a bijection between Y-interpretations and Z-interpretations of a word.]

(d) Let X be a finite maximal biprefix code. Let $x = w^2$ be a pure square for X and $Y = \gamma_w(X)$. Show that $d(X) = d(Y)$.
[Hint: Show that $\{1, w\}$ is a maximal set of left contexts and use Proposition 4.2.]

(e) Let X be a finite maximal biprefix code. Let $x = w^2$ be a pure square for X and let $Y = \gamma_w(X)$. By (b) the word x^2 is a pure square for Y. Let $Z = \delta_x(Y)$. Show that $d(Z) = d(X)$.
[Hint: Show that $\{1, w, w^2, w^4\}$ is a maximal set of left contexts for $T = \gamma_x(Y)$. Deduce from Proposition 4.2 that $d(T) = d(X)$. Then use (c) to show that $d(Z) = d(T)$.]

(f) Show that if $d(X)$ is a prime number and $d(X) > 2$, the code Z of (e) does not admit any decomposition over a suffix or a prefix code.

(g) Use the above construction to show that for each prime number $d \geq 3$, there exist finite maximal codes of degree d which are indecomposable and are neither prefix nor suffix.

SECTION 6

6.1. Let $X \subset A^+$ be a circular code. Show that the series

$$\log \underline{A}^* - \log \underline{X}^*$$

has nonnegative coefficients (use Proposition VII.1.5). Show that X is commutatively prefix.

6.2. Let X be the circular code $X = \{a, ab, c, acb\}$. Show that there is no bijection $\alpha: X \to Y$ of X onto a prefix code Y such that $\alpha(x)$ is a conjugate of x for all $x \in X$.

6.3. Let $X \subset A^+$ be a finite set and assume there is a letter $a \in A$ such that $X \cap a^* = a^n$ for some $n \geq 1$. Let $b \in A - \{a\}$ be another letter.

(a) Show that if X is a code, then $\text{Card}(X \cap a^*ba^*) \leq n$.

(b) Show that if X is complete, then $\text{Card}(X \cap a^*ba^*) \geq n$.

(c) Show that if X is a maximal code, then $\text{Card}(X \cap a^*ba^*) = n$.

SECTION 7

7.1. Let $\mathscr{A} = (Q, i, T)$ be a finite automaton. The aim of this exercise is to construct the syntactic representation of the series $\sigma = |\mathscr{A}| \in \mathbb{N}\langle\langle A \rangle\rangle$.

Let φ be the representation associated with $\mathscr{A}$ and let $M = \varphi(A^*)$. We may assume $Q = \{1, 2, \ldots, n\}$ and $i = 1$.

Let $E = \mathbb{Q}^n$, let E_0 be the subspace of E generated by the vectors m_{1*}, $m \in \varphi A^*)$. Let E_{-1} be the subspace of E_0 composed of all vectors $l \in E_0$ such that for all $m \in M$, $\sum_{t \in T}(lm)_t = 0$.

Show that the linear function $\alpha: E_0 \to V_\sigma$ defined by $\alpha: \varphi(u)_{1*} \mapsto \sigma \cdot u$ has kernel E_{-1}. Deduce from this fact a method for computing a basis of V_σ and the matrices of $\psi_\sigma(a)$ in this basis for $a \in A$.

7.2. Let $S \subset A^+$ and $\sigma = \underline{S}$. Show that V_σ has finite dimension iff S is recognizable (use Exercise 7.1).

7.3. Let K be a commutative field and let $\sigma \in K\langle\langle A \rangle\rangle$. The syntactic representation of σ over K is defined as in the special case $K = \mathbb{Q}$. Recall that the characteristic of a field is the greatest common divisor of all integers n such that $n \cdot 1 = 0$ in K.

Let X be a very thin biprefix code. Let K be a field of characteristic 0 or which is prime to the order of $G(X)$. Show that the syntactic representation of X^* over K is completely reducible.

7.4. Let X be a very thin biprefix code. Show that if X is synchronizing, then $\psi_{X^*}(A^*)$ is irreducible.

NOTES

Theorem 1.1 is due to Schützenberger (1965b). The proof given here is essentially that of this paper with some additions from Hansel *et al.* (1984).

The problem of characterizing commutatively prefix codes has an equivalent formulation in terms of optimality of prefix codes with respect to some cost functions, namely, the average length of the code for a given weight distribution on the letters. In this context it has been treated in several papers and in particular in (Carter and Gill, 1961; Karp, 1961). The codes of Example 6.3 have been studied more recently under the name of *bayonet codes* (Hansel, 1982; Pin and Simon 1982; De Felice, 1983). Example 6.4 is due to Shor (1983). It is a counterexample to a conjecture of Perrin and Schützenberger (1981). A particular case of commutatively prefix codes is studied in Mauceri and Restivo (1981).

Results of Section 7 are due to Reutenauer (1981). The syntactic representation appears for the first time in Schützenberger (1961a). It has been developed more systematically in Fliess (1974) and in Reutenauer (1980). Theorem 7.2 is Maschke's theorem. The property for an algebra of matrices to be completely reducible is equivalent to that of being semisimple (see, e.g., Herstein, 1969). Thus Theorem 7.3 expresses that the syntactic algebra $\psi_\sigma(A^*)$ for $\sigma = \underline{X}^*$, $\underline{X}$ a thin biprefix code, is semisimple. This theorem can be considered a generalization of Maschke's theorem.

Exercises 1.1 and 1.5 are from Boë (1981), 1.3 from (Restivo 1977), 1.4 from (Boë 1978), 2.2 from Hansel *et al.* (1984), 4.1 from Perrin (1977a) and Vincent (1982), 6.1 from Perrin and Schützenberger (1977) and 6.3 from Perrin and Schützenberger (1976).

A new proof of Theorem 1.1 has been obtained recently by Reutenauer (1983a). Further developments can be found in (Reutenauer, 1984a,b) where the following result is proved: for any finite maximal code $X \subset A^+$ there exist polynomials $P, Q \in \mathbb{Z}\langle A \rangle$ such that

$$1 - \underline{X} = P(1 - \underline{A})Q.$$

If one could prove that, in fact, P, Q can be chosen in $\mathbb{N}\langle A \rangle$, it would imply that any finite maximal code is factorizing and, therefore, commutatively prefix. This is the main question left open in the theory of codes.

References

Aho, A., Hopcroft, J., and Ullman, J., 1975. "The Design and Analysis of Computer Algorithms." Reading, Massachusetts: Addison Wesley.

Apostolico, A., and Giancarlo, R., 1984. Pattern matching implementation of a fast test for unique decipherability. *Information Processing Letters* (to appear).

Arnold, A., and Latteux, M. 1981. A new proof of two theorems about rational transductions. *Theoret. Comput. Sci.* **8,** 261-263.

Ash, R. B. 1965. "Information Theory." New York: Wiley (Interscience).

Bandyopadhyay, G. 1963. A simple proof of the decipherability criterion of Sardinas and Patterson. *Inform. and Control* **6,** 331–336.

Berstel, J. 1979. "Transductions and Context-Free Languages." Stuttgart: Teubner.

Berstel, J., and Reutenauer, C., 1984. "Les series rationnelles et leurs langages." Paris: Masson.

Berstel, J., Perrin, D., Perrot, J. F., and Restivo, A. 1979. Sur le théorème du defaut. *J. Algebra* **60,** 169–180.

Blanchard, F., and Perrin, D. 1980. Relèvement d'une mesure ergodique par un codage. *Z. Wahsch. Verw. Gebiete* **54,** 303–311.

Blum, E. K. 1965. Free subsemigroups of a free semigroup. *Michigan Math. J.* **12,** 179–182.

Bobrow, L. S., and Hakimi, S. L. 1969. Graph theoretic prefix codes and their synchronization properties. *Inform. and Control* **15,** 70–94.

Boë, J. M. 1972. Sur les codes d'inclusion. *Inform. and Control* **4,** 291–299.

Boë, J. M. 1976. "Representations des monoïdes: Applications à la théorie des codes." Thèse de 3e cycle, Montpellier.

Boë, J. M. 1978. Une famille remarquable de codes indécomposables. *In* "Automata, Languages and Programming Lecture Notes in Comput. Sci., 105–112.

Boë, J. M. 1981. Sur les codes synchronisants coupants. *In* "Non-commutative Structures in Algebra and Geometric Combinatorics" (A. De Luca, ed.). *Quaderni de la ricerca scientifica,* **109** 7–10.

Boë, J. M., Boyat J., Bordat, J. P., and Césari Y. 1979. Une caractérisation des sous-monoïdes libérables. *In* "Théorie des codes" (D. Perrin, ed.). 9–20. LITP.

Boë, J. M., De Luca A., and Restivo, A. 1980. Minimal completable sets of words. *Theoret. Comput. Sci.* **12,** 325–332.

Brzozowski, J. A. 1967. Roots of star events. *J. Assoc. Comput. Mach.* **14,** 466–477.

Carter, L., and Gill, J. 1961. Conjectures on uniquely decipherable codes, *IRE Trans. Inform. Theory* **IT7,** 27–38.

Cerny, J. 1964. Poznamka K homogenym s Konecnymi automati. *Mat.-fyz. cas. SAV.*, 14, 208–215.

Césari, Y. 1982. Sur un algorithme donnant les codes bipréfixes finis. *Math. Systems Theory* **6,** 221–225.

Césari, Y. 1974. Sur l'application du théorème de Suschkevitch à l'étude des codes rationnels complets. *In* "Automata, Languages and Programming." Lecture Notes in Comput. Sci., 342–350. Berlin and New York: Springer-Verlag.

Césari, Y. 1979. Propriétés combinatoires des codes biprefixes. *In* "Théorie des codes" (D. Perrin, ed.). 20–46. Paris: LITP.

Choffrut, C. 1979. Une caractérisation des codes ă délai borné par leur fonction de décodage. *In* "Theorie des Codes" (D. Perrin, ed). LITP.

Clifford, A. H., and Preston, G. B. 1961. "The algebraic theory of semigroups." Vol. 1. Providence, R. I.: Amer. Math. Soc.

Cohn, P. M. 1962. On subsemigroups of free semigroups. *Proc. Amer. Math. Soc.* **63,** 347–351.

Cohn, P. M. 1971. "Free Rings and Their Relations," New York: Academic Press.

Csiszár, I., and Körner, J. 1981. "Information Theory: Coding Theorems for Discrete Memoryless Systems." New York: Academic Press.

De Felice, C. 1983. A note on the triangle conjecture. *Inform. Process. Lett.* **14,** 197–200.

De Felice, C., and Restivo, A., 1984. Some results on finite maximal codes. *RAIRO Informat. Théor.* (to appear).

De Luca, A. 1976. A note on variable length codes. *Inform. and Control* **32,** 263–271.

De Luca, A., and Restivo, A. 1980a. On some properties of very pure codes. *Theoret. Comput. Sci.* **10,** 157–170.

Devitt, J. S., and Jackson, D. M. 1981. Comma-free codes: An extension of certain enumerative techniques to recursively defined sequences. *J. Combin. Theory Ser. A* **30,** 1–18.

Eastman, W. L. 1965. On the construction of common free codes. *IEEE Trans. Inform. Theory* **IT-11,** 2, 263–267.

Ehrenfeucht, A., and Rozenberg, G. 1978. Elementary homomorphisms and a solution to the DOL sequence equivalence problem. *Theoret. Comput. Sci.* **7,** 169–184.

Ehrenfeucht, A., and Rozenberg, G. 1983. Each regular code is included in a regular maximal code RAIRO Informat. Théor. (to appear).

Eilenberg, S. 1974. "Automata, Languages, and Machines." Vol. A. New York: Academic Press.

Eilenberg, S. 1976. "Automata, Languages, and Machines." Vol. B. New York: Academic Press.

Elgot, C., and Mezei, G. 1965. On relations defined by generalized finite automata. *IBM J. Res. Develop.* **9,** 47–65.

Feller, W. 1957. "An Introduction to Probability Theory and Its Applications." New York: Wiley.

Fliess, M. 1974. Matrices de Hankel. *J. Math. Pures Appl.* **53,** 197–222.

Gilbert, E. N. 1960. Synchronization of binary messages. *IRE Trans. Inform. Theory* **IT-6,** 470–477.

Gilbert, E. N. and Moore, E. F. 1959. Variable length binary encodings. *Bell System Tech. J.* **38,** 933–967.

Golomb, S. W., and Gordon, B. 1965. Codes with bounded synchronization delay. *Inform. and Control* **8,** 355–372

Golomb, S. W., Gordon, B., and Welch, L. R. 1958. Comma free codes. *Canad. J. Math.* **10,** 202–209.

Greenander, U. 1963. "Probabilities on Algebraic Structures." New York: Wiley.
Guibas, J. L., and Odlyzko, A. 1978. Maximal prefix synchronized codes. *SIAM J. Appl. Math.* **35,** 401–418.
Hansel, G. 1982. Baïonettes et cardinaux. *Discrete Math.* **39,** 331–335.
Hansel, G., and Perrin, D. 1983. Codes and Bernoulli partitions. *Math. Systems Theory.* **16,** 133–157.
Hansel, G., Perrin, D., and Reutenauer, C. 1984. Factorizing the commutative polynomial of a code. *Trans. Amer. Math. Soc.* **285,** 91–105.
Hashiguchi, K., and Honda, N. 1976a. Homomorphisms that preserve star height. *Inform. and Control* **30,** 247–266.
Hashiguchi, K., and Honda, N. 1976b. Properties of code events and homomorphisms over regular events, *J. Comput. System Sci.* **12,** 352–367.
Herstein, I. N. 1969. "Non-commutative Rings," Carus Mathematical Monographs. New York: Wiley.
Huppert, B. 1967. "Endliche Gruppen." Berlin and New York: Springer-Verlag.
Huppert, B., and Blackburn, N. 1982. "Finite groups II and III." Berlin and New York: Springer-Verlag.
Jiggs, B. H. 1963. Recent results in comma free codes. *Canad. J. Math,* **15,** 178–187.
Karhumaki, J. 1984. A property of three element codes, *in* "STACS 84," Lecture Notes in Computer Science. **166,** 305–313.
Karp, R. M. 1961. Minimum redundancy codes for the discrete noiseless channel. *IRE Trans. Inform. Theory.* **IT-7,** 27–38.
Knuth, D. 1973. "The Art of Computer Programming. Vol. 1. Fundamental Algorithms." Reading, Massachusetts: Addison-Wesley.
Lallement, G. 1979. "Semigroups and Combinatorial Applications." New York: Wiley.
Lallement, G., and Perrin, D. 1981. A graph covering construction of all the finite complete biprefix codes. *Discrete Math.* **36,** 261–271.
Lassez, J. L. 1973. Prefix codes and isomorphic automata. *Internat. J. Comput. Math.* **3,** 309–314.
Lassez, J. L., 1976. Circular codes and synchronization. *International Journal of Computer and System Sciences,* **5,** 201–208.
Lentin, A. 1972. Equations dans les Monoides Libres." Paris: Gauthier-Villars.
Lentin, A., and Schützenberger, M. P. 1967. A combinatorial problem in the theory of free monoids. *In* "Combinatorial Mathematics and Its Applications." (R. C. Bose and T. A. Dowlings, eds.). 128–144. Chapell Hill: North Carolina Press.
Lerest, E., and Lerest M. 1980. Une représentation fidèle des groupes d'un monoïde de relations sur un ensemble fini. *Semigroup Forum* **21,** 167–172.
Levenshtein, V. I. 1964. Some properties of coding and self-adjusting automata for decoding messages. *Problemy Kirbernet.* **11,** 63–121. [Russian]
Levi, F. W. 1944. On semigroups. *Bull. Calcutta Math. Soc.* **36,** 141–146.
Lothaire, M. 1983. "Combinatorics on Words." Reading, Massachusetts: Addison-Wesley.
McEliece, R. 1977. "The Theory of Information and Coding." Reading, Massachusetts: Addison-Wesley.
McMillan, B. 1956. Two inequalities implied by unique decipherability. *IRE Trans. Inform. Theory* **IT-2,** 115–116.
McWilliams, F. and Sloane, J. 1977. "The Theory of Error Correcting Codes." Amsterdam: North-Holland.
Makanin, G. S. 1976. On the rank of equations in four unknowns in a free semigroup. *Mat. Sb.* (*N.S.*) **100,** 285–311; English translation *Math. USSR-Sb.* **29,** 257–280.
Margolis, S. W. 1982. On the syntactic transformation semigroup of a language generated by a finite biprefix code. *Theoret. Comput. Sci.* **21,** 225–230.
Markov, Al. A. 1962. On alphabet coding. *Soviet. Phys. Dokl.* **6,** 553–554. [Russian]

Martin-Löf, P. 1965. Probability theory on discrete semigroups, *Z. Wahrsch* **4,** 78–102.

Mauceri, S., and Restivo, A., 1981. A family of codes commutatively equivalent to prefix codes. *Inform. Process. Lett.* **12,** 1–4.

Moore, E. F. 1956. Gedanken Experiments *In* "Automata Studies," *Ann. of Math. Stud.* **34,** 129–153.

Nivat, M. 1966. Elements de la théorie générale des codeś. *In* "Automata Theory." (E. Caianiello, ed.). 278–294, New York: Academic Press.

Perles, M., Rabin, M., and Shamir, E. 1963. The theory of definite automata. *IEEE Trans* Electronic Computers, **12,** 233–243.

Perrin, D. 1975. "Codes bipréfixes et groupes de permutations," Thèse. Université Paris 7.

Perrin, D. 1977a. Codes asynchrones. *Bull. Soc. Math. France* **105,** 385–404.

Perrin, D. 1977b. La transitivité du groupe d'un code bipréfixe fini. *Math. Z.* **153,** 283–287.

Perrin, D. 1978. Le degré minimal du groupe d'un code bipréfixe fini *J. Combin. Theory Ser. A* **25,** 163–173.

Perrin, D. 1979. La représentation ergodique d'un automate fini. *Theoret. Comput. Sci.* **9,** 221–241.

Perrin, D. 1982. Completing biprefix codes. *In* "Automata, Languages and Programming." Lecture Notes in Computer Science. **140,** 397–406.

Perrin, D., and Schützenberger, M. P. 1976. Codes et sous-monoïdes possédant des mots neutres. *In* "Theoretical Computer Science." Lecture Notes in Computer Science **48,** 270–281.

Perrin, D. and Schützenberger, M. P. 1981. A conjecture on sets of differences of integer pairs. *J. Combin. Theory. Ser. B* **30,** 91–93.

Perrot, J. F. 1972. "Contribution ă l'étude des monoïdes syntaxiques et de certains groupes associés aux automates finis." Thèse. Université de Paris.

Perrot, J. F. 1974. Groupes de permutations associes aux codes préfixes finis. *In* "Permutations," 19–35. Paris: Gauthier-Villars.

Perrot, J. F. 1977. Informatique et algèbre: la théorie des codes ă longueur variable. *In* "Theoretical Computer Science." Lecture Notes in Computer Science. **48,** 27–44.

Pin, J. E. 1978. "Le problème de la synchronisation; contribution ă l'étude de la conjecture de Cerny." Thèse de 3 cycle. Université Paris 6.

Pin, J. E. 1979. Une caractérisation de trois variétés de langages bien connues. *In* "Theoretical Computer Science." Lecture Notes in Computer Science. **67,** 233–243.

Pin, J. E. 1984. Variétés de langages formels, Paris: Masson.

Pin, J. E., and Sakarovitch, J. 1983. Some operations and transductions that preserve rationality. In "Theoretical Computer Science." Lecture Notes in Computer Science. **145,** 277–288.

Pin, J. E., and Simon, I. 1982. A note on the triangle conjecture. *J. Combin. Theory Ser. A* **32,** 106–109.

Reis, C., and Thierrin, G. 1979. Reflective star languages and codes. *Inform. and Control* **42,** 1–9.

Restivo, A. 1974. On a question of McNaughton and Pappert. *Inform. and Control* **25,** 1.

Restivo, A. 1975. A combinatorial property of codes having finite synchronization delay. *Theoret. Comput. Sci.* **1,** 95–101.

Restivo, A. 1977. On codes having no finite completions. *Discrete Math.* **17,** 309–316.

Reutenauer, C. 1980. Séries formelles et algèbres syntaxiques. *J. Algebra* **66,** 448–483.

Reutenauer, C. 1981. Semisimplicity of the algebra associated to a biprefix code. *Semigroup Forum* **23,** 327–342.

Reutenauer, C. 1983. Sur un théorème de Schützenberger, *C. R. Acad. Sci. Paris* 296, 619–621.

Reutenauer, C. 1984a. Sulla fattorizzazione dei codici. *Richerche di Matematica,* **XXXII,** 115–130.

Reutenauer, C. 1984b. Non commutative factorization of variable length codes *J. Pure and Applied Algebra.* (to appear)

Riley, J. A. 1967. The Sardinas–Patterson and Levenshtein theorems. *Inform. and Control* **10,** 120–136.

Rindone, G. 1983. "Groupes finis et monoides syntaxiques." These de 3 cycle. Universite Paris 7.

Rodeh, M., 1982. A fast test for unique decipherability based on suffix trees. *IEEE Trans. on Inf. Theor.*, **IT-28,** 648–651.

Salomaa, A. 1981. "Jewels of Formal Language Theory." Washington, D.C.: Computer Science Press.

Sardinas, A. A., and Patterson, C. W. 1953. A necessary and sufficient condition for the unique decomposition of coded messages. *IRE Internat. Conv. Rec.* **8,** 104–108.

Scholtz, R. A. 1966. Codes with synchronization capability. *IEEE Trans. Inform. Theory.* **IT-2,** 135–142.

Scholtz, R. A. 1969. Maximal and variable length comma free codes. *IEEE Trans. Inform. Theory.* **IT-15** 300–306.

Schützenberger, M. P. 1955. "Une théorie algébrique du codage." Séminaire Dubreil-Pisot, 1955–1956. Expose No. 15.

Schützenberger, M. P. 1956. On an application of semigroup methods to some problems in coding. *IRE Trans. Inform. Theory.* **IT-2,** 47–60.

Schützenberger, M. P. 1961a. On the definition of a family of automata. *Inform. and Control* **4,** 245–270.

Schützenberger, M. P. 1961b. On a special class of recurrent events. *Ann. Math. Statist.* **32,** 1201–1213.

Schützenberger, M. P. 1961c. On a family of submonoids. *Publ. Math. Inst. Hunger. Acad. Sci. Ser. A* **VI,** 381–391.

Schützenberger, M. P. 1964. On the synchronizing properties of certain prefix codes. *Inform. and Control* **7,** 23–36.

Schützenberger, M. P. 1965a. On a factorization of free monoids. *Proc. Amer. Math. Soc.* **16,** 21–24.

Schützenberger, M. P. 1965b. Sur certains sous-monoïdes libres. *Bull. Soc. Math. France.* **93,** 209–223.

Schützenberger, M. P. 1965c. Sur une question concernant certains sous-monoïdes libres. *C. R. Acad. Sci. Paris* **261,** 2419–2420.

Schützenberger, M. P. 1966. On a question concerning certain free submonoids. *J. Combin. Theory.* **1,** 437–422.

Schützenberger, M. P. 1967. On synchronizing prefix codes. *Inform and Control* **11,** 396–401.

Schützenberger, M. P. 1979. A property of finitely generated submonoids of free monoids. *In* "Algebraic Theory of Semigroups" (G. Pollak, ed.). 545–576. Amsterdam: North-Holland.

Shevrin, L. N. 1960. On subsemigroups of free semigroups, *Soviet Math. Dokl.* **1,** 892–894.

Shor, P. W. 1983. A counterexample to the triangle conjecture. *J. Combin. Theory Ser. A.*

Spehner, J. C. 1975. Quelques constructions et algorithmes relatifs aux sous-monoides d'un monoide libre. *Semigroup Forum* **9,** 334–353.

Spehner, J. C. 1976. "Quelques problèmes d'extension, de conjugaison et de présentation des sous-monóïdes d'un monoïde libre. Thèse. Université Paris 7.

Stryer, L. 1975. "Biochemistry," San Francisco: Freeman.

Tilson, B. 1972. The intersection of free submonoids is free. *Semigroup Forum* **4,** 345–350.

Van Lindt, 1982. "Introduction to Coding Theory," Berlin and New York: Springer-Verlag.

Viennot, G. 1974. "Algèbres de Lie libres et monoides libres." Thèse. Universite Paris 7.

Viennot. G. 1978. "Algèbres de lie et monoides libres". Lecture Notes in Mathematics **691**.

Vincent, M. 1982. "Une famille de codes indécomposables." Thèse de 3e cycle. Montpellier.

Wielandt, H. 1964. "Finite Permutation Groups." New York: Academic Press.

Yčas, M. 1969. "The Biological Code." Amsterdam. North-Holland.

Index

Pure and Applied Mathematics

A Series of Monographs and Textbooks

Editors **Samuel Eilenberg and Hyman Bass**

Columbia University, New York

RECENT TITLES

CARL L. DEVITO. Functional Analysis

MICHIEL HAZEWINKEL. Formal Groups and Applications

SIGURDUR HELGASON. Differential Geometry, Lie Groups, and Symmetric Spaces

ROBERT B. BURCKEL. An Introduction to Classical Complex Analysis: Volume 1

JOSEPH J. ROTMAN. An Introduction to Homological Algebra

C. TRUESDELL AND R. G. MUNCASTER. Fundamentals of Maxwell's Kinetic Theory of a Simple Monatomic Gas: Treated as a Branch of Rational Mechanics

BARRY SIMON. Functional Integration and Quantum Physics

GRZEGORZ ROZENBERG AND ARTO SALOMAA. The Mathematical Theory of L Systems

DAVID KINDERLEHRER AND GUIDO STAMPACCHIA. An Introduction to Variational Inequalities and Their Applications

H. SEIFERT AND W. THRELFALL. A Textbook of Topology; H. SEIFERT. Topology of 3-Dimensional Fibered Spaces

LOUIS HALLE ROWEN. Polynominal Identities in Ring Theory

DONALD W. KAHN. Introduction to Global Analysis

DRAGOS M. CVETKOVIC, MICHAEL DOOB, AND HORST SACHS. Spectra of Graphs

ROBERT M. YOUNG. An Introduction to Nonharmonic Fourier Series

MICHAEL C. IRWIN. Smooth Dynamical Systems

JOHN B. GARNETT. Bounded Analytic Functions

EDUARD PRUGOVECKI. Quantum Mechanics in Hilbert Space, Second Edition

M. SCOTT OSBORNE AND GARTH WARNER. The Theory of Eisenstein Systems

K. A. ZHEVLAKOV, A. M. SLIN'KO, I. P. SHESTAKOV, AND A. I. SHIRSHOV. Translated by Harry Smith. Rings That Are Nearly Associative

JEAN DIEUDONNÉ. A Panorama of Pure Mathematics; Translated by I. Macdonald

JOSEPH G. ROSENSTEIN. Linear Orderings

AVRAHAM FEINTUCH AND RICHARD SAEKS. System Theory: A Hilbert Space Approach

ULF GRENANDER. Mathematical Experiments on the Computer

HOWARD OSBORN. Vector Bundles: Volume 1, Foundations and Stiefel-Whitney Classes

K. P. S. BHASKARA RAO AND M. BHASKARA RAO. Theory of Charges

RICHARD V. KADISON AND JOHN R. RINGROSE. Fundamentals of the Theory of Operator Algebras, Volume I

EDWARD B. MANOUKIAN. Renormalization

BARRETT O'NEILL. Semi-Riemannian Geometry: With Applications to Relativity

LARRY C. GROVE. Algebra

E. J. MCSHANE. Unified Integration

STEVEN ROMAN. The Umbral Calculus

JOHN W. MORGAN AND HYMAN BASS (Eds.). The Smith Conjecture

SIGURDUR HELGASON. Groups and Geometric Analysis: Integral Geometry, Invariant Differential Operators, and Spherical Functions

ISAAC CHAVEL. Eigenvalues in Riemannian Geometry

W. D. CURTIS AND F. R. MILLER. Differential Manifolds and Theoretical Physics

JEAN BERSTEL AND DOMINIQUE PERRIN. Theory of Codes

IN PREPARATION

ROBERT B. BURCKEL. An Introduction to Classical Complex Analysis: Volume 2

RICHARD V. KADISON AND JOHN R. RINGROSE. Fundamentals of the Theory of Operator Algebras, Volume II

A. P. MORSE. A Theory of Sets, Second Edition

E. R. KOLCHIN. Differential Algebraic Groups